Baedeker's
JAPAN

A SPECTRUM BOOK

PRENTICE-HALL, Inc., Englewood Cliffs, New Jersey 07632

Cover picture: Fujiyama (Fuji-san) at cherry-blossom time

193 coloured photographs
48 maps and plans
1 large map

Text:
Dr Walter Giesen, St Blasien
(Religion, in part; Literature; Music)
Prof. Dr Wolfgang Hassenpflug, Kiel
(Climate)
Karin Khan, Frankfurt am Main
(introductory chapters, in part; Japan from A to Z;
Practical Information)

Editorial work:
Baedeker Stuttgart
English Language: Alec Court

Cartography:
Ingenieurbüro für Kartographie
Huber & Oberländer, Munich
(maps, plans and diagrams in text)
Georg Schiffner, Lahr
(large map)

Design and layout:
Creativ Verlagsgesellschaft mbH, Stuttgart

Conception and general direction:
Dr Peter Baumgarten, Baedeker Stuttgart

English translation:
James Hogarth

© Baedeker Stuttgart
Original German edition

© The Automobile Association
United Kingdom and Ireland 1983/57257

© Jarrold & Sons Ltd
English language edition worldwide

Licensed user:
Mairs Georgraphischer Verlag GmbH & Co.,
Ostfildern-Kemnat bei Stuttgart

Reproductions:
Gölz Repro-Service GmbH,
Ludwigsburg

The name Baedeker is a registered trademark

Source of illustrations:

Most of the illustrations were supplied by the Japan National Tourist Organisation and Frau Karin Khan, Frankfurt am Main.

Others:
Deutsche Presse-Agentur GmbH (dpa), Frankfurt am Main (pp. 11, top right; 12, top; 21, top left and bottom right; 22, left; 32, left; 36, left; 53; 61, both; 179, 185, 229, 230; 274, below; 275, left; 276–277, top and middle; 277, bottom right; 298, 299; 308, above; 327, 329, 330; 331, left and bottom right)
Siegfried J. Gragnato, Stuttgart (p. 49)
Japan Air Lines, Frankfurt am Main (p. 81)
Hans Kirchmann, Hamburg (pp. 21, middle, first three; 32, right; 77, all three; 114, 285)
Foto-Messerschmidt, Berlin (pp. 21, top right, middle right and bottom left; 22, right; 36, right; 270; 282–283, below; 317)

How to Use this Guide

The principal towns and areas of tourist interest are described in alphabetical order. The names of other places referred to under these general headings can be found in the Index.

Following the tradition established by Karl Baedeker in 1844, sights of particular interest and hotels and restaurants of particular quality are distinguished by either one or two asterisks.

In the lists of hotels and other accommodation r. = rooms, b. = beds and SP= swimming pool. The types of hotels and other accommodations are described on pp. 325–7.

The symbol ⓘ at the beginning of an entry or on a town plan indicates the tourist information offices or other organisations from which further information can be obtained: see, however, the note on p. 341. The post-horn symbol on a town plan indicates a post office.

Only a selection of hotels and restaurants can be given: no reflection is implied, therefore, on establishments not included.

Following Japanese practice, personal names are given with the surname first.

It should be noted that Japanese place-names frequently incorporate an affix denoting the type of geographical feature or structure, where English uses a separate word: -ji/temple, -kyo/gorge, -mon/gate, -shima/island, -yama/mountain, etc. For the convenience of the reader, however, names are often given in this Guide in the form Todaiji Temple, Sounkyo Gorge, etc., even though this involves reduplication.

In a time of rapid change it is difficult to ensure that all the information given is entirely accurate and up to date, and the possibility of error can never be entirely eliminated. Although the publishers can accept no responsibility for inaccuracies and omissions, they are always grateful for corrections and suggestions for improvement.

Printed in Great Britain by Jarrold & Sons Ltd, Norwich **
Japanese script in headings printed by LibroSatz Johannes Witt GmbH & Co. KG, Kriftel

013–056382–X

This guidebook forms part of a completely new series of the world-famous Baedeker Guides to Europe.

Each volume is the result of long and careful preparation and, true to the traditions of Baedeker, is designed in every respect to meet the needs and expectations of the modern traveller.

The name of Baedeker has long been identified in the field of guidebooks with reliable, comprehensive and up-to-date information, prepared by expert writers who work from detailed, first-hand knowledge of the country concerned. Following a tradition that goes back over 150 years to the date when Karl Baedeker published the first of his handbooks for travellers, these guides have been planned to give the tourist all the essential information about the country and its inhabitants: where to go, how to get there and what to see. Baedeker's account of a country was always based on his personal observation and experience during his travels in that country. This tradition of writing a guidebook in the field rather than at an office desk has been maintained by Baedeker ever since.

Lavishly illustrated with superb colour photographs and numerous specially drawn maps and street plans of the major towns, the new Baedeker Guides concentrate on making available to the modern traveller all the information he needs in a format that is both attractive and easy to follow. For every place that appears in the gazetteer, the principal features of architectural, artistic and historic interest are described, as are its main areas of scenic beauty. Selected hotels and restaurants are also included. Features of exceptional merit are indicated by either one or two asterisks.

A special section at the end of each book contains practical information, details of leisure activities and useful addresses. The separate road map will prove an invaluable aid to planning your route and your travel within the country.

Introduction to Japan

Torii of the Itsukushima Shrine on Miyajima

Japan
Nippon / Nihon

日本

—— **Boundaries of regions**
—— **Boundaries of prefectures**

Hokkaid

Sea of Japan

Sado

Niig

Kanazawa
Oki
16
Toyama
17
KANSAI
18
CHUB
Matsue
19
Gifu
31
27
26
25
CHUGOKU
34
32
Himeji
Kyoto
Nagoya
Tsushima
Okayama
Kobe
Nara
23
Hiroshima
28
24
Shimonoseki
33
36
29
Ise
Hamam
Kitakyushu
35
Takamatsu
Osaka
40
Matsuyama
30
Fukuoka
41
39
Wakayama
44
38
Goto Islands
Kumamoto
SHIKOKU
45
Shikoku
Naga-
43
42
saki
Kyushu
KYUSHU
Kagoshima
46
Tanegashima

*East China
Sea*
Yakushima

Ryu- kyu Islands
47
Naha
Okinawa

Pacific

REGION Prefecture	Land area in sq. miles (sq. km)	Population[1]	Chief town
HOKKAIDO			
1 Hokkaido	32,245 (83.515[2])	5,974,600	Sapporo
TOHOKU			
2 Aomori	3,713 (9,616)	1,635,100	Aomori
3 Akita	4,483 (11,611)	1,351,100	Akita
4 Iwate	5,899 (15,278)	1,523,900	Morioka
5 Yamagata	3,601 (9,327)	1,340,300	Yamagata
6 Miyagi	2,815 (7,291)	2,218,300	Sendai
7 Fukushima	5,321 (13,782)	2,176,200	Fukushima
KANTO			
8 Tochigi	2,476 (6,414)	1,909,400	Utsunomiya
9 Gumma	2,454 (6,356)	1,972,000	Maebashi
10 Ibaraki	2,351 (6,090)	2,703,200	Mito
11 Saitama	1,467 (3,800)	5,733,700	Urawa
12 Chiba	1,982 (5,133)	4,986,400	Chiba
13 Tokyo[3]	832 (2,154)	12,523,700	Tokyo
14 Kanagawa	925 (2,397)	7,353,700	Yokohama
CHUBU			
15 Niigata	4,856 (12,578)	2,632,000	Niigata
16 Toyama	1,642 (4,252)	1,185,800	Toyama
17 Ishikawa	1,620 (4,196)	1,198,800	Kanazawa
18 Fukui	1,617 (4,189)	855,400	Fukui
19 Gifu	4,091 (10,596)	2,100,600	Gifu
20 Nagano	5,245 (13,585)	2,236,700	Nagano
21 Yamanashi	1,724 (4,464)	858,600	Kofu
22 Shizuoka	3,001 (7,773)	3,693,600	Shizuoka
23 Aichi	1,980 (5,127)	6,670,000	Nagoya
KANSAI			
24 Mie	2,230 (5,776)	1,808,000	Tsu
25 Shiga	1,551 (4,016)	1,148,000	Otsu
26 Kyoto[4]	1,781 (4,613)	2,716,200	Kyoto
27 Hyogo	3,232 (8,372)	5,550,100	Kobe
28 Osaka[4]	719 (1,863)	9,166,000	Osaka
29 Nara	1,425 (3,692)	1,285,200	Nara
30 Wakayama	1,824 (4,723)	1,177,200	Wakayama
CHUGOKU			
31 Tottori	1,348 (3,492)	646,900	Tottori
32 Okayama	2,736 (7,086)	2,014,200	Okayama
33 Hiroshima	3,268 (8,463)	2,940,800	Hiroshima
34 Shimane	2,559 (6,627)	844,600	Matsue
35 Yamaguchi	2,355 (6,100)	1,715,000	Yamaguchi
SHIKOKU			
36 Kagawa	726 (1,880)	1,074,600	Takamatsu
37 Tokushima	1,600 (4,145)	886,700	Tokushima
38 Kochi	2,744 (7,107)	894,200	Kochi
39 Ehime	2,188 (5,667)	1,619,900	Matsuyama
KYUSHU			
40 Fukuoka	1,912 (4.953)	4,834,100	Fukuoka
41 Oita	2,445 (6,332)	1,321,900	Oita
42 Miyazaki	2,986 (7,734)	1,232,300	Miyazaki
43 Kumamoto	2,861 (7,410)	1,918,100	Kumamoto
44 Saga	939 (2,432)	927,700	Saga
45 Nagasaki	1,585 (4,106)	1,719,400	Nagasaki
46 Kagoshima	3,538 (9,163)	1,911,600	Kagoshima
47 Okinawa	869 (2,250)	1,183,700	Naha
Japan	145,823 (377,682[5])	125,369,500	Tokyo

[1] Projection for 1982–83.

[2] Including the Southern Kuriles (Kunashiri, Etorofu, Shikotan, Habomai and associated smaller islands), occupied by the Soviet Union since the end of the Second World War, which are claimed by Japan.

[3] Included within the administrative area (*to*) of Tokyo are the Bonin or Ogasawara Islands, far to the S in the Pacific, and Marcus Island (Miniami Torishima).

[4] Special status as city prefecture (*fu*).

[5] Differs slightly from total of figures for prefectures as a result of rounding of these figures.

Japan is a land of contrasts. After deliberately isolating itself from the outside world until the latter half of the 19th century, then seeking to establish relations with other countries, particularly in Europe, and finally developing into one of the world's great economic powers, it is now the most "Western" State in the Far East and at the same time the State in the Western World (taken in its widest sense) which is most intimately imbued with the mentality of Eastern Asia.

On the one hand, as a result of its rapid industrialization and the dominating position thus achieved by its economy, Japan appears to have taken on thoroughly European and American characteristics; but on the other these influences have been confined to externals, and behind the Westernized façade Japan's conception of itself, established by centuries of tradition, survives unchanged. It is precisely this mingling of different elements that makes the "Land of the Rising Sun" such a fascinating country to visit.

The visitor to Japan should not be too hasty in reaching conclusions about Japan, if only because of the difficulties posed by the language and script and by the totally different mental attitudes of the Japanese. They are a sensitive people, and emotions play a greater part in their make-up than soberly rational reflection and action.

The Meiji constitution of 1889 was superseded on May 3, 1947 by the present constitution (Nihon Koku Kempo; promulgated November .3, 1946), which provided the basis for the development of a democratic society in Japan (**Nippon** or **Nihon**, "land of the sun's origin"). Under this constitution the **Emperor** (*Tenno*; since 1926 Hirohito, b.1901), previously the titular head of the Empire, became merely a symbol of the state and of the unity of the nation, performing purely representational functions within the framework of a parliamentary and democratic monarchy: the sovereign authority is now the Japanese people. Other important principles enshrined in the constitution are the separation of legislative, executive and judicial powers, the guarantee of human rights and the renunciation of war except in self-defense.

The highest organ of the state is the **Parliament** or **Diet** (*Kokkai*), which is elected by universal suffrage and secret ballot. It consists of two houses – the *Lower House* (*Shugi-in*; 511 members elected for a four-year term), in which legislative power is vested, and the *Upper House* (*Sangi-in*; 252 members elected for a six-year term), a deliberative body. The Prime Minister is elected by Parliament and appoints the members of his Cabinet, which exercises executive power. The Cabinet is responsible to Parliament, not to the Emperor, and can be compelled to resign by a vote of no confidence. – The electorate consists of men and women over 20. There is no compulsory military service in Japan.

All political *parties* were dissolved during the Second World War but were again permitted after 1945. In 1955 the two largest parties, the Liberals and the Democrats, combined to form the conservatively oriented Liberal Democratic Party (Jiyu Minshuto commonly known as Jiminto), which is at present in power and enjoys a majority in both Houses of Parliament. There are a number of opposition parties – the Socialist Party (Shakaito), the right-wing party Komeito and the moderate Democratic Socialist Party (Minshu Shakaito). The next largest parties in Parliament are the Communist Party (Nihon Kyosanto) and the New Liberal Club (Shin-Jiya Korubu), followed by a few independents and various splinter groups of both the right and the left. Outside the party system there are a variety of nationalist bodies whose aim is the establishment of an authoritarian and anti-Western system of government.

Japan is a unified and centralised State divided for local government purposes into 47 **prefectures** – 43 rural prefectures (*ken*), roughly equivalent to counties, the two city prefectures (*fu*) of Kyoto and Osaka, the national capital (*to*) of Tokyo and the island territory (*do*) of Hokkaido. The prefectures in turn are divided into towns (*shi*), small towns (*cho*) and rural districts (*son*). Each prefecture is headed by a directly elected prefect, who puts forward the interests of his prefecture to the central government.

Japan is a member of the United Nations, the Organization for Economic Cooperation and Development (OECD), the General Agreement on Tariffs and Trade (GATT), the Food and Agriculture Organization (FAO) and numerous other international organizations and institutions.

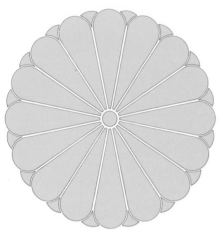

The imperial emblem

The national flag

Geography

The territory of Japan consists of a group of islands off the east coast of the Eurasian land mass extending in an arc from north-east to south-west for a distance of 1735 miles/2790 km between latitude 45° 33′ and 20° 25′ N and longitude 123° and 149° (claimed) E. The maximum breadth of the group is 250 miles/400 km, the average 145 miles/230 km. The main islands, accounting for 97% of the total area, are **Hokkaido** (30,077 sq. miles/ 77,900 sq. km) in the north, **Honshu** (89,124 sq. miles/230,832 sq. km), *Shikoku* (7258 sq. miles/18,799 sq. km) and *Kyushu* (17,135 sq. miles/44,380 sq. km), lying opposite the Korean peninsula. The rest of Japan's land area, totaling 145,823 sq. miles/377,682 sq. km, is made up of 3918 smaller islands, islets and rocks, some of them very small indeed and largely uninhabited.

Broken up in this way, the territory of Japan has an extraordinarily long coast-line (18,450 miles/29,700 km) and an intimate interrelationship with the surrounding sea. Off the north-east coast of Hokkaido is the Sea of Okhotsk, extending between the Soviet island of Sakhalin and the *Kurile chain* (USSR; southern part claimed by Japan); between Honshu and the mainland of Asia (USSR, China, Korea) is the *Sea of Japan*; the islands of Kyushu and Shikoku are separated from Honshu by the *Inland Sea*; and to the east and south is the great expanse of the **Pacific Ocean**, into which extend two chains of small islets – the *Southerly Islands* to the south of Tokyo and the

Ryukyu Islands (South-west Islands) south-west of Kyushu, with the island of Okinawa which was occupied by the United States until May 15, 1972. This last arc of islands reaches south-westwards almost to the island of Taiwan (Formosa), separating the *East China Sea* from the Pacific.

The Japanese islands are the summit areas of a much-folded range of submarine mountains which rises steeply out of the Pacific from the Japan Trench (27,600 ft/8412 m below sea-level) and the Bonin Trench (33,926 ft/10,340 m below sea-level) to heights of over 9800 ft/3000 m above sea-level and is separated from the mainland of Asia by the 9800 ft/3000 m deep trough of the Sea of Japan. The northern part of the arc, opposite the island of Sakhalin, is traversed by the Fossa Magna, which with its numerous volcanoes sets the topographical pattern of central Japan. The chain of islands was originally joined to the mainland but was detached in the Lower Miocene (Aquitanian stage) by the

The Inland Sea

gradual sinking of the Sea of Japan. Japan's close link with the mainland, which has influenced its development in many ways, is still very evident: Hokkaido is only 28 miles from Sakhalin, and it is only 125 miles from Kyushu to the Korean peninsula.

Mountains (Japanese *-yama, -sen, -san, -zan, -dake, -take, -mine*). – Japan is a country of markedly mountainous character, with some 70% of its total area covered by well-wooded massifs. Some 7% of its area ranks as totally inaccessible. Although there are a number of extensive lowland areas only some 16% of Japan's total area is permanently cultivable; 11% consists of pastureland and grazing; and human settlement is effectively confined to some 3% of the total area.

Fujiyama and Lake Ashi

The highest and steepest peaks are to be found in central Honshu, across which runs the rift valley of the Fossa Magna. Hokkaido, less affected by movements of the earth's crust, has gentler slopes and rounded heights.

Japan's Highest Mountains	
Fujiyama (Fuji-san)	12,389 ft/3776 m
Shirane	10,473 ft/3192 m
Hotaka-dake	10,466 ft/3190 m
Yari-ga-take	10,434 ft/3180 m
On-take	10,050 ft/3063 m
Norikura-dake	9928 ft/3026 m
Tate-yama	9892 ft/3015 m
Asama-yama	8340 ft/2542 m
Myoko-san	8025 ft/2446 m
Daisetsu-zan	7513 ft/2290 m
Zao-zan	6040 ft/1841 m
Dai-sen	5614 ft/1711 m
Aso-san	5223 ft/1592 m

Japan lies within the *circum-Pacific earthquake belt,* and as a relatively young land formation shows continuing activity. Of Japan's 265 **volcanoes** 36 are still regarded as active, although only 20 are recorded as having erupted since 1900. New volcanic formations can also be observed, such as the Showa-Shinzan volcano on Hokkaido, which came into being in 1944–45. The finest and best-known Japanese volcano is Mount *Fuji*, which last erupted in 1707 and is now dormant. Particularly active volcanoes are Asama (central Honshu), Aso (central Kyushu), Sakurajima (southern Kyushu) and

Mihara (Oshima). Notable for their beauty are Fuji with its classical conical form (which has lent its name to many conical volcanoes in other parts of Japan, such as Satsuma-Fuji) and Aso, which ranks as the largest volcano in the world, with beautiful expanses of plain and whole villages enclosed within its crater. The highland areas of Japan are regions of dense forest, crater lakes and countless hot springs (*onsen*), round which many attractive health resorts have grown up.

Plains (*heiya*), **basins** (*bonchi*) and **plateaus** (*daichi*). – Japan's great ranges of mountains leave little room for lowland areas such as the Kanto and Nobi plains on Honshu, the Tsukushi plain on Kyushu and the Ishikari and Konsen plains on Hokkaido, and there is usually only a narrow strip of low-lying ground between the foothills of the central uplands and the sea. In the lower courses of the rivers there are fertile plains which offer scope for agriculture (rice), including the Kanto Plain in central Honshu (River Tone), the Niigata Plain, also in central Honshu (rivers Shinano and Agano), the Nobi Plain near Nagoya, which is watered by

Rapids on the River Kiso

the Kiso, the "Japan Rhine", the Ishikari Plain in Hokkaido (River Ishikari) and the Sendai Plain in northern Honshu (River Kitakami).

The largest basins in Japan are the Yamagata Basin and Yokote Basin in northern Honshu, the Kofu Basin in central Honshu and the Kyoto Basin, each based on the town after which it is named.

In the upland regions which cover so much of Japan there are many plateau regions which are among the most popular holiday areas in the country from early summer to the fall (autumn).

Rivers (*-kawa, -gawa*). – Given the narrowness of the Japanese islands (average width 145 miles/230 km) and the mountainous character of the country, the rivers are relatively short and steeply graded. As a result of the steep gradients, massive deposits of detritus and seasonal variations in volume (snow meltwater in spring, typhoons in the fall (autumn)) considerable stretches of the rivers, particularly those flowing down from the central mountains of Honshu (the "Japanese Alps"), are unsuitable for navigation.

Kurobe Gorge in the Japanese Alps

Lakes (*-ko, -numa, -ike*). – Most of the Japanese lakes – mainly lying within National Parks – were formed as a result of volcanic activity, and many of them are of outstanding beauty. Lakes Inawashiro (northern Honshu) and Chuzenji (Nikko) and the five Fuji Lakes, like many others, were formed as a result of the damming of a river by lava flows. Thanks to their situation in the mountains most of the lakes – often notable for the unusual intensity of their coloring – have remained almost intact and unspoiled, such as Lakes Mashu (claimed to be the world's clearest lake), Akan and Shikotsu, all on Hokkaido.

Japan's Longest Rivers	
Shinano-gawa	228 miles/367 km
Tone-gawa	200 miles/322 km
Ishikari-gawa	163 miles/262 km
Teshio-gawa	162 miles/261 km
Tenryu-gawa	155 miles/250 km
Kitakami-gawa	155 miles/249 km
Abukuma-gawa	149 miles/239 km
Mogami-gawa	142 miles/229 km
Agano-gawa	130 miles/210 km

The rivers do, however, offer visitors the opportunity of exciting boat trips through long stretches of rapids and magnificent gorges flanked by dense forests and bizarrely shaped rock formations. The best-known rapids are those on the rivers Kiso (Nagoya), Hozu (Kyoto), Tenryu (Shizuoka prefecture) and Kuma (Kumamoto prefecture); among the finest gorges (*kyo*) are the Kurobe-kyo and Tenryu-kyo in central Honshu, the Soun-kyo on Hokkaido and the Takachiho-kyo on Kyushu. Of the three longest rivers, the Shinano and Tone in central Honshu and the Ishikari on Hokkaido, it is the Ishikari that forms the largest plain.

Japan's Largest Lakes	
Biwa-ko	260 sq. miles/673·8 sq. km
Kasumi-ga-ura	65 sq. miles/167·7 sq. km
Saroma-ko	59 sq. miles/151·7 sq. km
Inawashiro-ko	40 sq. miles/103·9 sq. km
Naka-no-umi	38 sq. miles/98.5 sq. km
Shinji-ko	31 sq. miles/79·7 sq. km
Kutcharo-ko	31 sq. miles/79·5 sq. km
Toya-ko	27 sq. miles/69·4 sq. km
Hamana-ko	27 sq. miles/68·9 sq. km
Towada-ko	23 sq. miles/59·8 sq. km
Hachiro-gata	19 sq. miles/48·1 sq. km
Suwa-ko	5 sq. miles/14·1 sq. km

Among the finest of the lakes, notable both for their scenic beauty and their abundance of very tasty fish, are the northern crater lakes of Tazawa (Japan's deepest lake, 1395 ft/425 m) and Towada, the naturally dammed lakes

Lake Towada

Islands west of Kyushu and the Ryukyu Islands in the extreme south-west and the islands in Matsushima Bay (Honshu) reckoned to be among the most beautiful scenery in Japan.

Most of these islands have beautiful beaches of white sand, alternating here and there with rugged rock formations and sheer cliffs. In the Inland Sea (Setonaikai), the narrow arm of the sea between Honshu, Shikoku and Kyushu there are about a thousand islands and islets with attractive beaches; and there are many such beaches on the main islands themselves. Some of the finest stretches of coast on the main Japanese islands, with beautiful crescent-shaped beaches and bizarrely contorted rias, are to be found around Sanriku (Iwate prefecture), Kumano (Kii Peninsula) Capes Muroto and Ashizuri (Shikoku) and the Shima Peninsula (Mie prefecture). In contrast to these are the extensive white beaches of Uchiura Bay (Hokkaido), Kujukarihama (Chiba prefecture), Miho-no-Matsubara (Shizuoka prefecture), Nijo-no-Matsubara (Saga prefecture) and many more.

already mentioned, Lake Ashi in the beautiful Hakone region near Tokyo and Lake Biwa near Kyoto, the largest of the Japanese.

Coastal regions. – Around the four main islands or in island chains reaching out for hundreds of miles into the Pacific are innumerable lesser islands, some of them large enough to accommodate several towns, others no more than a few rocks covered with trees. Among the largest of these other islands are Sado in the Sea of Japan, Awaji and Shodojima in the Inland Sea, the Tsushima Islands between southern Japan and Korea, Tanegashima, Yakushima and Okinawa, as well as such enchanting archipelagos as the Goto

There are also very beautiful stretches of coast on the peninsulas of Oga (Akita prefecture), Noto (Ishikawa prefecture) and Sotomo (Fukui prefecture) – all on the west coast of Honshu (Sea of Japan) – the Oki Islands (Daisen-Oki National Park, Sea of Japan) and the Kujukushima Islands (Saikai National Park, Kyushu).

Climate

The climate of Japan is determined by its situation off the east coast of the world's largest continent (Asia) and on the edge of its largest ocean (the Pacific). In the regular alternation of the seasons it is subject in winter to cold continental air masses coming from the north and west, in summer to maritime and tropical influences from the south (the monsoon climate of Eastern Asia). Japan thus has colder summers and milder winters than would normally be expected in the latitude in which it lies.

The **climatic variation** within the territory of Japan results from its great length from north to south (extending from 20° to almost 46° of northern latitude) and the long mountain ranges extending along its longitudinal axis, dividing the country into Ura-Nihon (Rearward Japan), facing the Sea of Japan and the mainland of Asia, and Omote-Nihon (Frontal Japan) on the Pacific.

Japan has four clearly differentiated seasons comparable to those of Europe and North America, with very settled weather conditions during the summer and winter months and more changeable weather during the transitional seasons of spring and fall (autumn).

Winter begins at almost the same time all over Japan, about the middle of December, when cold Siberian air masses move down from the north-west. The duration and intensity of the winter decline from north to south. In northern Japan (Hokkaido) winter brings severe cold, while in the south-west (Okinawa) temperatures remain above freezing-point throughout the year.

From mid February temperatures begin to rise all over the country. In southern Kyushu and Shikoku spring begins in March with the *plum blossom*, while on Hokkaido and the west side of the country (Ura-Nihon) the weather is still cold and changeable. By the end of April the cherry blossom has reached northern Honshu. May is pleasantly warm, with temperatures comparable with those of a European summer.

At the end of May begins the *summer rainy season* associated with the front of maritime and tropical air masses which now drives back the polar air masses to the north and west. Accordingly the rain begins earlier in the south, lasts longer and is more abundant (Okinawa, second half of May; southern Kyushu, first half of June; Tokyo, ten days later; Hokkaido, July). During this period it is oppressively sultry, there is almost a total absence of wind, the sky is overcast, air humidity is high and the rain is fine and penetrating; leather, paper, etc., tend to be affected by mildew.

About the middle of July the rain stops and stable tropical air masses prevail over the whole of Japan. The weather is predominantly fine and warm, only occasionally interrupted by thunderstorms and typhoon rain (in the south in July). It is now warm in the north as well, so that even on Hokkaido rice can be grown. – The second half of July and the month of August can often be oppressively hot: these are the *dog days,* with high temperatures (maximum about 95°F/35°C) and relatively high air humidity, when everyone who can makes for the cooler summer resorts and spas in the upland regions.

Summer comes to an end in mid September, when cooler air masses from the mainland of Asia drive the maritime-tropical air masses south again. Along the front between the two there is wind and rain, bringing the *typhoon rainy season.*

From July to the middle of September is the period when the **typhoons** which approach Okinawa from the south-east and then turn north-east are most likely to pass over Japan. Most of the 30 or so typhoons which arise in the north-west Pacific every year, however, do not directly affect Japan. When a typhoon does come it brings with it some 12 in./300 mm of rainfall in south-western Japan, 6 in./150 mm in central Japan and still less than this farther north – representing in each case a substantial proportion of total annual rainfall. Storm tides, breaches in dikes and flooding caused by typhoons are very real dangers in low-lying and densely populated areas (including part of Tokyo), which in the past have cost thousands of lives and much destruction of property.

October brings the fall weather which is frequently clear, vivid *autumn colors* and occasional night frosts. The first snow falls in the highlands of central Japan. In mid December comes winter.

The duration of daylight season by season – a matter of concern for photographers – is approximately the same as in the Mediterranean regions of Europe.

In the *far north* of Japan the sun rises in winter between 7 and 7.30 and sets between 4.30 and 5. The longest day in summer lasts from 4.15 a.m. to 7.45 p.m., with a good half-hour of half-light or twilight at each end of the day.

In *Tokyo* the day is half an hour longer at each end in winter, and half an hour shorter in summer.

On *Okinawa* – just north of the Tropic of Cancer – the differences between the seasons are still smaller. In December the day lasts from shortly before 7 to shortly before 5.30, in June from shortly before 5 to shortly before 7 p.m., in each case with a bare half-hour of half-light in the morning and twilight in the evening. In summer the sun is almost at the zenith at noon.

The climatic characteristics of different parts of Japan are shown in the **climatic diagrams** on pp. 16–17,

which give month-by-month figures for temperature and precipitation recorded at selected weather stations.

The blue columns show the precipitation (rainfall and snow) in inches, in accordance with the scale in the right-hand margin. The orange band shows the temperature in °F, the upper edge giving the average maximum day temperature, the lower edge the average minimum night temperature, in accordance with the orange scale in the margin.

By way of comparison the corresponding figures for Kassel in north-western Germany (latitude 51°N) are shown by broken lines in the diagram for Tokyo. This may help visitors from similar latitudes to put the climatic differences in perspective and to adjust to them (e.g. in deciding what to wear).

Omote-Nihon (Japan east of the central highlands)
Tokyo weather station

Tokyo weather station is taken as representative of the Kanto plain, the centre of Omote-Nihon, with its concentration of population in a series of great cities and the most popular tourist areas in Japan.

The beginning of winter in December is marked by a simultaneous fall in temperature and reduction in precipitation. The cold continental air masses coming from the north-west, after taking up moisture while passing over the Sea of Japan, have discharged it over Ura-Nihon (to the west of the central highlands) in the form of snow; while in Omote-Nihon, on the lee side of the mountains, the weather is windy and cool but sunny. The duration of sunshine in December (170 hours) is greater than in June (150 hours); the minimum is in September and October (136 hours). – In particularly warm and sheltered areas on the Pacific coast it is even possible to grow flowers and vegetables in winter, especially with the additional protection provided by plastic sheeting supported on arches of bamboo.

In spring both temperature and precipitation rises again. During this transitional season temperatures fluctuate considerably over the day and from day to day, and there are recurring night frosts. The advance of tropical air masses from the south, combined with predominantly south winds, brings the early summer rainy season (*bai-u*) in June, with hot and sultry weather. The height of summer is tropically hot, interrupted by occasional days with rain; after which comes the fall (autumn), with a second rainy period (*shu-u*).

Comparison with European figures shows that daily temperature fluctuations in Tokyo are almost twice as great as in Europe and that annual fluctuations are also greater. Thus a European visitor going to Tokyo in April for the cherry-blossom season will encounter minimum night temperatures comparable with those of Europe but day maximum temperatures fully 18°F/10°C higher than in Europe.

Ura-Nihon (Japan west of the central highlands)
Niigata weather station

Niigata weather station is taken as representative of this region, in which winters with an abundance of snow alternate with tropically hot summers. The pattern of weather over the year is almost exactly contrary to that of Omote-Nihon. Along the 750 mile/1 200 km

Climate in Japan

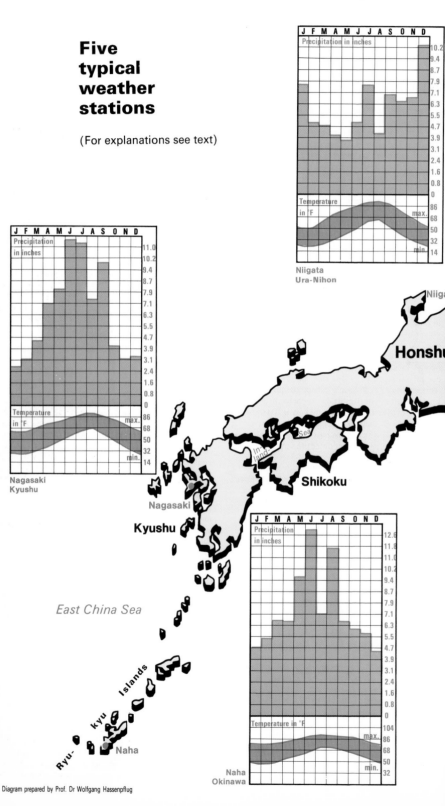

Sea of Japan

Five typical weather stations

(For explanations see text)

Niigata
Ura-Nihon

Nagasaki
Kyushu

Honshu

Shikoku

Nagasaki

Kyushu

East China Sea

Ryu-kyu Islands

Naha

Naha
Okinawa

Diagram prepared by Prof. Dr Wolfgang Hassenpflug

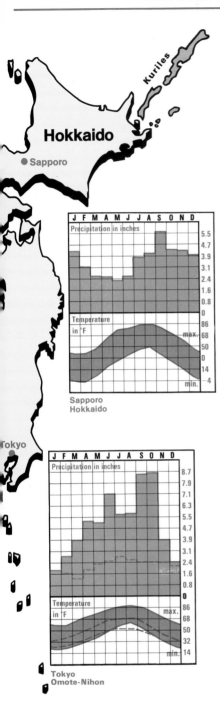

Hokkaido

● Sapporo

Sapporo
Hokkaido

Tokyo

Tokyo
Omote-Nihon

Pacific

Ocean

coastline of this climatic province there is a steady transition from the relatively mild winters of the south-west to the longer and severer cold in the north.

Winter begins in mid December, when the air masses from Siberia, originally dry and cold, move out over the Sea of Japan and take up moisture, which is then discharged on the coastal regions and the slopes of the mountains in the form of heavy snowfall. The sky is dark and overcast, and there is snow almost every day. December and January have only 60–70 hours of sunshine; the maximum is reached in August, with 254 hours.

The massive winter snowfalls make it necessary for buildings to have extra strong roofs and frequently bring all traffic to a standstill. It is only within recent years that the snow has been seen to have counter-vailing advantages as the basis for an increasing development of winter sports and a reserve of water for the summer, meeting the needs of industry and the large cities.

From the middle of February the temperatures begin to rise again and the precipitation falls off. The wind blows more strongly from the south, sometimes driving over the central highlands like a warm dry föhn wind, bringing higher temperatures and drought, with the danger of forest fires.

After a sunny spring and early summer the rainy period in July brings higher precipitation. The highest tem-peratures – of tropical heat – and the longest periods of sunshine are reached in August, and after this comes the autumn cooling-off, followed in mid December by the onset of winter.

Hokkaido
Sapporo weather station

In the climate of Hokkaido the proximity of Siberia makes itself felt. Lying so far north, this is the coldest part of Japan. The contrast with the more southerly islands of Japan is most marked in winter, when even the maximum day temperature frequently remains below freezing-point. In the mountainous areas the cold is even more severe than on the coast. While the west coast of Hokkaido is warmed by the Tsushima Current, the east coast is made colder still by the cold Oyashio Current.

As in Ura-Nihon, temperatures rise and precipitation decreases in spring, beginning to rise again only in July and reaching their maximum in September. Thus in this region the summer is not enclosed, as it is farther south, between the two rainy seasons, *bai-u* and *shu-u*. Although it brings hot days, with maximum temperatures above 86 °F/30 °C, the tem-perature falls sharply at night to below 50 °F/10 °C. – As the fall (autumn) comes on there is a rapid drop in temperature, and the first frosts occur in October, presaging the coming of winter.

Kyushu
Nagasaki weather station

Nagasaki weather station is representative of western Kyushu. Like the rest of the island, it has a warm climate with a good deal of rain, but experiences a sharp fall in temperature, with frost and snow, in win-ter, when cold air comes in from the north-west. The southern part of the island, around Kagoshima, is least affected by these intrusions of cold air and is also warmed by the Kuroshio current. – From the middle of February there is a distinct rise in temperature; the first intimations of spring come with the plum blossom; and spring itself arrives at the end of March when the cherry trees come into blossom.

June and July are the months of highest rainfall. At the height of summmer, in August, the weather is hot and sometimes sultry, with brief cooler periods during the passage of extra-tropical and tropical depressions (typhoons).

On average between 12 and 14 typhoons hit the island a year. The likeliest time is the beginning of September, when the autumn rains also come, bringing about a second rainy period. – During the fall temperatures drop and rainfall declines, with pleasantly warm days continuing into November but with nights which are already cool.

Okinawa
Naha weather station

The climate of Okinawa is almost tropical, with high temperatures and rainfall throughout the year. Minimum temperatures in winter are well above freezing-point; and in general, thanks to Okinawa's oceanic situation, temperatures over the year are fairly even.

In April the wind veers from north to south, and in May rainfall begins to increase considerably. Passing typhoons, particularly in September, also bring high rainfall. Sunshine is at its maximum in July (279 hours) and at its minimum in the winter months with less than 120 hours (cf. Tokyo).

Plant and Animal Life

As a result of its great length from north to south, extending over 25 degrees of latitude and several climatic zones, its rainy oceanic climate and its varied pattern of mountainous and upland regions Japan has an unusually wide range of plant and animal life. The original vegetation pattern has, of course, been much changed by the busy farming and other activities of man, so that the endemic plants and trees of Japan are now to be found only in remote and inaccessible areas or on marginal land of no use for cultivation.

The **vegetation** is strongly differentiated according to climatic zone. Particularly striking is what has been called the "three-dimensional" stratification of vegetation zones according to latitude and altitude, with vegetation specific to warmer regions growing in the lowland areas and that of colder regions growing at higher altitudes. Thus in the "Japan Alps" in northern Honshu all the various vegetation zones represented in Japan, from the subtropical to the sub-Arctic, are found superimposed at their various levels of altitude.

Some two-thirds of the total land area of Japan is covered with forest. In the coastal regions the commonest type is the evergreen deciduous forest of the temperate zone, with laurels (*Calophyllum inophyllum,* Japanese *teriha-boku*), various species of oak (*Quercus, kashi*), golden chestnuts (*Castanopsis, shii*) and camellias (*Camellia japonica*), in-creasingly interspersed towards the south with palms, tree ferns, camphor trees (*Cinnamomum camphora, kusunoki; Cinnamomum japonicum, yabunikkei*) and in river basins with bamboo groves (on Honshu and Shikoku, in parts of Kyushu, etc.). On the southern Ryukyu Islands, as far south as Okinawa, evergreen *Castanopsis* forest predominates. The coasts are fringed by mangrove swamps (*Bruguiera coniugata* and *Kandella Candel, hirugi*) and, farther inland, thickets of pandanus (*Pandanus tectorius, adan*), wild figs (*Ficus retusa, gajumaru*) and fern palms (*Cycas revoluta, sotetsu*).

In the transitional climatic zones of northern Honshu, between the warm temperate and the subtropical regions, deciduous and mixed forests predominate. These continue towards the south at ever higher levels, and are found even on Kyushu at altitudes of 3300–4900 ft/1000–1500 m. They consist mainly of oaks, golden chestnuts and pines (*Pinus, matsu*), undemanding trees which are found all over the country in every climatic zone. In the forests of the temperate zone the Japanese red cedar (*Cryptomeria japonica, sugi*), the country's principal source of timber, is over-abundantly represented as a result of deliberate afforestation. Other common species are the maple (*Bischofia javanica, akagi*) with its marvellous coloring, the Japanese cypress (*Chamaecyparis obtusa, hinoki*), the birch, the beech and the paulownia (*Hermandia ovigera, giri*). In the north, on Hokkaido, the forests consist of sub-arctic conifers, in particular the mountain pine (*Pinus pumila, haimatsu*).

Rape-field in flower

In central Honshu above 8200 ft/2500 m dense forests of dwarf pines alternate with rich Alpine vegetation, but there are no Alpine meadows similar to those found in Europe. Towards the north the limit of vegetation falls, and on Hokkaido is as low as 4900 ft/1500 m.

About half the other plants found in Japan, whether wild or cultivated, are believed to have been introduced from the mainland of Asia, even though they are frequently described as "Japanese", *japonica* or *nipponica* (e.g. Japanese almonds, quinces, cherries, etc.).

The **animal life** of Japan, like its vegetation, shows a wide range of species, varying according to region and altitude, the development of which has been promoted by the variety of habitats, the immense expanses of forest and the meeting of warm and cold marine currents. Another factor of major importance in producing Japan's variety of species was the fact that the country was comparatively little affected by the Ice Ages, so that some very ancient species were able to survive. The finds of ancient animal bones showing similarities to those found on the mainland of Asia have also provided evidence of Japan's former attachment to the mainland.

Lines of separation between the habitats of particular species and genera were identified by two zoologists, Watase and Blakiston. The "Watase Line", running between the islands of Yakushima and Amami-Oshima, to the south of Kyushu (lat. 30° N), marks the boundary between the animal life of Japan and that of the tropical islands of the southern Pacific; notable among the animals living to the south of this line are the Ryukyu rabbit (a protected species) and the spiny mouse of Amami. The northern boundary for certain species is the "Blakiston Line", in the Tsugaru Strait between Honshu and Hokkaido. The animal life of Hokkaido, which shows affinities with that of Siberia, includes black bears, red deer, sables, ground squirrels, various species of mice and hares and a number of northern species of birds (the Kamchatka raven, Blakiston's eagle owl, etc.).

The animals living between these two lines of division are mainly species related to the fauna of north-eastern China, whose ancestors reached Japan by way of the old land bridge linking it with the mainland of Asia. They include the fox, the Japanese monkey, the chamois, the wild pig, the collared bear, the dormouse and a variety of birds, among them the Japanese green woodpecker, the green game pheasant, the ring-necked pheasant and the thrush. Among statutorily protected species are the East Asian ibis, now found only in small numbers on the island of Sado; the black-billed stork, another rare species occasionally seen in Hyogo prefecture; and the giant salamander, a survival from the Tertiary era found in the mountain streams of western Honshu and northern Kyushu. The territory of various species of reptiles and insects (the latter including the popular cicada) is bounded on the north by the Blakiston Line.

The *marine life* of Japan is also of great variety and beauty, developing a particular abundance of forms and richness of color in southern Japanese waters, with their coral-fringed islands. Special mention may be made of the sea-snakes (Hydrophiidae), relatively small poisonous snakes found only in the warm water on the coasts of the Pacific and the Indian Ocean.

Population

The first census of the population of Japan was carried out by the Tokugawa Shogunate in 1721, and thereafter censuses were held at six-yearly intervals, making it possible to follow the development of population over a period of more than two and a half centuries. Until the middle of the 19th century the population remained fairly constant at a level of 25–27 million, reaching the 30 million mark only towards the end of the Tokugawa era. The industrialization of the country which began with the Meiji Restoration (1868) promoted a rapid increase to 60 million by 1920; and over the hundred years from 1875 to 1975 the population of Japan was multiplied more than threefold, from 35·3 million to 112 million. The increase is all the more striking in view of the fact that during this period there was no significant immigration into Japan from other countries. With its present population of some 125 million Japan is now the world's sixth most populous country. The population is expected to continue increasing during the 1980s by about a million a year, though with a gradual reduction in the rate of increase. Projections by the Japanese Ministry of Health put the population at 135 million in the year 2000 and 145 million by 2050.

Estimates for the year 1981 put the *population density* of Japan at 818 inhabitants to the sq. mile (312 to the sq. kilometre). This is of course a statistical average which conceals very wide variations in different parts of the country. While in the upland regions only the valleys are populated and under cultivation, the great mass of the population of Japan is crowded together in the industrial concentrations in the few plains and basins. Hokkaido, with only 171 inhabitants to the sq. mile (66 to the sq. kilometre), was the most thinly populated region, giving rise to considerable problems in the provision of social services. In the plain areas the density was about 3100 to the sq. mile (1200 to the sq. kilometre); in Tokyo it is now as high as 15,000 to the sq. mile (5800 to the sq. kilometre). – This imbalance has been aggravated by the *flight from the land* and the movement of country people into the towns, attracted by the much higher wages to be earned there. The urban population of Japan rose from 38% of the total in 1940 to 68% in 1975, and more than 80% of all Japanese now live in towns – some 20% in cities of over half a million inhabitants. It must be added, however, that on the outskirts of the towns, where small landholders combine farming with other occupations, the rural way of life has largely been preserved.

While the *birth rate* was as high as 32·4 per 1000 in 1930, and in the post-war "baby boom" reached a peak of 34·3 per 1000 in 1947, it fell rapidly thereafter to the level normal in highly industrialized countries; the figure for 1981 was 17·1 per 1000. The trend nowadays is clearly towards the two-child family. – The *expectation of life*, in 1935 only 47 years for men and 50 years for women, has risen rapidly to 72·2 years for men and 77·9 years for women in 1974. The *death rate,* which before the war was still about 17–18 per 1000, has been brought down to 6·3 per 1000 in 1981 thanks to an excellent system of medical care. – Falling death rates and increased life expectancy have brought about a radical change in the age structure of the population. The proportion of children (0–14 years) fell from 36·5% in 1920 to 24% in 1975, while the population of working age (15–64) rose from 58% to 68% and the proportion of old people (65 and over) from 5·3% to 7·9%.

Of the total population of Japan 99·5% are **Japanese**; the others are predominantly Asian minorities who do not stand out from the rest of the population. – On Hokkaido there are an estimated 15,000 *Ainu,* now fully assimilated. Probably descended from the original inhabitants of the Japanese islands, they show physical characteristics which are rather Caucasian than Asian (tall stature, light skin, considerable growth of beard). Until the beginning of the 19th c. they constituted a majority of the population of northern Japan, gaining their subsistence by hunting and fishing. Only a few thousand of them still maintain their ancient way of life. – Other minorities include some 650,000 Koreans and 48,000 Chinese, together with rather more than 20,000 Americans, Europeans and incomers from South-East Asia in the large conurbations.

Although the 1947 constitution laid down that men and women have equal rights the traditional view that women's role is to concern herself with the home and the family remains deeply entrenched. For the most part married women go out to work only after their children have grown up and, lacking any specialized training, are confined mainly to subaltern and poorly paid employment. While the wife devotes herself to her domestic duties her husband's life is bound up with his job, which encroaches even on his leisure time. Marriage as a relationship between equal partners, regular in the West, is still the exception in Japan.

The Japanese *educational system,* originally based on European models, was

In the Asakusa-Kannon Temple, Tokyo

In the Shinkansen "super-express"

replaced after the Second World War by the United States system. Education is compulsory between the ages of 6 and 15. Six years in the elementary school are followed by three years in the middle school; then come three years of high school (not compulsory), which lead to a qualification for university entrance. – Since the end of the war there has been a vast expansion of university education. The prestige attached to a university train-ing combined with the good job pros-pects for academically qualified special-ists in a rapidly expanding economy had led to an increase in the number of students from 10% of the annual age group in 1950 to 40% in 1977. In the latter year Japan had a total of 431 universities (310 of them privately run), 515 colleges (435 privately run) and 65 technical colleges (7 private).

History

PREHISTORY

Fossils of marine creatures found on the territory of Japan show that during the *Palaeozoic* era the islands lay under the sea; then, towards the end of the Palaeo-zoic, they were thrust upwards by violent volcanic activity. The simultaneous occurrence of fossils of early forms of the elephant and later of the hairy Arctic mammoth shows that at least during the *mesozoic* era Japan was connected with the mainland of Asia. The land bridge was probably across what is now the Korea Strait, and the island of Tsushima may be a relic of this phase. – Although large numbers of stone im-plements, mainly of agate, slate and obsidian, have been found, it is difficult because of the uncertainty of their dating to classify them as Palaeolithic. Material of the Neolithic period can more readily be fitted into the archaeological sequence.

Modern scholars (e.g. John W. Hall) put the begin-ning of the **pre-pottery phase** at about 150000 B.C – A find of axes and stone knives in the Kanto plain (Iwajuku, Gumma prefecture) can be fairly securely dated by the geological strata to before 8000 B.C. The form of the axes is similar to forms dated to compar-able periods on the southern Asian mainland, that of the knives to forms found in Siberia and northern China. This points to a mingling of the spheres of influence of northern and southern cultures in Japan at this period. There is still, however, no firm evidence of permanent settlement in the early pre-pottery phase.

Between about 7000 and about 250 B.C. the **Jomon culture** or **cord-impressed pottery culture** developed in Japan. Important finds of material belonging to this culture have been made in northern Honshu and the Kanto plain. The people who produced it, still at the hunting and food-gathering stage, lived in pit dwellings with tent-like roofs. In the Middle Jomon period houses without a central post were built, frequently being protected by moats. The dog is now found, no doubt playing its part in the hunting of food. Soon clay vessels of colossal size appear, and pottery hearths sometimes replace the earlier fire-pits. On the evidence of the weapons (wooden swords, bows, arrowheads) and imple-ments (fishing-hooks, harpoons, axes, hammers) this period can be considered a kind of belated neolithic – soon, however, overlaid by a Bronze Age culture.

From the Western point of view Japanese historical writing, particularly on the prehistoric and early periods, long suffered from the fact that the Japanese – partly out of reverence for their ancestors, partly from lack of interest – carried out hardly any archaeological investigation, preferring to regard mythological accounts as having historical value.

Since then, however, scholars from the United States, Britain, France and Germany, together with a new generation of Japanese archaeologists, have gathered much evidence on the earlier phases of human development in Japan, though the chronology still presents difficulties and contradictions. Unfortunately, too many of the excavation sites in the great built-up areas had to be covered over with concrete soon after their discovery.

There are also still difficulties over the dating of the dynasties of the early period and the transition to the medieval period. This is because the traditionally minded Japanese, out of respect for any written document and for the supposedly divine origin of the Imperial House, have tended to place implicit faith in early chronicles such as the "Wajin-den", "Kojiki", "Nihon-shoki", "Weilüeh" and "Sankuo". Unfortunately this attitude is sometimes still found in works by Western writers, although the various chronicles – most written by Japanese courtiers on the basis of Chinese annals – are almost all readily available, in whole or in part, in English translations with an extensive critical apparatus.

The unhistorical character of such traditions emerges very clearly from the table on p. 24 showing the comparative chronology of Japanese emperors before the introduction of Buddhism. A comparison of the dates given in the "Kojiki" and the "Nihon-shoki" with the corrected dates based on modern research speaks for itself. It should be added, too, that some reputable scholars consign all the early emperors down to and including Ojin to the realm of legend.

From about 250 B.C. to the 3rd c. A.D. the **Yayoi culture** reached the Japanese islands from the south. The potter's wheel and agricultural techniques (in particular irrigated rice culture) were introduced. Bronze objects of Japanese manufacture now begin to appear. But since tombs of the Middle Yayoi period in northern Kyushu have been found to contain bronze mirrors and weapons from China, which had already experienced the flowering of Han culture (202 B.C. to A.D. 220), it is improbable that the new techniques, developed at a considerably earlier period, were the result of an independent development in Japan. Moreover both Korean and Chinese chroniclers agree that about the period of the conquest of Korea by the Han dynasty there was a Japanese settlement at Mimana on the south coast of Korea.

Yayoi pottery, a thin reddish ware, shows less variety of form than the pottery of the Late Jomon period. The cord-impressed decoration now gives place to painted, incised or comb-impressed patterns. – Recently almost identical ware has been found near Seoul in South Korea (Karakuri, on the Han River); and linguistic study (e.g. by Susumo Ohno) of the terms for simple cultural techniques in Korean and Japanese confirms the theory of Korean influence.

The horses of the Yayoi period were of medium size, similar to those of the Korean Stone Age; the Jomon horses, of which only a few remains have been found, were smaller.

Among typical items found in tombs are imported bronze mirrors (later regarded in Japan as symbols of the solar disc and of divine origin), bronze weapons and reproductions of such weapons in stone, and bell-shaped ritual objects (*dotaku*), perhaps buried as votive offerings, which in the late phase have fine figural decoration. Burials are mostly in pottery jars and stone cists, but some dolmens are also found.

EARLY PERIOD

During the **Kofun period** (late 3rd–6th c. A.D.), the period of the large **burial mounds**, the population of Japan – much increased as a result of the introduction of new farming techniques – was organized in ever larger units or lordships, and finally united under the Yamato dynasty into a single large empire. The peaceful village communities presided over by a religious head were now transformed into petty kingdoms rigidly organized on a military basis, centered on a fortified town or equipped with powerful armed forces.

Kingdoms of this kind, such as the kingdom of Yamatai-koku under its legendary queen Himiko, are described in the Chinese chronicle "Wajin-den". Its account of the transition from a theocratic to a dynastic régime may well be near the truth, but the names and dates belong to the realm of fable rather than history. – The chronicles which were already being written in Japan at this time, using the Chinese characters as a phonetic script – in particular the "Kojiki" and the "Nihon-shoki", which in many respects are to be considered as literature rather than history – also throw some light on the period in their anecdotal accounts. In these chronicles the Empress Jingo (Jingu), whose regnal period is traditionally given as A.D. 201–269, features as a shamanist prophetess who after a successful campaign of conquest in Korea gives birth to the future Emperor Ojin. In fact the military and political relationships between Japan and Korea at that period were, if anything, the other way round: it is not until the second half of the 4th century that there is firm evidence for Japanese military expeditions in Korea. What seems to have happened here is that out of patriotic motives the Japanese chroniclers took an actual military enterprise of the Empress Saimei (mid 7th c.) and antedated it to the Kofun period, embroidering their account with details from the legendary kingdom of Queen Himiko which they took from Chinese chronicles. It is certain at any rate that soon after these legendary events – Ojin is frequently regarded as the founder of the Yamato dynasty – the unification of most of the Japanese islands was achieved.

The archaeological evidence for this period is provided by the famous **burial mounds** (*kofun*), which first appeared in the Kansai area in the late 3rd or early 4th century. It is highly probable that they were based on Korean models and were constructed on a larger scale by the Yamato rulers, who were able to assemble the necessary manpower, as a symbol of their royal power. The giants among these mounds were raised in the 5th century; among them were the tombs of the Emperors Nintoku and Richu, whose existence as historical figures seems reasonably probable. The later burial mounds date from the 6th and 7th centuries: i.e. they overlap the introduction of Buddhism.

Chronology of Japanese Emperors before the Introduction of Buddhism

Emperor	Traditional dates of reign	Duration of life (years) according to "Kojiki"	Duration of life (years) according to "Nihon-shoki"	Duration of reign (years) according to "Kojiki" or "Nihon-shoki"	Corrected period (approximate)
Jimmu	660–585 B.C.	137	127		Beginning of Christian era
Suizei	581–549	45	80		1st c. A.D.
Annei	548–511	49	57		1st c.
Itoku	510–477	45	77		1st c.
Kosho	475–393	93	113		1st c.
Koan	392–291	123		102	2nd c.
Korei	290–215	106		76	2nd c.
Kogen	214–158	57		57	2nd c.
Kaika	157–98	63		60	3rd c.
Sujin	97–30	168	120		219–249
Suinin	29 B.C.–A.D. 70	153	140		249–280
Keiko	A.D. 71–130	137	106		280–316
Seimu	131–190	95	107		316–343
Chuai	191–200	52	52		343–346
Jingo (Empress)	201–269	100	100	68	
Ojin	270–310	130	110		346–395
Nintoku	313–399	83		87	395–427
Richu	400–405	64	70		427–432
Hanzei	406–411	60		6	433–438
Ingyo	412–453	78		42	438–453
Anko	454–456	56		3	
Yuryaku	457–479	124		23	
Seinei	480–484			5	
Kenzo	485–487	38		3	
Ninken	488–498			11	
Buretsu	499–506			8	
Keitai	507–531	43	82		
Ankan	534–535		70		
Senkuwa	536–539		73		
Kimmei	540–571			32	

The *kofun* are constructed on varying ground-plans. Some are circular, others are rectangular; but the characteristic form is a circular mound with a rectangular or trapezoid appendage, producing a "keyhole" shape. Many of the mounds are surrounded by ditches or moats. The dead were laid in hollowed-out tree-trunks in the early period, later in stone sarcophagi of rounded form reminiscent of the original tree-trunks, and finally in cube- or house-shaped cists formed of stone slabs.

The grave-goods originally consisted of simple metal implements and arrowheads. The curious practice also developed of replacing iron, bronze or wooden objects by stone copies, the making of which must have been a more laborious process than the manufacture of the originals. The warlike period of the unification of the empire under the Yamato dynasty is reflected in the finds of arms and armor, shields and swords. – The commonest grave-goods, and from the point of view of the historian the most informative, are the pottery figures and sculptured objects known as *haniwa*, after which the whole period is often named by art historians. Simple and realistic in style, they include house models ranging from a peasant's store-house to a lord's reception hall, replicas of everyday objects, animals and many human figures dressed according to their trade or class. Together with the wall-paintings and incised or relief decoration on metal articles (particularly mirrors) which are occasionally found, the *haniwa* figures give an excellent picture of the everyday life of the period, which otherwise would be known only from the later legendary accounts.

Asuka and Hakuho periods (552–710). – *Buddhism* and *Confucianism* come to Japan, in the first place by way of Korea. They initiate a major spiritual and cultural development, but give rise to conflicts between secular and priestly interests.

538 and 552   The kingdom of Paeckche (Korea) sends Buddha statues and sutra manuscripts to Japan.

562   The Korean kingdom of Silla captures the Japanese base in Korea.

587   The introduction of **Buddhism** leads to conflicts between the *Mononobe* clan, who hold fast to the national religion of Shintoism, and the *Soga*, who support the cause of Buddhism. The struggle ends in the victory of the Soga clan and the accession to power of Prince *Shotoku-taishi* (574–622), the strongest advocate of the new faith.

593   During the Regency of Shotoku-taishi the building of the Shitennoji Temple is begun.

594   Buddhism is declared the State religion.

604   First Japanese "constitution", with 17 articles, which become the basis of political reforms and the concentration of political power in the Imperial

House. Shotoku-taishi adopts the Chinese system of a centralized State run by officials and the Chinese calendar and promotes Chinese cultural influence in Japan.

607 Japanese envoys are sent to the Court of the Chinese Sui dynasty, and many Japanese go to China to study Buddhism. Building of the Horyuji Temple, and creation of other major works of architecture, sculpture and painting.

645 The *Taika reform*, carried through by Prince *Nakano-oe* (626–671; posthumously named Emperor *Tenchi*) and *Nakatomi-no-Kamatari* (614–669; ancestor of the *Fujiwara* clan), completes the reforms initiated by Shotoku-taishi. The new code, following a Chinese model, provides among other things for land reform, the introduction of a school system and the establishment of the central authority of the Emperor. Later the new order becomes the instrument of political interests; the clan system is destroyed.

663 End of the Japanese presence in Korea.

701 The Taiho legal code is introduced, extending the Taika code to cover procedural and civil law. The code itself, produced in the reign of the Emperor *Mommu* (683–707), has not been preserved, but it can be partly reconstructed with the help of the Yoro code (757).

708 The first copper and silver coins are minted.

Nara and Heian periods (710–1192). – The town of Nara, which gives its name to the first of these two periods, becomes the center of a great cultural flowering, but is soon compelled to yield up its leading role to Heiankyo (present-day Kyoto). – During the Heian period, the heyday of courtly culture, the Court displays the utmost luxury, while the rural areas become increasingly impoverished. The peasants' need to provide for their own protection leads to the formation of the *samurai* class, whose members gain increasing authority in the State.

710 Foundation of the national capital, HEIJOKYO (Nara), planned on the Chinese model: the first permanent capital (previously the capital had been changed after the death of every Emperor, since the Emperor's residence was polluted by his death). – Building of the Kofukuji Temple. – Heijokyo remains the capital for 74 years.

712 Compilation of the "Kojiki", a chronicle which records both legends and historical events.

713 The "Fudoki", the first topography of Japan, is written.

718 The Yakushiji Temple, built in 680, is moved to Nara.

720 Compilation of the "Nihon-shoki" (or "Nihon-gi"), which ranks with the "Kojiki" as a major source on the early history of Japan.

724–749 Reign of **Shomu-tenno**. Great flowering of Buddhism; building of provincial temples (*kokubunji*) with monasteries and nunneries. The power of the priesthood increases; the "Seven Great Temples of Nara" in particular are a threat to the authority of the Imperial House. The population of Japan is about 3·5 million.

733 Building of the Todaiji Temple in Nara begins (completed 752).

754 The Chinese priest *Ganjin* (Chinese name Chien-chen) comes to Japan from the court of the T'ang dynasty; other Chinese priests teach Buddhism in Japan.

759 Completion of the "Manyoshu" ("Collection of Ten Thousand Leaves"), the oldest Japanese anthology (begun in the 5th century).

764–770 Reign of the Empress *Shotoku-tenno* (during a previous period of rule Empress *Koken*). She is under the influence of a priest named *Dokyo* (d. 772), who is appointed Grand Chancellor in 765 and as the "Monk-Emperor" (from 762) exemplifies the striving of the Buddhist priesthood for political power. After the Empress's death in 770 he is exiled.

781–806 Reign of **Kammu-tenno**, one of the strongest Emperors of the period.

784 The seat of government is moved to Nagaoka.

794 Establishment of a permanent capital at HEIANKYO (Kyoto). The power of the priesthood is broken, and, with a new national consciousness, Japan develops its own cultural forms and its own syllabary (characters representing syllables) – Katakana and Hiragana. After the fall of the T'ang dynasty contacts with China decline.
The Emperor's attempts to achieve independence are frustrated by the **Fujiwara** clan, who acquire influence over the Imperial House by marriage connections and reduce it to political insignificance. The Taika reform begun in 645 finally comes to nothing; governors, high officials and monasteries acquire feudal lordships. The military nobility appointed to protect them gains in influence.

801 Victory over the **Ainu** of northern Honshu and incorporation of this region in the Japanese Empire.

805 The priest *Saicho* (Dengyo-daishi, 776–822) returns to Japan from China and founds the Tendai sect. In the following year another priest returning from China, *Kukai* (Kobo-daishi, 774–835), founds the Shingon sect. Both sects play a major part in the propagation of esoteric Buddhism.

From 859 The Fujiwara clan becomes increasingly powerful and influential. Its members rule as "shadow emperors" (guardians of the Emperor during his minority).

901 After an unsuccessful attempt to break the power of the Fujiwara the statesman *Sugawara Michizane* is exiled to Dazaifu.

About 1000–1020 Refinement of courtly culture. A lady of the court, *Sei Shonagon*, writes the "Pillow Book"; *Murasaki Shikibu* writes the "Tale of Prince Genji", the masterpiece of classical Japanese prose.

1016 *Fujiwara Michinaga* (966–1027) receives the title of Regent (Kampaku).

From 1050 The decentralization of power leads to unrest. The military clans increase in power, particularly the **Minamoto** or *Genji* family in the east of the country and the **Taira** or *Heike* family in the west. The Taira gradually take over power from the Fujiwara. The two families become involved in violent conflict 1083–87, fighting in the Tohoku region in which the Minamoto are victorious.

1156–59 *Heiji War* between the Taira and the Minamoto; victory of *Taira-no-Kiyomori*, who in 1167 is appointed Grand Chancellor (Dajodaijin). Heyday of the Taira family.

1175 The priest *Honen-shonin* (1133–1212) founds the Jodo ("Pure Land") sect.

1180–85 **Gempei War**, in which the Minamoto, under the leadership of *Minamoto Yoritomo*

(1147–99), are victorious. In the decisive Battle of Dannoura the Taira are annihilated and the boy Emperor *Antoku* is killed.

MEDIEVAL PERIOD

Kamakura and Yoshino periods (1185–1392). – During these two centuries the Emperor loses all authority and power falls into the hands of the *Shoguns* (military regents), who govern the country in accordance with the strict ethical principles of the warrior caste.

1191 The priest *Eisai* brings **Zen Buddhism**, originally Chinese, to Japan (Rinzai sect).

1192 **Minamoto Yoritomo** becomes Regent, moves the seat of government to KAMAKURA in order to get away from the luxurious life of the Court, and founds the **Kamakura Shogunate**. He establishes a firm government and stations troops to maintain the security of the country's frontiers. His policy, later continued by the **Hojo**, is based on the ethic of Bushido (loyalty, courage, self-discipline), which also gains influence on Japanese society. The offices of *Shugo* (provincial governor) and *Jito* (military governor) are established.

1199 After Yoritomo's death his widow *Hojo Masako* and her father *Hojo Tokimasa* assume power.

Zen and the Way of the Samurai

Zen Buddhism was introduced into Japan during the warlike Kamakura period (1185–1333), the beginning of the Japanese feudal age, when the power of the Shoguns was consolidated after the Gempei War. This power rested on a rising warrior caste whose members called themselves **samurai**. The samurai were rough military men lacking the literary culture of the Court nobility, whose soft and luxurious life they despised: hence the great interest taken by the samurai in the new teaching which saw all book-learning merely as an obstacle on the path that led to final truth. The *Rinzai sect* in particular, with its ascetic way of life and its sudden spontaneous moment of enlightenment, found many adherents among the new knightly class.

After a first invasion attempt by the Mongols in 1274 was frustrated by a sudden storm, when the inadequacy of the Japanese defensive forces was revealed, the Hojo Regents entrusted the training of their fighting men to Zen monks. The success of this policy was demonstrated when the Mongols attempted another landing in 1281: for seven weeks the samurai held out against superior Mongol forces, until once again the enemy fleet was destroyed by a typhoon, to which the name of *kamikaze* ("divine wind") was given.

In addition to the general practice of spiritual discipline the Zen training concentrated particularly on *sword-fighting* and *archery*. The sword-fighter who had attained the state known as *mushin* ("not thinking" or "no consciousness") by the mental exercise called *koan* and the practice of *zazen* meditation acted intuitively: his spirit was free of all feeling, free of fear and even of the desire for victory. The warrior's body and his sword became a unity, a single instrument of the unconscious; and this gave him superiority over an opponent who had first to plan his actions rationally and then put them into effect.

For the samurai, however, the sword was not only a weapon: it was also a symbol of the code of honour known as "Bushido". This called for fearlessness in the face of death, loyalty to the warrior's lord, contempt for money and possessions and resolute defense of his own honor and that of his family. If that honor was attacked the samurai must be ready at any time to restore it by the ritual suicide known as *seppuku* (harakiri), for which purpose he carried a second, shorter, sword in his belt.

The samurai swords were made in accordance with a traditional procedure which remained unchanged for centuries. Before beginning work the smith, who wore a white robe while making a sword, and his workshop underwent ritual purification; then, starting with a length of steel made up of layers of varying degrees of hardness, he subjected it to repeated heating and folding until he had produced a blade made up of innumerable layers of metal, soft and tough in the core and increasing in hardness to reach a maximum of strength in the cutting edge.

The Japanese bow, made from several strips of bamboo and the wood of the wax tree, was asymmetrical, with the grip not in the middle but in the lower third of its length. The Zen technique of archery, like *zazen* meditation, was based mainly on correct breathing. The drawing of the bow was accompanied by exactly timed rhythmical breaths, and the release of the cord, like the thrust of the samurai's sword, was an intuitive act independent of the will. If the archer carried out the action correctly he need not consciously concern himself with the accuracy of his aim: this would come about of itself, for his hand would, without any apparent intention on his part, release the arrow at the precise moment when its point was directed towards the target.

The martial arts of medieval Zen have been preserved down to the present day. *Kyudo* (archery) is still practiced in the same way as in the heyday of the samurai. In present-day *kendo* (sword-fighting) the contestants are trained in attack and defense with bamboo swords. *Iaido* is a kind of shadow fighting in which the practitioner beats off an attack, draws his sword, kills his imaginary opponent, shakes the blood off the blade and sheathes the sword again – all at such lightning pace that the eye can hardly follow his movements. These old fighting techniques are not practiced nowadays for the sake of the physical exercise but as a means of attaining self-knowledge and a change in consciousness. Carried out in the spirit of Zen, they lead to the state of *kensho*: i.e. knowledge of one's self and insight into one's own nature.

1205 *Hojo Yoshitoki*, Tokimasa's son, becomes *Shikken* (chief administrator of the Empire), an office which continues to be held by the Hojo family.

1207 The priests *Honen* and *Shinran*, whose sects (Jodo and Jodo-shin-shu) have gained many adherents, are exiled.

1219 The murder of *Minamoto Sanetomo*, Yoritomo's son, brings the period of Minamoto rule to an end.

1221 Civil war, resulting from an unsuccessful attempt by the Imperial House to regain power.

1232 *Hojo Yasutoki* promulgates the Goseibaishikimo-ku, a legal code regulating the status of the samurai.

About 1250 "Heike-monogatari", a history of the Taira (Heike) clan.

1253 Foundation of the Nichiren sect.

1274 and 1281 Mongol attacks on Kyushu. On both occasions the Mongol fleet is destroyed by a sudden typhoon (*kamikaze*, "divine wind"). National solidarity is strengthened, but the samurai show increasing discontent.

1325 A Japanese embassy is sent to China for the first time since the fall of the T'ang dynasty.

1333 *Godaigo-tenno* takes advantage of the weakness of the Kamakura Shogunate to overthrow the Hojo.

1334 Godaigo-tenno sends his forces, led by *Ashikaga Takauji*, against the Kamakura Shogunate, which is defeated after ten years' fighting. The Emperor reassumes power, but is then expelled by Takauji, who in 1336 sets up *Komyo-tenno* as Emperor. Komyo founds the *Northern Dynasty* and appoints Takauji as Shogun. Godaigo flees with the Imperial insignia to Yoshino, where he establishes the *Southern Dynasty*. This is the "period of the two imperial courts" (*Namboku-cho*).

From the Muromachi period to the Azuchi-Momoyama period (1338–1600). – During this phase the power of the Shoguns declines. The country is involved in *civil wars* lasting many years, the result of attempts by regional princes and monasteries to gain increased power and of conflicts between supporters of the rival Imperial dynasties. In spite of these difficulties Japan develops new art forms during these centuries (No and Kabuki plays, the tea ceremony, etc.).

1392 *Gokameyama*, third successor to Godaigo, abdicates and hands over the Imperial insignia to the northern Emperor.

1401 Diplomatic contacts established with the Ming dynasty in China. – *Ashikaga Yoshimitsu*, third of the Ashikaga shoguns, transfers his residence to MUROMACHI (Kyoto) and initiates a flowering of culture. The period of peace after the unification of the two Imperial Courts is of brief duration.

1402 *Zeami* writes the "Kadensho", one of the great works of the No theatre, which is now in its heyday.

1403 *Do-ikki*, a rising by peasants and the lesser samurai.

1467–1590 **Daimyo Wars (Sengoku period).** 1467–77, *Onin Wars*, caused by fighting for the succession between members of the Ashikaga family. – The increasing decentralization of power strengthens the · position of the *daimyates* (domains of the local magnates known as *daimyos*), which seek to achieve the status of independent principalities. Artists and scholars flee to the remoter provinces, where new cultural centers develop.

1543 Portuguese landing on Tanegashima, bringing the first firearms to Japan. These soon spread throughout the country.

1549 *Francisco de Xavier* (St Francis Xavier) brings *Christianity* to Japan. He is supported by the daimyos, who see the new religion as a means of increasing their power. European medicine and science also become known in Japan, and there are the first trading contacts with the West.

1568 **Oda Nobunaga** comes to power in Kyoto. He succeeds in breaking the power of the monasteries and the daimyos and bringing peace to the Empire. He allows Christian missionaries to propagate their faith, seeing it as a counterweight to the Buddhist monasteries.

1571 Nagasaki is thrown open to trade with foreign countries.

1573 The last Ashikaga is deposed and the Ashikaga Shogunate comes to an end. Nobunaga consolidates his power and in 1576 transfers his residence to Azuchi Castle, Omi.

1582 Japanese embassy to the Holy See. – Nobunaga is murdered by his vassal *Akechi Mitsukide*, but the unification of the Empire which he had begun is continued by *Toyotomi Hideyoshi*, who reorganizes the administrative system and paves the way for the **feudal age**.

1586 Hideyoshi becomes Grand Chancellor (Dajodaijin). In the following year he expels the Christian missionaries.

1588 In order to obviate further risings peasants are forbidden to carry arms.

1590 Hideyoshi defeats the Hojo forces at Odawara; the country is now finally unified.

1592–93 First campaign of conquest in Korea. Japanese forces advance to the Chinese frontier with the aim of overthrowing the Ming dynasty.

1597 First persecutions of Christians.

1597–98 Second Korean campaign, which, like the first, ends in an armistice.

1600 *Battle of Sekigahara*: Tokugawa Ieyasu defeats Hideyoshi's son *Hideyori* and establishes the **Tokugawa Shogunate**, which is to rule Japan until 1867. – The population of Japan is about 25 million.

MODERN TIMES

Edo period (1600–1867). – After a brief period of contact with the West, Japan is completely shut off from the outer world. During these two and a half centuries of peace the Shogunate establishes a tight control over every field of Japanese life which prevents the development of any major concentration of political or economic power.

1603 Ieyasu is appointed Shogun by the Emperor Tenno and transfers his seat of government to EDO (Tokyo). Strict regulation of the social structure, with segregation of classes (warriors, peasants, craftsmen, merchants). Buddhism and Confucianism are fostered by the Government.

1605 Ieyasu abdicates in favor of his son *Hidetada*. Development of trade and stabilization of the economy.

1609 Establishment of a Dutch factory (trading-post) on Hirado.

1614 Renewed *persecutions of Christians*.

1614–15 *Battle of Osaka*: siege of the castle. Ieyasu is victorious; Hideyori, the last of the Toyotomi, commits suicide.

1616 Ieyasu dies of a wound received in the Battle of Osaka.

1616–24 Relations with Britain and Spain are broken off.

1633 Ban on travel to foreign countries and restriction of trade with Europe.

1637–38 *Shimabara Rising*: the subjects of the Christian daimyos, made subject to new masters, rebel against oppressive taxation. The rising – a reflection of the general economic distress – is repressed, and is followed by the final *ban on Christianity*.

1639 The Portuguese are expelled from Japan; only the Dutch and the Chinese are still tolerated. All contacts with foreign countries are brought to an end, and for more than 200 years Japan is a closed country. This is a period of peace during which there is a flowering of culture.

1641 The Dutch factory is moved from Hirado to Dejima; it is Japan's only contact with the outside world.

1707 Last eruption of Mount Fuji.

1720 The bringing in of Western books (except Christian works) is permitted.

1774 Three Japanese doctors translate Dutch medical works.

1792 A Russian embassy arrives in Matsumae (Hokkaido) seeking to establish trading relations. The proposal is rejected by the Shogunate.

1853 Commodore *Matthew Perry* anchors in Uraga Bay with a United States squadron with the object of opening Japan up to foreign trade.

1854 Perry returns with a larger fleet and compels the Shogunate to give way. The *Treaty of Kanagawa*, under which Shimoda and Hakodate are opened up to American vessels, is followed by other treaties with Britain and Russia.

1855 Under the *Treaty of Shimoda* with Russia the Russian-Japanese frontier in the Kuriles is drawn between the islands of Uruppu and Etorofu; the island of Sakhalin (Japanese Karafuto) is regarded as belonging to both countries in common.

1856 *Townsend Harris* becomes the first United States diplomatic representative in Japan.

1859 Opening of the ports of Yokohama, Nagasaki and Hakodate to foreign trade, marking the end of the period of closure.

1860 Japanese embassy established in the United States. Murder of an official of the Shogunate by supporters of the Emperor who are opposed to the opening up of Japan.

1861 Treaty between Japan and Prussia.

1863–64 Daimyo rising against the Shogunate in south-western Japan; after foreign vessels are fired on Kagoshima is bombarded as a reprisal.

1867 Under heavy political pressure the Shogun abdicates and hands over power to the Emperor **Meiji**; end of the Shogunate.

SINCE THE MEIJI RESTORATION

Meiji period (1867–1912). – In the "Meiji restoration" the Emperor recovers his authority. This is a period of *reform*, in which Japan is opened up to relations with the outer world. Great efforts are made to develop industry and catch up with other modern states. The Government system is reorganized under a new constitution.

1868 **Meiji reforms**: a five-point plan, the main thrust of which is directed towards coming into line with other countries in the field of science and modern thought. The Emperor Meiji moves the capital to Edo, which is renamed TOKYO ("Eastern Capital").

1869 The daimyos surrender their feudal authority to the Emperor.

1870 Abolition of the division into classes and introduction of civil surnames.

1871 The old provinces are replaced by prefectures headed by Government-appointed governors.

1872 Establishment of public elementary schools; opening of railway line from Tokyo to Yokohama.

1873 Adoption of the solar calendar; ban on the wearing of swords.

1875 Under a treaty with Russia, signed in St Petersburg, Japan abandons its claim to the island of Sakhalin and receives in return the whole of the Kurile chain.

1877 The *Seinan Revolt*, headed by *Saigo Takamori*, is repressed by the Government.

1889 Promulgation of a new **Constitution** on the Prussian model: Japan becomes a **constitutional monarchy** with a bicameral Parliament.

1894–95 *First Sino-Japanese War*: China cedes Formosa (Taiwan) and the Pescadores to Japan.

1902 Treaty with Britain: an alliance directed against Russian expansion in East Asia.

1904–05 *Russo-Japanese War*, won by Japan, which under the Treaty of Portsmouth (New Hampshire) secures the southern half of Sakhalin (Karafuto) and recognition of its paramount interest in Korea.

1910 Japan annexes Korea.

1911 Commercial treaty with the United States.

1912 Death of the Emperor Meiji, who is succeeded by his son *Yoshihito* as the Emperor **Taisho**.

Taisho and Showa periods (from 1912). – Japan increasingly pursues an expansionist policy in East Asia. During the First World War it sides with the Allies, and the production of armaments promotes the development of heavy industry. The post-war period brings growing social tensions and a grave economic crisis. – During the Second World War Japan joins the Axis Powers and gains control of the whole of South-East Asia. After bitter fighting on land and sea and in the air, with heavy losses, Japanese forces are everywhere driven back, and after heavy bombing of Japanese cities, culminating in the dropping of atomic bombs on Hiroshima and Nagasaki, Japan is forced to surrender; it is then compelled to give up all its conquered territories and is itself occupied for the first time in its history. – After the war the Allies insist on the *democratization* of Japan, which recovers relatively rapidly from its annihilating defeat and develops within a few decades into a leading world economic power, at the same time establishing close links with the Western World.

1914–18 During the *First World War* Japan captures German possessions in China (Tsingtao) and the Pacific.

1920 Japan becomes a member of the League of Nations.

1923 A severe earthquake devastates the Tokyo and Yokohama area.

1926 The Emperor Taisho dies and is succeeded by **Hirohito** (b. 1901).

1929 The *world economic crisis* brings Japan a brief boom in the export of low-priced goods.

1931 Japan occupies Manchuria.

1932 Manchuria becomes a Japanese protectorate under the name of Manchukuo.

1933 Following international criticism of the occupation of Manchuria Japan leaves the League of Nations.

1937 *Second Sino-Japanese War*: Japan pushes into the interior of China, taking Nanking, Peking, Canton and other cities, and blockades the whole of the Chinese coast.

1938 Law providing for general mobilization and proclaiming a "New Order" in Asia (expansion on to the Chinese mainland). – Fighting on the Sino-Soviet frontier.

1941 Japan, allied with Germany and Italy under the Three Power Pact, becomes involved in the **Second World War**. Neutrality agreement with the Soviet Union. Raw materials boycott by the United States. – The Japanese **attack on Pearl Harbor** (December 7) sparks off the *Pacific War*. The United States and Britain declare war on Japan (December 8).

1941–42 With the object of creating a "Greater Asian Co-Prosperity Sphere", Japanese forces advance along the coast of Asia, taking Hong Kong (December 25, 1941), Singapore (February 15, 1942) and Rangoon (March 7, 1942). At the same time they attack the Philippines (capture of Manila, January 2, 1942) and the Dutch East Indies (occupation of Celebes and Borneo, end of January 1942; Java and Lesser Sunda Islands, February–March 1942), occupy the island of Guam (December 10, 1941) and launch air attacks on northern Australia (February 1942). Japanese expansion reaches its peak with landings on the Aleutians and New Guinea, giving Japan control of territories with a population of more than 450 million.

1942 Heavy losses in the air and sea battles in the Coral Sea and at Midway Island considerably weaken Japan and mark the turning-point in the war; major Allied offensive in the South Pacific.

1943 After bitter fighting Allied forces recapture the Japanese air base of Guadalcanal (British Solomon Islands) in the south-western Pacific.

1945 The Allied demand for unconditional surrender, agreed on at the Potsdam Conference, is rejected by Japan. The Soviet Union declares war on Japan (August 8) and occupies the southern Kuriles.

After bloody battles for the islands of Iwojima (Volcano Island) and Okinawa (Ryukyu group)

Japanese resistance is finally broken when the US Air Force drops **atomic bombs** on Hiroshima (August 6) and Nagasaki (August 9). The Japanese sign the document of **surrender** on board the US battleship "Missouri" on September 2. American forces enter Tokyo on September 8. For the first time in its history Japan is occupied by a foreign power; it is compelled to give up all its conquered territories and is reduced to its 1868 frontiers.

The US military government headed by General Douglas MacArthur seeks to destroy Japanese militarism (trials of war criminals) and democratize public life.

1946 The Emperor Hirohito, in a speech on January 1, renounces the Imperial claim to divinity, and under a new constitution the Emperor is left with a purely figurehead function as symbol of the State and the unity of the nation. Women are given the vote; Japan renounces war.

From 1949 After the lifting of Japan's obligation to pay reparations the reconstruction of Japanese industry begins, with American help.

1951 Under the *peace treaty* with the United States signed at San Francisco on September 8 Japan gives up Korea, Taiwan (Formosa), the Pescadores, the Kuriles and southern Sakhalin; security pact with the United States. – Japanese relations with the Soviet Union and China remain unresolved.

1952 Japan recovers full sovereignty. Conclusion of a peace treaty with Chiang Kai-shek, recognized as the legitimate representative of China.

1954 Japan joins the Colombo Plan (devised in 1950 to provide development assistance for the countries of South and South-East Asia).

1956 Japan becomes a member of the United Nations. – Agreement on ending the state of war with the Soviet Union, which undertakes to return to Japan, after the ratification of a peace treaty, the southern Kurile islands of Shikotan and Habomai, with their subsidiary islands; resumption of diplomatic relations with the Soviet Union.

1960 Security pact with the United States, giving the US the right to establish military bases on Japanese territory. Violent anti-American demonstrations.

1964 As a result of the country's meteoric economic growth the Japanese yen becomes fully convertible. Japan joins the Organization for Economic Co-operation and Development. (OECD).

1966 Japan becomes a founder-member of the Asian and Pacific Council (ASPAC), designed to promote economic and cultural co-operation between states in Asia and the Pacific.

1969 Agreement on the return to Japan of the island of Okinawa, which had remained under American occupation since the end of the war and had been used as a supply base during the war in Vietnam (1964 onwards).

1972 Okinawa is returned to Japanese sovereignty. – Establishment of diplomatic relations with the Chinese People's Republic (involving the annulment of the 1952 peace treaty with Chiang Kai-shek).

1973 The world-wide *energy crisis* caused by steep increases in the price of oil involves Japan, which is almost wholly dependent on oil imports, in grave economic difficulties.

1974 Long-term commercial agreement with the People's Republic of China.

1975 Japan in economic recession. – Emperor Hirohito pays a State visit to the United States.

1976 Following a corruption scandal involving the US aircraft firm of Lockheed the Government resigns. In the subsequent election the Liberal Democratic Party loses its majority in the Lower House, but recovers it by the accession of independent members. The new Government is headed by *Fukuda Takeo*.

1978 Fruitless negotiations with the Soviet Union on a peace treaty (the sticking-point being the return of the southern Kuriles). – Treaty of peace and friendship with the People's Republic of China. – Fukuda Takeo, the Prime Minister, resigns and is succeeded by *Ohira Masayoshi*.

1979 World economic conference in Tokyo (United States, European Community, Japan, Canada) on energy problems and the "North–South dialogue". – The Liberal Democratic Party loses seats in elections to the Lower House. – Ohira Masayoshi, the Prime Minister, visits the Chinese People's Republic.

1980 *Hua Guofeng*, head of the Chinese Government and Communist Party, pays a State visit to Japan. – The Ohira Government falls, Parliament is dissolved and a General Election is called. After Ohira's death *Suzuki Zenko* becomes Prime Minister.

1981 *Pope John Paul II* visits Japan (Hiroshima, Nagasaki). – Japan renews its claim to the southern Kuriles, occupied by the Soviet Union since the end of the war. In spite of attempts to keep down national expenditure there is a marked increase in defense spending. – A Japanese freighter sinks after colliding with an American nuclear submarine in the East China Sea. – The European Community tries to persuade Japan to adopt a more moderate export policy.

1982 The Prime Minister of the Chinese People's Republic, Zhao Ziyang, visits Japan for political discussions. – The Japanese Foreign Minister, *Sakurauchi Yoshio*, represents Japan at the World Economic Conference in Versailles. – The island of Kyushu is ravaged by a typhoon, the Nagasaki area being worst affected. – *Nakasone Yasuhiro* becomes Prime Minister (November).

Religion

Creeds and Confessions

The religious beliefs current in Japan during the prehistoric and early historical periods, down to the age of the burial mounds (*kofun*), were still at the stage of **animism**. Incarnations of the forces of nature, known as *kami*, were invoked by shamans in order to ensure success in hunting and fishing or, later, good harvests. There were also sorceress-priestesses (reflecting the influence of a matriarchal system) who were credited with prophetic gifts. These tribal priests or sorceresses occupied the leading role in their kinship groups in virtue of their magical powers, giving place at a later stage to military leaders such as the Yamato.

It was only under the influence of the advanced culture of China that this Japanese natural religion acquired a spiritual context, a ritual, a religious architecture in the true sense of the term and figural representation of the personified forces of nature which had previously been revered (and nowadays to some extent are again being revered) in the form of fetishes.

In its early days the cult later known as Shintoism took over from the social and political philosophy of *Confucius* (the Latinized form of the Chinese name Kung fu-tse, or Master Kung; original name Kung Chin; *c.* 550–*c.* 479 B.C.) the doctrine of ancestor worship and the idea of the "Son of Heaven" (i.e. of the divine descent of the ruling house), which had been developed under the Chou dynasty in China. Both of these conceptions were readily adopted by the Yamato emperors, anxious to find some presentable philosphical basis for their claim to rule the whole of Japan.

Later the dualist principle of *yin* and *yang* (i.e. a passive female and an active male element) was taken over from **Taoism** (named after the mystical aphorisms, the "Tao-te-ching" of Lao-tse, 4th–3rd centuries B.C.), in particular from the "Book of Changes", and combined with the old rituals of natural religion and the art of divination. – Finally the sun goddess Amaterasu was taken over from earlier cults, declared to be the ancestress of the Imperial House and set at the head of an elaborate hierarchy of natural and ancestor divinities.

At the beginning of the 6th century B.C. a Korean embassy brought the first effigy of

Buddha to Japan. This was followed by a constant flow of information, at first probably coming through Korea but later direct from China, and **Buddhism** began to gain a foothold in Japan, particularly among the nobility.

Buddha (the "Awakened One" or "Enlightened One") is the honorific style of the founder of the religion, who is also known as *Gautama* or Gotama, after a family of seers in his home area in northern India, and as *Shakyamuni* (i.e. the "ascetic of the House of Shakya"), after his own family name of Shakya. He was born about 560 B.C. to an old princely family in the region below the Nepalese Himalayas, but at the age of 29 he gave up wealth, power and noble status in order to become a pilgrim and study the doctrine of renunciation. Disappointed by his teachers, he gathered his own disciples round him and devoted himself to asceticism, remote from all book wisdom. While meditating under a fig tree (*bodhi*) he attained Enlightenment, and thereafter taught the "Four Truths": all existence is incessant suffering; the cause of this suffering is selfish desire; the killing of desire brings release from suffering; the way to achieve this renunciation is the "Eightfold Path", the elements in which are right knowledge, right thought, right speech, right conduct, right means of livelihood, right effort, right mind control and right meditation.

After some initial resistance by supporters of the traditional natural religion Buddhism was accepted by the upper classes of Japanese society. In 594 it was declared the State religion by Prince Shotoku, and thereafter was a major formative influence on Japanese cultural life for many centuries. The Buddhism which came to Japan, however, had already departed from the original teaching of Gautama. This contained no reference to either God or an afterlife, and its path to salvation demanded absolute self-discipline and self-denial from every believer. But since only a small élite could be expected to show such qualities the doctrine of the "Great Vehicle" (Mahayana) had become popular among ordinary people in preference to the more demanding "Lesser Vehicle" (Hinayana), whose adepts held to the full rigour of Shakyamuni's demands; and since to ordinary people, caught up in the fetters of everyday life, it seemed impossible to meet the requirements of the Eightfold Path, assistance was provided for them in the form of *Bodhisattwas* (a Sanskrit term meaning "those whose being is Enlightenment" Japanese *Bosatsu*), who performed a role akin to that of the Christian auxiliary saints. These were ascetics who had attained a degree of perfection enabling them to achieve release and entry into Nirvana but, out of compassion for imperfect believers, remained in a kind of intermediate world and acted as mediators.

Images of Bodhisattwas brought in from China were set up in the earliest temples and pagodas, built at the beginning of the 7th century A.D. Impressed by the artistic and spiritual superiority of Chinese culture, then supported by the prestige of a powerful empire, the Japanese ruling classes followed this foreign model almost slavishly – concentrating, however, on external appearances. In 710 the first real town in Japan was founded at Nara, modelled on Ch'ang-an, the capital of the T'ang dynasty. In the new Japanese capital Buddhism exerted a powerful influence on the courtiers; but with them, as with the newly ordained priests, it was probably lip-service rather than true understanding of the new doctrine, which came only later. Japan's real contribution to the religious history of Asia lay in the later development of Zen Buddhism.

The idea of the mediating influence of the Bodhisattwas was mingled in popular faith with the deeply rooted belief in protective spirits of nature which must be propitiated by offerings and rites of purification. This *syncretism* (attempt at unification) of Buddhist symbolic figures and Shintoist rituals is found throughout the whole of Japanese mythology, and still finds expression in many old customs whose origins are lost in the mists of time. – Under Chinese influence, too, Japanese courtly society refined not only its ceremonial (soon to be governed by an etiquette even more highly stylized than in China) but also its psychological and metaphysical conceptions – thus paving the way for the later development of Zen culture in Japan.

Although Buddhism is wholly undogmatic, considering all other religions and philosophies with relaxed tolerance, schools (Japanese *shu*, usually translated, rather unhappily, as "sects") had already developed in India and China which sought to mitigate or circumvent the world-denying demands of Buddha in order to make the doctrine more accessible to ordinary people, and other such "schools" grew up in Japan. Of the six sects of the Nara period three – the *Hosso, Ritsu* and *Kegon* sects – still have adherents, though their numbers are relatively small.

The priests at the Court of Nara, trained in China, based themselves on the sutras of the eclectic Mahayana canon. They

Buddhist priest   Members of the Soka Gakkei

enjoyed high reputation and acquired great wealth: the cost of gilding a gigantic Buddha statue four storeys high brought the National Exchequer to the verge of bankruptcy. This circumstance and the undue influence of the priesthood on the Government of the country are believed to have been the reasons for the transfer of the imperial capital to Heiankyo (Kyoto), after which Nara with its sumptuous temples became a mere ghost city.

In order to counter still more effectively the striving for power of the priestly caste embassies were sent to China to bring back Buddhists of other schools and thus fight the Nara sect with their own weapons. For this purpose the choice fell on the Tien-tai school, whose founder Chih-i (538–597) – no doubt influenced by his experience during a period of military turmoil – had derived from the meaninglessness of existence a conception of hell totally alien to the original teachings of Buddhism, which later gave rise to a whole system of demonology. In the Chinese doctrine this idea of hell could be seen to have some spiritual and psychological basis: of the ten stages of existence through which men must pass, six are spent in a dark world full of suffering.

The Japanese **Tendai sect**, founded in 805 by *Saicho* (767–822; posthumously known as Dengyo-daishi), later developed the inner torments associated with man's involvement in the trials of the world into demons in bodily form, whose evil influence had to be countered by special rituals and offerings. The ruling classes were naturally very ready to use the fear of hell as a psychological deterrent useful in controlling the mass of the people, whose living conditions had deteriorated as a result of the increasing density of population and the luxury of the Heian Court.

The Tendai priest *Genshin* (942–1017) carried the process of giving concrete form to abstract conceptions of Buddhism one stage further by adding to the demoniac underworld a paradisiac Hereafter. In this he was a forerunner of the **Jodo school** founded by *Shinran* (1173–1262), which soon attracted many adherents by its denial of the existence of hell. This school derived from the doctrine of the "Pure Land" which was evolved in India in the 1st century A.D. and later became very popular – probably under the influence of a misunderstanding of the Christian idea of salvation – in virtue of its simplicity. The practice of the Jodo school centered on the invocation of curiously sexless representations of a Bodhisattwa known as *Amida*, who had little more to do with Buddha than the fact that the name was derived from one of the invocations of Buddha, Amitayus (the "Buddha of the immeasurable light"). By paying reverence to the image of Amida the believer was assured of the wiping out of all sins and impurities and of a passage into the "Pure Land".

Still more appealing to ordinary people was the teaching of **Nichiren** (1222–82), who so far reduced the demands of religion as to hold that, out of all the innumerable Buddhist writings, one sentence from the Lotus Sutra (known in Japanese as Hokke-kyo: hence the name of Hokke-shu by which the sect is also known) was sufficient to ensure salvation: the worshipper had only to pray in the words ''All reverence to the Sutra of the Lotus of the wondrous Law'' for his soul at once to achieve the state of perfection. In spite of – or rather because of – this enormous simplification the sect is still popular among simple people in Japan. – Nichiren was also a keen would-be politician, chauvinistic in his views and with a fanatical sense of mission. Of himself he asserted: ''I shall be the pillar of Japan. I shall be the eyes of Japan. I shall be the great vessel of Japan.''

In these views Nichiren was the forerunner of the *Soka Gakkai*, the ''Value-Creating Society'' of the present day. This body holds meetings of its members in large sports arenas at which the prayer in praise of the Lotus Sutra is accompanied by brass bands and mass gymnastics – a parody of Buddhist practice which the serious Buddhist, for all his tolerance, must surely regard as blasphemous. Thanks to generous contributions from industrial sources, however, the Soka Gakkai is able to erect huge ''temples'' in a pompous style quite at variance with the uncluttered style of Japanese architecture. In recent years the militant political arm of this ''religion'', the right-wing conservative Komeito Party, has become increasingly influential in Japan.

Far removed from this trivializing of one of the boldest and profoundest conceptions ever evolved by the human mind – for so the true Buddhist doctrine must be considered – is the distinctive Japanese contribution to meditative Buddhism; **Zen Buddhism**, which has not only pervaded the whole spiritual and intellectual life of Japan but has also had an enduring influence on Western thinkers.

The Japanese word **Zen**, a shortened form of *zenna* (later *zazen*), means the practice of meditation, in particular a form of contemplation in a seated position (Sanskrit *dhyana*) which passed from India to China together with Buddhism in its original form. There it became known as *Ch'an* or *ch'an-na*, but in consequence of the strong influence of the eclectic Mahayana schools and the rational attitudes of the Chinese it was at first thrust into the background by the ''official'' custodians of the new faith.

Nevertheless it is known that as early as the 5th–6th centuries there was in China a school of itinerant meditating monks who for the most part passed on their teachings orally and attributed their doctrine to the ''Patriarch'' *Bodhidharma*, claimed to be the 28th master in a chain of ancestors (no doubt partly fictitious) in India and the first master of the doctrine in China.

Ch'an found more support among the Chinese Taoists than it had received from the adherents of Mahayana Buddhism. Their mystical doctrine of withdrawal from the world, the *Tao* or Way, had existed alongside Confucianism and Buddhism for many centuries and had produced a succession of ascetic hermits who withdrew to the solitude of the mountains, remote from the busy activities of the world, to meditate on the essence of nature and the origin and objects of existence.

About the beginning of the T'ang period (618–907) the Indian doctrine of contemplation fused with some elements of Taoism. At the same time the adepts of Ch'an founded their first monasteries, which brought them more adherents; for itinerant mendicant monks had never had the same status in China as they enjoyed in India. Thus under the T'ang dynasty the Ch'an doctrine prospered in China, although – or perhaps precisely because – its teachings were diametrically opposed to the prevailing respect for the intellect and for intellectuals. The most original thinkers came from the southern school which was later to be the major influence on the development of Zen in Japan. Its founder, *Hui-neng* (638–713) is traditionally described as illiterate – reflecting the contempt in which his school held tradition and book-learning.

Like Taoism, Ch'an and its later development Zen are not religions in the normal sense, nor even in the etymological sense of binding together: it does not seek to bind men together but to release them from all bonds. It has no theological conception of divinity, no rites, no dogmas and no sacred texts. It does not call for analysis or rational comprehension, but rather a direct intuitive perception. The world of material things is treated in the way the world of belief and thought is often treated in the West – as a conventional way of looking at things which stands for something unreal.

The novice must free himself, by strict self-discipline, from all the distinctions drawn by logical, discursive thought. His aim is to achieve the transcendental wisdom which dissolves all contradictions between the individual and the All. This central concept of Buddhism, the process of becoming one with all creation, was known in India as *prajnag*. It betokens the same state of enlightenment which Gautama attained under the bodhi tree, and is thus to be equated with the attainment of the Buddhahood which is believed to lie deep within all men.

For this state the Japanese later coined the term *satori*. This state of consciousness and the path towards its attainment are not to be described in words and logical concepts, since they lie beyond the bounds of the rational. Thus the Zen master who has reached the state of *satori* is faced with the problem of how to bring his pupil closer to enlightenment other than by training him in the technique of sitting in contemplation (*zazen*). A solution was found in the alogical riddles known in Japan as *koan*. In one of the best known of these the master claps his hands and says, "That is the sound of two hands: what is the sound of only one?" The pupil is then expected to find an answer which corresponds spontaneously and intuitively to the illogicality of the riddle, without becoming lost in rational explanations. This sometimes develops into a rapid series of questions and answers, known to the Japanese as *mondo*. These techniques destroy the novice's confidence in discursive patterns of thought and are designed to free him from the fetters of the rather simplistic logic of the syllogism. Originally, when the monks were fewer in number, the Ch'an masters presented each pupil with a *koan* composed specially for him, but later, when the monasteries attracted more aspirants, use was made of well-tried riddles of the T'ang period, collections of which had already been compiled. From these collections of classical *koan* a suitable one was selected and put to a large number of adepts. But the collections of riddles, which grew to considerable size, were not regarded as sacred texts with the status of dogma, since the only dogma of Zen was that there were no dogmas.

The leading Chinese masters of Ch'an founded their own schools, the teachings of which later reached Japan. The doctrine of *Lin-chi* (d. 867), known in Japan as **Rinzai**, preferred the "sudden" path to *satori* by the use of the *koan* technique. The school of *Tung-shan* (807–869) and *Tsao-shan* (840–901), the Japanese name of which is **Soto** (a combination of Tsao and Tung), relied rather on the "gradual" route by the practice of sitting in contemplation.

The first Zen master in Japan was a monk named *Eisai* (1141–1214), a former adherent of the Tendai school, who had studied the techniques of Ch'an on two journeys to China and believed himself to have attained Enlightenment. After his return from China he founded a Rinzai monastery on Kyushu (1191). The founder of the Japanese Soto section was *Dogen* (1200–53), also from a Tendai monastery, who travelled to China to study the new doctrine and after his return spent several years as an itinerant monk before founding his own monastery in 1236.

It was only in the 18th century that **Shintoism**, which as noted above developed out of a syncretism of natural religion and Chinese ritual, was seen by undogmatic Japanese as being in essence typically Japanese.

Archaeological remains of the Jomon culture (from about the 5th millennium B.C.) point to totemism, the worship of nature and the cult of a fertility and mother goddess. Features characteristic of a matriarchal society were preserved in the role played by shamanist priestesses and sacred dancing-girls in later Shintoism. In the Yayoi period (to A.D. 300) there is evidence of sun worship. Chinese annals of the 4th century refer to various kinship groups and their divinities (e.g. the clan gods known as Ujigami), cults of nature and the souls of the dead, shamanism and the worship of divine forces which dispensed sustenance to men. During the centuries which elapsed before the compilation of written chronicles ("Kojiki", 712; "Nihon-shoki", 720), the cult of ancestral divinities developed, probably influenced from an early stage by the Confucian writings. The cult of clan divinities was matched on a wider scale by the worship of the sun goddess Amaterasu in the national sanctuary, the Great Shrine of Ise. It was only after the introduction of Buddhism that the indigenous cult of the "eight hundred myriads of *kami* [divinities]" was given the distinctive name of **Shinto** ("Way of the Gods").

In subsequent centuries Shintoism was closely bound up in the Imperial Palace with the Emperor's State functions and with Government affairs. A kind of symbiosis (mutually advantageous association) with Buddhism was achieved in *Ryobu-Shinto* ("Way of the Gods of Both Provinces"): the *kami* were regarded as reincarnations of Buddha and Bodhisattwas, and the sun god was equated with Dainichi Nyorai, the Buddha of Light.

From the 14th century attempts were made to restore the archaic *Yuiitso-Shinto* and to purify it of all Confucian adjuncts.

During the Meiji restoration patriotically minded intellectuals sought to have the "National Doctrine" (*Kokugaku*) devised by Motoori Norinaga (1730–1801) on the basis of the mythological passages in the "Kojiki" officially accepted as representing the "Japanese spirit" (*Yamato gokoro*) and, later, declared the State religion; and, in their chauvinistic zeal, they either rejected altogether or dismissed as "superficial Chinese thinking" the Chinese elements with which Shintoism, like Buddhism, was riddled. When such features could not be got rid of by the doctoring of the texts which was not infrequently undertaken they were merely ignored as "un-Japanese". – Alongside State Shintoism ("shrine Shinto") there grew up in the second half of the 19th century various communities of religious bent incorporating elements from other creeds ("sect Shinto").

After Japan's annihilating defeat in the Second World War the Emperor was obliged to renounce his claim to divinity, and State Shintoism was abolished: the shrines and their priests, deprived of State financial support, now depend solely on contributions from believers. Nevertheless many politicians, whatever their private views, still appear at Shinto shrines on great festival occasions; for although since the war Shintoism has been on an equal footing with other religions it is still very popular with large sections of the population.

Shinto worship makes no great demands on the worshipper – the purification of his hands and mouth, pulling on the hempen rope and clapping his hands to attract the divinity's attention, prayer, the giving of money, the purchase of an amulet. On the occasion of a festival (*matsuri*) the actions required of the priest (*kannushi*) and the congregation are more elaborate: after the invocation of the god comes the solemn purification (*harai*) or the simpler "washing off" (*misogi*) of moral and ritual impurity, followed by offerings of foodstuffs and sake; after which, for the entertainment of the gods, the Kagura (originally a shamanist (priest's) trance dance) and courtly dances (Bugaku) are danced. There may also be various part-sacred events, the most spectacular of which is a procession with a portable shrine (*mikoshi*). In the portable shrine and in the main hall of the shrine proper, concealed from the eyes of the faithful, are symbols representing the divinity (*shintai*, "divine body"). A striking feature of any shrine is the *torii* (gateway), usually red, with two uprights topped by (usually two) horizontal beams.

Roman Catholic **Christianity** was brought to Kyushu in 1549 by the Spanish missionary *Francisco de Xavier* or Javier (St Francis Xavier). This was the beginning of the "Christian century", during which southern and western Japan were introduced to the Christian faith and liturgy, and also to the culture, way of life and technology of the West. Christian literature and painting developed in Japan, and Western musical instruments enjoyed a brief period of popularity. The feudal lords of south-western Japan, however, fostered the growth of Christianity mainly on economic grounds and as a means of supporting their own power; and this led to the banning of Christianity by the shogunal authorities in 1614, followed by bloody persecutions which led by 1638 to the almost total extirpation of the Christian community. Thereafter it was possible only for a few "crypto-Christians" (*kakure-kirishitan*) to survive in the remoter parts of the country, transmitting the beliefs and practices of their faith by word of mouth. The ban on Christianity was not lifted until 1873; but even after freedom of religious belief was enshrined in the 1889 constitution Christian missionaries found it difficult to make headway against the indigenous religions and traditional prejudices. It was only after the post-1945 democratization of the country that Christian influence again made itself felt in Japan, which now has some 750,000 Protestants, 400,000 Roman Catholics and 25,000 Orthodox Christians.

Since the middle of the 19th century many **new religions**, some of them lying outwith traditional doctrines, have come to the fore in Japan, usually founded by some charismatic individual and frequently syncretistic in character, or sometimes monotheistic. Of more than 300 such religions the following are worthy of particular note:

Tenrikyo ("Doctrine of Heavenly Reason"), founded by Nakayama Miki (1798–1887): Shintoist, Messianic, monotheistic.

P. L. Kyodan ("Perfect Liberty Group"), a refoundation in 1946 of the former Hito-no-michi Kyodan: humanist, liberal.

Mukyokai ("without a church"), a Protestant group which preaches a non-institutionalized and purely Japanese

Shinto priest

Changing-room in a shrine

form of Christianity based solely on the Bible.

Two neo-Buddhist sects derive from Nichiren: the *Rissho Koseikai* ("Society for Righteousness and Comradeship"), a branch, founded in 1938, of the *Reiyukai* ("Friends of the Ancestral Spirits"), and the *Nichiren Shoshu* ("True School of Nichiren"), founded in 1913, which, with its lay organization the **Soka Gakkai** (more than 10 million members) and the *Komeito* ("Justice Party"), seeks to make the belief in Nichiren as the Buddha of the present last days of the world (*Mappo*) into a universal religion centered on Japan and the Japanese State religion.

Syncretism and Religious Feeling

These various creeds, with the exception of Christianity, are not seen in Japan as mutually exclusive: they supplement and overlie one another. Although Shintoist philosophers and learned Buddhist monks erected astonishingly detailed structures of ideas, these lacked the aggressive hair-splitting which has so often led to religious wars. It is true that during the medieval and early modern periods the great Buddhist temples were frequently involved in conflicts over prestige and privileges, over economic and political power, and maintained huge armies of

monkish warriors; but these struggles did not arise from doctrinal controversies and were usually justified on general moral grounds. Even the ruthless persecution of Christians at the beginning of the Edo period had political causes: in the eyes of the Tokugawa the Christians were terrorists who endangered the peace of the Empire and the power of the Shogunate.

Japanese thought and feeling was – and to some extent still is – directed towards achieving harmony rather than creating discrimination. This basic attitude leads in the religious field to a **syncretism** which leaves the individual free to belong to different confessional groups. Japan owes to **Shintoism** the firm involvement of the individual in the family and the State, given dogmatic form and a political dimension by **Confucianism**. The spiritual and speculative element, with a touch of transcendence and a dawning of personal awareness, was added by **Buddhism**; and finally the stimulus towards the development of a social consciousness overriding the traditional boundaries was given by **Christianity**.

A further characteristic of Japanese religious feeling is its concern with life as it is lived on earth. The Japanese are by nature attached to the world and to their native soil; they are optimistic and practical, more interested in pragmatic aims than in theories. For them the divine is present in the visible natural world and does not have to be sought behind the phenomena by laborious thought. The spirit beings of Shinto and the invisible auxiliary divinities of Buddhism are anthropomorphic and anthropocentric – they attribute human forms to god and regard man as central fact of universe – and the worshipper's commerce with them, achieved by magical invocations and prayer, has almost always a concrete purpose related to the life of this world. Vengeful spirits and demons have the power to harm men, but they may be propitiated by prayer, offerings and due reverence. Good deeds earn a more fortunate rebirth, but even a scoundrel may – according to the popular belief in the Saviour Buddha, Amida – enter paradise merely by calling on Amida in the hour of death. Thus the believer's relationship to the divinity is based on conditions which are reasonable, often perhaps schematic but always within his own control.

This closeness to everyday life explains many features of Japanese religious life: the blurring of the boundary between the sacred and the profane, as seen for example in the popular religious festivals (*matsuri*); the great popularity of amulets and devotional objects of all kinds and the high regard in which works of religious art and other visible and tangible symbols of the divine are held; and finally the sense of community provided by the "new religions", which offer the individual lost in modern mass society a new spiritual home.

Out of the great mass of doctrines and articles of belief contained within the Buddhism of the "Great Vehicle" the Japanese selected those elements which best suited their basic religious attitudes: among them the cult of the auxiliary divinities, the conception of the Saviour Buddha and the Bodhisattwa, certain magical and esoteric practices (consecration of a building site, exorcism), the use of devotional objects, the rituals of burial and the ceremonies in honor of the dead. Buddhist philosophy and concepts like the detachment from the Self (*muga*) which is attainable by meditation – however great their influence on art and intellectual life – never had such a durable impact on the everyday life of all classes of the population as the system of conjurations, burial rites, amulets, taboos and fortune-telling (hand-reading). – The ascetic doctrines of Zen, which during the feudal period became the ideology of the warrior caste and taught them to be ready to face death unafraid, may seem a negative creed, but in the circumstances of the samurai served a practical purpose, since death to them was an everyday event. The same doctrines enabled the ordinary citizen, once he had attained the moment of enlightenment (*satori*), to carry on with his life as before in spite of its illusory nature.

Certain basic Japanese attitudes are found in similar form both in Shintoism and in the beliefs of the Buddhist sects. The Buddhist conception of the world is more developed than that of Shintoism, but in both creeds the universe is seen as consisting of three parts. Shintoism teaches that above the earth there is a heaven and below it the realm of the dead and of demons, the dark and impure land of Yomitsukuni; in early times there was also the distant land of the dead known as Toyoko or Jodo, which was also seen as paradise. In Buddhist belief there is also, below the world of men, an underworld consisting of hells of varying degree; but both of these belong to the same world of desires, above which are the World of Pure Forms, inhabited by divinities purged of all desire, and the World of Non-Form inhabited by pure spirits without material form. Both systems dispense with the idea of an original creator or director of the universe. Shintoism holds that Japan and its inhabitants originally stemmed from an island and a pair of divinities of unknown origin; the island is believed to have been formed from primeval mud, which itself was without origin. There is in Shintoism no plan for human salvation nor any conception of the end of all things. In the Buddhist view time is cyclical: worlds come into being, go out of existence and come into being again in an eternal cycle which obeys cosmic and moral laws. Shintoism takes the material world as something which is "given" and does not inquire into its essence, while Buddhism denies its reality or, in view of its participation in the Absolute, postulates the identity of existence and non-existence (the Void).

As well as great differences there are also common features in the Shintoist and Buddhist conceptions of *death and the hereafter*. To the Japanese mind death was not really a transcendental event. According to the oldest Shinto beliefs the dead passed into the underworld, but could also pursue a continued existence on earth, living in hiding as *goryoshin* (avenging or protective spirits) and intervening in the life of men, or could rise into heaven. The Buddhist teaching was that human life is only one link in the chain of rebirths: the dead could be reborn, according to their merits, either in hell (*Jigoku*) or in a higher existence, perhaps in the World of Pure Forms. The only transcendental state was Nirvana (the extinction of man's transitory and illusory existence in the Absolute); but this lofty concept was beyond the reach of most believers. Its place was taken towards the end of the Heian period by the conception of a paradise (*Gokuraku*) into which the believer yearned to be reborn. This paradise, also known as the Pure Land (*Jodo*), was merely the antechamber to Nirvana; but once arrived there, there was no return to the cycle of rebirths. The Buddhist idea of rebirth had its counterpart in the Shinto concept of the migration of souls, which held that the souls of the dead could take up their lodgings in animals (usually birds). Behind the Shintoist cult of the dead and of ancestors, however, there lay fear of the vengeful spirits of the dead and concrete expectations of good fortune, since the deified dead and the ancestral gods protected the living; this was matched in Buddhism only by a form of piety based on general moral considerations (the well known *O-bon* festival in honor of the dead is the result of syncretism).

In Japanese thought the concepts of the *gods* and of the *divine* are barely separable. In Shintoism nature and the forces manifested in it have a spiritual (numinous) quality, personified in the *kami* (divine beings: the word is etymologically connected with many Asian terms for the supreme and numinous, for shamans and exorcists). The Shinto gods and the Buddhist protective divinities are immanent in the world and, like the world, are not eternal: the brother and sister known as Izanagi and Izanami came into being spontaneously, and from them the other gods and ancestral divinities are descended; while even the high Hindu divinities like Bonten (Brahma), who are deified in the Buddhist pantheon, are transitory and subject to the law of Karma.

A special category of Shinto divinities consists of the clan and ancestral gods. The sun goddess *Amaterasu-omikami* ("Illustrious Great Divinity Radiant in the Sky"), daughter of Izanagi, became the clan divinity of the Imperial House (Jimmu-tenno, the legendary founder of the Empire, being her descendant) and thus the Japanese national divinity. According to a myth recorded in the "Kojiki" and the "Nihon-shoki" she was victorious in a conflict with her brother Susanoo, god of the sea. This probably reflects a struggle between two immigrant peoples: one, represented by Amaterasu, coming from southern China and the Pacific islands, gained political power, while the other, represented by Susanoo, coming from Central Asia and Korea, became established as a religious and spiritual power, thanks to their shamanist skills, in the Izumo region. The ancestors of great families became ancestral gods, the pioneers of technical skills protective gods of particular professional groups, while great artists and scholars became saviour gods after their death, patrons of their particular artistic or intellectual discipline. – Within the framework of Buddhism, too, many Saviour Buddhas of the "Great Vehicle", particularly those in the higher worlds, took on the qualities of divinity; endowed with supernatural spiritual power, they also enjoyed unusually long lives. The *Dainichi Nyorai* ("Great Sun-Buddha"), a strongly monotheistical conception, incarnated universal reason and absolute wisdom. – Popular worship, however, was directed towards divinities of nature, ancestral gods and a host of other gods and goddesses who, like the Seven Gods of Good Fortune (*Shichi-fukushin*), combined Buddhist, Shintoist and Taoist elements and in their nature and manifestations were very much of the earth.

Neither Shintoism nor Buddhism made much contribution to *ethics* and *morals*. The ethics of Shinto were relatively undeveloped: its moral rules were concerned with the religious field – the offerings to be made to ancestors, the practices of purification and the avoidance of impurity (and of the evil influences associated with it). The basic commandments and prohibitions of Buddhism were binding on the believer, but they were mainly confined to the private actions of the individual and were much qualified by Zen and the cult of the Saviour Buddha

Amida. – In the social life of Japan, however, with its strong emphasis on the clan and the family, the Confucian moral code for the five human relationships (*gorin*: subject/lord, child/parents, wife/husband, younger/older children in a family, friend/friend) imposed more rigorous requirements than any religious commandments. Medieval religious feeling was dominated by the principle of guilt and atonement, combined with magical conceptions and the belief in spirits: the souls of dead people who had been wronged during life might return as avenging spirits and must be appeased by appropriate offerings.

The Japanese Pantheon

Aizen Myoo	God of passion
Amaterasu-omikami	Sun goddess; mythological ancestress of the Imperial House
Amida	Buddha of Light; ruler of the Western Paradise
Bato	Horse-headed figure of Kannon
Benten, Benzaiten	Goddess of love and good fortune
Binzuru	One of the sixteen disciples of Buddha; healer of sickness
Bishamon	One of the four kings of heaven; god of wealth and good fortune
Bodhisattwa	Bosatsu; one who has attained Enlightenment but has not yet entered Nirvana; a helper or auxiliary
Bonten	Japanese name of the Hindu god Brahma; temple guardian (*dewa*)
Bosatsu	Bodhisattwa (see above)
Buddha	The "Awakened One" or "Enlightened One"; honorific title of Shakyamuni, the founder of Buddhism
Butsu	Japanese name of Buddha
Daibutsu	Great Buddha
Daikoku	God of rice-growing and of wealth
Dainichi	Buddha of Light
Dainichi Nyorai	Buddha of Light; usually represented as part of a Trinity
Dewa	The two guardian gods represented at the entrances to temples
Ebisu	God of good fortune; patron of workers and fishermen
Emma-O	Ruler of the underworld
Fudo	God of light
Fugen	Buddhist helper or auxiliary figure
Fukurokuju	God of good fortune and wisdom
Gakko-bosatsu	Moon goddess
Gochi Nyorai	The five Buddhas of Wisdom and Contemplation
Gongen	Earthly manifestations of Buddha
Hachiman	Clan god of the Minamoto; revered as a war god
Hotei	God of good fortune
Inari	Rice divinity
Izanagi and Izanami	The primal divine couple; creators of the land of Japan
Jizo-bosatsu	Patron god of travelers, expectant mothers and children
Jurojin	God of good fortune
Kannon (Kwannon)	Bodhisattwa of Compassion; usually represented in female form
Kappa	Water spirits
Kompira	Mountain divinity, revered by seamen and travelers
Koshin	God of the monkey triad
Miroku-bosatsu	Bodhisattwa, future Buddha
Ninigi-no-mikoto	Grandson of Amaterasu-omikami; legendary founder of the Empire
Nio	Kings of heaven; guardian figures (Indra and Brahma)
Nyoirin-Kannon	Divinity who fulfils wishes
Nyorai	"Enlightened One", honorific title of Buddha
Oni	Demons of the underworld
Rakan	Disciples of Buddha
Sengen	Goddess of Mount Fuji
Shaka-nyorai	Buddha's earthly existence
Shakyamuni	Buddha
Shichi-fukushin	Seven Gods of Good Fortune
Shiki	Demon of black magic
Shitenno	Four kings of heaven
Shoden	God of wisdom
Susanoo	Moon, sea and storm god
Taishakuten	Guardian figure at temple entrance
Tenjin	God of learning
Ujigami	Clan gods
Yakushi-nyorai	Healing Buddha; ruler of the Eastern Paradise

Art and Culture

Westerners thinking of Japanese art usually have in mind the art of the 17th and 18th centuries, which they tend to see as merely a variant of Chinese art. But although Chinese influences play an important part Japan also received artistic impulses from India – evidence of the far-reaching influence of the Far Eastern religions, which were always closely bound up with artistic creation and led in Japan to the development of distinctively national styles.

History of Japanese Art

The archaic phase of Japanese art extends to the historically established foundation of the Empire in the 1st century A.D. The **Jomon period** (7th millennium to 3rd century B.C.) saw the appearance of pottery in a wealth of forms which demonstrates the high level of craftsmanship of the potters. The wide distribution of **Jomon ware** with its cord-impressed patterns is shown by its occurrence on more than 70,000 sites. There are also terracottas of male and female figures and masks in the form of animals' heads. The potter's wheel was still unknown.

Japan's geographical isolation meant that the craft of bronze-working arrived there (probably from China) relatively late, perhaps in the 3rd century B.C. The incomers who brought this culture drove the Jomon peoples back into northern Japan. The techniques of pottery manufacture were now improved, and the potter's wheel came into use. This **Yayoi ware** is fired to a red color; sometimes also it has painted, cord-impressed or comb-impressed decoration. Bronze was now used to make mirrors, weapons, etc., and also cylindrical bells edged with a metal band (*dotaku*). The dead were buried in stone cists or pottery urns.

About A.D. 300 the **Kofun culture** developed. Its most striking remains are the huge keyhole-shaped burial mounds which are found particularly in the Kinki area. The tombs show an increasingly marked social differentiation; in the richer tombs the grave-goods include not only arms and armor but also Chinese jade jewelry. In order to protect it from erosion the sarcophagus was surrounded by

haniwa – originally plain pottery cylinders, later developing into representations of houses, animals and, finally, human figures. The finest achievements of this culture are the tombs of the Emperors Ojin and Nintoku. Stylistic study of the grave-goods suggest that the tombs belonged to a horse-riding people who had come to Japan by way of Korea. In the mid 4th century contacts with Korea increased: new techniques now came to Japan (iron-casting, weaving, hard-fired Sue pottery) and the architecture became more elaborate.

The coming of Buddhism marked the beginning of the **Asuka period** (522–645), in which the cult of anthropomorphic divinities came to the fore alongside the Shintoist worship of nature. Japanese artists and craftsmen took over from China features of the advanced cultures of Greece, Persia and India and created a great flowering of art. Japanese temple architecture began to develop a character of its own, and there was a proliferation of cult images. A particularly notable work of this period is the Shakya Trinity (623) by *Tori-busshi,* the first Japanese artist who is known to us by name. This still shows Chinese influence, while the gilded wooden figure of Guze-Kannon, strongly individualized, already has the makings of a specifically Japanese style. The Miroku statues in the Chuguji Monastery and the Koryuji Temple – representations of Buddha sunk in meditation – are remarkable for the vigorous physical presence which the sculptor has coaxed out of the wood. A new technique now introduced was dry lacquerwork on a wooden core. – From the mid 7th century dates the Tamamushi-no-zushi, a domestic altar which is the earliest example of Japanese painting. The technique of lacquerware now also developed.

The **Hakuho period** was also under the influence of Buddhism. The Japanese embassies to the Chinese Court (Sui and T'ang dynasties), then the cultural center of East Asia, brought back with them a variety of new stylistic elements. Sculpture now develops a lively vigor; and the flexible and flowing forms also betray Indian influence. Characteristic of the work of this period are the bronze Buddha head (685) in the Kofukuji Temple at Nara and the Yakushi Trinity (central figure end of 7th century, the others 720), which since the loss of its gilding stands out all the more prominently against the gilded aureole added in the Edo period. A similar degree of perfection is attained by the wall-paintings in the hall of the Horyuji Temple (destroyed by fire in 1949). Here, too, similarities to Indian models can be detected, but the Japanese style is dominant. – During this period artistic creation spread to the remoter parts of the country, developing characteristic local forms, particularly in the field of religious art.

The **Nara period** (710–794) produced the magnificent bronze statue of the Great Buddha (Daibutsu). The best examples of the high aesthetic quality and truth to nature of the works of art of this period – now increasingly showing distinctively individual characteristics – are the statues of the Nikko-bosatsu and Gakko-bosatsu (Bodhisattwas) in the Todaiji Temple (Nara), the Yakushi Trinity, the terracotta guardian figures and the figures of the six disciples of Buddha and the guardian divinity in the Kofukuji Temple (Nara), which, like the figure of Fukukensaku-Kannon in the Todaiji Temple, are in dry lacquer technique. The seated figure of the blind priest Ganjin, who founded the Toshodaiji Temple in or after 753, shows a degree of spiritualization which is in sharp contrast to the work of the Hakuho period. – The Gigaku masks, probably intended for wear by actors on the stage, are notable for their caricatural exaggeration of facial characteristics. The increased individualization now aimed at in representations of the human figure led to the development of portrait-painting: a good example is a likeness of Kichijo-ten, goddess of fortune, on a hempen fabric. – From the Nara period date the collection of objets d'art from all over eastern Japan – said to number 10,000 in all – assembled by the Emperor Shomu which is now housed in the treasury of the Todaiji Temple. A small selection from this collection is displayed in the National Museum in Nara.

During the Early **Heian period** (794–c. 900) Japanese culture and art were much influenced by two rapidly growing new sects of esoteric Buddhism, the Tendai and Shingon sects. The mystical tenets of these sects led to the development of quite new artistic forms, which broke away from the realism of the preceding period and downgraded artistic creativity in favour of an almost schematic symbolism. Great prominence was now given to the *mandara* (mandala, a mystical diagram), a representation of the esoteric Buddhist conception of the world in the form of numerous compartments and sub-compartments grouped round a Buddha (the Enlightened One) or Bodhisattwa (one awaiting Enlightenment), designed to help the beholder to understand the complex tenets of the faith by setting them out in graphic form.

During this period wood was the preferred material for sculpture, which in the early days was carved from a single block. The limits set by the requirements of symbolism were overcome, for example, by the vigorous expressiveness given to the terrifying faces of the gods of light. In general the statues now lack the earlier nearness to the world of the beholder: they have a remote dignity, an aura of spiritualization, which can be comprehended only through meditation. Good examples are the Yakushi-nyorai in the Jingoji Temple in Kyoto and the Nyoirin-Kannon in the Kanshinji Temple in Osaka. – Shintoism now also turned to the anthropomorphic representation of divinities. Less confined by strict iconographic rules than the sculpture of Buddhism, however, the Shinto images still show the realism of the Nara period.

In the *Late Heian period* (c. 900–1184) the new imperial capital, Heiankyo (Kyoto), became the cultural hub of the Empire. The break with China at the end of the 9th century brought a new sense of national awareness, and there was a great flowering of art in which specifically Japanese aspects were stressed. Major literary works were written at the Imperial Court in the newly devised Kana script. The emperors, having lost their power to the Fujiwara clan, devoted themselves to the refined cultural and artistic life of the Court. Palace architecture became more magnificent (Shinden-zukuri style) and developed into a new symbolic representation of the Buddhist system of beliefs as set out in the mandala images. This change reflected the replacement of the school of esoteric Buddhism which concerned itself with the life of this world by the doctrine of the Pure Land (*Jodo*), a readily comprehensible other-worldly promise of salvation based on the belief in Amida and the invocation of his name.

The high standard of achievement reached by the sculpture of this period is exemplified by the statue of Amida by *Jocho* (d. 1057). The new technique of building up a work of sculpture in wood from a number of separate pieces made possible an increased dynamism. At the same time the fearsome aspect of earlier figures gave place to the tranquil expression of the Amida statues. The sculptors emerged from their previous monastic seclusion and established their own workshops and schools, thus becoming involved in the changing cultural currents of the period. Religious symbolism was now overlaid by an aesthetic realism which found expression in softer, almost feminine forms. Examples of this sensitive style of sculpture are the statues of Kannon, the statue of Kichijo-ten in the Joruri Temple at Nara, and the figure of the seven-year-old Shotoku-taishi in the Horyuji Temple (Nara basin).

The lavish use of gold leaf in sculpture and the elaborately detailed painting have their counterpart in the national school of painting, very different from the Chinese style, known as **Yamato-e**, which reaches its peak of achievement in the *emaki* – picture scrolls on religious and more especially on historical themes, mostly based on literary works. One of the best-known scrolls, the "Genji-monogatari", depicts courtly life in the 12th century; characteristic features are the use of parallel perspective, the practice of omitting the roofs of houses so as to give a view of the interior, and the stylized representation of human figures. – In religious painting, under the influence of the Pure Land doctrine, the predominant themes are the entry of believers into paradise and the return of Amida-Buddha. – The lacquerwork of this period, having developed a considerable degree of independence, is also of high quality, making use of the *makie* technique (in which the patterns were created by sprinkling gold- or silver-dust on the fresh lacquer).

The art of the **Kamakura period** (1192–1333), a time marked in the political field by the increased strength of the warrior caste in the provinces, has a simplicity and vigour of expression which hark back to the art of the Nara period. Sculpture now reached a peak which was never to be surpassed. The principal representatives of the new style were *Unkei* (d. 1223), *Kukei* (late 12th century) and *Jokei* (c. 1200). Unkei's early works, such as the Dainichi-nyorai (1176) in the Enjoji Temple in Nara, already show a turning away from the style of the Heian period. The new naturalism produced portraits of secular figures showing a strongly individual stamp. Among representative works in the new style to be seen in Nara are the Nio statues on the Nandaimon Gate of the Todaiji Temple and the statues of the priests Muchaku and Seshin in the Kofukuji Temple, which are among Unkei's finest works. The statues of Jizo-bosatsu and the Shinto god Hachiman are by *Kaikei*.

The resumption of contacts with China (Sung dynasty) brought Japan Zen Buddhism, which was very much in line with the spirit of the Kamakura period. The new doctrine rejected all external means of finding salvation and held out the prospect of release only by looking inward. In art this attitude led to a drastic limitation of the means of expression, which on the one hand brought a certain stagnation but on the other carried the expressive power of calligraphy and ink-wash painting to a high degree of perfection. Picture scrolls and portraits became increasingly popular, as the feudal society of the time in a sense began to discover itself. The aim of the artist was to achieve an exact likeness, as in the portrait of Minamoto Yoritomo by *Fujiwara Takanobu* (1142–1205). The picture scrolls produced in large numbers in this period might be anything up to 80 ft/25 m long; their subject-matter now included biographies, accounts of the origin of temples and shrines, heroic representations of the ruling warrior class (as in the "Heiji-monogatari") and also satirical works like the "Choju-giga" (in the Kozanji Temple, Kyoto), in which the life of the Court is caricatured in animal form.

The applied arts flourished particularly during this period. Damascened swords of superb quality were produced; the traditions of lacquerware and woven fabrics were developed further; and after returning from China the potter *Toshiro* began to produce notably fine ware about 1230, establishing his workshop at Seto, where it was followed by some 200 others.

In the **Muromachi period** the courtly elegance of the Heian period, now rediscovered, mingled with Zen influences. Zen had the effect of sharply reducing the means of artistic expression, replacing the colorful Yamato-e style by monochrome ink-wash painting, in which detailed representation gives place to suggestion; the artist no longer seeks to depict his subject as it is, but rather its quintessence, revealed to him in a flash of illumination. The ink-wash painting is restricted to a few bold strokes of the brush, the dynamic force of which is enhanced by shading. Leading exponents of this technique were *Mokuan* and *Kao* (14th century); favourite subjects were imaginary portraits of the Chinese monks

Zen and the Art of Landscape-Painting in Ink Wash

What appealed to Zen adepts in **ink-wash painting** Sumie was the spontaneity of the technique, which was in tune with their direct and immediate approach. In ink-wash painting the ink is immediately absorbed by the porous rice-paper, and every brush-stroke must be exactly right. Even retouching by overpainting above shows up, since the ink then appears duller when it dries. The second quality which appealed to Zen monks in monochrome ink-wash painting was its capacity to achieve the greatest possible effect with the simplest means. The use of shading, from the white of the paper through various tones of grey to deep black, expressed not only the distribution of light and shade but also that of the colors which it called up in the mind of the beholder.

The technical problems of landscape-painting had been solved in China towards the end of the T'ang period. The effect of perspective was achieved, not by converging lines as in Western art but by disposing the elements of the picture in three planes, one above the other. The aim was not to achieve a realistic representation of the landscape but to reproduce the impression which it conveyed to the artist. At the beginning of the Sung period (960–1279) the rules, at first flexible, were set down in a rigid canon of conventions which was observed both in China and in Japan for many centuries.

A northern and a southern school of painting developed at roughly the same time. The *northern school* of Sung landscape-painting produced formally composed symmetrical works marked by sharp, jagged outlines, particularly in the foreground; while the mountains in the upper plane are usually just as distinctly represented as the rocks in the lower one. The *southern school,* on the other hand, preferred soft, blurred outlines, rounded hills and misty valleys; the mountains in the background are merely suggested by shading. After the Sung Court moved south in 1127 the two styles were combined: the foreground was frequently depicted in the hard northern manner while the background was executed in the diffuse technique of the south. This mingling of the two styles, known as the Ma-Hsia style after its two leading exponents, *Ma Yäan* and *Hsai Kuai,* became the model for the Zen painting of the Ashikaga period in Japan. The Japanese painters were at first influenced by the spontaneous Expressionist style introduced in the 13th century by the monk *Mu-chi,* a scorner of all conventions, in the Ch'an monasteries in southern China, where the Japanese first encountered landscape-painting in the form of his work.

In the time of the Ashikaga shogun *Yoshimitsu,* a great patron of Zen art, an academy of painting was established in the Shokoku-ji Temple under the direction of the Zen master *Josetsu,* who was active from about 1400 to 1413. His paintings and those of his pupils demonstrate the considerable mastery of the Ma-Hsia style they had achieved by study of the Sung originals. Josetsu was succeeded by his pupil *Shubun,* who between about 1420 and his death in 1460 produced a large number of fine picture scrolls and wall screens. He did not merely imitate the Sung style: his works are new and original creations breathing the very spirit of the Ma-Hsia school. Shubun was followed by *Sotan* (1414–81), who lacked his originality; and under his direction the academy produced mere copies of the Sung paintings.

A new breakthrough was achieved by one of Shubun's pupils, **Sesshu Toyo** (1420–1506), who is regarded as the greatest master of Zen art. He had become an adept of Zen at an early age and was soon appointed to a senior position in the Shokoku-ji Temple. He then visited China, but returned disappointed: in his own words, he had found no worthy teachers there apart from the mountains and the rivers. Features of his technique which do, however, stem from China are the realistic elements and the "broken wash" style evolved in the Ch'an schools. Sesshu became famous through the two styles which he developed in his later years. In the first of these, known as the Shin style, the picture is built up from angular planes reminiscent of Cubism, bounded by sharp and vigorous outlines. In the other there is practically no use of line: it shows a mingling of the blurred shading of the southern Sung school with the technique of "broken wash" (*haboku*), in which the landscape is composed of little dabs of wash merging into one another. This is known as the So or Haboku-sansui style.

Sessho was offered the post of Director of the Kyoto Academy, but preferred to paint and to meditate in a village on the west coast. Sotan was then succeeded as Director by *Kano Masanobu* (1434–1530), who, together with his son *Kano Motonobu* (1476–1559), introduced the decorative Kano style. This school, which turned away from the spirit of Zen, thereafter enjoyed a long period of predominance in Japanese art.

Sesshu provided a model for painters outside the academy such as *So-ami,* who practiced the So style, and *Sesson,* who was proficient in both the So and the Shin styles. Their works show a certain smooth elegance, but lack the depth and vigorous originality of Sesshu Toyo's painting. Thus ended, after a brief flowering, the Zen school of landscape-painting, which gave consummate expression to mystical intuitions in the simple techniques of monochrome ink-wash painting.

Kanzan and Jittoku (T'ang period, 618–907), who are depicted in a tranquil state of Enlightenment, contrasting with the intellectual pretensions of other sects.

Landscape-painting also reached a peak of perfection in the 14th and 15th centuries. Notable artists of the period were *Josetsu* (14th century), one of the greatest teachers of his time, *Mincho* (1352–1431) and *Shubun* (early 15th century). Models were provided by the paintings of the Sung and Early Ming dynasties in China (10th–15th centuries), which exerted a powerful influence on the work of *Noami* (1397–1471), his son *Geiami* (1431–95) and his grandson *Soami* (1472–1525). – Incontestably the greatest landscape-painter of his time was *Sesshu Toyo* (1420–1506), who found enormously rich sources of inspiration during a visit to China in 1468–69. With a skill unequalled by any of his contemporaries he combined the Chinese technique with a distinctively Japanese choice of subject-matter, recording the timeless quality of the Japanese landscape in such works as his "Ama-no-hashidate", "Hoboku" (National Museum, Tokyo) and the "Great Landscape Picture Scroll", which follows Chinese models of the Sung dynasty and is in marked contrast to the scrolls of the Heian and Kamakura periods.

The tea ceremony became increasingly popular during this period, and its complex refinements had a fertilizing influence on ceramics, painting and landscape-gardening. The closeness to nature of Zen Buddhism led to the emergence of a number of priests among the leading garden architects of the day, among them *Muso Kokushi,* who designed the garden of the Saihoji Temple in Kyoto. The great extent and variety of nature were now given expression in a restricted space by the use of symbolism and abstraction carried to its highest point, as in the gardens of the Ryoanji and Daitokuji Temples in Kyoto.

In the *Late Muromachi period* there was a counter-current to the art of Zen Buddhism in which decorative elements came to the fore. The new trend centered on the **Kano school**, founded by *Kano Masanobu* (1434–1530) and carried on by his son *Kano Motonobu* (1476–1559). Art now broke away from its association with religion and was of thoroughly secular cast. During its existence of more than three centuries the new school was responsible for the interior decoration of most of the new palaces and temples which were now being built, and its landscapes and animal pictures are still to be seen in Kyoto and many other places. In the 15th century there was a revival, outside Kyoto, of the Yamato-e style, which now turned also to genre scenes.

Sculpture was completely neglected, since Zen Buddhism, looking inward rather than outward, attached no importance to cult images.

In the second half of the 16th century peace was restored in Japan by the shoguns Nobunaga, Hideyoshi and Ieyasu. This period of political renewal was accompanied by a reorientation of Japanese culture, which during the **Momoyama period** (1573–1603) lost its courtly character and was influenced by middle-class tastes. The Kano school now devoted itself to the interior decoration of the mighty castles which were being built in this period, combining the linearity of ink-wash painting with the Yamato-e style's delight in color to produce a sumptuous new style in which the figures stood out against a background of gold leaf.

Towards the end of the 16th century the fusion of the Kano school with the **Tosa school** which carried on the traditions of the Yamato-e style was achieved. *Kano Eitoku* (1543–90) was responsible for the painting of folding screens and sliding doors in Azuchi Castle. Leading representatives of the Tosa school were *Mitsumoto* (1530–59) and *Mitsuyoshi* (1539–1613). Other artists of the period were *Kaiho Yusho* (1533–1615) and *Hasegawa Tohaku* (1539–1610), the latter of whom was responsible for the wall-paintings in the Chishakuin Temple in Kyoto.

Ink-wash painting, now rather in the background, was represented by *Shokado* (1584–1639) and *Miyamoto Niten* (1584–1645). – The **Namban school** depicted the arrival of the first Europeans in Japan. With the development of genre painting there was a greater interest in the individual: large gatherings gave place to small groups, and in the subsequent period to individual figures – a total novelty in this genre.

The applied arts and crafts now developed on an increasing scale. Lacquerware and metalwork became symbols of status and prosperity in the houses of the rising middle classes, particularly the merchants. Contacts with foreign countries took Japan out of its isolation and brought in the technique of oil-painting and new aspects of art and art appreciation. The manufacture of porcelain received fresh stimulus from the Korean potters brought to Japan as a result of the Korean campaigns; *Chojiro* (1515–92) made the first *raku* tea-bowls in the preferred tones of black and red in Kyoto, and new manufactories were established (Seto-yaki, Oribe-yaki, Shino-yaki).

During the **Edo period (Tokugawa era**, 1603–1868) middle-class culture became firmly established. Cut off from all contact with other countries and confined within the bounds of the strict social stratification, the middle classes turned to art and developed an elegant and costly life-style. All religious, philosophical or courtly standards of value lost their authority, and the impoverishment of the samurai class reflected the casting off of the medieval system of ethics. This development culminated in the *Genroku era* (1688–1704).

The Kano school had begun to show signs, towards the end of the Momoyama period, of stagnating, falling into mere routine and losing its creative power; and it was now overtaken by fresh styles and techniques. New schools arose, such as the **Korin (Rimpa) school** founded by *Honami Koetsu* (1558–1637). Among its members was *Ogata Korin* (1658–1716), who developed a highly decorative style of painting with typically Japanese subjects. His best-known works include the folding screen "Red and White Plum Blossom" and "Sword Lilies". Another member of the group, whose members worked north of Kyoto, was the painter *Tawaraya Sotatsu* (c. 1600–1640), also an adherent of the Yamato-e and Tosa schools, whose surviving works include folding screens depicting the story of Genji and a Bugaku scene. Honami Koetsu produced lacquerware and porcelain of high quality. Another potter belonging to the group was *Ogata Kenzen* (1663–1743), Korin's brother and a pupil of *Ninsei*. – These versatile artists gave fresh impulses to the whole of the Japanese art world. In addition to

Chinese influences increased European influence can now be detected, with the previous system of parallel perspective giving place to centralized (convergent) perspective.

At the beginning of the 17th century there developed the *Bunjinga* school, in which scholars and calligraphers supplied illustrations to works of literature, producing work of the highest quality which owed allegiance to no previous artistic traditions. – The art of the woodcut, previously only used for illustrations in books, now achieved independence in the *Ukiyo-e* technique, which soon achieved wide popularity and after the introduction of color printing (1765) developed into the *Nishiki-e* technique. The themes included erotic subjects, scenes in the theater and places of

Technical Terms

Byobu	Folding screen
Dotaku	Bronze bell
Emakimono	Picture scroll
Fusuma	Sliding wall
Haniwa	Pottery figures (animals, human figures, houses)
Jomon	Cord-impressed pottery
Kakemono	Picture scroll (vertical)
Kannon	Representation of the Compassionate Buddha
Kodo	Porch of temple
Kofun	Burial mound
Kongo rikishi	Guardian figures at entrance to temples
Makimono	Picture scroll (horizontal)
Mandara	Symbolic and highly abstract cult picture (mandala)
Mikoshi	Portable shrine
Mudra	Position of hands in Buddha image
Netsuke	Small sculptured object designed for use as a toggle on a belt
Nise-e	Portrait-painting
Nishiki-e	Colored woodcut
Nuri-mono	Lacquerware
Obi	Sash worn by a woman over her kimono
Shoji	Sliding wall
Suiboku	Ink-wash painting
Sumi-e	Ink-wash painting
Tokonoma	Ornamental recess for picture scroll
Torii	Entrance gate of a Shinto shrine
Ukiyo-e	Colored woodcut
Yaki-mono	Porcelain

entertainment, female portraits, etc. In the late phase of Ukiyo-e many landscape-prints of outstanding quality were produced by *Hokusai* (1760–1849), *Hiroshige* (1797–1858) and others. – The potters of this period produced glazed ware painted with vitrifiable pigments. About 1600 the discovery of deposits of kaolin led to a rapid expansion of porcelain manufacture. Nabeshima porcelain was reserved for imperial and aristocratic use; coarser ware designed for export to foreign (including European) countries was made at Imari.

The **Meiji period** saw Japan's first great step forward into the modern age, and the rapidly developing contacts with the West also influenced Japanese art. Painting was split between two trends – the **Nipponga** school of traditional Japanese painting and the **Yoga** school, which adopted Western techniques and forms of expression, in particular painting in oils. To this latter group, which mainly followed Paris models, belonged *Kuroda Kiyoteru* (1866–1924), *Ishida Ryusai* (1891–1926) and *Yasui Sotaro* (1880–1935). About 1900 there was a revival of traditional Japanese styles, including the Kano and Shijo schools, ink-wash painting and colored woodcuts. Side by side with the fine arts, traditional arts and crafts (porcelain, lacquerware, metalwork) continued to flourish.

Arts and Crafts

Pottery and ceramics. – The Jomon period (7th millennium to 3rd century B.C.; Neolithic) produced Japan's earliest pottery. This was a dark-colored ware, made without a wheel and decorated with a variety of cord-impressed patterns. Between 300 B.C. and A.D. 300 there appeared the light-colored, wheel-turned and simply decorated Yayoi ware. This was followed by Sue ware, a style imported from Korea – thin-walled, dark-colored vessels with sparse linear decoration, which continued in production until the Heian period (8th–12th centuries). During this period there also appeared the first *haniwa*, pottery cylinders found as grave-goods, which later developed into figural forms. As early as the Nara period (8th century) Chinese ceramics were much esteemed in Japan, being imported and imitated in the form of glazed ware (e.g. tiles for the roofs of temples). This

Chinese influence increased during the Kamakura period (12th–14th century). The glazed ware produced at Seto (near Nagoya), in colors ranging from yellowish to dark brown, was particularly favored by tea-masters. Pots and vases were also produced in olive-green and brown glazes (celadon).

The main centers of ceramic production in this and the following Muromachi period (13th–16th centuries) were in the provinces of Mino and Owari (Aichi prefecture). The best-known manufactories were the "Six Old Kilns" – Echizen (Fukui prefecture), Shigaraki (Shiga prefecture), Tamba (Hyogo prefecture), Bizen (Okayama prefecture) and Ko Seto and Tokoname (Aichi prefecture) – which produced mainly robust unglazed ware for everyday use, later very popular with tea-masters. Only the light to dark brown and greenish-yellow Ko Seto ware (*ko* = "old", to distinguish this ware from later Seto products) was glazed, sometimes with transparent ash glazes. The influence of the Korean potters which was already making itself felt during this period became predominant at the end of the 16th century. Kyushu was the first great center of production of Korean-influenced ceramics, typical products being the wares known as *Karatsu-yaki* and *Satsuma-yaki,* notable for their simplicity of form and quiet coloring.

Hagi (Yamaguchi prefecture) now became an increasingly important center of production. The tea-bowls produced here, shaped by hand and roughly finished, appealed to the tea-masters as showing the aesthetic characteristics prized by Zen Buddhism. The arbitrary character of their form and color, the accidental effects, even bad firing, were seen as the highest artistic merit because they were entirely natural and spontaneous. The *raku* tea-bowls originally produced by Chojiro (1515–92) – so called after a seal with the inscription *raku* ("joy") which Toyotomi Hideyoshi presented to Chojiro's son Jokei – were particularly esteemed; they were decorated with a thick glaze in colors ranging from black through brown and reddish brown to red, with lighter patches. Among noted *raku* masters were Ninsei (d. 1678 or 1695) and Kenzan (1664–1743) – the latter a member of a group of artists founded by Koetsu (1558–1637) at Takagamine, north of Kyoto.

Kutani-yaki

Koetsu himself produced tea-bowls of outstanding quality. Ninsei, Kenzan's teacher, used the vitrified glaze technique which came into use in the 17th century to produce ware of consummate artistry. At this period ceramic wares were manufactured mainly for use in the tea ceremony, which required not only tea-bowls but other utensils, including tea-caskets, flower-vases and water-containers.

Japanese ceramics also became of great importance in the aesthetics of Zen Buddhism; and they have retained their reputation down to the present day, thanks to the work of such well-known artists as Kawai Kanjiro (1890–1966), who worked in Kyoto, and Hamada Shoji (1884–1978), who made Mashiko one of the most popular ceramic towns in Japan – which can justly claim to be *the* country for porcelain.

Japanese porcelain (*yaki*), to be found nowadays in countless small shops, manufactories (many of which are open to visitors) and in antique shops, owes its character and quality largely to the influence of the Korean potters who settled in Japan after the Korean campaigns of Toyotomi Hideyoshi between 1592 and 1598. – The characteristics of this ware are its unshowy beauty, its unpretentious simplicity and its freedom from all artificial effects. The irregularity produced by the artist's free and unmechanical use of form and color gives it a distinctive and satisfying quality, expressed in every creative detail, which appeals to the collector, the lover of fine porcelain and the souvenir-hunter alike.

Many of the manufactories established over the centuries and still carrying on an unbroken tradition, with their varying firing techniques and their characteristic forms and colors, welcome visitors, who are shown the production processes and can visit an exhibition of the manufactory's products. In some cases there are facilities for amateurs to practice the craft. – The following are among the leading manufactories (in alphabetical order):

Bizen (Okayama prefecture). – Unglazed ware, in dark grey to reddish tones, with natural glazes produced by falling ash; irregular bands of glazing produced by wrapping rice straw round the vessel. Originally made for everyday use, Bizen-yaki was later much used in the tea ceremony. One of the "Six Old Kilns". 12th–16th centuries.

Echizen (Fukui prefecture). – Large thick-walled stoneware vessels in greyish-brown to reddish-brown tones, with greenish ash glaze. One of the "Six Old Kilns". 12th–17th centuries.

Hagi (Yamaguchi prefecture). – Produced in unbroken tradition from the 17th century to the present day. Ware with thick crackle glaze in milky to greyish-yellow tones. First produced by a Korean potter, Li Kyong.

Mino (Aichi prefecture). – The Mino kilns, operating from the end of the Muromachi period (16th century), produced white Shino ware, Seto ware and green Oribe ware.

Seto (Aichi prefecture). – The oldest center of ceramic production in Japan, manufacturing glazed ware from the Kamakura period (12th–14th centuries). Dark brown to black glazes from the 16th century; later yellowish crackle glazes (Ki Seto) and various other types. Seto is now Japan's largest ceramic center, and the name *Seto-mono* (Seto ware) has become a synonym for porcelain. One of the "Six Old Kilns".

Shigaraki (Shiga prefecture). – Transparent yellowish-grey to greyish-green ash glazes on greyish-brown to dark brown fabric with light-colored grain. One of the "Six Old Kilns", operating from the Kamakura period (12th–14th centuries). The ware favored by the 16th-century tea-masters.

Shino (Aichi prefecture). – Ware produced from the 16th century for the tea ceremony, in yellowish to bright red tones with a greyish-white glaze. Still produced in unbroken tradition. The name comes from the great tea-master Shino Soshui (16th–17th century).

Takatori (Fukuoka prefecture). – Greyish-brown fabric with speckled glaze in brown to reddish-brown tones. Much influenced by the tea-master Kobori Enshu (1579–1647).

Tamba (Hyogo prefecture). – Dark brown to reddish-brown fabric, the result of long firing, with a thick ash glaze. One of the "Six Old Kilns", operating from the 16th century. Now made at Tachikui, near Sasayama.

Tokoname (Aichi prefecture). – Brown fabric with natural green glaze. After the end of the 16th century much reduced output; from the 19th century ceramics for use in building. One of the "Six Old Kilns".

Metalwork. – The earliest evidence of metalworking in Japan dates from the Yayoi period (c. 300 B.C.–A.D. 300), in the form of elongated bells (dotaku), jewelry and cult instruments of bronze or iron. In the 6th century new and more refined techniques came to Japan from the mainland with Buddhism, and the art of bronze-casting in particular reached a high degree of perfection. Under the influence of Chinese and Korean teachers jewelry, cult instruments, vessels and sculpture were produced by a variety of different processes: bronze was cast, hammered, beaten, chased, inlaid with gold or silver, punched or perforated to produce an openwork effect. The finest example of the bronze-casting of this period is the Shaka Trinity by Tori-busshi in the Horyuji Temple (623).

The Nara period (8th century), under the influence of the T'ang dynasty in China, produced realistic monumental sculpture in cast bronze, notably the "Great Buddha" (752) in the Todaiji Temple at Nara. It was only after 800 that Japanese metalworking broke away from the influence of the mainland and produced its own distinctive forms. With the flowering of sculpture in wood the craft of bronze-casting took second place, and metalworkers increasingly concentrated on the production of articles for everyday use, jewelry and ornaments in the nobler metals, already showing a typically Japanese use of natural decoration.

In the war-torn Kamakura period (12th–14th centuries) the work of the weapon-smiths took pride of place. Their finest achievements date from the beginning of the 14th century, when they had developed increasingly refined techniques and forms of decoration. The classic type of Japanese sword was evolved by the Myochin family of armorers. Until the 9th century the type of straight-bladed sword, either single-edged or two-edged, used on the mainland (tsurugi) was still in general use in Japan; then, at the beginning of the 10th century, a single-edged sword with a slightly curved blade (nihonto), found only in Japan, came into use. These were made by the process known as damascening, in which several layers of metal were welded, folded or twisted together and then hammered into shape. As in other cultures, the weapon-smiths enjoyed a high status in Japanese society, and their work was accompanied by prescribed ritual actions. – Japanese swords can be seen in various historical museums, but the best collection is that of the Sword Museum in Tokyo.

In the Muromachi period (14th–16th centuries) iron-casting increasingly came to the fore again. Articles of everyday use, cauldrons, vases and vessels for the tea ceremony, ornamental fittings and handles were produced, predominantly by the "cire perdue" process (rogata). – The opening up of Japan in the Meiji period (1867 onwards) brought in industrial metal-processing, heralding the decline of the traditional metalworking crafts. In order to preserve the techniques of these crafts for future generations the Government is making special efforts to foster them, and leading craftsmen teach at colleges and in craft workshops with the honorific title of "guardians of important and sacrosanct cultural traditions".

Textiles. – There is evidence of the use of the loom in Japan as early as the Yayoi period (c. 300 B.C.–A.D. 300), and this period probably also saw the beginnings of silkworm culture. In addition to silk the weavers worked with hemp, nettle fibers and various forms of bast (raffia). By the Nara period (8th century) a variety of refined weaving techniques, all taken over from China and Korea, were already in use, and the fabrics now widely manufactured included twill, damask and simple brocades and gauzes. With the rise in prosperity under the Shogunate in the 13th century other advanced weaving techniques came to Japan from the mainland, including silver and gold brocades and satin. Cotton began to be woven only in the 15th century.

The craft of dyeing was also of great importance from early times. Since the cut of the traditional Japanese garments changed little over the centuries, developments in fashion and style found expression mainly in color and pattern. As early as the 8th century the three basic dyeing processes, still used in textile production, were already in full use – the batik technique, the use of stencils and tie-dyeing. From the 13th century sumptuous effects were produced by the combination of various dyeing techniques, embroidering with gold and silver thread and rubbing with gold and silver leaf.

With the opening up of Japan in the Meiji period industrial weaving and textile printing processes came in and soon displaced the old techniques. These still retain their place in craft production, and are also used in the making of particularly costly fabrics for the much sought after and very expensive silk kimonos which are still worn by women on ceremonial occasions or for important family events. Both natural and artificial fibers are used, new techniques are developed and old ones revived. The most popular fabrics are now produced on Okinawa and Amami-Oshima, in the prefectures of Kumamoto, Fukuoka (Kurume) and Kagoshima and at Matsuyama (Ehime prefecture); other centers of production are in Shimane and Niigata prefectures. – Leading centers of the dyeing industry are Kyoto and Kanazawa, Miyagi and Yamagata prefectures and Tokyo.

Northern Japan, particularly Aomori, is noted for its embroidery, with geometric patterns on a dark ground. On Hokkaido, particularly around Sapporo and in the Ainu villages of Chikabumi and Shiraoi, fabrics with appliqué decoration of the type formerly made by the Ainu can still be found. – The Silk Museum in Yokohama and the Nishijin Textile Museum in Kyoto offer excellent surveys of Japanese textile production.

Tattooing – i.e. the drawing of patterns on the human skin by pricking and injecting indelible colors – was practiced from the earliest times by many primitive peoples, particularly in the islands of the South Seas. A Chinese account of Japan at the end of the 3rd century B.C. records that the inhabitants of western Japan tattooed their bodies and faces, partly for ornament and partly to indicate their clan and social class. Later tattooing became a form of judicial punishment (*irezumi*, to inject ink; provided for in a statute of 1720). During the Edo period the tattooing of designs and after 1750 of pictures (*horimono*, the incising of patterns) became a great fashion, particularly in the demi-monde; and in spite of repeated prohibitions during the 19th and 20th century the practice of tattooing is still popular in certain Japanese circles.

For some Japanese the human body is beautiful only if it is tattooed; and tattooing can also serve to indicate membership of a particular social group. The most

Japanese tattoos

favored parts of the body are the back, the upper arms, the breast, the upper part of the thighs and the buttocks. In contrast to the subjects commonly found in other countries (anchors, lighthouses, girls, butterflies, etc.), Japanese aficionados prefer an over-all decorative scheme covering as large an area as possible. This preference can be traced back to models provided by famous woodcut artists and painters of the 18th and 19th centuries (scenes from heroic epics); and tattooing patterns are also influenced by ink-wash painting and the decorative patterns on kimonos and on the backs of the sleeveless tunics worn by samurai warriors (dragons, demons, etc.).

The traditional tattooing technique involves sticking into the subject's skin one or more needles containing colored dyes fastened to a stick about the size of a pencil; modern techniques make the painful and very taxing process more tolerable. Since the victims of this torture – who include women as well as men – can stand no more than one or two hours of it at a time, the time-consuming and expensive process of tattooing a large design can extend over several months. The classic colors are black (which produces a bluish shimmer under the skin), vermilion and brown; more recently yellow, orange and green have been added. – The pictures produced by the tattoo artists, which are always signed, can be seen at temple festivals and in bath-houses.

Lacquerware. – The craft of lacquerwork, which originated on the mainland of Asia, reached the Japanese islands, in its simplest form, in prehistoric times. The sap of the varnish tree (*Rhus verniciflua*), which when dry is resistant to acids, heat and humidity, was used to coat everyday articles for protective purposes; and it was soon realized that with the addition of natural pigments it also served as a simple form of decoration.

With the coming of Buddhism in the 6th century A.D. highly developed lacquer techniques were brought from China to Japan, where they were subsequently further refined. Soon Japanese lacquer-workers began to produce lacquerware of high quality which surpassed Chinese work both technically and artistically. Boxes and caskets, tableware, cult utensils, small items of furniture, jewelry, sculpture and other objects made of wood, bamboo, leather, metal, terracotta, fabrics and even paper were protected and decorated at the same time by the application of delicate lacquer ornament; and when Japan was opened up to trade with foreign countries in the mid 19th century Japanese lacquerware became world-famed. Young lacquer-workers now worked in Europe and America and passed on their skills. At the present time the finest lacquer-workers of the day, with the style of "guardians of sacrosanct cultural traditions", work and teach at Japanese art schools and in specialized workshops.

Japanese lacquerware is produced by three different processes, each with a number of variants: flat, inlaid and carved. – Among the *flat lacquer* techniques were the *makie* ("sprinkle picture") gold lacquer techniques – the principal Japanese innovation – which achieved a high standard of technical and artistic achievement as early as the Heian period (8th–12th centuries). In the *togidashi* process the pattern was produced by sprinkling gold and silver dust on a still-wet coat of lacquer, which was then covered with several further coats of black lacquer; after which the surface was polished with charcoal until the delicate underlying pattern was revealed. In the *hiramakie* process the gold or silver dust was sprinkled directly on to the surface of the lacquer to produce the pattern. *Takamakie* was a form of "sprinkle" technique which produced raised patterns. In *okibirame* the metal dust was replaced by small pieces of metal sheet. – Another of the flat lacquer techniques was lacquer-painting, which was much practiced in the 7th century but declined in importance in the 8th. *Negoro-nuri* was a flat lacquer technique in which a red upper coat was polished away until the black undercoat appeared in patches; it began to be practiced in the Muromachi period and is still very popular.

Inlaid lacquerwork, which is first recorded during the Nara period (8th century), is frequently combined with the *makie* technique. The favorite inlays were mother-of-pearl in the early days, later followed by gold and silver foil, coral, ivory and various semi-precious stones. – *Carved lacquerware* (*tsui-shu*) did not appear until the 15th century, when it followed Chinese models and was difficult to distinguish from Chinese work. A distinctive Japanese style developed only in the 17th century. Alongside the very time-consuming genuine carved lacquer, which involved cutting the thick lacquer coating, there soon came into being the simpler *Kamakura-bori* process, in which the wood was first carved and then coated with lacquer. – All lacquerware gets its high gloss through repeated polishing of the surface, a laborious and time-consuming process.

In consequence of the labor and great care required for its production lacquerware was always costly, exceeding even porcelain in value. – The craft of lacquerwork is still practiced in the old production centers of Tokyo, Kyoto and Kanazawa; and there are other traditional workshops at Takamatsu and Nagoya and throughout Japan (e.g. Wakasa and Wajima). Simpler ware for domestic use is produced mainly in the prefectures of Fukushima, Ishikawa, Toyama and Wakayama.

Netsuke. – The *netsuke* (from *ne,* "root-wood", and *tsuke,* "peg") which first appeared in the 15th century and gained great popularity in the 17th, are toggles carved in the form of human figures, animals, plants and a variety of other objects which served to attach purses and pockets carried at the belt for holding everyday requisites such as writing-materials, money, medicines or tobacco. They have either one or two holes for the cords from which the purse was suspended, and which when inserted under the *obi* (sash, belt) prevented it from slipping down. A good netsuke must be suitable for its function and must also be convenient to hold, with no sharp points or edges. Originally these small objects were carved from root-wood, but later increasing use was made of other materials including ivory, horn, bamboo, nutshells, lacquerware, pottery, semi-precious stones or metal. There were no restrictions on the choice of motifs, which might come from any aspect of life, mythology, religion, legend or poetry or might spring from the artist's imagination.

In terms of form several types can be distinguished. The oldest are the button-shaped *manju; sashi* are elongated, with a single hole; the sickle-shaped *obihasami* were hooked over the sash; the *kagamibuta* ("mirror ceiling") have a small metal inset; the *katabori* are figures fully carved in the round. – In addition to netsuke, which serve only as a toggle from which to suspend something, there are others which can themselves contain small objects.

Paper. – The use of paper and the various ways of making it probably came to Japan from China by way of Korea in the 7th century. Thereafter it was manufactured in great variety and used for a wide range of purposes – delicate paper dolls, brightly coloured boxes, wallets with printed decoration, partition walls and sliding doors, calligraphy and the miniature masterpieces of paper-folding known under the name *origami.* Originally reserved for the use of Court circles, paper came into general use in the Japanese middle classes in the Edo period, from the mid 17th century.

Japan paper or Japan vellum is a stout long-fibered paper made from the fibers of the paper mulberry plant (*Broussonetia papyrifera*). *Rice-paper,* a delicate but astonishingly tough material, is made from the white pith of the araliaceous plant *Tetrapanax papyrifera.* The fine *Misumata paper* is made from the bark of *Edgeworthia chrysantha,* a shrub of the Daphne family.

These traditional types of paper are still made by hand but are also produced industrially, like all other kinds of paper and cardboard. Japan is the world's largest paper-producer after the United States. The main centers of the paper industry are a number of towns in Iwate prefecture, including particularly Higashiyama and Yanagifu, together with Oguni (Niigata prefecture), Matsumoto (Nagano prefecture), Tokyo and the neighboring prefecture of Saitama, Mino (Gifu prefecture), Fukui and Kanazawa prefectures, Kyoto, northern Shikoku and the prefecture of Fukuoka on Kyushu. – The interesting Paper Museum in Tokyo contains not only a wide range of different papers and printed material but also paper-making machinery and implements.

Packaging. – Another Japanese craft with a long tradition behind it is the art of packing or packaging (*tsutsumi*), which gives expression to the national love of harmony. The idea behind it is that "pure" things should not be displayed openly but should be covered up as attractively as possible. Originally it was mainly foodstuffs that were packed for transport and keeping; but to this practical aspect was added a desire to achieve beauty as well as utility, and in course of time there developed a regular art form, mainly now practiced in the wrapping of gifts.

The favorite natural packing materials have from time immemorial been rice straw, bamboo and cedarwood. Since rice is one of the staple foods of the Japanese, straw is available in abundance; and since it is both tough and elastic it is very suitable for use in wickerwork or the making of cord. Thus dried fish will keep for months if it is wrapped in seasoned straw rope, through the gaps in which air can circulate; containers for eggs or rice patties are plaited from rice straw; and rice-wine containers are wrapped up in mats of rice straw. – The leaves and stems of the rapidly growing bamboo – a symbol of strength and fruitfulness – make useful packing and containers for a variety of foodstuffs, and bamboo grass is much used in basketwork. – Wooden boxes of varying shape and size are used for the packaging of fish, rice, etc., with elaborately corded press-on lids.

But packing materials are useful not only for keeping foodstuffs: they may also add a flavor. Rice cakes are wrapped in cherry leaves in spring, in oak leaves in early summer, in camellia leaves in winter; and leaves of bamboo, reeds or water-grown rice can impart still other flavors. – A curious example of the Japanese art of packaging is the practice of heating a large cuttlefish in hot ashes and shaping it for use as a rice-wine bottle; then, after being used for this purpose, sometimes several times, the "bottle" can be grilled and eaten.

The Japanese clearly take a great delight in packing and unpacking gifts, whether on religious or family festivals, on other ceremonial occasions or in the course of business. More valuable gifts are always carefully and tastefully packed; and also money is not infrequently wrapped up in tissue paper.

Both in the craftsman-produced traditional forms of gift-packing and in the mechanically produced versions which have developed out of them only natural materials are used; but in the field of industrial packaging the use of man-made materials – paper, cardboard, plastics, etc. – continues to increase. In Japan as in other countries the demands of convenience, prosperity and a consumption-oriented society prevail, leading to the loss of a traditional craft, time-consuming and labor-intensive though it may be.

Landscape-gardening *(Zoen)*. – With its restful atmosphere, its harmony and the complexity it achieves within the most restricted space a Japanese garden exerts an extraordinary charm on the beholder. In Japanese gardens, unlike the gardens and parks of the West, the hand of the gardener is concealed: the measure of a garden's perfection lies in its apparently accidental form, in the naturalness with which its various elements fall into place. Japanese garden architecture was influenced by Japanese painting, and has the same status as a work of art of symbolic content created in accordance with strict aesthetic principles as an object for contemplation by the spectator. Its connection with religion was, from its earliest days, equally close.

The earliest Japanese landscaped gardens were based on Chinese models. The first gardens in China are said to have been created in the Han period as representations of the legendary "Isles of the Immortals". Later, under the influence of Buddhism, they symbolized Amida's Western Paradise. The spread of Taoist ideas led to a deeper feeling for unspoiled nature; and since Taoist scholars often sought solitude in remote mountain gorges the designers of gardens liked to set them against mountain backgrounds or to build up artificial crags on islands.

The Nara period (8th century) saw the creation of beautiful gardens based on Chinese models, with miniature lakes containing islands which were linked with one another and with the shore by small arched bridges. During the Heian period (8th–12th centuries) gardens were laid out in association with buildings in the splendid and elegant Shinden-zukuri style. The Court nobility acquired pleasure gardens with a varied pattern of lakes, waterfalls, man-made islands and pavilions in Chinese style. These large private parks, however, were designed for the pleasures of walking and boating, and were without any religious or symbolic significance. In the 11th century the art of landscape-gardening had achieved a perfection of which some inkling can still be gained in the garden of the Byodoin Temple at Uji, near Kyoto; other examples dating from this period are the gardens of the Motsuji Temple (Iwate prefecture) and the Joruri-ji at Kyoto.

A very different pattern was set by Zen Buddhism, exerting a powerful influence on Japanese life during the Kamakura period (12th–14th centuries) which soon extended to garden architecture and replaced courtly elegance by severity and simplicity. Whereas hitherto the garden had served mainly as a place for walking, playing and edification, it was now seen as the expression of a system of symbolism – not to be walked in but contemplated from a veranda. The formal principles of garden layout were derived mainly from the monochrome landscape-painting of the Sung period in China; and the principal object of the Zen landscape-gardener was to create the appearance of limitless space within a small area.

In order to achieve this effect of space, use was made of optical illusions to make the distances appear greater. The natural perspective was accentuated by putting large and strikingly shaped rocks and light-colored plants with large leaves in the foreground, while the background had small smooth stones and low trees, often artificially stunted, with small dark leaves. The paths and streams were narrower towards the far end of the garden, their winding course made them seem longer than they were and they finally disappeared behind rocks and shrubs, so that they appeared to be continuing into the distance. The boundary walls were built of dark-colored natural materials or concealed behind bushes, so that any sign of human intervention was carefully camouflaged. Thus the impression of unspoiled nature, untouched by the hand of man, was created; and at the same time the layout was so skilfully composed that it appeared to the observer like a picture formed from natural materials. – The most famous landscaped gardens in the Zen style are to be seen in Kyoto – the gardens of the Saiho-ji (*c.*1339) and the Tenryu-ji (*c.* 1343), designed by the Zen master Muso in the time of the Takauji; the garden of the Golden Pavilion (1397), laid out by Shogun Yoshimitsu; and the garden of the Silver Pavilion (1484), which dates from the time of Yoshimasa.

In the landscaped gardens there was a mingling of reality and abstract form, but in the *rock gardens (kare sansui)* pure abstraction was achieved. These are dry gardens without water or vegetation, consisting only of rocks and sand, and yet they contrive within a narrow space to represent wide landscapes, with the carefully raked sand taking on the form of watercourses and seas, out of which the rocks rear up like rugged islands. In their sparse simplicity these gardens are the form of artistic expression which comes closest to the teachings of Zen; and at the same time many of them are the most perfect spatial representations of the ink-wash landscapes of the Sung period which had such an enduring influence on the arts of Zen. The best examples of this type of garden are likewise to be found in Kyoto.

The classic simplicity of the rock gardens is found also in the *tea-gardens (roji)* of the Momoyama period (16th century); here the austerity is relaxed and nature, though compressed into a small space, appears to flourish without any artificial intervention. The same conscious naturalness is expressed, in a different way, in the tea-houses set in these gardens. The Momoyama period, however, was a time of down-to-earth zest for life in which the abstract symbolism of the Zen gardens gave place to the magnificence and variety of spacious pleasure gardens, such as the gardens of Nijo Castle in Kyoto.

Two Famous Zen Rock Gardens in Kyoto

The garden of the Daitokuji Temple in Kyoto, the **Daisen-in**, is the prototype of the "ink-wash painting garden". A band of sand and rocks surrounds the four sides of the temple like a panorama of Chinese landscape scenes of the Sung period. The most "picturesque" part is in a corner where two tall vertical rocks rear up like distant mountain peaks. Over some lower rocks the sand streams down like a waterfall and then becomes a river, flowing under a stone bridge and washing round flatter rocks which represent boats and islands. The "water" appears to continue under the veranda from which spectators observe the panorama and spreads out on the other side like a sea. Laid out in 1513, probably by the painter Kogaku Soko (1465–1548), the Daisen-in as a whole shows a very close resemblance to the ink-wash paintings of Zen art: the carefully selected angular rocks correspond to the energetic brush-strokes with which the painters drew the rugged outlines of mountains.

Very different in this respect is the rock garden of the **Ryoanji Temple**, which was laid out at about the same time. While the Daisen-in can be described as a landscape-painting executed in sand and stone, the Ryoanji garden is an abstract work of art constructed of the same materials. It consists of a level area of sand within which fifteen rocks are set – one group of five, two groups of three and two groups of two. Here there is no resemblance to a mountain landscape, merely an abstract arrangement of objects in space. Each group of rocks is carefully composed, and there is an optical balance between the two groups on the left and the three on the right. The longitudinal axis

Zen rock garden in the Ryoanji Temple

of the rocks is the same as that of the garden; and the sand, too, is raked in the same direction. Thus the spectator's eye is also drawn in this direction and receives a feeling of movement. The contrast between the empty areas of sand and the contours of the rocks gives rise in the mind of the meditating observer to the idea of infinite space and thus to the state aimed at by Zen – spiritual emptiness and non-attachment.

Ikebana – the art of flower arrangement

The Edo period (17th century onwards) brought little that was new in the way of stylistic elements, but the beginning of the period saw the creation of a number of very beautiful gardens, including those of the imperial villa of Katsura and the Nanzenji Temple in Kyoto. The increase in the size of the gardens laid out during this period (e.g. the Korakuen and Rikugien gardens in Tokyo) led to the creation of delightful pleasure grounds, but also reflected a decline in this typically Japanese art form, which appeared for the time being to have come to a dead end before the beginning of the contemporary period.

Ikebana. – The art of *flower arrangement* as an expression of aesthetic sensibility is deeply rooted in the cultural life of Japan. Originally introduced from China as a floral decoration in front of Buddhist statues, flower arrangement broke free of this religious application and developed into an independent art form.

As early as the Heian period (8th–12th centuries) flower-arrangement competitions (*hana-awase*) were popular in Court circles, and during the Muromachi period (14th–16th centuries) the art became widely practiced among ordinary people, gaining increased expressive force from the later inclusion of a vase or bowl in the arrangement.

The linear structure of the flower arrangement, symbolizing in its philosophical interpretation the trinity of heaven, man and earth, soon showed the typically Japanese leaning towards naturalism, as expressed in the natural-looking disposition of the flowers and stems. Ikebana played a supplementary part in the tea ceremony which was particularly popular in the 15th and 16th centuries, but was largely relieved of this subordinate function by later masters and developed on its own. The art reached a peak of popularity during the Edo period (17th–19th centuries); new techniques were evolved, and the effect of the arrangements – set in the ornamental niches known as *tokonoma* – was varied and enhanced by the use of new materials and new types of vases or containers such as shallow plates and bamboo baskets.

There are now a number of different schools of ikebana – Ikenobo, Nisho, Enshu, Ohara, Sogetsu, etc. – which are concerned both to carry on the old traditions and to develop new creative ideas. Long an essential part of the education of Japanese girls, it is still the province of male teachers. The art has also become increasingly popular in other countries.

Bonsai. – Bonsai, the art of growing miniature trees, now famed throughout the world as a Japanese speciality, was probably of Chinese origin, though it is known to have been practiced in Japan since the 11th century. It was much influenced by Zen Buddhism.

The miniature *bonsai* trees, ranging in height between 8 inches/20 cm and 2 feet/60 cm, are produced by planting seeds or cuttings of suitable species such as juniper, pine, spruce, Japanese red cedar (*Cryptomeria japonica*) and various maples in a small quantity of firm soil, feeding them with small and carefully calculated amounts of nourishment, pruning the roots and shoots and training the branches on wires. The pruning must be done in such a way that the cuts heal properly and remain invisible. The wires are removed after a year to prevent them from cutting into the bark. Under the careful hand of the bonsai expert the tree, growing in a shallow bowl, on a piece of bark or on a stone slab, develops into a work of art which, in complete harmony with its setting, imitates a natural situation. In the course of years and decades this treatment produces wind-blown, gnarled and twisted trees, miniature groves of trees and shrubs or delicate little bushes bearing flowers and fruit and, like their prototypes of normal size, changing their aspect from season to season.

Bonsai trees can reach an age of several hundred years, and, grown by almost every Japanese family, are handed down from generation to generation. The main centers of production are Omiya (near Tokyo), Kurume, Nagoya and Takamatsu (Kinashi).

Bonsai are bought and sold like antiques, at prices which vary according to their age and aesthetic quality.

Tea Ceremony

The tea ceremony (*chanoyu*) is, superficially considered, the traditional way of preparing and serving green tea (*matcha*), made from finely grated tea-leaves; but although often seen as no more than one of the traditional accomplishments expected of Japanese women, it has its roots in the aesthetic sense and religious feeling of the Japanese. In order to understand something of the procedure and the significance of the tea ceremony it is necessary to consider the historical and religious developments which have led to the form of the tea ceremony as it is now practiced.

Behind an abundance of formal requirements, from the need for the participants in the ceremony to be suitably dressed by way of the prescribed set of vessels and implements to the precisely specified movements of the tea-master and the appropriate subjects for conversation during the ceremony, which lasts several hours, lies the real purpose of the occasion, transcending the particular place and time – to enable the individual to achieve composure and purification in an atmosphere of seclusion, simplicity and tranquility, in which the externals and actions involved in the ceremony combine in perfect harmony.

The desired all-embracing consciousness is not to be achieved by great flights of thought: the union with nature and with the universe is attained by a meditative concentration on what seems to the Western mind the inconsequential course of the ceremony. This reflects the status of the tea ceremony as an art form strongly influenced by Zen Buddhism and incorporating the Buddhist ideals of tranquility, harmony and simplicity which are expressed in Japanese by the term *wabi*.

Important criteria for the proper performance of the tea ceremony are the maintenance of inner and outer purity (*sei*), reverence for all life (*kei*), harmony (*wa* – contained in the word *wabi*) and tranquility (*jaku*). These requirements are secured by detailed rules, which may differ in certain respects between one school and another but in essence are the same.

Over the centuries the tea ceremony exerted strong influence on various other Japanese art forms. The integration of the room in which it took place, the interior decoration, the garden and the vessels and implements used into the requirements of the ceremony enabled great tea-masters to influence the form of the tea-room, the layout of the tea-garden, the vessels and implements and even the arrangement of the floral decoration and the style of the picture scrolls. Many of the tea-masters themselves became creative artists, designing tea-houses and tea-gardens of high artistic quality. Even the manners and social forms of the Japanese were stamped with the principles of the tea ceremony, as indeed they still are; and there are many different schools still active to this day. One of the best known is the Ura-Senke school, founded by a great-grandson of the tea-master *Sen-no-Rikyu* (1522–91) and still carried on in the 15th generation. Other major schools are the Omote-Senke, Mushakoji-Senke and Enshu schools.

Tea, used in China from the end of the Han dynasty (A.D. 25–220) as a medicine as well as a drink, came to Japan in 805, when the priest *Saicho* (767–822) the founder of the Tendai sect, brought seed back from a study visit to China and planted it on Mount Hiei, north-east of Kyoto. For long, however, green tea made little headway in Japan, being used less as a drink than as a medicine and a means of refreshing Buddhist monks during the long hours in which they practiced meditation. Later the drinking of tea moved out of the Zen monasteries and became increasingly popular in aristocratic circles. Among those who promoted and fostered this early form of the tea ceremony was the Ashikaga shogun *Yoshimitsu* (1358–1408). During the cultural flowering of the Higashiyama period, under the rule of the 8th Ashikaga shogun, *Yoshimasa* (1443–74), the tea ceremony became a widely practiced art, and a game taken over from China (*tocha*) in which the players had to decide which was the best of a number of teas tasted, rapidly became popular. During the period tea plantations were established in many parts of the country, e.g. at Uji, south of Kyoto. Tea-drinking now changed from a game to a social occasion, strongly influenced by the spartan way of life of the samurai class which was then becoming increasingly powerful.

The real foundations of the tea ceremony as it is now practiced were laid by *Noami* (1397–1471) and *Murata Shuko* (1423–1502). While Noami became the leading master of the tea ceremony in the aristocratic circles of Kyoto, Shuko founded a school at Nara which shunned the lavish details and sumptuous show of Noami's ceremonies and aimed at simplicity and closeness to everyday life. This desire for tranquility and modesty led Shuko to adopt the principles of Zen Buddhism, which taught that the soul could find satisfaction in the performance of everyday actions. *Sado*, the "Way of Tea", seemed to Shuko a way of achieving this aim. Noami, who had been Shuko's teacher, later adopted his ideas, and this led to a combination of the elegant external setting of the one school with the philosophical content of the other which was fundamental to the later development of the tea ceremony. This tradition was later carried on by *Takeno Jo-o* (1502–55). The final form of the tea ceremony, which has been preserved unaltered down to the present day, was established by *Sen-no-Rikyu* (1522–91), a pupil of Takeno Jo-o, who combined the various schools and practices of his day into a formally defined art form which served as a counterweight to the Baroque art forms of the Azuchi–Momoyama period (1573–1600).

Among surviving examples of historic old **tea-houses** are the tea-house of the Ginkakuji Temple in Kyoto (1482), which was designed by Shuko, and the tea-room in the Shokin-tei, within the grounds of the Imperial villa of Katsura (1624) in Kyoto, which is attributed to the tea-master *Kobori Enshu* (1579–1647). Enshu is believed to have been responsible also for the Shinjuan and Kohoan tea-houses belonging to the Daitokuji Temple (1324) in Kyoto. This temple preserves a number of works of art by both Sen-no-Rikyu and Kobori Enshu, who are buried within the temple precincts.

Tea-house, Matsue

Sen-no-Rikyu designed the tea-house of the Myokian Temple at Yamazaki (near Osaka), which is now recognized as a national treasure. Another notable tea-house, Rokusan, is in the National Museum in Tokyo.

Tea ceremony

The tea ceremony begins with the assembly of the participants (who because of the limited space in a tea-house rarely number more than five) in the *yorit-suki* (waiting-room). The role of *shokyaku*, chief guest or guest of honor, is assigned by the host and tea-master, after due deliberation, to one of the participants, who retains this role until the end of the ceremony.

From the waiting-room the guests proceed through the front part of the tea-garden (*soto-roji*) to a covered bench (*koshikake*) at the entrance to the inner part of the garden (*uchi-roji*), where they are greeted by the host, who invites them with a bow, but without saying a word, to approach the tea-house. Within its restricted area the garden reproduces a complex natural pattern, carefully designed to achieve an effect of complete naturalness and to prepare the guests, by its consummate beauty of form, for the atmosphere of the tea ceremony. The path to the tea-house leads past trees, bushes and a stone lantern (*ishi-doro*) and over stepping-stones (*tobi-ishi*) set in the moss which covers the soil to a stone water-basin (*chozubachi*), in which the guests, beginning with the principal guest, wash their mouth and hands. – The tea-house (*sukiya*), at the far end of the inner garden, is an unpretentious structure of rustic type with a thatched roof, both the style and the materials used being of the greatest simplicity. An air of freshness and coolness is given to the setting by the water which has just previously been sprinkled on the stones, the bushes and the moss.

The guest of honor precedes the other guests into the tea-room (*chashitsu*), the low doorway of which obliges them to enter it on their knees – symbolizing the equality of all the participants and the humility of each individual. The room is usually just under 9 feet (2·7 m) square, the floor being covered with four and a half straw mats (*tatami*). Here, too, the simplicity of the constructional materials is very evident, particularly in the timbers supporting the roof, which have been left in their natural state. The sliding screen (*shoji*) and the windows with their covering of thin bamboo canes repeat the rectangular pattern of the mats.

The guests first admire, one after the other, the picture scroll (*kakemono*) – either an ink-wash painting or an example of calligraphy – which hangs in a special niche (*tokonoma*). Let into the floor in the middle of the room is a small hearth, and beside this are the vessels and implements used in the tea ceremony – a tea-bowl (*chaire*), the tea-casket or tea-caddy (*chasen*), a small bamboo brush for stirring the tea and a bamboo ladle (*hishaku*). After the guests have had time to admire the room, the decoration and the apparatus of the ceremony the tea-master enters the room from the *mizuya*, the side room in which the tea is prepared, and welcomes them with a bow. During the ceremony the sliding door is kept closed across the low doorway.

The tea-master then serves the guests with *kaiseki*, a meal specially prepared for the tea ceremony, and custom requires that the whole of it should be eaten, leaving nothing over. Thereafter sweets are served, and this marks the end of the first part of the ceremony.

The guests are then invited to go out into the garden for a brief interval. They sit on a bench in the garden until they are summoned back to the tea-room, which they enter after once again using the hishaku to pour water over their hands. In the meantime the picture scroll in the niche has been replaced by a flower display. Now begins the main part of the tea ceremony (*gozairi*). The tea-master brings from the preparation room a dish containing cakes, which he places in front of the principal guest, and then sets about preparing the thick viscous tea (*koicha*). After cleaning his apparatus with a silk cloth provided for the purpose (*fukusa*), he pours two or three ladle scoops of the finely grated green tea into the tea-bowl, adds hot water with a different ladle and whisks the tea to a slightly frothy consistency with the bamboo whisk. (The tea usually consists of young leaves from tea plants at least 20 years old – often more than 50.)

When the tea is ready the bowl is put down in a particular place by the hearth. The principal guest, who by this time has eaten his cake, takes up the bowl, with a bow to the other guests. He must hold it in the prescribed way, taking it into his left hand and supporting it with his right hand on one side. After the first sip he compliments the tea-master, and after two further sips he expresses his admiration for the tea-bowl and passes it on to the next guest, after first carefully wiping the place from which he drank with a paper napkin (*kaishi*). After the last guest has drunk the bowl is returned to the principal guest, who hands it back to the tea-master. The guests then, in turn, say a few words in praise of the artistic quality of the vessels and implements used in the ceremony, and the *gozairi* comes to an end.

The final stage of the tea ceremony (*usucha*) is less formal than the main part. In this stage a thinner tea (*matcha*) is drunk, made from leaves from tea plants between 3 and 15 years old. The tea is prepared separately for each guest, using a smaller bowl into which two ladle scoops of tea are put; and each bowl must be completely drained. When the last guest has returned his bowl the tea-master carries out the utensils and indicates with a deep bow that the ceremony is over. The guests then take their leave with a bow. They must not omit to express their thanks to the tea-master and host on the following day, either by letter or in person.

Architecture

Japanese architecture is notable particularly for its simplicity, functional quality and harmony with its natural setting. The same concern to match the proportions of a building to its function has been shown in the West only since the beginning of the 20th century. Apart from the architecture of the large cities in the contemporary period the predominant type of building is a single-storey structure, often with a clear separation between the different functions of daily life. The rooms, with movable screens and sliding walls, are very flexible in use, and the "open-plan" layout produces an interaction between inside and outside the house which would be inconceivable in a more massive structure. The favorite building material in this forest-covered land has from time immemorial been wood, the structure of which plays a major part in the aesthetic effect of the building as a whole. Practical considerations also argue in favour of wood; for in a country still very much subject to the risk of earthquakes the elasticity of a timber structure offers a considerably higher safety factor than a rigid stone building. – Japan's architecture, like its art, shows clear evidence of the Chinese influence which determined the character of Japanese architecture in the 7th and 8th centuries, gave fresh impulses in the 13th century and was later fully assimilated, leading to the development of distinctively Japanese architectural styles.

The earliest evidence on indigenous Japanese architecture is given by the *haniwa* of the **Kofun period** (3rd–7th centuries) – pottery models of one- and two-storey buildings with characteristic saddle roofs. These early examples, influenced by the pile-borne buildings of the southern Pacific, show practically no difference between the architectural form of dwelling-houses, shrines and temples. Thus the earliest Japanese architectural style, *Taisha-zukuri*, which can be seen in the Shinto shrines of Izumo-Taisha (Izumo) and Sumiyoshi (Osaka), can probably be taken as characteristic of other buildings of this period as well. Its essential features are the widely projecting saddle roof familiar from the *haniwa*, the entrance on the gable side, the four square corner pillars and the single central pillar. – Out of this style developed the *Shimmei-zukuri* style, represented by the

outer and inner shrines (Geku and Naiku) of the Ise Shrine (both originally erected on other sites). The entrance is now on the eaves side; the crossed beams on the gable (*chigi*) and the rounded transverse timbers above the gable designed to keep the thatched roof in place (*katsuogi*) stand out prominently. Simplicity of form and straightness of line are characteristic features of Shinto architecture to this day. Another very ancient element is the *torii* (entrance gate to the shrine), the origin and function of which have not been established with certainty.

At the beginning of the **Asuka period** (6th–7th centuries), during the reign of the Empress Suiko, Buddhism came to Japan, bringing with it an architecture of previously unknown complexity developed by an advanced civilization. The earlier rigidity of form now gave place to softer lines, and for the first time purely decorative features came into use. In the center of the Buddhist temple complex, which was fundamentally different from secular buildings and the Shinto shrines which closely resembled them, stands the *pagoda* (*to*), which is in essence a reliquary shrine. An early example of this is the pagoda, built in 588, which is the central feature of the Shitennoji Temple in Osaka. Its architecture follows a strict symbolic pattern: the central pillar represents the axis of the world, the five storeys stand for the five Chinese elements (fire, water, air,

Pagoda of the Yakushiji Temple, Nara

earth and empty space), the summit pinnacle (*sorinto*) for the nine celestial
spheres. The Horyuji Temple in the Nara
basin shows the classic layout: in the center is the pagoda and adjoining this the
Golden Hall (Kondo), both surrounded by
galleries or corridors enclosing the inner
courtyard, on the north side of which is
the Lecture Hall (Kodo), flanked by the
Library (Kyozo) and Bell-Tower (Shoro).
The priests' lodgings, temple offices and
treasury lie outside the central courtyard,
likewise enclosed within a wall. – In the
new form of construction the thatched
roof gave place to a shingle roof, the
beams and joists showed more variation
and the timber structures had added
decorative features. The walls were now
revetted with clay and painted red. The
importance attached to symmetry was
reflected in the introduction of a second
pagoda, as exemplified by the original
form of the Yakushiji Temple, originally
erected at Asuka in 680 and later transferred to Nara, of which only one pagoda
now survives. This three-storey pagoda is
unique in having decorative intermediate
storeys (*mokoshi*) which give it the appearance of a six-storey structure. The
typical 8th-century pagodas (e.g. in the
Taimadera Temple) are simple three-
storey structures.

During the **Nara period** (8th century)
the temples increased in size and the
buildings were set on stone bases. Under
Chinese influence, the roof-line became
curved; hipped roofs came into fashion,
often overlying pent-roofs terminating in
decorative features (*shibi*). The most important temples of this period in Nara,
then the capital, are the Kofukuji Temple
(710) and the Todaiji Temple (745–752).
The latter is a classic example of the architecture of the period and possesses in the
Daibutsuden what was originally the largest temple hall ever built in Japan and is
still, even in the smaller reconstruction of
1708, the largest timber building in the
world.

In this period the influence of the Early
T'ang era in China can be detected, being
particularly evident in the Golden Hall of
the Toshodaiji Temple with its classical
colonnade. The Lecture Hall of this
temple, once part of the Imperial Palace, is
the only surviving example of 8th-century
feudal architecture, with its typical hipped
roof (*irimoya*). Other notable buildings of
this period are the Sangatsudo Hall and

Todaiji Temple, Nara

the Treasury (Shosoin) of the Todaiji
Temple and the octagonal Yumedono
Hall of the Horyuji Temple, a unique
structure in the style of a Chinese pavilion.

During the **Heian period** (8th–12th centuries) the temple complexes lost their
symmetrical form. The rising Tendai and
Shingon sects of Buddhism preferred to
site their temples in hilly regions, and the
layout of the temple had to be adapted to
the local topography. The only surviving
buildings of this period belonging to the
esoteric Buddhist sects are the five-storey
pagoda (824) and the Golden Hall of the
Muroji Temple at Yamato. Both the Tendai and Shingon sects segregated monks
and laymen; and this required an
additional veranda, which in the 11th
century developed into a separate Cult
Hall (Raido).

Even the Shinto shrines of this period took
over Buddhist features. The previous strict
linearity was relaxed, and timber structures were painted. The introduction of
corridors and the building of two-storey
torii (e.g. at the Kasuga Shrine in Nara and
the Usa Shrine on Kyushu) also undoubtedly reflected Buddhist influence.

Residential buildings were much less
affected by Chinese influence and largely
preserved the simplicity of the *Shinden-
zukuri* style. Pile-built halls of varying size
were linked by corridors, while the sober
external lines were relieved by the
displacement of the various parts of the
building, thus achieving a characteristic
lightness. The interiors were splendidly
decorated.

The **Kamakura period** (12th–14th centuries) brought three new styles of military
severity and massiveness. On the one
hand the native Japanese architectural
manner developed into the *Wa-yo* style;
on the other the *Tenjiku-yo* style (a name

of Indian origin, though the style itself came from southern China) enjoyed a brief vogue. This massive and imposing style, contrasting sharply with the light and elegant buildings of the Heian period, was unable to establish itself in Japan, though a representative example survives in the South Gate (Nandaimon; rebuilt 1195) of the Todaiji Temple at Nara. The *Kara-yo* ("Chinese") style, which came to Japan along with Zen Buddhism, now became predominant in Zen architecture. This style, also of imposing effect, is represented by the Kenchoji Temple (1253) in Kamakura, the Nanzenji Temple (1293) and the Daitokuji Temple (1319) and the Relic Hall (1285) of the Engakuji Temple in Kamakura.

The palace and residential architecture in the Shinden-zukuri style of the Heian period showed little change during the Kamakura period, but the needs of defense led to the development of the more compact style known as *Buke-zukuri* ("warrior's dwelling").

The influence of Zen Buddhism as the source of a new aesthetic continued into the Early **Muromachi period** (14th century onwards), promoting the further development of the Kara-yo style, which now increasingly incorporated Japanese stylistic elements and finally achieved a perfect synthesis between the majestic style of Chinese origin and the lightness and grace of the native Japanese style in the Kinkakuji Temple (1397). Zen architecture also influenced Shintoism, which now built shrines consisting of a number of separate buildings. – The Buke-zukuri style of secular architecture, influenced by the abbots' lodgings in the monasteries, developed into the *Shoin-zukuri* style, the name of which is derived from the oriel windows of the study (*shoin*). The floors of these buildings were covered with straw mats (*tatami*); the ornamental niche for picture scrolls (*tokonoma*) now served a purely decorative purpose. This style formed the basis of the classic style of Japanese *domestic architecture*, characteristic features of which are the use of timber as a building material, sliding partition walls (*fusuma*) and sliding doors into the garden (*shoji*). A forerunner of this deliberately simple style, which was influenced by the great Japanese tea-masters, was the Togu-do Hall in the Ginkakuji Temple (by Shuko, 1483), which in spite of later alterations still gives a com-

prehensive impression of the architecture of this period.

During the **Momoyama period** (16th–17th centuries) the Shoin-zukuri style reached its peak, achieving its finest expression in the Katsura Imperial Villa (early 17th century) near Kyoto and in the Kohoan of the Daitokuji Temple and the Hiankaku of the Nishihonganji Temple, both in Kyoto – all buildings of notable harmony and austerity. This severe simplicity was carried to an extreme in the tea-houses (*chashitsu, sukiya*) of this period, which turned back to traditional Japanese forms and materials. At the same time the native style developed a rich interior decoration: functional elements were enriched by ornament, walls and doors were covered with splendid paintings and metal fittings were richly ornamented.

Prominent in the building activity of this period were the imposing *castles* now built, which gradually lost their military character and became sumptuous princely mansions with tall principal towers (*tenshukaku*) and numbers of decorated curving gables. The best examples are Himeji Castle (late 16th century, Kumanoto Castle (*c.* 1600) and Nagoya Castle (1610), together with the finest of them all, the magnificent Nijo Castle (1603) in Kyoto.

Equally sumptuous are the shrines of the Momoyama period, in the *Gongen* style. These adopt the architectural canon of Chinese Buddhism, in which the shrine consisted of a cult hall, an intermediate building and the sanctuary. This type is also represented in the **Edo period** (17th century onwards) by the Toshogu Shrine, the mausoleum of the Tokugawa shoguns in Nikko, with its overcharged decoration of carving, gilding and brilliantly colored painting.

After the **Meiji Restoration** (1868), when Japan became exposed to Western influences, there was a break in the development of Japanese architecture, reflecting the changes that were taking place in Japanese life. Thus in the early years of the new age the British style of Neo-Gothic architecture in brick was imitated, and it was some time before architects came back to traditional Japanese forms. Industrial architecture and civil engineering, serving a functional

Nijo Palace, Kyoto

Tower blocks in Shinjuku ward, Tokyo

purpose, followed international practice and international models.

During the 1920s a modern school of architecture developed in Japan, inevitably influenced by the new trends then coming to the fore in Europe (the Bauhaus, Le Corbusier). Among notable Japanese architects of the period were *Sutemi Horiguchi*, whose finest work was produced between the twenties and the forties; *Tetsuro Yoshida*, who worked successfully in the international style of the day; *Kunio Maekawa*, who was trained in the Bauhaus; and *Junzo Sakakura*, who worked for a time with Le Corbusier and designed the Japanese Pavilion at the Paris International Exhibition of 1937. *Kenzo Tange* is particularly well known in the West, having done work of outstanding quality not only in Japan (buildings for the 1964 Olympics; Peace Center in Hiroshima, 1946–56; planning for Osaka International Exhibition, 1970) but also abroad (reconstruction of Skopje, Yugoslavia, 1965). – The group known as the Metabolists have devoted themselves since 1960 mainly to urban planning, with a tendency towards Utopian and futuristic designs.

Literature

The Western reader can as a rule get to know Japanese literature, whether modern literature or the even less accessible older literature, only through the medium of translations. These translations must seek to bridge the gap between two radically different cultures, with different ways of thinking and feeling and different linguistic structures, and it cannot be expected that in addition to correctly rendering the content of a Japanese work and setting it in the right cultural and linguistic context they will also invariably be able to convey the linguistic beauties of the original, its nuances of sensibility and the impression it makes on the Japanese reader. The differences between the semantic connotations of words in Japanese and English are usually great, and particular things or ideas may play quite different parts in Japanese and in Western life; and a further difficulty is created by the prevalence of allusions and direct or indirect quotations in the Japanese literary language, comprehensible to the Western reader only with the help of a footnote. The principal difficulty, however, is created by the very different character of the Japanese language and script.

The Japanese originally had no **script** of their own. In the 4th century A.D. they adopted the *Chinese script*, the ideographic characters of which, designed for the monosyllabic Chinese language (with each character representing a one-syllable, non-inflected word), were ill suited to the polysyllabic Japanese language (with inflected words of one or more syllables). Accordingly it is necessary to add to the **Kanji** (Chinese) character which gives the semantic content or root meaning of the word a character or characters from the Japanese syllabic script known as **Kana** to represent the flexional ending and any affixed particles. This system requires a greater effort of attention from the reader than an alphabetic script, and has always constituted a major element in the curriculum of Japanese primary schools. This is perhaps the explanation of the traditional reverence of the Japanese for any written matter and their tendency towards discursive, non-abstract and non-dialectic modes of thought which seek constantly to define and to classify; the ability to record something in writing then becomes an art in its own right – a fact which may explain the amount of space taken up by descriptive passages in Japanese literature.

The *differences between the written and the spoken language* became marked at an early stage. A written language which called for so much effort to learn it was inevitably unusually resistant to change; and accordingly the classical Japanese written language remained in all essentials the language of Japanese literature until the beginning of the 20th century. The adoption of colloqial words and turns of phrase into the literary language which took place regularly over the years, marking the different phases of linguistic development, gives many works a linguistic pattern full of contrasts which is difficult to render adequately in translation. Efforts were made in the late 19th century to unify the written and spoken languagues (*Gembun-itchi* movement), and from about 1900 literature was written only in the colloquial language.

The **classic Japanese written language,** formed during the Heian period, largely through the work of noble ladies at the Imperial Court, is characterized by a relatively small vocabulary which is given variety and flexibility by a great range of prefixes and suffixes. While the characters involved in a story or historical account often remain vague and undefined – perhaps identifiable only by the form of the verb – actions, events and facts are precisely specified by reference to the time at which they take place, their development over time, their reality, possibility or probability; an abundance of particles and predicates make it possible to define precisely the social position and relationships of the characters and their participation in the action or event that is taking place. The language, rich in rhetorical questions, real and unreal conditional clauses, concessive and presumptive turns of phrase, renders with great subtlety both external and internal realities – always concerned lest too categorical a statement should destroy their inner truth. – A language of this kind was best suited to poetry, a psychological novel, a diary, a loosely structured story, a brief improvisatory essay, an epic or ballad-style work; the terse short story, the tightly plotted novel are modern innovations influenced by Western literature. A properly constructed dramatic plot is found only in the bourgeois tragedies (*sewamono*) of the Edo period: other dramatic forms tend to take after the mystery play or resemble a dramatic version of a popular illustrated broadsheet. If a translator set out to render word for word the elaborate nuances of a language operating within such narrow bounds he would inevitably weary and put off his readers; and the regional and social dialects which provide a lively contrast to the standard language and are found in Japanese literature from the early medieval period onwards, cannot be satisfactorily rendered by the use of English dialect words and turns of phrase.

A special problem for the translator is provided by what is called *Sino-Japanese*. Together with the Chinese script the Japanese also learned the Chinese language; in reading Chinese texts or texts in Chinese by Japanese writers, however, the Chinese syllables are rendered by the Japanese phonetic equivalents, but in the sequence required by Japanese syntax. Since the rules of word order are different in the two languages, the Japanese order was indicated in the Chinese text by additional signs and aids to the reader; and the artificial reading language which was thus evolved became known as **Kambun** ("Han script"). A page of Kambun, with its intricate Kanji characters, looks quite different from a page in the elegant cursive, **Hiragana** ("smooth Kana'), devised by the Japanese in the 8th century; and the difference between literature written in pure Japanese (*Wabun*) and Kambun, with its monosyllabic Sino-Japanese words, is equally evident in spoken form. Kambun was a masculine idiom used by the Emperor, the Court nobility and monks from the 9th century onwards for writing poems, essays, chronicles and philosophical treatises, and it did not finally disappear from official administrative and military language until the end of the Second World War. During the 9th century a more angular phonetic script known as **Katakana** ("part-Kana") was devised by monks, using parts of selected Kanji characters. Kanji, Kambun and Katakana were long regarded as characteristically masculine, Wabun and Hiragana as feminine. – After the landed and warrior nobility rose to power in the early medieval period increasing numbers of Sino-Japanese words (*kango*) were taken into the literary language, and the mixed style thus created (*Wakan-konkobun*) has dominated the written language down to the present day. These *kango* turns of phrase and forms taken over from Kambun, when used in a Japanese text, give it a tone of masculine concision, philosophical profundity and pregnant meaning, and sometimes also of bureaucratic formality – all of which creates problems for the translator.

The possibility of conveying his meaning by the use of Japanese or Sino-Japanese words, using Kana or Kanji script, gives the Japanese writer a very special stylistic resource which can be called semantic polyphony. Since a Kanji character may be read in a number of different ways in Japanese and Sino-Japanese, the particular reading intended is frequently indicated by adding to the Kanji character a Kana character in smaller print (*Furigana*). The writer can thus use a current Japanese word, written in Furigana, to convey the literal sense, and is then free to select a specific Kanji character, often a recondite and complex one, to indicate the intellectual and sometimes the socio-cultural background of what he wants to say. Where this device is used in a passage of some length the primary text acquires a secondary semantic level which the educated reader takes in at the same time. Special techniques of semantic polyphony are *engo* (words with particular associations) and *kake-kotoba* (homonymous doubles), which were widely used in poetry, in No plays and in the bourgeois prose writing of the Edo period. When such fine-spun stylistic devices are employed the translator must acknowledge defeat: the effect of the secondary semantic text can be conveyed only by long-winded paraphrases or footnotes which necessarily lose the concision and pregnancy of the original.

All of these considerations should be borne in mind when reading an English translation of a Japanese text. A long passage which seems monotonous and tedious in English may to the Japanese reader be full of interest and stimulation, thanks to the nuances and contrasts which cannot be conveyed in translation.

Nara and Heian periods. – In the early period before the art of writing reached Japan myths and legends were preserved and handed on orally by professional story-tellers (*kataribe*), and some of this material later found its way into the *chronicles* which are the earliest surviving examples of Japanese writing. The "Kojiki" ("Record of Things Past", 712) was a codified version by a Court official named *O-na-Yasumaro* of material transmitted orally by *Hieda-no-Are*, written in Kambun with numerous Japanese passages. The "Nihongi" or "Nihon-shoki" ("Japanese Annals"), compiled in 720 by Prince *Toneri*, is written in pure Kambun. In both of these works the myths about gods and the early emperors are followed by a record of events in the more recent past. The earlier parts are primarily of interest as folk traditions, while the later parts are of some historical value. Both of these chronicles include many poems and songs, so that although intended as historical works they are also the earliest sources of Japanese legends, folk traditions and poetry. The "Nihongi" was the first of the "Six Histories of the Empire" ("Rikkokushi"), the other five of which, also written in Kambun, are of interest only to the historian. After the sixth of these, the "Sandai-jitsuroku" ("Chronicle of the Reigns of Three Emperors", 901), official histories gave place to narrative history by private persons, such as the "Eiga-monogatari" ("Narration of Splendour and Magnificence"; to end of the 11th century) and "O-kagami" ("Great Mirror"; beginning of 12th century), both written in Japanese, and other works of what is known as Kagami literature.

The *lyric poetry* of the earliest period (from the 5th to the 6th centuries A.D.) is recorded in the "Manyoshu" ("Collection of Ten Thousand Leaves"), an anthology compiled in the second half of the 8th century by *Otomo-no-Yakamochi* and others which contains some 4500 poems by 800 authors, some of them anonymous and a fifth of them women, from all classes of the population. The Japanese texts of the songs – folk-songs, love-songs and ceremonial prize-songs – are written in Kanji, sometimes rendering the meaning and sometimes the sound (*Manyogana*). Lines of five syllables alternate with lines of seven syllables; there is no rhyme in Japanese poetry. Apart from a small number of longer poems (*choka*) of up to a hundred or more lines the predominant type is the typically Japanese short poem (*tanka*) with the five lines of 5, 7, 5, 7 and 7 syllables which thereafter became standard. The artistic effect is enhanced by the use of stock poetic figures of, often, five syllables (*makura-kotoba*, "pillow words"), or sometimes longer (*jo*, "introduction"); phrases with contrasting meanings are coupled by the use of homonyms (*kake-kotoba*).

During the 8th and 9th centuries emperors and courtiers wrote Chinese poems (*kanshi*) on the model of the *shih* of the T'ang period, usually of four or eight lines, with parallelism between the lines and end rhymes (earliest collection: "Kaifuso", 751); but thereafter the short poem (*uta*, "song", or *waka*, "poem") remained the characteristic Japanese form of lyric poetry. The close association of poetry with politics and society is indicated by the fact that the emperor ordered anthologies of *kanshi* and *waka* to be compiled, and that it was one of the spiritual functions of the divine emperor to compose poems in order to maintain order and peace in the Empire. At banquets it was the custom for guests to recite poems of their own composition, and there were poetic contests (*uta-awase*) at which the contestants extemporized poems in presence of a judge. The ritualized life of the Court required officials and ladies-in-waiting to be able to improvise and recite *waka* on every conceivable occasion, even during the act of love or on their death-bed. – Of the seven official anthologies (*chokusenshu*) produced during the Heian period the most important is the "Kokinshu" or "Kokin-waka-shu" ("Collection of the *Waka* of Times Past and Present"; about 914), with an authoritative foreword by its chief compiler, *Ki-no-Tsurayuki*. In the *waka* in this collection the expression of feeling sublimated in the contemplation of nature reaches its peak of refinement, without falling into the academic rigidity of later periods.

The history of Japanese literary prose begins – apart from the earlier Shinto ritual prayers known as *norito*, ceremonial and declamatory in style – with the *narrative tales* (*monogatari*) of the 10th century. The earliest of these was the "Taketori-monogatari" ("Tale of the Bamboo Collector"; end of 9th century, anonymous), the story of a beautiful moon fairy who rejects all her suitors, with many features characteristic of a fairy-tale. In later tales the prose narrative is interwoven with numbers of *waka*: in the "Ise-monogatari" ("Tales from Ise"; mid 10th century, anonymous), for example, 209 *waka* alternate with 125 short love-stories, while verse tales such the "Utsuo-monogatari" ("Tale of the Cave") and "Ochikubo-monogatari" ("Tale of the Young Lady in the Dungeon") – both anonymous works of the mid 10th century – form the framework of a single plot. The outstanding work in this genre is the "Genji-monogatari" ("Tale of Prince Genji"), written between 1000 and 1010 by a lady of the Court, *Murasaki Shikibu*. In the story of the brilliant Genji and his son the authoress, a woman of culture and education, paints a broad picture of Court life, though already with a romantically tinged backward look. Both for its artistic quality and its content this is a repository of the traditional arts of Japan.

A more realistic view of Court life can be obtained from the *diaries* (*nikki*) usually written by ladies of the Court. The "Kagero-nikki" (about 974) and "Sarashina-nikki" (about 1060) are not so much diaries as autobiographies by noble ladies of the Fujiwara and Sugawara clans. In the "Tosa-nikki" (935), a travel diary, Ki-no-Tsurayuki, compiler of the "Kokinshu", writes in the character of a lady of the Court; like other diaries written by emperors and Court officials, it is a valuable historical source. In the "Makura-no-Soshi" ("Pillow Book", about 1100) the witty but super-ficial *Sei Shonagon* abandons the diary form and strings together in no particular order a series of sketches, notes and observations, thus founding the genre known as *miscellany literature* (*zuihitsu*, "collection of essays").

Kamakura and Muromachi periods. – From the mid 12th century onwards political power, and with it the intellectual and cultural initiative, passed to the war-rior nobility. The Wabun used by the ladies of the Court now began to incorporate increasing numbers of Sino-Japanese expressions from the military and Buddhist spheres, giving rise to the style known as *Wakan-konkobun*. The "Konjaku-monogatari" ("Once-upon-a-Time Stories"; by Minamoto-no-Takakuni and others, beginning of 12th century), a collection of legends and tales

from India, China and Japan, had already shown a leaning towards a more popular vein: the style of this work is plain and unadorned and the characters come from all classes of the population. This founded the genre of popular tales (*setsuwa*), to which the "Ujishui-monogatari" ("Further Uji Tales" – referring back to the early-13th-century "Konjaku") and the didactic and moralizing "Jikkinsho" ("Outline of the Ten Moral Rules", 1252) also belong. Later, in the 15th and 16th centuries, a genuine type of popular literature was produced in the form of the *otogizoshi*, naïve moralizing "tracts for the entertainment of women and children" written in highly colloquial language.

Miscellany literature produced during this period included the "Hojoki" ("Notes from my Cell", 1212) of *Kamo-no-Chomei*, which breathes the very spirit of the Buddhist withdrawal from the world, and the "Tsurezuregusa" ("Leaves from Leisure Hours", 1331) of *Yoshida Kenko*, in which the very conservative author sets down a series of sensitive maxims and reflections. – The martial spirit of the times is reflected in the genre of *tales of war* (*gunki-monogatari*), the most famous of which is the "Heike-monogatari" ("Tale of the House of Taira"). This heroic epic, written and orally transmitted versions of which appeared in the 13th century, describes the great days of the warrior Taira clan and their final annihilation by the Minamoto. In scenes of battle and of love it paints a broad picture of medieval Japan and the political and personal fates of families and individuals in all classes of society. The basic idea of the work is the Buddhist insight into the transitoriness of all earthly power.

In *courtly poetry* the "Shin-kokin" or "Shin-wakashu" ("New Kokinshu"; 1205), compiled by ex-Emperor Gotoba, marks a final high point. The ideals ex-pressed are *ushin* and *yugen* (genuine feeling and deeply mysterious beauty), and many poems hark back deliberately to earlier ones, enhancing the content of the new work by the juxtaposition with the old (*honkadori*). New impulses came from the practice of reciting poems by guests at a social gathering: the first three lines and the last two lines of a *waka* were composed by two different persons, and this process was carried further in the "chain poems" (*renka*), extemporised by two or more authors, which might consist of a hundred more thematically linked verses. In the *haikai-no-renka* ("joking *renka*") an unexpected and humorous linking of the verses was aimed at. Finally, in the 16th century, the first three lines of the *waka* achieved independent status as the *haikai-no-hokku*, a brief poem of 17 syllables. – A development characteristic of the 15th and 16th centuries was the *lyrical No play*, the recited text of which (*yokyoku*) followed the pattern of the *waka* with its alternation of 5 and 7 syllables but achieved a highly complex variability of rhythm by the alternating length of line combined with the varying relationship between the poetry and the musical accompaniment.

Edo period. – In the period of late feudalism, beginning in the 17th century, the warrior class was recognized as holding the political leadership of the country; but the real economic – and therefore the social – power lay with the merchants, formally a lower caste, who together with the craftsmen and those employed in the service trades made up the population of the large cities of Osaka, Kyoto and Edo (Tokyo). The townspeople's thirst for education and culture and their need of entertainment on the one hand, together with the development of printing from the early 17th century onwards on the other, led to the development of a middle-class or bourgeois literature (*chonin-bungaku*; from *chonin*, "townsman") which already showed some of the characteristics of modern mass literature and the contemporary literary world. The new self-confidence and down-to-earth attitudes of the townspeople found expression mainly in prose; and the focal point of the literature of the Edo period was no longer the Imperial Court, as in earlier days, but the red-light district (particularly the Yoshiwara district in Edo). This may seem at first a surprising statement; but it should be remembered that Yoshiwara offered not only low-price prostitution and dubious places of entertainment but also refined artistic pleasures and more discriminating relationships with highly cultured courtesans. Moreover in the strictly regulated class society of the Tokugawa Shogunate the red-light district was the only place where the different classes could meet and communicate with one another. While the philosophical and political works of the day were imbued with Confucianism and

Shintoism with a nationalist slant, the sole objective of belletristic (fine letters) literature was entertainment. The originally didactic *kanazoshi* ("Kana tracts": printed in the Kana syllabary so that the less educated could read them) soon switched to humorous stories aiming purely at entertainment and finally to tales of considerable literary quality, such as the "Ukiyozoshi" ("Stories of the Floating World") by *Ihara Saikaku* (1642–93), a master of the erotic novel and the novel of manners.

New genres arose in the 18th century, including the *sharebon* (from *share*, which meant both a mocking play on words and an elegant life-style), depicting everyday life in Yoshiwara in a humorous light, and *kibyoshi* ("yellow bindings"), the contemporary equivalent of our modern comic books. Of more literary merit were the *yomihon* ("reading books", in which illustrations played a subordinate role), a genre founded by *Ueda Akinari* (1734–1809) with his collection of ghost stories, Ugetsu-monogatari" ("Tales in Rain and Moonlight", 1768). The great master of the genre was the enormously productive *Takizawa Bakin* (1767–1848). The last notable prose works of the Edo period apart from Bakin's stories were the *kokkeibon* ("fun books") of *Jippensha Ikku* (1765–1831) and *Shikitei Samba* (1766–1822) and the realistic and sentimental love romances (*ninjobon*) of *Tamenaga Shunsui* (1790–1843).

In lyric poetry the 17-syllable *haikai-no-renka* now occupied a dominant place. At first limited to epigrams and plays on words, as in the poems of *Matsunaga Teitoku* (1571–1653), it was then released from this restricted choice of subject and from the linguistic and other rules which had previously confined it by *Nishiyama Soin* (1605–82). His pupil *Matsuo Basho* (1644–94) raised the *haikai-no-hokku*, or *haiku* for short, to the plane of serious art. Subject to strict rules in the choice of words denoting the seasons (*kigo*) and the place where the caesura could fall (*kireji*), his haikus evoke the universal in a miniature form, the eternal in a momentary glimpse, thanks to an extraordinarily dense language which can convey man's profoundest thoughts with simplicity and truth. Basho established the tradition of haiku-writing which has continued down to the present day; his best-known successors during the Edo period were *Yosa Buson* (1716–83) and *Kobayashi Issa* (1763–1827).

The *theater* of the Edo period was dominated by the *Joruri* play, which was acted by puppets, and the *Kabuki* play, in which the actors were human. In the Kabuki theater the text and its author were subordinate to the other artistic elements; only in the Joruri theater, where the recitative by the singer played a central part, could the text aspire to literary quality. Japan's greatest dramatist, *Chikamatsu Monzaemon* (1653–1724), wrote his plays for the puppet theater. His *jidaimono*, historical plays of war and bloody revenge, were highly popular with the middle-class audiences of the Edo period – the contemporary equivalent of the "Western". On a higher artistic level, with well-constructed plots, were the *sewamono* ("plays of the present day"), depicting ordinary people in conflict with the Confucian norms of a class society – a conflict which in a case of illicit love, for example, could be resolved only by the death of the lovers (*shinju*). The end was always tragic, inevitably frustrating the individual and his striving for happiness. The present-day critical view is that if Chikamatsu himself had been able to break free of the norms of contemporary society and resolve the conflict formulated in his plays – a step which admittedly was impossible on both personal and external grounds – he might have become what his mastery of language entitled him to be, a Japanese Shakespeare.

Since the Meiji Restoration. The rapid adoption of Western cultural and intellectual values after the Meiji Restoration in 1868 at once faced Japanese literature with the necessity of deciding whether to support or oppose the new ideas. The decision was favorable to Western ideas, and the result was a new *realism* closely following Western models. The ground was prepared by a wave of didactic literature which sought to educate the Japanese public through the medium of the political novel (*seiji-shosetsu*) and a mass campaign of translation from Western literatures. *Tsubouchi Shoyo* (1859–1935) introduced Japan to Shakespeare's plays and the new theory of the novel ("Shosetsu-shinzui", 1886), which taught that literature must be taken seriously as an art and man taken seriously as an individual. He and *Futabatei Shimei*

(1864–1909), the translator of Turgenev and novelist ("Ukingomo", 1889), are regarded as the forerunners of the modern Japanese novel. – The nationalist and reactionary school which opposed the Westernization of Japanese literature, though looking back to the culture of the Edo period, also depicted the conflict between the individual and the world in which he lived: *Ozaki Koyo* (1867–1903), *Yamada Bimyo* (1868–1903). Other attitudes were represented by the romantic transfiguration of masculine chivalry in the novels of *Koda Rohan* (1867–1947) and the mystical symbolism of *Izumi Kyoka* (1873–1939).

In *lyric poetry* there was a revolutionary break with the formal and structural rules of the waka and the haiku. The "new-style poem" (*shintai-shi*) even allowed free rhythms, as in the work of *Kitahara Hakushu* (1885–1942); but experiments with end-rhyme were soon abandoned. The *shintaishi* poets *Kambara Ariake* (1875–1952) and *Hagiwara Sakutaro* (1886–1942) took the French Symbolists as their models, while later *Nishiwaki Junzaburo* (1894–1982) followed the Surrealists. – From 1893, when the "Akasha" group was founded by *Ochiai Naobumi* (1861–1903), efforts were also made to bring the traditional *waka* into line with the new aesthetic sensibilities. The best-known practitioner of the new *waka* was the poetess *Yosano Akiko* (1878–1942), who broke away from many of the old traditional rules. The old name of *tanka* had by this time come into use again.

From the early years of the 20th century Japanese literature was much influenced by Naturalism – though *Hirotsu Ryuro* (1861–1928) had already discovered the world of the ugly and the tragic. Taking Zola as their model, but also reflecting Christian and Socialist ideas, writers criticized the faults of both traditional Japanese society and the modern society which had developed under Western influence: *Kosugi Tengai* (1865–1952), *Kunikida Doppa* (1871–1908). Shortly before the Russo-Japanese War (1904–05) *Kinoshita Naoe* (1869–1937) paid for his uncompromising attitude to capitalism and war with a period of imprisonment. An "objective" school of Naturalism, without direct commitment to social militancy, was represented by *Tayama Katai* (1871–1930) and *Tokuda*

Shusei (1871–1943). – A remarkable number of novels took the Japanese family as their subject or showed markedly autobiographical features: *Tokutomi Roka* (1868–1927), *Kikuchi Yuho* (1870–1947), *Tayama Katai*. Both characteristics are found in the novel "Ie" ("The Family", 1910) by *Shimazaki Toson* (1872–1943), who was also a considerable lyric poet. The novel had by now begun to deal with the position of women as independent individuals – at first in the work of *Suehiro Tetcho* (1849–96), an early representative of the political novel, who was followed by Tokutomi Roka and later by the pessimistic *Masamune Hakucho* (1879–1962) and the aesthetician *Nagai Kafu* (1879–1959).

Nagai Kafu belonged to the anti-Naturalism school, which had many aspects but for the most part held to the Japanese tradition, combining this with social criticism: *Natsume Soseki* (1867–1916), *Mori Ogai* (1862–1922).

The "Shirakaba" group, founded in 1910, with *Musanokoji Saneatsu, Shiga Naoya* and the Anarchic Socialist *Arishima Takeo* (1878–1923) among its members, propagated an idealistic humanism in the tradition of Tolstoy. The "Satanist" *Tanizaki Junichiro* (1886–1965), an aesthetician and a writer of great talent, glorified sex and its mysterious power in a way unusual in Japan.

After Naturalism and up to the end of the Second World War Japanese literature broke up into a variety of different trends and individual personalities, among which two groups, the writers of the Left and the Sensualists, can be distinguished. The *literature of the Left* took its subject-matter and its tone from the everyday life of workers and peasants: its heroes were no longer individuals but groups. The writers of the Left did not confine themselves to social criticism but sought to achieve concrete political objectives: *Hayama Yoshiki* (1894–1945) and *Kobayashi Takiji* (1903–33), for example, described conditions in the merchant navy and the seamen's struggle to improve their lot. Kobayashi's novel "Kanikosen" ("The Prawn Boat", 1929) is regarded as the leading work of proletarian literature in Japan; its author died in prison as a political prisoner. *Tokunaga Sunao* (1899–1958) wrote the first working-class novel, "Taiyo-no-nai machi" ("Street without Sun", 1929). From about 1930, during the period of increasing militarism, writers of the Left were suppressed, reduced to silence or "converted" (*tengo-bungaku*, "literature of the converted"). During the Second World War only patriotic or apolitical literature was tolerated. The influence of left-wing literature, however, has persisted throughout the post-war period down to the present day, though there is a certain reluctance to have this widely known abroad. – Better known in the West through translations is the work of *Sensualists*, including the aesthetician and Nobel Prize winner *Kawabata Yasunari* (1899–1972), who looked back nostalgically to the world of the "Genji-monogatari", and *Yokomitsu Riichi* (1898–1947), who introduced the "stream of consciousness" technique into Japanese literature. – Standing apart from all current trends is *Akutagawa Ryunosuke* (1892–1927), heir to the psychologically oriented school of Objective Naturalism.

Post-1945 literature was at first entirely concerned with assimilating and overcoming the experience of the war, with criticism of post-war society – as in the work of *Dazai Osamu* (1909–48) and *Oda Sakunosuke* (1913–47) – and with the quest for new forms of expression. The members of the "Democratic Literature" group, among them the Marxist woman writer *Miyamoto Yuriko* (1899–1951), sought to achieve an intellectual and social reorientation. – Since the 1950s Japanese literature has entered the age of *internationalism*, and novels, films, radio plays and television series are no longer confined to specifically Japanese subjects. The literary scene is now dominated by the mass market and the best-seller list; and writers have adapted themselves to the realities of the situation and beome adepts of the literary trade. A notable example of this is *Mishima Yukio* (1925–70), who even contrived to commercialize his suicide by advance publicity. An extraordinarily versatile and fertile writer of wide culture, Mishima combined Western and Eastern themes and old and modern forms. His intellectual development took him from the European "art for art's sake" school by way of a pessimistic nihilism to an "active" nihilism which preached the ideals of Bushido, the "way of the warrior", harking back to Japan's feudal past. *Kaiko Ken* (b. 1930) is concerned with the gulf between the individual and society; in his "Natsu-no-yami" ("Summer Darkness", 1972) a Japanese living abroad casts a critical eye on both Japan and the West. *Oe Kenzaburo* (b. 1935) shows the influence of Sartre, while the Surrealism of *Abe Kobo* (b. 1924) is reminiscent of Kafka. *Inoue Yasushi* (b. 1907) deals with Existentialist themes, sometimes set in the Japanese past. Political criticism came to the fore again from 1960 onwards (mass movement against the agreement with the United States), as in the work of *Shibata Sho* (b. 1935) and *Kurahashi Yumiko* (b. 1935). The problems of old people were dealt with by *Ariyoshi Sawako* (b. 1931) in his successful novel "Kokotsu-no-hito" (1972). Since the 1970s a sceptical group of writers hostile to all ideologies, the "Introvert Generation" (Naiko-no-sedai), have made a name for themselves. Among the members of the group are *Furui Yoshikichi* (b. 1937) and *Ogawa Kunio* (b. 1927).

Drama

The traditional Japanese dramatic forms, still vigorous today, were originally derived from the ritual dances of prehistoric times, which were closely concerned with human life and human needs. The incantations designed to secure success in the hunt, the reverence paid to the sun goddess Amaterasu who dispensed light and life, the sacrifice and glorification of the stag (both as the hunters' prey and the messenger of the gods) and the act of thanksgiving for an abundant catch of fish: these all formed the content of the dances performed by priests and shamans, varying in character in the different parts of the country, which still survive in fragmentary form in Japanese folk-dances, in courtly dances and in the theatre.

The 8th-century chronicles "Kojiki" and "Nihon-shoki" recount the myths which lay at the origin of some of these dances. They tell how the goddess Amaterasu-omikami withdrew to a cave to escape the wrath of her brother, the storm god Susanoo-no-mikoto, and how with her disappearance light also disappeared from the world. It was only after the goddess Ama-no-Uzume had danced in front of the cave that the sun goddess was induced to leave her hiding-place and bring the sun back into the world of men. This was the origin of the oldest Japanese ritual dance, the Kagura, danced at Court in a ceremony (Mikagura) honoring the divine Imperial ancestress, Amaterasu. Archaic forms of this dance are preserved in village dance rituals in the Takachiho Gorge (Kyushu), and it is still danced in the Iwato Shrine (Iwato-kagura). Similarly stylized pantomimic dances (Sato-kagura) were developed for performance in Shintoist shrines, originally by dancing-girls and later by priests. They began with the invocation of the gods (Kami-oroshi); this was followed by dances for the entertainment of the gods (Kami-asobi) and the presentation of the worshippers' requests; and the dance concluded with the sending away of the gods (Kami-okuri). These dances formed the basis of later dramatic forms and other types of performance (*gigaku*) which reached Japan from China in the 7th century and on an increased scale in the 8th, combining with the introduction of musical instruments and Buddhist ideas to produce early forms of folk-dance-plays and singspiels (*sarugaku*).

The sarugaku actor *Kan'ami* (1333–84) and his son *Zeami Motokiyo* (1363–1443) developed the sarugaku plays into the lyrical and melodramatic **No theatre**, a highly refined and stylized dramatic form which reaches its climax in a dance and abandons all realism in favor of a powerful symbolism. Of the 240 surviving No plays about half are attributed to Kan'ami and Zeami. Zeami also wrote important theoretical works which laid down the aesthetic principles of No drama and made a major contribution to the flowering of the art. Zeami's work enjoyed the patronage of the Shogun and art patron *Ashikaga Yoshimitsu*.

There has been little change in the method of presentation of No plays during the subsequent 600 years, and they are still widely popular. Their roots lie in the old *sangaku* ("music for entertainment"), which developed into *sarugaku* ("monkey music'') during the Heian period. This popular form of entertainment was a kind of farce, incorporating various artistic turns and dances, in which Buddhist and Shintoist priests were satirized, frequently in a burlesque or even obscene fashion. It was also influenced by the *dengaku* (''field music'') which had developed out of rural harvest dances. In the 13th century these crude popular entertainments were given more serious substance and strict dramatic form, and were now performed by professional actors. The plays were now known as *sarugaku-no-No* (''artistic *sarugaku*'') or *dengaku-no-No*; later the abbreviated form *No* came into use. During this period the No play was similar in function to the European mystery plays, though in essence it was still a form of popular drama designed to appeal to the mass of the population.

The No theater developed into a serious and aristocratic art form only in the time of the Ashikaga shogun Yoshimitsu, being given its definitive poetic form by Zeami. Under Yoshimitsu's patronage and the influence of the Zen aestheticians who also enjoyed the Shogun's favour Zeami wrote a series of plays which are still unsurpassed. – There are now five schools of No drama: *Kanze* (the largest), *Komparu, Hosho, Kongo* and *Kita*. All of these except Kita, which was founded in the 17th century, have a family tradition going back to the 14th century.

No plays are performed on a covered stage 18 ft/ 5·4 m square, plainly constructed of cypress wood, which projects into the auditorium, imitating the open-air stage on which the plays were originally performed. The permanent backdrop is the painting of a pine, and in front of this are the musicians (a flautist accompanied by three drummers) who accompany the recitative of the chorus, seated in two rows on the right-hand side of the stage. On the left-hand side of the stage, to the rear, is a gangway, flanked by three pines arranged to give an effect of perspective, by which there enter the principal actor (*shite*), his attendant (*tsure*) and the second actor (*waki*) – all men. While the two subsidiary players, sometimes with masks and sometimes without, explain the story of the play, the principal actor, wearing an appropriate character mask, carries on the action, having first put himself into the right frame of mind for his role – which may be that of a divinity, the spirit of a dead knight or even a beautiful woman – by meditation in the ''mirror room'' (*kagami-no-ma*). The introductory explanations of the *waki* are followed by the entrance of the *shite*, who is always elegantly and magnificently clad even if this is not appropriate to his role. His acting, with its symbolic movements and gestures, is almost abstract in form, in accordance with Zeami's basic principles of bloom (*hana*), elegant beauty (*yugen*) and the charm of the moment (*mezura-shi*). Even dramatic events do not disturb these principles, which leave no room for any kind of realism.

No theater

The classical programme of five No plays in succession is now generally reduced to two, which are accompanied by the farcical interludes known as *kyogen* (see below) to relieve the tension. The plays are classified by subject-matter in five groups: *kami-mono* or *waki-no*, light-hearted stories about divinities; *shura-mono* or *otoko-mono*, tragic heroic epics; *katsura-mono* or *onna-mono*, stories about beautiful women; *kyoran-mono*, stories about mentally confused persons; and *oni-mono*, stories about supernatural beings (which are presented as the concluding item in a No programme).

The **kyogen** are humorous interludes which are closely related to the No plays but have a distinctive form of their own. Using the popular language of the 16th century, they caricature society and its weaknesses, sometimes approaching the tragi-comic in their handling of this wide field. They differ from the No plays in their pattern of a dialogue between two characters or groups, in their very rare use of masks and in their realistic style of acting.

The **Bunraku puppet theater** dates from the 16th century, when recitals by blind musicians (*biwa-hoshi*) of tales from the great warrior chronicles such as the ''Heike-monogatari'', accompanied by *biwa* music, enjoyed great popularity. In the second half of the century this popularity was increased by the inclusion in the repertoire of the type of love romance known as *joruri-junidanzoshi*, after which the recitations were called *joruri*. At the same time the *biwa* gave place to the *shamisen*, introduced from Okinawa; and towards the end of the century the first primitive puppets made their appearance.

Bunraku enjoyed a great flowering in the 17th and 18th centuries thanks to *Chikamatsu Monzaemon* (1653–1724), Japan's first great dramatist, who wrote many famous Bunraku plays; the *joruri* singer *Takemoto Gidayu* (1651–1714), whose name (*gidayu*) became a synonym for *joruri*; and the puppet-master *Yoshida Bunzaburo*, who refined the technique of puppetry to such an extent that from 1734 three operators were required to make full use of the flexible acting capacity of a puppet.

More sharply than the No play, Bunraku reflected the circumstances of the day, subject to the strict moral code of Confucianism, with its presentation of the confrontation between human emotion and an inflexible philosophy of the State. The plays concentrated on historical and contemporary events and by avoiding legendary or fairy-tale themes avoided also the air of unreality inherent in puppets; and as a result achieved a success which lasted into the 18th century and almost displaced the Kabuki play in popular favour. By 1780, however, Bunraku was showing signs of decline – a decline which was arrested by *Uemura Bunrakuken*, who established a puppet theater in Osaka (Bunraku-za, now Asahi-za). Today, Bunraku thrives.

The **Kabuki theater** (*ka* = "singing", *bu* = "dancing", *ki* = "performing art") originated during the Edo period (17th–19th centuries). It incorporates elements from various dramatic forms, welding them into an independent art form which has continued to flourish. A combination of acting, dancing and music, also confined to male performers, Kabuki achieves great variety and dynamic force and accordingly now appeals to a wider public than the classically formal No theater.

The Kabuki theater traces its origin from a religious folk-dance (Nembutsu-odori) which was performed in Kyoto by *Okuni*, a dancing-girl from the Izumo Shrine and soon gave rise to the *onna-kabuki*, popular singing and dancing shows which in 1623 (barely 30 years after they originated) were condemned by the Shogunate as immoral and forbidden to women. Boys under 15 then took their place in playing the Kabuki parts (*wakashu-kabuki*); but this seemed to the Shogunate equally dangerous to public morals, and accordingly only men were permitted to act in Kabuki and the subject-matter was restricted to realistic themes and plots, thus laying the foundations of the Kabuki theater as it still exists. Women were now banned from the Japanese stage for some 260 years; and even since the relaxation of the ban in 1891 male actors have largely retained their predominance. – About the middle of the 17th century the first two-act plays appeared. The stage was enlarged from the size prescribed for the No theater, and the "flower walk" (*hanmichi*) was

introduced – a gangway reaching from the stage across the auditorium by which the actors entered and exited and on which some of the most dramatic scenes were played. The roofing-over of the auditorium (from 1717) brought a further departure from the pattern of the No theater and a closer approach to a modern theater. The introduction of a revolving stage (1758) opened up further technical possibilities.

Kabuki flourished particularly during the Genroku period (1688–1704), when there was a flowering of middle-class culture. It achieved greater variety by the introduction of new characters – Wagoto, the handsome youth seeking to win a bride; Onnagata, a female part conceived with great sensitivity which is still one of the most admired roles in Kabuki; and Aragoto, a heroic figure of superhuman strength. The heavy make-up known as *kumadori* – particularly favoured by Aragoto – came into use; and the dramatic device called *mie* was introduced – a pose adopted by an actor at some climax in the action or in the final scene, when he froze into picturesque immobility, inciting the audience to frantic ovations. The great dramatist *Chikamatsu Monzaemon* (1653–1724) wrote Kabuki plays of enduring quality which were performed by such outstanding actors as *Ichikawa Danjuro I* (1660–1704) and *Yoshizawa Ayame* (1673–1729), famous for his playing of Onnagata.

After the death of the great Kabuki actors and Chikamatsu's switch to writing for the Bunraku puppet theater Kabuki went

Bunraku puppet theater

Kabuki theater

through a difficult period of some 50 years when it was largely displaced by Bunraku. It was finally able to gain a new lease of life by taking over popular Bunraku plays and developing the musical accompaniment (with the *shamisen* as the leading instrument). The creation of magnificently colorful stage settings and the selection of subjects which appealed to the middle classes, now increasingly prosperous and subordinate only in terms of the class hierarchy to the impoverished samurai, brought Kabuki a further heyday towards the end of the 18th century, with the work of dramatists including *Namiki Shozo* (1730–73), *Namiki Gohei* (1747–1808)

and *Sakurada Jisuke* (1734–1806) who established the classical form of this musical drama.

The Kabuki classical repertoire of some 300 plays consists of *jidai-mono* (historical dramas, usually tragic), *sewa-mono* (stories of middle-class life) and *buyo-geki* (dance-plays). Although basically realistic, the plays have a number of features which have a "distancing" effect, such as the declamatory recitative, certain refinements of stage technique and, not least, the *mie* pose; but it is precisely these contrasts that give the Kabuki theater its invariability and attraction.

Music

Traditional Japanese music is radically different from the polyphonic music of the West with its fixed time structure, and is almost impossible, therefore, to grasp at first hearing. The completely different melodic system and the unfamiliarity of the sound, together with the monotonous-seeming economy of resources, create major obstacles to understanding. The scales either have no semitone steps or have them at unfamiliar places. Some types of music have no measured pitch or exact intervals; others have only one or two notes of fixed pitch in a pattern of glides and grace notes in quarter-tones or micro-tones. As a rule a note is not hit exactly but approached from a lower note. To Western ears this all

seems wrong and out of tune, although the music is merely following different rules, no less strict and logical than those of Western music. Economy of means is a feature common to all Japanese art forms, and accordingly the music lacks resonance and volume. The differences in the sound produced by similar instruments are small and are perceptible only to those familiar with Japanese music. An instrument made differently from the norm, or even played differently, might give rise to a new type. To appreciate Japanese music it is necessary to be able to perceive a wide and subtly nuanced range of musical elements within a narrow compass. The absence of harmony and polyphony makes it necessary to approach the appreciation of music in a quite different way: rests are "quiet notes", dissonances have the quality of tone color. The melodic and rhythmic possibilities are thus richer than in Western music.

Musical notations and theoretical treatises on the performance of music have survived from as early as the 8th century A.D.; but oral transmission (based on learning by heart) was always regarded as the only authentic method. A master would select his most gifted pupil to be his successor. The ideal was to hand on what had been learned without change: any unauthorized interference endangered the tradition and the unity of the work. The structure of a composition was subject to the same conditions. The music consisted of more or less fixed melodic and rhythmic forms, the juxtaposition and superimposition of which made up the composition; and any changes in the forms, in their sequence or in the work as a whole – for example by the use of new instruments calling for a different technique – led to a cleavage in the tradition and in the school which fostered it and to the foundation of a new branch of the tradition. Changes of this kind led, particularly during the Edo period, to the establishment of many new schools, and it is sometimes difficult to determine how far they were reworking old compositions or creating new ones. Thanks to the system of musical training and the practice of oral transmission the complexity of a composition was always adjusted to the capacity of the listener: anyone who had learned the language of traditional music could follow it without the need to puzzle out its mysteries with the help of a score.

Traditional Music

The various kinds of traditional music show differences which reflect the divergent values of the different social classes for whom it was performed. In the **music of the Imperial Court** at Kyoto elegance was the essential quality, and the music of the Court was known as **gagaku**, "elegant music". The orchestral music (*kangen*, "pipes and strings") played by Court musicians (*gakunin*) in the Imperial Palace and the great temples originally stemmed from South and South-East Asia (*rin'yugaku*, "music from Lin-yi"), China (*togaku*, "music of the T'ang") and Korea (*komagaku*, from Koma, the old name for Korea). – The

music, instruments, notation and musical theory reached Japan in the 7th century A.D. or perhaps even earlier. In the 9th century the repertoire began to be augmented by Japanese compositions, and thereafter underwent many changes.

The dominant instrument in the orchestra was a type of oboe, the high-pitched *hichiriki* (Chinese *pi-li*), though the melody was mainly carried by a transverse flute, the *yokobue* (also known as the *ryuteki*, "dragon flute"). The melody was played by these two instruments, each dissonant with the other, against a background of dissonant chords from the mouth-organ (*sho*, Chinese *sheng*; not used in *komagaku*). The themes consisted of short melodies, usually rising and falling, of four to eight binary bars, with a rhythmic accompaniment by the *taiko* (a large frame drum), *shoko* (a small hanging gong) and *kakko* (side-drum), which was replaced in *komagaku* by the hourglass-shaped *san-no-tsuzumi*. In addition to the three wind instruments (*sankan*) and the three percussion instruments (*sanko*) there were two plucked string instruments, the *so* (also known as *gakuso*), a round-bellied zither with 13 strings, and the biwa (Chinese *pi-pa*), a four-stringed bass lute played with a plectrum, which accentuated the beat with short figures and arpeggios. Orchestral music accompanying dances (*bugaku*, "dance music") dispensed with the stringed instruments, but was reinforced by a huge drum (*dadaiko*) which marked various climaxes in the dance. – In addition to the "State music" played by the Court musicians there were also compositions by aristocratic amateurs. The solo music for the koto and the biwa ceased to be played, although the *saibara* (folk-songs arranged for playing by Court musicians) and *roei* (settings of Chinese poems) were revived in the 19th century.

The **music of the feudal age** developed when political power passed to the landed and warrior nobility towards the end of the 12th century. The tone of this music was dramatic and declamatory, the sound cruder and more expressive. While the Imperial Court, following a philosophical tenet of Confucian China, attached importance to exact pitch and pure notes, the music favored by the warrior class, which was derived from the folk-music of the rural areas, had no precise pitch or exact intervals.

The history of the No theater is discussed in the previous section (Drama). **No music** is primarily vocal; instrumental pieces (*hayashi*) were used only at the entrance of the actors and to accompany dances, the most important of which was the dance performed by the principal character (*shite*) in the second part of the play. In addition to recitative (*sashi*) there were declamation (*kotoba*) and the more melodious *utai*, resembling the arioso of Italian opera. The *utai* had three ranges (upper, middle and lower), which extended over two octaves in the "gentle" mode (*yowagin*) but only one in the "strong" mode (*tsuyogin*); each range had a basic note, the basic notes of adjoining ranges being a fourth apart. The basic metrical unit was a *hyoshi* of 8 beats; the *utai* was usually subject to this rhythmic discipline (*hyoshi-ai*), while the *kotoba* and *sashi* were rhythmically free (*hyoshi-fu-ai*). A chorus of 8 to 12 singers (*ji-utai*) accompanied the *shite*. A flute (*fue* or *nokan*) also accompanied the *shite* and led the orchestra, providing the melody while the rhythm came from three snare-drums, the *taiko* or big drum and two hourglass-shaped drums (*o-tsuzumi* and *ko-tsuzumi*, the "large" and the "small" drum).

In later centuries the No theater became a stylized form of drama favored by the shoguns and the local feudal lords (daimyos), and musical creativity centered in the towns of Osaka and Edo (Tokyo), where a new **middle-class or bourgeois music**, with new musical genres and forms, developed under the patronage of the wealthy merchant class. The instruments used in the music of the Edo period (17th–19th centuries) were the *shamisen* (a long-necked three-stringed lute, played with a plectrum, which was introduced from China by way of Okinawa), the 13-stringed *koto* (now known as the *zokuso*, "secular *koto*", to distinguish it from the *gakuso* used by the Court musicians) and the *shakuhachi*, an end-blown bamboo flute. The dominant instrument was the *shamisen*, played by blind musicians and geishas; the *koto* was played by blind musicians and amateurs (young ladies of good family), the *shakuhachi* by mendicant monks.

Vocal music (*ji-uta*, "local songs", and *kumi-uta*, suites of six songs) at first developed separately in the different musical fields of the *koto* and the *shamisen* until the two instruments were brought together by *Ikuta* (1656–1715), a *koto*-player. The voice and instrumental parts were heterophonic (offering different versions of the melody), sometimes getting out of step with one another in a form of syncopation which produced dissonances and rhythmic cadences. Thereafter interludes of increasing length (*aino-te* or *tegoto*) were introduced, and the orchestra was reinforced by additional instruments (first and second *koto* and/or first and second *shamisen*). If the *shakuhachi* (or more rarely the *kokyu*, the only Japanese string instrument played with a bow) was added to the *koto* and *shamisen* the ensemble was known as *sankokyu* ("three parts"). – Perhaps as early as the 17th century the few purely instrumental pieces for the *koto* were played in the form of *sankyoku*. These pieces (*shirabe-mono*, "play pieces", or *dan-mono*, "partitas") usually consisted of six sections (*rokudan*) with recurring variations on the theme.

The samurai favored the music of the *biwa* and the *shakuhachi*. Towards the end of the 16th century there developed at Satsuma (Kyushu) the *Satsuma-biwa*, a more advanced version of the *heikyoku*, the tales from the "Heike-monogatari" which were recited by blind monks and minstrels (*biwa-hoshi*). *Kurozawa Kinko* (1710–71) put into proper musical form the *shakuhachi* melodies of the itinerant mendicant monks (masterless samurai) and raised them to the level of an art.

During the Edo period **theater music** also played an important part in Japanese musical life. The music which accompanied the Joruri puppet plays was in the *katari-mono* style (songs of epic or ballad type accompanied by the *shamisen*). The movements of the puppets were accompanied by a vocalist and an instrumentalist, the singer putting on a different voice for each of the parts and miming at the same time; the style of singing was full and highly expressive. *Takemoto Gidayu* (1651–1714), along with the famous dramatist *Chikamatsu Monzaemon* (1653–1724) and the puppet-master *Yoshida Bunzaburo*, raised puppet-playing to an art, and the leading Joruri style is named after him (*gidayu-bushi*). This style was also adopted in the Kabuki theater, which in addition to several *katari-mono* styles (*kiyomoto-bushi*, *tokiwazu-bushi*, etc.) had a lieder-like style (*utai-mono*) known as *nagauta* which was used in lyrical scenes and as an accompaniment to dances. An interesting feature of the Kabuki theater is the *geza* ("lower seats"), an ensemble, concealed from the audience by a lattice screen, consisting of singers, *shamisen* players, flautists and percussion which provides background music.

Religious music, a musical field with its own aesthetic rules and without attachment to any particular social class, occupied a special position in the sense that the form of the music and the singing were frequently beyond the grasp of the worshippers, who received only a general impression of something solemn and magical (conveyed by the "gliding" or legato singing and the use of instruments reputedly magical – the drum, the jingle-bells, the flute). The *norito* (prayers – simple recitatives, sometimes with responses) which formed part of the *kagura* ("divine music", played in the Imperial Palace or at the Great Ise Shrine) and songs for the invocation or entertainment of gods (*torimono, saibari*) are among the oldest forms of Japanese music, but were arranged in the *gagaku* style. In this music the orchestral accompaniment was provided by *wagon* (six-stringed round-bellied zithers, probably of Japanese origin), *shakubyoshi* (wooden rattles), *kagurabue* (flutes) and *hichiriki* (oboe-like instruments). – **Shinto music** also included sacred dances (*mikomai*) performed by female shamans (*miko*) and semi-sacred dances (*shirabyoshi*).

Shomyo, a form of ritual singing which is the oldest **Buddhist music**, was practiced by the Tendai and Shingon sects and adopted by later sects with minor modifications. Chinese transliterations of Sanskrit hymns (*bonsan*) and purely Chinese hymns (*kansan*) were introduced into Japan from China in the 9th century; and songs and recitatives with Japanese texts and increasingly Japanese melodies (*wasan*) began to appear in the 11th century. While the essential elements in the ceremony were the reading of sutras and the recital of prayers, the introductory psalms (*bai*: e.g. *nyorai-bai, sange* or *unga-bai*) and hymns (*san, shichi-bongosan*) are musically richer.

Many semi-liturgical types of music were popular in the precincts of temples and shrines from early times, and in many places these have been preserved or have become part of the varied range of folk-music. – At the present time religious music of Western type predominates in Christian communities and also in many Buddhist sects. In some remote areas in south-western Japan Latin and Japanese chorales originally introduced by the crypto-Christians (see under Religion, p. 35) have been preserved by oral tradition.

Modern Music

Since the Meiji Government, for political reasons, introduced **Western music** in schools and barracks about 1880 several generations of musicologists and music-teachers have made European classical music so familiar in Japan that the time for mere imitation is long past. At the beginning of the period *shoka* ("school songs") and *gunka* ("soldiers' songs") became popular. The *shoka*, with words and tunes based on Western and earlier Japanese folk-songs, a pentatonic scale and Western harmonies, are still very much alive; the *gunka* are used as background music in gambling arcades.

Japanese composers devoted themselves in the first place to vocal and piano music. Among leading figures were the talented *Taki Rentaro* (1879–1903) and the pioneer of orchestral music, *Yamada Kosaku* (1886–1965), who composed the popular "Akatombo". Since 1925 there have been regular concerts and recitals in Japan. The first composers of the contemporary period had studied abroad and fell into various schools – German (*Moroi Saburo*, 1903–77), French (*Ikenouchi Tomojiro*, b. 1906) and a national (or Russian) school (*Ifukube Akira*, b. 1914). The next generation – *Ishii Kan* (1887–1962), *Dan Ikuma* (b. 1924) broke away from this academism. After 1955 Japanese composers rallied to the international avant-garde. From atonality (*Dan; Moroi Makoto*, b. 1930; *Matsushita Shin'ichi*, b. 1922) the development proceeded by way of dodecaphony (*Mayuzumi Toshiro*, b. 1929; *Fukushima Kazuo*, b. 1930) and experimental compositions (*Takemitsu Toru*, b. 1930; *Suzuki Hiroyoshi*, b. 1931) to "musique concrète" (*Mayuzmi, Takemitsu, Moroi Makoto; Shibata Minao*, b. 1916) and computer- or chance-produced music (*Takahashi Yuji*, b. 1938; *Matsudaira*

Yoriaki, b. 1931). More recently there have been an interest in improvisation and a return to the patterns and aesthetic principles of traditional Japanese music in the quest for a conception of music going beyond the purely musical (*Takemitsu, Fukushima; Ishii Make*, b. 1936; *Noda Teruyuki*, b. 1940).

Early forms and styles of **jazz** were known in Japan from 1916; and the use of the word *jazu* and the typical jazz sound can be firmly dated to 1923. Banned from 1940 onwards as "enemy music", jazz enjoyed a great revival after the war under American patronage. First came bebop (Japanese *bappu*); and from 1955 onwards all the styles of the international jazz avant-garde, from cool jazz to free jazz, reached Japan with practically no time-lag. Until then Japanese jazz had merely imitated the American model, occasionally adding an exotic touch with a dash of pentatonic scale, and the boundaries between jazz and commercial dance music were fairly fluid. From about 1968, however – the year of the first Japanese Jazz Festival – Japanese jazz musicians began to go their own way. Among leading figures whose reputation extends beyond Japan are the composer, flute-player and saxophonist *Watanabe Sadao* (b. 1933), the composer and trumpet-player *Hino Terumasa* (b. 1942) and the pianist *Yamashita Yosuke* (b. 1942). More recently there has been a tendency to branch out beyond the bounds of conventional jazz in the direction of Brazilian jazz, the folk-music of black Africa (Watanabe Sadao), mixed forms combining rock and folk-music (*nyumyujikku*; Watanabe Kazumi and others), or electronic music (Sato Masahiko).

In the field of **pop music** the Japanese have developed their own form of hit-song. The general term for a pop song, mostly applied to foreign products, is *ryukoka* ("fashion song"); the term *kayokyoku* is applied to a Japanese song with an original Japanese text, composed, arranged and performed by Japanese, which is usually more restrained than its Western counterpart. The melody with its frequent use of the pentatonic scale, harmonized and orchestrated in the Western manner, gives it a touch of the exoticism which to the Western ear seems characteristic of Japanese music. The purely Japanese hit-song has gone through some vicissitudes since it was first commercialized by the record industry about 1927. Immediately after the Second World War its melodic system was adjusted to fit into the Western major/minor harmonic pattern, with the addition of melodic elements from Japanese folk-songs or from jazz; thereafter it moved closer to folk, pop, rock and disco music. The subject-matter, however, remained fairly constant – unhappiness, loneliness, homesickness, memories of the past. Common to all the tunes is a basic structure linked to the scales of traditional Japanese music, with frequent tetrachords, falling in semitones and rising in full tones, usually in the Western minor keys, since the major is too alien to traditional Japanese music.

Economy

With a gross national product of 1,117 billion US dollars in 1980, Japan was second only to the United States among the nations of the world. The achievement which this represents can be appreciated when it is remembered that Japan's development into a modern industrial state began only with the accession of the Emperor Meiji in 1868. The Second World War cost Japan not only the loss of its overseas territories but also enormous destruction of industrial plant. By 1951, however, as a consequence of the Korean War, it had reached the pre-war level of output and was able to dispense with American economic aid. Between 1951 and 1955 the Japanese industrial structure was thoroughly modernized, and consumption per head and the real value of incomes reached pre-war levels. The year 1956 marked the beginning of a period of active investment in private industry, supported and promoted by various Government measures. The main aims were to build up an efficient iron and steel industry, to ensure an adequate energy supply and to expand the ship-building industry.

Between 1959 and 1969 the gross national product rose by an average of 17·5% a year – a result of the increase in capital investment already referred to. In

1956 alone investment increased by 57·4%, and five years later it had multiplied fourfold. In November the Ikeda Government announced a plan to double the national income by the end of the 1960s, involving an annual growth rate of 7·2%. The prerequisites for a development on this scale were the provision of the necessary financial resources and the continued improvement and modernization of the industrial structure. In fact the plan's objectives were achieved by 1964. The main thrust was now transferred from light to heavy industry, the products of which played an increasingly important part in the Japanese export trade.

Between 1965 and 1970 capital investment increased 2·4 times, consumption expenditure 1·6 times and the gross national product 1·8 times. Japan's competitiveness in international markets increased during this period, since industrial production costs were reduced by the systematic application of technical advances. The rapid growth of the Japanese economy was slowed only by the fourfold increase in the price of oil in 1973–74; and in 1974, for the first time since the war, it showed a decline. A year later, however, the growth rate in real terms had risen again to 1·4%, and thereafter it increased to 6·5% in 1976, 5·4% in 1977 and 5·6% in 1978. The current economic plan (1979–85) is aimed at an average annual growth rate in real terms of 3·4% with micro-miniaturization, information technology and the automation of industrial production as the main fields of technological development. In the view of the Japanese Office of Economic Planning Japan is well on the way to becoming the richest industrial nation in the world by the end of the century.

The figures show that the rate of industrial growth in Japan – admittedly starting from a lower base – is almost twice that of the countries of western Europe. The principal reason for this lies in the fact that investment has remained at a very high level in Japan, even during the recent recession. Of the gross domestic product roughly a third had gone to capital investment, compared with 20% in western Europe and even less than this in the United States. The satisfactory development of the economy as a whole, however, has been accompanied by a high bankruptcy rate among small and medium-sized firms, some 70,000 of which went out of business between 1974 and 1979.

Here we encounter the dual face of the Japanese economy. On the one hand only 0·1% of Japan's industrial firms had more than 1000 employees in 1976; and these firms, with 15% of the total number of employed persons, accounted for 26·2% of total national output. On the other hand 76·1% of firms had fewer than ten employees and, with 18·9% of the total national labour force, produced only 6·7% of total output. There are many reasons for this preponderance of small and medium-sized firms, but one major factor is undoubtedly the fact that the large Japanese industrial corporations deliberately eschew vertical concentration and rely in the main on a large number of suppliers, thus hiving off the labor-intensive processes to smaller firms and retaining the capital-intensive processes "in house". There is also a considerable difference in wage levels between large and small .enterprises, amounting not infrequently to as much as 30% or more, and there are also substantial disparities in other conditions of employment: in firms employing more than 1000 workers, for example, 44% of all employees do not work on Saturdays, while in firms with between 30 and 99 employees the proportion is only 2·8%. – A major factor in the success of the Japanese economy has been the steady increase in productivity. Between 1970 and 1975 there was an increase of 33·3% – considerably above the rate for other industrial nations.

In 1980 the total number of employed persons was 56·5 million, of whom 11% worked in the primary sector, 37% in industry and 52% in the service trades. The relatively high figure for the primary sector is explained by the fact that fishing is an activity of considerable importance and that Japanese agriculture, with its very small holdings, is highly labor-intensive. In January 1978 there were 4·79 million farm holdings, with an average size of only 3 acres; only 31·4% of these were run as full-time occupations, while 68·4% were part-time activities subordinate to, or associated with, some other occupation.

With the continuing economic growth of the 1950s and early 1960s the massive drift away from the land gave rise to no difficulties in the labor market. During the second half of the 1960s and the early 1970s, however, there were employment problems. The unemployment rate fell from 2·5% in 1955 to between 1·1% and 1·4% in 1970–74, but since then it has risen again to about 2·4%. In addition many firms are faced with the problem of overmanning; and it is difficult to reduce the labor force because of the "life-time employment" which is the normal practice in Japan. The school-leavers and university graduates who are taken on by a firm once a year can reckon on remaining in the same firm until they reach pensionable age (usually at 60). A system of pay and promotion based on seniority fosters a strong sense of loyalty to the firm;

and this complete identification of the employee with the firm which employs him is no doubt the explanation of the highly effective quality control and low rate of absenteeism in Japan. The very high life expectancy of the Japanese population, the still inadequate development of the system of social security and the relatively slow rate of population growth create particular problems for the traditional system of employment – though in the past it has always been possible to overcome them. So far, however, the Japanese trade union pattern – each enterprise having its own union, which maintains close contact with the management – has played a major part in avoiding excessive labor costs which

Protection of the Environment

The reconstruction of Japanese industry after the Second World War led to developments which have since been recognized as highly damaging to the environment. Conspicuous examples are the massive industrial installations, the towering concrete monsters in the cities and the road development which has eaten up so much land. As a result of the very high population densities in the great urban areas, however, a high degree of awareness of the need to protect the environment developed in Japan at a time when other industrial countries were paying little attention to the problem.

In the field of *industry* the Japanese regulations on the control of noise and the emission of harmful substances are broadly comparable with those applying in western Europe and North America; the regulations controlling automobile exhaust gases, however, are considerably stricter. – The regulations are less rigorously applied to the innumerable small firms, although these are not infrequently situated within residential areas.

After experiencing the horrors of Hiroshima and Nagasaki in 1945 the Japanese are naturally very sensitive to the possible dangers of *nuclear power* and radioactivity.

There is also much concern about the pollution of the environment by Japan's heavy *rail and air traffic,* and accordingly new projects such as the development of the Shinkansen "super-express" system and the construction or extension of airports now tend to encounter resistance and give rise to protest movements.

Although there is so far no general legislation on the *protection of nature,* a number of National Parks, Quasi National Parks and Nature Parks have been established to protect areas of outstanding natural beauty; and in 1974 a forest of Japanese red cedars (*Cryptomeria japonica,* Japanese *sugi*) over a thousand years old covering an area of some 4 sq. miles/10 sq. km on the island of Yakushima, south of Kyushu, was given full statutory protection.

Road and rail ...   ... in Tokyo

Terraced rice-fields

Tea harvest

might have involved the Japanese economy in some difficulty.

The rapid economic changes which have taken place since 1945 have completely altered the Japanese attitude to consumption. The modest way of life and high rate of saving which formerly characterized Japan have lost ground to an increasing urge towards consumption. Nevertheless Japan is still the country with the highest rate of private saving, now running at almost 20% of disposable income. This reflects the fact that provision for the future is still largely the responsibility of the family. In consequence the State accounts for a considerably smaller proportion of the gross national product than in other industrial nations (21%). The highly developed Japanese group consciousness resulting from the homogeneity of the population has so far prevented the development of any conflict between the State and the private sector or between labor and capital; and the national consensus thus achieved is reflected in the low frequency of strikes, which have not increased in spite of the fall in real incomes.

Only some 16% of the land area of Japan is suitable for **agriculture**, though this average conceals wide regional variations (the island of Hokkaido, for example is predominantly agricultural). Before the Second World War some 50% of all employed persons worked in the primary sector of the economy – a proportion reduced to 10% by the tremendous industrial development of recent decades.

There has also been a decline in the area under cultivation (15·1 million acres in 1957, 14·1 million acres in 1978) and in the number of full-time farm holdings (3·1 million in 1950, 595,000 in 1979). On the other hand there has been an increase in the number of holdings worked on a part-time basis (over 3 million in 1950, 4·2 million in 1979), particularly around the large industrial cities, where the agricultural workers have opportunities of finding part-time employment in some other job.

Japan's most important agricultural crop is *rice,* which occupies an area of some 9650 sq. miles (almost half the country's cultivable land) and yields an annual total of over 12 million tons – far more than enough to meet domestic consumption. The main rice-growing areas are on the island of Honshu. Other major crops are wheat, barley and other cereals, fruit, vegetables, such as pulses, and potatoes, and tea. – *Stock-farming* is of less importance, but is increasingly being developed on an intensive basis. The numbers of sheep and goats are declining, but poultry-farming is being steadily expanded. – Nor should the importance of *silkworm-culture* be underestimated. It flourishes particularly in central Honshu, where there are large plantations of mulberry trees.

Japanese agriculture is now able to meet some three-quarters of the country's needs. Thanks to intensive and efficient farming this proportion is steadily increasing in spite of the reduction in the area under cultivation. – Japan has some

94,550 sq. miles of *forests,* roughly a third of this area being under statutory protection. The yield of timber in 1980 was almost 48 million cubic yards/37 million cubic metres.

Fishing has long played a major role in the Japanese economy. With annual catches of almost 10 million tons of sea fish, roughly 15% of the total world catch, Japan is the leading fishing nation in the world. In recent years the 200-mile fishing limits introduced by many countries have severely hampered the Japanese fisheries. Japan has so far opposed the restriction of whaling (a total ban on which, beginning in 1985, has been proposed). – The once-famous Japanese *pearl fisheries* are now in decline.

Pearl-divers

Japan has a variety of **minerals**, but the available reserves are small, with an output amounting to only 1% of the world total. The country is therefore almost wholly dependent on imports – to the extent of 85% for coking coal, 92% for copper ore and 100% for bauxite, iron ore and crude oil. Japan has thus become the principal purchaser of these raw materials in world markets. It is at pains, however, to avoid becoming dependent on individual supplying countries.

The principal contribution to the economy is made by the production of **industrial goods**, in which Japan takes third place in the world league, after the United States and the Soviet Union. The most important fields of production are steel-making (Japan is the No. 1 producer of raw steel in the Western world), motor-vehicle manufacture (world leader in the production of private automobiles, largely automated; motor-cycles), shipbuilding, the manufacture of pharmaceuticals

(world leader), paper, optical apparatus and toys, entertainment electronics (audio systems), electrical and computer technology. – Industry is concentrated in the coastal areas, particularly in the old port towns on the Pacific and their immediate surroundings. These areas have the advantage of minimizing transport costs, and this factor has been kept very much in mind in the siting of new steel plants, so that the necessary raw materials can be brought into a deep-water harbor and the finished products exported by sea without costly and time-consuming intermediate transport.

Foreign trade is of great importance to Japan, even though the country's dependence on it appears relatively small (only some 12% of total output was exported in 1979). Since the end of the Second World War, however, Japan's foreign trade has grown almost twice as fast as total international trade.

In the early post-war years exports consisted mainly – as they had before the war – of textiles, household goods and other products of light industry. It soon became clear, however, that Japan would be unable by this means to achieve a satisfactory balance of trade: it had the greatest difficulty in accumulating the foreign currency required to purchase raw materials and acquire production licenses. It was obliged, therefore, to alter its export structure: a process facilitated by the rapid build-up of heavy industry and the chemical industry and by the measures taken to increase productivity, reduce costs, improve quality and extend the range of products. The contribution made to exports by heavy industry and the chemical industry accordingly rose from 36% in 1955 to 75% in 1971. With high-technology methods of production and high-quality products Japan established a good sales image throughout the world, and in 1980 the value of exports amounted to almost 130 billion US dollars. The principal exports were machinery, iron and steel products, automobiles, ships, optical appliances (cameras), radio, television and video sets, record-players, cassette recorders, quartz watches, pocket calculators, computers, cotton and artificial fibre goods, raw silk, porcelain, glass, toys and fish products. – Almost a quarter of total exports went to the United States, 12·8% to the European Community and 6% to the Eastern Bloc countries.

The Shinkansen "super-express" at Himeji

In contrast to other industrial nations, the Japanese import structure shows an unusually high proportion of raw materials compared with finished products (some 60% in Japan against no more than 20–30% in other industrial countries).

The Large Commercial Houses (Shosha)

The largest Japanese commercial houses play a major part in the country's export and import trade, marketing in foreign countries the products both of their own subsidiaries and of other firms and importing foreign raw materials and industrial products for the domestic market. They also operate successfully throughout the world as dealers and brokers between producers and purchasers in other countries.

The nine largest Japanese commercial houses are:

	Turnover 1980–81 (£ billion)
Mitsubishi	37
Mitsui & Co.	34
C. Itoh & Co.	28
Marubeni	27
Sumitomo	26
Nissho-Iwai	18
Toyo Menka	9
Kanematsu-Gosho	8
Nichimen	7

In the field of **energy supply** – primarily in the case of oil – Japan's dependence on imports is particularly marked. In 1980 some 40% of total Japanese imports was accounted for by oil, which supplied roughly 72% of the country's energy requirements. The main consumer of energy is industry, which takes over 60% of the energy generated, while domestic use and consumption by small-scale producers account for under 20% (compared with some 35% in the United States). In order to reduce its dependence on oil Japan has invested in the large-scale development of *atomic energy*. More than 20 nuclear power stations (including one at Fukushima which is the largest in the world) are at present in operation, and their number is to be increased to 60 by 1995. The Government is also devoting large resources to the promotion of research into *alternative sources of energy,* and experimental power-stations using the warmth of sea-water and solar energy are at the trial stage.

In the last few years Japanese firms have increased their activities in other countries, seeking new markets for their products, cheaper labor and additional sources of supply of raw materials. Their efforts in these directions are directed mainly towards the United States, Central and South America, Europe and, not least, Asia and Australia.

The Japanese **transport system** has barely been able to keep pace with the rapid development of the economy. With some 20 million private automobiles and 10 million trucks in 1980, Japan had more than 620,000 miles/1,000,000 km of *roads,* including 1600 miles/2600 km of motorway. – The *rail system* also makes a major contribution to passenger transport. The State-run Japanese National Railways (JNR) have more than 13,000 miles/21,000 km of track, and there are also various private companies with another 3750 miles/6000 km of track. Spectacular efforts have been made to attract increased custom to the railways by higher speed, greater frequency of services and higher standards of comfort – most notably by the introduction of the Shinkansen super-expresses ("bullet trains") from 1964 onwards. The first of these was the Tokaido Express on the important Tokyo–Osaka–Fukuoka route (just under 750 miles/1200 km), which reached speeds of up to 130 miles/210 km an hour. In 1982 two attached Shinkansen routes came into operation: the Tohoku Express on the Tokyo–Fukushima–Morioka route (310 miles/500 km) and the Joetsu Express between Tokyo and Niigata (170 miles/270 km), running through the central highlands. Further "super-express" routes are to follow, including the extension of the Tohoku line to Sapporo on the northern island of Hokkaido (tunnel over 30 miles/50 km long under the Tsugaru Strait now under construction) and of the Tokaido line to Kagoshima, at the southern tip of Kyushu.

A large number of domestic *air routes* provide reliable and rapid communications between practically all parts of the country. Frequent services are flown not only by the national airline, Japan Air Lines (JAL), in addition to its international services from Narita and Osaka airports, but also by a number of regional and local companies.

In 1981 Japan had the world's third largest *merchant navy,* with 38 million GRT, predominantly consisting of tankers.

Tourism is now making an increasingly important contribution to the Japanese economy, with a growth rate which reached double figures in the early 1970s. The European countries in particular have been showing increased interest in visiting Japan. The largest numbers of visitors (over 1·5 million in 1981) come from the United States, Taiwan, South Korea and Britain (with many from Hong Kong).

JAL Jumbo jet at Mount Fuji

Japan
A to Z

Tourist information. – At most of the places described in this Guide there are local information bureaus. Almost invariably, however, the staff of these bureaus speak only Japanese (though they may understand English very well if written down), and the tourist literature they provide is in Japanese. Wherever possible, therefore, each entry also gives the address of a central tourist information office, usually in Tokyo, which is likely to have staff speaking foreign languages. Foreign visitors will be well advised to apply to these offices for information in the first place.

Daibutsu (large Buddha figure) in Kotokuin Temple, Kamakura

Abashiri
あばしり

Prefecture: Hokkaido. – Population: 44,000.
Post code: J-093. – Telephone code: 01524.

(i) (local)
Abashiri-shi Kanko Kyokai,
Abashiri Bus Terminal,
Nishi 1, Minami 2-jo;
tel. 4 5849.
Abashiri Tourist Section,
Higashi 4-chome, Minami 6-jo;
tel. 4 6111.
Japan Travel Bureau,
Nishi 1–15, Minami 2-jo;
tel. 4 5205.

HOTELS. – **Western style:** *Sakuraso,* 24, Omagari,
8 r.; *Morisanso,* Higashi 2–13, Minami 3-jo, 7 r. –
YOUTH HOSTELS: *Abashiri YH,* Higashi 1-chome,
250 b.; *Gensei-kaen YH,* 208–2, Kitahama, 52 b.;
Bihoro YH, 15 miles/25 km SW in Bihoro, 31, Motomachi, 120 b.; *Higashi-mokoto YH,* 25 miles/40 km S
in Higashi-mokoto, 394, Suehiro, 52 b.

EVENTS. – *Ryuhyo-matsuri* (Drift Ice Festival; beginning of February); *Orochon Fire Festival* (third Sunday in July), in Katsuragaoka Park.

TRANSPORTATION. – **Rail:** from SAPPORO Hakodate
main line (JNR) and Sekihoku main line (JNR: 6
hours); from ASAHIKAWA Sekihoku main line (JNR: 4
hours); from KUSHIRO Semmo main line (JNR: 3
hours).

**The town of Abashiri lies on the Sea
of Okhotsk in the eastern half of the
island of Hokkaido, in the center of
the Quasi National Park of Abashiri,
which takes in the coastal areas to N
and S of the town. Two thousand
years ago the region was occupied
by the Ainu and Moyoro** *peoples.*
**Abashiri is now a marketing center
for the agricultural produce of the
Abashiri plain, a fishing port and a
center of the fish-processing
industry and the site of Japan's top
security prison.**

SIGHTS. – To the E of the station (10
minutes by bus) is the **Municipal
Museum** (natural history; culture of the
Ainu and Moyoro peoples). – 1 mile/
1·5 km NE of the station rises the shell
mound of **Moyoro-kaizuka,** with many
remains of occupation by the Moyoro,
predecessors of the Ainu (material from
site in Municipal Museum). – 15 minutes'
walk from the station is the *Okhotsk
Aquarium.*

SURROUNDINGS. – SW of the town lies *Lake
Abashiri* (circumference 25 miles/40 km), part of the

Quasi National Park of Abashiri (10 minutes by bus
from Abashiri Station). From the hill of *Tentozan*
(679 ft/207 m), on the NE shore of the lake, there are
fine views of the town, the lakes in the surrounding
area and the sea. On the S side of the lake are the
resorts of **Memambetsu-onsen** and **Abashiri
Kotan-onsen.**

6 miles/10 km NW of Abashiri, in the coastal region,
is **Notoro Lagoon** (bus to Ubaranai), which has an
area of 22 sq. miles/58 sq. km. Beyond this is **Saroma
Lagoon,** the largest on Hokkaido (circumference
45 miles/72 km).

See also **Akan National Park.**

Aizu-Wakamatsu
あいずわかまつ

Prefecture: Fukushima. – Population: 115,000.
Post code: J-965. – Telephone code: 02422.

(i) (local)
Aizu-Wakamatsu-shi Kankoka,
Town Hall,
Higashi-Sakae-cho 3-46.

HOTELS. – **Western style:** *Green Hotel Aizu,*
opposite station, 59 r.; *Izumiya,* 6-35, Minami-
Sengoku-cho, 19 r.; *Business Central Hotel,* 2-20,
Naka-machi, 20 r. – **Ryokan:** *Tsuru-ya Ryokan,*
20 r.; *Osaka-ya,* 19 r.

TRANSPORTATION. – **Rail:** from TOKYO (Ueno
Station) Ban-etsu-saisen line (JNR: 4 hours).

**Aizu-Wakamatsu, situated in the
center of Fukushima prefecture
(eastern central Honshu) and the
second largest town in the prefecture, is noted for its lacquerware,
which has a tradition going back 300
years. To the E of the town extends
the Bandai-Asahi National Park,
which offers a wide range of excursions into country of great interest
and beauty. The view from Mount
Bandai (5000 ft/1819 m) is especially
breath-taking.**

HISTORY. – Thanks to its central situation the 14th c.
castle of Tsuruga or Wakamatsu, commanding the
town which was then known as *Aizu,* developed into
a fortress of great strategic importance, the most
powerful stronghold in north-eastern Japan. The
granting of this fief to Hoshina Masayuki (1611–72),
half-brother of the Tokugawa ruler Iemitsu, in 1643
ensured the loyalty of this politically important region
to the central government. In the armed conflicts
during the transition from the Tokugawa era to the
Meiji period the Tokugawa régime found strong support here. After a month's siege by Imperial forces,
however, the castle was compelled to surrender, and
in 1868 both the castle and the town were razed to the
ground. The Aizu clan was banished to the small fief
of Tonami, the present town of Mutsu (Aomori
prefecture).

SIGHTS. – **Tsuruga Castle,** 2 miles/ 3 km S of the station, was built by Ashina Naomori in 1384, but only the ramparts and the moat survived the destruction of the castle by the Imperial forces. The main tower was rebuilt in 1965. – On *Iimori Hill,* 2 miles/3 km E of the station (15 minutes by bus, then 20 minutes on foot), are the tombs of members of the Byakkotai (Corps of White Tigers). Here, true to their vows, 19 young men who remained loyal to the Shogunate committed suicide when they saw the castle go up in flames.

SURROUNDINGS. – To the E of the town (10 minutes by bus) is **Aizu bukeyashiki,** a complex of old samurai houses and museums. Among them is the *Karo-yashiki,* a faithful reproduction of a military commander's house, with 35 rooms, a richly decorated reception hall (modelled on the Nijo Palace in Kyoto) and a garden. – In the village of **Nakahata** stands the Nakahata-jinya, the only surviving example in northern Japan of a governor's residence (transferred here from the town of Yakubi in Fukushima prefecture).

The **Aizu Historical Museum,** housed in a former arsenal, contains interesting terracotta material, Buddhist sculpture, etc. – The *Reinan-an* tea-house was built to the design of the tea-master Sen-no-Rikyu (1522–91). – The *Lacquer Museum* contains fine examples of Aizu-nuri ware; it also displays products of local folk art (Aizubuke-yashiki), with demonstrations of their manufacture.

3 miles/5 km SE of Aizu-Wakamatsu (20 minutes by bus) is the health resort of **Higashiyama-onsen** (springs at temperatures of 113 °F/45 °C and 154 °F/ 68 °C, situated in a west-facing valley surrounded by hills. This popular spa lies on both banks of the *Yugawa* stream.

SE of Higashiyama-onsen is *Seaburi Mountain* (2841 ft/866 m), with two cableways (winter sports; panoramic views).

See also **Bandai-Asahi National Park**.

Akan National Park
あかん国立公園

Prefecture: Hokkaido.
Area: 338 sq. miles/875 sq. km.
(i) (central)
National Parks Association of Japan
Toranomon Denki Building,
8-1, Toranomon 2-chome, Minato-ku,
J-105 **Tokyo;**
tel. (03) 502 0488.

(local)
Akan National Park Tourist Association,
2, Urami-cho,
J-085 **Kushiro;**
tel. (0154) 41 1131.

HOTELS. – IN AND AROUND TESHIKAGA. – **Western style:** *Kawayu Grand Hotel,* Aza Kawayu, 144 r., SP, thermal bath; *Mashu Grand Hotel,* 120, Aza Teshikaga, 44 r., thermal bath; *Hotel Mashu,* 120, Aza Teshikaga, 29 r., thermal bath. – **Ryokan:** *Mashu-Kaku,* Aza Teshikaga, 43 r., thermal bath; *Hakuun-so,* Aza Teshikaga, 32 r., thermal bath; *Tachibana-ya,* Aza Teshikaga, 23 r., thermal bath. – YOUTH HOSTELS: *Nomura Kawayu YH,* Kawayu, 72 b., thermal bath; *Teshikaga Seinen-no-Ie,* 169, Tobetsu, 80 b.; *Mashu-Ko YH,* 883, Genya, 112 b.

ON LAKE AKAN. – **Ryokan:** *Hotel Akankoso,* Akanko-onsen, 97 r.; *New Akan Hotel,* Akanko-onsen, 175 r.; *Hotel Ichikawa,* Akanko-onsen, 95 r. – YOUTH HOSTELS: *Akan-kohan YH,* Akan-kohan, 58 b.; *Choritsu Akan YH,* Akan-kohan-bangaichi, 60 b.; *Akan Angel YH,* 5-1, Shurikomabetsu, 90 b.

TRANSPORTATION. – **Rail:** from ABASHIRI or KUSHIRO Semmo main line (JNR) to Kawayu and Teshikaga. – **Bus:** from ABASHIRI via Mokoto-onsen to Kawayu-onsen; from BIHORO via Kitami-Aioi to Akan-kohan; from BIHORO via Wakoto-hanto, Kawayu-onsen, Lake Mashu and Teshikaga to Akan-onsen; from KUSHIRO to Akan-kohan and via Teshikaga to Kawayu-onsen; from OBIHIRO via Ashoro to Akan-kohan; from TESHIKAGA to Wakoto-hanto; from KAWAYU to Kawayu-onsen. – **Boat:** cruises on Lake Akan.

The * **Akan National Park, in eastern Hokkaido, extends around three lakes, Kutcharo, Akan and Mashu. On either side of Lake Akan are the volcanoes Me-Akan and O-Akan. Much of the park is covered by sub-Arctic primeval forests and is particularly attractive in the fall with its brilliantly colored foliage.**

In the western part of the National Park lies ** **Lake Akan** (alt. 1375 ft/419 m), which has a circumference of 14 miles/ 22·5 km and a maximum depth of 118 ft/ 36 m. The lake is noted for its abundance of fish (trout, salmon) and for a waterweed known as the marimo, which can reach a diameter of 6 inches/15 cm. Normally growing on the bottom, the plants rise to the surface when the sun shines, giving the lake a shimmering green colour. The marimo, which is found also in Lake Yamanaka (Yamanashi prefecture) and Lake Sakyo (Aomori prefecture), is a statutorily protected species. – On the S side of the lake rises *Me-Akan* (4931 ft/ 1503 m), on the E side *O-Akan* (4498 ft/ 1371 m) – two volcanoes which form a magnificent backdrop to the lake with its many small islands.

On the S side of the lake is the health resort of **Akan-kohan-onsen,** a junction for the various bus services which run through the park. From here Me-Akan can be climbed (7 miles/11·5 km to summit;

On Lake Akan

1½ miles/2·5 km from Me-Akan-onsen). The *view from the summit takes in the Sea of Okhotsk, the Pacific and the Tokachi and Nemuro plains. – From Akan-kohan-onsen the *Akan Transverse Road* leads to **O-Akan-onsen,** starting-point for the ascent of the extinct volcano of O-Akan (7 miles/11 km). The road continues E to **Teshikaga,** passing the viewpoints of *Sogakudai* (view of Me-Akan and O-Akan) and *Sokodai* (view of the little lakes of Penketo and Panketo).

12½ miles/20 km N of Teshikaga (35 minutes by bus) is the magnificent ****Lake Mashu** (alt. 1152 ft/351 m). Steep rock faces rising to 650 ft/200 m and dense forests make the shores of this crater lake (circumference 12½ miles/20 km, depth 696 ft/212 m) almost inaccessible, but there is a superb view of the lake from the outlook terrace high above its shores. Lake Mashu is claimed to be the clearest lake in the world, with visibility reaching down to over 130 ft/40 m. On the E side of the lake rises Mount *Kamui-Nupuri* (2815 ft/858 m) and on the W side the still-active volcano of *Io* (1673 ft/510 m) with its numerous solfataras (vents emitting vapor). The best starting-point for a trip to the foot of the volcano is the romantically situated health resort of **Kawayu-onsen** (hot springs at temperatures of 104–140 °F/40–60 °C; railway station). From here it is 1 mile/1·5 km to the base of the volcano, where sul-phurous vapors emerge from numerous vents, coloring the rocks yellowish green with their deposits.

NW of Kawayu-onsen we find the largest lake in the Akan National Park, **Lake Kutcharo** (alt. 397 ft/121 m, area 30 sq. miles/77·5 sq. km, depth 395 ft/120 m). In the middle of the lake is the wooded island of *Tomoshiri,* on the S side is the resort of **Wakoto-onsen**, with subterranean hot springs warming the waters of the lake and the sand on its shores (camp sites). Here, too, is the source of the River *Kushiro,* which flows S. – There is a very fine view of the lake from the *Bihoro Pass* (1723 ft/525 m; bus from Wakoto-onsen or Bihoro), which carries the road from Teshikaga to *Bihoro* and **Abashiri** (see entry).

The volcano of Io

Lake Mashu

Akita
あきた

Prefecture: Akita. – Population: 290,000.
Post code: J-010. – Telephone code: 0188.

ⓘ (central)
Akita-ken Tokyo Bussan Kanko Assensho,
Tetsudo Kaikan,
1-9-1, Marunouchi, Chiyoda-ku,
J-100 **Tokyo**;
tel. (03) 211 1775.

(local)
Akita-ken Tourist Information Center,
4-1-1, Sanno;
tel. 60 1702.

HOTELS. – **Western style**: *Akita Dai-Ichi Hotel*, 1-
3-5, Naka-dori, 101 r., beach, skiing area; *Akita New
Grand Hotel*, 5-2-1, Naka-dori, 59 r., Japanese gar-
den; *Hotel Sun Route Akita*, Omachi 3-chome, 113 r.;
Park Hotel, 3-7-1, Sanno, 72 r. – YOUTH HOSTEL:
YH Yabase Seinen-no-Ie, 86, Yabase, 92 b.

RESTAURANTS. – *Akita Club*, 5-2-30, Naka-dori;
Kamata Kaikan, 4-16-4, Naka-dori; *Kappo Soshu*, 5-
1-11, Omachi; *Suginoya*, 4-1-15, Naka-dori.

EVENTS. – IN AKITA: *Kanto-matsuri* (beginning of
August), Akita-Hachiman Shrine (young men carrying long bamboo poles with up to 50 lanterns on
each). – IN YOKOTE: *Bonten-matsuri* (mid January),
procession to the Asahi Shrine with gaily decorated
poles; *Kamakura Festival* (mid February), when children build snow houses in which altars are set up.

TRANSPORTATION. – **Air**: from TOKYO (Haneda Airport; 1 hour); from OSAKA (2 hours). – **Rail**: from
TOKYO (Ueno Station) Ou main line (JNR: 7¾ hours);
from OSAKA Hokuriku, Shin-etsu and U-etsu lines

(JNR: 12 hours); from MORIOKA Tazawako line (JNR:
2½ hours); from SENDAI Tohoku and Kitakami line
(JNR: 4 hours).

**Akita, chief town of the prefecture
of that name, lies on the NW coast of
Honshu in a plain surrounded on
three sides by mountain ranges and
bounded on the W by the Sea of
Japan. It is the agricultural and cultural center of the surrounding area
and the seat of a university. The girls
of Akita are renowned throughout
Japan for their beauty (Akita-
obako).**

The town's main products are articles
made from Japanese cedar wood (Akita-
sugi), silks, chased metalwork (precious
and other metals), rice and sake (rice
wine; about 100 breweries).

HISTORY. – With the construction of its castle in 733,
Akita became a place of importance in the colonization of the northern region and a stronghold against
the Emishi of the Ou district (now Tohoku). From
1602 until the beginning of the Meiji Reform in 1868
Akita was the principal castle of the Satake family.

SIGHTS. – In **Senshu Park**, ¾ mile/
1·2 km NW of the station, are the remains
of *Akita Castle* and the **Akita-Hachiman
Shrine**, which is dedicated to Satake
Yoshinobu (1570–1633), ancestor of the
Satake family. Near by stands a statue of
Satake Yoshitake. Also in the park are the
Prefectural Museum of Art (*Kenritsu-
bijitsukan*) and another *Art Museum*

(Hirano Masakichi-bijitsukan: works by Fujita Tsuguharo, Van Gogh, Cézanne, etc.). – 20 minutes' walk from the park we come to the *Mineralogical Museum* (Kobutsu-hakubutsukan).

In 25 minutes by bus from the station we reach the **Zenryoji Temple**, with a military cemetery for those who fell in 1868, and the **Hotoji Temple**, with a five-storey stone-built pagoda.

SURROUNDINGS. – 8 miles/13 km from Akita on the Ou railway line (JNR) or the Oga line is **Oiwake**, with the Prefectural Museum (Akita-kenritsu-hakubutsukan). Still farther N lies the *Hachirogata Lagoon*, once Japan's second largest lake, with an area of 85 sq. miles/220 sq. km, but now largely drained. – From Oiwake the Oga line runs NW to the *Oga Peninsula* (see separate entry).

7½ miles/12 km NE of Akita rises Mount **Taihei** (3842 ft/1171 m; skiing) from the summit of which a fine*view of the town and the island of Sado far to the S may be enjoyed.

SE of Akita, on the Kitami line (JNR), is the town of **Omagari**, from which the Kakunodate line (JNR) continues to **Kakunodate**. This sleepy little town surrounded by mountains, known as the "Kyoto of the north", was once a stronghold of the Tozawa and later of the Satake family. It has interesting old samurai houses, and is one of the best-known cherry-blossom areas in northern Japan (end of April). It is also noted for the production of boxes and caskets of polished cherry-tree bark (*Kaba-zaiku*). – To the N lies *Lake Tazawa* (see under Towada-Hachimantai National Park).

To the S of Omagari, on the Ou line (JNR) from Akita, is **Yokote**. During the Edo period (1603–1868) the ancestral stronghold of the Satake family, the town is now the agricultural, commercial and cultural center of the surrounding area. The abundance of snow in winter allows the local children to celebrate the well-known Kamakura festival, when they build snow houses in which altars are set up and they then gather round a bonfire in the evening. – The Bonten-matsuri festival (mid January) involves a procession to the *Asahi Shrine*, carrying gaily decorated poles which are phallic symbols.

1¼ miles/2 km from Yokote Station is *Yokote Park*, with the ruins of the old castle and an outlook tower modelled on the tower of Tenshukaku Castle. – Near *Hagurocho* (¾ mile/1 km from the station) are a number of old samurai houses; morning market.

Amami Islands
See Satsunan Islands

Ama-no-hashidate
あまのはしだて

Prefecture: Kyoto.
(central)
(i) **Kyoto-fu Tourist Information Center,**
Tokyoseimei Building,
Karasuma-shijo-nishikado,
Shimogyo-ku,
J-600 **Kyoto**;
tel. (075) 371 2226.

HOTELS. – **Ryokan**: *Gemmyoan*, Monju, Miyazu-shi, 32 r.; *Monjuso*, Monju, Miyazu-shi, 21 r. – YOUTH HOSTELS: *Amanohashidate YH*, 905, Manai, Nakano, Miyazu-shi, 60 b.; *YH Amanohashidate Kanko Kaikan*, 22, Ogaki, Miyazu-shi, 70 b.

TRANSPORTATION. – **Rail**: from KYOTO San-in (JNR) and Maizuru line (3¼ hours). – **Bus**: from Ama-no-hashidate and Miyazu to Ichinomiya (15 and 30 minutes). – **Boat**: ferry from Ama-no-hashidate to Ichinomiya (15 minutes).

Ama-no-hashidate ("Bridge of Heaven") a spit of land at the W end of Wakasa Bay, on the Sea of Japan in western Honshu, is an area long famed as one of the finest stretches of coastal scenery in Japan. Bizarrely shaped pines are a notable feature of the landscape.

This tongue of land 2¼ miles/3·6 km long and 120–360 ft/37–110 m wide separates the *Aso-no-umi Lagoon* from *Miyazu Bay* (part of Wakasa Bay). The name is derived from Ama-no-ukihashi ("floating bridge of heaven"), reflecting the tradition that the divine couple Izanagi and Izanami stood here during the creation of Japan. In the narrow arm of the sea between the spit of land and the mainland is a small island, linked with both sides by bridges.

Monju, near Ama-no-hashidate Station, is the best starting-point for a walk along the spit of land. In the town stands the *Chion-ji Temple*; to the S a cableway ascends Mount *Monju*. – In the southern part of the spit of land, a little way N of Monju, we find the **Hashidate-Myojin Shrine**; at its N end the town of **Ichinomiya** lies at the foot of Mount *Nariai*. Half-way up the hill, from the *Kasamatsu Park* (cableway), there is a magnificent*view of the lagoon and the spit of land – it is customary to view the spit, or sand-bar, upside-down, that is through one's legs. – From the Kasamatsu terminus a bus service (2 miles/3 km) goes to the **Nariaiji**, a temple of the Shingon sect founded in the 8th c. (the 28th of the 33 pilgrimage temples of Kannon in the western region of Kansai). – There is also a fine *view from the *Ochi Pass*, near *Iwataki* (bus from Ama-no-hashidate Station).

An attractive EXCURSION is by boat from Ama-no-hashidate through the lagoon to Ichinomiya; from here a detour to Kasamatsu Park and then return on foot along the spit of land to Ama-no-hashidate. – The coastal region, extending 4 miles/6 km S to the little fishing port of *Miyazu*, is a popular resort within easy reach of Kyoto, Osaka and Kobe.

Aomori

あおもり

Nebuta festival

Prefecture: Aomori. – Population: 290,000.
Post code: J-030. – Telephone code: 0177.

ⓘ (central)
Aomori-ken Tokyo Kanko Bussan Assensho,
Kokusai Kanko Kaikan,
1-8-3, Marunouchi, Chiyoda-ku,
J-100 **Tokyo**;
tel. (03) 216 6010.

(local)
Aomori-ken Tourist Information Center,
1-1-1, Nagashima;
tel. 22 5080.

HOTELS. – **Western style:** *Aomori Grand Hotel,* 1-1-23, Shin-machi, 150 r., Japanese garden; *Hotel Aomori,* 1-1-23, Tsutsumi-machi, 102 r., beach; *Hotel Universe Aomori,* 2-4-7, Hon-machi, 144 r.; *Hotel Sun Route Aomori,* 1-9-10, Shin-machi, 124 r.; *Aomori Green Hotel,* 1-11-22, Shin-machi, 89 r.; *Aomori Dai-ichi Hotel,* 2-5-6, Shin-machi, 89 r. – YOUTH HOSTEL: *Uto YH,* 13-9, Chaya-machi, 160 b.

EVENTS. – *Nebuta-matsuri* (beginning of August), great procession with illuminated papier-mâché figures.

TRANSPORTATION. – **Air:** from TOKYO (Haneda Airport; 1¼ hours). – **Rail:** from TOKYO (Ueno Station) to Omiya (30 minutes), then New Tohoku-Shinkansen line (JNR) to Morioka (3¼ hours) and on to Aomori (2½ hours); also Tohoku line (JNR) via Sendai (9 hours).

Aomori, chief town of the prefecture of that name, lies on Aomori Bay, the western part of Mutsu Bay, in the extreme NE of the island of Honshu. It is a good base from which to explore the region to the S. The town – opened up to trade with other countries in 1906 – has many modern buildings. The economy of the surrounding area depends largely on forestry and fruit-growing (particularly apples).

SIGHTS. – From the station it is a 5-minute bus ride to the **Prefectural Museum** (*Aomori-kenritsu-kyodokan*: natural history, folk traditions, archaeological material). – The **Museum of Folk Art** (*Keikokan*) contains, among much else, examples of the well-known Tsugaru-nuri lacquerware, the hardness of which is achieved by the application of up to 48 coats of lacquer, and dolls representing the Haneto dancing-girls of the Nebuta festival. There are also mementos of the writer Dazai Osamu. – Near the station an interesting fish market is held daily.

The *Nebuta-matsuri* procession is one of the biggest festivals in the prefecture. When darkness falls huge illuminated papier-mâché figures (*nebuta*) are paraded through the streets of the town. The festival recalls a stratagem attributed to Sakanoue-no-Tamuramaro (758–811), who, seeking to deceive the hostile Emishi forces about the strength and disposition of his troops, caused figures of this kind to be moved about the town.

In **Nebuta-kaikan** (35 minutes by bus from the station) ten of these huge *nebuta* figures are displayed. Nebuta-kaikan belongs to the **Nebuta-no-Sato** complex, which also includes various sports facilities.

SURROUNDINGS. – 12½ miles/20 km NE (45 minutes by bus; 25 minutes by the JNR Tohoku line) is the health resort of *Asamushi-onsen* (springs at temperatures of 136–174 °F/58–79 °C). N of this, on the coast of the **Natsudomari Peninsula** (Asadokoro Beach) swans from colder regions spend the winter. Camellia flowers in spring. Offshore lies the little island of *Oshima*.

Mutsu Bay, the western part of which is known as Aomori Bay, is bounded on the E and N by the **Shimokita Peninsula**, which projects into the *Tsugaru Strait* (access from Aomori on the JNR Tohoku line, then Ominato line to Ominato). – The largest town on the peninsula is **Mutsu** (pop. 46,000), a fishing and agricultural center. NE of the town rises the extinct volcano of *Osorezan* or *Usorisan* (2717 ft/828 m; from May to October bus service from Tanabu Station) which has been regarded as sacred since the 9th c. On the N side of the crater lake (numerous solfataras) stands the **Entsuji Temple**, believed to have been founded by a priest named Ennin or Jikaku-daishi (794–864), the scene of a great annual festival on July 20–24. It is believed that during this festival worshippers can establish contact with their ancestors.

Old women, most of them blind, perform in the temple precincts a shamanist ritual which can be traced back to the 3rd c., enabling them to bring about this contact through trances and with the help of objects associated with the particular protective spirit who is invoked.

Farther N is the quiet health resort of *Yagen-onsen* (a 30-minute bus ride from Ohata Station, then 30 minutes on foot). On the N coast is *Shimofuro-onsen* (30 minutes by bus from Ohata).

See also **Towada-Hachimantai National Park**.

Arita
ありた

Prefecture: Saga. – Population: 15,000.
Post code: J-844. – Telephone code: 09554.

ⓘ (central)
Saga-ken Tokyo Kanko Bussan Assensho,
Kokusai Kanko Kaikan,
1-8-3, Marunouchi, Chiyoda-ku,
J-100 **Tokyo**;
tel. (03) 216 6596.

(local)
Saga-ken Tourist Information Center,
1-1-59, Jyonai,
J-840 **Saga**;
tel. (0952) 25 2148.

EVENTS. – *Porcelain Fair* (beginning of May).

VISITS TO FACTORIES. – Arita Bussan Co. Ltd; Koransha Co. Ltd; Fukagawa; Kakiemon; Gen-emon; Imaemon.

TRANSPORTATION. – Rail: from FUKUOKA Sasebo line (JNR: 1½ hours).

Arita, in the extreme NW of the island of Kyushu, lies in a long straggling valley surrounded by densely wooded hills at the foot of Mount Kurokami. Characteristic features of the town are the many porcelain shops and the tall chimneys of the 300 or so *porcelain factories in the town and surrounding area, some of which are centuries old and are the basis of the town's economy. The porcelain of Arita already had an international reputation in the 17th c.

Many of the factories still fire their wares in the traditional way. Clay of the highest quality is found in the surrounding area. Tiles and industrial porcelain are produced as well as the traditional porcelain ware. Since 1979 Arita has been twinned with the town of Meissen in the German Democratic Republic.

HISTORY. – During the expansionist campaigns of Toyotomi Hideyoshi (1536–98) in Korea (1592–95) Korean potters were brought to Japan and settled in the then province of Hizen (Saga prefecture) and elsewhere. In 1616 a Korean named Ri-Sampei (in Korean Yi Samp'yong) discovered the rich deposits of kaolin on Mount Izumiyama and established in Tengudani – where previously only ordinary pottery had been produced – the oldest known porcelain factory in Japan. The discovery of this source of raw material, combined with the decline of the Ming dynasty which had hitherto been the main supplier of porcelain to the European market, led to the rapid development of porcelain manufacture in Arita, which had 41 establishments producing porcelain by 1620. The trading-post of the Dutch East India Company in Nagasaki Bay, the only foreign agency operating in Japan during the "closed" period, handled the export of the Arita-yaki ware, which soon acquired a great reputation and exerted great influence on European centers, including Meissen in Germany. In 1628 Daimyo Nabeshima Katsushige established the first State-sponsored factory, the output of which was not exported but was reserved for princely houses and the Imperial Court. Nabeshima ware is now rated the finest Japanese porcelain.

Three different types of porcelain are distinguished:

Kakiemon (principal colors red, blue and yellow), which reached its greatest perfection in the second half of the 17th c. (1659–91) under the 5th and 6th Kakiemon generations.

Iro-Nabeshima (*iro* = "coloured"), with the vitrifiable colors red, yellow, light green and cobalt-blue. Its finest period was between 1688 and 1735, in the time of the Imaizumi family of porcelain-painters.

Ko-Imari, sometimes with luxuriant decorative patterns, using a blue underglaze and the colors red and gold. It achieved its finest flowering during the Genroku period (1680–1709), the heyday of Japanese middle-class culture.

Kakiemon and Nabeshima are now reckoned among the finest ancient porcelains.

Arita-yaki porcelain

The original type of decoration, in blue on a white ground (Sometsuke), gave place from 1644 onwards, under the influence of Sakaide Kakiemon (1595–1666), to polychrome firing techniques with vitrifiable colors, the dense reddish tones of Kakiemon being particularly characteristic. This style was soon copied, and in course of time the various factories produced distinctive patterns of their own. Arita-yaki ware became known in the West under the name of Ko-Imari (ko = "old"), after the port of Imari, 7½ miles/12 km N of Arita, from which the porcelain was exported. The Nabeshima kilns in Okawachi-yama were closed down in 1871 during the replacement of the Daimyate by the Meiji régime, and it was another 40 years before production was resumed in accordance with old traditions by Imaemon in 1912. There are now some 20 factories in Okawachi-yama.

SIGHTS. – To the E of the station is the *Arita Pottery Museum (*Arita Toji-bijutsukan*), which houses magnificent examples of the work of earlier and present-day potters. *Arita Park* to the S of the Museum contains the tomb of Ri-Sampei and the **Tozan Shrine**, which has the largest ceramic *torii* (Shinto gateway) in Japan.

SURROUNDINGS. – 3 miles/5 km N is Mount *Kurokami*, with the Kurokami Nature Park. – 7½ miles/12 km N lies the port of **Imari** (reached from Arita on the JNR Matsuura line). Scattered about in the bay are the beautiful **Iroha Islands**.

9 miles/15 km E (JNR Sasebo line) in the health resort of **Takeo-onsen** stands an old gate tower. Toyotomi Hideyoshi is said to have stayed in the historic old posting-station. The Mifunegaoka plum orchard is very beautiful when the trees are in blossom (begin-

ning of March). Takeo-onsen which is a popular holiday place has attractive footpaths around the foot of Mount *Horai*. – 9 miles/14 km S (bus from Arita, 40 minutes) is a beautiful region of wooded hills in the valley of the River *Ureshino*, with extensive tea plantations (Ureshino tea). The resort of **Ureshino-onsen** (hot springs, 97–208 °F/36–98 °C) has a number of good hotels and *ryokan*. There is a bus service to *Sonogi*, continuing to **Nagasaki** and the **Unzen-Amakusa National Park** (see separate entries).

Asahikawa
あさひかわ

Prefecture: Hokkaido. – Population: 357,000.
Post code: J-070. – Telephone code: 0166.
(i) (local)
Asahikawa Tourist Section,
9-chome, Rokujo-dori;
tel. 26 1111.
Japan Travel Bureau,
Sumitomo Seimei Building,
8-1704, Sanjo-dori;
tel. 24 3571.

HOTELS. – **Western style**: *New Hokkai Hotel*, 6, Gojo-dori, 98 r., Japanese garden; *Hotel New Kikuya*, 6, Ichijo-dori, 98 r.; *Asahikawa Prince Hotel*, Hidari 1-go, 7-chome, Ichijo-dori, 127 r.; *Green Hotel*, Hidari, 6-go, Ichijo-dori, 8-chome, 113 r. – YOUTH HOSTEL: *Asahikawa YH*, Inosawa-ski-jo-nai, 18-chome, 7-jo, Kamui-cho, 178 b.

RESTAURANT. – *Kagetsu Kaikan*, 7-8, Sanjo-dori.

EVENTS. – *Fuyu-matsuri* (Winter Festival; beginning of February), display of snow sculpture in Tokiwa Park; *Cherry Blossom Festival* (mid May); *Kotan-matsuri* (Ainu Festival; beginning of October), in Kamui-Kotan.

TRANSPORTATION. – **Air**: from TOKYO (Haneda Airport), 2¾ hours. – **Rail**: from SAPPORO JNR Hakodate main line (1¾ hours).

Asahikawa lies in the center of the island of Hokkaido, in the southern part of the Kamikawa Basin and the upper reaches of the Ishikari Valley. It is the second largest city on the island, the administrative, cultural and economic hub of central Hokkaido and an important railway junction. It has a markedly continental climate, with pleasant summers but very cold winters (down to −40°F/−40°C). The town's main output consists of agricultural produce, paper, timber and – thanks to its excellent water – brewery products and sake.

The town, which is divided into a northern and a southern part by the Ishikari, Hokkaido's longest river, was a garrison of the

Tonden-hei pioneers, who during the 19th c. colonization period steadily drove back the Ainu who then occupied the region. The present name ("river of the sunrise") is derived from a translation of the Ainu phrase *chupu petsu*, which was confused with the name of the River Chubetsu.

SIGHTS. – On the left bank of the Ishikari, 1 mile/1·5 km N of the station, lies the **Tokiwa Park**, a recreational center with various sports facilities and an observatory. In the **Regional Museum** (*Asahi-kawa-Kyodo-shiryokan*) are displays illustrating the history of the Ainu and the Tonden-hei pioneers.

SURROUNDINGS. – 2¾ miles/4 km NW of the station (20 minutes by bus) is **Chikabumi**, with the Kawamura Ainu Museum, where Ainu dances are performed and examples of Ainu folk art offered for sale. 2 miles/3 km W of Chikabumi Station is an old Ainu settlement (Arashiyama Park).

A very attractive excursion is to the *Kamui-kotan Gorge*, 8 miles/13 km W of the town (30 minutes by bus). This narrow gorge, carved by the Ishikari through the *Yubari Hills*, is particularly beautiful at cherry-blossom time and in the fall. Once the home of the Ainu, it is a place of many legends. 6 miles/9 km from *Ino* Station are cliffs in which some 200 prehistoric cave-dwellings were discovered, with fragments of stone and iron implements and pottery.

E of Asahikawa in the beautiful *Sounkyo Gorge* lies the **Daisetsusan National Park** (see separate entry).

2 miles/3 km SE of Asahikawa Station (20 minutes by bus) is **Kaguragaoka Park** (area 110 acres), a nature park in the valley of the *Chubetsu*, a tributary of the Ishikari. In the park can be seen the **Kamikawa Shrine**, dedicated to the town's protective divinity. From this hilly country there are fine *views of the town and the Kamikawa Basin; skiing in winter.

Ashizuri-Uwakai National Park

あしずり うわかい 国立公園

Prefectures: Kochi and Ehime.
Area: 42 sq. miles/109 sq. km.
(i) (central)
National Parks Association of Japan,
Toranomon Denki Building,
8-1, Toranomon 2-chome, Minato-ku,
J-105 **Tokyo**;
tel. (03) 502 0488.

Cape Ashizuri, at the southern tip of Shikoku

HOTELS. – IN TOSA-SHIMIZU. – **Western style**: *Ashizuri Kokusai Hotel*, 662, Ashizuri-misaki, 62 r., beach; *Hotel Ashizurien*, 478-5, Ashizuri-misaki, 39 r., beach; *Business Hotel Daiei*, 11-23, Shiomi-cho, 18 r. – YOUTH HOSTELS: *YH Kongoji* (temple), 214-1, Ashizuri-misaki, 80 b.; *Shirao Jinja YH* (shrine), 1351-3, Ashizuri-misaki, 20 b.; *YH Fuji-dera* (temple), 3940, Misaki, 21 b.

TRANSPORTATION. – **Rail**: from KOCHI Nakamura line to Nakamura (2½ hours). – **Bus**: from Nakamura to Tosa-Shimizu (1¼ hours); from Tosa-Shimizu to Tatsukushi and Cape Ashizuri.

The *Ashizuri-Uwakai National Park, established in 1972, takes in the coastal region of southern Shikoku, extending around the towns of Tatsukushi and Minokoshi and reaching down to Cape Ashizuri, the southernmost tip of the island. The rugged SW coast of Shikoku and the offshore islands are also included within the park.

This region, with its sleepy little fishing villages, offers some of the finest coastal scenery in Japan. It is still largely unspoiled and in its natural state, with crystal-clear water and long beaches of white sand. – The best centers from which to explore the park are the towns of Tosa-Shimizu and **Uwajima** (see separate entry). The road from Uwajima runs parallel to the coast, affording magnificent views.

Tosa-Shimizu (pop. 26,000), on the E side of the park, is a port with considerable deep-sea fisheries. From here a road 8 miles/13 km long, the *Ashizuri Skyline*, runs S to Cape Ashizuri (bus services), where there is a lighthouse (the subject of very popular songs in Japan) (far-ranging views).

The buses to *Cape Ashizuri take two different routes, one along the W coast, the other through the middle of the promontory; there is also a road along the E coast (journey time between 30 and 50 minutes). In the bays to the N of the promontory, with cliffs rising to 260 ft/80 m, there is very heavy surf. The vegetation is subtropical (many camellias).

From Mount *Shiraozan* (1421 ft/433 m) there is a magnificent *view of the sea. – Near the white light-house stands the **Kongofukuji Temple**, first built by Kobo-daishi in 822. The present buildings date from 1662. The temple, dedicated to the Thousand-Handed Kannon, is the 38th of the 88 pilgrimage temples on Shikoku. It contains a statue of John Manjiro (Japanese name Nakaham Manjiro), who was saved from the shipwreck of an American ship in 1841 and after living in the United States for many years returned to Japan.

8 miles/13 km W of Tosa-Shimizu are the towns of **Tatsukushi** and **Minokoshi** (40 mi.ıutes by bus). On the coast is the *Ashizuri Marine Park* (Ashizuri Kaichu Koen), with long banks of coral and color-ful marine life (trips in glass-bottomed boats, 30 minutes). Tatsukushi Bay has a beautiful beach of white sand. In the town, near the bus station, are an interest-ing Shell Museum and a Coral Museum (Sango Hakubutsukan), with a sales counter and a restaurant. – To the W of Tatsukushi, at *Nagashima*, the 80 ft/25 m high Kaiteikan Underwater Observatory has an observation chamber 23 ft/7 m below the surface. 10 minutes' walk away is the Kaiyokan Aquarium, with many rare species of fish.

Along the coast to the N we reach the *Uwanoumi Underwater Park* (Uwanoumi Kaichu Koen). From the town of *Funakoshi* there is a ferry service (10 minutes) to the little island of **Kashima**, in the center of the park. Trips in glass-bottomed boats enable visitors to see the teeming underwater life. There are many troops of monkeys on the island.

Other attractive trips are to the beautiful islands of *Hiburi* and *Okinoshima*.

Aso National Park
あそ国立公園

Prefectures: Kumamoto and Oita.
Area: 282 sq. miles/731 sq. km.
(central)
ⓘ **National Parks Association of Japan**,
Toranomon Denki Building,
8-1, Toranomon 2-chome, Minato-ku,
J-105 **Tokyo**;
tel. (03) 5020488.

HOTELS. – IN ASO. - **Ryokan**: *Hotel Kadoman*, 82 r.; *Asonotsukasa*, 66 r.; *Hotel Soyokaku*, 56 r.; *Aso Hotel*, 56 r.; *Ryokan Sanrakuso*, 37 r.; *Kamenoya Ryokan*, 24 r. – YOUTH HOSTELS: *Aso YH*, 922-2, Bochu, 60 b.; *YH Kumamoto YMCA Aso Camp*, Kuruma-gaeri, 35 b.; *YH Murataya-Ryokan*, 1660, Takamori (S of Mount Aso), 35 b.

TRANSPORTATION. – **Rail**: from KUMAMOTO or OITA JNR Hohi main line (stations at Tateno, Akamizu and Aso/Uchinomaki). – **Bus**: from BEPPU via Yufuin-onsen to Aso (and on to Kumamoto).

*Aso National Park, in the center of Kyushu, the most southerly of the main Japanese islands, is a region of scenic contrasts in which lush green meadows and dense forests alter-nate with bare blackish-brown lava-fields and bizarrely shaped moun-tain ranges. This beautiful tract of country is very characteristic of the scenery of the volcanic island of Kyushu.

The National Park takes in the massifs of the volcano, Mount Aso, and Mount Kuju, together with the Tsurumi, Yufu and Takasakiyama summits to the W of Beppu. The crater region of Mount Aso is bounded on the N by the River Kurokawa and on the S by the Shirakawa, which have their sources in the park and join at Toshita, on the W side of the volcano.

The most notable feature in Aso National Park is the **crater basin of Mount Aso, one of the largest calderas in the world (diameter 11–15 miles/18–24 km). Within the basin five volcanic cones have been formed in recent times; one of these is still active, the most recent recorded eruptions being in 1933, 1953 and 1958–65, when it spewed out great masses of ash which darkened the sky over Kumamoto, 30 miles/50 km to the W. Aso National Park has been developed as a holiday and recreational area with many scenic attractions and an extensive system of mountain paths.

A convenient approach to the park from *Beppu* (see separate entry; bus service) is by way of the Trans-Kyushu road (Yamanami Highway), which runs W to Nagasaki. At the resort of *Yufuin-onsen* the road to the Kuju Plateau turns S and goes over the *Makinoto Pass* (4331 ft/ 1320 m) to reach Mount Kuju and the *Senomoto Plateau*, where a country road branches off for the *Kuju Plateau*. A good base from which to explore the plateau and the heights of Kuju is the town of *Kanno-jigoku* (bus from Beppu, 1¾ hours; also bus to Miyaji Station, 1 hour).

The caldera of Mount Aso

The **Kuju Plateau** is a popular holiday area, covered in summer with great tracts of red azaleas and frequented in winter by large numbers of skiers. A major element in the economy of the area is stock-farming. – To the N are the **Kuju Mountains**, covered with forest at the lower levels and with varied Alpine vegetation higher up. The most southerly and highest peak is **Mount Kuju** (5840 ft/1780 m), which is also the highest point on the island of Kyushu. Other considerable peaks are *Daisen, Waita, Hossho, Ogihana* and *Mimata*. The gateway to this region from the S is the town of *Miyaji* (railway station).

There are a number of different routes up Mount Kuju. Below the N side of the mountain is *Kuju-Tozanguchi* (Kyudai railway line from Oita to Bungo-Nakamura, then bus), from which it is 4 miles/6 km to the summit (2 hours). – There is also a route from *Minami-Tozanguchi* (JNR Hohi line to Bungo-Taketa, then bus). – The most popular route starts from *Shuchikujo* (bus from Bungo-Taketa), below the S side of the mountain. From here it is a 4 hours' climb by way of the *Tembodai* viewpoint to the summit, from which there are fine views of the Aso region and Beppu Bay to the E.

To the S of Mount Kuju rises the ****Mount Aso** Massif. Within the old crater, lying at an average height of 2625–2950 ft/800–900 m, are the volcano's five cones – *Takadake*, the highest (5223 ft/1592 m); *Nekodake* (4620 ft/1408 m); *Eboshidake* (4387 ft/1337 m); *Nakadake* (4341 ft/1323 m), the only one which is still active; and *Kishimadake* (4334 ft/1321 m). The crater area extends for 14 miles/23 km from N to S and 10 miles/16 km from E to W, with a total area of 98 sq. miles/255 sq. km, making it one of the largest craters in the world. This

area, with the spacious Asodani Valley and the towns of *Aso* and *Ichinomiya* in the N and the Nangodani Valley and the town of *Takamori* in the S, is now densely populated (some 70,000 inhabitants), and the volcanic soil provides good agricultural land.

There are two routes to the summit of **Nakadake**, the crater of which is 650 yds/600 m across and 525 ft/160 m deep. From **Aso** Station (JNR Hohi main line) the Aso Kanko Toll Road (bus service, 50 minutes) crosses the *Kusasenri Plateau* to **Asosan-Nishi**, from which a cableway runs up to the rim of the crater. – From **Miyaji** Station the Sensuikyo Gorge Toll Road (bus service, 15 minutes) leads to **Asosan-Higashi**, from which there is a cableway to the rim of the crater. There is a bus service between the lower stations of the two cableways, so that it is possible to go up by one route and come down by the other. When an eruption is imminent the cableways cease to run; there are underground shelters (bunkers) at various points on the road.

Very different from the rugged beauty of the seething crater and its surrounding lava-fields is the green landscape of the Mount Aso Basin, with its gentle rounded summits, its evergreen forests and its little villages. In the northern part of the region, ¾ mile/1 km N of Miyaji Station, we find the **Aso Shrine**, dedicated to the divinity Takeiwatatsu-no-Mikoto. Legend has it that the shrine was founded in the year A.D. 100, making it the oldest in the historic province of Higo (now Kumamoto prefecture). The present buildings (main hall and gate) date from 1842. From early times this was the starting-point of the pilgrimage to the Sanjo Shrine on Mount Nakadake.

One of the finest viewpoints in the Aso region is the charming resort of **Aso-onsen** (*Uchinomaki*), NW of Aso Station. From here the bus takes 20 minutes to reach Mount *Daikambo* (3071 ft/936 m), the northern summit of the old crater rim, from which there are extensive views of the crater with its five peaks.

There are a number of thermal springs in the Aso area which have made it a busy holiday region. 4 miles/6 km SE of Akamizu Station, half-way up Mount Eboshidake, is **Yunotani-onsen** (2625 ft/800 m), the highest health resort in the crater area, and from which there are views of the Kumamoto Plain, Ariake Bay and the area round Unzen.

On the SW slopes of Mount Eboshidake, at an altitude of 2188 ft/667 m, lies the summer resort of *Tarutama-onsen* (Takamori railway line from Aso-Shimoda Station, 30 minutes), from which a beautiful road continues to the *Kusasenri Plateau*. To the S of the town is *Jigoku-onsen* (2460 ft/750 m), and to the W of this *Tochinoki-onsen*. Near by can be seen the impressive waterfall of *Ayugaeri-no-Taki*, and at the junction of the rivers *Kurokawa* and *Shirakawa* lies the idyllic little town of *Toshita-onsen*.

Awaji Shima
あわじ

Prefecture: Hyogo.
Area: 229 sq. miles/593 sq. km
ⓘ (local)
Hyogo-ken Tourist Information Center,
Kenmin-kaikan,
4-57-4, Yamate-dori,
Inkuta-ku,
J-650 **Kobe**;
tel. (078) 321 2958.

HOTELS. – IN SUMOTO. Ryokan: *Kaigetsu Kan,* 1-3-11, Kaigan-dori, 114 r., thermal bath; *Mikuma Kan,* 1-1-50, Yamate, 97 r., SP, thermal bath; *Shishuen,* 1052, Orodani, 82 r., SP, thermal bath; *Awaji-shima Kanko Hotel,* 1053, Orodani, 70 r., thermal bath; *Hotel New Awaji,* Komoe, 50 r., SP, thermal bath; *Awaji Shima Grand Hotel,* 23-1, Orodani, 48 r., thermal bath; *Ryuguen,* 2379, Shimofuno, 48 r.; *Matsuei Kan Bekkan,* 1-2-8, Kaigan-dori, 44 r., thermal bath; *Shishuen Ohama Bekkan,* 2-2-30, Kaigon-dori, 38 r., thermal bath; *Kanko Hotel Awasu,* 1-7-2, Kaigan-

dori, 24 r., thermal bath; *Nagisa Bekkan,* 1053, Orodani, 22 r., thermal bath. – YOUTH HOSTELS: *Awaji YH,* in Nandan (12½ miles/20 km W), Ama, 116 b.; *Asahi-ryokan YH,* in Ichinomiya (NW coast), 239, Gunge, 150 b.

EVENTS. – *Awaji-ningyoza* (puppet theater), in Fukura, performances daily.

TRANSPORTATION. – **Boat:** ferry services from KOBE and NARUTO. **Bus:** several routes on island.

The densely populated island of Awaji lies at the eastern end of the Inland Sea. Separated from Honshu to the N by the narrow Akashi Strait and from Shikoku to the S by the Naruto Strait, only 1500 yd/1·4 km wide (bridge under construction), Awaji forms a link between the largest and the smallest of the main Japanese islands.

The largest island in the Inland Sea (circumference 100 miles/160 km), Awaji consists mainly of flat agricultural land and has few facilities for tourists. The island's main sources of income are stock-farming (about 20,000 head of cattle) and fishing.

Awaji is renowned as the place of origin of the Japanese puppet theater, and the popular puppet plays (Awaji-ningyo-joruri) are still performed here by amateurs, mainly peasants. The only other puppet theaters still operating are in Osaka (Bunraku-za) and Tokyo (National Theater).

The chief place on the island and the principal tourist center is **Sumoto** (pop. 46,000), situated half-way along the E coast. From here there are bus services to all parts of the island; national highway No. 28 runs N to *Iwaya* and SW to Fukura. The area around Sumoto is a favorite holiday region, with beaches of white sand, groves of bizarrely shaped pines and a variety of recreational facilities.

4 miles/6 km NW of Sumoto (10 minutes by bus) is Mount **Senzan** (1470 ft/448 m), on the summit of which stands the *Senkoji Temple,* belonging to the Shingon sect. The temple, dedicated to the Thousand-Handed Kannon, contains a bell cast in 1283 and a gong which is thought to date from the Muromachi period (1338–1573). From the top of the hill there are impressive views of the mountains of Shikoku to the W and the Kitan Strait to the E.

To the S of Sumoto lies the **Mikuma Park**, with the remains of an old castle. Immediately S of this is *Ohama Beach,* one of the most beautiful beaches in the Kansai region, with white sand, deep blue water and a fringe of green pine groves. There are a number of attractive smaller resorts on the E coast, in Osaka Bay and on the W coast (Lake Harimanade). **Yura** is an attractive little fishing port, in the bay of which is situated the little island of *Narugashima.* – The port of **Fukura** (40 minutes by bus from Sumoto), the gateway to the island from the W, is the home of the Awaji puppet theater, which has a 400-year-old tradition. Fine * view of the *Naruto* whirlpool (see separate entry).

The highest point on the island is Mount *Yuzuhara* (1998 ft/609 m), to the S. – Among the finest beaches on the W coast are **Goshikihama** (bus from Sumoto, 50 minutes), a 2½ mile/4 km-long beach which takes its name from its brightly colored shingle (Go-shiki-hama = "beach of five colors"), and *Kei-no-Matsubara,* a 2 mile/3 km-long beach of white sand.

Bandai-Asahi National Park

ばんだいあさひ 国立公園

Prefectures: Fukushima, Yamagata and Niigata.
Area: 732 sq. miles/1897 sq. km.

(i) (central)
National Parks Association of Japan,
Toranomon Denki Building,
8-1, Toranomon 2-chome, Minato-ku,
J-105 **Tokyo;**
tel. (03) 502 0488.

HOTELS. – IN FUKUSHIMA. – **Western style:** *Ebisu Grand Hotel,* 10-6, Soneda-cho, 79 r. – YOUTH HOSTEL: *Azuma-Kogen Fukushima YH,* a little way W in Takayu-onsen, 1-49, Jin-no-mori, Machiniwasaka, 96 b. – IN ATAMI. – **Western style:** *Bandai Grand Hotel,* 2-27, Atami, 284 r., SP, thermal bath. – IN INAWASHIRO. – YOUTH HOSTELS: *YH Bandai Yuaisanso,* in Hayama, 70 b.; *YH Bandai-so,* in Yokomuki-onsen, 200 b.; *Urabandai YH,* in Ura-Bandai, to N, 100 b. – IN AIZU-WAKAMATSU: see separate entry.

TRANSPORTATION. – **Rail:** from TOKYO (Ueno Station) to Omiya (30 minutes), then JNR New Tohoku–Shinkansen line to Koriyama or Fukushima (3¼ hours); branch lines from Koriyama to Inawashiro and Aizu-Wakamatsu. – **Bus:** from Fukushima, Inawashiro and Yamato to various places in the National Park.

The * **Bandai-Asahi National Park, in northern Honshu, consists of four separate and unconnected parts. The most southerly part is Lake Inawashiro with its immediate surroundings; to the E are the Bandai-Azuma Mountains; NW of the lake rises Mount Iide; and far to the N the largest section of the park contains the Asahi Massif and the three sacred hills of Dewa-Sanzan.**

Lake Inawashiro is in Fukushima prefecture; the Bandai-Azuma Mountains extend into the southern part of Yamagata prefecture; Mount Iide lies at the junction of Fukushima, Niigata and Yamagata prefectures; and the Asahi Mountains are in Yamagata prefecture. – Access to the National Park is facilitated by excellent roads and a dense network of bus services.

The region around Lake Inawashiro is most easily reached from the town of *Koriyama,* to the E, from which the JNR Ban-etsu-saisen line runs via **Bandai-Atami** to **Lake Inawashiro** (alt. 1686 ft/ 514 m, area 40 sq. miles/105 sq. km), Japan's fourth largest lake. The lake was formed by the deposit of masses of lava from the *Bandai* and *Nekoma* volcanoes, and now supplies water for irrigation in the Koriyama area and for the provision of hydroelectric power. The finest *view of the lake is from the *Kohiragata-Tenjin Shrine,* 1 mile/1·5 km from Sekito Station.

To the N of the lake is **Inawashiro**, a marketing center for rice and timber. 1¼ miles/2 km N of the station lies the beautiful Kamegajo Park, a site once occupied by Kamegajo Castle. – From Inawashiro there are buses (30 minutes) to *Numajiri-onsen,* 12 miles/19 km NE, which with the neighboring resort of *Nakanozawa-onsen* is one of the most popular skiing centers in the region. Numajiri-onsen is the starting-point for the ascent of Mount *Adatara* (5580 ft/ 1700 m), in the Bandai-Azuma Mountains; the climb (6 miles/10 km) takes about 4 hours. – 8 miles/13 km N is *Noji-onsen,* near the *Tsuchitu Pass,* the starting-point of the *Bandai-Azuma Skyline Drive,* a ridge road some 19 miles/ 30 km long. The road has an average height of about 4265 ft/1300 m, reaching its highest point at 5322 ft/1622 m, and affords magnificent views. It ends at *Azuma-Takayu-onsen*, near Fukushima.

Inawashiro is also a good base from which to climb Mount *Bandai* (5968 ft/ 1819 m), a massif containing a number of peaks.

There are buses (20 minutes) to *Omote Bandai Tozanguchi*, starting-point of the most popular of the three routes up Mount Bandai (bus service). The route leads via the *Hanitsu Shrine* and *Umagaeshi* to one of the peaks, **Akahani**, from which it is a short distance down to another peak, **Numanotaira**, and up to **Tengu-Iwa**. Fine° view of the northern slopes of the mountain, with the lakes and craters formed by the 1888 eruption. – Another popular approach route is the new *Bandai Gold Line*, a toll road (11 miles/ 18 km) which runs from *Bandaimachi* over the Bandai Plateau to the summit. – The best descent route is by way of *Funkayu* and the skiing region of *Urabandai* to the Bandai Plateau.

The **Bandai-Kogen** Plain (alt. c. 2625 ft/800 m), below the N side of Mount Bandai, is covered by more than a hundred lakes, with water of many different hues, formed by the great eruption of 1888. The largest of the lakes are *Hibara*, *Onogawa* and *Akimoto*. This beautiful area is well provided with footpaths, camp sites and a variety of recreational facilities.

2½ miles/4 km SW of Inawashiro, near the lake, is **Okinajima**, birthplace of the bacteriologist Noguchi Hideyo, who discovered the yellow fever virus. 2 miles/ 3 km SE of the station stands a small memorial. – From here there are buses to the idyllic resort of **Ottate-onsen**, 2¼ miles/3·5 km on *Nagahama Beach*.

The Azuma Mountains, NE of the Bandai Massif, are best approached from the university town of **Fukushima**, capital of Fukushima prefecture, 19 miles/30 km E on the JNR Tohoku line. – The **Azuma Mountains** are divided by the River *Okura* into the *Higashi-Azuma* (Eastern Azuma) and the *Nishi-Azuma* (Western Azuma). They are reached by way of the Bandai-Skyline (bus service), a toll road opened in 1959 (see above). The highest point in the eastern part of these volcanic mountains is **Higashi-Azuma** (6480 ft/ 1975 m), and near this are **Azuma-Kofuji** (5594 ft/1705 m), also known as *Azuma-Fuji* on account of its resemblance to Fujiyama, and **Issaikyo** (6395 ft/1949 m), which last erupted in 1893. These majestic peaks are almost entirely barren of vegetation.

The starting-point for the ascent of **Azuma-Kofuji** and **Issaikyo** is *Jododaira*, near the summit of Azuma-Kofuji on the Bandai-Azuma Skyline (see above), between Mount *Azuma-Takayu* and the *Tsuchiyu Pass*. The climb to the summit of Azuma-Kofuji takes 30 minutes, the climb to the summit of Issaikyo and back about an hour.

W of Fukushima lies the health resort of *Azuma-Takayu-onsen* (2460 ft/750 m; bus from Fukushima or Jododaira, 45 minutes), from where there is a° view of the Fukushima Basin. Near by, on the eastern slopes of Azuma-Kofuji, can be found the quiet little resort of *Nuruyu-onsen*.

One of the most attractive little towns in this region is *Tsuchiyu-onsen* (1427 ft/ 435 m; bus from Fukushima, 30 minutes), traversed by a rushing mountain stream. – There are impressive views from the *Tsuchiyu Pass*, which carries the road from Fukushima to Inawashiro.

A pleasant ROUND TRIP is by bus from Fukushima via *Azuma-Takayu-onsen*, *Jododaira*, the *Tsuchiyu Pass* and *Iizaka-onsen* to *Bandai-Kogen* (about 3 hours) and return.

The northern part of the Azuma region is formed by the **Tengendai Plateau**, on the N side of Mount **Nishi-Azuma** (6641 ft/2024 m). The plateau, lying at an average height of 4265 ft/1300 m, is reached by way of **Shirabu-onsen** (cableway, 7 minutes), a popular summer and winter resort. – Nishi-Azuma is flanked by **Nishi-Daiten** (6503 ft/ 1982 m) and **Higashi-Daiten** (6326 ft/ 1928 m).

On the north-eastern outliers of this group are the attractive health resorts of *Nuruyu-onsen*, *Azuma-Takayu-onsen* and *Goshiki-onsen*.

The best center for exploring the most westerly part of the Bandai-Asahi National Park is the town of *Yamato* (rail from Niigata and Koriyama), from which there is a bus service to the S side of Mount **Iide** (6907 ft/2105 m).

The most northerly and the largest section of the National Park takes in the **Dewa-Sanzan** (the "three hills of Dewa"), with the three peaks of Gassan, Yudono and Haguro. The best bases from which to approach these hills are the towns of **Yamagata** (see separate entry), to the S, and *Tsuruoka* (see under Sakata).

The highest of the Dewa-Sanzan hills is Mount **Gassan** (6496 ft/1980 m). The best ascent route is from the SW by way of Mount *Yudono* (4935 ft/1504 m), which can be reached from Tsuruoka by bus (1¾ hours). Mount Yudono is believed to be the home of the divinity Oyamat-sumi-no-mikoto, who is honoured at a waterfall fed by a thermal spring. On the summit of Mount Gassan stands a shrine dedicated to the moon divinity Tsukiyomi-no-mikoto; extensive ˚ views of the surrounding heights and the Sea of Japan.

E of Tsuruoka (45 minutes by bus) is Mount **Haguro** (1375 ft/419 m), with the *Dewa Shrine,* which is dedicated to the divinity Ideha-no-mikoto. The shrine is approached by a long flight of steps flanked by ancient trees, and contains what is said to be the oldest pagoda in the Tohoku district.

Dewa Shrine on Mount Haguro

All three hills are regarded as sacred by the ascetic Shugendo sect, whose creed shows Buddhist influence, and every year, particularly during the festival of the Dewa Shrine in mid July, pilgrims clad as *yamabushi* (itinerant monks) flock to the shrines. As their precursor they honour En no Gyoja; but the founder of the sect was a priest of the Shingon sect named Shobo (832–909), who gave authoritative form to a corpus of ascetic and magical beliefs. – A visit to this remote mountain region, still unfrequented in spite of the pilgrims, is one of the highlights of a journey through northern Japan.

Beppu

Prefecture: Oita. – Population: 138,000.
Post code: J-874. – Telephone code: 0977.
(i) (local)
Beppu Kanko Kyokai,
Beppu Station,
Eki-mae-cho.

HOTELS. – **Western style:** *Suginoi Hotel,* Kankaiji, 606 r., Japanese garden, SP, thermal bath, beach; *Hotel Hakuunsanso,* Kankaiji, 131 r., Japanese gar-

den, thermal bath, beach; *Beppu New Grand Hotel,* Kijima-kogen, 111 r., Japanese garden, SP, thermal bath; *Kamenoi Hotel,* 5-17, Chuo-machi, 88 r., Japanese garden, SP, thermal bath, beach; *Nippaku Hotel,* 3-12-26, Kitahama, 73 r., thermal bath; *Hinago Hotel,* 7-24, Akiba-cho, 131 r., Japanese garden, beach. – **Ryokan:** *Hanabishi Hotel,* Kitahama, 120 r.; *Hotel Shiragiku,* Kamitanoyu-cho, 93 r.; *Beppu Fujikando Hotel,* Wakakusa-cho, 91 r.; *Hotel Kodama,* Tsurumi, 76 r.; *Oniyama Hotel,* Kannawa, 68 r.; *Ryokan Bokaiso,* Kitahama, 67 r.; *Takenoi Hotel,* Kitahama, 56 r.; *Hotel New Tsuruta,* Kitahama, 53 r.; *Hotel Sansenkaku,* Kitahama, 71 r. – YOUTH HOSTEL: *Beppu YH,* Kankaiji-onsen, 150 b.

TRANSPORTATION. – **Air:** from TOKYO (Haneda Airport) to Oita (1½ hours; then bus or hovercraft). – **Rail:** from TOKYO (Central Station) JNR Sanyo-Shinkansen line to Kokura (6½ hours), then JNR Nippo line (2 hours). – **Bus:** from Oita to Beppu (1 hour); several local services. – **Boat:** from OSAKA/KOBE Kansai Steamship through the Inland Sea (15 hours); other services from HIROSHIMA (8 hours) and UWAJIMA (6 hours).

˚**Beppu, one of the best-known spas and seaside resorts in Japan, lies on a narrow strip of low-lying land on the NE coast of the island of Kyushu. Inland are Mount Tsurumi (4511 ft/ 1375 m) and Mount Takasakiyama (2060 ft/628 m), to the lower slopes of which the city area extends. The town's harbor lies at the innermost tip of Beppu Bay. The resort area includes, in addition to Beppu itself, the little towns of Hamawaki-onsen, Kamegawa-onsen, Shibaseki-onsen, Kannawa-onsen, Myoban-onsen, Horita-onsen and Kankaiji-onsen.**

The Beppu region, which draws several million visitors every year, owes its reputation to its ˚˚ hot springs, more than 3000 in number, with temperatures of up to 212 °F/100 °C and a daily flow of 22,000,000 gallons/100,000 cu. m, which supply numerous spa establishments. The columns of steam rising from the hot springs shroud the area in perpetual mist. Beppu has a number of geothermal research laboratories and a Balneo-Therapeutic Institute attached to Kyushu University. – There are bus trips through the hot-spring area (Jigoku-Meguri), starting from the railway station and Kamenoi bus station (3–8 hours).

SIGHTS. – In the center of the town, 10 minutes from the station, is the *Takegawara Spa Establishment,* the best known of the many such places in Beppu. Also 10 minutes from the station is the *Beppu-Furusato-kan Museum* (archaeological material excavated in the area, displays on the subject of the thermal springs). – On the coast to the E of the station stands the **Beppu Tower**; from the public bath on one of the upper storeys there are panoramic views of the town and the bay.

¾ mile/1 km W of the station lies *Beppu Park* and on the slopes of a hill 2 miles/3 km SW of the station in **Rakutenchi Park** are beautiful footpaths, a swimming pool and a chair-lift.

To the W of Beppu Park (2 miles/3·5 km from the station), in an idyllic setting on the slopes of Mount *Tsurumi,* we come to the spa of *Kankaiji-onsen, with a magnificent *view of the bay. – A little way N is the *Suginoi Leisure Center,* with several large swimming pools and other facilities, surrounded by plant arrangements.

4½ miles/7 km NW of Beppu,* **Kannawaonsen** has four hot springs (known as Jigoku, "Hell") which supply the town with hot water. The largest of the springs is *Umi-jigoku,* estimated to be 395 ft/ 120 m deep, an emerald-green pool with a daily flow of 79,000 gallons/360 cu. m of water at a temperature of 201 °F/94 °C. Near by is the *Oniyama-jigoku* Spring, with an alligator-breeding farm, and to the SW is the *Bozu-jigoku* Spring, filled with viscous white mud.

"Hell", Beppu

Farther N are the *Chinoike-jigoku* Spring, a pool of blood-red mud (199 °F/93 °C; *c.* 540 ft/165 m deep) which supplies the adjoining large mud-bath establishments, and the *Tatsumaki-jigoku* Geyser, which ejects a spout of hot water every 20 minutes. In Kannawa-onsen a research institute, sponsored by Oita prefecture, is concerned with investigating the possibility of using the hot springs for agricultural purposes.

4 miles/6 km N of Beppu, near the coast, **Kamegawa-onsen** has well-known sand baths in the nearby bay.

SURROUNDINGS of Beppu

SE of the town, on the road to Oita, rises Mount *Takasakiyama* (2060 ft/628 m), on the slopes of which live more than 2000 tame monkeys. Near here are an Aquarium and *Fauna Land,* with many rare animals (stuffed and preserved). – SW of Beppu (4 miles/6 km from the station) lies *Lake Shidaka,* an area of great natural beauty with a riding-school and a natural ice-rink. Beyond this, between the two extinct volcanoes *Yufu* (5197 ft/1584 m) and *Tsurumi* (4511 ft/1375 m), extends the *Kijima Plateau,* a holiday and recreation area.

30 miles/48 km SE (JNR Nippo line via Oita) is the port and commercial town of **Usuki** (pop. 40,000), in Usuki Bay. This old castle town, once a stronghold of the princely Otomo family, played an important part in the trade with Portugal. Here, too, Otomo Sorin (1530–87), who became a Christian in 1578, contributed to the spread of Christianity in Japan. – 5 miles/8 km inland (20 minutes by bus) there once stood the Mangetsuji Temple, the site of which is marked by some 60 *Sekibutsu statues* (Buddha figures) carved from the local tuff. Most of the figures date from the Heian period (784–1192), some from the Kamakura period (1192–1333). Particularly notable is the head of Dainichi-nyorai, which still shows traces of the original painting.

To the W of Beppu (30 minutes by bus) is the lower station of a cableway up *Mount Tsurumi (4511 ft/ 1375 m). From the summit (restaurant, park, zoo) there are fine * views of the town and the sea. – Beyond Tsurumi, 22 miles/35 km W of Beppu (JNR Kyudai line from Oita), extends a large resort area with many hot springs. **Yunohira-onsen** (1988 ft/606 m), on the River *Hananokawa,* is a small town with saline springs (128–183 °F/59–84 °C) which are used internally. To the S rise the Kuju Hills and the Handa Plateau. – To the NW, in the romantic basin of the River *Yufukawa,* is the spa and holiday resort of *Yufuin-onsen (1575 ft/480 m; JNR Kyudai line or bus from Oita; also rail services from Fukuoka/ Hakata). It lies at the foot of Mount *Yufu* (5197 ft/ 1584 m) and has several hot springs. Notable features are the Konsen-in Temple (1370), with old stone figures, and the Oga-sha Shrine, where there is an old cedar with a circumference of more than 43 ft/13 m. To the N of the station is the idyllic little Lake Kirinko, where swarms of glow-worms are to be seen from May onwards. The hill of *Namiyanagi-no-oka,* W of the station, was a Christian burial-place during the period of persecution of Christians in Japan.

From Beppu the JNR Nippo line runs N along the bay, turns inland and in 45 minutes reachs **Usa,** in the NW of the Kunisaki Peninsula. From the station there is a bus (10 minutes) to the Usa Shrine (also reached on a pleasant footpath, 20 minutes).

The* *Usa Shrine** (Shintoist), built in 725, is a classic example of the religious architecture of the period. It was originally dedicated to the god Hirohata Yahata and the goddess Himekami; but Yahata was later equated with the Emperor Ojin, who lived about A.D. 400, and during the Kamakura period (1192– 1333) this divinity was transformed into the war god Hachiman. When Buddhism began to spread in Japan

Rock-cut sculpture, Usuki

– about 719 – 28 Buddhist temples were erected here. The Usa Shrine is the principal shrine of more than 10,000 dedicated to Hachiman throughout Japan. – The three buildings which form the main part of the shrine are a reconstruction of 1861. Note particularly the woodcarving. The temple's annual festival is celebrated on March 18.

From Usa it is worth making a visit to the *Kunisaki Peninsula,* the north-eastern tip of the island of Kyushu. This remote and beautiful area, with its quiet gorges, chains of hills and streams tumbling down to the sea, reaches its highest point in Mount *Futago* (2366 ft/721 m). Scattered over the rugged country of the peninsula are some 70 Buddhist temples of the Nara and Kamakura periods, showing the fusion of Shintoism and Buddhism characteristic of these periods. Particularly notable are the *Tennenji Temple* and the *Misogi Shrine* W of Mount Futago.

Numerous ancient stone sculptures make this region a kind of open-air museum. The 140 pagoda-like stone towers to be seen here are of a type unique in Japan.

In the NW of the peninsula is the town of **Bungo-Takada** (pop. 21,000), where the Horan-enya boat festival is celebrated annually in May. There are a number of places of interest within easy reach of the town, including the *Choanji Temple,* the *Tennenji Temple,* the *Monjusenji Temple* and the *Sentoji Temple,* as well as the ° **Makino-odo Temple Hall** (bus from Bungo-Takada, 40 minutes), built in the 12th c., which contains ancient sculpture. Also of interest is the ° **Fukiji Temple** (Heian period), the main hall of which is the oldest surviving building on Kyushu.

Lake Biwa
びわ湖

Prefecture: Shiga.
Area: 260 sq. miles/674·4 sq. km.
ⓘ (central)
Shiga-ken Tokyo Kanko Bussan Assensho,
Kokusai Kanko Kaikan,
1-8-3, Marunouchi, Chiyoda-ku,
J-100 **Tokyo;**
tel. (03) 231 6131.

(local)
Shiga-ken Kanko-ka,
4-1-1, Kyomachi,
J-520 **Otsu;**
tel. (0775) 24 1121.

HOTELS. – **Western style:** *Omi Plaza Hotel,* in Hikone (E side of lake), 1911, Matsubara-cho, 75 r., Japanese garden, SP, beach. – **Ryokan** (all in Otsu, S end of lake): *Hotel Koyo,* Chagasaki, 245 r.; *Biwako Hotel,* Yanagasaki, 84 r.; *Kokkaso,* Ogotocho, 68 r.; *Hogetsuro,* Ogotocho, 36 r.; *Hakkeikan,* Hama-Otsu, 32 r. – YOUTH HOSTELS: *Otsu YH Center,* in Otsu, 18-1, Yamagami-cho, 310 b.; *YH Wanihama Seinen-Kaikan,* in Shiga (W side of lake), 403, Minamihama, 150 b.; *YH Saikyo-ji,* in Otsu, 3210, Sakamoto-hon-machi, 100 b.; *YH Hikone Seishonen Kensyu Center,* in Hikone (E side of lake), 1103, Ohora, 30 b.; *Kajuji YH,* in Omi-Hachiman (E side of lake), 610, Maruyama-cho, 30 b.

EVENTS. – *Shrine festivals* (mid April) in Hie Shrine, Otsu (S end of lake) and Taga Shrine, Hikone (E side of lake).

TRANSPORTATION. – **Rail:** from KYOTO JNR Shin-kansen line to Maibara (30 minutes); JNR Kosei line to Omi-Shiozu and JNR Hokuriku line from there to Maibara; also JNR Tokaido line from Maibara to Otsu. – **Boat:** from Hama-Otsu (S end of lake) to Ishiyama-dera, Biwako-Ohashi, Biwako-Hakkei and Chikubu; from Hikone and Imazu to Chikubu; from Ogoto-onsen via Hama-Otsu to Ishiyama-dera, and via Biwako-Hakkei to Hama-Otsu. – Round trips from Hama-Otsu and Hikone.

**Lake Biwa, occupying a collapse basin NE of Kyoto, is Japan's largest lake, with an area of 260 sq. miles/ 674·4 sq. km. Tradition has it that an earthquake in the year 286 B.C. created both the lake and Mount Fuji; and it is true that the islands of Chikubu, Take, Shiraishi and Okinoshima are of volcanic origin. Lying near the old cultural and political centers of Nara and Kyoto, the region was settled at an early stage. – The lake and the surrounding area now form the Lake Biwa Quasi National Park (area 425 sq. miles/1100 sq. km).

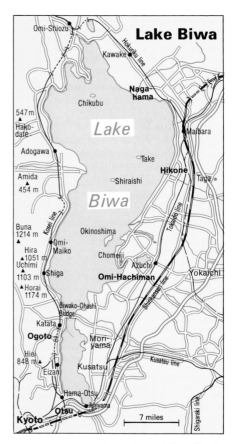

The name is derived from that of the Japanese lute (*biwa*), which the lake resembles in shape. In the 15th c. Japanese artists listed the eight classic beauties of the local landscape (*Omi-hakkei*) – evening snow on Mount Hira, a skein of wild geese over Katata, nocturnal rain in Karasaki, the evening bell in the Miidera Temple, a breeze in Awazu on a clear day, the red evening sky on the River Seta, the autumn moon over Ishiyama, the sails of vessels returning to Yabase. Later eight other special beauties (Biwako-hakkei) were identified – the view of Mount Shizugatake, the granite cliffs at Kaizu-Osaki, a peaceful view of the island of Chikubu, the old Castle of Hikone, the white beach of Omatsuzaki, the coastal villages at Azuchi-Hachiman, dense foliage on Mount Hiei (on which is the center of the Tendai sect of Buddhism), gentle waves at Seta-Ishiyama.

Around Lake Biwa

At the S end of the lake is the industrial town and tourist center of **Otsu** (pop. 210,000). About 1600 the painter Iwasa Matabei developed the Otsu-e style here, producing genre and heroic pictures notable for their vigorous line and lively colors which are still popular souvenirs. – The various places of interest around the lake can be seen by rail, bus or boat services, starting from the outlying district of *Hama-Otsu*. Near the station is the *Miidera Temple* (also known as Onjoji), belonging to the Tendai-Jimon sect, which was founded in 674. Of the original complex of 859 buildings some 60 still survive. Opposite the main hall is the bell which features in one of the classic views of Lake Biwa (*Omi-hakkei*). The Kannon-do Hall (also known as Shoho-ji), rebuilt in 1689, is one of the 33 traditional places of pilgrimage in the Kansai region; from here there is a superb view of the lake. – near by stands the **Homyoin Temple**, with the tomb of an American, Francisco Fenollosa (1853–1908), who taught for some time at the Imperial University in Tokyo and whose remains were brought here from London.

Farther N (15 minutes by bus from Hama-Otsu Station) is another temple of the Tendai sect, the *Shojuraigoji Temple*, founded in 790 by a priest named Saicho (767–822) and renovated in the 11th c. It contains a number of art treasures (statues, etc.).

From Hama-Otsu the JNR Kosei line follows the SW shores of Lake Biwa. To the E of **Karasaki** Station there once stood a mighty fir tree – well known from a woodcut by Hiroshige (1797–1858) – which featured in the classic view of "nocturnal rain at Karasaki". 1¼ miles/ 2 km N of the station, in the **Inari Shrine**, is a descendant of the original fir.

The **Saikyoji Temple** of the Tendai sect 1¼ miles/2 km NE of **Sakamoto** Station (Keihan–Ishisaka private line), was founded in the 7th c. by Shotoku-taishi and is famous for its art treasures of the Momoyama period (1573–1600). – Near by is the** **Hie Shrine** (1586), dedicated to the protective divinities of Mount Hiei (annual festival, the Sanno-matsuri, in mid April).

The JNR Kosei line continues to the resort of **Ogoto-onsen**, now a popular holiday center offering excellent facilities for fishermen, water-sports enthusiasts and walkers. In the background is Mount *Hiei* (2782 ft/848 m), with a cableway ascending from the shores of the lake to the summit (see under Kyoto).

The Keihan–Ishisaka private railway line leads to the town of **Ishiba**, near which is the **Gichuji Temple**, founded in 1553 in honor of the 12th c. military leader Kiso Yoshinaka (1154–84). Within the precincts of the temple is the tomb of the haiku-writer Matsuo Basho (1644–94).

The JNR Kosei line continues N to *Katata*. In the lake, built on piles, stands the **Ukimi-do Temple** (also known as *Mangetsu-ji*) of the Rinzai sect. This is another of the classic views of Lake Biwa (*Omi-hakkei*), "wild geese coming down over Katata". From Katata the toll bridge, *Biwako-Ohashi Bridge*, 1480 yd/1350 m long, crosses the lake to the E shore and the town of Moriyama.

Near *Shiga* Station rises Mount *Horai* (3852 ft/1174 m), from which there is a panoramic* view of the lake. Mount Horai can also be reached from Otsu Station on the bus to the winter-sports resort of *Biwako Valley*, from which a cableway runs up Mount **Uchimi** (3619 ft/ 1103 m); then chair-lift to the summit of Mount **Horai**. To the N of Mount **Hira** (3448 ft/1051 m; chair-lift to summit) is another of the classic views of Lake Biwa, "evening snow on Mount Hira".

Near the N end of the lake lies the island of **Chikubu**, bounded by high steep cliffs and covered with bamboo and cedar forests. Notable features on the island are

the *Tsukubusuma Shrine*, built by Toyotomi Hideyoshi in 1603, probably with material from the famous Fushimi Castle, and the *Hogenji Temple*, dedicated to the goddesses of mercy and good fortune. The temple was founded by a priest named Gyoki (670–749) at the behest of Shomu-tenno (i.e. the Emperor Shomu).

From *Omi-Shiozu* Station, at the N end of the lake, the JNR Hokuriku line skirts the eastern shore. From *Maibara* Station, 6 miles/9 km SE, Mount *Ryozen* (3557 ft/ 1084 m) can be climbed; fine panoramic views from the summit.

Beyond this is the old castle town of **Hikone** (pop. 89,000), once a staging-point on the Tokaido Highway and after the building of the castle the seat of the Ii family, who fought on the side of Tokugawa Ieyasu in the Battle of Sekigahara.

** **Hikone Castle** (completed 1622), ¾ mile/1 km W of the station, consists of a three-storey *main tower* and the *Sanju* and *Tempin Towers*. The Tempin Tower houses a museum containing items which belonged to the Ii family, including a** screen (*Hikone-byobu*, copy) of the Kano school (17th c.). Other features of the castle are the *Gate of the Drums* (Taiko-mon) and the *Sawaguchi-tamon Tower*. The view of the castle by moonlight (*Biwako-hakkei*) is particularly fine.

At the foot of the castle stands the residence of the Ii family (Rakuraku-en), built in 1677, and its garden (Kenkyu-en). In the adjoining Konki Park is a bronze statue of Naosuke, who was instrumental in opening Japan to trade in the 1860s. – At *Matsubara* lies *Hikone Beach*. On Mount Ohara can be found the *Ryotan-ji Temple* (transferred to this site in 1614), with a beautiful Zen garden, and the *Seiryoji Temple*, with the tombs of the Ii family.

SE of Hikone (Omi private railway: change at Takamiya) is the **Taga Shrine**, dedicated to the divine couple Izanagi and Izanami. It is believed to be as old as the Ise shrines, and is one of the most important shrines in the Kinki region.

From Hikone the JNR Tokaido line continues S, keeping close to the lake, to **Omi-Hachiman** (pop. 59,000). NW of the town (25 minutes by bus, then a 15-minute walk), above the lake, stands the **Chomeiji Temple**, probably founded by Shotoku-taishi (573–621) which was rebuilt in the 16th c. The surrounding area is depicted in the view "coastal villages at Azuchi-Hachiman". – Opposite here is the island of *Okinoshima*.

E of Omi-Hachiman lies **Azuchi**, site of the once-splendid Castle of Oda Nobunaga, of which only some fragments of wall survive. Here, too, are Nobunaga's tomb and the Sokenji Temple, with his statue.

From *Ishiyama*, at the S end of the lake, the Keihan private railway line runs S (10 minutes) to the **Ishiyama Temple**, belonging to the Toji school of the Shingon sect. It was founded in the 8th c. by a priest named Roben and rebuilt in the 12th and 16th c. It is one of the 33 pilgrimage temples of Kansai.

Among the main features of the temple are the *Todai-mon Gate*, with Nio figures by the famous sculptor Unkei and his son Tankei; the main hall, **Hondo**, has a statue of Nyorai-Kannon; in the adjoining room, known as *Genji-no-ma*, Murasaki Shikibu (975–1031), a lady-in-waiting at the Court, is said to have written the famous novel "Genji-monogatari" ("Tale of Genji"). The *Tahoto Pagoda* dates in its present form from 1190. – From the temple precincts there is a fine* view of the lake (one of the classic views, *Omi-hakkei*).

The tour ends in **Otsu**, a short distance W.

Bonin Islands (Ogasawara Islands)
See under Tokyo

Boso
See under Narita

Chichibu-Tama National Park

ちちぶたま
国立公園

Prefectures: Saitama, Yamanashi and Nagano.
Area: 469 sq. miles/1216 sq. km.
(central)
National Parks Association of Japan,
Toranomon Denki Building,
8-1, Toranomon 2-chome, Minato-ku,
J-105 **Tokyo**;
tel. (03) 502 0488.

YOUTH HOSTELS. – *Mitake YH,* in Mitake, 60 b.; *Chichibu YH,* in Otaki, 50 b.

MOUNTAIN HUTS. – *Kumotori Sanso,* open all year (take own food); *Kumotori Hut,* May–October (take own food); *Shiraiwa Goya,* March–November.

EVENTS. – *Plum Festival* (March), in Yoshino Baigo; *Hinode-matsuri* (beginning of May), procession with portable shrines at Mitake Shrine, Fujimine; *Kawase-matsuri* (mid July) and *Chichibu-Yo-matsuri* (beginning of December), shrine festivals in Chichibu.

TRANSPORTATION. – **Rail:** from TOKYO (Shinjuku Station) JNR Chuo line to Tachikawa (30 minutes), then JNR Ome line to Okutama (1¼ hours); from TOKYO (Ikebukuro Station) Seibu-Ikebukuro line to Seibu-Chichibu (1½ hours), then Chichibu Railway to Mitsumineguchi (20 minutes); from TOKYO (Ikebukuro Station) Tobu-Tojo line to Ogawamachi (1¼ hours). – **Bus:** several regional services.

The beautiful *Chichibu-Tama National Park**, established in 1950, extends over the Kanto Mountains, NW of Tokyo. This upland region, lying at an average altitude of some 3300 ft/1000 m, is traversed by numerous rivers and gorges and is attractively wooded. It is a very popular recreational area, particularly with the people of Tokyo and Yokohama.

The principal gateways to the National Park are the towns of Ome, in the Upper Valley of the Tama (Okutama), to the E, and Chichibu, to the N. The highest peaks in the area are *Kimpu* (8514 ft/2595 m) and *Kokushi* (8504 ft/2592 m); and these mountains, together with *Ryogami* (5656 ft/1724 m), *Mikuni* (5998 ft/ 1828 m) and *Mizugaki,* offer much good walking and climbing. On the southern periphery rises Mount *Daibosatsu* (6749 ft/2057 m). – Among the finest gorges and valleys are *Shosenkyo* to the SW, *Okutama* to the SE and the Valley of the River *Chikuma.* The best-known spa is *Masutomi-onsen,* to the SW, from which Mount Mizugaki and Mount Kimpu and the Shosenkyo Gorge can be reached.

Ome (pop. 80,000), on the SE fringe of the National Park, is a center of the textile industry. In Hikawa Park (15 minutes' walk from the station) is the *Ome Railway Park,* opened in 1962 on the 90th anniversary of the Japanese railway system. An exhibition hall contains railway models and old steam locomotives and rolling stock. – The next station to the E is *Hina-tawada.* ½ mile/800 m away, reached by way of the Jindaibashi Bridge over the River Tama, are the plum orchards of

Yoshino Baigo, with a magnificent show of blossom from the end of February to mid March (when special excursions are run). During the whole of March the traditional Plum Festival is celebrated here. – Features of interest in the immediate surroundings are the *Yoshino Gorge, Temma Park,* the *Taisei-in Temple* and the *Atago Shrine.*

On the JNR Ome line is a station at the foot of the densely wooded Mount **Mitake** (3051 ft/930 m). The rivers *Tama* (to the N) and *Yozawa* (to the S) form romantic gorges, and along the slopes are beautiful footpaths edged with cherry trees, azaleas and maples. From Mitake Station there is a bus service (10 minutes) to *Takimoto,* with the lower station of a cableway which runs up in 6 minutes to the upper station at *Mitakesan* (also reached from Takimoto on a footpath, 2½ hours); from here there is a chair-lift to **Fujimine**, with an outlook terrace above *Mitake-daira.* From the summit of Mount Mitake the ˚view extends on clear days to the mountains of Nikko and Tsukuba to the NE and E. – Near the summit (footpath from Fujimine, 30 minutes) is the **Mitake Shrine**, founded about 800, in the Shimmei-zukuri style; the main shrine was rebuilt during the Meiji period. It contains many works of art, weapons, documents, etc. During the Hinode-matsuri festival (beginning of May) there are processions with portable shrines in which men in samurai armor take part.

Saiwai Station is the starting-point of a delightful walk through the **Mitake Gorge** to Mitake Station (about 45 minutes), near which one finds the **Gyokudo Museum of Art**, with works by the painter Kawai Gyokudo (1873–1957).

The JNR Ome line ends in the town of **Okutama**, near *Lake Okutama* (bus from station, 20 minutes), formed by the *Ogochi Dam* (489 ft/149 m high, 585 yds/535 m long); the lake is well stocked with fish. On the N side of the lake are some 6000 cherry trees (in blossom in mid April). Okutama is a good base from which to explore the *Tama Alps.*

9 miles/15 km NW of Okutama (bus, 40 minutes) is **Nippara**, notable for its *stalactitic cave,* the largest in the Kanto region, 1640 ft/500 m deep. A length of some 920 ft/280 m is lit and open to

visitors. – In the surrounding area there are bizarre rock formations. Beautiful autumn foliage in October.

The north-eastern gateway to the National Park is the town of **Chichibu** (pop. 61,000), which is noted for its silks (*Chichibu-meisen*). In a grove of centuries-old trees is the Chichibu Shrine, which ranks with the Hodo Shrine at Nagatoro and the Mitsumine Shrine on Mount Mitsumine as one of the most important shrines in the region. In July the shrine festival, Kawase-matsuri, is celebrated with lively processions, and on the evening of December 3 the Chichibu-Yo-matsuri festival is the occasion for a procession of splendidly illuminated floats and a great firework display. There is an interesting Municipal Museum (Chichibu-Shiritsu-minzoku-hakubutsu-kan). – The town's principal landmark is Mount *Buko* (4383 ft/1336 m), to the S. To the W (15 minutes' walk from Urayamaguchi Station) is the *Hashidate Stalactitic Cave.*

The terminus of the Chichibu Railway is **Mitsumineguchi**, from which there is a bus service to Owa, at the foot of Mount *Mitsumine* (3612 ft/1101 m); cableway (2080 yds/1900 m) to the summit. The **Mitsumine Shrine**, said to have been founded 2000 years ago, was a center of the mountain ascetics of the Tendai sect during the Tokugawa period; it contains some notable pieces of sculpture. During the summer months accommodation for climbers (huts, chalets, tents) is available near the summit.

Below the NW side of Mount Mitsumine is the man-made *Lake Chichibu,* spanned by two suspension bridges. On the shores of the lake stands a youth hostel. This is a popular area with fishermen and walkers. The *Mitsumine Ridgeway* leads from the lake to the *Treasury* of the Mitsumine Shrine, 4 miles/6 km away.

For a **round trip** the following route is recommended: bus from Mitsumineguchi to Owa – cableway to summit of Mount Mitsumine – walk to shrine (20 minutes) – on to Lake Chichibu (1½ hours) – back to Mitsumineguchi (40 minutes).

In the Upper Valley of the *Arakawa* (lower down called the Sumida) lies **Nagatoro** (pop. 9000). The valley is renowned for its beautiful scenery and its unusual rock formations. The *avenue of cherry trees,* 1 mile/1·5 km long, which links the town with Kami-Nagatoro is a magnificent sight in spring; equally beautiful are the display of azalea blossom in summer and the foliage of the maples in the fall.

The *Chichibu Natural History Museum* near **Kami-Nagatoro** Station is devoted to plant and animal life of the region. At Nogami Station, N of Nagatoro, is the *Nagatoro Synthetic Museum* (minerals, fossils).

A bus runs from Nagatoro to the foot of *Mount Hodo* (1631 ft/497 m); there is a cableway to the summit from which there are fine views of the surrounding hills, Nagatoro Gorge and the Chichibu Basin. On the summit is the *Hodo Shrine*.

From the *Oyabana-bashi* Bridge, 750 yds/700 m from Kami-Nagatoro Station, there are boat trips (starting from both banks of the Arakawa) through the rapids to the *Takasago-bashi* Bridge (30 minutes).

Also of interest is the little town of **Ogawa** (Tobu-Tojo line from Tokyo, Ikebukuro Station), with several factories producing hand-made paper. The Prefectural Industrial Laboratory of Paper and the Kubo Shotaro and Tanaka Shosaku factories can be visited.

Chiran
ちらん

Prefecture: Kagoshima. – Population: 15,000.
Post code: J-897-03. – Telephone code: 09938.
(i) (central)
Kagoshima-ken Tokyo Kanko Bussan Assensho,
Olympic Building,
2-7-17 Ginza, Chuo-ku,
J-100 **Tokyo**;
tel. (03) 561 6701.

(local)
Kagoshima-ken Kanko Renmei,
9-1, Nayama-cho,
J-890 **Kagoshima**;
tel. (0992) 23 9171.

TRANSPORTATION. – **Bus**: from KAGOSHIMA (Bus Center; 1¼ hours) and IBUSUKI.

The town of *Chiran lies in southwestern Kyushu, some 19 miles/ 30 km S of Kagoshima, chief town of the prefecture. It is surrounded by enchantingly beautiful hills covered with extensive tea plantations. During the Edo period it was one of the 102 castle towns on the borders of the province of Satsuma. In the Second World War it was a military air base, with a flying school. Chiran is now an idyllic little town with something of the atmosphere of a large village, renowned for its old gardens and its excellent green tea.

HISTORY. – About the middle of the 18th c. Shimazu Hisamine, Castellan of Chiran, visited Kyoto, then capital of Japan, and was so impressed by the beauty of the gardens there that he invited gardeners to come to Chiran and caused them to lay out a series of beautiful dry gardens (*karesansui*) on plots of land carved out of the estates of the samurai.

SIGHTS. – The six old gardens and samurai houses which have been preserved unaltered all lie on one or other of the streets, laid out on a grid plan, to the S of the Town Hall. The gardens are shut off from the street by walls of undressed stone and hedges, enhancing the medieval atmosphere of the town. In accordance with the classic principles of Japanese landscape architecture, trees, rocks and sand are arranged in complex patterns within an area of only 240–335 sq. yds/ 200–280 sq. m against the background of the bright green hills.

The *Garden of Saigo Ikkei* (250 sq. yds/ 208 sq. m), in the *karesansui* style, is a composition of moss, rocks and raked sand symbolizing a sheet of water. The *Garden of Hirayama Soyo* (330 sq. yds/ 277 sq. m) was laid out between 1751 and 1772. The *Garden of Hirayama Shoin* (1781–89) is in the Shakkei style, which incorporated the background in the total picture, on the principle of the "borrowed landscape". Also worth seeing are the *Garden of Sata Minshi*, the *Garden of Sata Naotada* (330 sq. yds/277 sq. m) and the *Garden of the Mori Family* (237 sq. yds/ 198 sq. m). The Mori garden, in contrast to the others, is in the Tsukiyama style

Dry garden, Chiran

("hill gardens"), with a small pool. Laid
out in 1741, it has preserved the dwelling-
house and warehouse of the Edo period.

Chubu-Sangaku National Park/ Japan Alps

中部山岳 国立公園 日本アルプス

The River Azusa at Kamikochi

Prefectures: Nagano, Gifu, Toyama and Niigata.
Area: 656 sq. miles/1699 sq. km.

ⓘ (central)
National Parks Association of Japan,
Toranomon Denki Building,
8-1, Toranomon 2-chome, Minato-Ku,
J-105 Tokyo;
tel. (03) 502 0488.

(local)
Kita Alps Tourist Association,
Kita-Azumi Chihojimusho,
J-398 Omachi;
tel. (02612) 2 1570.
Kamikochi General Information Center,
J-390-15 Kamikochi.

HOTELS. – IN MATSUMOTO AND TAKAYAMA: see separate
entries. – IN KAMIKOCHI. – Western style: Kamikochi
Onsen Hotel, Kamikochi, 62 r., thermal bath; Hotel
Shirakaba-so, 4468, Kamikochi, 57 r.; Shimizu-ya
Hotel, 22 r. – Ryokan: Gosenjo Ryokan, 58 r.;
Yamano-Hida, 19 r.

IN NATIONAL PARK. – Western style: Tateyama
Kokusai Hotel, in Hara, 98 r., Japanese garden;
Hakuba Tokyo Hotel, in Happo, 83 r., Japanese gar-
den; Hotel Tateyama, in Murodo-daira, 85 r. –
Ryokan: Hosono-Kan, in Happo, 25 r.; Bijodaira
Hotel, in Bijodaira, 19 r.; Kawachi-ya Omachi An, in
Omachi, 2884-7, Higashihara, 45 r.; Kawachi-ya
Omachi Annex, in Omachi, Inunokubo, 44 r., thermal
bath; Seiryu-so, in Senjugahara-onsen, 15 r., thermal
bath; Mikuriga-ike-onsen, in Mikuriga-ike-onsen, 25
r.; New Fusaji, in Jigokudani-onsen, 29 r., thermal
bath. – YOUTH HOSTELS: Azumino YH, in Hotaka,
4509, Kashiwabara, 20 b.; Norikura Kogen YH, in
Norikura-kogen, 50 b.; YH Sugita, in Senjugahara-
onsen, 44 b.

EVENTS. – Yama-biraki (July 1), opening of the
climbing season, Kamikochi.

TRANSPORTATION. – Rail: from TOKYO (Shinjuku
Station) JNR Chuo line to Matsumoto (3¾ hours),
then JNR Oito line to Omachi; also private line to
Shin-Shimashima. – Bus: from Matsumoto to
Kamikochi (3 hours) and Kiso-Fukushima (3 hours)
from Shin-Shimashima to Kamikochi (1½ hours:
summer only) and Shirahone-onsen (1¼ hours);
several local routes.

The ** Chubu-Sangaku National
Park, in the center of Honshu, takes
in the northern (Hida Mountains)
and central regions of the mountains
known as the "Japan Alps" and contains the highest peaks in Japan
after Fujiyama. The Japan Alps are
very similar to the Alps of Central
Europe both in the character of the
landscape and in the abundance of
snow in winter.

The mountains attract large numbers of
walkers and climbers in summer and of
skiers in winter. The plant life is varied,
differing in pattern with altitude. Ptar-
migan and mountain antelopes are found
at the higher altitudes.

The highest peaks in the National Park,
from N to S, are Norikura (9928 ft/
3026 m), the active volcano Yake
(8055 ft/2455 m), Hotaka (10,466 ft/
3190 m), Yari (10,434 ft/3180 m), Tateyama (9892 ft/3015 m) and Shirouma
(9623 ft/2933 m). The many hot springs
all over the park have led to the development of various spas and holiday resorts,
the best known of which is Kamikochi
(alt. 4920 ft/1500 m). The River Kurobe
flows through the mountains from S to N,
and the construction of the Kurobe Dam
has created a large lake which adds to the
beauty of the scenery.

The most important center of communications near the National Park is the city
of Matsumoto (pop. 191,000) (see
separate entry) to the E of the Hida Mountains.

The Kamikochi Valley, enclosed by
mighty peaks, is traversed by the River

Azusa, which lower down, after junctions with various tributaries, flows through the Matsumoto Basin as the River *Sai*. – The town of **Kamikochi** (4920 ft/1500 m) has the best facilities for visitors and is a good base from which to climb the surrounding heights; it tends to be overcrowded in summer. Near the town is *Lake Taisho*, formed in 1915 when the River Azusa was blocked by debris ejected during an eruption of the volcano *Yake*.

Farther upstream is the *Kappa Suspension Bridge*, from which there is a fine view of Mount *Hotaka* (10,466 ft/3190 m). Halfway to the bridge stands a monument to Walter Weston, one of the first foreigners to explore this mountain region. The opening of the climbing season is marked by the Yama-biraki ceremony in Kamikochi on July 1.

Recommended WALKS from the Kappa Bridge:

Kappa Bridge–Weston Monument–Tashiro Bridge–Lake Taisho–Lake Tashiro–bus terminus at Imperial Hotel–Kappa Bridge (2 hours).

Kappa Bridge–Konashidaira–Myojin Bridge–Lake Myojin–Kappa Bridge (2 hours).

Kappa Bridge–Konashidaira–Lake Myojin–Tokusawa (4 hours).

SW of Kamikochi is the extinct volcano **Norikura** (9928 ft/3026 m), which forms the southern part of the National Park. The summit region with its many lakes is particularly beautiful.

The mountain is brought within easy reach by a bus service which runs almost to the summit. Starting from Kamikochi, the bus climbs a toll road (9 miles/ 14·4 km), with magnificent views. via *Nakanoyu-onsen, Hirayu-onsen* and the *Hirayu Pass* to *Norikura*

Tatamidaira; the journey to the Norikura Hut takes 2½ hours. There is also a bus service, of about the same length, from the town of **Takayama** (see separate entry), to the W of the mountain. – The climb from the hut to the summit (2 miles/3 km) takes about 1½ hours. The eastern slopes of the mountain offer excellent skiing.

NE of Mount Norikura is the holiday resort of **Shirahone-onsen**, reached by bus (1¼ hours) from *Shin-Shimashima*, to the E.

NW of Kamikochi rises the majestic ⁎⁎**Mount Hotaka** (10,466 ft/3190 m), Japan's third highest mountain. There are four peaks – *Mae-Hotaka, Nishi-Hotaka, Oku-Hotaka* (the main peak) and *Kita-Hotaka*. The ascent of Mae-Hotaka, starting from Kamikochi, takes about 7 hours, and from there to Oku-Hotaka takes another 1½ hours. The climbing season is from May to November 5. – To the N is Mount **Yari** (10,434 ft/3180 m); the name means "spear", from the mountain's characteristic silhouette. The ascent, starting from Kamikochi, takes about 9 hours.

22 miles/35 km N of Matsumoto (JNR Oito line) is **Omachi** (pop. 33,000), another gateway to the National Park and a popular climbing center. This quiet little country town has a small Alpine Museum.

From the Kurobe Dam ...

... the view of the river below

Toyama Castle

From Shinano-Omachi the railway line continues N, passing *Lakes Kizaki, Nakatsuna* and *Aoki*, to **Hakuba**, starting-point of a trip to the mountain ridge of **Happoone**, which has one of the largest skiing areas in Japan. There is a bus service (10 minutes) from Hakuba Station to *Hosono*, at the foot of the mountains. Ranging in height between 2460 ft/750 m and 5415 ft/1650 m, the skiing area has a cableway 1¼ miles/2 km long and 21 chair-lifts and ski-tows. The winter-sports season lasts from December to March. – An alternative route (1 hour by bus) is from Hakuba Station via Hosono to the *Sarukura Hut* on the flank of Mount **Shirouma** (9623 ft/2933 m), at the N end of the National Park.

Of the other routes to the Sarukura Hut one of the most impressive is from *Omachi* by way of the spa of *Shirouma-Yari-onsen*, the highest in Japan (6890 ft/ 2100 m).

The ascent of Mount **Shirouma** from the Sarukura Hut (5 miles/7·5 km) takes about 6½ hours. The route goes past an ice field 1¼ miles/2 km long and the *Ohana-batake* Plain, renowned for its profusion of Alpine plants, seen at their best in July and August. From the summit there is a magnificent panoramic view of Mount Myoko (8025 ft/2446 m) and Mount Togakushi (6270 ft/1911 m) to the E, Mount Tsurugi (9853 ft/3003 m) and Mount Tateyama (9892 ft/ 3015 m) to the SW and the Sea of Japan to the N. Overnight accommodation is available in two huts on the summit.

– There is a bus service (40 minutes) from *Shinano-Omachi* to *Ogisawa*, from which the Kuroyon Dam, 15 miles/25 km NW, can be visited. From Ogisawa a tunnel 3¼ miles/5·4 km long (bus service) cuts through the rock to the **Kuroyon Dam** (*Kurobe Dam No. 4*), the fifth largest in the world (610 ft/186 m high, 540 yds/ 495 m long). The lake formed by the dam contains 44,000 million gallons/200 million cu. m of water. Visitors can walk along the top of the dam to the lower station of a cableway to the summit of *Kurobe-daira*, from which there is an impressive view of the dam and the River Kurobe below. – It is well worth while continuing W from here, taking the cableway to *Daikanbo* (7 minutes), then by bus to *Murodo* (10 minutes) and *Bijodaira* (5 minutes), and finally by cableway to *Tateyama* (7 minutes). On the way there are magnificent views of the mountains and valleys with their colorful vegetation. Instead of returning by the same route it is a good plan to continue W to the town of **Toyama** (pop. 305,000), situated outside the National Park in Toyama Bay on the Sea of Japan. From here there are excellent communications in all directions.

Daisen-Oki National Park
だいせんおき
国立公園

Prefectures: Tottori and Shimane.
Area: 123 sq. miles/319 sq. km.
ⓘ (central)
National Parks Association of Japan,
Toranomon Denki Building,
8-1, Toranomon 2-chome, Minato-ku,
J-105 **Tokyo**;
tel. (03) 502 0488.

(local)
Daisen-cho Tourist Information Center,
J-689-33 **Daisen**;
tel. (085952) 2327.
Oki Tourist Association,
J-679-11 **Nakamachi**;
tel. (08512) 2 1577.

HOTELS. – IN IZUMO AND MATSU: see separate entries. – ON OKI ISLANDS. – **Western style**: *Oki Plaza Hotel*, in Saigo, Minato-machi, 35 r., Japanese garden, beach. – *Ryokan*: *Oki Seaside Hotel Tsurumaru*, in Nishi-no-shima, 17 r., beach; *Hotel Oki*, in Nishi-no-shima, 16 r.; *Chokai*, in Saigo, 18 r.; *Takanashi Ryokan*, in Saigo, 14 r. – YOUTH HOSTELS: *Okino Shima YH*, in Fuse, 60 b., beach; *YH Oki Jinja* (shrine), in Ama, 37 b.; *YH Mizuwakasu* (shrine), in Goka-mura, 30 b.

EVENTS. – *Shrine festivals* (mid May, June 1, mid October, mid November) in Izumo-Taisha Shrine.

TRANSPORTATION. – To IZUMO and MATSUE: see separate entries. – **Air**: from OSAKA to Saigo (Dogo island; 2 hours); from Yonago to Saigo (30 minutes). – **Rail**: from KYOTO JNR San-in line to Daisenguchi, Yonago, Matsue and Izumo; Ichihata private line from Izumo-shi to the Izumo-Taisha Shrine and Matsue-onsen; branch line from Yonago to Sakaiminato. – **Bus**: from Daisenguchi to the Daisenji Temple (35 minutes); from Matsue to Mihonoseki and Kaga (1¼ hours). – **Boat**: from Sakaiminato to Saigo (Dozo island) and Beppu (Dozen island).

The * **Daisen-Oki National Park occupies an area of land and sea on the N coast of western Honshu, including part of the Shimane Peninsula and the Oki island group. It is a region of wooded hills and wide strips of coastal scenery, with the added charm of a remote and secluded group of islands.**

The various parts of the National Park are separated from one another. At the western end of the Shimane Peninsula is the area around the Taisha Shrine at Izumo; to the S, inland, rises the extinct volcano of Sambe; in the NE of the peninsula extends the stretch of the coast between Kashima and Mihonoseki; farther E, inland, is the region around the extinct volcano of Daisen; and some 45 miles/72 km off the coast are the Oki Islands.

Mount **Daisen** (5620 ft/1713 m), in the eastern part of the National Park, also known as the "Fuji of Hoki province" is the highest peak in the Chugoku district. From the station (JNR San-in line) of *Daisenguchi*, near the coast, a bus runs (35 minutes) to the **Daisenji Temple** on the slopes of the mountain. The temple, founded in 718, was one of the leading centers of the Tendai sect, with more than a hundred subordinate temples and convents. Later, however, all the buildings were destroyed by fire, leaving only scanty remains. The temple contains a bronze * statue of the Eleven-Headed Kannon, six other Buddhist sculptures and a fine miniature shrine. – From here it

is a 3½ hours' climb (3¼ miles/5·5 km) to the summit, which affords fine * views of the National Park, extending on clear days to the island of Shikoku to the S. In winter Mount Daisen offers ideal skiing conditions.

A panoramic road coming from the SE over the *Hiruzen Plateau* cuts across Mount Daisen and continues to Sakaiminato, providing an excellent link with the central part of the park. The road, from which there are magnificent views, runs along a narrow tongue of land between *Miho Bay* to the E and the *Naka-no-umi Lagoon*, skirts the pine-fringed coastal strip of *Yumigahama* and continues to **Sakaiminato** (pop. 36,000), an important port in the San-in district. From here there are boats to the Oki Islands (3 hours). Along the coast are beautiful beaches.

The **Oki Islands**, the most northerly part of the National Park, lie some 45 miles off the coast. Of volcanic origin, the archipelago comprises the two main groups, **Dozen** and **Dogo**, and a large number of smaller islands and islets. The boats from Sakaiminato put in at *Saigo* (Dogo island) and *Beppu* (Dozen island). There are also air services from Osaka and Yonato. The 31,000 inhabitants of the islands live mainly by farming, forestry and fishing. The islands themselves offer the double attraction of beautiful and varied scenery and a number of historic old buildings dating from the period when they served as a place of banishment.

In 838 the statesman and poet Ono Takamura was exiled to the islands. Later Gotoba-tenno (1180–1239) was deported to Dozen after the failure of his attempt to wrest power from the Hojo dynasty, and died on the island. In 1332 the Emperor Godaigo was also exiled here.

From Sakaiminato the **Shimane Peninsula** can be reached either by boat or by a bridge 1875 yds/1714 m long spanning the natural channel which links the lagoon with the sea. At the eastern tip of the peninsula lies the fishing port of **Mihonoseki**, perhaps the most charming of the coastal towns in the National Park. The name means "barrier at Miho", and refers to the existence at some time in the past of a control post here. To the E of the town stands the *Miho Shrine*, one of the oldest in the region, dedicated to the divinity Kotoshironushi. Outside the town (15 minutes' walk) is the *Gohon-Matsu*

Park; the name is derived from five ancient pines, one of which still survives (13 ft/ 4 m in circumference, about 250 years old). From the park there are fine views of Mount Daisen and the coastal area.

W of Mihonoseki, on a picturesque stretch of the N coast which can be reached by bus from Matsue (see separate entry), we come to the **Kaga-no-kukedo Cave** which can be entered by

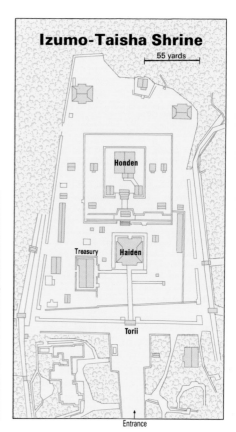

Izumo-Taisha Shrine

55 yards

Honden

Treasury   Haiden

Torii

Entrance

Izumo-Taisha Shrine

boat through a narrow opening on the seaward side.

The best starting-point for a visit to the section of the National Park in the western part of the Shimane Peninsula is the town of **Izumo** (see separate entry). To the NW is the celebrated ** **Izumo-Taisha Shrine** (bus, 7 minutes), the oldest Shinto shrine in Japan. It is dedicated to Okuninushi-no-mikoto, god of agriculture and healing. The legend has it that the god founded a State in the Izumo area and later withdrew to the shrine, originally designed as a large palace, in which his descendants served as priests in an unbroken line. The shrine now ranks with the Ise Shrine and the Kompira Shrine (Shikoku) as the largest Shinto pilgrimage center in Japan. It attracts large numbers of pilgrims, particularly during the shrine festivals.

The SHRINE, covering an area of 40½ acres, contains many buildings in the Taisha-zukuri style, an early Japanese architectural style. Characteristic features of this style are a projecting saddle roof, cylindrical ridge beams, crossed gable joists and an entrance on the gable side. The present buildings date mainly from 1874, the * **Honden** (main hall) from 1744. The roofs

are covered with cypress bark. The shrine, which is approached by an avenue of cedars, is surrounded by a double enclosure wall. On either side of the main shrine are two long buildings in which, according to Shintoist teaching, all the Shinto gods assemble once every year, in the tenth lunar month (October). Accordingly October is known as the "godless month" (Kannazuki) throughout Japan, except at Izumo, where it is known as the "month of the assembled divinities" (Kamiarizuki). To the left of the entrance is the **Treasury** (museum), and beyond this the hall for sacred dances (Kagura-den). The wooded hills of *Yakumo* and *Tsuruyama* form a backdrop to the shrine.

765 yds/700 m W of the shrine is the beach of *Inasanohama* (1¼ miles/2 km S of Taisha Station; bus service). To the NW lies *Cape Hino-misaki*, the western tip of the Shimane Peninsula, reaching out into the Sea of Japan (bus from Taisha, 35 minutes). On the cape are the *Hinomisaki Shrine* and what is claimed to be the tallest lighthouse in Asia.

The most westerly section of the National Park is the region around the extinct volcano of *Sambe*. Below the S side of the hill is the spa of *Sambe-onsen*, with hot saline springs at temperatures of up to 109 °F/43 °C. The beauty of the surrounding area has made this one of the most popular holiday resorts in the San-in district, and the slopes of Mount Sambe offer excellent facilities for winter sports.

Mount **Sambe** (3694 ft/1126 m), also known as *Iwami-Fuji*, is brought within easy reach by a toll road (bus services).

Daisetsuzan National Park

だいせつ山 国立公園

Prefecture: Hokkaido.
Area: 895 sq. miles/2319 sq. km.
(i) (central)
National Parks Association of Japan,
Toranomon Denki Building,
8-1, Toranomon 2-chome, Minato-ku,
J-105 **Tokyo**;
tel. (03) 502 0488.

(local)
Daisetsuzan Tourist Association,
Asahikawa-Shiyakusho,
6-jodori 9,
J-070 **Asahikawa**;
tel. (0166) 26 1111.

HOTELS. – IN ASAHIKAWA: see separate entry. – IN NATIONAL PARK. – **Ryokan**: *Sounkyo Grand Hotel*, Sounkyo, 245 r.; *Hotel Soun*, Sounkyo, 150 r.; *Sounkyo Kanko Hotel*, Sounkyo, 133 r.; *Tenninkaku*, Tenninkyo, 126 r. – YOUTH HOSTELS: *Sounkyo YH*, Sounkyo, 90 b.; *YH Ginsenkaku*, Sounkyo, 84 b. (closed November–April).

TRANSPORTATION. – TO ASAHIKAWA: see separate entry. – **Rail**: from SAPPORO JNR Nemuro line to Obihiro (3 hours), then JNR Shihoro line to Nukabira (1¾ hours); from Asahikawa JNR Sekihoku line to Kamikawa (2 hours); from Asahikawa JNR Furano line to Biei (NW of Shirogane-onsen). – **Bus**: from Asahikawa to Sounkyo-onsen; to Yukomambetsu-onsen (2 hours) and Tenninkyo-onsen (1¼ hours); from Sounkyo-onsen to the Sekihoku Pass (1 hour).

The * **Daisetsuzan National Park lies in the center of the most northerly of the main Japanese islands, Hokkaido. Its imposing series of peaks have earned it the name of the "roof of Hokkaido". The park contains three volcanic massifs with the highest peaks on the island – Mount Asahi (7513 ft/2290 m), Mount Tomuraushi (7025 ft/2141 m) and Mount Tokachi (6815 ft/2077 m). In the eastern part of the park are Mount Ishikari (6437 ft/1962 m) and Lakes Shikaribetsu and Nukabira.**

At the higher altitudes there is mountain vegetation of extraordinary richness. At the foot of the hills, between areas of virgin forest and on the banks of crystal-clear streams, are numbers of small mountain villages.

Within the National Park are the sources of the rivers *Tokachi*, *Ishikari* and *Chubetsu*, which form beautiful gorges, the best known of which is the Sounkyo Gorge 30 miles/50 km E of Asahikawa. – Asahikawa is the best starting-point for a visit to the National Park, which is entered here from the NW. The southern gateway to the park is the town of *Obihiro*.

The **Sounkyo Gorge**, in the N of the National Park, extends for 15 miles/24 km between the northern outlier of Daisetsu and Obako to the S. The road which winds its way through the gorge affords superb * views of the beautiful area (sightseeing buses). On either side the rock walls rise to a height of 500 ft/150 m, with waterfalls tumbling down at intervals (Ryusei-no-taki, Ginga-no-taki). At the upper end of the gorge are two basins, *Kobako* ("little box") and *Obako* ("big box"), so called because anyone standing within the vertical walls of these depressions feels he is enclosed within a box.

Half-way along the gorge is **Sounkyo-onsen**, one of the most popular holiday resorts in Hokkaido, with a cableway running up in several stages to a height of 4265 ft/1300 m, from which a chair-lift continues the ascent. From the top there is a panoramic * view of the surrounding mountains and the wooded countryside with its idyllic little villages. At the higher altitudes there are many species of mountain vegetation.

The *Daisetsu Highway*, which provides a link with the Akan National Park (see separate entry), runs E from the gorge to the *Sekihoko Pass* (3445 ft/1050 m), on the E side of the Daisetsuzan National Park. To the W of the pass, 25 miles/40 km SE of Asahikawa, lies the health resort of **Tenninkyo**, from which Mount *Tomuraushi* (7025 ft/2141 m), to the S, and Mount *Asahi* (7513 ft/2290 m), to the N (via Yukomambetsu), can be climbed. Near Tenninkyo (5 minutes' walk) are the *Hagoromo Falls* ("feather cloak"), 820 ft/250 m high and enclosed between steep rock walls. The valley adjoining the falls is known as the Ten-ninkyo Gorge.

To the E of this gorge, on the southern slopes of Mount Asahi, is the health resort of **Yukomambetsu-onsen** (3445 ft/ 1050 m), 27 miles/43 km E of Asahikawa. This is a good base from which to climb Mount *Asahi* (4 hours), Mount **Hoku-chin** (7369 ft/2246 m) and Mount *Kuro* (6510 ft/1984 m), to the N, and Mount *Aka* (6818 ft/2078 m), to the E, as well as being a popular winter-sports center.

The south-western part of the National Park can be reached from Asahikawa by rail, via *Shirogane-onsen*. 5 miles/8 km from this attractive resort is the volcano of **Tokachi**, which last erupted in 1962; its slopes are considered to be one of the four best skiing areas on Hokkaido. Near the volcano are Mount *Biei* (6733 ft/ 2052 m), to the N, and Mount *Kami-Horokamettoku* (6191 ft/1887 m), to the S.

To the E of this range of mountains, beyond the River *Tokachi*, is another range, with Mount *Nipesotsu* (6605 ft/2013 m) and Mount *Upepesanke* (6135 ft/ 1870 m) on the E side of which lies **Lake Nukabira** (1970 ft/600 m), a man-made lake with a circumference of 20 miles/ 33 km and an area of 3 sq. miles/8·2 sq. km through which flows the River *Otofuke*. This is a very attractive vacation area with beautiful little towns and villages. **Nukabira-onsen**, near the lake, has hot saline springs at temperatures of up to 140°F/60°C. A road running SW from here comes in 14 miles/23 km to **Lake Shikaribetsu**, on the W side of Mount *Tembo* (3852 ft/1174 m), which can also be reached by bus from Obihiro (2 hours). The lake (alt. 2618 ft/798 m, area 1½ sq. miles/3·7 sq. km, depth 340 ft/ 104 m) lies in the middle of a forest, which is particularly attractive in the fall with its vividly coloured foliage. On the shores of the lake are the resorts of *Shikaribetsu Kohan-onsen* (to the W) and Yamada-onsen (to the N).

Fuji-goko
See Fuji Lakes

Fuji-Hakone-Izu National Park
ふじはこねいず 国立公園

Prefectures: Yamanashi, Shizuoka and Kanagawa.
Area: 472 sq. miles/1223 sq. km.
(i) (central)
National Parks Association of Japan,
Toranomon Denki Building,
8-1, Toranomon 2-chome, Minato-ku,
J-105 **Tokyo**;
tel. (03) 502 0488.

The ** **Fuji-Hakone-Izu National Park, on the S coast of central Hon-shu, consists of four separate and unconnected sections. The most northerly part includes the area**

Lake Ashi and Fuji-san

around Mount Fuji and the Fuji Lakes; the central part consists of the Hakone region with Lake Ashi and a number of health resorts; while to the S are two areas taking in the Izu Peninsula and the seven Izu islands.

See also **Fuji Lakes, Fujiyama, Hakone** and **Izu**.

Fuji Lakes/ Fuji-goko

ふじ五湖

Prefecture: Yamanashi.

(i) (local)
Fuji-gogome Tourist Association,
Fuji Kyuko, 331-1, Matsuyama,
J-401-05 **Fuji-Yoshida;**
tel. (0555) 2 2171.

HOTELS. – **Western style:** *Fuji View Hotel,* on Lake Kawaguchi, 511, Katsuyama-mura, 66 r.; *Hotel Mount Fuji,* on Lake Yamanaka, 1360-82, Yamanakako-mura, 111 r.; *Yamanakako Hotel,* on Lake Yamanaka, 506-1, Yamanakako-mura, 71 r. – YOUTH HOSTELS: *Fuji-Saiko YH,* on Lake Saiko, 2068, Saiko, 68 b.; *Fuji Yoshida YH,* in Fuji-Yoshida, 2-chome, 30 b.; *Kawaguchi-ko YH,* on Lake Kamaguchi, 2128, Funazu, 58 b.; *Gotemba YH,* in Gotemba, 3857, Higashiyama, 52 b.

EVENTS. – *Himatsuri* (ending of climbing season: end August) in Fuji-Yoshida.

TRANSPORTATION. – To GOTEMBA and KAWA-GUCHIKO: see under Fujiyama. – **Rail:** from TOKYO JNR Tokaido line to Fuji, then JNR Minobu line to Fujinomiya. – **Bus:** from Kawaguchiko via Koyodai, Fugaku Fugetsu, Lake Shoji, Lake Motosu and the Fujinomiya Toll Road to Fujinomiya (1 hour); from Kawaguchiko to Gotemba (1¼ hours) and Mishima (2 hours); from Numazu (Izu Peninsula).

Below the N side of Mount Fuji is the beautiful region of the five * * **Fuji Lakes (Fuji-goko), a popular resort of the people of Tokyo at every time of year and a region much frequented by foreign visitors. The climate of this lake district, lying at an altitude of over 2000 ft/600 m, is pleasantly fresh; in spring the cherry trees and azaleas offer a magnificent display of blossom, and in the fall the forests take on a vivid coloring. In summer the region attracts large numbers of water-sports enthusiasts, in winter skiers and skaters. The lakes lie within the Fuji-Hakone-Izu National Park.**

The lake district extends around the N side of Mount Fuji in a wide arc. To the E lies Lake Yamanaka, followed towards the W by Lakes Kawaguchi, Saiko, Shoji and Motosu. For visitors coming from the Tokyo direction the most convenient base is the town of Gotemba, for visitors coming from the Osaka, Kyoto and Nagoya area the town of Fujinomiya, to the W of Mount Fuji.

From Gotemba to Fujinomiya. – This route take in all five of the Fuji Lakes as well as the starting-points of the routes for the ascent of **Fujiyama** (see separate entry).

Lake Yamanaka is the highest of the lakes (alt. 3222 ft/982 m) and also the largest (area 2½ sq. miles/6·5 sq. km). The area around the lake is one of the most popular health resorts in Japan. On the S side of the lake is **Asahigaoka**, which can be reached from Gotemba or direct from Tokyo by bus. There are boat trips on the lake, and near the town are the Fuji golf-course and a number of camp sites. The globular green pond-weed called marimo (also found in Lake Akan on Hokkaido) grows in the lake, which also contains eels, carp and fish of the salmon family. A popular sport in winter is fishing under the ice for a species of fish known as wakasagi. The nearby River *Katsura* is an excellent trout stream.

The town of **Fuji-Yoshida** (pop. 51,000; rail and bus services from Tokyo), to the N of Lake Yamanaka, is noted for its silks (*kaiki*). The end of the official climbing season on Mount Fuji is marked by the Himatsuri festival, celebrated here on August 26, when torches and beacons are lit along the Fuji–Yoshida road (see under Fujiyama) and there is a procession with a portable shrine weighing 2475 lb/ 1125 kg. – To the S of the town is the **Fujikyu Highland Amusement Park**, one of the largest in the region (reached on Fuji–Kyuko Railway; overnight accommodation).

NW of Fuji-Yoshida (bus service; rail service from Tokyo) we find the second largest and most beautiful of the lakes, **Kawaguchi-ko** (alt. 2697 ft/822 m, area 2½ sq. miles/6·1 sq. km). From the E side of the lake a cableway ascends Mount **Tenjo** (3557 ft/1084 m), from which there is an impressive * view of Fujiyama reflected in the lake. – In the center of the lake lies the densely wooded island of *Unoshima*, with a shrine dedicated to the goddess of fortune, Benten, and a variety of recreational and leisure facilities. ¾ mile/ 1 km NW of *Kawaguchiko* Station is the **Fuji Museum** (local history, a collection of erotica). Near the toll point on the Fuji-Subaru road (see under Fujiyama) is the **Visitor Center** *of Yamanashi prefecture* (formerly the Fuji National Park Museum), where a collection illustrating the natural history of Mount Fuji can be seen. Kawaguchiko is the starting-point of a route up Fujiyama (see separate entry); boat trips on the lake (1 hour). The E end of the lake is spanned by the *Kawaguchiko O-hashi* Bridge (1380 yds/ 1260 m long; toll).

The next lake to the W is **Lake Saiko** (area ¾ sq. mile/2 sq. km; bus from Kawaguchiko), which attracts many fishermen in spring and in the fall (trout). Like Lakes Shoji and Motosu, this lake has no visible outflow; it is supposed that these three lakes are drained by underground channels leading to the source of the River *Shiba*. There is a boat service between *Saiko* on the NE side of the lake and *Neba* on the NW side. Attractive excursions can be made in the area S of the lake, for example to **Koyodai** ("maple hill"; bus or 20 minutes' walk from Kawaguchiko Station), from which there are fine *views of the surrounding forests. A short distance SW we reach the *Narisawa Hyoketsu* ice cave, and farther W (20 minutes' walk or bus from Kawaguchiko Station) the **Fugaku Fuketsu Cave** contains lava and ice formations (NB: interior extremely cold).

Between Lake Saiko and the next lake to the W, Lake Shoji, is an area of primeval forest known as **Jukai** ("Sea of Trees"). In this wilderness (circumference 10 miles/16 km) the magnetism in the eruptive rocks affects the accuracy of compasses, so that walkers in this area frequently go astray.

Lake Shoji, surrounded on three sides by gentle wooded hills but open to the S, is the most idyllic and the smallest (area ¾ sq. mile/·75 sq. km) of the five lakes (bus services from Fuji-Yoshida, Kawaguchiko and Fujinomiya). Here in winter wakasagi, a fish of the salmon family can be caught. – From the N side of the lake it is a 1½ hours' climb to the summit of Mount **Eboshi**, also known as *Shoji-Panorama-dai* (4124 ft/1257 m), from which there are magnificent *views of the lake, Mount Fuji and the "Sea of Trees".

The most westerly of the lakes is the deep-blue **Lake Motosu** (bus services from Fuji-Yoshida and Fujinomiya). It is the deepest of the lakes (413 ft/126 m) and does not freeze over in winter.

The *Fujinomiya Toll Road* beyond Fujinomiya (14 miles/22 km long; bus, 1¼

hours) affords superb *views of Mount Fuji. Half-way along the road are the **Shiraito Falls**, where the River *Shiba*, here 140 yds/130 m wide, plunges down a sheer rock face 85 ft/26 m high. On the other side of the road are the *Otodome-no-taki Falls*. – To the S is the **Taisekiji Temple**, founded in 1290, one of the principal shrines of the Nichiren sect and the headquarters of the associated Soka Gakkai organization. Modern assembly hall seating 6000.

At **Fujinomiya** (pop. 95,000), ¾ mile/1 km NW of the station, stands the *Sengen Shrine*, built in 1604, the principal Sengen shrine in the Fuji area. It is dedicated to the goddess Konohana-Sakuyahime-no-mikoto. – From Fujinomiya the JNR Minobu line runs S to *Fuji* Station, from which the Tokaido line continues to Tokyo.

Fujiyama/Fuji-san

ふじ山

Prefectures: Yamanashi and Shizuoka.
Altitude: 12,389 ft/3776 m.
(i) (local)
Fuji Gogome Tourist Association,
Fuji Kyuko, 331-1, Matsuyama,
J-401-05 **Fuji-Yoshida**;
tel. (0555) 2 2171.

MOUNTAIN HUTS. – 1st to 4th stations, open April 1 to November 23; 5th to 9th stations, open July 1 to August 31.

EVENTS. – *Himatsuri* (end of the climbing season; end August) in Fuji-Yoshida.

TRANSPORTATION. – **Rail**: from TOKYO (Shinjuku Station) JNR Chuo line via Fuji-Yoshida to Kawaguchiko (2 hours; through coach from Otsuki); from OSAKA JNR Tokaido-Shinkansen line to Mishima (3¼ hours); from KOZU or NUMAZU JNR line to Gotemba. – **Bus**: from TOKYO (Hamamatsucho or Shinjuku Bus Terminal) to 5th station (2½–3 hours); from Mishima (Fujinomiya route) to new 5th station (Shingogome; 2 hours); from Fuji-Yoshida (Fuji-Yoshida route) to Fuji-Sengen Shrine (5 minutes); from Gotemba (Gotemba route) to new 2nd station (Shinnigome; 45 minutes).

Mount **Fuji is the highest peak in the Fuji volcanic chain in central Japan and Japan's highest and most beautiful mountain. Its regular form has been celebrated since early times in poetry and painting, for example in the verses of Yamabe Akahito (8th c.) and the series of woodcuts, "Views of Fuji" by

Hokusai (1760–1849). The very symbol and emblem of Japan, it can be seen on clear days from as far away as Tokyo. It lies within the Fuji-Hakone-Izu National Park.

The correct Japanese name for the mountain is **Fuji-san**; the usual English form, Fujiyama, is not commonly used in Japan. In early times it was revered as a sacred mountain, the home of the gods, and from the 12th c. Buddhist teaching held that it was the gateway to another world. Until 1868, like other natural shrines, it was banned to women. Nowadays Fuji is climbed during the months of July and August by more than a million people, for whom the ascent is an almost religious act, the culmination of which is the observation of sunrise on the summit (*Goraiko*). The beginning and ending of the official climbing season are celebrated on July 1 and August 31 with solemn ceremonies, but climbers do go up all year round.

Fuji is a strato-volcano which came into being in the Quaternary era, some 300,000 years ago. Its almost exactly circular base has a diameter of 22–25 miles/ 35–40 km. The name is believed to come from the Ainu word for fire. Eighteen eruptions have been recorded in historical times, the most violent being those of 800, 864 and 1707. During the 1707 eruption the town of Edo (Tokyo), 60 miles/ 100 km away, was covered with a thick layer of ash and the lateral crater of Hoeizan (8865 ft/2702 m) was formed. Since then the volcano has been quiescent. – On the northern flank of Fuji are the five **Fuji Lakes** (see separate entry).

There are five routes up Mount Fuji, each divided into ten stages (*gome*) of varying length (*ichi-gome* = first stage, *ni-gome* = second stage, etc.). At the end of each stage are stone direction signs and sometimes a mountain hut. During the season all the huts are open, so that climbers can spend the night at one of the intermediate "stations". Stout footwear, a pocket-torch, warm clothing and protection against bad weather are essential: the average temperature on the summit even in the height of summer (July–August) is only 41–43 °F/5–6 °C. Unless Japanese food is acceptable, provisions for the climb should also be taken: as a rule only Japanese food can be obtained on the climbing routes.

The ascent is usually begun in the early afternoon, so as to reach the 7th or 8th station before nightfall. Then early the following morning climbers continue to the summit and walk round the crater (diameter 550 yds/ 500 m). The descent is begun about midday, returning to base in the late afternoon. – An increasingly popular variant is to make the ascent in one go, starting about 4 p.m. and reaching the summit at sunrise. The advantages of this method are that it takes less time and avoids the heat of the day. In any event the view down into the valley is obstructed by clouds after 9 a.m. – Fuji should not be climbed in winter in view of the danger of **avalanches**.

Ascent to the Rim of the Crater

Of the five routes to the summit – **Kawaguchiko, Fuji-Yoshida, Gotemba, Subashiri** and **Fujinomiya** – the most convenient for climbers coming from Tokyo are the Kawaguchiko route for the ascent and the Subashiri route for the descent. For those coming from Osaka or Kyoto the Fujinomiya route is best.

Kawaguchiko route. – From *Kawaguchiko* Station (JNR Fujikyuko line from Tokyo, 2 hours) there is a bus service to the *5th station* (*go-gome*), affording fine· views of the Fuji Lakes. The ascent begins at the 5th station. At the 6th station this route is joined by the Fuji-Yoshida route. The climb to the summit (4 miles/6 km) takes 4–5 hours. – A variant of this route is the **Subashiri route**, usually preferred for the descent, which leads to the *new 5th station* (*shin-gogome*), to the E of the summit. From here there are buses to *Subashiri* and *Gotemba* Station, from which there are trains to Tokyo (1¾ hours). This route joins the Fuji-Yoshida route at the 8th station.

Fuji-Yoshida route. – From *Fuji-Yoshida* Station, below the N side of Fuji, there is a bus service to the **Fuji-Sengen Shrine**, from which it is a 2½ hours' walk to *Umagaeshi* (or road, about 30 minutes), and from there a 6½ hours' climb to the summit. At the end of the route is the **Kusushi Shrine**. – The descent to the *5th station* takes about 2 hours.

Gotemba route. – From *Gotemba* Station (JNR Gotemba line from Tokyo) there are buses (45 minutes) to the *new 2nd station* (*shin-ni-gogome*), from which it is a 6½ hours' climb to the summit (7 miles/11 km). This stony route is more suitable for the return journey. The descent to the 7th station takes an hour, and from there a short cut can be taken (*suna-*

bashiri, "sand-sliding"), "scree-running" down 4½ miles/7 km of volcanic ash in half an hour. – ¾ mile/1 km S of the *5th station* on this route is the lateral crater of **Hoeizan**. Like the Subashiri route, this route affords a fine * view of the sunrise (above the 3rd station).

Fujinomiya route. – From *Fujinomiya* Station (JNR Minobu line) there are buses to the *new 5th station* (*shin-gogome*), from which it is a 4–5 hours' climb (3 miles/5 km) to the rim of the crater. Above the *8th station* (*manatsuki-hatcho*) the route becomes fairly steep, leading direct to the *Okunoin* (the inner shrine of the Sengo Shrine) on the summit. – There is also a bus service to the 5th station from *Mishima* (2 hours).

Summit Region

The summit region of Fuji consists of the crater, known as the *Naiin* ("shrine"), with a diameter of 550 yds/500 m. The crater rim is formed by eight peaks – *Kengamine, Hakusan* (or *Shaka*), *Kusushi, Dainichi* (or *Asahi*), *Izu, Joju* (or *Seishigadake*), *Komagatake* and *Mishi-madake*. From Kengamine there are two variants of the route round the crater (*ohachi-meguri*). Easier than the steep

Fujiyama, Japan's sacred mountain

direct route along the crest is the shorter (2 miles/3·5 km) path round the inner rim of the crater. To the N of Komagatake, at the end of the Fujinomiya route, stands the **Sengen Shrine**, and a short distance E, on the outer flank of the crater, is the *Gimmeisui* Spring ("silver-shimmering water"). Near the shrine can be found a post office, and there is now also a telephone service. – A few hundred yards W is a *weather station*, where the meteorologist Nonaka Itaru recorded his first observations in 1895. At the foot of the Hakusan peak, on the N side of the crater, rises the *Kimmeisui* Spring ("golden-shimmering water").

From the summit there are extensive views, taking in almost the whole of mainland Japan.

Around the Lower Slopes of Fuji

A footpath, *Ochudo-meguri*, encircles the mountain at about the level of the 5th and 6th stations on the access routes (about 8200 ft/2500 m). The complete circuit (12½ miles/20 km) takes 8–10 hours, starting from any convenient point. The most difficult stretches are **Hoeizan**, on the E side, and the **Osawa Gorge** (the

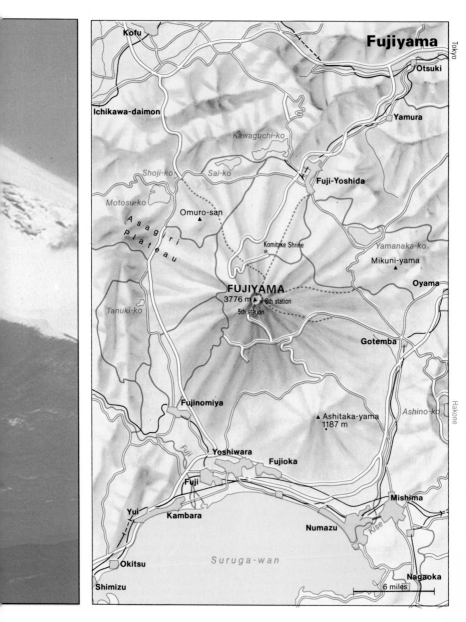

Winter on Fuji

largest gorge of Mount Fuji) on the W side. The path is known as the "boundary between heaven and earth".

Fukui

Prefecture: Fukui. – Population: 245,000.
Post code: J-910. – Telephone code: 0776.
(i) (central)
Fukui-ken Tokyo Kanko Bussan Assensho,
Kokusai Kanko Kaikan,
1-8-3, Marunouchi, Chiyoda-ku,
J-100 **Tokyo;**
tel. (03) 211 8054.

(local)
Fukui-ken Tourist Information Center,
3-17-1, Ote-machi;
tel. 23 3677.

HOTELS. – **Western style:** *Fukui Palace Hotel,* 2-1-3, Junka, 40 r., Japanese garden; *Hotel New Nawaya,* 3-11-28, Chuo, 39 r.; *Hotel Akebono,* 3-10-12, Chuo, 29 r., sauna. – **Minshuku:** *New Echizen,* Shuku, Mikuni-machi, 80 r., SP; *Nagata-so,* Miyama, Mikata-cho, 80 r.; *Itaya,* in Obama, Anoukaigan, 85 r., SP; *Yoshioka,* in Shuku, Mikuni-machi, 50 r., SP. – YOUTH HOSTELS: *Fukui YH,* 31-2, Nishitani-cho, 80 b.; *YH Fukui Fujin-Seinen Kaikan,* 3-11-17, Ote, 40 b.

TRANSPORTATION. – **Air:** from TOKYO (Haneda Airport) to Komatsu (1 hour), then bus to Komatsu Station (10 minutes) and train from there to Fukui (30 minutes). – **Rail:** from TOKYO (Central Station) JNR Tokaido–Shinkansen line to Maibara (3½ hours), then JNR Hokuriku line (1 hour); from OSAKA JNR Kosei line and Hokuriku line (2½ hours).

Fukui, chief town of a prefecture, situated on the N coast of central Honshu, is one of the main centers of the Japanese textile industry. The manufacture of silk here dates back to the 10th c. During the 17th c. Fukui was a place of some consequence as a seat of the Mat-sudaira family, the first of whom was the daimyo Matsudaira Hideyasu.

SIGHTS. – On a hill ¾ mile/1 km SW of the station is **Asuwayama Park** (or *Atagoyama Park*), from which there is a fine view of the town and Mount Kakusan. In the park stands the *Fujishima Shrine,* dedicated to Nitta Yoshisada (d. 1338), who supported the Southern Dynasty of the Emperor Godaigo. Near by can be found a **Historical Museum,** a **Regional Museum** and a *Botanic Garden.* – The **Okajima Memorial Gallery,** ¾ mile/1 km N of the station, houses a private art collection.

SURROUNDINGS. – The principal sight in the neighborhood of the town is the **Eiheiji Temple,** one of the two principal temples of the Soto sect, in the little village of *Shibidani,* 10 miles/16 km E (rail service on Keifuku private line; also buses). Within the temple precincts are more than 70 buildings, including the seven principal buildings (*shichido-garan*) of a complete temple complex. The site of the temple (founded 1243), planted with centuries-old cedars, was presented by the provincial governor of the day, Hatano Yoshishige, to the Zen priest Dogen (posthumously known as Joyo-daishi).

The temple enclosure is entered by the *Dragon Gate* (Ryu-mon), beyond which a flight of stone steps leads up to the *Chokushi-mon* Gate, which can be entered only by emissaries of the Emperor (doors with the Imperial emblem). From here visitors go left by way of the temple offices to the *Chushaku-mon* Gate, between the two-storey main gate, **Sammon** (1749), and the **Butsuden** (Buddha Hall), originally built in 1338. This hall, in the center of the main group of seven buildings, contains the statues of the Buddhas of the Three Worlds (Sanzebutsu); restored in 1902, it is the finest building within the temple precincts. Beyond this is the Dharma Hall, *Hatto*, which can accommodate a congregation of 1000; rebuilt in 1843, it is, like the Butsuden, a fine example of the architecture of the Sung period (10th–13th c.). To the right of the Buddha Hall are the kitchen and refectory, Ku-in (vegetarian meals), to the left the Meditation Hall, *Sodo* (or Zazen-do), built in 1902 on the model of a Zen temple of the Sung period (open to visitors only when not in use). Obliquely beyond this (turn left twice at the Hatto) is the Founder's Hall (*Joyo-den*), a memorial to Dogen and other abbots of the temple as well as to the founder, Hatano (services in honour of Dogen begin at 2 a.m.). Also in the main group of buildings are the bath-house, *Yokushitsu* (to right of main gate), and the lavatory (to left). When using either of these establishments monks must refrain from speech and devote themselves to contemplation. – Among the art treasures in the temple are pictures and sculpture, including a * * painting by Dogen. Near the entrance is the *Temple Museum.*

7½ miles/12 km N of Fukui is **Maruoka** (JNR Hokuriku line). Outside the town (bus service) is *Maruoka Castle (or *Kasumi-ga-jo*, "Castle in the Clouds"), one of the oldest surviving castles in Japan, built in 1575 by Shibata Katsuie, one of Oda Nobunaga's generals. – 19 miles/30 km farther NW (Keifuku private railway to Mikuni-Minato, then bus) is the beautiful coastal area of *Tojimbo*, with columnar basalt formations up to 295 ft/90 m high. Offshore, linked with the mainland by a bridge, lies the island of **Ojima**, on which there is a small shrine (boat trips around the island). This stretch of coast is in the *Echizen-Kaga-kaigan Quasi National Park.*

Fukuoka

Prefecture: Fukuoka. – Population: 1,110,000.
Post code: J-810-815. – Telephone code: 092.

(i) (central)
Fukuoka-ken Tokyo Kanko Bussan Assensho,
Kokusai Kanko Kaikan,
1-8-3, Marunouchi, Chiyoda-ku,
J-100 **Tokyo**;
tel. (03) 231 1750.

(local)
Fukuoka City Tourist Information Office,
JNR Hakata Station,
Chuo-guchi Office;
tel. 431 3003.
Chikushi-guchi Office;
tel. 451 5731.

HOTELS. – **Western style**: *Hakata Green Hotel*, 4-4, Chuo-gai, Hakata-eki-higashi, 500 r.; *Central Hotel*, 12, Watanabe-dori 4-chome, Chuo-ku, 361 r.; *Hakata Zennikku Hotel*, 3-3, 3-chome, Hakata-ekimae, Hakata-ku, 358 r., Japanese garden, SP; *Nishitetsu Grand Hotel*, 6-60, Daimyo 2-chome, Chuo-ku, 308 r., Japanese garden, SP; *Hakata UI Hotel*, 15, 3-chome, Hakata-ekimae, Hakata-ku, 320 r.; *Hokke Club Fukuoka-ten*, 3-1-90, Sumiyoshi, Hakata-ku, 303 r.; *Hakata Miyako Hotel*, 2-1-1, Hakataeki Higashi, 269 r.; *Hakata Tokyu Hotel*, 1-16-1, Tenjin, Chuo-ku, 266 r.; *Tokyo Dai-ichi Hotel Fukuoka*, 5-2-18, Nakasu, Hakata-ku, 229 r.; *Hotel Rich Hakata*, 3-27-15, Hakata-ekimae, Hakata-ku, 178 r.; *Hakata Shiroyama Hotel*, 5-3-4, Nakasu, Hakata-ku, 118 r.; *Fukuoka Oriental Hotel*, 12-17, Nishi-nakazu, Chuo-ku, 118 r.; *Hakata Dai-ichi Hotel*, 2-1-17, Hakata-eki-higashi, 117 r.; *Hotel Takakura*, 2-7-21, Watanabe-dori, Chuo-ku, 60 r.; *Business Heiwadai Hotel*, 1-3-26, Otemachi, Chuo-ku, 30 r. – **Ryokan**: *New Taisei Hotel*, 5-4-11, Nakasu, Hakata-ku, 114 r.; *Fukuoka Hotel*, 2-9-3, Takasago, Chuo-ku, 40 r.; *Fukuoka Kanko Hotel Marumeikan*, 5-6-1, Nakasu, Hakata-ku, 32 r.; *Ryokan Gekkoen*, 2-3-15, Kiyokawa, Chuo-ku, 24 r. – YOUTH HOSTELS: *Sefuri Yuai-sanso YH*, 1184-5, Shiiba, Nishi-ku, 50 b.; *Dazaifu YH*, in Dazaifu (SE of town), 1553-3, Dazaifu, 24 b.

ON TSUSHIMA ISLANDS. – **Western style**: *Tsutaya Hotel*, Izuhara-cho, 21 r. – **Ryokan**: *Ryukiso Bekkan*, Izuhara-cho, 17 r.; *Ryokan Kakiya*, Izuhara-cho, 14 r. – YOUTH HOSTELS: *YH Tsushima-Seizanji* (temple), 1453, Kokubu, Izuhara-machi, 16 b., beach; *Kita-Tsushima YH*, Otsu Sasuna, Kamigata-cho, 20 b., beach.

RESTAURANTS. – *Fuyo Bekkan*, 3-1-13, Tenjin, Chuo-ku; *Haginomiya-sanso*, 1-18-1, Takamiya, Minami-ku; *Royal*, 603, Naka, Hakata-ku; *Sangen Hakata Miyako Hotel-ten*, in Hakata Miyako Hotel, 2-2-1, Hakata-Higashi; *Shin Miura*, 21-12, Sekijoma-chi; *Wadamon*, 5-15, Nishi-Nakasu, Chuo-ku.

EVENTS. – *Tamaseseri* (contest for a ball which brings good luck; beginning of January), Hakozaki Shrine; *Hakata-dontaku* (ceremonial procession; beginning of May); *Hojo-e* (shrine festival; mid September), Hakozaki Shrine; *Annual Festival* (mid October), Sumiyoshi Shrine.

TRANSPORTATION. – **Air**: from TOKYO (Haneda Airport), 1½ hours; from OSAKA (1 hour). – **Rail**: from TOKYO (Central Station) JNR Tokaido-Shinkansen line via OSAKA (7 hours); local lines from Fukuoka into surrounding area. – **Bus**: from Fukuoka Station to city center (15 minutes); from airport to station (15 minutes). – **Boat**: ferry service to island of Iki (2¾ hours); to Izuhara, Tsushima Islands (5 hours). – *Subway* under construction.

*Fukuoka, chief town of a prefecture and Japan's tenth largest city, is the administrative, economic and cultural center of the island of Kyushu and one of the most progressive cities in the S of Japan. Situated in Hakata Bay, it is the northern gateway to Kyushu.**

The territory of present-day Fukuoka is divided into two by the River *Naka*. Hakata, the older eastern part of the town, was formerly known as Nanotsu, a port and commercial center. To the W of Hakata the castle town of Fukuoka grew up in the 17th c. The two towns were amalgamated in 1889, but Hakata is still mainly the business center, while banks and administrative offices are concentrated in Fukuoka. The city's principal products are electrical appliances, tools, textiles and foodstuffs; it is also famed for its porcelain dolls (Hakata-ningyo).

HISTORY. – Archaeological excavations in northern Kyushu indicate that as early as the 2nd c. B.C. this area had contacts with China, one result of which was the introduction of rice-growing. During the T'ang period (618–906) Nanotsu (Hakata), like Bonotsu (Kagoshima prefecture) and Anotsu (Mie prefecture), was an important commercial port. After the unification of Japan in the 7th c. the central government established an administrative and military base at Dazaifu, SE of the present town, which controlled Kyushu and its foreign contacts until the 14th c. – In 901 Sugawara Michizane (845–903), Chancellor of the Right at the Imperial Court in Kyoto, was stripped of his functions as a result of intrigues by the Fujiwara family and relegated to the Governor-Generalship of Dazaifu. When he died he left collections of Chinese poems (Kanke-bunso, Kanke-koso) and historical writings. He is now revered throughout Japan as the god of literature.

In the second half of the 13th c. Fukuoka was the scene of bitter fighting against the Mongol forces of Kublai Khan. A first attempt at invasion by the Mongols in 1274 was beaten off, but in 1281 they returned to the attack with an army of 100,000 men. The invaders were brought to a halt by a defensive wall 10 ft/3 m high which had been built between Hakozaki and Imazu in Hakata Bay, and a sudden typhoon (subsequently named kamikaze, the "divine wind") destroyed the whole Mongol fleet. – Fukuoka Castle was constructed by Kuroda Nagamasa in 1607.

SIGHTS. – ¾ mile/1 km NW of Hakata Station (Fukuoka's main station, SE of the city center) is the Shofukuji Temple, the oldest Zen temple in Japan; it is believed to have been founded in 1195 by a priest named Eisai (1141–1215) at the behest of Minamoto Yoritomo. Eisai had brought Zen Buddhism to Japan from the Court of the Sung dynasty in China. The temple, which belongs to the Rinzai sect, has a *bronze bell of Korean type.

A little way N of the temple lies Higashi Park (the Eastern Park; area 80 acres), with a monument commemorating the two Mongol invasions and statues of Nichiren (1222–82), founder of the sect named after him, and the Emperor Kameyama (1249–1305). – Farther N is the Hakozaki Shrine (or Hakozaki-Hachiman Shrine; tram from station), one of the best-known Hachiman shrines in Japan, founded in 923. The *Prayer Hall

(Haiden) and Main Hall (Honden) were built in 1546, the stone *torii in 1609. The two-storey gate-tower, built entirely of wood without the use of a single nail, dates from 1594. The temple festivals are Tamaseseri (January) and Hojo-e (September).

Some ½ mile/800 m SW of Hakata Station is the *Sumiyoshi Shrine, one of the oldest shrines on Kyushu, which, like the one at Osaka, is dedicated to the protective divinities of seafarers. Particularly impressive is the main building, in classical style (rebuilt 1623). From the shrine, which is surrounded by a grove of Japanese cedars and camphor trees, there is a fine *view of the River Naka. The shrine festival in October includes displays of sumo wrestling.

Fukuoka Center

Some ¾ mile/1200 m NW of the Sumiyoshi Shrine, in the administrative banking and commercial district of TENJIN-CHO, stands the **Historical Museum** (*Kyushu Rekishi-shiryokan*; beyond the Tokyu Hotel), with an excellent collection of material, mainly of the Jomon, Yayoi and Kofun periods. In this part of the town is the station of the Nishitetsu private railway line (to Dazaifu). – To the E, on an island between two arms of the River Naka, lies the district of NAKASU, the entertainment quarter of Fukuoka, with many cinemas, restaurants and other places of entertainment.

Following the river downstream we come to **Hakata Harbor**, in Hakata Bay. From *Hakata Pier* there are ferry services to the islands of Iki, Tsushima and Hirado, the Goto Archipelago and Yobuko and Shikanoshima. Near here is the **Hakata Playland** leisure complex (tram from Hakata Station), with a hotel, an outlook tower with a revolving platform, etc.; hovercraft trips in the bay.

On the coast W of the harbor (3 miles/ 4·5 km from the station) is **Nishi Park** (the **Western Park**), in which are the ruins of the old defensive wall and some 4000 cherry trees; from the hills there are fine *views of the bay. – Some ½ mile/ 800 m S of this park (bus from station) is **Ohori Park**, with the remains (gate and watch-tower) of **Maizuru Castle**, a stronghold of the Kuroda family. In the western part of the park, in a large lake (rental of boats), are three islands linked by bridges. On the shores of the lake

The Temmangu Shrine ...

... in Dazaifu

stands the **Fukuoka Museum of Art**, with items which belonged to the Kuroda family, Buddhist works of art, utensils for the tea ceremony and modern art. A gold seal of A.D. 57, a present from China to the then ruler of Na (a province of Japan) which was excavated in Hakata Bay in 1874, is now in the National Museum in Tokyo. In the eastern part of the park are various sports facilities. – To the W of the park is the **Kinryuji Temple**, with the tomb of Kaibara Ekiken (1630–1714), whose Confucian writings remained influential into the 19th c.

SURROUNDINGS of Fukuoka

To the N of the city the **Shikanoshima Peninsula** extends westward for some 7½ miles/12 km and encloses Hakata Bay. The beautiful coastal area of *Uminonakamichi*, ending at *Cape Saitozaki*, is fringed by pine woods and has long sandy beaches. Ferry service from Fukuoka to *Saitozaki* (20 minutes); also buses (1 hour).

The coast to the N of Fukuoka is part of the **Genkai Quasi National Park** (area 43 sq. miles/111 sq. km), which extends for 55 miles/90 km along the S side of the *Genkai-Nada Sea* (Fukuoka and Saga prefectures). The coast and the 20 or so offshore islands have beaches of white sand, bizarre rock formations and picturesque groves of pines, and from the cliffs there are beautiful views of the sea and the Tsushima Islands to the NW. The basalt rocks, eroded by the heavy surf, give the coastal scenery a particular charm; and here and there can be seen remains of the defensive wall built to provide protection from Mongol attack. At the W end of the **Itoshima Peninsula** is the *Keya-no-Oto* Cave (bus from Hakata Station), gouged out of a 200 ft/60 m-high cliff. In calm weather boats can penetrate into the cave for a distance of 55 yds/50 m through an entrance 30 ft/9 m high and 60 ft/18 m wide.

Some 9 miles/14 km S of Fukuoka (reached by bus or the Nishitetsu railway line) is the resort of *Futsukaichi* and beyond this **Dazaifu**, which was the seat of the governor-general of Kyushu from the early 7th to the 14th c. Dazaifu has close associations with Sugawara Michizane (845–903), who spent the last years of his life here and prayed for the Emperor Daigo on Mount

Tempaizan (846 ft/258 m); as the god Tenjin he is particularly revered by schoolchildren and students.

According to tradition the animals transporting Michizane's body stopped at the spot where the **Dazaifu-Temmangu Shrine** was built in 905. The present buildings date from 1590. Within the precincts of the shrine are several hundred plum trees and in front of the prayer-hall is the Tobi-ume ("flying plum tree"), which is said to have flown through the air from Michizane's garden in Kyoto. The temple possesses writings and other objects belonging to Michizane. Shrine festivals on January 7 (at night) and September 23–25.

¾ mile/1 km W of the shrine is the ** **Kanzeonji Temple**, belonging to the Tendai sect. Built in 746, this was once the center of Buddhism on Kyushu. In spite of repeated destruction – the present buildings date from 1690 – the temple has preserved a * bell of the Nara period and some fine examples of * sculpture of the Heian and Kamakura periods, including statues of Batto-kannon, goddess of mercy, and Kichijo-ten, goddess of good fortune. To the W of the temple are the excavated foundations of the former governor's residence, Tofuro.

To Iki and the Tsushima Islands. – There are regular ferry services from Hakata Harbor to these islands, which lie within Nagasaki prefecture.

10 miles/16 km N of Fukuoka we come to **Iki** (area 54 sq. miles/139 sq. km; pop. 44,000; crossing time 2 hours 40 minutes). The main sources of income of this hilly and wooded island are fishing and farming. Near the port of **Gonoura**, in the SW of the island, are the remains of a *castle* built by Toyotomi Hideyoshi in 1592–95 during his Korean campaigns. – In the N of the island (bus service) the town of **Shinjo** has a shrine dedicated to Taira Kagetaka, Governor of Iki, who died fighting the Mongols.

There is also a ferry service from Fukuoka to the **Tsushima Islands**, 40 miles NW of Iki. The southern island, Shimo, is separated from its northern neighbor, Kami, by the *Manzeki Strait*, now spanned by a bridge. Since the 4th c., when Japan gained control of part of southern Korea, the islands have been regarded as a bridge to the mainland of Asia. The main source of revenue for the 56,000 inhabitants is fishing.

The port of **Shimo** (area 95 sq. miles/247 sq. km) is **Izuhara** (ferry from Fukuoka, 5 hours; by air 30 minutes), for 700 years a castle town belonging to the princely So family, whose tombs are in the Banshoin Temple. On the outskirts of the town are the remains of the old castle; there are also remains of some old samurai houses. – Beautiful and much-indented coasts, particularly in Aso Bay, between the two islands.

The largest settlement on **Kami** (area 168 sq. miles/435 sq. km) is **Kami-Tsushima**, in the N of the island. The rugged coasts on either side of the town, with many small coves, are strikingly beautiful.

Gifu
See under Nagoya

Goto Islands
See under Saikai National Park

Hagi
はぎ

Prefecture: Yamaguchi. – Population: 55,000.
Post code: J-758. – Telephone code: 08382.
(i) (central)
Yamaguchi-ken Tokyo Kanko Bussan Assensho,
Kokusai Kanko Kaikan,
1-8-3, Marunouchi, Chiyoda-ku,
J-1000 **Tokyo;**
tel. (03) 231 4980.

HOTELS. – **Western style:** *Hagi Grand Hotel*, 25, Huruhagi-cho, 150 r. – **Ryokan:** *Hagi Tanaka Hotel*, Koshigahama, 97 r.; *Hagi Kokusai Kanko Hotel*, Rakutenchi, Koshigahama, 92 r.; *Hagi Kanko Hotel*, Koshigahama, 86 r. – **Minshuku:** *Senjuan*, 351, Hijiwara, 60 r.; *Shigeeda Ryokan*, 58, Hashimoto-cho, 40 r. – YOUTH HOSTEL: *Hagi Shizuki YH*, 109-22, Jonai, Horinouchi, 74 b.

EVENTS. – *Mandarin Blossom Festival* (May–June).

TRANSPORTATION. – **Rail:** from TOKYO (Central Station) JNR Sanyo-Shinkansen line to Ogori (6 hours). – **Bus:** from Ogori to Hagi; from YAMAGUCHI to Hagi; from TSUWANO to Hagi.

The quiet fishing town and port of Hagi lies in south-western Honshu at the mouth of the River Abu, which here flows into the Sea of Japan. Its narrow little streets still preserve much of the atmosphere of the past. Situated on a beautiful stretch of coast against a backdrop of green hills, Hagi is an attractive town, with the additional interest of a 300-year-old tradition of pottery manufacture which is still maintained today.

HISTORY. – At the beginning of the 17th c. Mori Terumoto (1553–1625), having been exiled from Yamaguchi, settled in Hagi, then a fishing village situated in a marshy area overgrown with reeds, and in 1604 built a castle which was to be the seat of his family for 263 years. Terumoto brought in Korean potters who laid the foundations of the craft in which Hagi later gained a leading place. In 1857–60 the patriot Yoshida Shoin (1831–60) was a teacher in the town, and his school produced a number of major statesmen of the Meiji period – Kido Koin (1834–77), Yamada Akiyoshi (1844–92) and Ito Hirobumi (1841–1909), first Prime Minister of the Meiji era. The 1000 yen banknote bears Ito's portrait.

SIGHTS. – A good way of seeing the town is by bicycle (which can be rented at the station). Some 3 miles/4·5 km from the Higashi-Hagi Station is **Shizuki Park**, on the way to which are numerous potters' workshops (Shiroyama, Shogetsu, Hagijo). In the park are ramparts and moats, relics of the castle built in 1604 which was destroyed during the Meiji Reform in 1871, together with the *Shizuki Shrine* and the *Hananoe-tei* tea-house (1889).

Some ¾ mile/1·2 km SE of the station is the **Shoin Shrine**, dedicated to Yoshida Shoin, who taught in a school within the precincts of the shrine (Shoka-sonjuku) until his execution by the Tokugawa Shogunate. Near the shrine are the workshops of the famous potters Miwa, Shodo, Renkozan and Saka. The simple forms of this pottery, with its milk-white to rose-pink glaze, soon came into favor for the tea ceremony, and Hagi-yaki ware is still much sought after.

Shoin Shrine

¾ mile/1 km E of the Shoin Shrine is the **Tokoji Temple**, in Chinese Buddhist style, built in 1691. Here is the burial-place of the Mori family, decorated with some 500 stone lanterns.

1½ miles/2·5 km SW of the station are the old *Kikuya*, *Iseya* and *Edoya* Streets, in which can be seen a number of old

Tokoji Temple

samurai houses, including one which belonged to Kido Koin, first Prime Minister of the Meiji period.

1½ miles/2·5 km NE of the station is the *Senrusan* pottery workshop, with old kilns (open to visitors).

SURROUNDINGS. – 3 miles/5 km N of the station lies the **Koshigahama Peninsula**, with the extinct volcano of *Kasayama* (367 ft/112 m). To the E of this, in an area of great natural beauty, are the Myojin Lagoon and a small lake, *Myojin-ike*. This coastal region, together with the coast W of Hagi, forms the **Kita-Nagato-kaigan Quasi National Park** (area 31 sq. miles/80 sq. km), which also includes some 60 islands. The largest of these is **Omishima** (area 7 sq. miles/18 sq. km), to the W of Hagi, which is linked with the mainland by a bridge (JNR San-in line from Hagi to Senzaki, then bus to Odomari, on the island). It is well worth making an excursion to the island for the sake of its beautiful and varied scenery. The chief place on the island is *Ohibi*, with the Saienji Temple (separate entrances for men and women). In the "Whales' Tomb" (1962) in the Seigetsuan Temple, in accordance with an old custom, embryos found in the bodies of whales caught by the local fishermen were buried. – There are 2-hour trips round the island from *Senzaki*.

Another attractive excursion from Hagi is to the large limestone cave of **Akiyoshi-do**, SW of the town, one of the many stalactitic caves on the Akiyoshi Plateau. The cave system, some 6 miles/10 km long, is open to visitors for a distance of ¾ mile/1 km (bus from Hagi via Yuda-onsen). – It is possible (and worth while) to continue by bus via **Yamaguchi** (see separate entry) to *Ogori*, on the Shinkansen line from Hiroshima to Kyushu.

Hakodate
はこだて

Prefecture: Hokkaido. – Population: 321,000.
Post code: J-040. – Telephone code: 0138.
ⓘ (central)
Hokkaido Tokyo Kanka Bussan Assensho,
Kokusai Kanko Kaikan,
1-8-3, Marunouchi, Chiyoda-ku,
J-100 **Tokyo**;
tel. (03) 214 2481.

(local)
Tourist Section of the City,
4-13, Shinonome-cho;
tel. 23 6161.
Japan Travel Bureau,
in Wako department store,
20-1, Wakamatsu-cho;
tel. 22 4185.

HOTELS. – **Western style:** *Hotel Hakodate Royal,* 16-9, Omori-cho, 117 r.; *Hakodate Kokusai Hotel,* 5-10, Ote-machi, 131 r. – YOUTH HOSTEL: *Hokusei-so YH,* 1-16-23, Yunokawa-machi, 42 b.

EVENTS. – *Cherry Blossom Festival* (beginning of May); *Port Festival* (beginning of August), with fireworks and folk-dancing; *Summer Festival* (second Saturday in August), in Yunokawa-onsen.

TRANSPORTATION. – **Air:** from TOKYO (Haneda Airport), 1½ hours; from SAPPORO (Okadama Airport), 40 minutes. – **Rail:** from TOKYO (Ueno Station) to Omiya (30 minutes), then JNR New Tohoku–Shinkansen line (7 hours); also JNR Tohoku line to Aomori (8½ hours), then ferry; from SAPPORO JNR Hakodate line (4½ hours). – **Boat:** ferry from Aomori to Hakodate.

The port of Hakodate lies at the S end of the Oshima Peninsula on the Tsugaru Strait, which separates the islands of Honshu and Hokkaido. It is the southern gateway to Hokkaido and its third largest town. The city, dominated on the S by Mount Hakodate, contains many features of historical interest.

Hakodate is the principal center of the Japanese fisheries in the North Pacific (fishing season July to December). The city's other industries are closely bound up with the fisheries – shipbuilding, fish-processing plants, etc.

HISTORY. – The name of the town is first recorded in the 15th c. in connection with the building of a castle by the Kono family. Hakodate is thus older than the city of Sapporo. Commodore Perry, who opened up Japan to foreign trade, visited the town in 1854, and in the following year, under the Treaty of Kanagawa, it became a supply point for foreign ships. In 1859, under the peace treaty between Japan and the United States, Hakodate and four other ports were authorized to trade with foreign countries. Thereafter it developed into the principal port on Hokkaido, and as late as 1930 had a larger population than the island's capital, Sapporo.

View of Hakodate

SIGHTS. – Near the station is the interesting market (held every morning except Sunday), with some 600 stalls. – 2 miles/ 3 km SW of the station (bus) rises Mount **Hakodate** (1099 ft/335 m), from which there is a magnificent * view (particularly fine at night) of the harbor bay and the Tsugaru Strait. The hill was formed by the eruption of a submarine volcano; its highest point is the northern peak, *Gotenyama*. From 1899 to the end of the Second World War the hill formed part of the town's fortifications; thereafter it became a popular place of recreation.

From the foot of the hill a *cableway* runs up to the summit where a fine **viewpoint** affords an extensive prospect of the Sea of Japan, the Pacific and the island of Honshu. Set in the wall is a bust of Ino Tadataka (1745–1818), who produced the first reliable map of Japan. – On the summit can be seen a monument to Thomas W. Blakiston (1832–91), who lived in Japan from 1861 to 1884 and built up a large ornithological collection (now in the Botanic Garden in Sapporo). Blakiston discovered that the Tsugaru Strait marked the line of division (now known as the Blakiston Line) between different animal species.

On the eastern slopes of the hill 1½ miles/ 2·5 km from station; tram to Aoyagicho stop) is **Hakodate Park**, renowned for the beauty of its numerous cherry and plum trees. – In the park are the *Municipal Library* and the **Hakodate Museum** (*Hakubutsukan*), opened in 1879 on the initiative of Horace Capron (1804–85), an American adviser who was involved in the colonization of Hokkaido. It contains works by the well-known poet Ishikawa

Takuboku (1886–1912), prehistoric material and exhibits illustrating Ainu culture. – Adjoining the museum, in old timber buildings, are the *Museum of Archaeology* and the *Museum of Fisheries*.

Farther SE (¾ mile/1 km from the Yachigashira tram stop) is *Cape Tachimachi*, from which there are fine views of the sea. Near by are the tombs of three poets, Yosano Akiko and Hiroshi (husband and wife) and Ishikawa Takuboku.

In the MOTOMACHI district, 2½ miles/ 4 km SW of the station (tram to Suehirocho stop, then 10 minutes' walk) stands the Russian Orthodox *Church of the Resurrection*, founded in 1862 by a Russian priest named Nikolay (1836–1912); the present building, in Byzantine style, dates from 1916. The church is not open to visitors. – 3 minutes' walk from the tram stop is the *Kyodo-shiryokan* (1880), a local museum, and near this the *Kyu-Hakodate-Kokaido* (Civic Hall), built in 1910. From here it is a 20 minutes' walk to the **Koryuji Temple** (1633), believed to be the oldest temple on Hokkaido. Near this, on the outskirts of the town, is the *Gaijin Bochi Foreigners' Cemetery* (fine * view of the harbor area). – A walk through Motomachi (about 2 miles/3 km) will reveal a number of old Western-style houses built after the opening-up of the port to foreign shipping.

2 miles/3 km NE of the station (bus, 15 minutes) we come to* **Fort Goryokaku**, a star-shaped structure based on European models. It was designed by Takeda Ayasaburo, who had made a thorough study of Dutch military engineering. Completed in 1864 after a building period of eight years, the fort was intended to protect the town, then controlled by the Tokugawa dynasty. Here in 1868 Admiral Enomoto Takeaki (1836–1908), a supporter of the Tokugawa Shogunate, made a last vain attempt to oppose the Imperial forces. The walls and moats of the old fort now enclose a park which attracts large numbers of visitors during the cherry-blossom season in May. Near the fort are a 200 ft/ 60 km high *outlook tower* and a small *museum* with relics of the fighting in 1868.

SURROUNDINGS of Hakodate

4¼ miles/7 km E (trams and buses from station) lies the idyllic spa of **Yunokawa-onsen** (hot springs at temperatures of up to 151 °F/66 °C), one of the oldest spas on Hokkaido, frequented since 1654. 2 miles/ 3 km E of the town is a **convent of Trappist nuns** (buses from Yunokawa-onsen and Hakodate), founded in 1898, which produces butter and cheeses of typical Hokkaido type.

30 miles/50 km E of Hakodate (bus, 2¼ hours) rises Mount **Esan** (2028 ft/618 m), at the south-eastern tip of the Oshima Peninsula. From the summit of this still-active volcano there are superb views of the surrounding countryside. The mountain vegetation includes some 150 rare species. To the SE is **Cape Esan**, with the resorts of *Esan-onsen* and *Ishida-onsen*.

To the N of Hakodate (JNR Hakodate line, 17 miles/ 27 km) extends the **Onuma Quasi National Park** (area 37 sq. miles/95 sq. km), with Mount Koma and Lakes Onuma, Konuma and Junsai. Scattered about in the lakes are about a hundred small wooded islands. The best* view of this beautiful area is from Mount *Konuma*, between Lakes Konuma and Junsai. The largest of the three lakes, **Lake Onuma** is linked with Lake Konuma by a river; with a circumference of 12½ miles/20 km and a depth of 46 ft/14 m, it offers excellent fishing (trout, carp). There are attractive footpaths in the surrounding area. – SW of Lake Onuma, **Lake Konuma** (circumference 10 miles/16 km, depth 75 ft/23 m) has more than 30 small islands; fine * views from Mount **Higure** (994 ft/303 m). – NW of Lake Konuma is **Lake Junsai**, the smallest of the lakes (circumference 4½ miles/7·3 km), which is linked with Lake Konuma by the River *Yadonobe*. – The most northerly point in the park is Mount **Koma** (or *Komagatake*), an active volcano with three peaks, *Sahara* (3658 ft/1115 m), *Kengamine* (3740 ft/ 1140 m) and *Sumidamori* (2887 ft/880 m). The summit crater measures 1¼ miles/2 km from E to W and 1 mile/1·5 km from N to S. The lower slopes are covered with deciduous and coniferous trees, while above 1970 ft/600 m Alpine plants (including mountain azaleas) predominate. The volcano's conical form (best seen from the N) has earned it the name of Oshima-Fuji.

16 miles/26 km W of Hakodate (JNR Esashi line to Oshima-Tobetsu, then 30 minutes' walk) is a **Trappist monastery**, founded in 1895 by Okada Furie, a Frenchman who became a Japanese citizen. This and the convent of Trappist nuns at Yunokawa-onsen are the only Roman Catholic religious houses in Japan. Like the convent, the monastery makes dairy products.

The fishing port of **Esashi** (pop. 14,000), on the W coast of the Oshima Peninsula (52 miles/83 km from Hakodate; JNR Esashi line, 2 hours), had a population of some 30,000 in the Edo period. From this period it preserves a number of old houses, including the residences of the Nakamura and Yokoyama families (about 100 years old). In the little local museum are cannon from the warship "Kaiyomaru", which sank during a battle between Tokugawa and Imperial forces in 1868. – From the station there is a bus service to *Kaminokuni*, which is famous for its azalea blossom.

There are boat services from Esashi to the island of **Okushiri** (area 55 sq. miles/143 sq. km), 38 miles/ 61 km to the NW. This beautiful wooded island was formerly a penal colony. The 6300 inhabitants live mainly by fishing and farming. The island offers magnificent scope for fishermen and campers. From the coasts there are superb* views of the sea, the best viewpoints being *Nabetsuru-Iwa*, *Cape Inaho* (northern tip of the island) and *Cape Aonae* (southern tip). There is a popular beach at *Muenjima-kaigan*. The only health resort on the island is *Horonai-onsen* (to the S).

57 miles/92 km SW of Hakodate (JNR Matsumae line) is **Matsumae**, known as Fukuyama during the Edo period. Now a fishing port, it was then the only castle town (seat of the Matsumae family) on Hokkaido and the island's political center.

Hakone
はこね

Prefectures: Kanagawa and Shizuoka.
ⓘ (central)
　　Kanagawa-ken Tokyo Kanko Bussan Assensho,
　　Kokusai Kanko Kaikan,
　　1-8-3, Marunouchi, Chiyoda-ku,
　　J-100 **Tokyo**;
　　tel. (03) 231 3901.

HOTELS. – **Western style**: *Fujiya Hotel*, 359, Miyanoshita, 155 r., Japanese garden, SP, thermal bath; *Hotel Kowaki-en*, 1297, Ninotaira, 256 r., Japanese garden, SP, thermal bath; *Hakone Kanko Hotel*, 1245, Sengokuhara, 113 r., SP, thermal bath; *Yumoto Fujiya Hotel*, 256, Yumoto, 101 r., Japanese garden, SP, thermal bath; *Hakone Prince Hotel*, 144, Moto-Hakone, 238 r. (incl. cottages); *Yamano Hotel*, Moto-Hakone, 93 r.; *Hotel Kagetsu-en*, 1244 Itari, Sengokuhara, 73 r., Japanese garden, thermal bath; *Gora Hotel*, 1300, Gora 62 r., Japanese garden, thermal bath; *Odakyu Hakone Highland Hotel*, 940 Shinanoki, Sengokuhara, 60 r., Japanese garden; *Hakone Hotel*, 65, Hakone-machi, 34 r., Japanese garden. – **Ryokan**: *Tenseien*, Yumoto, 96 r.; *Chokoku-no-mori Hotel*, Ninodaira, 60 r.; *Ichinoyu*, Tonosawa, 21 r.; *Naraya Ryokan*, Miyanoshita, 23 r.; *Senkyoro*, Sengokuhara, 60 r.; *Suizanso*, Yumoto, 26 r. – YOUTH HOSTEL: *Hakone-Sounzan YH*, 1320, Goura, 28 b.

EVENTS. – *Ume-matsuri* (beginning of February), Plum Blossom Festival, Odawara; *Sakura-matsuri* (beginning of April), Cherry Blossom Festival, Odawara; *O-shiro-matsuri* (beginning of May), procession with old costumes, Odawara; *Kintoki-matsuri* (beginning of May), with climbing competition and "Lion Dance", Sengokuhara; *Tsutsuji-matsuri* (mid May), Azalea Festival, Kowakidani; *Kojo-sai* (end of July), Lake Festival in Hakone Shrine; *Taiko-hyotan-matsuri* (beginning of August), commemorating the siege of Odawara Castle in 1590, Miyanoshita; *Torii-matsuri* and *Ryuto-sai* (beginning of August), Festival of Lights on Lake Ashi; *Daimonji-yaki* (mid August), Festival of Lights, when the Chinese character for *dai* ("great") is displayed by torches on the hillside; *Daimyo-gyoretsu* (beginning of November), procession in historical costumes, Hakone-Yumoto.

TRANSPORTATION. – **Rail**: from TOKYO (Central Station) JNR Tokaido–Shinkansen line or JNR Tokaido line to Odawara (45 minutes or 1½ hours); from TOKYO (Shinjuku Station) Odakyu private line to Hakone-Yumoto via Odawara (1½ hours).

The Odakyu line offers an all-in ticket, the *Hakone Free Pass*, which covers the journey from Tokyo (Shinjuku Station) and travel in the Hakone area by the Hakone–Tozan railway, buses, cableways and boats.

The ** Hakone region, bounded on the N by Mount Fuji and on the S by the Izu Peninsula, is one of the most popular holiday areas in Japan, attracting large numbers of visitors in both summer and winter. It is a region of volcanoes and health resorts with a variety of sights of historical interest. One of its outstanding beauty-spots is Lake Ashi. The region lies within the Fuji-Hakone-Izu National Park.

Hakone lies within the crater area (circumference 25 miles/40 km) of a dormant

Excursion boat in the Hakone region

Transport Services in the Hakone Region

Hakone–Tozan Railway from Odawara via Hakone-Yumoto, Tonosawa, Miyanoshita and Kowakidani to Gora (about 1 hour).

Hakone–Tozan bus service from Odawara via Hakone-Yumoto, Tonosawa, Miyanoshita, Sengoku and Sengoku-kogen to Togendai (about 1 hour).

Izu-Hakone railway bus service from Odawara via Hakone-Yumoto, Tonosawa, Miyanoshita, Kowakien, Ashinoyu, Moto-Hakone, Hakone-machi, Gora, Sounzan, Owakudani and Ubako to Togendai (about 2 hours).

Izu-Hakone cableways from Hakone-en up Mount Komagatake (8 minutes). Also cableway from Gora to Togendai.

Boat services on Lake Ashi: from Hakonemachi, via Moto-Hakone and Hakone-en to Kojiri (about 45 minutes); from Hakonemachi via Moto-Hakone to Togendai (about 45 minutes).

Recommended tour: from Tokyo (Shinjuku Station) Odakyu line to Hakone-Yumoto; Hakone–Tozan line to Gora; cableway to Togendai; boat to Moto-Hakone; walk by way of the Hakone Museum to Hakonemachi; bus to Atami; JNR to Tokyo (about 6 hours).

---

volcano, Mount Hakone, the center of which collapsed some 400,000 years ago to form a caldera. Later eruptions formed the volcanoes of Kamiyama (4718 ft/1438 m), the highest peak in the Hakone region, Komagatake (4354 ft/1327 m) and Futago (3580 ft/1091 m). The crater lake became Lake Ashi, drained by the rivers Hayakawa and Sukumo, which have carved out romantic gorges.

The pleasant climate and excellent facilities for visitors make this a favorite recreation area for the people of Tokyo, Yokohama, Kobe and Osaka. The abundant thermal springs were already frequented by invalids seeking a cure during the Heian period (8th–12th c.). Many artists (including Ando Hiroshige) have depicted the beauty of the scenery. The traditional craft products of the Hakone region are wooden articles decorated with mosaic-work (*Hakone-zaiku*).

There are 17 communes (local government units) within the crater area. Among the many health resorts of old-established reputation the "twelve spas of Hakone" are particularly notable; the oldest of these resorts is Yumoto. The most popular places with foreign visitors, however, are Miyanoshita, Gora and Kowakidani, together with Tonosawa, Dogashima, Sokokura, Kiga, Ubako, Sengokuhara, Ashinoyu and Yunohanazawa.

Tour of Hakone

The following tour can easily be made by public transport, since the region is well served by railways, buses, cableways and boat services.

The starting-point is **Odawara** (pop. 170,000), which can be reached from Tokyo on the Shinkansen line or the Odakyu Electric Railway. This old castle town, once a stronghold of the Hojo family, lies in *Sagami Bay* below the E side of the Hakone Massif. During the Edo period it was regarded as one of the best defended points on the Tokaido Highway. 440 yds/400 m from the station (10 minutes' walk) stands the castle, the five-storey principal tower of which was restored in 1960 and now houses a museum (weapons, local history). Within the precincts of the castle, now laid out as a park, are a Zoo and a Museum of Folk Art. On the coast between Odawara and *Kozu* (the next-but-one station in the direction of Tokyo) there are good beaches. – 7½ miles/12 km NW (Izu–Hakone Railway) we reach *Daiyuzan*, from where there is a bus service (20 minutes) to the **Saijoji Temple** (also known as the *Doryoson*), on the NE slopes of the densely wooded Mount *Myojin* (3835 ft/1169 m). This is one of the largest temples of the Soto sect of Zen Buddhism. In the main hall is a statue of the Eleven-Headed Kannon.

To the W of Odawara (rail and bus services) is **Yumoto**, the oldest health resort in the region, situated at the junction of the rivers *Hayakawa* and *Sukumo*, with hot springs at temperatures of 95–133 °F/ 35–74 °C. This is the starting-point of the Daimyo-gyoretsu procession. S of the station can be seen the Sounji Temple of the Rinzai sect, founded by Hojo Soun (1432–1519), once one of the most important temples in eastern Japan. Toyotomi Hideyoshi had his headquarters here during the Siege of Odawara Castle (1590). Only a few buildings have been preserved. There is a fine * portrait on silk of the founder. Within the precincts of the temple are Hojo family tombs.

W of Yumoto, at the mouth of a beautiful gorge on the River *Hayakawa*, is

Tonosawa. 1¼ miles/2 km N (footpath, 40 minutes) is Mount *Tonomine* (1824 ft/ 556 m), with the *Amida Temple* (17th c.); beautiful view of the surrounding area.

7½ miles/12 km W of Odawara we come to **Miyanoshita**, a traffic junction and, together with Sokokura and Dogashima, one of the liveliest towns in the region. The climate is equable even in summer, and there are many thermal springs at temperatures of 143–172 °F/62–78 °C. There are good hotels and shops, and a dense network of roads and paths providing excellent facilities for both motorists and walkers. To the N of the station stands the Fujiya Hotel, the oldest Western-style hotel in Japan, open in 1878. S of the hotel is Mount *Sengen* (2631 ft/802 m) which can be climbed in an hour (fine view of Hakone). The route down on the western side of the hill passes the **Chisuji-no-taki Falls** towards *Kowakidani*. To the N of the hotel, beyond **Dogashima**, is Mount **Myojo** (3032 ft/ 924 m; 1½ hours' climb), on the slopes of which the Daimonji-yaki festival is celebrated on August 16.

550 yds/500 m NW of Miyanoshita is **Sokokura**, with the Kozan Park, which belongs to the Kozan-en-Tsutaya Ryokan. In the park are a monument to General Nitta Yoshinori (d. 1403) and an old bath-house which is said to have been used by Hideyoshi's troops during the Siege of Odawara. – From here a bus runs NW to *Sengokuhara*, in the middle of a dense forest in the Sengokuhara Plain. The plain is bounded on the N and W by the outer rim of the crater, with Mounts *Kintoki*, *Nagao* and *Maru*. There are 20 golf-courses in this area.

The **Kowakien Garden Leisure Center** near the *Kowakien-mae* bus stop (2 minutes from Kowakidani) has a *ryokan*, open-air baths, a Botanic Garden and a *Children's Village*. Close by is the Ryokan Mikawaya, with the *Horaien Garden*, which is famous for its azalea blossom (Azalea Festival in May). Other fine displays of azaleas are to be seen in the garden of the Yamano Hotel in Moto-Hakone and in Gora Park in Gora.

To the N of Kowakidani is **Gora** (2625 ft/ 800 m), on the eastern slopes of Mount *Sounzan*. From here there is a beautiful * view of the Upper Valley of the Hayakawa. From Owakudani (''valley of

Lake Ashi and Fujiyama

the great steam") hot water is piped to Gora. To the S of the town the *Hakone Open-Air Museum* (Chokoku-no-mori) houses sculpture by modern artists (Moore, Rodin, Bourdelle, etc.). SW of the town, in **Gora Park** (also famous for its azalea blossom), is the *Hakone Museum of Art* (Japanese and Chinese porcelain, old pictures).

From Gora a cableway runs W to the northern shore of Lake Ashi, with a number of intermediate stations. – The first section goes up to the **Sounzan** Station (change), near which is the Hakone-Sounzan Youth Hostel. – From an outlook terrace at **Owakudani** Station one can enjoy a fine* view of Mount Fuji. Near this station are numerous solfataras. The *Natural History Museum* (opened 1972) gives an excellent survey of the local plant and animal life and geology. – From **Ubako**, a remotely situated spa on the slopes of Mount *Kanmuri-gadake*, there is a bus service to Kojiri, on the N side of Lake Ashi. – The cableway ends at **Togendai**, on the northern shore of the lake. From here and from *Kojiri* there are boat services to Hakone-en, on the E side of the lake and to Moto-Hakone and Hakone-machi, on the S shore.

Lake Ashi, or *Lake Hakone* (alt. 2372 ft/ 723 m, circumference 11 miles/17·5 km, area 2¾ sq. miles/6·9 sq. km, depth 138 ft/ 42 m) is the most notable beauty-spot in

the Hakone region, renowned particularly for the view of Mount Fuji reflected in its waters. It also offers good fishing (trout, perch) and facilities for water sports. Along its W side runs a 7½ mile/12 km-long toll road, the *Ashinoko Skyline Drive*, from which there are fine* views of Mount Fuji and Sagami and Suruga Bays. – The busiest places at the N end of the lake are *Togendai* and *Kojiri*. The road along the E side leads to **Hakone-en** and the large **Hakone-en Park Leisure Center**, with swimming pools, ice-rinks, golf-courses and camp sites, an "International Village" with typical houses from 29 countries and an exhibition of folk art. To the NE is Mount *Komagatake* (4354 ft/1327 m), with cableways running up to the summit (ice-rink) from Hakone-en and from the SE side of the mountain; far-ranging * views of Mount Fuji and the Izu Peninsula. – Near Hakone-en, below the W side of the hill, is the *Hakone Picnic Garden*, with 140 log cabins and a camp site.

At the S end of the lake lies **Moto-Hakone** (bus services from Miyanoshita and Odawara, and from Yugawara, Atami, Mishima and Numazu, outside the Hakone region), one of the ports of call of the boats plying on the lake. Together with Hakone-machi, 1 mile/1·5 km S, it is an important tourist center. On a densely wooded hill NW of the town (footpath, 15 minutes) is the **Hakone Shrine** (or *Hakone-Gongen*), founded in 757 by a priest named Mangan and dedicated to the god Ninigi, his wife Konohana-sakuya-hime and their son Hiko-hohodemi. In the treasury adjoining the main hall can be seen a picture scroll on the foundation of the shrine, a wooden statue of the founder and a sword which belonged to Soga Goro, one of the Soga brothers who revenged their father's death and were themselves killed (12th c.). The shrine later became a place of refuge for Minamoto Yoritomo, who tried in 1180 to wrest power from the hands of the Taira family. The annual shrine festival is celebrated on July 31 and August 1.

From the old posting-station of Moto-Hakone there is a 1¼ mile/2 km long avenue of Japanese red cedars leading to **Hakone-machi.** This was once part of the Tokaido Highway from Kyoto to Tokyo and an important control point for the passage of the daimyos, who were required to appear before the Shogun in Edo every two years, their wives being kept in the capital as a guarantee of their loyalty to the Government. A little way outside the town (5 minutes' walk) are reconstructions of the *control post* and *guard-room*, originally built by the Tokugawa in 1618 to protect the capital, Edo (Tokyo), and closed down in 1869. Close by is the **Hakone Palace Garden**, originally belonging to an Imperial Villa. At the entrance is the **Historical Museum** (*Hakone-shiryokan*), with exhibits illustrating the history of the Tokaido Highway and the control post. Opposite the Hakone Hotel is the **Hakone Museum** (old coins, seals, documents, maps). The holiday region around Hakone-machi attracts many visitors both in summer and in winter.

From Hakone-machi the *Hakone Bypass* (bus service) returns through the beautiful Valley of the River *Sukumo* to Odawara.

Himeji
ひめじ

Prefecture: Hyogo. – Population: 450,000.
Post code: J-670. – Telephone code: 0792.
(i) (local)
Hyogo-ken Tourist Information Center,
Kenminkaikan,
4-57-4, Yamatedori,
Ikuta-ku,
J-650 **Kobe**;
tel. (078) 321 2958.

HOTELS. – **Western style:** *Himeji New Osaka Hotel,* 198-1, Ekimae-cho, 38 r.; *Himeji Castle Hotel,* 207, Hojo, 243 r. – **Ryokan:** *Banryu,* Shimodera-machi, 18 r. – YOUTH HOSTEL: *YH Tegarayama-Seinen-No-Ie,* 58, Nishi-nobuse, 48 b.

EVENTS. – *Rice-Planting Ceremony* (beginning of April) and *Spring Festival* (mid April), at Hiromine Shrine; *Kenka-matsuri* (mid October), with portable shrines which are banged noisily against one another in order to delight the gods, at Matsubara-Hachiman Shrine.

TRANSPORTATION. – **Rail**: from TOKYO JNR Sanyo–Shinkansen line via KOBE (4 hours); from HYOGO San-Yo private line (1 hour).

The town of Himeji, situated NW of Kobe in western Honshu, is the industrial and commercial center of the Himeji Plain and an important port on the Inland Sea. The ** castle, standing high above the town, is one of the few which have survived complete.

HISTORY. – The first castle in Himeji was built in 1333 by a member of the princely Akamatsu family to provide protection from the Hoyo clan. In 1581 it was the main base for Toyotomi Hideyoshi's campaigns of conquest in the Chugoku district, and in 1600 it became the seat of Ikeda Terumasa, one of Hideyoshi's generals, who in 1608 heightened the main tower to five storeys. The castle was extended to its present size between 1615 and 1624. It was restored in 1958–64.

SIGHTS. – In the heart of the town, conspicuously situated on Mount *Himeyama* (N of station; 10 minutes' walk), stands the ** **Shirasagi-jo Castle**, or *Hakuro-jo*, "Castle of the White Heron". It is the supreme achievement of medieval Japanese military architecture. The five-storey main tower is connected with the three-storey outer towers by a series of passages; altogether there are 38 separate buildings and 21 gates, the whitewashed façades contrasting effectively with the walls of grey stone. In the main tower is a collection of old arms and armor, and from the top storey there are fine * views of the

Castle of the White Heron, Himeji

surrounding area. The north-eastern part of the castle precincts is laid out as a park (particularly beautiful when the cherry trees are in blossom).

NW of the town (bus from station, 15 minutes) is the *Nagoyama Cemetery*, with a pagoda built in 1960 containing the ashes of Buddha, a present from the then Indian Prime Minister, Jawaharlal Nehru.

2 miles/3 km N of the station (bus, 25 minutes) is Mount *Hiromine* at the foot of which is a beautiful grove of plum trees, and on the summit is the *Hiromine Shrine*, founded in the 8th c. and dedicated to the storm god Susanoo and his son Itakeru, which attracts many worshippers, particularly to the shrine festivals.

SURROUNDINGS. – On Mount *Sosha* (1191 ft/363 m), 5 miles/8 km NW of the station (bus service), is the **Enkyo-ji Temple**, founded in 966 by a priest named Shoku, which was one of the three largest seminaries of the Tendai sect. From the top of the hill (cableway) there are extensive* views.

Half-way between Himeji and the port of *Aioi*, to the W, is the *Ikagura Temple* of the Tendai sect, founded by Shotoku (573–621), which contains fine sculpture and paintings. The three-storey pagoda dates from 1565.

10 miles/16 km E of Himeji (JNR Sanyo line) lies the town of **Kakogawa**. A short distance away (JNR Takasago line, 6 minutes), in an old cedar grove, stands the **Kakurin-ji Temple**, founded by Shotoku in 587. The finest of the temple buildings are the main hall (Hondo) and the Princes' Hall (Taishido). The temple festival is celebrated at the end of March. – At the end of the Takasago line (4 miles/6·5 km) is the town of **Takasago** (pop. 73,000), situated at the mouth of the River *Kako*, which here flows into the Harima-Nada Sea, the eastern part of the Inland Sea. Within the precincts of the Takasago Shrine (550 yds/500 m S of the station) grows a pine tree, descendant of an older pine which provided the inspiration for a No play named after the town.

Himeji

Shirasagi-jo

110 yards

A Hommaru   B Ninomaru   C Nishinomaru
D Harakirimaru   E Sannomaru

TOWERS
1 Daitenshu (main tower)
2 Higashi Kotenshu
3 Inui Kotenshu
4 Nishi Kotenshu

GATES
5 Bizemmon Gate
6 Hanomon Gate
7 Ronomon Gate
8 Inomon Gate
9 Hishinomon Gate

10 Well   11 Shrine   12 Himeyama Park

Hirado
See under Saikai National Park

Hiraizumi
ひらいずみ

Prefecture: Iwate. – Population: 10,000.
Post code: J-029-41. – Telephone code: 01946.
ⓘ (local)
Hiraizumi Machiyakuba Kankoka.
45-2, Hiraizumi Shirayama.

HOTELS. – **Ryokan:** *Hotel Hiraizumi Kinkei-so*, 28 r.; *Matsuda Ryokan*, 23 r.; *Ryoso Hana-Yakata*, 14 r. – **Minshuku:** *Chiba-so*, in Koromogawa, 13 r. – YOUTH HOSTEL: *Motsu-ji* (temple), 58, Osawa, 90 b.

EVENTS. – *Ennen no Mai* (mid January), dances of the Heian period, in Motsuji Temple; *Azuma Kudari Gyoretsu* (beginning of May), procession in historical costume to commemorate the flight of Minamoto Yoshitsune, between the Chusonji and Motsuji Temples; *performances of No plays* (May and October) at Hakusan Shrine; *Daimonji-okuribi* (mid August), lighting of fires in the form of the Chinese character meaning "great" on Mount Tabashine.

TRANSPORTATION. – **Rail:** from TOKYO (Ueno Station) JNR Tohoku line via SENDAI to Ichinoseki (5½ hours); from MORIOKA JNR Tohoku line to Ichinoseki (1 hour). – **Bus:** from Ichinoseki to Hiraizumi and the Chusonji Temple (30 minutes).

Hiraizumi is a sleepy little town in the Middle Valley of the River Kitagami, which flows through north-eastern Honshu. In the 12th c. it was the seat of a branch of the Fujiwara clan, and the famous Chusonji Temple was built during this period.

HISTORY. – In the 7th c. the Hiraizumi region was still inhabited by Ainu tribes. Towards the end of the 11th c. members of the Ou-Fujiwara family, a branch of the Fujiwara clan named after the old designation for Tohoku, settled here and in the course of four generations erected a series of buildings which were in no way inferior to those of Kyoto. The town's heyday lasted from 1090 to 1189.

The decline of the Ou-Fujiwara began when Minamoto Yoshitsune, fleeing from his brother Minamoto Yoritomo, was given shelter in Hiraizumi. After Fujiwara Yasuhira had killed the young Yoshitsune at Yoritomo's behest, Yoritomo took this as a pretext for a punitive expedition against the Ou-Fujiwara, in the course of which most of the buildings in Hiraizumi were destroyed (1189). Yasuhira, fleeing, was killed by his own people. Among the few surviving buildings in the town are the Chusonji and Motsuji Temples.

SIGHTS. – NW of the station (4 minutes by bus) is the large **Chusonji Temple**, founded in 1005 by the Fujiwara. In 1108 it comprised more than 40 buildings, but very few of these have survived.

The Golden Hall, *Konjiki-do* (or Hikari-do), a building only 18 ft/5·5 m square erected in 1109, is famous for its rich decoration. The outer walls were originally covered with lacquer and faced with gold leaf. To protect these the hall was rebuilt in 1288, and it is now contained within a modern concrete structure (1962–68); the interior has been restored. The inner chamber (Naijin) contains three altars, each with eleven Buddhist sculptures, together with three Amida statues, six Jizo statues and two Niten statues. Below the central altar are the mummified bodies of Fujiwara Kiyohira, Motohira and Hidehira. The main columns and beams are covered with lacquer, inlaid with mother-of-pearl and decorated with Buddhist pictures.

The Sutra Hall, *Kyozo*, is also of small size, measuring 18 ft/5·5 m square. Built in 1108, the building was originally of two storeys, but the upper floor was destroyed by fire in 1337. In the central chamber is an altar with a statue of Monju-bosatsu, god of wisdom. The 3000 sutra scrolls formerly kept here are now in the temple treasury, leaving in the Kyozo only a few lacquered scroll-cases inlaid with mother-of-pearl.

The Treasury, *Sankozo*, opposite the Golden Hall is a recent structure (1955). Here are preserved the temple's most precious possessions, including the coffins and grave-goods of members of the Fujiwara family, sculpture and liturgical utensils. – The museum in front of the temple, **Hiraizumi Bunkashi-kan**, contains further antiquities.

To the N of the temple is the **Hakusan Shrine**, with a *No theatre* (performances in May and October).

1 mile/1·5 km SE of the Golden Hall (¾ mile/1 km N of the station) a small hall, the **Yoshitsune-do**, stands on the site of Yoshitsune's house, in which he was murdered.

550 yds/500 m W of the station we come to the *Motsuji Temple*, founded in the 12th c., which in the time of the Fujiwara was the most important temple in the region. All that now survives, however, is some foundation walls and moats. After visiting the ruins the famous poet Basho wrote a well-known poem (haiku) on the transitoriness of mortal things. The temple garden, Jodo-Teien, is notable as one of the few examples of the "paradise pool" gardens of the Heian period.

SURROUNDINGS. – From the station a bus runs (20 minutes) to the cave of **Takkoku-no-Iwaya**, to the SW. Here Sakanoue-no-Tamuramaro (758–811), who had been sent to this region to repress rebel tribes, built a temple dedicated to the patron god of warriors, Bishamonten. The original building was burned down in 1946; the present temple is a reconstruction of 1961. In a crag near the cave is a figure of Dainichi Nyorai, probably carved in 1087. – A short distance SW is the enchantingly beautiful **Gembikei Gorge** (bus from Hiraizumi, 40 minutes), through which the River *Iwai* pursues a winding course.

To the S of Hiraizumi, reached by way of *Ichinoseki* (bus from Hiraizumi), is the extinct volcano of **Kurikoma** (5338 ft/1627 m; bus from Ichinoseki, 2¼ hours, to Sukawa-onsen, below the NW side, 3 hours), which lies at the junction of Iwate, Akita and Miyagi prefectures. The ascent from *Sukawa-onsen* (3 miles/5 km) takes 1½ hours. From the summit of this densely wooded mountain there are fine *views of the surrounding country.

E of Ichinoseki (JNR Ofunato line) is the **Rikuchu-kaigan National Park** (see separate entry).

Hirosaki

ひろさき

Prefecture: Aomori. – Population: 178,000.
Post code: J-036. – Telephone code: 0172.

(i) (central)
Aomori-ken Tokyo Kanko Bussan Assensho,
Kokusai Kanko Kaikan,
1-8-3, Marunouchi, Chiyoda-ku,
J-100 **Tokyo;**
tel. (03) 216 6010.

(local)
Aomori-ken Tourist Information Office,
1-1-1, Nagashima,
J-030 **Aomori;**
tel. (0177) 22 5080.

HOTELS. – **Western style:** *Hotel New Castle,* 24-1, Kami-Sayashi-machi, 61 r.; *Hirosaki Plaza Hotel,* 101-1, Daikan-cho, 73 r.; *Hirosaki Dai-ichi Hotel,* 7-1, Ekimae-machi, 33 r. – YOUTH HOSTEL: *Hirosaki YH,* 11, Mori-cho, 40 b.

EVENTS. – *Nebuta-matsuri* (beginning of July), a nocturnal procession with huge illuminated figures on decorated floats. The festival commemorates a strategem by which Sakanoue-no-Tamuramaro sought to deceive the enemy about the strength of his forces.

TRANSPORTATION. – **Rail:** from TOKYO (Ueno Station) JNR Ou line via AKITA (10 hours); from OSAKA JNR Hokuriku and Uetsu lines (13 hours); from AOMORI JNR Ou line (40 minutes).

The town of Hirosaki lies at the N end of Honshu, at the most southerly point of the Iwaki Basin, which extends northward up the Tsugaru Peninsula, and is enclosed on the S and W by high ground. This old castle town, once held by the Tsugaru family, is now the third largest town in Aomori prefecture, a university town and the cultural and economic center of the western part of the prefecture.

Around the town is a well known apple-growing area. Hirosaki is renowned for its lacquerware, produced here for the last 200 years, the quality of which depends on the application of up to 48 coats of lacquer.

SIGHTS. – In the center of the town (1¼ miles/2 km W of the station) is **Hirosaki Park** (or *Oyo Park*), in which are the remains of the **Tsugaru Castle** – five gates, an old wooden bridge and the main tower (1610). The tower contains a small collection of old arms and armor. The park has one of the best-known displays of cherry blossom in Japan (end of April to mid May). To the N of the park is the **Hachiman Shrine,** and 1 mile/1·5 km SW the 17th c. **Choshoji Temple.**

1 mile/1·5 km W of the station (bus, 10 minutes) stands the **Saishoin Temple,** with a fine five-storey pagoda built in 1672.

SURROUNDINGS. – 8 miles/13 km NW (bus, 40 minutes) lies the health resort of **Hyakuzawa-onsen,** with the magnificent Iwakiyama Shrine, originally built in 770–781; the present buildings date mainly from the 17th c. The rich decoration and appointments have earned the shrine the name of the "Nikko of the north". The shrine festival is celebrated at the beginning of August. – Above the town rises Mount **Iwaki** (5332 ft/1625 m), the summit of which can be reached by a panoramic road and a cableway. Here is the innermost sanctuary of the Iwakiyama Shrine. The mountain, regarded as the residence of a divinity, is visited by large numbers of believers between July 25 and August 15. The slopes of the mountain and the area around Hyakuzawa-onsen and *Dake-onsen* are popular with walkers and winter sports enthusiasts.

N of Hirosaki (10 minutes by rail) is *Kawabe,* from which a road leads SE to *Nenokuchi,* on the S side of *Lake Towada.* The lake lies within the **Towada-Hachimantai National Park** (see separate entry).

Hiroshima

ひろしま

Prefecture: Hiroshima. – Population: 905,000.
Post code: J-730. – Telephone code: 0822.

(i) (local)
Hiroshima City Tourist Information Office,
in Central Station,
Minami-ku;
tel. 61 1877 (English spoken).

HOTELS – **Western style:** *Hiroshima Grand Hotel,* 4-4, Kami-Hatchobori, 398 r., Japanese garden; *Hiroshima City Hotel,* 1-4, Kyobashi-cho, 171 r.; *Hiroshima Station Hotel,* 2-37, Matsubara-cho, 156 r.; *Hiroshima River Side Hotel,* 7-14, Kaminobori-cho, 92 r.; *Hiroshima Kokusai Hotel,* 3-13, Tate-machi, 84 r.; *Hokke Club Hiroshimaten,* 7-7, Nakamachi, 388 r.; *Hotel New Hiroden,* 14-9, Osugacho, 353 r.; *Tokyu Inn,* 17, Komachi-cho 3-chome, 286 r.; *Hotel Union,* 3-27 Inari-machi, 270 r.; *Hotel Silk Plaza,* 14-1, Hatchobori, 233 r.; *Hiroshima Central Hotel,* 1-8, Kanayama-cho, 137 r.; *Hotel Yamato,* 10-11, Matsubaracho, 84 r.; *Hiroshima Diamond Hotel,* 2-4-6, Kannonshinmachi, 80 r. – **Ryokan:** *Fuyo Besso,* Futabanosato, 23 r.; *Mitakiso,* Mitaki-cho, 16 r. – **Minshuku:** *Ikeda-ya,* 6-36, Dobashi-cho, 56 r., SP. – YOUTH HOSTELS: *Hiroshima YH,* 1-13-6, Ushitashin-machi, 104 b.; *Hiroshima Saka-Machi YH,* Ueda, Sakamachi, 25 b.

RESTAURANTS. – *Amagi,* 10-10, Kami-Noboricho; *Hanbei* (garden restaurant), 8-12, Hon-Uracho; *Hada Besso,* 26, Funairicho; *Hyotei,* 6-16, Dobashicho; *Sunday's Sun Ebisu-ten,* Ebisu Building, 4-1, Horikawacho; *Supper Club Shiro,* Chogin Building, Tatemachi.

EVENTS. – *Peace Festival* (August 6), commemorating the dropping of the atomic bomb; first celebrated in 1947.

TRANSPORTATION. – **Air:** from TOKYO (Haneda Airport), 1¼ hours. – **Rail:** from TOKYO (Central Station) JNR Sanyo–Shinkansen line via KYOTO and OSAKA (2 hours). – **Bus:** from Hiroshima Airport to city centre (35 minutes). – **Boat:** ferry service from OSAKA (Minami-ko Ferry Terminal) to Hiroshima (Dejima Harbor), 11½ hours; regular services to Kure, Takamatsu and Imabari (Shikoku).

Hiroshima, chief town of a prefecture, lies on the Inland Sea in western Honshu. Traversed by six arms of the River Ota, the city extends into Hiroshima Bay in the pattern of a human hand. Hiroshima gained a melancholy place in history when it became the target of an atomic bomb in 1945. Now rebuilt, it is the largest city and the administrative, educational and tourist center of the Chugoku district.

On the coast to the S of the town are large industrial installations (petrochemicals, metalworking, shipbuilding and

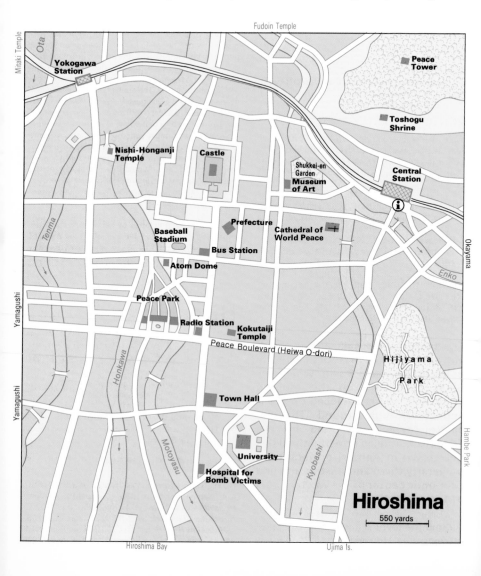

automobile manufacture, together with agricultural products and fish-processing).

HISTORY. – In 1593 Mori Terumoto (1553–1625) built a castle at the mouth of the Ota, naming it Hiroshima-jo ("far-stretching islands"); and this name soon began to be applied to the whole of the settlement which grew up here. The town was the seat of the Mori and Fukushima families and later of the Asano, who laid the foundations of its further development.

After the Asano family fell from power under the Meiji Reforms the harbor was enlarged by the municipality; and a further impetus was given to its town's development by the construction of the railway from Kobe to Shimonoseki, which passed through Hiroshima (1894). Conveniently situated as it was, Hiroshima became the Imperial Headquarters during the war with China in 1894–95; and the stationing of troops here during this war and later led to the establishment of various institutions and industrial installations in the town, which by 1940 had become Japan's seventh largest town, with a population of 344,000.

On August 6, 1945, at 8.15 a.m. local time, the United States Air force dropped the first **atomic bomb** on Hiroshima, completely destroying the city, killing an estimated 260,000 people and injuring more than 160,000. It was then thought that the site would remain uninhabitable for decades, but in fact reconstruction began in 1949, and by 1974 the city had doubled its pre-war population.

SIGHTS. – On the banks of the River *Ota* (770 yds/700 m W of the station, 5 minutes by bus) is the* **Shukkei-en Garden**, laid out by Asano Nagaakira in 1620 in imitation of the famous landscaped garden on the Western Lake of the old South Chinese capital of Hangchow (Sung dynasty). The pools and streams in the garden draw their water from the Ota. – 1¼ miles/2 km W of the station (bus, 10 minutes) stands the **Castle** (*Ri-jo*, "Castle of the Carp"), built in 1593, which became the residence of Fukushima Masanori in 1600 and passed into the possession of Asano Nagaakira in 1619. The five-storey main tower, reconstructed in 1958, contains a local museum. From the top floor there are fine *views of the city, the harbor and the island of Miyajima.

To the S of the Castle is the **Atom Dome**, the ruin of the Chamber of Industry and Commerce, which lay at the epicenter of the explosion (total destruction within a radius of 2 miles/3 km). – To the W, at the northern tip of an island lying between the *Honkawa* and the *Motoyasu,* two arms of the River Ota, is the **Peace Memorial Park** (buses and trams from station). In the park are the **Peace Memorial Hall,**

Park of Peace   **Hiroshima**

1 Miyekichi Suzuki	9 Children's Memorial
2 Tamiki Hara	10 Peace Flame
3 Students' Cenotaph	11 Cenotaph
4 Bell-Tower	12 Sculpture, "Prayer"
5 Peace Bell	13 Sankichi Tooge
6 Memorial to Unknown Victims	14 Prayer Fountain
7 Statue of Kannon	15 "Mother and Child in Storm"
8 Peace Foundation	16 Flower Clock

the **Peace Memorial Museum**, the Monument to the Victims of the Atomic Bomb, the *Civic Auditorium* and the New Hiroshima Hotel.

The **Monument to the Victims of the Atomic Bomb** was designed by the well-known architect Tange Kenzo. Through the concrete arch the Atom Dome can be seen. Under a stone slab is a list of the victims, and on the slab is the inscription "Rest in peace, for this error shall not be repeated."

From the S side of the Park of Peace the 330 ft/100 m wide *Peace Boulevard* (Heiwa Odori) runs E to **Hijiyama Park** (1 mile/1·5 km S of the station), on a hill planted with cherry trees from which there is a fine view of the city.

NW of the park (¾ mile/1 km W of the station) stands the **Memorial Cathedral of World Peace**, built in 1954 on the initiative of a German Jesuit named Hugo Lassalle, who had experienced the explosion of the atomic bomb. This is one of the largest Roman Catholic churches in Asia, and many countries contributed to the cost of construction. The four bells in the 150 ft/46 m high tower were presented by the German town of Bochum, the organ by Cologne and the bronze doors by Düsseldorf. The altar was presented by Belgium.

Offshore, to the S, is the island of **Ujina** (bus from station, 30 minutes), on which is the beautiful **Moto-Ujina Park** (bridge from harbor area).

On the north-western outskirts of the city, to the W of the main arm of the River Ota, can be found the **Mitaki Temple**, situated at the foot of Mount Mitaki (bus from Kamiyacho stop, 15 minutes; also railway station). The temple is notable for its red-lacquered pagoda (Tahoto). Near by are three waterfalls and beautiful wooded country. – In the extreme N of the city, above the right bank of the Ota (bus from station, 20 minutes), is the **Fudoin Temple**, a particularly fine example of the architecture of the Muromachi period (14th–16th c.). The Main Hall contains a fine carved statue. – To the N of the city (bus, 1 hour) is the **Asa Zoo**.

SURROUNDINGS. – NW of Hiroshima, in the beautiful valley of the River *Minochi,* lies the health resort of **Yuki-onsen** (bus, 1½ hours), and near this are the resorts of **Yunoyama-onsen** and **Iwakura-onsen** (bus, 1¼ hours), in beautiful walking country. – 47 miles/ 75 km N of Hiroshima (bus, 2¼ hours) we reach the magnificent *Sandankyo Gorge*, with beautiful waterfalls on the River Ota. At the S end of the gorge, which lies within the **Nishi-Chugoku Quasi National Park**, is *Togochi.*

The most attractive excursion from Hiroshima is to the island of **Miyajima** (see separate entry), to the S.

Hokkaido
北海道

Area of island: 30,312 sq. miles/78,509 sq. km
Population: 5,300,000.

Hokkaido, the most northerly of the large Japanese islands, is separated from Honshu by the Tsugaru Strait and from the Soviet island of Sakhalin to the N by the Soya Strait. There is still dispute about the ownership of the Southern Kuriles (Etorofu and Kunashiri) and the islands of Habomai and Shikotan, NE of Hokkaido: they were assigned to the Soviet Union by the Yalta Conference in 1945 but are claimed by Japan. – A railway tunnel connecting Hokkaido with Honshu, to the S, is under construction.

Hokkaido, with 21·2% of Japan's area, has only 5% of its population; but although it is sparsely populated it is still, in terms of population, the country's fifth largest prefecture. The chief town of the island and the prefecture is **Sapporo** (see separate entry), on the W side of the island. There are 14 subordinate local government units (*shicho*) – Abashiri, Hidaka, Hiyama, Iburi, Ishikari, Kamikawa, Kushiro, Nemuro, Oshima, Rumoi, Shiribeshi, Sorachi, Soya and Tokachi.

Much of the island is still in an unspoiled natural state. The topographical pattern is made up of mighty mountain ranges (central Hokkaido), volcanoes (in the SW and E), impenetrable forests and beautiful lakes (in the E). The highest peak, in the center of the island, is Mount **Asahi** (7513 ft/2290 m), part of the chain of volcanic mountains which runs S from the Kuriles. The outliers of the Nasu volcanic belt of Honshu reach into south-western Hokkaido, and in this area there are numerous hot springs, which have led to the development of large spas and tourist centers including *Jozankei, Noboribetsu* and *Yunokawa.* – Through the Tsugaru Strait runs the "Blakiston Line", which marks the northern boundary of the habitat of many Japanese species of animals. Hokkaido is noted for its snow monkeys, which during the winter come down to bathe in the hot springs.

On Hokkaido are the *Shikotsu-Toya, Daisetsuzan, Akan, Shiretoko* and *Rishiri-Rebun-Sarobetsu* National Parks (see separate entries).

CLIMATE. – Hokkaido lies within the temperate climatic zone. Average summer temperatures are about 70°F/21°C; the winters are long, bringing intense cold to the central area and the Pacific coast. Spring comes late, and the trees come into blossom only in May and June. The foliage takes on its autumn coloring in September and October. – The best times to visit Hokkaido are spring, summer (the main season) and autumn. During the winter, which lasts 4–5 months, the west of the island in particular is a popular winter sports region, with snow up to 10 ft/ 3 m deep.

HISTORY. – The original inhabitants of Hokkaido were the *Ezo* (Emishi), after whom the island was formerly known as Ezo or Ezochi. Ezo territory also extended into northern Honshu (Tohoku district), Sakhalin and the Kuriles. The **Ainu**, who are of a completely different racial type from the Japanese, are now thought to be the descendants of these tribes, though no proof of this has yet been adduced. – Contact with the Japanese was established as early as the 7th c., when Abe-no-Hirafu pushed N on to the Oshima Peninsula (658). Later Japanese fishermen

Lake Mashu, Hokkaido

Mount Io, Hokkaido

landed on the island of *Watarishima*; but Japanese colonization of Hokkaido began only during the Heian period (749–1192). In 1457 an Ainu chieftain named Koshamain tried to drive out the intruders; the rising was repressed by Takeda Nobuhiro, but fighting continued. In 1599 Yoshihiro, a descendant of Nobuhiro, was granted the fief of Ezo, and in 1600, having taken the name of Matsumae, he built Fukuyama Castle at what is now the town of Matsumae. This became the base for the further colonization of the island and the repression of the Ainu, who rebelled again in 1669. During the 17th c. the Japanese also began to prospect the island of Sakhalin, where they established a bridgehead at Nemuro in 1754, and from there advanced into the Southern Kuriles. In face of continuing conflicts with the Ainu and increasing Russian penetration Hokkaido was brought under the direct control of the Shogunate towards the end of the 18th c. Even before Japan finally emerged from its centuries of isolation the Treaty of Kanagawa with the United States (1854) provided for the opening of the port of Hakodate, which together with Matsumae and Esashi had become a place of some importance. In 1869 the name of the island was officially changed from Ezo to Hokkaido, and in 1886 Sapporo, a former Ainu settlement, became its administrative center. The headquarters of Kaitakushi, the agency responsible for the development of Hokkaido, was transferred from Hakodate to Sapporo in 1871.

ECONOMY. – Hokkaido's main sources of revenue are farming and forestry (rice, wheat, potatoes), fishing (20% of the total Japanese catch) and dairying. The island's main mineral resource is coal (50% of total Japanese output); oil is worked in very limited quantities. The principal branches of industry are mining, heavy industry and papermaking.

Honshu
本州

Area of island: 89,185 sq. miles/230,988 sq. km
Population: 93,350,000.

Honshu is the largest and most populous of the Japanese islands and from the earliest times was the scene of the most important events in the country's history. It is still the main source of new impulses in the political, economic and cultural life of Japan. The great cities of Tokyo, Yokohama, Nagoya, Kyoto, Osaka, Kobe and Hiroshima are all on Honshu. – A rail tunnel linking Honshu with its northern neighbor island, Hokkaido, is in course of construction.

The island is divided into **Omote-Nihon**, the "front side" – the eastern half, facing on to the Pacific, with the largest industrial centers and concentrations of population – and **Ura-Nihon**, the "rear side", the western half on the Sea of Japan, which long lay in the shadow of historical events and still consists mainly of agricultural land.

Honshu is divided into five regions: in the N **Tohoku**, with the prefectures of *Akita, Aomori, Fukushima, Iwate, Miyagi* and *Yamagata*; in eastern central Honshu

Kanto, with the national capital, *Tokyo,* and the prefectures of *Chiba, Gumma, Ibaraki, Kanagawa, Saitama* and *Tochigi*; in central Honshu **Chubu**, with the prefectures of *Aichi, Fukui, Gifu, Ishikawa, Nagano, Niigata, Shizuoka, Toyama* and *Yamanashi*; in western central Honshu **Kansai**, with the prefectures of *Hyogo, Kyoto, Mie, Nara, Osaka, Shiga* and *Wakayama*; and in the W **Chugoku**, with the prefectures of *Hiroshima, Okayama, Shimane, Tottori* and *Yamaguchi.*

The **Kanto** region, which contains the capital, *Tokyo,* is the heartland of present-day Japan. In the center of the region is the *Kanto Plain,* the largest lowland area in Japan, bounded on the E and S by the Pacific and on the N and W by mountain ranges. The rivers *Tone, Naka, Arakawa* and *Tama* flow eastward through the region into the Pacific; and in this area are the main industrial centers. To the S the region merges into the mountain world of *Fuji,* the *Hakone* area and the uplands of the *Izu* Peninsula, to the W into the *Chichibu* Hills. The climate of the region is characterized by hot and humid summers; during the winter less rain falls than in the central area or on the W coast.

Unlike Kansai, which became a region of some political consequence at an early stage, Kanto – lying to the E of the control post at Hakone – was wrested from the indigenous inhabitants of eastern and northern Honshu, the Emishi, only at a fairly late period, and until the 12th c. was an area of no importance or influence. Thereafter, however, the Taira family and later the Minamoto contrived to build up their dynastic authority and become a predominant political force. In 1192 the seat of government was transferred to Kamakura; then in the time of Tokugawa Ieyasu the Shogunate moved to Edo (now Tokyo), giving impetus to the development of the country, the building of roads and the emergence of Kanto as the most important region in Japan. At the end of the 16th c. the greater part of Kanto was granted as a fief to Tokugawa Ieyasu, later to become Shogun.

Chubu, the central section of Honshu and the broadest part of the Japanese island chain, is the "roof of Japan", with the great massif of the *Japan Alps.* It is divided into the *Central Highlands,* the *Tokai district* along the Pacific coast and the *Hokuriku district* on the Sea of Japan. Climatic conditions vary in the different parts of the region: while the Tokai district to the E has a climate similar to that of the Kanto region, though with less cold winters, the Central Highlands and particularly the Hokuriku district have temperate dry summers and very cold winters with an abundance of snow. – The coastal topography also varies. On the Sea of Japan (Hokuriku district) the coasts are fairly regular; the Pacific coast (Tokai district) is much more indented, with numerous bays and inlets, the most beautiful of which are those on the Izu Peninsula and Ise Bay.

The ＊＊**Japan Alps** are divided into the *Northern, Central* and *Southern Alps.* Large parts of this area have been declared National Parks (Chubu-Sangaku, Joshin-etsu, Southern Alps). There are several peaks over 9800 ft/3000 m, including *Kita-dake* (10,473 ft/ 3192 m: Japan's highest mountain after Fuji) and *Akaishi-dake* (10,237 ft/3120 m). In addition to the mountains and volcanoes there are extensive plateaus, such as *Tateshina-kogen* (3900–4600 ft/ 1200–1400 m), *Shiga-kogen* (4900 ft/1500 m) and *Utsukushigahara* (6500 ft/2000 m). Of the rivers which rise in the central uplands the *Toyokawa, Ibi* and *Kiso* flow into the Pacific, the *Kurobe* and *Shinano* into the Sea of Japan.

Thanks to their moderate summer temperatures and their abundance of snow in winter the Central Highlands are a very popular holiday region, and there are excellent connections between Tokyo, Nagoya and other centers and the principal resorts.

The Hokuriku district attracts fewer visitors than the Tokai district, but it offers attractive excursions to *Fukui* and *Kanazawa* and along the coast of the *Noto* Peninsula (see the entries for these places).

The largest city in the Chubu region is **Nagoya** (see separate entry), also known as *Chukyo* ("intermediate capital") since it lies between Tokyo and Kyoto. Nagoya, with the Nobi Plain around the Delta of the River Ibi, was important as the home of Oda Nobunaga, Tokugawa Ieyasu and Toyotomo Hideyoshi, who guided Japan out of the period of civil wars and unified it politically by the beginning of the 17th c.

The **Kansai** region, to the W of the control barrier on Lake Biwa includes the area around *Nara,* which is regarded as the cradle of Japanese culture, *Kyoto* and *Lake Biwa, Osaka, Kobe* and the whole of the *Kii Peninsula.* In the NW it extends to the rugged coast of *Wakasa Bay,* in the SW to the *Chugoku Mountains.* The most striking scenery is in the central part of the region (Yoshino-Kumano National Park, Koya-san: see separate entries) and along the coasts of the Kii Peninsula (Ise-Shima National Park: see separate entry). Wakasa Bay is reached from *Tsuruga.* Major tourist attractions are *Kyoto* and *Nara* (see separate entries), which are now part of the great Kyoto-Osaka-Kobe urban complex and are thronged with visitors throughout the year but have much to offer, not least because of their situation in very beautiful valley basins. – The Kii Peninsula has a climate typical of the Pacific coast (rainy summers, mild winters), very different from that of the interior of the region with its hot dry summers and cold winters.

From the foundation of the Yamato kingdom (probably 3rd c. A.D. to the beginning of the Meiji period Kansai was the cultural and political center of Japan. Its main importance is now economic, thanks particularly to the Hanshin industrial zone in the Osaka and Kobe area.

The **Chugoku** region (western Honshu) is bounded on the W by the Sea of Japan and on the E by the Inland Sea, and is separated from Kyushu, the most southerly of the main Japanese islands, by the Shimonoseki Strait or Kammon Strait. The chain of the *Chugoku Mountains* (Dogoyama, 4160 ft/1268 m; Kammuriyama, 4393 ft/1339 m) divides the region into the district of **San-in**, extending parallel to the Inland Sea coast, and the district of **San-yo**, along the coast of the Inland Sea. While the predominantly agricultural San-in district has lagged behind eastern Honshu in economic development, San-yo is relatively prosperous, thanks to its excellent infrastructure. This district is also favoured climatically (hot dry summers and mild winters). Although industrialization has created environmental problems, particularly around Hiroshima and Iwakuni, the Inland Sea still offers great attractions to visitors, with its beautiful coastal scenery and numerous islands. – Of particular tourist interest are the picturesque *Onomichi* and *Miyajima* areas and towns such as *Kurashiki*. The largest town in the region is *Hiroshima* (see separate entry).

The San-in district has a fairly regular coastline, with no major indentations. A region of historical interest is the area around *Izumo* (see separate entry), which had contacts with the mainland of Asia at an early period (5th–6th c.). Other places of interest are *Matsue* and the little pottery town of *Hagi* (see separate entries).

In north-eastern Honshu is the **Tokohu** region, also divided into two by a mountain range, the *Ou Mountains* (Iwate, 6697 ft/2041 m), which extend into the Nasu volcanic chain in the S. The region is bounded on the W by the Sea of Japan and on the E by the Pacific, and is separated from the northern island of Hokkaido by the Tsugaru Strait. Tohoku is one of the lesser known parts of Honshu. In early times it was known as Michinoku, the remote "inner side of the road", referring to the rugged nature and comparatively cool climate of this upland region. In contrast to the regular coastline on the W side of the island, the E coast is hilly and much indented, with high cliffs falling sheer down to the sea in many places. The two coasts also differ climatically: in the W the summers are hot and the winters have an abundance of snow, while in the E most of the rain falls in summer.

The scenic high points of Tohoku are the *Towada-Hachimantai*, *Rikuchu-kaigan* and *Bandai-Asahi* National Parks (see separate entries). Mount *Zao* (6040 ft/1841 m) is one of the finest skiing areas in Japan.

The Japanese central government took a long time to subdue the indigenous inhabitants of Tohoku, the Emishi. Fierce fighting during the 7th–9th c. prepared the way for the advance to the Tsugaru Strait in the 10th c. Long known as the rice granary of Japan, this region is still predominantly agricultural (mainly fruit-growing). There is little industry, and minerals are worked only on a small scale.

Ibusuki
いぶすき

Prefecture: Kagoshima. – Population: 33,000.
Post code: J-891-04. – Telephone code: 09932.

 (central)
Kagoshima-ken Tokyo Kanko Bussan Assensho,
Olympic Building,
2-7-17, Ginza, Chuo-ku,
J-100 **Tokyo**;
tel. (03) 561 6701.

(local)
Kagoshima-ken Kanko Renmei,
9-1, Nayama-cho,
J-890 **Kagoshima**;
tel. (0992) 23 9171.

HOTELS. – **Western style:** *Ibusuki Kanko Hotel,* 3755, Juni-cho, 639 r., SP, thermal bath, beach; *Ibusuki Royal Hotel,* 4232, Juni-cho, 70 r., Japanese garden, SP, thermal bath, beach. – **Ryokan:** *Ibusuki Hakusuikan,* Higashikata, 237 r.; *Ibusuki Phoenix Hotel,* Juni-cho, 150 r.; *Ibusuki Seaside Hotel,* Juni-cho, 127 r.; *Ibusuki Kaijo Hotel,* Juni-cho, 118 r.; *Ibusuki Coral Beach Hotel,* Juni-cho, 66 r.; *Hotel Kairakuen,* Juni-cho, 65 r.; *Hotel Shusuien,* Juni-cho, 45 r.; *Ibusuki Oriental Hotel,* Juni-cho, 28 r. – YOUTH HOSTELS: *Tamaya YH,* 3739, Juni-cho, 130 b.; *Ibusuki YH,* 1850, Juni-cho, 96 b.

TRANSPORTATION. – **Rail:** from KAGOSHIMA (Nishi-Kagoshima Station) JNR Ibusuki–Makurazaki line (60–80 minutes). – **Bus:** from KAGOSHIMA (Bus Center) to Ibusuki Kanko Hotel (2 hours).

The seaside resort and spa of Ibusuki lies in south-western Kyushu on the Satsuma Peninsula, which flanks the W side of Kagoshima Bay, surrounded by extensive tobacco plantations. In this subtropical region palms flourish, and a wide range of other plants provide a colorful display of blossom throughout the year. The resort, which is noted for its hot chalybeate springs (118–210 °F/48–99 °C), extends along a 6 mile/10 km stretch of romantically beautiful coast, lined with a series of excellent hotels.

The best known of the local hot springs, *Surigahama,* is supplied by underground channels which warm the beach area. "Sand baths" (*sunamushi*), in which the "bather" is buried in the warm black sand, leaving only his head exposed, are very popular here. – Among local sources of income are the manufacture of articles of bamboo and boxwood and the growing of vegetables.

Ibusuki . . .

. . . and its sand baths

The public **Natural Sand Baths** are the only establishment of the kind in Japan. The large *Ibusuki Health Center* has 26 pools, surrounded by tropical plants. Adjoining is the Ibusuki Kanko Hotel, with an enclosed sand bath, a theater-restaurant and numerous shops. – There is good fishing around the harbor. Bicycles can be rented at the railway station.

SURROUNDINGS. – 6 miles/10 km S (bus from Ibusuki) is the port of **Yamakawa**, from which there are coach excursions to *Cape Nagasakibana* and Mount **Kaimon** (3025 ft/922 m; also reached by JNR Ibusuki–Makurazaki line from Ibusuki, 45 minutes). To the N of Mount Kaimon is **Lake Ikeda**, a caldera filled with water of unusual clarity.

Another attractive excursion from Ibusuki is to the **Osumi Peninsula**, a region of densely wooded hills and bizarre rock formations along the coast, to the E of Kagoshima Bay (ferry service between Yamakawa and Nejime). To the S of *Nejime* are the town of **Sata** and *Cape Sata,* the most southerly point on Kyushu, lying in the same latitude as Miami and Morocco. In the rich subtropical vegetation palms and cactuses predominate. From the outlook terrace there are * views of the rocky coast and the lighthouse (erected 1871).

See also **Chiran** and **Kirishima-Yaku National Park**.

Iki
See under Fukuoka

Inland Sea/ Setonaikai
せと内海

TRANSPORTATION. – **Boat:** from OSAKA via Kobe, Takamatsu, Imabari and Matsuyama to Beppu (about 15 hours); from HIROSHIMA (direct or via Kure) to Matsuyama (1–2¾ hours), and via Kure, Oosaki-Shimojima and Toyoshima to Imabari (1½ hours); many shorter services.

The ** Inland Sea (Setonaikai) is a wide arm of the sea extending between the islands of Honshu, Shikoku and Kyushu, with about a thousand small islands and islets, magnificent beaches and quiet little coves containing small fishing villages. The exceptionally mild climate ensures a rich and varied pattern of vegetation. The Inland Sea is linked to the Sea of Japan by the Kammon Strait and to the Pacific by the Straits of Kii, Kitan, Naruto, Hoyo and Bungo. Over most of its area the Inland Sea is no more than 130 ft/40 m deep. There are strong tidal movements and counter-currents in the various straits.

Much of the area was declared a National Park in 1934, including part of the island of *Shodojima*, the *Yashima Peninsula,* the island of *Sensui, Cape Abuto* and Mount *Washuzan.* The **Inland Sea National Park** (land area 254 sq. miles/659 sq. km) now extends much farther SW, reaching as far as the coasts of northeastern Kyushu. In the E it extends to the island of *Awaji.*

On the S coast of Honshu is the port of **Mihara** (population 84,000; JNR Sanyo–Shinkansen line from Hiroshima, 30 minutes), an industrial town noted for the production of sake. There are some remains of a castle built by Kobayakawa Takakage in 1582. – 7½ miles off the coast lies the island of **Ikuchi**, with the **Kon-sanji Temple**, built in 1946, which incorporates stylistic elements of the Asuka, Nara, Heian, Kamakura, Muromachi and Edo periods. The over-elaborately decorated main gate, resembling the gate of the Toshogu Shrine at Nikko, has earned the temple the name of the "Nikko of the west". The temple contains many Buddhist statues and antiquities.

The Inland Sea (Setonaikai)

From the port of **Imabari**, on the N coast of Shikoku, there is a boat service to **Miyaura** on the island of **Omishima**. ¾mile/1 km E of Miyaura is the well-known *Oyamazumi Shrine*, the foundation of which is ascribed to the legendary Jimmu-tenno. The present buildings of the temple, which is dedicated to the god of seafarers, date from the Muromachi period (1387). The temple contains a *collection of arms and armor, covering most of the types used in ancient Japan.

See also **Awaji, Himeji, Hiroshima, Kobe, Kurashiki, Matsuyama, Miyajima, Naruto, Okayama, Osaka, Shodo, Takamatsu** and **Yamaguchi.**

Ise-Shima National Park

いせしま
国立公園

Prefecture: Mie.
Area: 200 sq. miles/520 sq. km
(i) (central)
Mie-ken Bussan Kanko Assen Center,
Tetsudo Kaikan,
1-9-1, Marunouchi, Chiyoda-ku,
J-100 **Tokyo;**
tel. (03) 211 2737.

National Parks Association of Japan,
Toranomon Denki Building,
8-1, Toranomon 2-chome, Minato-ku,
J-105 **Tokyo;**
tel. (03) 502 0488.

HOTELS. – IN TOBA. – **Western style:** *Toba Hotel International,* 1-23-1, Toba, 124 r., SP. – **Ryokan:** *Todaya Toba Bekkan,* 1-24-26, Toba, 123 r.; *Fujita Toba Kowakien,* 1061, Arashimacho, 122 r.; *Toba Seaside Hotel,* Arashimacho, 109 r.; *Pearl Palace Hotel Shoto,* 300-1, Ohamacho, 78 r.; *New Mishima,* 1069, Sakadecho, 77 r.; *Toba Royal Hotel,* Arashimacho, 75 r.; *Toba Grand Hotel,* Ohamacho, 65 r.; *Hotel Taiike,* Ohamacho, 60 r.; *Toba Kokusai Hotel Bekkan,* 1-23-1, Toba, 54 r.; *Kogaso,* 237-1, Ohamacho, 44 r.; *Kinkairo,* 1-13-1, Toba, 41 r.; *Kimpokan,* 1-10-38, Toba, 38 r. – YOUTH HOSTELS: *Kontai-ji YH* (temple), 3-24-1, Toba, 7 b.; *Taiko-ji YH* (temple), at Futami, NW of Toba, 28 b.; *Ise-shima YH,* at Anagawa, S of Toba, 120 b.

TRANSPORTATION. – **Rail:** from NAGOYA or OSAKA and via KYOTO Kinki Nippon Railway to Uji-Yamada (1½ or 2 hours), then via Toba to Kashikojima. – **Boat:** ferry from IRAKO (Atsumi Peninsula) to Toba (Isewan Ferry Line; 1 hour).

Transportation in Ise-Shima National Park

Buses from Uji-Yamada via Naiku and Toba to Kashikojima (2½ hours).

Ferries from Kashikojima to Wagu, Goza and Hamajima (each about 30 minutes); from Hamajima to Goza (15 minutes).

The * **Ise-Shima National Park lies on the Shima Peninsula, which forms the south-eastern part of Mie prefecture on Honshu. The beautiful** coast facing on to the Pacific is indented by many bays and inlets; offshore are many small islands; the coastal region is covered with subtropical vegetation; and inland are dense forests. The main feature of interest is the ** Ise Shrines revered as one of the most sacred places in Japan.

The northern gateway to the National Park is the town of Ise (pop. 106,000), formed by the amalgamation of Uji and Yamada, wth the administrative offices of the Ise Shrines and their library, richly stocked with Shinto literature. Also in the town are the Chokokan Museum (antiquities) and the Nogyokan Museum (agriculture). A traditional local dance, the Ise-ondo, is performed to the music of *shamisen* and *kokyu* (similar to guitars and fiddles).

To the S of the town are the ** **Great Shrines of Ise**, set among magnificent trees.

HISTORY AND ARCHITECTURE. – The two shrines, the Outer Shrine (Geku) and the Inner Shrine (Naiku), are some 3 miles/5 km from one another. They were originally erected on other sites and later transferred to their present positions. The **Geku** is believed to have been originally built at Manai (historical province of Tamba, now Kyoto prefecture) and moved to Ise in 478, during the reign of the Emperor Yuryaku (457–479). The **Naiku** was originally part of the Imperial Palace; in the time of the Emperor Sujin (3rd c.), or perhaps later, it was moved to Kasanui (Yamato province) and subsequently transferred to its present site. The same priest serves both shrines; originally a sister of Tenno was priestess here.

The shrines, built of fine cedar and cypress wood, are in the Shimmei-zukuri style, the characteristic features of which are the saddle roof, the crossed gable joists (*chigi*) and the cylindrical beam (*katsuogi*) which forms the roof-ridge. The only decorative elements are the finely worked gold and copper facing of the beams and the doors. The Ise Shrines and the Izumo-Taisha Shrine are the only Shinto shrines in Japan which show no trace of Buddhist architectural influence.

Every twenty years the shrines are pulled down and the wood distributed to shrines throughout Japan, where it is used as consecrated building material. The 65 buildings of the shrines are then rebuilt in exactly the same form on sites immediately adjoining those of the demolished buildings, and the divinity is transferred to the new shrine. This ceremony (*Sengu-shiki*) was last performed in October 1973.

The Ise Shrines became of great importance as a result of the movement to restore Shintoism, which for centuries had become mingled with Buddhism, to its original form. Efforts in this direction which began in the 18th c. led in the latter part of the 19th c. to the reestablishment of the Imperial authority on a Shintoist basis and the recognition of Shintoism as the State religion. After the Second World War Shintoism lost this official status, but the shrines in Ise still attract great numbers of pilgrims. – Foreign visitors should behave with proper reverence and should observe the ban on photography.

The * **Outer Shrine (Geku)** lies a short distance SW of Uji-Yamada Station (Kinki–Nippon Railway). The precincts of the shrine, occupying 220 acres, are approached by a bridge. Beyond the first *torii*, on the right, are the residences occupied by the Imperial family when they come to Ise – **Anzaisho**, the

Shima Peninsula

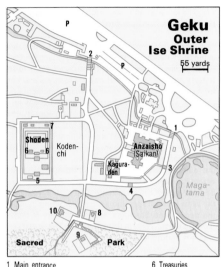

Geku
Outer
Ise Shrine

55 yards

1 Main entrance	6 Treasuries
2 North entrance	7 Mike-den
3 First torii	8 Kazenomiya Shrine
4 Second torii	9 Taganomiya Shrine
5 Itagaki	10 Tsuchinomiya Shrine

Emperor's house, and *Sanshujo*, for other members of the family. Beyond the second *torii*, on right, is the *Kagura-den*, a hall for cult dances.

The **Kagura** dance, widely performed before 1868, was restricted in the Meiji period to cult performances in the shrines. Here it is danced by young girls, on presentation of an appropriate offering. Since Shintoism ceased to be the State religion the Ise Shrines, like all other shrines, are dependent on offerings for their income; and the last rebuilding of the shrines was largely financed in this way. The shrines also gain some income from the sale of souvenirs and amulets.

Beyond the Kagura-den is the Cult Hall, and beyond this again is the main shrine, enclosed by four walls. The outermost wall (*Itagaki*), enclosing a rectangular area, is of cedar wood. At one end is the main entrance, with subsidiary entrances on the other three sides. The second enclosure (*Soto-tamagaki*), constructed of cedar wood planks, alternatively short and long, may be entered only by priests, the Emperor and emissaries of the Emperor; all other visitors may go only as far as the gate at the S end, with a white curtain which prevents them from seeing the interior of the shrine. Within this enclosure are the third (*Uchitamagaki*) and fourth (*Mizu-gaki*) enclosures, each with a gate at the S end. In the innermost court is the principal shrine, **Shoden**, built of natural-colored cypress wood with sparse metal decoration and a thatched roof. On either side of the gate are two treasuries (*Hoden*) containing cult utensils and ceremonial vestments.

Between the first and second walls, at the N end, is the *Mike-den*, a hall in which offerings of food are made twice daily. Within the second wall, on right, is another hall, the *Shijo-den*.

To the S of the main shrine lies the **Sacred Park** (*Geku-Jin-en*; area 11 acres), which contains a number of smaller shrines, including the *Kazenomiya Shrine* (dedicated to the wind god) and the *Taganomiya Shrine* (dedicated to the god Toyouke).

The ** **Inner Shrine (Naiku)**, 3 miles/ 5 km SE of the Geku, is Japan's greatest national shrine. It is entered by way of the *Uji Bridge* spanning the River *Isuzu*, beyond which is the *first torii*. From here a flight of steps leads down to the river, in which pilgrims ritually wash their hands and mouth. Beyond the *second torii* is an avenue of ancient cedars leading to the temple offices and the *Kagura-den* (hall for ritual dances). Near by are a rice-store and a number of smaller buildings, beyond which is the **Shoden** (main shrine) within its enclosing walls. This is similar in plan to the Geku and is likewise surrounded by four wooden enclosure walls, only the outermost one of which may be passed by visitors.

In the Naiku is preserved the mirror known as **Yata-no-kagami**, one of the three Imperial insignia of Japan. Tradition has it that the sun goddess Amaterasu gave the mirror to her grandson Ninigi-no-mikoto when he went down to earth to establish Im-

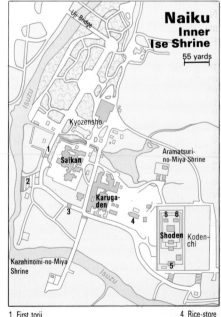

Naiku
Inner
Ise Shrine

55 yards

1 First torii	4 Rice-store
2 Steps to river	5 Itaki
3 Second torii	6 Treasuries

Inner Ise Shrine

perial rule in Japan. In early days the mirror, revered as a symbol of the sun goddess, was kept in the Imperial Palace under the charge of a princess who officiated as high priestess; then, during the reign of the legendary Sujin-tenno, the holy place was moved out of the palace, marking the separation of secular and spiritual power. Until 1339, however, the priestess was always a member of the Imperial House.

The Naiku stands in the middle of a forest of 165 acres which also contains the **Aramatsuri-no-miya** and **Kaza-hinomi-no-miya** shrines.

NE of the Naiku is the beginning of the 10 mile/16 km-long *Ise-Shima Skyline*, a toll road which runs E through the *Asama Hills* to Toba, affording magnificent *views of Toba and Ise Bays and the hills of the National Park. There are also fine views from Mount *Asama* (1814 ft/553 m), to the N of the road (bus from Naiku-mae, 40 minutes). On the summit stands the *Kongosho-ji Temple* of the Rinzai sect.

The temple contains a statue of **Kokuzobosatsu** attributed to Kobodaishi (774–835), sculpture by *Uho-Doji* and a *portrait of General Kuki Yoshitaka* (1542–1600). The date of building of the **Main Hall** is unknown.

9 miles/14 km W of Ise (Kinki–Nippon Railway, 15 minutes) lies the town of **Toba** (pop. 30,000). Near the station is an outlook tower 157 ft/48 m high (good view of the bay with its many little islands). 550 yds/500 m S of the station is the Toba Tourist Center (far-ranging views). Near the pier (boat trips round the bay) can be found the Toba Aquarium (diving demonstrations). Above the town rises Mount *Hiyori* (167 ft/51 m), a good viewpoint. – The Shirongo-matsuri festival is celebrated in mid June, when more than 200 women clad in white dive for abalone.

NW of Toba is **Futamiga-ura** (bus service), in the bay of the same name. Here there rise out of the sea the two rocks known as *Meoto-Iwa*, the Wedded Rocks, which are seen as symbolizing the divine couple who created the Japanese island kingdom, Izanagi and Izanami. The two rocks are linked by a long straw rope (*shimenawa*) which is renewed every year in a solemn ceremony at the beginning of January. On the larger rock, 30 ft/9 m high, is a *torii* (view finest at sunrise). – A little way E is the *Wedded Rocks Paradise*, a leisure center with an aquarium, a tropical garden, a reconstructed farmhouse in Gassho-zukuri style, etc. – On the bus route to Toba is another leisure center, *Beachland*.

From Toba a bridge 69 yds/63 m long leads on to **Pearl Island**, where Mikimoto Kokichi (1858–1954) established the first pearl-culture farm. (The process involves inserting a foreign body into the pearl oyster, which leads in the course of some 7 years to the formation of a pearl.) The great majority of the cultivated pearls now produced come from here. On the island are a monument to Mikimoto, a demonstration pearl-culture establishment (diving displays) and a number of stalls selling pearls. There is an interesting *Mikimoto Pearl Museum*, among the exhibits in which is a pagoda 4 ft/1·2 m high made of more than 10,000 pearls.

The 15 mile/25 km-long *Ise Toll Road* runs S to **Kashikojima** (also reached by the Kinki–Nippon Railway or by bus from Iseshi via Toba), on the N coast of *Ago Bay*, in the clear waters of which there are also large pearl culture beds. Here, too, the women divers (*ama*) can be seen at their work. In Kashikojima is the National Institute of Research into Pearl Culture. Near the station can be found Shima Marineland, an extraordinary structure in the form of an ammonite (aquarium, etc.) – A boat can be taken across Ago Bay (or bus from Toba) to **Goza**, at the W end of the Goza Peninsula. From Mount *Kompira* (325 ft/99 m), to the S of the town, there are fine *views of the bay and the Pacific. – To the E lies **Wagu**, known as the "town of the women divers", beyond which the road continues to *Cape Daido*, with steep cliffs and strong surf.

To the NW, outside the National Park, is **Matsusaka** (pop. 113,000; JNR line and Kinki–Nippon Railway from Nagoya), renowned for producing the best beef in Japan (the cattle are given beer to drink and are massaged). In Matsusaka Park, ¾ mile/1 km SW of the station, are the remains of an old castle and a house which belonged to the scholar Motoori

Norinaga (1730–1801), transferred here from its original site; it contains some of his possessions and manuscripts.

Motoori, a native of Matsusaka, was one of the leading members of the **Kokugaku**, a group of scholars whose work had considerable influence on the re-establishment of Imperial authority at the end of the 19th c. His works on the ancient literature of Japan promoted the recognition of Shintoism as the State religion. His most important work was a 44-volume commentary on the "Kojiki", the oldest surviving Japanese historical work (712).

Itsukushima
See Miyajima

Izu Peninsula
いず

Prefecture: Kanagawa.
(central)
Kanagawa-ken Tokyo Kanko Bussen Assensho,
Kokusai Kanko Kaiken,
1-8-3, Marunouchi, Chiyoda-ku,
J-100 **Tokyo;**
tel. (03) 231 3901.

HOTELS. – IN ATAMI. – **Western style:** *Atami Fujiya Hotel,* 13-8, Ginza-cho, 165 r., Japanese garden, SP, thermal bath; *New Fujiya Hotel,* 1-16, Ginza-cho, 318 r., SP, thermal bath, beach. – **Ryokan:** *Hotel New Akao,* 1993-250, Atami, 250 r.; *Tsuruya Hotel,* Higashi-Kaigancho, 166 r.; *Onoya Ryokan,* Wadahama-Minamicho, 131 r.; *Kinjokan,* Showacho, 111 r.; *Taikanso,* Hayashigaoka-cho, 45 r.; *Atami Sekitei,* Wadacho, 33 r.; *Kiunkaku Honkan,* 31 r.; *Happoen,* Minaguchicho, 20 r.

EVENTS. – *Atami ume-matsuri* (mid January), with geisha dances and tea ceremony, in Atami Apricot Garden; *Kurofune-matsuri* (mid May), commemorating the landing of Commodore Perry in 1853, with processions and fireworks, in Shimoda; *Genji-ayame-matsuri* (beginning of July), procession with portable shrines, dancing, in Izu-Nagaoka-onsen; *Tarai-nori kyoso* (first Sunday in July), contest in wooden tubs on the River Matsukawa, in Ito-onsen; *firework displays* (July–August) in Atami; *Ito Anjinsai* (beginning of August), commemorating William Adams, the English shipbuilder who worked for the Tokugawa, with processions and fireworks, in Ito; *Shrine Festival* (mid August) in Mishima-Taisha Shrine, parade with decorated floats.

TRANSPORTATION. – **Air:** from TOKYO (Haneda Airport) to the island of Oshima. – **Rail:** from TOKYO (Central Station) JNR Tokaido–Shinkansen line to Atami and Mishima (2¼ hours); also to Shimoda (2¾ hours); JNR Tokaido line to Atami, Mishima and Numazu; from TOKYO (Central Station) JNR Ito line via Atami to Ito, then Izu-Kyuko private line to

Shimoda; from MISHIMA Izu-Hakone private line to Shuzenji. – **Boat:** from TOKYO (Takeshiba Pier) to Okada (island of Oshima; 4–7 hours); from YOKOHAMA to Okada (6 hours); from Atami to Motomachi (1–2 hours); from Ito to Motomachi (1 hour); from Shimoda to Motomachi (1¼ hours) and to the islands of Kozu, Shikine, Niijima and Toshima.

The ✱✱**Izu Peninsula, to the S of Mount Fuji, projects into the Pacific; it is bounded on the W by Suruga Bay and on the E by Sagami Bay. With its mild climate throughout the year and its varied and beautiful scenery (coasts indented by many bays and inlets, wooded hills, hot springs, romantically situated spas) the peninsula is a popular holiday region. Much of it lies within the Fuji-Hakone-Izu National Park. The name is derived from the original form Yu-Izu (***yu*** = "hot water", ***izu*** = "spring").**

The **Amagi Mountains**, which run along the peninsula, are a continuation of the highlands of the Hakone region (see the entry for Hakone). Their highest peak is Mount *Amagi* (4616 ft/1407 m), with the source of the River *Kano,* which flows northwards down the peninsula to reach *Suruga Bay* at **Numazu.**

Good bases from which to explore the interior of the peninsula are **Atami, Mishima** and **Numazu,** all of which can be reached from Tokyo. The best road is the Tomei Express Highway, which runs past Mishima and Numazu. The peninsula is also served by the Izu-Kyuko and Izu-Hakone railway lines and by several bus services.

East Coast of the Izu Peninsula

At the extreme N end of the E coast of the peninsula is the seaside resort of **Atami** (pop. 52,000), situated on a beautiful stretch of coastal scenery. This is one of Japan's most modern resorts. It has a beautiful *Apricot Garden* (Atami-baien; bus from station, 15 minutes), with some 1300 trees. On the slopes of a hill from which there is a fine view of the town is the *Cactus Garden* (Atami saboten-koen; bus from station, 15 minutes), with large glasshouses. The ✱✱*Atami Museum of Art* (Atami-bijutsukan; bus from station), housed in the headquarters of the Church of World Messianity, displays the art of this "new religion", including colored woodcuts (*ukiyo-e*), pottery, objects of precious metals and lacquerware. Many of the exhibits are classified as "national

Atami, in Sagami Bay

stretch of coast of volcanic origin. – The *Ikeda Museum of 20th Century Art* (Ikeda-nijusseiki-bijutsukan) contains works by Picasso, Matisse, Chagall and others, together with Japanese colored woodcuts.

At the foot of Mount *Omuro* (1906 ft/ 581 m), to the S of the lake, we find the **Izu Cactus Garden** (*Izu-saboten-koen*; bus from Ito, 40 minutes), with an outlook terrace; peacocks are bred here.

At the S end of the E coast lies the port of **Shimoda** (pop. 32,000; Izu–Kyuko Railway, 1 hour from Ito), from which there are boat services to the Seven Izu Islands.

HISTORY of Shimoda. – The "black ships" of the American Admiral, Commodore Matthew Perry (1794–1858), anchored in Shimoda Bay in 1854, leading to the Treaty of Kanagawa (March 31, 1854) and the opening up of the ports of Shimoda and Hakodate to foreign ships. The first American diplomatic representative in Japan, Townsend Harris (1804–78), resided in Shimoda from 1856 to 1857 and then moved to Yokohama, which became available to foreign shipping under a new commercial treaty with the United States in 1858.

treasures" or "works of major cultural importance". The beautiful *Atami-Himenosawa Park* (bus from station, 20 minutes) is at its best when the azaleas and cherry trees are in blossom. – On *Cape Uomi* the *Atami Korakuen Leisure Center* (bus from station, 10 minutes) has a swimming pool, fishing-ponds, a reptile garden, etc. – The best view of the town is from the *Atami Pass*, to the N.

The beautiful coast road (with the railway running parallel to it) leads S to **Ito** (pop. 71,000), the second largest town on the peninsula. Here there are some 700 hot springs, which supply water to houses and spa establishments in the town; some of them have been used for several centuries. 1 mile/1·5 km S of the station is *Lake Jonoike,* and to the E of this stands the *Butsugenji Temple,* belonging to the Nichiren sect, whose founder lived in exile here from 1261 to 1263. – 1¼ miles/2 km SE of the station is a monument to William Adams (1564–1620), who built the first Western-type ship in Japan here (commemorative festival in August).

From Ito Station there is a bus service (20 minutes) to the **Omuroyama-shizenkoen Nature park**, around a volcanic hill 1053 ft/321 m high (beautiful views of the Amagi Mountains and the island of Oshima, to the E).

SW of the Nature Park the crater lake *Ippeki* (circumference 2½ miles/4 km) has the Amagi Mountains reflected in its waters. The lake is famous for the cherry blossom along its shores. To the E is *Jogasaki Beach,* a 6 mile/10 km-long

1¼ miles/2 km E of the town in the village of **Kakisaki** is the *Gyokusenji Temple,* where Townsend Harris had his headquarters. In addition to a portrait and some mementoes of the diplomat, the temple contains an eight-volume diary by an inhabitant of the village on Harris's life. Near by are the graves of American and Russian sailors. In mid May a three-day festival, the Kurofune-matsuri, is held in Shimoda to commemorate Commodore Perry's landing. – Opposite the temple is the little island of *Bentenjima,* with a temple dedicated to Benten, goddess of good fortune. From here the patriot Yoshida Shoin (1830–59) rowed out to the "black ships" to ask for a passage to America; but his enterprise failed, and the Tokugawa Shogunate condemned him to death. – On a hill near the harbor is *Shimoda Park,* with a fine view of Cape Suzaki to the E. At the railway station can be found the lower station of a cableway up Mount *Nesugata,* from which there is a view of the S end of the Izu Peninsula. Here there was an observation-post which watched over the movements of the "black ships" in the bay.

Near the station stands the *Hofukuji Temple,* dedicated to Okichi Tojin, who is said to have been Harris's mistress; there are a portrait and various mementoes in a

Cape Iro

building adjoining the temple. – To the S of the station is the *Ryosenji Temple,* in which the Japanese-American Treaty was negotiated. The temple contains an exhibition of documents illustrating the love-life of the Japanese. – In the adjoining *Chorakuji Temple* the Japanese-American Treaty and the agreement with Russia were signed.

The *Underwater Aquarium,* housed in a cave, contains an interesting collection of local marine life (several hundred species). – Near *Shirahama Beach,* to the E, is the *Shimoda Kaiko-Kinenkan,* a memorial hall containing mementoes of the period of the "black ships".

SW of Shimoda (bus from station, 20 minutes) we reach **Yumigahama Beach**, one of the finest beaches on the island, with white sand and large numbers of pine trees. Here there is a holiday village (Kokumin Kyuka-mura). – Farther SW (bus) is the resort of **Shimogamo-onsen**, with a Tropical Garden.

The most southerly point on the Izu Peninsula is **Cape Iro** (bus from Shimoda, 40 minutes), from which there is a fine *view of the Seven Izu Islands. Near the cape the *Jungle Park* (Jungle-koen; opposite the lighthouse) contains more than 3000 species of plants.

Central Izu

The starting-point of a tour of the central part of the peninsula is **Mishima** (pop. 94,000), with the *Mishima-Taisha Shrine* (bus from station, 5 minutes), the oldest shrine on Izu. Within the precincts of the

temple, which is surrounded by forest, is a treasury containing documents of the time of Minamoto Yoritomo (1147–99), founder of the Kamakura Shogunate, and a collection of old weapons. – S of the station (10 minutes' walk) lies the landscaped garden of *Rakuju-en,* laid out during the Meiji period on the site of the residence of the daimyo Mito Mitsukuni. The garden contains a pool which is fed by melt-water from the Fuji region. There is also a hall displaying folk art.

From Mishima the Izu–Hakone Railway runs S. On this line is the little resort of **Nirayama** (pop. 14,000), with the remains of a Hojo castle and a well-preserved forge for the manufacture of firearms; this was built in 1853 and directed by Egawa Tarozaemon (or Tanan), Provincial Administrator of Izu. – 1 mile/1·5 km E of the station is a residence of the Egawa family, *Egawa-no-ie,* 700 years old. – Still farther E we come to a large amusement center, **Izu-Fujimi Land** (also reached by bus from Mishima, 50 minutes), with tropical gardens, sports facilities, etc.

The Izu–Hakone Railway ends at **Shuzenji**. 2 miles/3 km SW (bus) is the spa of **Shuzenji-onsen** (pop. 18,000), beautifully situated in the Valley of the River *Katsura* and which has been frequented since the 9th c. It ranks with Atami and Ito as one of the most popular resorts on the peninsula. There are numerous hot springs (99–165 °F/37–74 °C). In the center of the town stands the Shuzenji Temple, believed to have been founded by Kobo-daishi at the beginning of the Heian period. The treasury contains mementoes of the House of Minamoto and an old No mask.

The mask features in the Kabuki play "Shuzenji-monogatari", which centers on the murder of Minamoto Yoriie (1182–1204), son of Yoritomo, by Hojo Tokimasa (1138–1215). The temple was also the scene of the murder of Minamoto Noriyori (1156–93) by his brother Yoritomo, founder of the Kamakura Shogunate. – Noriyori and Yoriie are buried here. Adjoining Yoriie's tomb, on the opposite bank of the river, is the little **Shigetsuden Temple**.

To the W of the town rises Mount *Daruma* (3222 ft/982 m; bus from Shuzenji Station to the foot, 30 minutes, then 1 hour's climb); from the top there are *views of Mount Fuji and Suruga Bay. An attractive footpath runs parallel to the road, the *Nishi-Izu Skyline Drive.*

From Shuzenji a road (bus service) runs S to the Amagi Mountains. Below the NW side of the hills is the little town of **Yugashima** (pop. 9000), with several hot springs (113–136 °F/45–58 °C). In the beautiful surrounding area (1½ miles/ 2·5 km S; bus) are the *Joren Falls,* which can be observed from a cave behind the curtain of water.

SE of Yugashima are the **Amagi Mountains**, a group of extinct volcanoes. The road from the N climbs to the *Amagi Pass* (2625 ft/800 m), from which a road runs E into the highlands. The highest peak is *Banzaburo* (4616 ft/1407 m); others are *Banjiro* (4265 ft/1300 m) and *Hoko* (3360 ft/1024 m). These densely wooded uplands, well stocked with game, are a popular hunting (shooting) area.

A rewarding WALK (about 6 hours) is from the *Amagi-kogen Golf-jo* (bus from Ito, 1 hour) to Mount Banjiro, then via Mount Banzaburo to the romantic mountain lake of *Hacho-ike,* near the summit (particularly beautiful in the fall), and from there to the Amagi Pass.

West Coast of the Izu Peninsula

The town of **Numazu** (pop. 206,000), in the NW of the peninsula, is a port used by coastal shipping and the starting-point of coach tours of the peninsula and the Fuji Lakes (see separate entry). 1 mile/1·5 km SW of the station is the beach of *Sembon Matsubara* ("beach of a thousand firs"). The trees are said to have been planted by a priest named Zoyo in the 16th c.

6 miles/10 km S of Numazu, on a small island in *Uchiura Bay,* lies the **Awashima Marine Park** (*Awashima-kaiyo-koen;* bus from Numazu, 35 minutes), with a wide range of recreational facilities. – Near here (on the same bus route) is **Mito**. On the beach *Mito Aquarium* (Mito-tennen-suizokokan) has a number of separate pools, a dolphin show and an area enclosed by nets in which fish can swim freely. Anchored off the coast is the hotel ship S.S. "Scandinavia".

An attractive EXCURSION from here is to **Cape Ose** (also reached by bus from Numazu, 1½ hours), a narrow promontory projecting far out into the sea from which there is a fine *view of Mount Fuji. Here, too, we find the *Ose Shrine,* dedicated to the god of seafarers. – A beautiful promenade encircles the cape.

The only health resort on the W coast is **Toi** (pop. 7000; boat from Numazu, 1½

hours; by rail from Shuzenji, 1 hour), which has a beautiful beach. From here it is well worth while taking the bus which runs S, through magnificent coastal scenery, to **Matsuzaki**, which is noted for its mild climate and its beaches. – 2½ miles/4 km S (bus, 10 minutes) the *Dogashima Orchid Center* (Dogashima-yoran-center) possesses 23 glasshouses. On the coast near by are bizarrely shaped rocks and caves gouged out by the sea, which are believed to have been inhabited in prehistoric times.

From Matsuzaki there are buses (twice daily; 40 minutes) and a coastal boat (45 minutes) to **Cape Hagachi**, with cliffs many hundred feet high which are inhabited by wild monkeys.

The Seven Izu Islands

The **Seven Izu Islands (Izu-Shichito)**, the continuation of the volcanic chain of Mount Fuji and Hakone, extend southward into the Pacific. Most of their land area was incorporated in the Fuji-Hakone-Izu National Park in 1964. The group, which is under the administrative authority of Tokyo, comprises (from N to S) the islands of *Oshima, Toshima, Niijima, Kozushima, Miyakejima, Mikurajima* and *Hachijojima.*

The largest of the islands (35 sq. miles/ 90 sq. km) is **Oshima** (pop. 35,000), 73 miles/117 km SW of Tokyo and 25 miles/ 40 km E of Shimoda. The boats from Tokyo put in at **Okada**, on the N coast, from which there are bus services to other places on the island. The administrative center of the island is the port of **Motomachi** (boat services from Atami and Ito). From both of these towns there are buses to Mount *Mihara* (2487 ft/ 758 m), a still-active volcano which is the island's highest peak. From the summit there are fine views of Mount Fuji and the seven islands.

From Okada it is a 15-minute bus ride to **Oshima Park** (zoo, camp site, recreational facilities). At the S end of the park in the *Gyoja Cave,* is a rock-cut figure of the ascetic En-no-Ozunu (7th–8th c.).

To the S **Habuminato**, the island's principal fishing port, lies in a bay formed by a submerged crater.

CRUISES round the islands (6 hours) are run daily, starting from Okada and Motomachi.

Toshima, 12½ miles/20 km SW of Oshima, can be reached by boat from Oshima three times weekly. *Maehama Beach,* on the N coast, offers good bathing. The island, with a circumference of only 5 miles/8 km, is famous for its display of camellia blossom (February–March).

Niijima (boats from Oshima three times weekly) also has good beaches, particularly on the N and W coasts.

Kozushima (boats from Oshima three times weekly; direct service from Tokyo in summer) has beaches at *Tako-wan* and *Nagahama* on the N coast and *Sawajiri* on the E coast, and is also a base for deep-sea fishing (apply to the office of the Boat Union in the little port of Maehama).

Miyakejima (boats from Oshima and direct from Tokyo) is built up of lava, and the beaches are covered with black sand. The best beaches are on the N coast; there are good fishing waters off the S coast. – From here the island of **Mikurajima**, with a population of only 200, can be reached. At the W end of the island is a 330 ft/100 m-high waterfall. The S coast is lined with sheer cliffs. There is no public transport on this island.

The most southerly of the islands is **Hachijojima** (pop. 11,000; boats from Oshima and direct from Tokyo; also air service from Tokyo), the second largest island in the archipelago (27 sq. miles/ 70 sq. km). The highest peak on the island is Mount **Nishi** (or *Hachijo-Fuji;* 2802 ft/ 854 m), which, like Mount **Higashi** (or *Mihara,* 2300 ft/701 m), is an extinct volcano. Ukita Hideie (1573–1655), a henchman of Toyotomi Hideyoshi, was exiled to this island by Tokugawa Ieyasu. – From *Hachijo* there are coach tours of the island.

Izumo

いずも

Prefecture: Shimane. – Population: 79,000.
Post code: J-693. – Telephone code: 0853.

(central)
Shimane-ken Tokyo Kanko Bussan Assensho,
Tetsudo Kaikan,
1-9-1, Marunouchi, Chiyoda-ku,
J-100 **Tokyo;**
tel. (03) 212 1091.

(local)
Shimane-ken Kanko Renmei,
1, Tonomachi,
J-690 **Matsue;**
tel. (0852) 22 5293.

HOTELS. – **Ryokan:** *Inaba-ya Ryokan,* in Taisha, 721, Oaza Kizuki-Higashi, 33 r.; *Takeno-ya,* in Taisha, Oaza Kizuki-Minami, 44 r.

TRANSPORTATION. – **Air:** from TOKYO (Haneda Airport), 1½ hours; from OSAKA (1 hour). – **Rail:** from TOKYO (Central Station) JNR Shinkansen line to OKAYAMA (4¼ hours), then JNR Hakubi line to YONAGO and JNR San-in line to Izumoshi (4 hours); from OSAKA JNR San-in line (7 hours). – **Bus:** from Izumo Airport to city center.

The town of Izumo lies on the N coast of western Honshu, at the point where the Shimane Peninsula projects into the Sea of Japan. To the W of the town the River Kando flows into the sea, while to the E the River Hii flows into Lake Shinji, which is situated between the peninsula and the main island. Izumo is an important traffic junction and commercial and agricultural center for the surrounding region.

The Izumo area was settled at an early stage, and still shows traces of a culture differing from the rest of Japan and marked by Korean influences. This difference can also be seen in the architecture of the old peasant houses and in the Izumo-Taisha Shrine to the NW of the town (see under Daisen-Oki National Park).

SURROUNDINGS. – 5 miles/8 km S of the station is the **Tachikue-kyo Gorge** (Ichihata private railway, 30 minutes), carved out by the River *Kando;* the gorge is particularly beautiful in autumn.

See also **Daisen-Oki National Park** and **Matsue.**

Japan Alps

See Chubu-Sangaku National Park

Kagoshima
かごしま

Prefecture: Kagoshima. – Population: 515,000.
Post code: J-890. – Telephone code: 0992.

ⓘ (central)
Kagoshima-ken Tokyo Kanko Bussan Assensho,
Olympic Building,
2-7-17, Ginza,
J-100 **Tokyo**;
tel. (03) 561 6701.

(local)
Kagoshima City Tourist Information Office,
1, Chuo-cho;
tel. 53 2500 (English spoken).
Tourist Section of Kagoshima Prefecture,
14-50, Yamashita-cho;
tel. 26 8111.

HOTELS. – **Western style:** *Shiroyama Kanko Hotel,* 41-1, Shinshoin-cho, 621 r., Japanese garden, SP; *Kagoshima Sun Royal Hotel,* 8–10, Yojiro 1-chome, 337 r., Japanese garden, SP, thermal bath; *Kagoshima Hayashida Hotel,* 12-22, Higashi-Sengoku-cho, 200 r., beach; *Hokke Club Kagoshimaten,* 3-22, Yamanoguchi-cho, 127 r.; *Kagoshima Gasutofu,* 7-3, Chucho, 87 r.; *Kagoshima Daiichi Hotel,* 1-41, Takashi, 40 r. – **Ryokan:** *Daiichiso,* 1-38-8, Shimoarata, 60 r.; *Hotel Fukiageso,* Terukuni-cho, 52 r.; *Kagoshima Kokusai Hotel Kakumeikan,* Shiroyama-cho, 53 r.; *Hotel Rakuzan-so,* Shimotatsuocho, 43 r. – YOUTH HOSTEL: *YH Kagoshima-ken Fujin Kaikan,* 2-27-12, Shimoarata, 45 b.

EVENTS. – *Soga-don no Kasayaki* (end of May), ceremonial burning of paper umbrellas; *Myoen-ji mairi* (end of September), procession of boys in samurai armor; *Ohara-matsuri* (begining of November), parade through the town, with folk-singing.

TRANSPORTATION. – **Air:** from TOKYO (Haneda Airport), 1½ hours; from OSAKA (1 hour); from NAGOYA (1¼ hours). – **Rail:** from TOKYO (Central Station) JNR Shinkansen line via NAGOYA, KYOTO, OSAKA, OKAYAMA and HIROSHIMA to Hakata (7 hours), then JNR Kagoshima line (4½ hours); from MIYAZAKI JNR Nippo line (1¾ hours).

Kagoshima, chief town of a prefecture and its principal center of communications, lies in southern Kyushu, on the W side of Kagoshima Bay, a wide inlet projecting far inland. In the bay is an active volcano, **Sakurajima, which is often compared with Vesuvius; Kagoshima has been twinned with Naples since 1960.

Kagoshima has a pleasant climate thanks to a warm marine current, *Kuroshio:* the average temperature is about 61–64 °F/ 16–18 °C. There are, however, frequently typhoons in the late summer and autumn. – The city's main sources of income are the manufacture of silk, glass and bamboo articles and above all the production of ceramics, a trade established here for 300 years.

HISTORY. – From the 13th c. onwards Kagoshima was the seat of 29 generations of the Shimazu family, which controlled the provinces of Satsuma, Osumi and Hyuga. – In 1549 the Jesuit Francisco de Javier (St Francis Xavier, 1506–52) landed in Kagoshima, where he began to preach the Gospel, at first with the support of Shimazu Takahisa (1514–71). After only ten months, however, he fell into disfavor and was obliged to leave the town; but in this short period more than 600 Japanese were converted to Christianity. – Nariakira, the 28th Shimazu (1809–58), laid the foundations of the town's industry by introducing Western technology. The first modern Japanese warship was built here, and in 1863 was involved in an engagement with a British fleet. – The town's best-known son was the samurai Saigo Takamori (1827–77), who retired to the town after coming into conflict with the Meiji régime in Tokyo. On February 15, 1877 he advanced on the capital with a force of 10,000 men in order to negotiate with the Government on the preservation of the ancient rights of the samurai order. After suffering heavy losses in fighting with superior Government forces he returned to Kagoshima and entrenched himself with a few faithful followers on Mount Shiroyama, where he committed suicide on September 24, 1877. This ended the rebellion known as the Seinan Rising. Saigo, posthumously rehabilitated, is still presented as a model of local patriotism in Kagoshima.

SIGHTS. – SW of Kagoshima Station is Mount *Shiroyama* (351 ft/107 m), with a stepped path leading up to the top. At the foot of the hill are the remains of the walls of **Tsurumaru-jo Castle,** destroyed by fire in 1874, and a bronze statue of Saigo, who committed suicide in the nearby cave (memorial). From the top of the hill there is a *view of the bay and the volcano of Sakurajima. To the S of the summit is the **Terukuni Shrine,** with a large stone *torii;* the shrine is dedicated to Shimazu Nariakira. To the left the four-storey *Cultural Center* (1966) has a planetarium and a natural history museum. To the S lies the **St Francis Xavier Park,** with a memorial to the missionary (bronze bust) and the remains of a Christian church, one of the

Mount Shiroyama, Kagoshima

first to be built on Japanese soil. Here, too, is the *St Francis Xavier Memorial Church*, built in 1949 on the 400th anniversary of Francis Xavier's landing.

¾ mile/1 km NW of Kagoshima Station is the **Nanshu Shrine**, dedicated to Saigo Takamori. In the graveyard of the nearby *Jokomyoji Temple* are the tombs of Saigo and his followers. – 1½ miles/2·5 km N of the station stands the **Shoko-Shuseikan Museum** (weapons, glass, ceramics, parts of ships, yarns), housed in a factory built in 1852, of a type then unique in Japan. The museum also contains a variety of material illustrating the 700-year history of the Shimazu family. – Beyond the railway line is the *Ijin-kan*, once the residence of British engineers working in the Shuseikan factory.

****Iso Park** farther N, was an old summer residence of the Shimazu family (17th c.). One of the most charming landscaped gardens on Kyushu, it affords the best *view of Sakurajima. From here a cableway runs up Mount *Isoyama*, on which there is a small amusement park.

SURROUNDINGS. – To the E of the town, in the bay, the still-active volcano ****Sakurajima** (ferry, 20 minutes), has three peaks – *Kita-dake* (3668 ft/ 1118 m), *Naka-dake* (3642 ft/1110 m) and *Minami-dake* (3478 ft/1060 m). The only crater still active is Minami-dake, above which there always hangs a column of smoke. Sakurajima lies within the *Kirishima-Yaku Nation Park* (see separate entry).

The eruptions of **Sakurajima** have been recorded as far back as the year 708. Particularly notable was the

Mount Sakurajima, Kagoshima

1914 eruption, in the course of which the arm of the sea, 440 yds/400 m wide and 235 ft/72 m deep, which had previously separated the volcano from the *Osumi* Peninsula to the E was filled up with great masses of lava, so that Sakurajima is now a peninsula which can be reached from Osumi by road. – The volcanic soil produces crops of giant horse-radishes (Sakurajima-daikon) weighing up to 99 lb/45 kg (harvested January–February).

A good road (coach tour, 1¾ hours) traverses the lava-fields from **Hakamagoshi**, on the W side of the peninsula. At the S end is the little town of **Kurokami**, with a stone *torii* which during the 1914 eruption was buried in lava up to its lintel.

See also **Chiran, Ibusuki** and **Kirishima-Yaku National Park**.

Kamakura
かまくら

Prefecture: Kanagawa. – Population: 175,000.
Post code: J-248. – Telephone code: 0467.
ⓘ (local)
   Kamakura Eki Kanto Information,
   Kamakura-eki
   (East Station);
   tel. 22 3350.

HOTEL. – **Western style**: *Kamakura Park Hotel*, 33-6, Sakanoshita, 41 r., SP, beach. – YOUTH HOSTEL: *YH Nihon Gakusei Kaikan*, 27-9, Sakanoshita, 400 b.

EVENTS. – *First visit to shrines* (January 1–3), including Tsurugaoka-Hachiman Shrine and Kamakura Shrine; *Setsubun* (beginning of February), driving out of winter, in Tsurugaoka, Kamakura, Kenchoji and other shrines; *Kamakura-matsuri* (beginning to middle of April), municipal festival with parades and tea ceremony; *Annual Festival of Tsurugaoka-Hachiman Shrine* (mid September), with Yabusame, equestrian festival and archery contests; *Menkake-gyoretsu* (mid September), masked procession at Gongoro Shrine; *Takigi-no* (end of September), evening performances of No plays in open air at Kamakura Shrine.

TRANSPORTATION. – **Rail**: from TOKYO (Central Station) JNR Yokosuka line via YOKOHAMA (1 hour).

****Kamakura, once capital of Japan, lies 25 miles/40 km SW of Tokyo in Sagami Bay. It is surrounded on three sides by wooded hills, and to the SE the Miura Peninsula extends into the Pacific. With its many temples and shrines and other features of interest, Kamakura is a busy tourist center and its mild climate and beaches attract many summer visitors from the Tokyo-Yokohama area.**

Only 30 years ago Kamakura was a small seaside resort. It has now developed into a residential suburb of Tokyo and Yokohama, favored particularly by many members of the intelligentsia.

Kamakura has no fewer than 65 temples and 19 shrines, together with many art treasures. – A major thoroughfare, the Wakamiya-oji, runs northward from the coast, dividing the town into two halves. – The best-known product of Kamakura is its lacquered woodcarving (*Kamakura-bori*; demonstration of process in Kamakura-bori-Kaikan Hall).

HISTORY. – Emerging victorious from the bloody battle between the Minamoto and the Taira at Dannoura (1185), Minamoto Yoritomo (1147–99) established his military government (*Kamakura-bakufu*) in Kamakura in 1192, thus distancing himself from the decadent Court life of Kyoto. This also enabled him to establish his authority over the eastern part of the country, now entirely under his control. He developed a strict knightly culture, and Kamakura remained until 1333 the central stronghold of the feudal order of warrior nobility. After Yorimoto's death his sons Yoriie and Sanetomo took over the shogunal authority, but with their murder the House of Minamoto became extinct and the Hojo clan seized power. The fall of the Hojo family was accompanied by fierce fighting, during which the town was largely destroyed. In the Muromachi period which followed (1338–1573) Kamakura enjoyed a period of prosperity under the Ashikaga shoguns as the administrative center of the eastern provinces, but the transfer of administrative authority to Odawara relegated it to the role of a quiet little fishing village.

SIGHTS. – 550 yds/500 m N of the station, situated in the city center, stands the **Jufukuji Temple** of the Rinzai sect, founded in 1200 by Masako, wife of Yoritomo, which was one of the five great Zen temples situated on hills (*Kamakura-gozan*) – the others being Kenchoji, Engakuji, Jochiji and Jomyoji. All that remains of the temple is the *Cult Hall* (rebuilt), with a wooden *statue of Jizo, the patron god of children. On the hill behind the temple are the tombs of Masako and her son Minamoto Sanetomo (1192–1219). – A little way N is the **Eishoji Temple**, with a nunnery of the Jodo sect founded in 1636 by Eisho, wife of Tokugawa Ieyasu.

To the W of the station (20 minutes' walk) is the **Zeniarai-Benten Shrine**, dedicated to Benten, goddess of good fortune. It is the popular belief that any sum of money washed in the spring here when the snake (one of the Oriental signs of the zodiac) is in the ascendant will be doubled or trebled. The *torii* leading to the

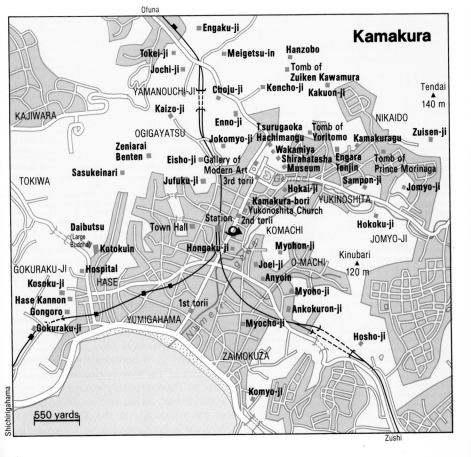

Tsurugaoka-Hachiman Shrine

consecrated cave were presented by grateful worshippers.

NE of the station (bus, 3 minutes) is the ****Tsurugaoka-Hachiman Shrine**. The street leading to the shrine, *Wakamiya-Oji*, with three *torii* set at intervals along its length, becomes narrower towards the N end, thus creating the effect of great distance. Between the second and third torii the street is lined with cherry trees and azaleas.

The ****Tsurugaoka-Hachiman Shrine** was founded in 1063 by Minamoto Yoriyoshi (998–1075) and was transferred to its present site by Yoritomo in 1191. It is dedicated to the war god Hachiman, who was particularly revered during the Kamakura period; identified with the legendary Ojin-tenno, he was the patron god of the Minamoto family. The present buildings of the shrine, which date from 1828, are in the sumptuous style of the Momoyama period (1573–1600). The shrine contains valuable *art treasures, including armor, swords and masks. To the left of the steps leading up to the shrine is a ginkgo tree 72 ft/22 m high with a girth of 23 ft/7 m. It marks the spot where Sanetomo, the third Kamakura Shogun, was murdered by his nephew Kugyo in 1219.

To the right of the steps is the subsidiary **Wakamiya Shrine** (1624), dedicated to Nintoku-tenno, son of Ojin. A favourite theme in Japanese literature is the dance which Shizuka, the beloved of Minamoto Yoshitsune (1159–89), was compelled to perform here for Yoshitsune's brother Yoritomo: the object was to force her to reveal the hiding-place of Yoshitsune.

Near the Wakamiya Shrine can be found the **Shirahatasha Shrine**, dedicated to the memory of Yoritomo and Sanetomo. The name ("white banner") refers to the banner of the Minamoto family. – To the

right of the shrine the ***Municipal Museum** (*Kamakura Kokuhokan*), built in 1928 in the style of the Shosoin at Nara, contains art treasures from local temples and shrines and private collections of material of the Kamakura and Muromachi periods. Adjoining is the **Museum of Modern Art**, built in 1951.

550 yds/500 m NE of the shrine a 5 ft/1·60 m-high *pagoda* surrounded by a stone wall, marks the tomb of Yoritomo, founder of the Kamakura-bakufu. To the E of this is the **Kamakura Shrine** (also reached by bus from the station, 10 minutes), set in a grove of trees. Built in 1869, it is dedicated to Prince Morinaga (1308–35); the treasury is worth seeing. Morinaga, son of Godaigo-tenno, attempted to re-establish the Emperor's authority and was murdered by the brother of the ruling Shogun in a nearby cave. His tomb is on the hill of *Richikozan*, 220 yds/200 m E.

770 yds/700 m N of the Kamakura Shrine is the **Kakuonji Temple** of the Shingon sect (Sen-yuji school), built in 1218, in the time of Hojo Yoshitoki.

In the *Aisendo Hall* are a seated wooden *statue of Yakushi-nyorai, flanked by two Bosatsus, and a *statue of Jizo, patron god of children.

The caves (*yagura*) in the hill behind the temple appear, on the evidence of bones found in them, to have been burial-places.

¾ mile/1 km E of the Kamakura Shrine, in a setting of verdant hills, is the **Zuisenji Temple**, a Zen temple of the Rinzai sect (Engakuji school). The *garden*, laid out by Muso-Kokushi (or Soseki, 1275–1351), is a famous example of the landscape architecture of the Late Kamakura period, showing the influence of Zen Buddhism. The temple, also founded by Muso-Kokushi, was rebuilt in the 14th c. The wooden *statue of Muso-Kokushi (40 inches/1 m high) in the Founder's Hall is one of the finest works of art of the Muromachi period. – From the hill behind the temple a fine *view of the town may be enjoyed.

To the S of the Kamakura Shrine (bus from station, 7 minutes) stands the **Samponji Temple** (or *Sugimoto-dera*), which is believed to have been founded in the 8th c. It contains three wooden *statues of the Eleven-Headed Kannon, two of them probably dating from the Heian period. As the former starting-point of the pilgrimage to the 33 temples of Kannon in the Kanto region the temple is still known as the Sugimoto-Kannon Temple. – 380 yds/350 m E (bus from station, 8 minutes) an avenue of cherry trees leads to the **Jomyoji Temple**, one of the five large Zen temples in Kamakura, founded in 1188 by Ashikaga Yoshikane (d. 1199).

SE of the station are a number of temples of the Nichiren sect. 10 minutes' walk from the station is the **Myohonji Temple**, founded by Hiki Yoshimoto (later a priest under the name of Nichigaku), a disciple of Nichiren. A little way S is the **Ankokuronji Temple** (bus from station, 5 minutes), built in 1274 on the site of Nichiren's hermitage, among the principal treasures of which is an early copy of "Rissho-ankokuron", a polemical work by Nichiren directed against other sects. – Close by, to the N, the **Myohoji Temple** contains the Hokke-do Hall.

Daibutsu (Great Buddha)

> **Nichiren Shonin** (1222–82), a native of Kominato on the Boso Peninsula, spent three years in a monastery in Kyoto and then began to propagate his doctrine in his home town. Having been expelled from Kominato, he founded the *Nichiren-Hokke sect* in 1253, established his hermitage and within a period of three years produced his "Rissho-ankokuron" and various other writings. His criticisms of the Government and his attacks on other sects led to his being exiled to the Izu Peninsula (1261–63). After his return he continued to promote his doctrine. Barely escaping execution, he was again exiled in 1271, this time to the island of Sado (see separate entry), where he wrote various other works, including the "Kaimokusho" (1272). From 1274 until his death he lived in the remote Kuon-ji Temple on the slopes of Mount Minobu (to the W of Mount Fuji) and in the Hommonji Temple which he founded in Ikegami (now Tokyo).

In the SE of the town (bus from station, 10 minutes) the **Komyoji Temple** of the Jodo sect, founded in 1243, contains a number of fine *pictures and *picture scrolls. Within the precincts of the temple is a beautiful lotus-pond.

The best-known sight in Kamakura, the ****Great Buddha** (*Daibutsu*) is at the Kotokuin Temple (Jodo sect) in the SW of the town (bus from station, 10 minutes).

> The ****Great Buddha**, a seated bronze figure of Amida, is the largest statue in Japan after the Daibutsu in the Todai-ji Temple at Nara (see separate entry); 37 ft/11·4 m high, it weighs 93 tons. It is rated the finest and most perfect of all Buddha statues in Japan.
>
> The statue, cast in 1252 by Ono Goroemon or Tanji Hisamoto, was originally enclosed in a large hall, but

this was destroyed in a storm in 1369 and its remains were washed away in a flood in 1495. – The position of the hands (*mudra*) expresses steadfastness of faith.

A short distance SW is the **Hase-Kannon Temple** (Jodo sect), with a statue of the Eleven-Headed Kannon in the main hall. This gilded wooden *statue, 30 ft/9.3 m high, is said to have been carved from one half of an old camphor tree by a priest named Tokudo in the year 721; the other half of the tree was used to make the statue of Kannon in the Hase-dera at Nara (see separate entry). The temple also possesses the third oldest *bell in the town, cast in 1264. From the temple there is a fine *view of the beaches S of Kamakura.

Farther SW is the **Gokurakuji Temple** (Enoden private railway from Kamakura Station). Apart from a number of treasures such as the *statue of Shakyamuni little is left of the temple, which was founded in 1259 by Hojo Shigetoki (1198–1261). – To the S, beyond the railway line, are the beaches of *Yumigahama* (to E) and *Shichirigahama* (to W); from the latter there is a fine view of Enoshima. Yumigahama Beach (1¼ miles/2 km long), one of the finest beaches around Tokyo, is the scene of a lively festival at the beginning of August.

From Kita-Kamakura Station, outside the city to the N, a bus (10 minutes) runs to the ****Engakuji Temple**, 1½ miles/2·5 km E. This temple of the Rinzai sect, the center of the Engakuji school, was founded

Engakuji Temple

in 1282 by Hojo Tokimune and put under the direction of a Chinese abbot.

In spite of the severe damage it suffered in the 1923 earthquake the **Relic Hall** (*Shariden*), built in 1285, remains the finest example of the vigorous architecture of the Kamakura period. It possesses a valuable quartz reliquary containing a tooth of the Buddha (seen only from January 1 to 3). – In the bell-tower to the right of the two-storey gate is a *bell* cast in 1301, the largest in Kamakura (8½ ft/2·6 m high). Behind the main building is the tomb of Tokumine. There is a beautifully situated **tea-house** (*butsunichi-an*), with the tea-chamber (*ensoku-an*) and a garden.

S of Kita-Kamakura Station a 5-minute walk brings one to the **Tokeiji Temple** of the Rinzai sect (Engakuji school). Under a law promulgated by Hojo Sadatoki (1271–1311) women maltreated by their husbands were regarded as divorced when they entered the nunnery here, and the temple accordingly became known as the Enkiridera ("Temple of Divorce"). The first Abbess was the foundress of the temple, Sadatoki's widow. In the main hall is a wooden *statue of Sho-Kannon. – From here a footpath leads S to the **Jochiji Temple** of the Rinzai sect, situated in an old cypress wood. Founded by Hojo Morotoki in 1283, this is one of the five great Zen temples of Kamakura. The wooden *statue of Jizo (patron god of children) by the sculptor Unkei was the only one of the temple's treasures to survive the 1923 earthquake. Adjoining the gate of the temple is one of the "ten clear springs" of Kamakura.

SE of Kita-Kamakura Station stands the **Kenchoji Temple** (bus, 4 minutes; also service to Tsurugaoka-Hachiman Shrine,

6 minutes), surrounded by tall cedars. The temple was founded by Hojo Tokiyori (1227–63) in 1253 for a Chinese priest named Tai Chiao (Japanese name Daigaku-zenji). It was burned down in 1415 but was rebuilt by the Tokugawa in the 17th c. The gate and main hall are in the Chinese style of the Sung period. Notable among the temple's treasures are the second oldest *bell in Kamakura (cast 1255) and a wooden statue of the founder, a masterpiece of the Kamakura period. On a hill behind the temple lies the tomb of Tai Chiao, who was active as a political adviser and spiritual guide to the Hojo family.

SURROUNDINGS of Kamakura

To the W of the town lies the popular seaside resort of **Katase**, at the mouth of the River Katase (private railway lines from Fujisawa and Kamakura). In Shonan Park, on the W side of the river, are Enoshima Marineland (whales, dolphins) and an Aquarium. Along the coast are numerous swimming pools, boat-rental agencies, etc. – 110 yds/100 m NE of Enoshima Station is the *Ryukoji Temple* of the Nichiren sect, built in 1288 on the spot where Nichiren was due to be executed but was pardoned when a flash of lightning shattered the executioner's sword. An emissary of Kublai Khan was executed on the same spot in 1275. The Oeshiki-matsuri festival is celebrated here in mid September.

The Benten-bashi Bridge (650 yds/600 m long) leads on to the wooded island of **Enoshima**. At the top of a flight of 300 stone steps is the **Enoshima Shrine**, built by Minamoto Yoritomo in 1182 as a temple of Benten, goddess of fortune, and converted to its present function in 1868.

There are fine *views of the island of Oshima (one of the Seven Izu Islands) and Mount Fuji from the *Peace Tower* (177 ft/54 m high), set in a recreational area of 17 acres which also includes a tropical garden and a zoo. To the SW, lower down, the **Benten Cave** (Dragon Cave) once contained the unclothed statue of Benten which is now in the Enoshima Shrine. – *Shonan Harbor* is a large yacht harbor constructed for the 1964 Olympic Games.

N of Katase, 2½ miles/4 km from the coast, lies the town of **Fujisawa** (pop. 293,000; Enoden Railway from Kamakura, 35 minutes; JNR Tokaido line or Odakyu private line from Tokyo, 1 hour), with the Yugyoji Temple (or Shojoko-ji), founded in 1235 as the principal temple of the Jishu sect. To the left of the main hall is a bell-tower with a bell cast in 1356.

SE of Kamakura the **Miura Peninsula** divides between *Tokyo Bay* to the E and *Sagami Bay* to the W. Its mild climate makes this a favored residential area for well-to-do citizens of Tokyo; it also has excellent beaches.

The town nearest to Kamakura on the peninsula is **Zushi** (bus, 20 minutes; Yokosuka private railway, 5 minutes). From here a bus service (15 minutes) goes to the seaside resort of **Hayama**, from which there are magnificent views of Sagami Bay and Mount Fuji. To the N of the town, at *Abuzuri*, is the Hayama Marina leisure center, with the hotel of the same name. Along the coast to the S extends Hayama Park.

On the E coast of the peninsula is the city of **Yokosuka** (pop. 419,000), the largest town in this coastal region, with a commercial and a fishing harbor. Until the end of the Second World War this was also a naval port, and there is now a United States naval base here. There are rail connections from Tokyo and Yokohama. The city extends over a number of hills (Mount Okusu, 794 ft/242 m; Mount Takatori, 456 ft/139 m). ¾ mile/1 km E of the station Mikasa Park (bus from station, 5 minutes) is well worth a visit. Offshore is the "Mikasa", launched in 1900, flagship of Admiral Togo during the Russo-Japanese War (1904–05), taken out of service in 1923 in terms of the Washington Disarmament Conference and recommissioned as a museum ship in 1961. From the park a ferry service (10 minutes) serves the little island of *Sarushima*, once occupied by coastal batteries and now a popular water-sports center. – To the W of Yokosuka lies the Tsukayama Park, in which are the graves of William Adams (1564–1620; Japanese name Miura Anjin) and his Japanese wife. Adams was an English pilot who was cast ashore in southern Japan and became an adviser and shipbuilder in the service of Tokugawa Ieyasu. – The castle of the Princes Miura formerly stood in Kinugasa Park, from which there is a fine *view of the peninsula; cherry blossom at the beginning of April.

The most easterly port on the Miura Peninsula is *Uraga*, in the south-eastern part of the Yokosuka city area. Under the Tokugawa Shogunate (1603–1867) shipping entering Tokyo Bay was watched over and controlled from here. Here in the year 1846 Commodore Biddle delivered a letter from the President of the United States, and seven years later Commodore Perry anchored outside the harbor and initiated the opening-up of Japan with the delivery of a further letter from the US President. The letter was handed over at **Kurihama**, to the S (bus from Uraga, 15 minutes), where there is a monument commemorating the event. Ferry across Tokyo Bay to the Boso Peninsula.

At the S end of the peninsula is the port of **Miura** (bus from Kurihama, 40 minutes), a deep-sea fishing center. A bridge 630 yds/575 m long leads on to the little island of *Jogashima*, with a lighthouse and associated museum; *view of the port of **Misaki** to the W. Farther N are many little coves and inlets offering good bathing, for example at *Aburabutso* (boat service from Misaki), with a "marine park".

Kanazawa
かなざわ

Prefecture: Ishikawa. – Population: 425,000.
Post code: J-920. – Telephone code: 0762.

ⓘ (central)
Ishikawa-ken Tokyo Kanko Bussan Assensho,
Kokusai Kanko Kaikan,
1-8-3, Marunouchi, Chiyoda-ku,
J-100 **Tokyo**;
tel. (03) 231 4030.

(local)
Ishikawa-ken Tourist Information Center,
2-1-1, Hirosaka;
tel. 61 1111.

HOTELS. – **Western style**: *Kanazawa Sky Hotel*, 15-1, Musachi-machi, 137 r.; *Kanazawa New Grand Hotel*, 1-50, Takaoka-machi, 122 r.; *Hotel New Kanazawa*, 2-14-10, Honmachi, 117 r., beach; *Kanazawa City Hotel*, 6-8, Showa-machi, 160 r.; *Hakuunro Hotel*, Yuwaku-machi, 100 r., SP; *Kanazawa Miyako Hotel*, 6-10, Konohana-cho, 88 r.; *Central Hotel Kanazawa*, 4-1, Horikawa-cho, 49 r.; *Business Hotel Mikage*, 2-11, Miage-cho, 49 r.; *Business Hotel Kotoji*, 22-7, Chuodori, 32 r.; *Kanazawa Plaza Hotel*, 11-18, Konohana-cho, 30 r. – **Minshuku**: *Ryokan Nogi*, 4-16, Konohana-cho, 68 r., SP; *Ginmatsu*, 1-17-18, Higashiyama, 50 r. – YOUTH HOSTELS: *Kanazawa YH*, 37, Suehiro-cho, 120 b.; *YH Kanazawa-Shi Seinen-No-Ie*, 11, Te-ko, 100 b.; *Matsuiya YH*, 1-9-3, Kata-machi, 15 b.; *Izuminodai YH*, 1-1-31, Izumigaoka, 15 b.

EVENTS. – *Hyaku-mangoku-matsuri* (mid June), parade with historical costumes.

TRANSPORTATION. – **Air**: from TOKYO (Haneda Airport) to Komatsu (1 hour). – **Rail**: from TOKYO (Central Station) JNR Tokaido–Shinkansen line to MAIBARA (3½ hours), then JNR Hokuriku line (2½ hours); from TOKYO (Ueno Station) JNR Shin-etsu and Hokuriku lines (6½ hours). – **Bus**: from Komatsu Airport to Kanazawa (50 minutes).

*Kanazawa, chief town of Ishikawa prefecture, lies on the NW coast of Honshu at the point where the Noto Peninsula projects into the Sea of Japan and the River Asano reaches the sea. It is the largest and finest city in the Hokuriku district and its cultural center. Many features of interest survive from its brilliant past, including one of the three most beautiful gardens in Japan, the **Kenroku-en Park in the heart of the city.*

Kanazawa is now an industrial center and a university town, with a college of art. Local products are hand-colored silks

Remains of Kanazawa Castle

(*kagayuzen*) and elegant porcelain (*Kutani-yaki*) with colorful decoration (on sale in the main shopping streets, Katamachi and Korinbo).

HISTORY. – The little village of *Tamazaki* developed towards the end of the 15th c., under the leadership of the Buddhist priesthood, into a center of political power which came under the control of Sakuma Morimasa in 1580 but three years later, during the civil wars, passed to Maeda Toshiie. During the subsequent three centuries of rule by the princely Maeda family, masters of the province of Kaga and the second most powerful dynasty of the Edo period, Kanazawa prospered as a center of culture and craft production.

SIGHTS. – In the middle of the city (bus from station, 15 minutes) are the remains of the *Castle*, destroyed by fire in 1881.

The surviving features are the *gate, Ishikawa-mon, and a *samurai house* (Sanjuken-nagaya), 180 ft/54 m long.

Across the street lies the magnificent **Kenroku-en Park**, the largest (25 acres) of the three most famous Japanese gardens. (The others are at Mito and Okayama: see separate entries.) The park, attached to the residence of the Maeda family, was completed in 1837. As its name indicates, it incorporates six (*roku*) qualities – dignity, festiveness, spaciousness, artistic form, coolness and scenic harmony.

At the N end of the park are the *information bureau* and car park. Going S from here, we come to two small

Kenroku-en Park, Kanazawa

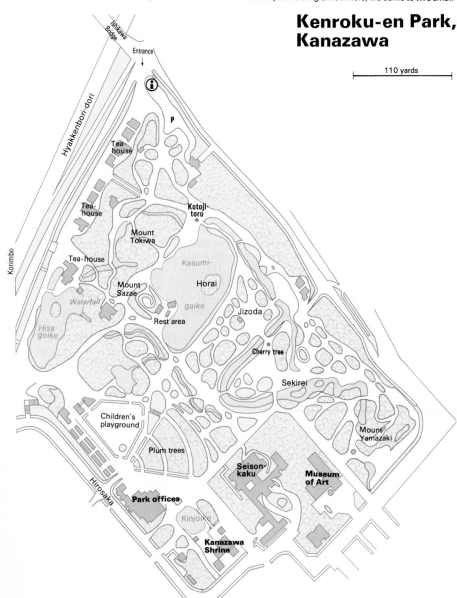

lakes, *Hisagoike* to the right and *Kasumigaike* to the left. At the E end of Hisagoike is a small waterfall, and beside Kasumigaike a *stone lantern*, Kotoji-toro. Farther E is a bronze statue of the legendary hero Yamato-takeru (see under Nagoya). SE of the lake grows a cherry tree famous for its magnificent show of blossom. – At the S end of the park stands the *Seison-kaku, a house built in 1863 for the Daimyo's mother, and to the E of this is the **Museum of Art**, with works by the artist Ninsei and a fine collection of Kutani-yaki porcelain. To the SW is the **Kanazawa Shrine**.

From the main shopping street, *Korinbo*, it is a 10 minutes' walk to the **Nakamura Art Gallery** (gold lacquerware, tea-services). In **Chuo Park** (also within easy reach of Korinbo) we find the **Municipal Museum** (*Kanazawa Kyodo-shiryo-kan*), housed in the brick buildings of the old University, with periodic exhibitions of No costumes. To the N of the museum (1¼ miles/2 km SE of station; Minami-cho bus stop) is the **Oyama Shrine**, dedicated to Maeda Toshiie. It was built on another site in 1599 and moved to its present position in 1873. The three-storey gate, designed in 1875 by a Dutch architect and incorporating both Eastern and Western features, is a fine example of Meiji architecture. – Near by (Musashi-ga-Tsuji bus stop) is the sumptuously decorated **Ozaki Shrine**, which is compared with the Toshogu Shrine at Nikko.

Performances of No plays in traditional style are given monthly in the **No-gakudo Theater** near the Civic Hall, one of the finest No theaters in Japan. The famous Kaga-Hosho school of No drama developed in Kanazawa.

To the NE of the town, beyond the River *Asano*, rises Mount *Utatsu* (463 ft/ 141 m), from which there are fine *views of the surrounding country. The area around the hill is a nature park, with an aquarium and a zoo. Here, too, are the **Utatsu** and **Gogoku Shrines** and monuments to the priests Nichiren and Rennyo and two writers born in Kanazawa, Izumi Kyoka (1873–1939) and Tokuda Shusei (1871–1943).

SW of the town (bus from station, 20 minutes) stands the **Myoryuji Temple** of the Nichiren sect, famous for its labyrinth of rooms and passages. The temple was also designed as a place of refuge, with an underground passage which is said to lead to the banks of the nearby River *Sai*. The temple can be seen by prior appointment (tel. 41 2877).

SURROUNDINGS. – SE of Kanazawa is the resort of **Yuwaku-onsen** (Hokuriku railway bus, 50 minutes), with the Edo-Mura Open-Air Museum. A variety of old buildings have been brought together on this 40 acre site – samurai houses, old town houses, a temple gate, a bell-tower of the Edo period, etc. – Mount *Io* (3081 ft/939 m) is a popular recreation and winter-sports area.

S of Kanazawa by way of *Komatsu* the quiet health resort of **Awazu-onsen** (JNR Hokuriku line, 40 minutes, then bus, 10 minutes), the oldest spa in the Hokuriku district, has hot springs at temperatures of 122–136 °F/50–58 °C. – The Hokuriku line continues to *Kaga*, from which there are buses (10 minutes) to the livelier resort of **Yamashiro-onsen**. Half-way between Kanazawa and here (rail, 40 minutes) is the *Kutani-yaki Hall*, with a fine collection of Kutani-yaki porcelain. Near by are a number of potters' workshops (facilities for amateur porcelain-painting: Kutani-Kaikan, Terai-machi, Ishikawa-ken, tel. 07615 – 7 0125).

In the middle of the 17th c. deposits of the kaolin required for the making of porcelain were discovered in the village of **Kutani**, S of Yamashiro. Skilled artists in Arita (see separate entry) soon became masters in the art of overglaze painting and established the reputation of Kutani-yaki porcelain, still much sought after today.

From Kanazawa Station a bus runs S to *Hakusanshita* (1 hour 20 minutes), in the **Hakusan National Park** (area 183 sq. miles/473 sq. km). Mount **Hakusan** (8865 ft/2702 m) is one of Japan's three sacred mountains. Of the five approach routes (Iwama, Chugu, Itoshiro, Hirase and Ichinose) the most popular, for climbers coming from Kanazawa, is the Ichinose route. From Hakusanshita it is a 40-minute bus run to *Ichinose* and the neighboring resort of *Hakusan-onsen*, the starting-points of two alternative routes which join at *Midagahara* (8038 ft/2450 m). Near here is the Murodo Hut, which is open during the summer. The route to the five peaks of Mount Hakusan (*views of the Tateyama Range to the SE and Mount Norikura) runs up through dense forests and rich Alpine vegetation. The highest of the five peaks is *Gozenmine* (8865 ft/2702 m), followed by *Tsurugigamine* (8714 ft/2656 m) and *Onanji* (8682 ft/2646 m); to the S are *Bessan* and *Sanno-mine*. On Gozenmine is the *Inner Shrine* (Okunoin) of the *Shirayamahime Shrine* (Kaga-Ichinomiya) at the foot of Mount Hakusan.

See also **Noto Peninsula**.

Karatsu

からつ

Pretecture: Saga. – Population: 79,000.
Post code: J-847. – Telephone code: 09557.
ⓘ (local)
Higashi Karatsu Kanko Information,
4, Higashi Karatsu
(Station);
tel. 2 4963.

HOTEL. – **Western style:** *Karatsu Seaside Hotel*, 4-182, Higashi Karatsu, 52 r., Japanese garden, SP, beach. – YOUTH HOSTEL: *Niji-no-Matsubara YH*, 4108, Kagami, 56 b.

Okunichi-matsuri festival, Karatsu

EVENTS. – *Castle Festival* (beginning of May); *Okunichi-matsuri* (beginning of November), procession with decorated floats.

TRANSPORTATION. – **Rail**: from FUKUOKA (Hakata) JNR Chikuhi line (1 hour); from SAGA JNR Karatsu line (1¼ hours).

The port of Karatsu lies on the N coast of Kyushu, the most westerly of the main Japanese islands. The town and the beautiful surrounding coastal region form the southern part of the Genkai Quasi National Park, which extends along the coast for a distance of some 55 miles/ 90 km.

Lying across the Tsushima Strait from the Korean mainland, Karatsu became a place of some consequence at an early stage as one of the largest ports in northern Kyushu and a gateway to the Asian continent, as its name indicates (*Kara* = "China", *tsu* = "port"). It is now one of the most popular seaside resorts on Kyushu and a good base for excursions to the wooded hills and extensive beaches of the surrounding area. It is also one of the best-known centers of Japanese ceramic production.

HISTORY. – Karatsu rose to importance in the 16th c. as a port for trade with Korea and a center of ceramic production (Karatsu-yaki) since the 14th c. During the Japanese campaigns in Korea Korean potters settled in the town and exerted great influence on the native artists. The rapidly increasing popularity of the tea ceremony in the 16th c. enabled Karatsu to rival Mino and Kyoto as one of the leading centers of manufacture of tea bowls (*chawan*), and the town also developed a considerable export trade in ceramics. – Terazawa Hirotaka (1563–1633) was appointed by Toyotomi Hideyoshi in 1587 to be the first Daimyo of Karatsu.

SIGHTS. – The town's principal landmark, 1 mile/1·5 km NE of the station, is the **Castle**, built in 1602 on a tongue of land at the mouth of the River *Matsuura* and

now surrounded by *Maizuru Park*. The five-storey main tower, demolished during the Meiji period, was rebuilt in 1966 and now houses a museum with an interesting collection of old porcelain. From the tower there are fine *views of the town and the beaches of Nishi-no-hama (to the W) and Higashi-no-hama (to the E), with the leisure park of Higashi-no-hama Koen.

660 yds/600 m NW of the station stands the **Kinshoji Temple** (Rinzai sect), built in 1599. It is also known as the Chikamatsu Temple after the well-known dramatist Chikamatsu Monzaemon (1653–1724), who was a novice here.

½ mile/800 m N of the station can be seen the **Karatsu Shrine**, founded in the Nara period (710–794). The shrine festival (Karatsu okunchi-matsuri), first celebrated in 1752, followed the pattern of the famous Gion-matsuri festival of Kyoto. The sumptuously decorated floats which take part in the ceremony are on show during the rest of the year in the nearby **Hikiyama Cultural Center**.

Also worth visiting are the *ceramic workshops* of two well-known potters, Nakazato-Taroemon and Nakano-Toki (respectively 10 and 15 minutes SE of the station). Both have interesting exhibitions of porcelain.

SURROUNDINGS. – 3 miles/5 km SE of Karatsu, at the foot of Mount *Kagamiyama*, is the **Einichi Temple** of the Soto sect, founded in 1375. A winding road runs up to the summit of the mountain, from which there is a fine view of Karatsu Bay. The temple, dedicated to Benten, goddess of fortune, recalls a legend associated with the mountain.

In the 6th c. Otomo-no-Sadehiko, a Japanese general, stayed in Matsuura (then in the province of Hizen) on his way to Korea and fell in love with a noble lady named Sayohime. When he sailed away she waved farewell to his ships with a cloth for so long that she turned into stone. To this legend the mount owes its other name of *Hlrefuruyama* (hire = "cloth", furu = "wave", yama = "hill").

To the N of Kagamiyama is the stretch of coast known as **Niji-no-Matsubara**, with the beautiful white beach of *Matsuuragata* and a grove of pines up to 200 years old, 3 miles/5 km long by ¾ mile/1 km wide.

9 miles/14 km NW of Karatsu, at **Minato Yakatashi**, are the interesting *Seven Caves* (Nanatsu-gama). These basalt caves carved out by erosion, the largest of which is some 10 ft/3 m high and wide and 120 yds/110 m long, can be visited by boat from Karatsu or Yobuko when the sea is calm.

The little fishing port of **Yobuko**, 8 miles/13 km NW of Karatsu (bus, 30 minutes), lies near the northern tip of the **Higashi-Matsuura Peninsula**; boats to the islands in the Genkai-Nada Sea. There is a colorful morning market at which the local fishermen and farmers sell their produce. Off the coast lies the island of **Kabeshima** (ferry, 10 minutes), with a shrine dedicated to a member of the Sayohime family. – There is also a ferry to the larger island of **Iki** or **Indoji** (area 54 sq. miles/139 sq. km, pop. 43,000), which achieved a place in history during the attempted invasion by Kublai Khan's Mongols (1274). The *Shinjo Shrine* at **Katsumoto** is dedicated to Taira Kagetaka, a Governor of Iki who was killed during the fighting. Near the port of **Gonoura**, in the SW of the island, are the ruins of a castle built by Toyotomi Hideyoshi as a base for his Korean campaigns. – There is a ferry from Gonoura to **Fukuoka** (see separate entry).

To the W of Yobuko, in *Nagoya-ura Bay*, lies the quiet little port of **Nagoya**, with a castle built by Toyotomi Hideyoshi in 1592. – On *Cape Hato*, situated on a tongue of land reaching far out into the sea, is the resort of **Genkai Kaichu-Koen**, with an underwater observatory.

Karuizawa
かるいざわ

Prefecture: Nagano. – Population: 14,000.
Post code: J-389-01. – Telephone code: 02674.
(i) (local)
Karuizawa Eki Kanko Information,
at Station;
tel. 2 2491.

HOTELS. – **Western style**: *Karuizawa Prince Hotel Seizan Honkan*, 1016, Karuizawa, 299 r., Japanese garden; *Mampei Hotel*, 925, Sakuranosawa, 127 r., Japanese garden; *Green Hotel*, 2147, Oaza-Nagakura, 39 r., Japanese garden. – **Ryokan**: *Shiotsubo Onsen Hotel*, Karuizawa-machi, 45 r. – **Minshuku**: *Yugawara-so*, 1117, Oaza Hotchi, 58 r. – YOUTH HOSTELS: *Karuizawa YH*, 1362, Kyu-Karuizawa, 50 b.; *YH Karuizawa Yuai-Sanso*, 1608, Karuizawa-machi, 60 b.

TRANSPORTATION. – **Rail**: from TOKYO (Ueno Station) JNR Shin-etsu line (2 hours).

Karuizawa lies NW of Tokyo in central Honshu, at the foot of the still-active volcano, Mount Asama (8340 ft/2542 m). Situated at an altitude of 3280 ft/1000 m), it is one of the most popular summer vacation resorts in Japan and also attracts large numbers of visitors during the winter. The average temperature in August is about 69°F/20.5°C; the winters are cold and severe.

In the northern part of the town are large numbers of week-end and holiday houses, hotels, etc. The newer southern part is at present being developed as a holiday resort. The first foreigners to visit Karuizawa were two guest lecturers at Tokyo University in 1886.

SIGHTS. – 1¼ miles/2 km N of Karuizawa Station is **Kyu-Karuizawa**, the oldest mountain holiday resort in Japan and the center of the region. During the summer season, when the town is crowded with visitors (mainly from the Tokyo region), many Tokyo and Yokohama businesses have branches here. – Near the main street stands *St Paul's Church*, designed by an American architect.

From Kyu-Karuizawa Station it is a half-hour climb to the **Usui Pass** (3133 ft/955 m), from which there are fine views of Mounts Asama, Haruna and Yatsugatake. Near the Sunset Point outlook terrace is the Kumano Shrine.

Near the spa of **Hoshino-onsen** is the "Wild Bird Wood" (bus from Naka-Karuizawa Station to Nishiku-Iriguchi stop, then 5 minutes' walk), with two observation huts. Farther N are the *Sengataki Falls* (bus from Naka-Karuizawa, 12 minutes), near which is situated the Karuizawa Skating Center (ice-rink with an area of 48,000 sq. yds/40,000 sq. m). – Still farther N are the *Shiraito Falls* (also reached by a footpath from Karuizawa Station, 30 minutes), 10 ft/3 m high and 75 yds/70 m wide.

The *Onioshidashi Highway* runs E past Mount Asama (8340 ft/2542 m) to the lava-fields of *Onioshidashi* (bus from Karuizawa or Naka-Karuizawa, 1 hour), the result of a great eruption of Mount Asama in 1783 when the lava flow covered the area below the N side of the volcano. A walk around the lava-fields takes about half an hour. There is also pleasant walking in the meadowland to the E, with large numbers of azaleas.

Mount*Asama ranks with Mount Aso on Kyushu as one of the most active volcanoes in Japan, although no major eruptions have been recorded since 1783. When it shows signs of increased activity access to the mountain is barred (information in Karuizawa or Komoro). Starting-points for the ascent of Mount Asama are the stations of *Karuizawa, Naka-Karuizawa, Shinano-Oiwake, Miyota* and *Komoro* on the JNR Shin-etsu line. The best routes for the ascent are from Karuizawa or Naka-Karuizawa; the best descent is to Komoro.

In the southern part of the area is *Lake Shiozawa* (a man-made lake formed by a dam); accommodation in private houses, tennis-courts. Also in the S is **Lake New**

Town, a recreation area with *Lake Leman* (a man-made lake), a swimming pool, tennis-courts and restaurants.

Kii
See under Wakayama

Kirishima-Yaku National Park

きりしまやく 国立公園

Prefectures: Kagoshima and Miyazaki.
Area: 176 sq. miles/456 sq. km.
(i) (central)
National Parks Association of Japan,
Toranomon Denki Building,
8–1, Toranomon 2-chome, Minato-Ku,
J-105 **Tokyo**;
tel. (03) 502 0488.

HOTELS. – **Western style**: *Hotel Hayashida-onsen*, 3958, Takachiho, Makizono-cho, 459 r., Japanese garden, SP, thermal bath; *Ebino Kogen Hotel*, 1495, Oaza-Suenaga, Ebino, 54 r., thermal bath; *Hayato Kanko Hotel*, 1487, Hayato-cho, 21 r., thermal bath. – **Ryokan**: *New Sorinkaku*, in Iodani-onsen, 61 r., thermal bath; *Kirishima Tachibana-so*, in Kirishima, 31 r.; *Matsunoe Ryokan*, in Miyakonojo, 27 r. – YOUTH HOSTELS: *Kirishima Kogen YH*, Kirishima-jingu-mae, 120 b.; *Ebino Kogen YH*, in Kobayashi, 8596, Tamakino, Minami-mishikata, 48 b.

ON YAKUSHIMA. – **Ryokan**: *Miyanoura Kanko Hotel*, Miyanoura, Kamiyaku-cho, 15 r., beach; *Anbo Kanko Hotel*, Anbo, Yaku-cho, 14 r., beach; *Hotel Pine*, 914, Harano, Yaku-cho, 22 r.; *Tashiro-kan*, Miyanoura, Kamiyaku-cho, 22 r., beach. – YOUTH HOSTEL: *Yakushima YH*, 4469-62, Anbo, Yaku-cho, 50 b., beach.

TRANSPORTATION. – **Rail**: from FUKUOKA (Hakata) JNR Kagoshima line to Yatsushiro (2 hours), then Hisatsu line to Kirishima–Nishiguchi. – **Bus**: several regional services in National Park. – **Boat**: ferry from KAGOSHIMA to Miyanoura (on Yakushima; 3½ hours).

The *Kirishima-Yaku National Park in southern Kyushu takes in the Kirishima mountain range, the island of Yakushima off the coast to the S, part of Kagoshima Bay including the Sakurajima Volcano, and the southern coasts of the Satsuma and Osumi peninsulas, at the southernmost tip of Kyushu. The predominant features of the National Park – the various parts of which are* separate from one another – are chains of volcanic mountains with lava-fields and beautiful crater lakes, extensive beaches and hot springs, most of them at busy health resorts. The countryside is at its most beautiful during the summer flowering season and in the fall when the foliage takes on its vivid coloring.

Excellent roads make the National Park easily accessible – from the N via *Yatsushiro* and *Hitoyoshi*, from the W via *Kagoshima* and *Hayato*, from the E via *Miyazaki* and *Kobayashi*. For visitors traveling by train the stations of *Kirishima-Nishiguchi* (Hisatsu line), *Kirishimajingu* (Nippo line) and *Takaharu* (Kitto line) make good centers.

The most northerly part of the National Park consists of the **Kirishima Range**, on the borders of Kagoshima and Miyazaki prefectures. The highest peaks are **Karakuni** (5580 ft/1700 m) in the N and **Takachiho** (5164 ft/1574 m) in the S. Between these two peaks are Mounts *Shishito* (4685 ft/1428 m), *Shimmoe* (4662 ft/1421 m) and *Nakadake* (4413 ft/1345 m). Among the most beautiful of the ten or so crater lakes in this area are Lakes *Onami, Fudo, Byakushi* and *Miike*, with water of varying hues. – There is rich vegetation, with dense primeval forests at lower altitudes, silver fir (*momi*) and red spruce (*aka-matsu*) at intermediate levels and an upper zone of scrub and deciduous forest. Many areas are renowned for the beauty of their vegetation, such as Lake Onami with its maples and firs and Mount Shimmoe with its great expanses of azaleas.

The Kirishima area features prominently in Japanese mythology. Mount Takachiho is the place where Ninigo-no-mikuto, grandson of the sun goddess Amaterasu-omikami, came down to earth to take possession of the "kingdom of reeds and corn" (the old name for Japan).

Kirishima-onsen is an extensive spa region on the south-western slopes of Mount *Karakuni*. Among the best-known resorts are **Hayashida-onsen, Iodani-onsen** and **Myoban-onsen**, all lying close together and accessible from *Kirishima-Nishiguchi* by bus (50 minutes). – 11 miles/18 km E of Kirishima-Nishiguchi is **Hayashida-onsen** (bus, 40 minutes), with sulphurous and chalybeate springs

(104–140 °F/40–60 °C). – In the center of the Kirishima area lies the idyllic resort of **Maruo-onsen**.

To the S of the Kirishima range rises Mount *Takachiho* (Takachiho-no-mine, 5164 ft/1574 m), scene of the god Ninigo-no-mikoto's descent to earth. It can be climbed from **Takachihogawara** (bus from Kirishima-Nishiguchi, 50 minutes), below the W side of the hill. The ascent (1½ miles/2·3 km) takes about 1½ hours. Near the summit is a still-active crater 280 ft/86 m deep and 220 yds/ 200 m in circumference, above which there rises a perpetual column of smoke. From the summit there are extensive *views of Kinko Bay and Lake Miike to the E.

Mount *Karakuni* (5580 ft/1700 m) can be climbed from **Tozanguchi** or **Onamiike-Tozanguchi**, both on the main Kirishima road. The ascent (2 miles/ 3·5 km) takes about 3¼ hours. Half-way up is *Lake Onami*, a crater lake surrounded by great expanses of azaleas. From the moss-covered summit crater there are fine *views of the surrounding area.

The northern part of the National Park consists of the **Ebino Plateau**, lying at an altitude of about 3900 ft/1200 m (bus from Kobayasho or Kirishima-onsen, 55 or 25 minutes). Bounded by Mounts *Karakuni*, *Koshiki* and *Kurino*, the plateau has many lakes and hot springs. To the S are large areas of scrub and pine woods. There is a magnificent show of azalea blossom (*Kirishima-tsutsuji*) in May. To the NE are the beautiful *Lake Byakushi* and *Lake Rokukannon*.

In the southern part of the National Park we find **Kirishimajingu**, near which is the *Kirishima Shrine* (bus 15 minutes), dedicated to Ninigi-no-mikoto, the legendary ancestor of the Japanese Imperial House. The shrine, set in a dense cedar forest, is believed to have been founded in the 6th c.; it was rebuilt in 1715.

The island of **Yakushima** (194 sq. miles/ 503 sq. km), some 45 miles/72 km off the southern tip of Kyushu, is served by a ferry from Kagoshima (daily, 3¼ hours). Its 32 extinct volcanoes, rising well above 3300 ft/1000 m, are known as the "Japanese Maritime Alps". The highest peak is *Miyanoura* (6349 ft/1935 m), its slopes covered with subtropical mountain vegetation; its mighty ancient cedars (*yaku-sugi*) are widely famed.

Kitakyushu
北九州

Prefecture: Fukuoka. – Population: 1,070,000.
Post code: J-800. – Telephone code: 093.

ⓘ (central)
Fukuoka-ken Tokyo Kanko Bussan Assensho,
Kokusai Kanko Kaikan,
1-8-3, Marunouchi, Chiyoda-ku,
J-100 **Tokyo**;
tel. (03) 231 1750.

(local)
Fukuoka-ken Kanko Renmei,
Fukuoka-ken Kankoka-nai,
1-1-1, Tenjin,
J-815 **Fukuoka**;
tel. (092) 751 2098.

HOTELS. – **Western style**: *Kokura Station Hotel*, 1-1-1, Asano, Kokurakita-ku, 182 r.; *Hotel New Tagawa*, 3-46, Furusenba-cho, Kokurakita-ku, 112 r.; Japanese garden; *Kokura Hotel*, 3-10, Semba-cho, Kokurakita-ku, 101 r.; *Kokura Castle Hotel*, 1-2-16, Muromachi, Kokurakita-ku, 58 r., beach; *Kitakyushu Daiichi Hotel*, 11-20, Konyacho, Kokurakita-ku, 105 r.; *Yukata Business Hotel*, 2-13-22, Asano, Kokurakita-ku, 96 r.; *Kokura Yayoi Kaikan*, 3-2-25, Muromachi, Kita-ku, 39 r. – YOUTH HOSTEL: *Kita-Kyushu YH*, 7, Hobashira, Yahata-higashi-ku, 96 b.

EVENTS. – *Mekari-shinji* (January 1), at Mekari Shrine; *Minato-matsuri* (beginning of May), a popular festival in the Moji district; *Numagaku* (beginning of May), historical festival in Kokura-minami district; *Gion-taiko* (mid July), parade, with drumming contest, at Yasaka Shrine; *Tobata Gion* and *Kurozaki Gion* (middle and end of July), Festivals of Lanterns.

TRANSPORTATION. – **Air**: from OSAKA (1½ hours). – **Rail**: from TOKYO (Central Station) JNR Sanyo-Shinkansen line to Kokura (6½ hours); from FUKUOKA (Hakata), 30 minutes. – **Boat**: ferry from OSAKA to Moji district (14 hours); regular service from KOBE (Higashi-Kobe) to Kokura district (14 hours).

The town of Kitakyushu lies on the Kammon Strait between the islands of Honshu and Kyushu. The largest city on Kyushu (area 180 sq. miles/ 466 sq. km), it was formed in 1963 by the amalgamation of the towns of Moji, Kokura, Tobata, Yahata and Wakamatsu, which then became wards or districts of the new city. In 1974 Yahata was divided into Yahata-Higashi and Yahata-Nishi (Eastern and Western Yahata) and Kokura into Kokura-Kita

and Kokura-Minami (Northern and Southern Kokura).

Industry began to develop in this region at the turn of the century, based on the coalfields to the S of the town and intensive commercial contacts with the mainland of Asia. A boost was given to industrial development when the Nippon Steel Corporation established a steelworks which ranks as one of the leading plants of the kind in the world.

The Yahata district is a center of chemical engineering and heavy industry; Tobata has fish-processing plants and a variety of other industry; the former castle town of Kokura is an important commercial and cultural center; Moji, once a small fishing village, established trading relations with foreign countries in 1899 and is now one of the most important commercial ports on Kyushu; and Wakamatsu, the most westerly of the city wards, has coal-shipping installations, engineering works and shipyards. Traditional products of the town are objects made of bamboo, paper dolls and sea grass.

SIGHTS. – In the NE of the city area is the district of MOJI, only 740 yds/680 m from Shimonoseki on Honshu. The Strait of Hayatomo-no-Seto is now spanned by the * Kammon Bridge, a suspension bridge 1170 yds/1068 m long leading to Dannoura (a ward of Shimonoseki). – The Kammon Strait was the scene of a naval battle in 1185 in which the Taira clan suffered a decisive defeat at the hands of the Minamoto. – The two islands are also linked by the Shin-Kammon Rail Tunnel, the third longest rail tunnel in the world (20,425 yds/18,675 m), and the Kammon Tunnel (3785 yds/3461 m) for road traffic and pedestrians, opened in 1958.

There is an impressive * view of the bridge and the surrounding area from Mekari Park, 1½ miles/2·5 km N of Mojiko Station (bus, 10 minutes). At the far end of Cape Mekari is the Mekari Shrine, traditionally believed to have been founded in the year 269 by the Empress Jingu on her return from a journey to Korea. At the annual shrine festival three Shinto priests gather seaweed in the early morning and present it as an offering to the divinity. – At the E end of the park stands the 100 ft/30 m high Peace Pagoda, presented by the Burmese Government in 1958 as a memorial to the dead of the Second World War.

SW of Moji in the KOKURA district. 550 yds/500 m from the station is * Kokura Castle (1602), once the seat of the Hosokawa family. Of the castle's 60 ft/ 18 m-high walls, 48 gates and 148 towers nothing now survives, following the destruction of the castle in 1856. Some parts of the castle (main tower, Tsukiji Rampart, Tsukimi Tower) were rebuilt in 1956. – Near the castle is the 15-storey glass structure of the Civic Hall, with an * outlook platform on the top floor.

To the W are the TOBATA and YAHATA districts. The TOBATA and WAKAMATSU districts are on the far side of the Dokai Channel, a narrow arm of the sea 4 miles/ 6 km long which is now spanned by the Wakato-o-hashi, a bridge 2262 yds/ 2068 m long.

Between the southern districts of YAHATA-NISHI and YAHATA-HIGASHI, 3 miles/5 km S of Yahata Station, lies the Kawachi Reservoir, which supplies water to the steelworks. The reservoir, with a circumference of 5 miles/ 8 km (large numbers of swans), is a favorite recreation area.

Near by is the Hobashira Nature Park (bus from Yahata Station, 20 minutes), with beautiful and varied scenery. A cableway ascends Mount Hobashira, from which there are extensive * views of the city and the Dokai Channel.

SURROUNDINGS. – To the S of the city extends the Hiraodai Plateau, a green and level area with numerous limestone crags. On the E side of the plateau is the very fine * Sembutsu Cave.

Kobe
こうべ

Prefecture: Hyogo. – Population: 1,400,000.
Post code: J-650-657. – Telephone code: 078.
 (local)
  Kobe City Tourist Information Office,
  Shinkansen Kobe Station Office;
  tel. 241 9550 (English spoken).
  Kokutetsu Sannomiya Station Office,
  Yannomiya Center Building;
  tel. 392 0020 (English spoken).

HOTELS. – Western style: Kobe Portopia Hotel, Boeki Building, 1-go, 123 Banchi, Higashimachi, Ikuta-ku, 560 r.; Oriental Hotel, 25, Kyo-machi, Ikuta-ku, 204 r.; New Port Hotel, 6-3-13, Hamabedori, Fukiai-ku, 204 r.; Rokkosan Hotel, 1034, Minami-Rokko, Rokkosan-cho, Nada-ku, 72 r.; Kobe Interna-

tional Hotel, 1-6, 8-chome, Goko-dori, Fukiai-ku, 48 r.; *Washington Hotel*, 2, Shimoyamate-dori, Chuo-ku, 216 r.; *Sannomiya Hotel*, Sannomiya-eki, Chuo-ku, 190 r.; *Kobe Tower Side Hotel*, 1, Hatobamachi, Ikuta-ku, 160 r.; *Kobe Ution Hotel*, 2-5, Nunobichiko, Fukiai-ku, 167 r.; *Kobe Plaza Hotel*, 1-41, Motomachi-dori, Ikuta-ku, 144 r.; *Green Hill Hotel*, 2-18-63, Kano-cho, Ikuta-ku, 100 r.; *Kobe Sunside Hotel*, 4-7-8, Kumoi-dori, Fukiai-ku, 104 r.; *Hotel Minakami*, 1-2-8, Mizuki-dori, Hyogo-ku, 64 r.; *Business Hotel Daini Kitagami*, 4-1, Kanomachi, Ikuta-ku, 54 r.; *Business Hotel Sanyo*, 2-15, Kitanagasa-dori, Ikuta-ku, 54 r.; *Business Hotel Kitagami*, 3-2-34, Kanomachi, Ikuta-ku, 35 r.

RESTAURANTS. – **Western cuisine**: *Dunie Boy*, 2-28, Nakayamate-dori, Ikuta-ku; *Fisherman's Port*, Port Terminal, Shin-Minatocho, Ikuta-ku; *Au Bec Fin*, 4-2-15, Iwayanaki-machi, Nada-ku; *Kitano Club*, 1-64, Kitanocho, Ikuta-ku; *Seaside Club Palace Shioya*, 179-6, Shioyamachi, Tarumi-ku; *Queen's Court*, 2-31, Yamato-dori, Ikuta-ku; *Restaurant Berg*, 5-1-14, Hamabe-dori, Fukiai-ku; *Restaurant Hook*, 2-24, Sakaemachi-dori, Ikuta-ku; *St George Japan*, 1-130, Kitanocho, Ikuta-ku. – **Japanese cuisine**: *Ichifuji*, 1-10-6, Aratocho, Hyogo-ku; *Iroriya*, 3-33, Kitanocho, Ikuta-ku; *Masaya Akatsukayamaten*, 1-10-6, Sumiyoshi-Yamate, Higashinada-ku; *Suma Kanko House*, Nishi-Suma, Aza Tekkai 7, Suma-ku; *Suzue*, 88, Hanakumacho, Ikuta-ku; *Torimitsu*, 1-1-39, Gyokomachi, Suma-ku; *Masaya Honten* (noodle dishes), 1-90-6, Nakayamate-dori, Ikuta-ku; *Okagawa* (tempura, sukiyaki), 1-115-2, Kitanocho, Ikuta-ku.

EVENTS. – *Tsuinashiki* (beginning of February), Dance of Spirits, in Nagata Shrine; *Shinkosai* (mid April), Spring Festival, in Ikuta Shrine; *Nanko-matsuri* (end of May), procession in historical costumes in honor of the popular hero Kusunoki Masashige, at Minatogawa Shrine; *Harbor Festival* (third week-end in May).

TRANSPORTATION. – **Air**: from TOKYO (Haneda Airport) to Osaka (1 hour). – **Rail**: from TOKYO (Central Station) JNR Tokaido and Sanyo–Shinkansen line to Shin-Kobe Station (3½ hours); from KYOTO JNR Tokaido line to Sannomiya Station (1 hour); local services (city line). – **Boat**: regular services from Beppu (Kyushu), Takamatsu, Imabari and Matsuyama (Shikoku); also to islands of Shodo and Awaji.

The city of Kobe, situated in Osaka Bay in south-western Honshu, is Japan's principal commercial port and an important industrial center as well as the chief town of Hyogo prefecture. While the city's industrial and port installations are on land reclaimed from the sea extending far into the bay to the S, the residential districts spread up to the lower slopes of the Rokko Hills which bound the city on the N. Kobe owes its mild climate to the shelter afforded by these hills, which lie within the Inland Sea National Park.

The town is divided into a number of wards – Fukiai, Higashi-Nada, Hyogo, Ikuta, Kita, Nada, Nagata, Suma and Tarumi. Between the residential area of Yamate (known as the Bluff) and the port area (known as the Bund) are the city's principal business and shopping streets, Motomachi-dori and Sannomiya-dori. The main entertainment district is in Shinkaichi.

About a quarter of Japanese imports and exports pass through Kobe. The main imports are raw materials; the main exports are iron and steel, textiles, synthetic fiber products and electronic apparatus. The Hanshin industrial zone between Kobe and Osaka has heavy industry, shipbuilding yards, engineering works, etc. – The city is also an important communications center. In addition to the excellent transportation facilities within the city itself (JNR lines, private lines, bus services) the Meishin motorway to Nagoya (118 miles/190 km) and the Hanshin motorway are important traffic routes. – There are shipping services from Kobe to Kyushu (Beppu), Shikoku (Takamatsu, Imabari, Matsuyama) and to the islands of Shodo and Awaji.

HISTORY. – The area around the natural harbor of *Muko-no-Minato* (to the W of the present city) was settled at a very early period, and in the 4th c. it was the gateway through which Chinese and Korean influences reached Japan. In an attempt to promote the development of Japan by an increase in foreign trade Taira Kiyomori (1118-81) moved the seat of government temporarily to *Fukuhara* (W of present-day Kobe); and although the capital was moved again only six months later the harbor established by Kiyomori at Hyogo developed into a considerable port which by 1788 had some 20,000 inhabitants. Resistance to the opening-up of this port to foreign trade enabled Kobe, hitherto a mere suburb of Hyogo, to take over its role in 1868. The result was that by 1889 Hyogo had been relegated to the position of a suburb of the rapidly growing city of Kobe. – Other major events in the development of the town were the opening of the railway line to Osaka (1874) and the line to Shimonoseki, at the western tip of Honshu. Kobe played an important part in the war with China in 1894–95 and the Russo-Japanese War (1904–05). During the Second World War two-thirds of the city was destroyed by air attack.

SIGHTS. – 440 yds/400 m NW of Sannomiya Station, in IKUTA ward, is the **Ikuta Shrine**, dedicated to the patron goddess of Kobe, Wakahirume-no-mikoto. According to legend the shrine was founded by the Empress Jingu after her return from a campaign in Korea. The name of Kobe is said to be derived from the Japanese word for serf (*kambe*), referring to the serfs who were presented to the shrine by the Imperial Court. The present buildings of the shrine are modern reconstructions. – To the SE, in the direction of SANNOMIYA ward, is a shopping and entertainment district. – W of the shrine is Mount *Suwayama* (525 ft/ 160 m), from which there is a fine view of the city.

At the **Port** stands the 354 ft/108 m-high *Port Tower*, with a revolving platform (view). Near by is the **International Port Museum**. The *Naka Pier* is used by the ships of the Kansai Steamship Company which ply in the Inland Sea; trips round the harbor and shorter cruises leave from the Meriken-Hatoba Pier. – Off the

harbor is the artificially built-up *Port Island* (reached from Sannomiya Station by the municipal railway, "Port Liner"). On the island are a hotel, a landscaped garden (Minami Park), an amusement park and the "Portopia '81" exhibition grounds. – NW of Pier 5 is the tower block occupied by the *Chamber of Industry and Commerce*, on the 26th floor of which is the "Sky Lobby", affording a fine view of Kobe.

To the NW the port area is bounded by three streets running parallel to the

seafront, *Kaigan-dori*, *Sakaemachi-dori* and *Motomachi-dori*, the city's principal shopping streets. In the street running N from the piers to Sannomiya Station stands a *totem pole* presented by the city of Seattle (Washington state, USA), which is twinned with Kobe.

330 yds/300 m N of Kobe Station is the **Minatogawa Shrine** (or *Nanko Shrine*), dedicated to Kusunoki Masashige (1294–1336), who was killed here fighting for the Emperor Godaigo against Ashikaga Takauji, founder of the Ashikaga Shogunate. The main hall of the shrine dates from 1953. To the SE of the precincts a gravestone, which was set up by Tokugawa Mitsukuni in 1692, commemorates Masashige.

In FUKIAI ward, NE of the port area, is the **Namban Museum of Art** (*Namban-bijutsukan*), with pictures by Japanese artists of schools influenced by the West. – To the W, beyond the Shinkansen railway line (Shin-Kobe Station), are the **Nunobiki Falls**. The *Odaki Fall* is 150 ft/ 45 m high, the *Medaki Fall* 60 ft/19 m. This wooded area is a favorite resort of the people of Kobe.

To the E of the Namban Museum, N of Nada Station in NADA ward, lies **Oji Park** (4½ acres), a recreation and amusement park with a zoo and large numbers of cherry trees. – Beyond this, to the NE, is HIGASHI-NADA ward. Near Sumiyoshi Station is the **Hon-Sumiyoshi Shrine**, on the site of the famous Sumiyoshi Shrine, founded in the year 202, which was later moved to Osaka. – ¾ mile/1·2 km N of the station, at the foot of Mount *Rokko* (3058 ft/932 m), we find the **Hakutsuru Museum of Art**, a modern building in the style of the Momoyama period containing Chinese and Japanese antiquities (bronzes, ceramics, lacquerware).

SW of the city center, in NAGATA ward, is the **Nagata Shrine**, dedicated to the divinity Kotoshironushi, which attracts many worshippers at the New Year and the shrine festivals. – In SUMA ward, to the SW, is Mount *Takatori* (1050 ft/ 320 m), at the foot of which is the **Zenshoji Temple**, founded in the mid 14th c. and dedicated to the Eleven-Headed Kannon. The main gate is attributed to Hidari Jingoro (17th c.). Within the temple precincts are large numbers of maple trees (particularly beautiful in the fall), after which the temple is also known as the *Momiji-dera*. – Farther W, 220 yds/200 m N of Sumadera Station, stands the **Fukushoji Temple** (or *Suma Temple*), believed to have been founded by the Emperor Koko in the year 886. It contains a statue of Sho-Kannon and a *statue of the Eleven-Headed Kannon of the Muromachi period. Within the precincts are many cherry trees (in blossom in mid April).

To the W is a large area with a variety of recreational facilities, within which, to the N of Sumaura-Koen Station (Sanyo

Falls · Namban Museum, Zoo · Sannomiya Station · Kumoi-dori · Onoe-dori · Isogami-dori · Town Hall · FUKIAI-KU · Hachiman-dori · Isobe-dori · dori · Office · Chamber of Industry and Commerce · Hamabe-dori · Hanshin motorway · Custom House · Kyoto · Pier 5 · Custom House · Marine · Pier 2 · Pier 3 · Pier 4 · Station · Port Island private line), is *Mount Hachibuse* (807 ft/ 246 m). A cableway runs up to the top, from which there are fine views of the hills, and sea and the island of Awaji. On the slopes of the hill are large numbers of cherry trees. – There is a chair-lift from the top of Mount Hachibuse to the summit of the neighboring Mount *Hatafuri*.

Mount Hachibuse is part of **Sumaura Park** (21 acres), which was the scene of a battle between the Taira and Minamoto clans. Also within the park is *Sumaura Beach*, with the municipally owned *Suma Aquarium*, one of the largest in Japan.

In the most westerly of the city's wards, TARUMI, near the station, can be found the **Wadatsumi Shrine**, dedicated to the patron goddess of seafarers and travelers. – There is a fine view of the island of Awaji from **Maiko Park**, at the W end of the city area. With its dark-colored ancient pines, its white sand and the blue water of the sea, this provided the inspiration for the colored woodcut by Ando Hiroshige (1797–1858), ''The Beach at Maiko''.

Outside the city limits to the W, 6 miles/ 10 km N of Akashi Station (JNR Sanyo line), is the **Taisanji Temple** of the Tendai sect (bus from station, 30 minutes), founded in 716 by Fujiwara Umakai, grandson of Kamatari. Particularly notable features are the **Hondo (Main Hall) of 1304; *Nio-mon*, a gate of the Muromachi period; and a seated *statue of Amida in the Amida Hall. Among the temple's treasures are 31 volumes of the ''Hokekyo Sutra'', old weapons and a number of pictures. The inner rooms of the temple are open only on one day in June (varying according to the lunar calendar).

SURROUNDINGS. – To the N of the city rise the **Rokko Hills**, an area of great scenic beauty much frequented by the people of Kobe; most of the area lies within the Inland Sea National Park. The highest point is Mount **Rokko** (932 m/3058 ft; bus from Rokko Station, 10 minutes). There is a cableway to the top, from which there are views of the sea and the island of Awaji; particularly impressive is the *view of Kobe by night. In the summit area, which offers ample space for recreation, are golf-courses, a botanic garden and a number of hotels. From the Rokksan Hotel a bus runs N to the health resort of **Arima-onsen** (also direct bus and rail connections from Kobe and Osaka). Situated in an idyllic setting at a height of 1191 ft/ 363 m, the resort is particularly attractive in the spring-blossom season and in the fall when the foliage takes on its vivid coloring. On account of its mild climate many visitors come to Arima-onsen from the neighboring cities. Thanks to its proximity to Nara and Kyoto this is one of the oldest health resorts in Japan.

The second highest peak in the Rokko Hills is Mount **Maya** (2293 ft/699 m; bus from Sannomiya Station, Kobe, to Mount Takao and cableway from there). On the summit there are recreational facilities and hotels. A flight of 400 stone steps leads up from the upper station of the cableway to the **Toritenjo-ji**, a temple of the Shingon sect which is believed to have been founded by a priest named Hodo in 646. It contains a statue of the Eleven-Headed Kannon.

SW of Mount Maya is Mount **Futatabi** (1536 ft/ 468 m), reached from the center of Kobe (Suwayama Park) on a ridge highway affording wide views. Near the summit stands the **Dairyuji**, a temple of the Shingon sect founded by Wake-no-Kiyomaro in 768 which contains a *statue of Nyoirin-Kannon, probably dating from the Nara period. The name of the hill (''twice visited hill'') refers to the two stays here by the founder of the sect, Kobo-daishi. The area around the densely wooded hill forms the **Futatabisan Park**. On its northern slopes lies *Lake Shuhogahara*.

See also **Awaji, Himeji** and **Osaka**.

Kochi

Prefecture: Kochi. – Population: 303,000.
Post code: J-780. – Telephone code: 0888.

(central)
Kochi-ken Tokyo Kanko Bussan Assensho,
Tetsudo Kaikan,
1-9-1, Marunouchi, Chiyoda-ku,
J-100 **Tokyo**;
tel. (03) 212 1981.

(local)
Kochi-ken Kanko Renmei,
Kochi-ken Kankoka-nai,
5, Marunouchi;
tel. 23 1111.

HOTELS. – **Western style**: *Kochi Dai-ichi Hotel*, 2-2-12, Kitahon-machi, 120 r.; *Hotel Sun Route*, 1-28, Kitahon-machi 1-chome, 110 r.; *Hotel New Kochi*, 1-1-2, Harimaya-cho, 53 r.; *Business Hotel Ichoo*, 3-11-12, Harimaya-cho, 55 r. – **Ryokan**: *San-suien Hotel*, Takajomachi, 133 r.; *Joseikan*, Kamimachi, 63 r. – **Minshuku**: *Kuroshio*, in Toza-Shimizu (to W), 480-2, Ashizuri-misaki, 74 r. – YOUTH HOSTELS: *Kochi-Ekimae YH*, 3-10-10, Kitahon-cho, 104 b.; *Hitsuzan YH*, 30-4, Koishiko-cho, 50 b.

EVENTS. – *Castle Festival* (end of March–beginning of April); *Doronko Festival* (beginning of April), in Wakamiya-Hachimangu Shrine; *Yosakoi Festival* (beginning of August), the town's principal festival, with processions: *Shinane-matsuri* (end of August), in Tosa Shrine; *Tachi-odori* (the fall), sword dance in Niida Shrine, Sagawa; *Ryoma-matsuri* (beginning of October), on Katsurahama Beach. – *Nichiyo-ichi* (weekly market, every Sunday), at Castle.

TRANSPORTATION. – **Air**: from TOKYO (Haneda Airport), 2¼ hours; from OSAKA (1 hour). – **Rail**: from TAKAMATSU JNR Dosan line (2¼ hours); from TOKUSHIMA (change at Awa Ikeda; 3 hours). – **Boat**: ferry from OSAKA (9½ hours) and from TOKYO (21 hours).

Kochi lies at the N end of Urado Bay, a narrow arm of the sea which extends inland from the wide expanse of Tosa Bay on the S coast of Shikoku. The town is surrounded on the N and E sides by hills and, thanks to the warm Kuroshio Current, has a notably mild climate. Kochi is the chief town of a prefecture and its economic and educational center (two colleges of higher education). The town's main sources of income are fishing and agriculture; other local products are coral jewelry, Japanese vellum and Odo-yaki pottery.

HISTORY. – Kochi's rise to become the political center of the old province of *Tosa* (now the prefecture of Kochi) began when Prince Chosokabe Motochika (1539–99) established his residence here in 1588. The province later passed into the hands of the Yamanouchi family, who controlled it for 16 generations. The castle was built in 1601 by Yamanouchi Kazutoyo, a vassal of the Tokugawa. A number of leading figures were born or worked in the town, including the politician Itagaki Taisuke (1837–1919) and Yoshida Shigeru (1878–1967), five times Prime Minister of Japan.

SIGHTS. – On Mount *Otakasakayama*, ¾ mile/1 km SW of the station, stands the **Castle**, Kochi's principal landmark. The five-storey main tower, built in 1748, now houses an archaeological museum; from the top there are extensive *views of the town and the sea. In front of the Castle is a statue of Chiyo, wife of its builder. In **Kochi Park**, in which the Castle is situated, are the **Municipal Museum** (*Kyodo-bunka-kaikan*), a *Zoo* and a monument to Itagaki Taisuke. To the E of the Castle a market is held every Sunday, as it has been for 300 years. – To the S of the Castle the *Museum of the Yamanouchi Shrine* (*Yamanouchi-Jinja homotsu shiryokan*) houses a variety of objects which belonged to the Yamanouchi family, including old weapons and a valuable collection of No masks of the Momoyama period. To the E of the Museum is the *Yamanouchi Shrine*.

In the center of the town, ¾ mile/1 km S of the station, is the red *Harimayabashi Bridge*, which features in an old Japanese folk-song, "Yosakoibushi". The Yosakoi Festival is celebrated here in summer. – ¾ mile/1 km W of the station the **Anrakuji Temple** has an impressive seated figure of the Amida-Nyorai Buddha.

2½ miles/4 km SE of the Harimayabashi Bridge (bus, 20 minutes), on a hill 475 ft/

145 m high, lies the **Godaisan Park** (cableway from *Aoyagi Bridge*, at the foot of the hill). From the top there is a fine *view of Urado Bay and the Pacific. There is a magnificent show of cherry and azalea blossom in spring. In the park, originally a garden of the Edo period, can be seen the **Chikurinji Temple** of the Shingon sect, the 31st of the 88 pilgrimage temples on Shikoku. Built in 724 by a priest named Gyoki, it is the oldest temple in the prefecture. Notable features are the main hall, Monjudo, and a collection of Buddhist sculpture. – At the foot of the flight of stone steps which leads up to the temple extends the **Botanic Garden** (*Shokobutsuen*; area 28,000 sq. yds/ 23,400 sq. m), dedicated to the memory of the botanist Makino Tomitaro (1862–1957): pools containing giant water-lilies, a wide range of tropical plants, small museum with a collection of fossils.

In an old cedar wood 3 miles/5 km NE of the station (bus, 10 minutes) is the *Tosa Shrine, some of the buildings of which date from the 16th c.

SURROUNDINGS. – From the station a bus runs S to the port of **Urado**, at the entrance to Urado Bay, here spanned by the *Urado-Ohashi Bridge* (1620 yds/ 1480 m long). In the town are the ruins of an old castle (1591) and a statue of the politician Sakamoto Ryoma, a native of Urado. – The whole of this coastal region is much frequented by water-sports enthusiasts. 5 miles/8 km S of Kochi (bus from Harimayabashi Bridge, 40 minutes) lies the seaside resort of **Katsurahama**, with pine woods, bizarre rock formations and a beach of white sand. In the town are an Aquarium and the Tosa Token Center, a stadium for dog-fights. From a small pavilion on a hillside above the town there are beautiful views of the surrounding area on moonlit nights in autumn.

6 miles/10 km E of Kochi (JNR Otochi bus service, 30 minutes) is **Nangoku** (pop. 45,000). The *Oshino* district is noted as a center for the breeding of *onagadori* (cocks with tail feathers 13–23 ft/4–7 m long). – 2½ miles/4 km NW of *Gomen*, the railway station for Nangoku, can be seen the *Kokubunji Temple of the Shingon sect, founded in 739 by the priest Gyoki. This is the 29th of the 88 pilgrimage temples on Shikoku. Notable features are the main hall and two wooden statues of Yakushi-nyorai. – To the E of Gomen lies the **Ryugado Cave** (bus from Kochi, 1 hour), discovered in 1931, with fine stalactites and sinter formations. Of the cave's total length of 2½ miles/4 km a stretch 1 mile/1·5 km long is open to visitors.

At the E end of Tosa Bay *Cape Muroto, the most southerly point in the Muroto-Anan Quasi National Park, reaches out into the Pacific (bus from Kochi, 2 hours). The wild and rugged coastal scenery merges farther inland into a zone of luxuriant subtropical vegetation. On the farthest point of the cape are a lighthouse (*view) and a weather station. The cape is known as Taifun-Ginza on account of the typhoons which occur frequently in the fall. – Near the cape is the *Hotsu-Misaki Temple, founded in 807 by Kobo-daishi, which has three Buddha figures of the Nara and Heian periods. This, too, is one of the 88 pilgrimage temples of Shikoku. – From the Muroto coast road there are fine *views of the coastal scenery.

From Kochi the JNR Dosan line runs N to **Osugi** (24 miles/39 km). ¾/1 km W of the station is the Yasaka Shrine, with two mighty cedars which are estimated to be 2000 years old. The larger of the two is 223 ft/68 m high and has a girth of 100 ft/30 m. – 5 miles/8 km farther N (Otaguchi Station) stands the *Burakuji Temple, the main hall (Yakushido) of which, built in 1151, is a notable example of the architecture of the Heian period. The temple contains a number of fine statues.

Koya-san
こうや山

Prefecture: Wakayama. – Population: 7000.
Post code: J-648-02. – Telephone code: 07365.

ⓘ (central)
Wakayama-ken Tokyo Kanko Bussan Assensho,
Kokusai Kanko Kaikan,
1-8-3, Marunouchi, Chiyoda-ku,
J-100 **Tokyo;**
tel. (03) 231 2041.

(local)
Wakayama-ken Kanko Renmei,
Wakayama-ken Kankoka-nai,
1-1, Komatsubara-dori,
J-640 **Wakayama;**
tel. (0734) 23 6111.

The temple hill of Koya-san

HOTELS. – **Ryokan:** *Koyasan Shukubo Kumia,* Koya-san, Koya-cho (arranges accommodation i, temples). – YOUTH HOSTEL: *Henjoson-in Y,* (temples), 303, Koya-san, Koya-cho, 100 b.

TRANSPORTATION. – **Rail:** from OSAKA (Nanba Sta tion) Nankai–Koya private line to Gokurakubashi (1. hours); from OSAKA (Tennoji Station) JNR Hanw. and Wakayama lines to Hashimoto (change a Wakayama), and from Osaka (morning and after noon) or Minatomachi (evening) JNR Kansai anc Wakayama lines to Hashimoto (via Tennoji; change a Oji). – **Cableway:** from Gokurakubashi to Koya-sa (5 minutes).

Lying at a height of some 2950 ft, 900 m, the Koya-san uplands, 4⁵ miles/70 km S of Osaka on the Ki Peninsula, are still largely off the tourist track in spite of the excellent communications to this area. Here, amid dense forest, are 125 **temples and shrines dating from the heyday of Japanese Buddhism in the 9th c.

The area extends for 1½ miles/2·2 km from N to S and 3½ miles/5·5 km from E to W or the eastern slopes of the *Takamine Hills* The complex of temples and monasteries is one of the leading centers for the study of Buddhism, and, as the place of origin of the Shingon sect, is visited by more than a million pilgrims every year.

HISTORY. – The first temples here were founded by a priest named Kukai (774–835), better known under his posthumous name of Kobo-daishi. After returning from China, where he had spent two years studying Buddhism, Kobo-daishi began in 806, at the Em- peror's behest, to propagate the doctrines of the Shin- gon sect. As the base for his missionary activity he selected the Koyo-san area, where in 816 he built the Kongobuji Temple, now the principal temple of the Shingon sect. In course of time other temples were built here, attracting large numbers of pilgrims, in- cluding emperors and nobles. Memorial temples were also built, e.g. for the Minamoto and Tokugawa families, and the area around Kobo-daishi's tomb became the last resting-place of numerous believers. – None of the original 9th c. buildings have survived: the oldest structure is the Fudo-do (1198).

Many of the temples are now threatened with ruin and rely for their income on providing accommoda- tion for visitors, who are housed in the priests' quar- ters; the food is purely vegetarian. Visitors have the opportunity of taking part in Buddhist ceremonies. It is advisable when visiting Koya-san to arrange to spend either one or two nights there.

From Gokurakubashi Station a cableway runs up to the plateau, and from there buses take visitors to the principal sights in the area. – The first place the bus comes to is the **Nyonindo** (Hall of the Women). Until 1873 women were not allowed beyond this point. The hall now houses an office which arranges accommodation for visitors in temples.

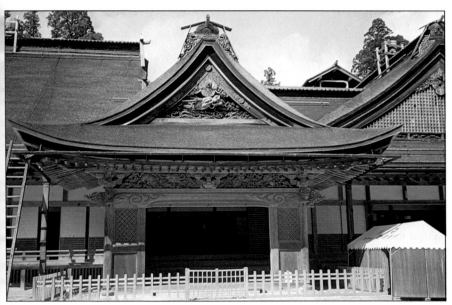

Kongobuji Temple

In ½ mile/800 m a side road goes off on the right to the **Kongobuji Temple**, the chief temple of the Koya-san Shingon sect, founded in 1861. The present buildings date from 1861.

> The founder of the temple was **Kobo-daishi**, known during his lifetime as *Kukai*. He was born on Shikoku on June 15, 774, and at the age of 24 wrote the "Sangoshiiki", a comparative study of Buddhism, Confucianism and Taoism. At the age of 25 he became a monk. In 804 he accompanied an Imperial mission to China, where he was exposed to decisive new influences. He studied for two years at Ch'an-an and was initiated into the secret teachings of Mi-tsung, a master of the Chinese Tantra school. After his return from China in 806 Kobo-daishi became Abbot of the Todaiji Temple at Nara, where he began to propagate his doctrines. His versatile talents also brought him fame as a poet, a calligrapher and a sculptor – although it is not always possible to prove the authenticity of works attributed to him. He is also credited with the introduction of the Hiragana syllabary. After his death in 835 Kukai was given the posthumous name of Kobo-daishi.

Near the temple are a number of schools of the Shingon sect and the *Buddhist University*. – To the SW, in a copse of ancient cedars and umbrella pines, stands the *Mieido* (Founder's Hall), which contains a portrait of Kobo-daishi and a **painting of 1086 depicting the entry of Buddha into Nirvana. Beyond this hall is the principal pagoda, the *Kompon-daito* (burned down several times: the present building dates from 1937), which contains five seated figures of Buddha. The **Kondo** (main hall) is also a modern

building (1932). To the E of this is the oldest building in the whole complex, the **Fudo-do** (1198).

SE of the main hall is the **Reiho-kan**, the monastery museum and treasury, built in 1920, which contains a variety of works of art, including sculpture, picture scrolls and documents of many centuries. – To the W of the main hall the *Daimon* or Great Gate (1705) has two guardian figures by the well-known sculptor Uncho. From here there is an extensive *view of the Kii Channel and the island of Awaji to the W.

The main road continues E towards the Mausoleum of Kobo-daishi. Beyond the *Ichinobashi* Bridge is the *Necropolis*, in a wood of ancient cedars which is traversed by a road 1¼ miles/2 km long. On either side of the road are numbers of stone monuments marking the graves of believers who desired to be buried near the founder of the sect. – The road passes

In the Kongobuji Temple

The Oku-no-in, Koya-san

the old **Gomado Temple**, which contains a seated wooden *statue of Fudo, one of the five light gods (Myoo). Close by are the **Gokusho** (Offerings Hall) and the **Torodo** (Hall of Lamps), with several thousand stone lanterns presented by worshippers, some of them very old. Adjoining is the **Nokotsudo**, an octagonal building in which the ashes of the dead are preserved. Finally the road comes to Kobo-daishi's Mausoleum, the *Oku-no-in, on a low hill planted with cedars.

Kumamoto

くまもと

Prefecture: Kumamoto. – Population: 540,000
Post code: J-860. – Telephone code: 0963.

(i) (central)
Kumamoto-ken Tokyo Kanko Bussan Assensho,
5-3-15, Ginza,
J-100 **Tokyo**;
tel. (03) 573 7825.

(local)
Kumamoto-ken Kanko Renmei,
Kumamoto-ken Kankoka-nai,
6-18-1, Saizenji;
tel. 66 1111.

HOTELS. – **Western style**: *Kumamoto Hotel Castle*, 4-2, Joto-machi, 225 r.; *New Sky Hotel*, 2, Higashi-Amidaji-machi, 201 r.; *Kumamoto Kotsu Center Hotel*, 3-10, Sakura-machi, 121 r.; *Togiya Hotel*, 1-8, Shimo, Senba-cho, 57 r., Japanese garden; *Hokke Club Kumamototen*, 20-1, Toorimachi, 147 r.; *Kumamoto Dai-ichi Hotel*, 356, Motoyama-machi, 84 r.; *Shin Kumamoto Hotel*, 1-11-17, Kuhonji, 51 r.; *Kumamoto City Hotel*, 1-9-3, Kuhonji, 29 r.; *Business Hotel Kurenai*, 1-16-14, Kasuga, 26 r.; *Business Hotel Konan*, 1-16-12, Kasuga, 21 r. – **Minshuka**: *Kotobuki*, 1-5-23, Suizenji, 100 r.; *Komatsu-so*, 1-8-13, Kasuga, 30 r. – YOUTH HOSTELS: *Kumamoto-Shiritsu YH*, 5-15-55, Shimazaki-machi, 64 b.; *YH Ryokan Shokaku*, 1-2-41, Nihongi, 50 b.; *Suizenji YH*, 1-2-20, Hakusan, 40 b.

RESTAURANT. – *Okumura*, 1-8, Shinmachi.

EVENTS. – *Taisai* (mid September), annual shrine festival at Fujisaki-Hachimangu Shrine, with procession in old armor.

TRANSPORTATION. – **Air**: from TOKYO (Haneda Airport), 1½ hours; from OSAKA (1 hour). – **Rail**: from TOKYO (Central Station) JNR Sanyo–Shinkansen line to FUKUOKA (Hakata; 7 hours), then JNR Kagoshima line (1½ hours); from BEPPU JNR Hohi line via OITA (3½ hours). – **Bus**: from BEPPU on Trans-Kyushu Expressway (4¼ hours).

Kumamoto, the "city of forests", lies in central Kyushu near Shimabara Bay, which comes in from the SW, forming a link between the open sea and the land-locked Ariake Sea. Chief town of its prefecture, it is the third largest city on Kyushu. Once a place of historical importance, it has developed into an important commercial and educational center serving the surrounding region.

Kumamoto is a marketing center for the agricultural produce of the surrounding area. Local craft products are inlaid metalwork (*Higo-zogan*; formerly artistically decorated swords), bamboo articles, pottery (*Shodai-yaki*) and wooden toys. Amakusa cultured pearls are much sought after.

HISTORY. – The town grew up around the castle, extending on to both sides of the River Shirakawa. The most notable ruler who resided in Kumamoto was Kato Kiyomasa (1562–1611), who won great fame in the Korean campaign of 1592. In the Battle of Sekigahara (1600) he fought at the side of Tokugawa Ieyasu, who rewarded him for his services with the grant of those parts of the province of Higo which he did not already control. In 1632 Kumamoto passed to the princely family of Hosokawa. During the Tokugawa era (1603–1867) the town became a strategically important base for the central government in their efforts to combat the powerful Satsuma princes of southern Kyushu. – During the Seinan Rising (1877) troops advanced against Kumamoto from Satsuma under the leadership of Saigo Takamori (1827–77) and besieged the castle for 50 days before it was relieved by Government forces. The castle was largely destroyed by bombardment and fire during the bitter fighting, from which the Government forces emerged victorious.

SIGHTS. – On Mount *Chausuyama*, 1¼ miles/2 km NE of the station, stand the **Castle**, built for Kato Kiyomasa in 1601–07 and severely damaged in 1877. There were originally three main buildings, 49 towers, 29 gates and 18 two-storey gatehouses, but all that now remains is the curtain wall and a number of gates and watch-towers, including one (the NW corner tower) which originally came from Uto Castle, to the S of the town, and was re-erected here in 1600. The castle walls are a typical example of the military engineering technique known as *mushagaeshi*, in which the wall has a slight batter (flattened slope) at the base but become steeper as it goes up, ending in an overhang at the top in order to make storming by an enemy more difficult. The *main tower*, rebuilt in reinforced concrete in 1960, now houses a Historical Museum. Near the tower grows a gingko tree said to have been planted by Kato, and so the castle is sometimes called Gingko Castle.

In Suizenji Park

To the N of the Castle is the **Kato Shrine**, which preserves Kato's helmet and sword. Within the precincts of the shrine is an old stone bridge, said to be a trophy from Kato's Korean campaign. From the shrine there is a view of the northern part of the town.

To the W of the Castle are **Museums** containing antiquities, material of regional and local interest and objects which once belonged to the Hosokawa family.

2 miles/3 km N of Kumamoto Station and ¾ mile/1 km W of Kami-Kumamoto Station stands the **Hommyoji Temple**, the principal temple of the Nichiren sect on Kyushu, founded by Kato in 1574. An avenue of cherry trees leads to the temple, with a flight of steps flanked by stone lanterns. To the N is Kato's tomb.

¾ mile/1 km NW of Kumamoto Station lies **Kitaoka Park**. Within the park is Mount *Hanaokayama* (436 ft/133 m), on which is the *Bussharito Pagoda*, built in 1954 as a memorial to those who died in the Second World War. It contains a portion of the ashes of Buddha, presented by Mr Nehru, then Prime Minister of India. From the hill there is a *view of the town.

2½ miles/4 km NE of Kumamoto Station (bus) and ¾ mile/1 km N of Suizenji Station is the **Fujisaki-Hachimangu Shrine**, the town's protective shrine, dedicated to the Emperor Ojin. Interesting shrine festival on September 15. – Near here in the *Tsukasa House* the winners of the sumo wrestling contests used to be honored; the building now contains a Sumo Museum.

3 miles/5 km E of the station (tram) is ***Suizenji Park** (160 acres), formerly known as the Joju-en Park. One of the most celebrated gardens in Japan, this was originally a landscaped garden attached to the summer residence of the Hosokawa family, laid out in 1632. It depicts on a miniature scale some of the 53 scenes on the Tokaido road represented in Hiroshige's woodcuts (e.g. Mount Fuji and Lake Biwa). Near a lake (fed by springs) is the **Izumi Shrine**, dedicated to the ancestors of the Hosokawa family, together with a *tea-house*. 4 miles/6 km S of the park is **Lake Ezu**, in a beautiful wooded setting. Near the lake is the municipal *Zoo*.

SURROUNDINGS. – NE of the town (bus, 20 minutes, then 20 minutes' walk) lies **Tatsuta Park**, with the Taishoji Temple, a protective temple of the Hosokawa family, and the Koshoken tea-house, built by Hosokawa Tadaoki (1563–1645).

15 miles/25 km N of Kumamoto, in the Valley of the River *Kikuchi*, which flows into the Ariake Sea, can be found a beautiful holiday and recreation area with many seaside resorts. Here, too, is the scene of the Battle of *Tabaruzaka*. – 15 miles/25 km away, on the Kumamoto Electric Railway (privately owned), is **Kikuchi-onsen**, from the 11th to the 16th c. a castle town held by the princely Kikuchi family; pleasant walks in the beautiful wooded country along the river. – 9 miles/15 km NW of Kikuchi-onsen, on the old national highway No. 3, is **Yamaga-onsen**, where the well-known Yamaga lanterns are made. – At the mouth of the Kikuchi is another health resort, **Tamana-onsen** or *Ryuganji-onsen* (pop. 45,000), with hot springs at temperatures of 113–120 °F/ 45–49 °C.

To the S of Kumamoto, reached by way of *Uto*, is the *Uto Peninsula*, at the SW tip of which is **Misumi** (JNR Kagoshima line to Uto, then Misumi line), a good base from which to explore the **Unzen-Amakusa National Park** (see separate entry). – The JNR Kagoshima line continues beyond Uto to **Yatsushiro** (pop. 107,000), the largest industrial center in Kumamoto prefecture (cement, paper), and which also produces the well-known Koda-yaki pottery. The harbor, on *Yatsushiro Bay*, is noted for the marine phosphorescence (*shiranui*) which appears in late summer.

From Yatsushiro the Hisatsu line runs 32 miles/52 km SE, inland, to **Hitoyoshi** (pop. 43,000), which is called the "Kyoto of Kyushu". This former castle town on the River *Kumakamu*, which flows through the *Hitoyoshi Basin*, is now a popular spa. 550 yds/500 m from the station the *Aoi-Aso Shrine has a main hall and a tower surviving from the original foundation. An attractive excursion from here is a boat trip down the *Kuma Rapids*, among the best known in Japan. The boats leave from the site of the castle (1 mile/1·5 km SE of station) and take 2½ hours to reach *Osakama* 11 miles/18 km W.

From Yatsushiro the Kagoshima main line continues 7½ miles/12 km S to **Hinagu-onsen**, with a mild climate and hot springs (108–113 °F/42–45 °C). From the coast roads there are *views of the Amakusa Islands.

Kurashiki
くらしき

Prefecture: Okayama. – Population: 407,000.
Post code: J-710. – Telephone code: 0864.
(i) (local)
Kurashiki-shi Kanko Kyokai Information,
Kurashiki eki
(Central Station);
tel. 22 0249.

HOTELS. – **Western style**: *Mizushima Kokusai Hotel*, 4-20, Mizushima-Aoba-cho, 74 r.; *Kurashiki Kokusai Hotel*, 1-44, Chuo 1-chome, 70 r., Japanese garden; *Station Hotel*, 2-8-1, Achi, 136 r.; *Young Inn*, 1-14-8, Achi, 42 r.; *Mizushima Grand Hotel*, 1-8, Minami-Saiwai-cho, Mizushima, 30 r. – **Minshuku**: *Kurashiki Tokusan Kan*, 8-33, Honmachi, 63 r. – YOUTH HOSTELS: *Kurashiki YH*, 1537-1, Mukai-yama, 80 b.; *Washu-zan YH*, 1666-1, Obatake, 60 b.

TRANSPORTATION. – **Air**: from TOKYO (Haneda Airport) to Okayama (2 hours). – **Rail**: from TOKYO (Central Station) JNR Sanyo–Shinkansen line via OSAKA and OKAYAMA (5¼ hours).

The town of Kurashiki lies in western Honshu near the Inland Sea. Although it is now part of the extensive industrial area around Mizushima the old town has largely preserved its original character. It has much of interest to offer the visitor with its old dwelling-houses and warehouses, its willow-fringed canals and stone bridges and a number of fine museums.

At the beginning of the 17th c. an administrative office of the Shogunate was established in Kurashiki, and the small village soon developed into an important marketing center for rice, sake and cotton. The warehouses then built gave the town its name (*kura* = "warehouse", *yashiki* = "village"). The town's economy now centers on textiles, petrochemicals, steel and engineering, together with the

production of ceramics (*Bizen-yaki* and *Ohara-yaki*). – When visiting the town it should be borne in mind that all museums and most shops are closed on Mondays.

SIGHTS. – ¾ mile/1 km SE of the station is the **Museum of Art** (*Ohara-bijutsukan*), housed in a building modelled on a Greek temple (by Ohara Magosaburo, 1930), which contains a collection of European art (El Greco, Corot, Gauguin, Picasso, Rodin) and – in a recent extension – modern Japanese art, Near Eastern and Far Eastern art, woodcuts, and ceramics.

To the E, on the River *Kurashiki*, the **Museum of Folk Art** (*Kurashiki-mingei-kan*), established, in 1949 in four former rice-stores, displays ceramics, textiles, bamboo articles, etc., primarily from Japan. – Beyond the river is the **Archaeological Museum** (*Koko-kan*), opened in 1950, with material recovered by excavation in the Kibi district (now Okayama prefecture), together with items from China and South America. A short distance NE is the **Historical Museum** (*Kurashiki-rekishi-kan*), with a large collection of material of the Kamakura period (weapons, Buddhist liturgical utensils, domestic furniture and furnishings). – Farther S are a 100-year-old brick *spinning-mill*, the remains of the mansion of *Daikan* and a small museum devoted to the town's early industrial period.

SURROUNDINGS. – 2 miles/3 km SW of Shin-Kurashiki Station (W of the town on the Shinkansen line) is the garden of **Entsuji-en**, with the Entsuji Temple, in which the well-known calligrapher Ryokan (1758–1831) lived as a monk for some years. From the hill on which the temple stands there is a fine view of the Inland Sea.

To the S of Kurashiki the *Kojima Peninsula* projects into the Inland Sea (bus to Washuzan, then footpath to Mount Washuzan). From Mount *Washuzan* (436 ft/133 m) there are panoramic *views of the sea with its many islands and of the main island of Shikoku (to which there is a ferry service from *Shimotsui*).

The JNR Hakubi line runs N from Kurashiki to **Soja** (pop. 50,000), birthplace of the famous priest and painter Sesshu (1420–1506), who spent his novitiate in the Hofukuji Temple 1 mile/1·5 km – of the station. – From the next station, *Gokei*, an excursion (particularly rewarding in the fall) can be made to the beautiful **Gokei-kyo Gorge** (bus, 25 minutes), carved out by the River *Makitani*.

The Hakubi line continues to **Takahashi** (pop. 28,000), on the River Takahashi, which teems with fish. Above the E bank of the river is Mount *Gagyuzan* (footpath, 10 minutes), with ** Matsuyama Castle, of which the three-storey main tower and an outer tower urvive. This is one of the few 17th c. castles built in the hills rather than in the plain. From the top of Mount Komatsu there are very fine views of the town and surrounding area. – At the foot of the hill is the Gagyuzan Wildlife Park, with troops of wild monkeys.

Kushiro
くしろ

Prefecture: Hokkaido. – Population: 219,000.
Post code: J-085. – Telephone code: 0154.
(local)
Kushiro Tourist Section,
7-5, Kurogane-cho;
tel. 23 5151.
Japan Travel Bureau,
Kanbayashi Building,
9, Kita-odori;
tel. 22 9181.

HOTELS. – **Western style:** *Kushiro Pacific Hotel,* 2-6, Sakae-cho, 135 r.; *Kushiro Parco Hotel,* 13-26, Kurogane-cho, 128 r.; *Kushiro Daiichi Hotel,* 3-2, Nichiki-cho, 61 r.; *Oriental Hotel,* 7-1, Saiwai-cho, 37 r.; *Hotel Suehiro,* 25 r.; *Kushiro Prince Hotel,* 21 r. – **Ryokan:** *Goto Ryokan,* 20 r.; *Murakami Ryokan,* 14 r. – YOUTH HOSTELS: *Kushiro YH,* 3-7-23, Tsurugadai, 50 b.; *Kushiro Makiba YH,* 7-23, Kawakita-cho, 44 b.

EVENTS. – *Port Festival* (beginning of August), on River Kushiro, with fireworks; *Snow Festival* (beginning of December) in Yone-machi Park, with snow sculpture.

TRANSPORTATION. – **Air:** from TOKYO (Haneda Airport), 1¾ hours; from SAPPORO (40 minutes). – **Rail:** from SAPPORO JNR Nemuro line (5 hours). – **Boat:** from TOKYO (30 hours).

The town of Kushiro, on the SE coast of Hokkaido, is the cultural, economic and political center of the eastern part of Hokkaido, the most northerly of the main Japanese islands. Only a hundred years ago the area was still occupied by the Ainu, the indigenous inhabitants of Hokkaido. – In spite of its severe climate and the low temperatures which prevail even in summer, Kushiro is the island's only ice-free port apart from Wakkanai, at the northern tip of Hokkaido.

The town's main industries are woodworking, paper-making and foodstuffs (particularly fish products).

SIGHTS. – 1¼ miles/2 km S of the station (bus, 10 minutes) is **Yonemachi Park,** from which there is a view of the Akan National Park (see separate entry). – 1 mile/1·5 km SE of the station is

Tsurugatai Park, in which is the *Municipal Museum* (Ainu culture). Near by is *Lake Harutori* (bus from station, 20 minutes), on the northern shore of which is an Ainu settlement.

SURROUNDINGS. – 12½ miles/20 km NW (bus from station, 1 hour) lies the **Nature Park of the White Cranes,** a bird sanctuary in a marshy area which is the last habitat of these rare and now statutorily protected birds.

30 miles/50 km E of Kushiro the **Akkeshi Peninsula** projects into Akkeshi Bay (JNR Nemuro line, 50 minutes). The town of **Akkeshi** is divided into a northern and a southern part (Shinryu and Honcho) by a lagoon, now spanned by the Great Akkeshi Bridge (510 yds/465 m long). The southern part began to develop during the Meiji period, the northern part only after the construction of the Nemuro railway line. The *Akkeshi Lagoon* (12½ sq. miles/32 sq. km) is an important center of oyster-culture; *Akkeshi Bay* is Japan's only herring-fishing area. – On the S coast of the peninsula the *Kokutaiji Temple* (Rinzai sect, Nanzenji school), was founded in 1802, and became in 1804 one of the three missionary temples on Hokkaido.

See also **Akan National Park** and **Daisetsuzan National Park.**

Kyoto
きょうと

Prefecture: Kyoto. – Population: 1,500,000.
Post code: J-600-606. – Telephone code: 075.
(local)
Tourist Information Center,
Kyoto Tower Building,
Higashi-Shiokojicho,
Shimogyo-ku;
tel. 371 5649.
Kyoto-shi Kanko Information,
Kyoto Ekimae
(at Central Station),
Sakyo-ku;
tel. 371 2108.

HOTELS. – IN SHIMOGYO WARD. – **Western style:** *Kyoto Station Hotel,* Higashi-no-Toin-dori, Shiokoji, 125 r.; *Kyoto Grand Hotel,* Horikawa-Shiokoji, 517 r., SP; *Kyoto Dai-Ni Tower Hotel,* Higashi-no-Toin-dori, Shiokoji-sagaru, 306 r.; *Kyoto Tower Hotel,* Karasuma Shichijo-sagaru, 148 r.; *Hokke Club,* Higashi-Shiokojicho, 138 r.; *Central Inn,* Nishi-iru, Shijo-Kawaramachi, 55 r.; *White Hotel,* Shiokoji Higashi-agaru, Higashino-Toin, 36 r. – **Ryokan:** *Kokusaikanko Hotel Hatoya,* Aburanokoji-Shiokoji-sagaru, 60 r.; *Hotel Sanoya,* Higashino-Toin-Shiokoji-agaru, 45 r., *Hizen-ya,* Ayanokoji-Karasuma-nishi-iru, 38 r.; *Kinta Ryokan,* Yanagionbanba-Shijo-sagaru, 28 r.; *Kaneiwaro Bekkan,* Kiyamachi-Matsubara-sagaru, 23 r.; *Ryokan Tsuruki,* Kiyamachi-Gojo-agaru, 16 r. – IN MINAMI WARD. – **Western style:** *New Miyako Hotel,* Nishi-Kujoincho, 714 r., Japanese garden.

IN HIGASHIYAMA WARD. – **Western style:** *Miyako Hotel,* Sanjo Keage, 480 r., Japanese garden, SP; *Tokyu Inn,* 35-1, Hanano-oka-cho, Kamikazan,

Yamashina, 156 r.; *Kyoto Park Hotel*, 644-2, San-jusangendo, Mawari-machi, 307 r., Japanese garden; *Kyoto Gion Hotel*, 555, Gion Minamigawa, 150 r. – **Ryokan**: *Tozankaku*, Myohoin-Maekawa-cho, 135 r.; *Seikoro*, Toiyamachi-Gojo-sagaru, 25 r.; *Kyoyamato*, Minami-masuya-cho, 14 r. – **Minshuku**: *Kodaiji*, 350-13, Masuya-cho, Kodaiji, 28 r.; *Masuya*, Konpirajinji-minami, Yasui, 20 r.

IN NAKAGYO WARD. – **Western style**: *Kyoto Hotel*, Oike, Kawara-machi, 507 r.; *International Hotel Kyoto*, 284, Nijo-Aburanokoji, 332 r., Japanese garden, SP; *Hotel Gimmond*, Takakura Oike-dori, 145 r.; *Kyoto Garden Hotel*, Miike Minami-iru, Muromachi-dori, 130 r.; *Kyoto Royal Hotel*, Kawara-machi, Sanjo, 395 r.; *Hotel Fujita*, Nishizume, Nijo-Ohashi, 195 r., Japanese garden; *Business Hotel*, Oike, Kiya-machi, 30 r. – **Ryokan**: *Chigiriya*, Takoyakushi-Tominokoji-nishi-iru, 46 r.; *Hiiragiya Ryokan*, Fuyacho-Anegakoji-agaru, 33 r.; *Sumiya Ryokan*, Fuyacho Sanjo-sagaru, 26 r.; *Daitomi Ryokan*, Gokomachi-Takoyakushi-agaru, 25 r.; *Ikumatsu*, Kiyamachi-Oike-agaru, 21 r.; *Tawaraya Ryokan*, Fuyacho-Anegakoji-agaru, 19 r.; *Matsukichi Ryokan*, Gokomachi-Sanjo-agaru, 17 r.

IN KAMIGYO WARD. – **Western style**: *Hotel New Kyoto*, Horikawa-Maruta-machi, 246 r.; *Hotel Palaceside Kyoto*, Shimodachiuri-agaru, Karasuma-dori, 120 r.; *Ladies' Hotel Nibakan*, Maruta-machi, Horikawa, 96 r.; *Ladies' Hotel Nishijin*, Nishiiru, Teranouchi, Horikawa-dori, 22 r. – **Minshuku**: *Tangoya*, Kudaru-higashigawa, Nakadate-uri, Senbon-dori, 25 r.

IN UKYO WARD. – **Western style**: *Arashiyama Ladies' Hotel*, 20-1, Tsukurimichi-cho, Sagatenryuji, 41 r. – **Minshuku**: *Ikuyo Ryokan*, 40, Suzukibaba-cho, Saga-Tenryuji, 19 r. – IN SAKYO WARD. – **Western style**: *Holiday Inn Kyoto*, 36, Nishihiraki-cho, Takano, 270 r., SP; *Kyoto Prince Hotel*, 43, Matsubara-cho, Shimogamo, 99 r.; *Hotel Sunflower Kyoto*, 51, Higashi-Tenno-cho, Okazaki, 77 r., Japanese garden; *Mount Hiei Hotel*, Ipponsugi, Hieizan, 73 r., SP; *Traveler's Inn*, 91, Okazaki-Enshoji-cho, 25 r. – **Ryokan**: *Yachiyo*, Nanzenji-Fukushi-cho, 27 r. – **Minshuku**: *Ohara-no-sato*, Ohara, Kusao-cho, 90 r.; *Miyama-so*, Ohara, 17, Kusao-cho, 60 r.

YOUTH HOSTELS. – *Higashiyama YH*, in Higashiyama ward, 112, Shirakawabashi-goken-cho, Sanjo-dori, 112 b.; *YH Matsusan*, in Nakagyo ward, 331, Ebiya-cho, Sanjo-sagaru, Goko-machi, 40 b.; *Utano YH*, in Ukyo ward, 29, Nakayama-cho, Uzumasa, 172 b.; *Oharago YH*, in Sakyo ward, 137, Ohara-todera-cho, 23 b.; *Ohara YH*, in Sakyo ward, 85, Ohara-todera-cho, 15 b.; *Kitayama YH*, in Kita ward, Hotori, Koetsuji, Takagamine, 38 b.

RESTAURANTS. – IN SHIMOGYO WARD. – **Western cuisine**: *Lipton Tea House*, Teramachi-kado, Shijo; *Manyoken* (French), Fuyacho, Higashi-iru, Shijo-dori. – **Japanese cuisine**: *Funatsuru*, 180, Minoya-cho, Matsubara-agaru. – IN HIGASHIYAMA WARD. – **Western cuisine**: *Restaurant Izutsu*, 33, Sanjo-sagaru, Yamato-oji. – **Japanese cuisine**: *Doi*, 353, Kodaiji Masuyacho; *Hiranoya Nishiten*, Maruyama-koen; *Kikunoi*, 459, Makuzugahara, Maruyama-koen; *Kiyomizu Tsuruya*, 2-216, Kiyomizu; *Kyoyamato*, Kodaiji-minami; *Nakamuraro*, 509, Gion-Minamigawa; *Jubei* (rice dishes), Shimbashi-agaru, Nawate-dori; *Junidanya Honten* (poultry), Gion Hanamikoji; *Matsuba* (noodle dishes), 192, Kawabatacho, Kawabata-higashi-iru, Shijo-dori; *Matsuno* (eel dishes), Yamato-oji, Nishi-iru, Shijo-

dori; *Mikaku* (sukiyaki), Shijo-agaru, Gion-Kawabata-dori; *Yasaka* (sukiyaki), Higashioji-Nishi-iru, Yasaka-dori; *Yotaro* (tempura), Sanjo-sagaru, Nawate-dori. – IN NAKAGYO WARD. – **Western cusine**: *Lipton Kawaramachi-ten*, 294, Naraya-machi, Sanjo-sagaru 3-chome, Kawaramachi-dori; *Lipton Shijo-ten*, Shijo-agaru, Higashinotoin. – **Japanese cuisine**: *Isecho*, Nishikino-koji-agaru, Shinmachi; *Izumoya*, Shijo-agaru, Pontocho-dori; *Tankuma*, Shijo-agaru, Kiyamachi-dori; *Mishimatei* (sukiyaki), Sanjo-Teramachi. – IN KAMIGYO WARD. – **Japanese cuisine**: *Mankamero*, 387, Demizu-agaru, Inokuma; *Uoshin*, Jofukuji-Nishi-iru, Nakasuji-dori; *Tenki* (tempura), Imadegawa-agaru-nishi, Senbon-dori.

EVENTS. – *First Shrine Visit* (beginning of January), at Yasaka Shrine (worshippers light a flame from the Sacred Fire with which they cook their first meal of the New Year); *Toka Ebisu* (beginning of January), a festival in honour of Ebisu, goddess of fortune, at Ebisu Shrine, Kita ward; *Ho-onko* (mid January) festival commemorating Shinran, founder of the sect, in Nishi-Honganji Temple; *Hadaka-odori* (mid January), dance by naked men in Hokaiji Temple; *Toshiya* (mid January), a traditional archery contest at the Sanjusangen-do; *Temple Festival* in Toji Temple (end of January) in honor of Kobo-daishi, founder of the sect; *Setsubun* (February 3), festival celebrating the end of winter, in several temples and shrines, including the Kamikamo Shrine and the Kurama Temple.

Baika-sai (end of February), Plum Blossom Festival at Kitano Shrine, with tea ceremony in open air; *Hina-matsuri* (beginning of March), Doll Festival in Hokyoji Temple; *Nehan-e* (mid March), Nirvana ceremony on day of Buddha's death, celebrated in several temples, including the Tofukuji and Seiryoji Temples; *Miyako-odori* (April–May), cherry-blossom dances in Gion-Kaburenjo Theater; *Hana-matsuri* (beginning of April), Buddha's birthday, celebrated in all temples; *Taiko-no-Hanami Gyoretsu* (second Sunday in April), cherry-blossom procession at Daigoji Temple; *Yasurai-matsuri* (second Sunday in April), dance to ward off demons, in Imamiya-Ebisu Shrine; *Jusan-mairi* (mid April), procession of 13-year-old children to Horinji Temple, whose divinity grants good fortune and wisdom; *Gyoki-e* (middle to end of April), festival commemorating Honen, founder of sect, in several temples, including the Chion-in; *Mibu-Kyogen* (end of April), 13th c. religious dance-plays, followed by the breaking of plates inscribed with good wishes, in Mibu Temple; *Matsunoo-matsuri* (fourth Sunday in April), procession with portable shrines at Matsunoo Shrine; *Kanogawa-odori* (beginning to middle of May), geisha dances in Pontocho-Kaburenjo Theater; *Aoi-matsuri* (mid May), procession in historical costumes and ceremonies in Kamikano and Shimokamo Shrines; *Goryo-e* (mid May), procession of palanquins, particularly at Shimokamo Shrine; *Shinran-Shonin Gotan-e* (end of May), festival in honor of Shinran, founder of sect, at Nishi-Honganji Temple; *Mifune-Matsuri* (third Sunday in May), boat festival on River Oi at Kurumazaki Shrine; *Takigi-no* (beginning of June), evening performances of No plays at Heian Shrine; *Takekiri-e* (end of June), ceremonial felling of bamboos at Kurama Temple.

Cormorant Fishing (July–August) at Gifu (at night, with trained cormorants); *Gion-matsuri* (mid July), procession of 29 large decorated floats from Yasaka Shrine (a festival dating from 876); *Motomiya-sai* (end of July), in Fushimi-Inari Shrine; *O-taue-matsuri* (end of July), rice-planting festival at Matsunoo Shrine; *Toki-matsuri* (beginning of August), pottery market in Gojo; *Daimonji-gozan-okuribi* (mid

August), lighting of fires on hillsides in the form of Chinese characters; *Toronagashi* (mid August), Lantern Festival in Arashiyama Park; *Matsuage* (end of August), Fire Festival on banks of river in Hanase; *Jizo-bon* (end of August), festival in honor of the patron divinity of children in several temples; *Rokusai Nebutsu-odori* (end of August), acrobatic folk-dances in Kisshoin-Temmangu Shrine; *Hassaku-sai* (first Sunday in September), Harvest Festival in Matsuo Shrine; *Karasu-sumo* (beginning of September), children's wrestling matches in Kamigamo Shrine; *Higan-e* (end of September), ceremony marking the equinox in all temples.

Zuiki-matsuri (beginning of October), procession with decorated floats at Kitano-Temmangu Shrine; *Kamogawa-odori* (October–November), geisha dances in Pontocho-Kaburenjo Theater; *Shamenchi-odori* (beginning of October), traditional folk-dances in Yase-Akimoto Shrine; *Ushi-matsuri* (mid October), play in traditional costumes in Koryuji Temple; *Jidai-matsuri* (end of October), festival commemorating the foundation of the town in 794, with a great procession in historical costumes, starting from Heian Shrine; *Kurama-no-hi-matsuri* (end of October), Fire Festival, with torchlight procession, at Yuki Shrine; *Momiji-matsuri* (second Sunday in November), boat trips in the style of the 10th c. in Arashiyama Park; *Ochatsubo Hokensai* (end of November), festival commemorating a tea ceremony celebrated by Toyotomi Hideyoshi in 1587, in Kitano-Temmangu Shrine; *Kaomise* (December), Kabuki performances in Minami-za Theater; *Shimai-Kobo* (end of December) ceremony in Toji Temple commemorating Kobo-daishi; *Shimai-Tenjin* (end of December), ceremony commemorating Tenjin, in Kitano-Temmangu Shrine.

THEATRES. – **No**: *Oe-nogakudo*, Yanaginobamba, Higashi-iru, Oshikoji, Nakagyo-ku; *Kongo-noga-kudo*, Muromachi, Shijo-aguru, Nakagyo-ku; *Kanze-kaikan*, Okazaki, Sakyo-ku. – **Kabuki**: *Minami-za*, Nakano-machi, Higashiyama-ku; *Kyoto-kaikan*,

The old Imperial city of Kyoto

Okazaki, Sakyo-ku; *Gion Kaburenjo*, Gionmachi, Higashiyama-ku; *Pontocho Kaburenjo*, Ishiya-machi, Nakagyo-ku.

SIGHTS SEEN ONLY BY APPOINTMENT. – **Imperial Palace**: apply 20 minutes in advance to Imperial Household Agency (to NW of Imperial Park), with passport. Conducted tours at 10 a.m. and 2 p.m. Closed on Saturday afternoons, Sundays and public holidays and from December 25 to January 5.

Katsura-rikyu, Shugakuin-rikyu and **Sento-gosho**: apply 5 days in advance in April, May, October and November, 2 days in advance in other months, to Imperial Household Agency (Kyoto Goen 3, Kamigyo-ku, Kyoto; tel. 211 1211-5); permit issued one day in advance on presentation of passport. Conducted tours: Katsura-rikyu at 10 a.m. and 2 p.m.; Shugakuin-rikyu at 9, 10 and 11 a.m., 1.30 and 3 p.m.; Sento-gosho 11 a.m. and 1.30 p.m. Persons under 20 not admitted. Closed on Saturday afternoons, Sundays and public holidays and from December 25 to January 5.

Saihoji Temple: apply in writing (with card for reply) at least two weeks in advance to Saihoji Temple, 56, Jingaya-cho, Matsuo, Nishikyo-ku, Kyoto.

TRANSPORTATION. – **Rail**: Kyoto is the junction of the JNR Tokaido–Shinkansen and Tokaido lines, the JNR San-in and Nara lines. From TOKYO (Central Station) JNR Tokaido–Shinkasen line (Hikari 3 hours, Kodama 4 hours); from NAGOYA JNR Tokaido–Shinkansen line (Hikari 50 minutes, Kodama 1 hour); from OSAKA JNR Tokaido–Shinkansen and Tokaido lines (20 minutes or 45 minutes); from NARA Kinki–Nippon private line (40 minutes) and JNR Nara line (1 hour). – **Bus**: from OSAKA (airport; 1½ hours).

Sightseeing walks in Kyoto

Higashiyama ward: from the Gojozaka bus stop to the Kiyomizu Temple. The route follows a curving street with many souvenir and antique shops; then N up Higashioji-dori to the Maruyama Park, around which is a maze of little streets with old houses, potters' workshops and small temples and shrines (particularly attractive during the cherry-blossom season and in the fall). Jingu-michi, running parallel to Higashioji-dori on the E, leads past the National Museum of Modern Art and the Municipal Museum of Art to the Heian Shrine. Time: 1 hour.

Along the Old Canal. – From the Nanzenji Temple (bus from station) Shishigatani-machi runs N to the Ginkakuji Temple. This route, following the canal, which is lined with cherry trees, is known as the "Philosophers' Way". Time: 50 minutes.

Arashiyama. – From Arashiyama Station (Keifuku–Arashiyama line from Shijoomiya Station), in the W of the city, it is possible to walk S to the river and N to the Tenryuji and Gioji Temples. During the Heian period this was a favorite resort of the Imperial Court, and the area has preserved an attractive old-world atmosphere. Time: 1½ hours.

Ohara. – From the Ohara bus stop there are various possible routes to the little Jakko-in Temple and the Sanzen-in Monastery, situated on a hill a few minutes' walk E of the temple. The autumn coloring of the maple trees is very beautiful (November). Time: 2 hours.

The city of ****Kyoto** lies, surrounded by hills, in central Honshu, near the SW end of Lake Biwa. Occupying an area of more than 230 sq. miles/600 sq. km in the south-facing basin between the rivers Katsura to the W and Kamo to the E, it is Japan's fifth largest city, the chief town of Kyoto prefecture and the educational hub of western Japan, with several universities and higher educational establishments. Although it is one of Japan's great tourist Meccas, attracting more than ten million visitors every year, it has preserved much of the atmosphere of the past, having been the only one of Japan's major cities to escape damage during the Second World War. – The climate of the Kyoto area shows marked differences between the seasons, with hot dry summers and relatively cold winters.

For almost 1100 years, from 794 to 1868, Kyoto was the residence of the Emperor and in consequence Japan's principal cultural center, where architecture, sculpture, painting and many other arts achieved a magnificent flowering. At an early stage the arts came under strong Buddhist influence, and as a result many of the surviving works of art are to be found in the old temples. In our own day Kyoto continues to play a dominant part in Japanese religion: thirty of the city's temples are centres of various Buddhist sects, and in addition there are some 200 Shinto shrines within the city limits.

HISTORY. – Ten years after the transfer of the seat of government from Nara to Nagaoka, in 794, the Emperor Kammu founded a new capital at the village of *Uda*, to the NE of Nagaoka. It was originally known as *Heiankyo* ("capital of peace"), later as *Miyako* ("imperial residence") and finally, after the Meiji reform, as *Kyoto* ("capital city").

Following Chinese models, the town was laid out on a regular grid, and was surrounded by walls and a double moat. From N to S it extended for 3¼ miles/5·2 km, from E to W for 2¾ miles/4·4 km. From the Imperial Palace (Dai-dairi) a street 272 ft/83 m wide, Suzaku-oji, ran S, dividing the town into an eastern half (Sakyo) and a western half (Ukyo). There were 18 gates. The town is said to have had a population of 400,000 in the very first year of its existence. On several occasions part of the town was destroyed by earthquakes and fires. The Imperial Palace was burned down in 960, 1177 and 1227, and after this last destruction was not rebuilt.

By the beginning of the 9th c. the Imperial House, increasingly involved in non-political matters, was overshadowed by the Fujiwara clan, which gained control of all the key positions of political power. Later

Kyoto has a long tradition of craft production. Among its best-known products are:

Nishijin silk. – Silk-weaving was practiced in Kyoto from its earliest days. Refined Chinese techniques soon came into use, and in the 17th c. the weaving-mills of the Nishijin district were granted a monopoly for the supply of the Imperial Court. The local silks are used in kimono girdles (*obis*) as well as table-cloths, curtains and clothing.

Printed fabrics. – The refined dyeing technique know as *Yuzen-zome* (or Kyo-zome) is said to have been devised by an artist named Yuzen Miyazaki in the late 17th c. Stencils are used to apply a wide range of patterns to silk. These fabrics are much used in kimonos.

Embroidery. – The technique of embroidery was acquired from China and Korea, and this form of decoration was used in combination with printed fabrics on costumes for wear at Court. This is still a characteristic Kyoto craft.

Porcelain. – The fine porcelain known as *Kyoyaki* (or *Kiyomize-yaki*) acquired its reputation in the 17th c. through the work of a potter named Ninsei Nonomura. It is used for everyday purposes and also in the tea ceremony.

Lacquerware. – Particularly sought after is the type of lacquerware known as *Maki-e*, in which gold and silver dust is incorporated in the coat of lacquer.

the Emperor came under increasing pressure from the militant monasteries in the surrounding area. After a period of unrest power was seized by the Taira family, but in 1185 the Taira suffered an annihilating defeat at the hands of the Minamoto clan in the Battle of Dannoura. Minamoto Yoritomo (1147–99), appointed Shogun by the Emperor, moved the seat of government to Kamakura, while the Imperial House, deprived of political power, was confined to the fostering of art, culture and religion. Court life now reached a high pitch of refinement.

The Emperor Godaigo (1288–1339), who came to the throne in 1318, set out to bring the Shogunate under control; but his general Ashigaka Takauji, after defeating the Shogunal forces, advanced on Kyoto in 1336, expelled Godaigo and set up Komyo (d. 1380) as a rival Emperor. In 1392 the Southern Dynasty which the exiled Godaigo had founded at Yoshino abandoned its claim to Imperial authority, leaving Kyoto as the undisputed capital. In 1467 further conflict arose over the succession to the Ashikaga dynasty, and at the end of the subsequent Onin Wars (1477) Kyoto had been reduced to ruins.

In 1568, at the request of the Emperor, Oda Nobunaga set about the task of rebuilding the Imperial Palace and the town, and his work was continued by Toyotomi Hideyoshi. The pacification of the Empire which Toyotomi achieved brought a fresh period of prosperity to Kyoto, which became the center of a Japanese renaissance. Governmental authority, however, still remained in the hands of the shoguns, and the political importance of Kyoto was finally extinguished when Tokugawa Ieyasu (1542–1616) transferred the seat of government to Edo (now Tokyo). –

Parts of the city were again destroyed by fire in 1708 and 1788, and in 1830 an earthquake caused much destruction.

The decision by the Shogunate in Edo to open up Japan to foreign trade after centuries of isolation strengthened the position of the Imperial House, which opposed this move, and in 1867 the Shogunate was abolished and the Emperor's authority restored. But since the Emperor Meiji moved his capital to Edo in 1869 Kyoto was no better off. though by Imperial decree it remained the place of coronation of the Emperor.

Sightseeing in Kyoto

Just N of the Central Station, in SHIMOGYO ward, rises the nine-storey **Kyoto Tower Building**, which has a total height of 430 ft/131 m including the Kyoto Tower on its roof. On the ground floor is the **Tourist Information Center** (English and other languages spoken). There are two outlook platforms (lift).

N of this again (Karasuma and Shichijo Streets) is the **Higashi-Honganji Temple** of the Jodo-shinshu sect, founded in 1602 and, after repeated destructions, last rebuilt in 1859.

The Jodo-shinshu sect was founded in 1224 by Shinran-shonin (or Keishin-daishi, 1173–1262), who had spent several years at the monastic center of Mount Hiei, NE of Kyoto. There he became a disciple of Ho-nen, founder of the Jodo sect, who encouraged him to found the Jodo-shinshu sect. The central features of the new sect were a belief in the Amida-Buddha, granter of salvation, and the rejection of celibacy. The increasing influence of this sect led Tokugawa Ieyasu in 1602 to divide the Honganji Temple into two and found the Otani school, a separate sect with its base in the Higashi-Honganji Temple.

The only parts of the temple freely open to the public are the Founder's Hall and the main Cult Hall. To see the other buildings and the Abbot's Lodging (Shosei-en) it is necessary to apply for permission at least one day in advance.

The great two-storey gate, *Daishido-mon*, gives access to the *Daishi-do* (Founder's Hall) with its massive wooden columns, which contains a statue of Shinran, said to have been carved by the founder himself. On either side of the statue are likenesses of abbots of the Otani school. To the S the hall is linked by a gallery with the **Hondo** (main hall), which contains a statue of Amida by Kaikei. – The smaller N gate, *Chokushi-mon*, which was used by Imperial emissaries (now closed), is a copy of a gate in Toyotomi Hideyoshi's Fushimi Castle. In addition to numerous works of art, including statues of Amida by Shotoku-taishi and Jocho and paintings by Eshin, the temple possesses the original text of the "Kyogyoshinsho", Shinran's exposition of the doctrines of his sect. – To the E of the temple, in Kawaramachi-dori, is the Abbot's Lodging, **Shosei-en** (or *Kikokutei*), which was orginally part of Fushimi Castle. There is a beautiful 17th c. garden laid out by Ishikawa Jozan and Kobori Enshu.

Takao
OMURO, Kitano Shrine
Kameoka ARASHIYAMA
Saiho-ji
Katsura-rikyu
Osaka

Sembon Sakado

Shokoku-ji

Doshisha University
Doshisha Church
Demachi-nayagi Station

Ur Ch

Jofuku-ji

Nishijin Textile Museum

Imadegawa-dori

Kankyuan

Shibunkak Museu

Chieko-in

International School

KAMIGYO-KU

Palace Treasury

Sembon-dori
Horikawa-dori

Old Imperial Palace

Karasuma-dori

Facult Medic

Goo Shrine
Sento Palace

Prefecture
YWCA

Univer Hospi

Marutamachi-dori

Chamber of Industry and Commerce

Nijo-jo

NAKAGYO-KU

Yanaginobanba-dori

Nijo Station
Shinsen-en

Oike-dori

Nijo Jinya

Sanjo-dori

Heian Museum

Honno-ji

Sanjo-keihan Station

YMCA

Rokkakudo

Pontocho-Kaburenjo Theater

Shijo-dori

Shijo-keihan Station

Shijoomiya Station

Omiya-dori

Gion-Kabure Theater

Mibudera Temple

Kennin-ji

GIO MA

Tanbaguchi Station

Gojo-dori

Gojo Station

SHIMOGYO-KU

Ota Mausole

Higashi-Hongan-ji

Kikokutei-en

Hoko-ji

Nishi-Hongan-ji

Toyokuni Shrine

Myoh

Shichijo-dori

Shichijo Station

National Museum

Chishaku-in
Imahiei Shri
Yogen-ir

Kyoto Tower

Sanjusangendo

College of Art

Hachijo-dori

Central Station

To-ji

Toji Station

Tofukuji Station

Kujo-dori

Tofuku-

Uji FUSHIMI-KU
Nara

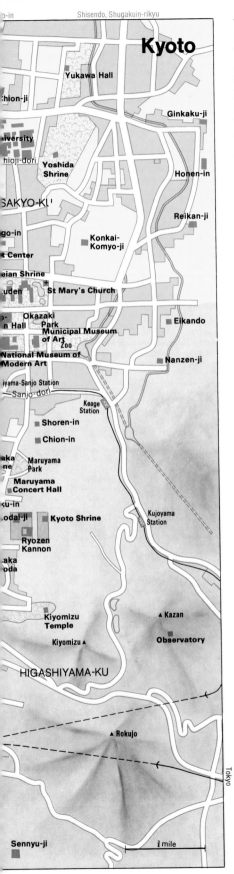

Kyoto

Shisendo, Shugakuin-rikyu

Yukawa Hall

:hion-ji

Ginkaku-ji

iversity

hioji-dori   Yoshida
              Shrine   Honen-in

SAKYO-KU¹

                                        Reikan-ji

go-in   Konkai-
               Komyo-ji
Center

eian Shrine
uden   St Mary's Church

)-   Okazaki
n Hall   Park   Eikando
          Municipal Museum
          of Art   Zoo
National Museum of
Modern Art   Nanzen-ji

iyama-Sanjo Station
—Sanjo-dori
                    Keage
                    Station
Shoren-in

Chion-in

aka   Maruyama
ne   Park
       Maruyama
       Concert Hall
ku-in   Kujoyama
odai-ji   Kyoto Shrine   Station
   Ryozen
   Kannon
aka
oda

       Kiyomizu   ▲ Kazan
       Temple
       Kiyomizu ▲   Observatory

HIGASHIYAMA-KU

       ▲ Rokujo

Sennyu-ji   ¾ mile

Tokyo

To the W, in Horikawa-dori (Nishi-Rokujo), stands the **Nishi-Honganji Temple**, chief temple of the original Jodo-shinshu sect and an outstanding example of Buddhist architecture. Only part of this temple is freely open to the public: to see the other parts application must be made in advance to the temple offices.

The *Hondo* (Main Hall), rebuilt in 1760, has a number of fine rooms decorated with paintings on a gold ground by unknown artists of the Kano school and contains a statue of Amida by a master of the Kasuga school. In the side-rooms are statues of Shotoku-taishi (573–621) and Ho-nen (1133–1212). The *Daishi-do* (Founder's Hall) has a much-revered statue of Shinran, probably carved by himself in 1244. After his death it was covered with a coat of lacquer mingled with his ashes. On either side are likenesses of later abbots. Above the entrance to the hall is an inscription in the hand of the Emperor Meiji consisting of two Chinese characters (*ken-shin*). In front of the Founder's Hall is a handsome gate, the *Seimon*. – Another notable building is the *Daishoin* or Treasury, originally part of Fushimi Castle, to the S of the town, which was transferred to its present site in 1632 together with the richly carved gateway, Kara-mon. The various rooms are named after the wall- and ceiling-paintings with which they are decorated (mostly of the Kano school). The Sparrow Room (Suzume-no-ma) was the work of Maruyama Ozui and Kano Ryokei. The (badly damaged) paintings in the Room of the Wild Geese (Gan-no-ma) are by Kano Ryokei. The Chrysanthemum Room (Kiku-no-ma) has flower pictures in gold and white by Kaiho Yusetsu (17th c.) and works by Kano Hidenobu and Kano Koi. The Stork Room (Ko-no-ma), decorated by Kano Tanyu, Kano Ryokei and Maruyama Okyo, was the Abbot's audience chamber. The room known as Shimei-no-ma or Siro-shoin, with works by Kano Koi, Kaiho Yusetsu and Kano Ryotaku, came from Fushimi Castle.

Near by are the *Kuro-Shoin* hall, with sliding doors painted by Kano Eitoku, and a *No theater* brought here from Fushimi Castle. – Some distance away, in the SE corner of the temple enclosure, is the *Hiun-kaku Pavilion* (16th c.), with paintings by Kano Tanyu, Tokuriki Zensetsu, Kano Eitoku, Kano Sanraku and Kano Motonobu; it contains Hideyoshi's tea-room.

To the S of the Nishi-Honganji Temple, beyond the railway line (MINAMI ward), stands the *Toji Temple (or Kyoo-gokoku-ji)*, founded in 796, which was made over to Kobo-daishi, founder of the Shingon sect, in 823. The temple was rebuilt after the destruction it suffered in the Civil War of the 15th c. The main hall, built by Toyotomi Hideyori in 1603, is one of the largest surviving Buddhist buildings of the Momoyama period. The 184 ft/56 m-high five-tiered *pagoda* was built by Tokugawa Iemitsu. Other notable features are the *Founder's Hall* (1380), the Rengemon gate (1191) and the *Lecture Hall* (1598). The *Temple Museum*, built in 1197 with the same kind of "air-conditioning" system as in the Azekura-zukuri style (see under Nara), contains some fine works of art.

To the E of the Central Station lies HIGASHIYAMA ward. Beyond the River *Kamo* is the **Sanjusangen-do** or *Rengyoin Temple*, founded in 1164 and rebuilt in 1266 after a fire. The name of the temple (*sanju-san* = "thirty-three") comes from the 33 chambers between the pillars supporting the roof. The temple's finest work of art is a seated wooden figure of the Thousand-Handed Kannon, which is flanked by statues of her 28 disciples and another 1001 small Kannon figures. All these works of sculpture are by Unkei, Tankei and their pupils. In the rear gallery is sculpture of the Heian and Kamakura periods.

NE of the temple stands the *National Museum*, established in 1897, with three departments (history, art, applied arts). – To the E, beyond the wide street Higashioji-dori, one finds the **Chishaku-in Temple**, the principal temple of the Chizan school of the Shingon sect. Originally erected in the province of Kii (now Wakayama prefecture), the temple was moved to its present site in 1598 by Tokugawa Ieyasu. In 1947 most of the old buildings were destroyed by fire. The temple garden was laid out by Sen-no-Rikyu (1522–91). – Immediately N is the **Myohoin Temple** of the Tendai sect, transferred here from its original site on Mount Hiei. In the Great Hall are paintings

by Kano Eitoku (1543–90) and Kano Shoei (1519–92). The temple also possesses various works of art which belonged to Toyotomi Hideyoshi. A flight of 500 stone steps leads up to the *Hokokubyo*, Hideyoshi's tomb, with a five-storey pagoda and the shrine containing his remains (restored 1897).

Farther NE, on Mount *Kiyomizu*, is the **Kiyomizu Temple**. In the street leading to it, Kiyomizu-zaka, there are many shops selling porcelain. The temple, dedicated to the Eleven-Headed Kannon, was founded in 798 and rebuilt by Tokugawa Iemitsu in 1633.

The **temple precincts** are entered by the *Seimon* (West Gate), which has guardian figures (*kongo-rikishi*) in lateral niches. Near by are the *bell-tower* and a three-storey *pagoda*. Beyond these are the *Hall of Writings* (Kyodo), the *Founder's Hall* (Tamurado) and the *Asakura Hall* (Asakurado), built by Asakura Sadagake (1473–1512). Then comes the **Hondo** (Main Hall), with a wooden veranda above the steep hillside from which there is a fine *view of Kyoto and the surrounding hills. The Japanese use the term "a

Kiyomizu Temple, Kyoto

jump from the veranda of the Kiyomizu Temple" to mean a particularly daring act. In front of the hall are two iron sandals, said to have belonged to the giant who was defeated by the dwarf Issun-boshi. In the interior is a statue of the Eleven-Headed Kannon. – At the E end of the temple precinct below two other halls, *Shakado* and *Amidado*, are the *Otowa Falls*, at which the god Fudo-Myo-o, who punishes evildoers, is honored.

Below the W side of the hill is the 128 ft/ 39 m-high five-storey *Yasaka Pagoda* (14th–15th c.; restored 1618), and a short distance away, to the NE, the **Kodaiji Temple**, built in 1606 by Toyotomi Hideyoshi's widow. The Founder's Hall (Kaisando) is decorated with pictures of the Kano school. The nearby funerary shrine (1606) has fine lacquer work (*tatamakie*). The two small pavilions on higher ground came from Fushimi Castle. There is a beautiful landscaped garden laid out by Kobori Enshu.

Kiyomizu Temple   Kyoto

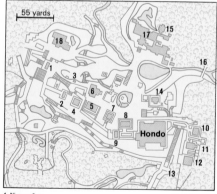

1 Niomon Gate
2 Seimon (West Gate)
3 Bell-tower
4 Three-storey pagoda
5 Hall of Writings (Kyodo)
6 Jishin-in
7 Founder's Hall (Tamurado)
8 Asakura Hall (Asakurado)
9 Todorokimon Gate
10 Shakado
11 Amidado
12 Okunoin
13 Otowa Falls
14 Jishu Shrine
15 Temple office
16 Joju Bridge
17 Jojuin
18 Hojoin

From the Central Station there are buses to the *Gionmachi district to the NE, with many places of entertainment, among them the **Minami-za Theater**, one of the oldest in Japan (early 17th c.), and the **Gion Corner** (displays of traditional arts including the tea ceremony, puppet plays, music and dancing, flower arrangement, etc.). In the narrow streets are a great number of restaurants. The night life in this area is very expensive.

To the S of Gionmachi is the **Kennin-ji Temple**, founded in 1202 by a priest named Eisai. Of the original buildings only one gate, the Chokushi-mon, still survives; the other buildings date from 1763. The temple possesses picture scrolls by Kaiho Yusho (1533–1615). – NE of this (Gion bus stop) is the **Yasaka Shrine** (or *Gion Shrine*), dedicated to the god Susanoo-no-mikoto, his wife Inadahime and their sons. The present buildings, erected in 1654, were modelled on the original architecture. To the S of the main shrine, which is roofed with cedar-wood shingles, stands a stone *torii* 30 ft/9·5 m high. Among the art treasures possessed by the shrine are wooden *koma-inu* figures (lion-like animals) by the well-known sculptor Unkei. The Gion-matsuri, celebrated in July, is one of the great Japanese festivals.

To the E of the Yasaka Shrine, at the foot of Mount Higashiyama, lies **Maruyama Park**, which is particularly beautiful during the cherry-blossom season (illuminated at night).

Going N along the street between the Yasaka Shrine and Maruyama Park, we come to the **Chion-in Temple**, with one of the largest precincts in Japan. The temple was founded by a priest named Genchi in 1234 as a center of the Jodo sect. The main hall and priests' lodgings date from the 17th c. The main gate (Sammon) is the tallest temple gate in Japan, 80 ft/ 24 m high. The main hall and the assembly hall are linked by a corridor with a floor so contrived that it squeaks when anyone walks on it – a means of ensuring that no one can approach unnoticed. Beyond the assembly hall, known as the "Hall of a Thousand Mats" (actually only 360), are the priests' lodgings, the wall screens in which are decorated with works of the Kano school. The adjoining garden is attributed to Kobori Enshu but is probably later. SE of the temple is a bell-tower with

what is claimed to be the largest bell in Japan, cast in 1633; it is rung about April 19 and at New Year in memory of the founder of the sect. The Kyozo (Sutra Library), built in 1616, contains sutras of the Sung period. Other features of interest are the Kara-mon Gate, also built in 1616, and the tomb of Ho-nen.

Just to the N of the Chion-in is the **Shoren-in Temple** or Awata Palace, formerly a residence of the abbots of the Enryakuji Temple (Mount Hisi). The main hall (rebuilt 1895) has wall screens with works by Kano Mitsunobu, Kano Motonobu and Sumiyoshi Gukei. There is a beautiful and carefully tended landscaped garden laid out by Soami and Kobori Enshu.

A short distance E of the Kumano-jinja-mae bus stop in SAKYO ward is the **Heian Shrine**, built in 1895 to commemorate the 1100th anniversary of the founding of Kyoto and dedicated to the founder, the Emperor Kammu, and the last Emperor to reside here, Komei. The shrine is a copy, on a smaller scale, of the first Imperial Palace of 794. The great entrance gate (reinforced concrete) and the red Ote-mon Gate give access to the Great State Hall (Daigokuden), the eastern and western Cult Halls (Honden) and the pagodas on either side. To the rear is a beautiful landscaped garden.

Immediately SE of the Heian Shrine we find **Okazaki Park** (21 acres), bounded by a stream which links Lake Biwa (see

Heian Shrine, Kyoto

separate entry) with the River Kamo. In the park are the **National Museum of Modern Art**, the **Municipal Museum of Art**, the *Civic Hall*, a *Library* and a *Zoo*.

E of Okazaki Park, in a grove of spruce, is the **Nanzenji Temple** of the Rinzai sect, founded in 1293. The present buildings are reconstructions dating from the time of Tokugawa Ieyasu. The main gateway (Sammon), built in 1628, has ceiling-paintings of the Kano school. The main hall was rebuilt in 1895 after a fire. The *Daihojo (priests' lodging), originally a residential hall of the Imperial Palace which passed into the possession of the temple in 1611, also contains works of the Kano school. The well-known picture by Kano Tanyu (1602–74), "Tiger in the Bamboo Grove", is in a smaller hall, the Shohojo, which came from Fushimi Castle. From the veranda there is a view of the famous *Zen garden (early 17th c.). Within the temple precincts are 12 smaller shrines, including the *Nanzen-in*, with a 14th c. garden; the Emperor Kameyama (1249–1305) lived for a time here. The garden of the *Konchi-in* was laid out in the 17th c. Beside the *Tenjuan Temple* are the tombs of Daimei-kokushi, founder of the Nanzenji, and Hosokawa Yusai.

A road continues N along the slopes of the hill to the **Ginkakuji Temple**, also known as the Silver Pavilion or Jishoji (Ginkakuji-mae bus stop).

Originally built in 1482 as a country residence for Ashikaga Yoshimasa, this was converted into a temple after Ashikaga's death. The facing of silver to which the temple owes its popular name was never in fact executed. The buildings are set round a *Zen garden* of white sand laid out by Soami. In the two-storey *pavilion* (not open to the public) is a gilded statue of Kannon, in the *Butsuden* (Buddha Hall) a figure of Buddha and in the *Togudo Hall* to the E a statue of Yoshimasa. The little tea-room in the north-eastern part of the hall is believed to be the oldest in Japan.

From the Ginkakuji-michi bus stop to the W of the temple a No. 5 bus can be taken to the Shugakuin-rikyu-michi stop. ¾ mile/1 km away from here, below the SW side of Mount Hiei, is the **Shugakuin-rikyu**, a former Imperial summer villa.

There are conducted tours of the villa (advance booking necessary: apply to Imperial Household Agency).

The villa was built and its **garden laid out for the Emperor Go-Mizunoo, who became a monk, under the name of Enjo, after his abdication in 1629. The garden is on three levels. Having found a suitable site in 1655, Enjo had the upper and lower gardens laid out by 1659. The middle garden, with the villa of the

Emperor's daughter Ake (which became the Rinkyuji Temple after she entered a nunnery), was a later addition, and was incorporated in the main complex, as the Middle Garden, only in 1855.

The visitors' entrance to the **Lower Garden** (Shimo-no-chaya) is a small gateway on the N side which leads to the second gate, Chumon. To the left is a roofed veranda, to the right an avenue leading to the Emperor's villa (1659, restored in the early 19th c.; not open to the public). – The East Gate and a path running through rice-fields and an avenue of firs lead to the **Middle Garden** (Naka-no-chaya), with the *Rinkyuji Temple* (garden with pool and waterfall). In the middle of the garden is the villa, with a reception hall (Kyaku-den) and a smaller building, the *Rakushi-ken* (1668). The reception hall has some fine paintings, including scenes from the Gion-matsuri festival and (on the wooden sliding doors) pictures of carp caught in a net. It is said that the net was added in the 18th c. by Maruyama Okyo because the painted fish always escaped into the garden pool during the night. – The **Upper Garden** (Kami-no-chaya), the largest of the three, is laid out on the principle of the "borrowed landscape" (*shakkei-zukuri*), which incorporates the surrounding area in the total composition. Standing on a higher level to the left of the entrance, beyond an earth rampart covered by a hedge, is the *Rinun-tei* Pavilion, from which there is a fine *view of the garden and its little lake. – On an island below the Rinun-tei stands a summer house, the *Kyusui-tei*, which was restored in its original form in 1824.

1 mile/1·5 km S of the villa is the *Shisendo Temple,* originally the residence of the poet and soldier Ishikawa Jozan (1583–1672). It contains paintings by Kano Tanyu, including portraits of 36 Japanese writers in the study (Shisen). In front of the temple is a sand garden of the Edo period. The temple stands in an area of quiet woodland.

On the north-eastern outskirts of Kyoto is the large **Takaragaike Park** (Keifuku–Eizan Railway to Takaragaike Station), in the northern part of which lies Lake Takaragaike. Near the lake is the **International Conference Hall** (1966). – The branch railway line which runs E from here ends in 3 miles/5 km at **Ohara** (also reached by bus from Central Station, 1 hour), with the **Sanzen-in Temple** of the Tendai sect, rebuilt in 860 by a priest named Joun. The main hall (Ojo-gokuraku-in, "Paradise of Rebirth") was built by another priest, Enshin (942–1017). The ceiling of the hall, in the form of a boat's keel, is decorated with 25 Bodhisattwas; on the walls are mandara pictures by Enshin; and the hall contains a gilded statue of Amida dating from 1148. Other buildings within the temple precincts were erected in the early 17th c., using material from the ceremonial hall of the Imperial Palace of Shishinden.

Garden of the Sanzen-in Temple, Kyoto

A little way W of the Sanzen-in is the **Jakko-in** Nunnery, to which the mother of the boy Emperor Antoku retired after the death of her son in the Battle of Dannoura (1185).

The western branch line of the Keifuku–Kurama Railway runs up to Mount *Kurama* (2460 ft/750 m), to the N of the city (Kurama Station). Half-way up the hill we reach the **Kurama Temple**, founded in 770 by the priest Kantei (re-

stored 1872; main hall destroyed 1945). The temple has a painting by Kano Motonobu.

From the Central Station buses 9 and 52 run N to NAKAGYO ward. Immediately W of the Nijojo-mae stop stands **Nijo Castle** (*Nijo-jo*), which has belonged to the city of Kyoto since 1939.

The castle was built by Tokugawa Ieyasu in 1603. At the beginning of the Meiji era it was for a time the seat of government, and it was from here that the Emperor issued the rescript abolishing the Shogunate. From 1871 to 1884 it was occupied by the prefectural administration, and during this period many of the works of art it contained were badly damaged.

The castle is surrounded by a moat and stone walls with corner towers. It is entered by the East Gate (*Higashi Otemon*) and an inner gate, *Karamon*, which has fine carving by Hidari Jingoro and decorative metalwork. This gate originally came from Fushimi Castle. Beyond it is still another gate, the *Mikuruma-yose*, also decorated by Hidari Jingoro, which gives access to the **Ninomaru Palace**. This consists of five separate buildings linked by corridors. The interiors are decorated with paintings by Kano Tanyu and his pupils. The principal apartment is the *Jodan-no-ma* (Hall of the Imperial Emissary); in the adjoining rooms, *Ni-no-ma* and *Tozamurai-no-ma*, are pictures of tigers. The linking corridors (like those in the Chion-in) have floors which creak when anyone walks on them, thus giving warning of the approach of a visitor.

Nijo Castle   Kyoto

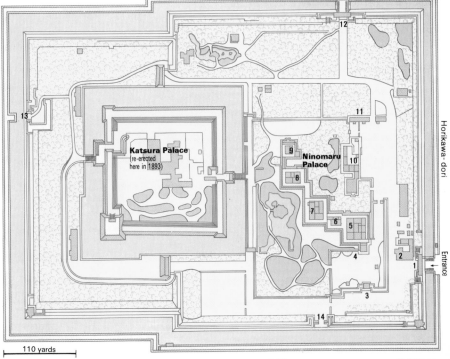

110 yards

1 Higashi Otemon
  (East Gate;
  main entrance)
2 Administration
3 Karamon (gate)

4 Mikuruma-yose (gate)
5 Tozamurai-no-ma
  (Samurai Hall)
6 Shikidai
  (Reception Hall)

7 Ohiroma
  (Audience Hall)
8 Kuro-shoin
9 Shiro-shoin
  (Private Apartments)

10 Kitchen
11 Rice-store
12 North Gate
13 West Gate
14 South Gate

Nijo Castle, Kyoto

The second building has three apartments, and beyond this is the third complex, the large *Audience Hall*, surrounded by a gallery or ambulatory. On the sliding doors are large paintings of larches on a gold ground; the subsidiary rooms have elaborate carvings by Hidari Jingoro. – The fourth building, the *Kuro-shoin*, has animal paintings by Kano Naonobu; in the Shogun's private apartments, beyond this, are paintings of mountain landscapes.

The *garden* to the W of the palace was originally designed without trees, since it was desired to avoid the impression of transitoriness created by their foliage. The trees which it now contains were planted in recent times.

¾ mile/1 km NE of Nijo Castle, in KAMIGYO ward, is the **Imperial Park** (area 207 acres/84 hectares; No. 36, 204 or 206B bus from Central Station), bounded by Karasuma-dori on the W, Marutamachi-dori on the S, Teramachi-dori on the E and Imadegawa-dori on the N. Within the park is the **Old Imperial Palace** (*Kyoto-gosho*).

To visit the palace it is necessary to apply in advance to the Imperial Household Agency (in the NW part of the park).

When he founded Kyoto the Emperor Kammu built the Daidairi Palace in the NW of the city. After being several times damaged by fire the palace was rebuilt in its original form on the present site in the late 18th c.; but this, too, was burned down and again rebuilt in 1855, still faithfully copying the original palace.

The rectangular area is surrounded by an earth rampart (Tsuijibei). Visitors enter by the West Gate (*Seisho-mon*): the South Gate (*Kenrei-mon*) was reserved for the Emperor, the East Gate (*Kensu-mon*) for the Empress and Dowager Empress, the South-West Gate (*Gishu-mon*) for princes and the North Gate (*Sakuhei-mon*) for the Emperor's junior wives and ladies of the Court. The 18 buildings which constitute the palace are linked by corridors or galleries; between them are charming gardens. After passing through the West Gate visitors turn right and in about 220 yds/ 200 m reach the *Shodaibu-no-ma,* with three waiting-rooms for nobles. To the E of this is the large Hall of Ceremonies (**Shishin-den** or *Shishii-den*), in which the Emperor was enthroned and the New Year celebrations took place. The central feature of the inner hall, which measures 72 ft/22 m by 108 ft/33 m, is the Throne (*Taka-mi-mura*), surmounted by an octagonal canopy bearing the figure of a phoenix, with a repository for the Imperial insignia on one side.

To the right is a smaller throne (*Michodai*) for the Empress. On the walls of the hall are portraits of Chinese sages, painted by Kano Sukenobu after 9th c. prototypes. – Outside the S front of the hall, in the inner courtyard, are an orange tree (Ukon-no-tachibana) and a cherry tree (Sakon-no-sakura), the names of which refer to the lodgings of the archers and horsemen which once stood on the site.

The **Seiryo-den** in the north-western part of the complex originally contained the residential apartments and later became a ceremonial hall. Since the ritual prescribed that during the ceremony of honoring the Imperial ancestors the Emperor must stand on natural soil, the floor in one corner of the hall is of beaten earth. The throne (*Michodai*) is flanked by two animal figures (*koma-inu*); the wall screens are decorated with paintings and calligraphy of the Tosa school. – The north-eastern part of the complex is occupied by the **Kogosho** (Little Palace; restored 1958), which consists of three apartments, and the Hall of Studies (**Gogakumonjo**), the exterior of which is in Shinden-zukuri style. The buildings to the N of this are for the most part not open to the public.

To the E is the *Oike-niwa Garden,* with a pool, which was not incorporated in the palace complex until the 17th c.

To the S of the palace enclosure, still within the park, are the remains of other old palace buildings (for permission to visit, apply to the Imperial Household Agency). Particularly attractive are the gardens of the **Sento-gosho** and the **Omiya-gosho**, which were the residence of ex-Emperors from 1629 to 1854. Of the residential buildings themselves little now remains. The gardens, with their pools and two tea-

Imperial Palace   (Heian)

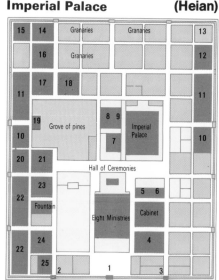

1 Gateway of the Scarlet Bird
2 Bifuko Gate
3 Koka Gate
4 Ministry of Population
5 Ministry of the Palace
6 Chancery of Divination
7 Cult Hall (Shinto)
8 Court Kitchen Department
9 Female attendants
10 Court Guard
11 Bodyguard
12 Court Office of the Dance
13 Tea-Garden
14 Armory
15 Lacquer Room
16 Ministry of Granaries
17 Library Chancery
18 Office for Poetry
19 Hall of Martial Virtue
20 Administration of
   Palace Workshops
21 Office for Sake Distilling
22 Chancery of Imperial Stables
23 Chancery for Medicines
24 Administration (Buddhism,
   the barbarians, imperial
   tombs)
25 Ministry of Justice

pavilions (*Seikatei* and *Yushintei*), were laid out by Kobori Enshu (17th c.).

To the N of the Imperial Park, beyond Imadegawa-dori, is the *Doshisha University*, and beyond this again the **Shokokuji Temple** of the Rinzai sect.

To the NE of the Shokokuji Temple, in SAKYO ward, is the **Shimogamo Shrine** (also reached by bus from Central Station, No. 4 or 214A). Most of the buildings date from 1628, the main hall from 1863. The shrine is renowned for the Aoi-matsuri festival, celebrated in mid May. – From here a No. 4 bus continues NW to the **Botanic Garden**, laid out in 1923 to commemorate the accession of the Emperor Taisho. To the S is the *University* of Kyoto prefecture.

To the W of the Doshisha University along Imadegawa-dori lies the weavers' quarter of **Nishijin** with its little old wooden houses, where this ancient traditional craft is still practiced. The **Nishijin Textile Museum** contains an interesting collection of textiles (shop; display of kimonos). – Immediately adjoining is the Horikawa-Imadegawa bus stop, from

which the No. 9 bus continues N. A short distance W of the next stop (Kitaoji-Horikawa), in KITA ward, stands the ****Daitokuji Temple**, one of the principal temples of the Rinzai sect.

The temple, founded in 1324, was destroyed during the Civil Wars of the 15th c.; the present structures date from the 16th and 17th c. Of the total of 22 buildings seven are open to the public. Of particular interest are the Zen gardens (dry gardens in kare sansui style).

The original main entrance to the temple precinct was the *Chokushi-mon* (now closed), originally the S gate of the Imperial Palace, which was moved here in 1640. Beyond this is the *kara-mon*, a Chinese-style gate with magnificent carving; an outstanding example of the architecture of the Momoyama period, it came from Fushimi Castle. The two-storey main gate (*Sammon*) was built by Sen-no-Rikyu in 1589. The ceiling-paintings on the lower floor were the work of Hasegawa Tohaku; on the upper floor are statues of Shakyamuni and the 16 Rakan (disciples of Buddha) – booty from Kato Kiyomasa's Korean campaign – and a portrait (said to be a self-portrait) of Rikyu.

The main hall, the **Butsuden** (or *Daiyu-den*), built in 1664, contains a statue of Shakyamuni with his disciples Anan and Kayo and a figure of Daito-kokushi, first Abbot of the temple. – Beyond the main hall is the Lecture Hall or *Hatto* (1636), which is based on Chinese models, and to the NE of this is the *Hojo* (Abbot's Lodging). This contains paintings by Kano Tanyu and a wooden tablet with an inscription ("Incomparable Temple of Zen") in the hand of the Emperor Godaigo. The adjoining garden was designed by Kobori Enshu.

The old Abbot's Lodging or **Shinju-an** (rebuilt 1638), once occupied by Ikkyu (1394–1481), can be seen only by prior arrangement. It contains a statue of Ikkyu and writings in his hand. The wall-paintings are by Soga Dasoku (d. 1483). Here too are the tombs of the *sarugaku* dancer Kan'ami (1333–84) and his son Zeami (1363–1443), who achieved a great reputation as a master of the No theater.

W of the Shinju-an is the **Daisen-in**, with a **garden – probably laid out in 1513 to the design of the founder, Kogaku Soko (1465–1548) – which is rated an outstanding example of a Zen garden. The models for these gardens were provided by Chinese paintings. The garden was divided into four parts, and – with only the most sparing use of plants – a mountain landscape with a waterfall was built up, mainly from rocks and sand, in a carefully contrived arrangement designed to produce an effect of space and depth. – The sliding doors in the interior of the building have paintings by Kano Motonobu, Soami and Kano Yukinobu; particularly interesting are the scenes of country life (*shikikosaku-zu*).

In the **Shuko-in**, to the W of the Abbot's Lodging, is the tomb of Sen-no-Rikyu, and to the W of this again, in the **Soken-in**, are the tombs of Oda Nobunaga and his sons and of Hideyoshi's widow. – The W end of the temple precinct is occupied by the *Koho-an*, a famous Zen garden designed by Kobori Enshu which contains the tombs of Enshu and his family.

1¼ miles/2 km N of the Daitokuji (No. 9 bus to Kamikamo-jinja-mae stop) is the

Old Imperial Palace   Kyoto

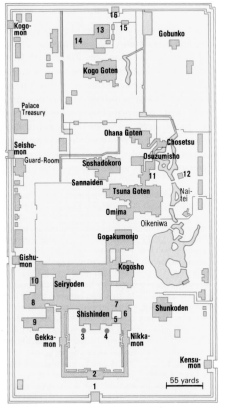

1 Kenrei-mon	9 Shin-Mikuruma-yose
2 Jomei-mon	10 Okuruma-yose
3 Ukon-no-Tachibana	11 Koshun-no-ma
4 Sakon-no-Sakura	12 Jishindono
5 Roofed corridor	13 Higyosha
6 Glyoden	14 Himemiya Goten
7 Jin-no-Zai	15 Genki-mon
8 Shodaibu-no-ma	16 Sakuhei-mon

Kamikamo Shrine, built at the time of the foundation of Kyoto and which is the scene in May of traditional horse-races and of the Aoi-matsuri festival.

From the Central Station the JNR Nara line runs S. Near Tofukuji Station is the **Tofukuji Temple** of the Rinzai sect, founded in 1236. The 13th c. gate (Sammon) has sculpture attributed to Jocho (d. 1057), and the ceiling-paintings are believed to be by Mincho (1352–1431) and his pupil Kandensu. In the extensive gardens are the Founder's Hall (with a portrait of the founder) and the Main Hall (burned down 1882, rebuilt 1932). Among the temple's treasures is a picture scroll (39 ft/11·9 m by 26 ft/7·9 m) by Mincho depicting Buddha's entrance into Nirvana (shown only on March 15).

The Nara line continues S into FUSHIMI ward, in which Toyotomi Hideyoshi's Fushimi Castle stood until the late 16th c. During the Tokugawa period the castle was demolished and used as a source of building material for various temples in Kyoto. No trace of the castle is now to be seen.

Fushimi-Inari Shrine, Kyoto

Immediately E of Inari Station, on the Nara line, is the ****Fushimi-Inari Shrine**, much frequented by merchants and tradesmen who pray for prosperity. One of the greatest shrines in Japan, founded in 711, it is dedicated to the goddess of rice-growing, Ukanomitama-no-mikoto. The main building (1499) is in typical Momoyama style. A notable feature is the 2½ mile/4 km-long avenue of red *torii* presented by worshippers. Here, too, are many sculptures of foxes (which are reputed to be messengers of the gods).

Near Momoyama Station is Mount *Momoyama,* planted with large numbers of cherry trees. This was the site of Fushimi Castle. A flight of 230 steps leads up to the mausoleum of the Emperor Meiji and his wife Shoken. The tomb, enclosed by three walls, is built of granite from the island of Shodo (see separate entry). – From the road to the mausoleum a side road goes off on the right to the *Nogi Shrine,* dedicated to General Nogi Maresuke, who had his headquarters here during the Russo-Japanese War (1904–05). When the Emperor Meiji died the General, who had been a loyal servant of the Emperor and had become a national hero as a result of his military achievements, committed suicide together with his wife.

The places of interest on the western and north-western outskirts of Kyoto can be reached from the city center by two private railway lines.

The terminus of the Hankyu line, which begins by running SW, is Hankyu-Omiya Station (buses Nos. 26, 28 and 38 from the Central Station). – A short distance E of Nishi-Kyogoku Station is the **Yuzen Hall of Culture**, where the Yuzen-zome technique of producing printed fabrics is demonstrated. – The next station is Katsura, in NISHIKYO ward, from which the Imperial Villa of ****Katsura-rikyu**, on the W bank of the River *Katsura,* can be visited.

Arrangements for visiting the villa must be made in advance through the Imperial Household Agency.

The villa was originally constructed for Prince Hachijo Toshihito (1579–1629), brother of the Emperor Goyozei. Much of it was built by 1624, and it was completed by 1658. The landscaped garden is said to have been designed by Kobori Enshu; and it was undoubtedly the work of either Kobori himself or some member of his circle. It is also believed that Prince Toshihito himself, a great art connoisseur, was involved in its planning. It is said that when Kobori accepted the commission he laid down three conditions designed to ensure that no changes were made in the original plan: first, no limit should be set to the cost of the work; second, no time limit for completion should be fixed; and third, neither the Prince nor anyone on his behalf should visit the site while work was in progress.

The garden is so designed that the visitor always sees things from the front. Around the pool are grouped a number of small gardens, and in the distance the summits of Mounts Arashiyama and Kameyama can be seen. The three parts of the building, offset from one another, have influenced modern architecture in

Kyoto Katsura-rikyū

Onari-mon
Miyuki-mon
Visitor Center
Machiai
Gepparo
Manji-tei
Shoin
Shokin-tei
Shoka-tei
Enrindo
Shoiken
55 yards
Katsura

Japan and even in other countries. The main buildings were thoroughly restored between 1974 and 1981.

The visitors' entrance is the *Miyuki-mon* Gate (1658). The garden paths, some of river pebbles and others of rectangular cobbles, are edged by mosses and bushes. Two further gates lead into the inner garden, in the centre of which is the group of buildings known as the **Goten**, consisting of three parts – Furu-shoin, Naka-shoin and Miyuki-den.

The veranda of the **Furu-shoin** was designed to permit observation of the moon. – The three rooms of the **Naka-shoin** contain fine paintings by Kano Tanyu (first room – including a well-known picture of a crow), Kano Naonobu (second room) and Kano Yusunobu (third room). – The **Miyuki-den**, the hall used by the Emperor, also contains a painting by Kano Tanyu. Notable, too, are the metal fittings (*kugi-kakushi*) in the form of flowers covering the heads of the nails used in the construction; they are attributed to a goldsmith named Kacho.

To the E of the main group of buildings, on higher ground, is the **Gepparo**, a building of plain and simple design. On the far side of the pool is the **Shokin-tei**, which contains a number of rooms including a tea-room so designed that natural light reaches into every corner. A small promontory covered with pebbles projects into the pool, in a highly stylized representation of the coastal scenery of Ama-no-hashidate (see separate entry). – In the SW corner of the garden is the **Shoiken**, with ten rooms.

From Katsura Station the Arashiyama section of the Hankyu railway line runs N. Near Kami-Katsura Station is the **Saihoji Temple** of the Rinzai sect, probably founded in the 12th c. and rebuilt in 1339 by a priest named Muso-kokushi, who was also a notable landscape-gardener. In the lower part of the **Zen garden* *surrounding the temple are a lake with a much-indented shoreline and a tea-house which probably dates from the Momoyama period. The garden is particularly noted for the 40 different species of moss which have earned it the name of the Kokedera ("Moss Temple"). In face of the increasing numbers of visitors it has

been found necessary to lay down a limit of 200 people a day, and accordingly prospective visitors must make written application at least three months in advance.

From the next station, Matsuno-jinja-mae, it is only a few minutes' walk westward to the **Matsunoo Shrine**, the scene of a well-known rice-planting ceremony (Otaue-matsuri). – Near the last station on the line, Arashiyama, stands the **Horinji Temple**, probably founded in 713, where the Jusan-mairi festival is celebrated in April.

From Arashiyama Station a bridge crosses the River *Katsura*, here also known as the Hozu or the Oi (direct route from Shijo-Omiya Station, near the Hankyu-Omiya Station, on the Arashiyama section of the Keifuku private railway line). The scenery in this part of the river's course is particularly beautiful. Above the river rises Mount *Arashiyama*, covered with cherry trees and dense thickets of maples; the hill is famous for its cherry blossom in spring and its vivid autumn foliage. Ex-Emperor Kameyama (1248–1304) caused cherry trees to be brought from Yoshino (see under Yoshino-Kumano National Park) and planted here. – From Arashiyama Station a road crosses the Togetsukyo Bridge and climbs the hill to a small lake, from which a side road leads to the **Daihikaku Temple**. This contains a figure of the Thousand-Handed Kannon and a wooden statue of Suminokura Ryoi (1554–1614), who made long stretches of the river navigable. Along the riverbank extends **Arashiyama Park** (or *Kameyama Park*). Farther downstream is the landing-stage used by the passenger-carrying boats which accompany the cormorant-fishing boats (beginning of July to mid August).

To the N, near the bridge over the Katsura, stands the **Tenryuji Temple**, the principal temple of the Tenryuji school of the Rinzai sect, founded in 1339 by Ashikaga Takauji, the first Ashikaga Shogun, in memory of the Emperor Godaigo. The garden behind the priests' lodgings was laid out by Muso-Kokushi, first Abbot of the temple. The present buildings date from about 1900.

From here a bus runs N to the **Seiryoji Temple** or *Shaka-do*, in the main hall of which is a sandalwood **statue of

Shakyamuni 5 ft 3 in/1·6 m high, said to have been carved in 987 by an Indian sculptor named Bishu Katsuma and brought from China to Japan by the priest Cho-nen. The statue can be seen only on April 8 (Buddha's birthday) and April 19 (purification ceremony).

Just N of the Seiryoji is the **Daikakuji Temple** originally a residence of the Emperor Saga and converted into a temple in 876. The main hall contains statues by Kobo-daishi (Godai Myo-o). The Kyaku-den (Reception hall) was originally a throne-room. The paintings in the temple are by Kano Motonobu, Kano Tanyu, Kano Sanraku and Watanabe Shiko.

From the terminus of the railway line the Keifuku private line runs a short distance E to Katabiranotsuji Station, near which is the **Koryuji Temple** or *Uzumasa-dera* (from the city center Keifuku line to Uzumasa Station).

The temple was founded by Hata Kawakatsu in 622, but the present buildings are later. The **Lecture Hall**, the second oldest building (1165) in Kyoto, contains three old *statues: in the center a seated figure of Buddha, flanked by figures of the Thousand-Handed Kannon and Fukukenjaku-Kannon. – In the rear hall (*Taishi-do*, 1720) is a wooden statue of Shotoku-taishi, probably a self-portrait (606).

An octagonal hall, the *Keigu-in or *Hakkaku-do* (1251), in the NW part of the temple precinct, contains a statue of the 16-year-old Shotoku-taishi and figures of Nyoirin-Kannon (presented by a king of Korea) and Amida. There is also some fine sculpture in the temple museum (*Reiho-kan*), including wooden statues of the Yakushi-nyorai (864) and **Miroku-bosatsu (the oldest work of sculpture in Kyoto, dating from the 6th–7th c.; said to be by Shotoku).

From Katabiranotsuji Station the Kitano branch line of the Keifuku private railway runs N to Omuro Station, just to the S of which is the **Myoshinji Temple**, the principal temple of the Myoshinji school of the Rinzai sect, which has many subordinate temples.

The temple was built in 1337 on the site of an earlier residence of the Emperor Hanazono. To the W of the Buddha Hall is a *bell-tower* with a *bell cast in 698. The Buddha Hall itself (**Butsuden**) contains a statue of Shakyamuni. The ceiling-paintings in the Lecture Hall (**Hatto**) are by Kano Tanyu. To the E the **Gyokuho-in** contains a likeness of Hanazono. To the W of the priests' lodgings are a number of smaller buildings, including the **Reiun-in** (also known as the Motonobu Temple), with many paintings by Kano Motonobu. The **Tenkuyan Temple** contains works by Kano Sanraku, while the **Kaifuku-in** has caricatural pictures by Kano Tanyu on the wall screens.

To the N of Omuro Station stands the *Ninnaji Temple**, originally the Omuro Palace (begun 886). After the abdication of the Emperor Uda (9th c.) the palace became a temple of which Uda was the first Abbot. – The present buildings date from the first half of the 17th c. To the right of the Middle Gate is a five-storey pagoda 108 ft/33 m high. The main hall contains a wooden statue of Amida. The temple precinct with its numerous cherry trees is a magnificent sight in the cherry-blossom season (April).

A short distance N of the Ninnaji is the **Ryoanji Temple**, which is famous for its **Zen garden* (dry garden), a highly stylized composition of rocks and raked white sand designed by an unknown artist. Within the temple precinct is the tomb of the founder, Hosokawa Katsumoto.

Zen garden of the Ryoanji Temple

To the SE, near the Toji-in Station (Keifuku private line), we come to the **Toji-in Temple**, founded in 1341 by Takauji, the first Ashikaga Shogun. The buildings were most recently restored in 1818. In the *Main Hall* are statues of all the Ashikaga shoguns except the fifth and tenth and paintings by Kano Sanraku (1559–1635). The temple is surrounded by a beautiful landscaped garden.

The Keifuku line (Kitano section) ends at Kitano-Hakubaicho Station. To the NE, in KAMIGYO ward, is the *Kitano Shrine or *Kitano-Tenjin,* the present buildings of which were erected by Toyotomi Hideyori in 1607.

The shrine, dedicated to Sugawara Michizane, was founded in 947. Michizane, appointed "Chancellor of the Right" in 899, was exiled in 901 to Dazaifu (Kyushu) on the basis of a false accusation and died there two years later. Following a series of catastrophes which beset Kyoto after his death he was posthumously rehabilitated in 933, and in order to pacify the spirit of the dead man he was honored as the god of learning, Tenjin.

The most notable buildings, in addition to three gates, are the *Honden (Main Hall) and *Haiden (Cult Hall). Among the temple's art treasures are a picture scroll by Tosa Yukimitsu (14th c.) depicting the history of the shrine and three other scrolls on the same subject by Tosa Mitsuoki (17th c.). The shrine is surrounded by large numbers of plum trees (Michizane's favorite trees).

From the Kitano-Hakubaicho Station a No. 204 or 214B bus can be taken to the **Kinkakuji Temple** (Kinkakuji-mae stop).

The temple, also known as the **Golden Pavilion,** lies at the foot of Mount Kinugasa (655 ft/200 m), its gilded façade reflected in a small lake. One of the finest examples of the architecture of the Muromachi period (14th–16th c.), it shows three different styles. The ground floor (Hosui-in) is in the Shinden-zukuri palace style of the Heian period, the first floor in the restrained Buke-zukuri style of the Kamakura period and the second floor in the Chinese Kara-yo temple style of the Muromachi period. The site was originally occupied by a villa belonging to a noble named Saion-ji Kitsune which passed into the hands of Ashikaga Yoshimitsu (1358–1408) after his retirement from active political life. It was he who built the Golden Pavilion and laid out the garden in 1394. After his death his son Yoshimochi converted the pavilion into a temple. It has several times been destroyed by fire, most recently in 1950 (arson). The present building is a faithful reconstruction of the original (1955).

Golden Pavilion (Kinkakuji Temple)

After passing through the entrance gateway (*Chuomon*) the visitor enters the temple garden with its lake, on the shores of which stands the temple, crowned by the bronze figure of a phoenix. To the right of the path is the **Main Hall**, with figures of the divinities Benten, Kannon and Taishakuten and statues of Ashikaga Yoshimitsu and the priest Muso-kokushi. In the forecourt of the hall is a 500-year-old fir tree. – On higher ground behind the temple is the *Sekka-tei,* a small tea-house dating from the reign of the Emperor Go-Mizunoo (restored 1874). In front of this is a stone basin with a lantern, from the Shogun's Palace of the Muromachi period. Near the rear gate can be seen a small **temple** with representations of Fudomyoo and his attendants.

From here a taxi can be taken to the **Koetsuji Temple,** to the N, which attracts many visitors in the fall with its vividly colored foliage. Within the temple precincts are the tomb of the artist Hon'ami Koetsu (1558–1637) and several tea-houses, including one built by Koetsu, the Daikyo-an.

SURROUNDINGS of Kyoto

NW of the city, on the lower slopes of Mount *Atago* and on the W bank of the *Kiyotaki,* a tributary of the Oi, are a number of interesting and attractive places. The area is particularly beautiful when the trees take on their autumn coloring.

At **Takao** (bus from Kyoto) is the Jingoji Temple, founded in 781; the present buildings date from the 12th c. The temple bell, cast in 875, has an inscription by Fujiwara Toshiyuki. – Farther upstream are **Makino-o,** with the Saimyoji Temple (1699), and **Togano-o,** with the Kazanji Temple, which contains six *picture scrolls by Fujiwara Nobuzane (1176–1265) on the history of the Kegon sect and a wooden figure of the Yakushi-nyorai.

On the south-eastern outskirts of the city (JNR Nara line) we find the **Daigoji Temple** of the Shingon sect, built by a priest named Shobo in 874 as one of two centers of the ascetic Shugendo doctrine. Notable among the temple buildings, some of which are very ancient, is the five-storey *pagoda, one of the oldest structures in Kyoto (951). – Adjoining the Daigoji is the **Sambo-in Temple,** principal temple of the Daigo school of the Shingon sect. Built in the time of Toyotomi Hideyoshi, this contains a fine **collection of paintings and calligraphy and has mural-paintings by Kano Sanraku. The **garden (16th c.) is particularly beautiful during the cherry-blossom season.

The Nara line continues to Kohata Station, 1 mile/1·5 km SE of which is the *Mampukuji Temple, the principal temple of the Obaku sect, founded in 1661 by a Chinese priest, Ingen. The Main Hall (Daiyuhoden) is built of Thai teak. In the Lecture Hall (Hatto) which lies beyond it are preserved the 60,000 wooden blocks with which the complete edition of the Obaku Sutras was printed in the 17th c.

11 miles/18 km S of Kyoto, on the JNR Nara line and the private Keihan-Uji line, lies **Uji** (pop. 151,000), noted for the production of green tea and sake.

On the island of *Tonoshima,* in the River Uji, is a *pagoda* built by a priest named Eison in the 13th c. Fishing with cormorants is practiced here on summer evenings. To the S of an old bridge spanning the river is the **Hojo-in Temple** (also known as the *Hashidera* or Bridge Temple), which contains a stone with an inscription referring to the construction of the first bridge in 646.

A short distance S is the °**Uji Shrine**, said to have been founded in 313 on the site of an earlier residence of Prince Uji-no-Wakiirakko (d. 312). It is dedicated to the Prince, his father the Emperor Ojin and his brother the Emperor Nintoku, and is in two parts, of which the Upper Shrine (10th c.) is older. In contrast to most other shrines, the buildings of the Uji shrine were not periodically pulled down, so that it is now the oldest shrine in Japan still surviving in its original form. In the forecourt is one of the seven springs of Uji, which are noted for the clarity of their water. The Lower Shrine dates from the Kamakura period. – Near by is the idyllically situated **Koshoji Temple**, the first shrine built by Dogen for the Soto sect (rebuilt 1646).

SE of the station stands the °°**Byodoin Temple**, a characteristic example of the temple architecture of the Heian period. The site was originally occupied by a country residence which belonged to Minamoto Toru, Fujiwara-no-Michinaga and Yorimichi. In 1052 Yorimichi made over the site for the building of a temple, and the main hall, **Hoo-do** (also known as the Phoenix Hall), was constructed in the following year. On the gable ends are two bronze phoenixes. The interior decoration (Heian period), much damaged, has been partly restored. The temple contains works

Byodoin Temple, Uji

by the 11th c. artist Takuma Tamenari and an imposing gilded °°*figure of Amida* (by Jocho, 11th c.). The altar and ceiling are inlaid with bronze and mother-of-pearl, but of the ceiling-paintings of the 25 Bosatsus little now survives. – Adjoining is the **Kannon-do**, a hall situated directly above the river and accordingly also known as the Tsuridono ("Fishing Hall"). Close by is a monument to Minamoto Yorimasa (1104–80), who took his own life here after suffering defeat at the hands of the Taira clan; his tomb is in the Saisho-in, behind the Byodo-in.

Opposite the Phoenix Hall stands a bell-tower, with a copy of one of the most famous bells in Japan, the original of which is in the temple museum (**Homotsu-den**).

The temple buildings and the garden form a unified composition symbolizing the paradise of the "Pure Land" proclaimed by the Jodo sect.

Near here is the **Agata Shrine**, dedicated to the goddess Konohana-Sakuyahime-no-mikoto (annual shrine festival at beginning of June).

Mount Hiei (2782 ft/848 m), NE of Kyoto, is an hour's bus ride from the city center, and can also be reached by rail (Keifuku-Eizen private line to *Yaseyuen*). From Yase-yuen Station a cableway runs up to the summit in two stages. Near the upper station of the cableway, at *Shimeigatake*, are a viewpoint with a revolving tower (°views of Kyoto and Lake Biwa), a natural history museum and a botanic garden. Here, too, is the °**Enryakuji Temple**, once one of the mightiest temples in Japan.

The temple was founded in 788, at the behest of the Emperor Kammu, by a Buddhist priest named Saicho (762–822), belonging to a family which had come to Japan from China, after his return from a stay in China. The site of the temple, lying NE of the city, was selected in order to ward off evil spirits coming from that direction. The growing political influence of the increasingly numerous monks, however, soon presented a threat to Kyoto, and accordingly Oda Nobunaga felt it necessary to destroy the temple. Although it was rebuilt by Toyotomi Hideyoshi and enlarged by Tokugawa Iemitsu the temple never recovered any degree of secular power.

In the eastern half of the temple precinct (Toto) are the °**Kaidan-in**, the hall for the ordination of priests; the **Amida Hall** (1937), approached by a flight of steps; the **Daiko-do** (Lecture Hall) of 1956; a *bell-tower*; the **Daikoku-do** (Hall of the Black God); a gateway, the *Monju-ro*; and the °**Konpon-chudo** (Middle Hall), which contains a wooden statue of Yakushi-nyorai by Saicho and other wood sculpture. – In the western half (Saito) are the °**Shaka-do** and a 33 ft/10 m high pagoda, the *Sorinto.*

From the summit of Mount Hiei a cableway leads down to **Lake Biwa** (see separate entry).

14 miles/22 km W of Kyoto (JNR San-in line, 30 minutes, or bus, 1 hour) lies **Kameoka** (pop. 69,000), a former castle town situated on the River Hozu in the *Kameoka Basin.* This is the starting-point of a 10 mile/16 km boat trip down the rapids to Arashiyama, on the western outskirts of Kyoto.

The TRIP DOWN THE RAPIDS, operated from March to November, takes about 2 hours. The rapids begin at Miyanoshita, and the river then follows a winding course between the Atagoyama range of hills on the left and the Arashiyama range on the right. This section of the river was opened up to navigation by Suminokura Ryoi in 1606. On its way down the river the boat passes *Kanagisone, Koayu-no-taki, Takase, Shishigakuchi* ("Lion's Jaws"), *Nagase* and *Gakugase.*

Kyushu

九州

Area of island: 17,103 sq. miles/44,296 sq. km.
Population: 12,960,000.

Kyushu, the "land of the nine provinces" (Chikuzen, Chikugo,

Cape Sata, the most southerly point on Kyushu

Hizen, Buzen, Bungo, Higo, Hyuga, Satsuma and Osumi), is the third largest of the main Japanese islands and the one which lies farthest to the SW. The Tsushima and Iki islands also belong to Kyushu for administrative purposes.

Kyushu is separated from Honshu, to the NE, by the **Kammon Strait**, but linked with it by rail and road tunnels and a suspension bridge. To the E, beyond the Bungo Strait, is the island of Shikoku.

Kyushu is divided into seven prefectures (Fukuoka, Saga, Nagasaki, Kumamoto, Oita, Miyazaki and Kagoshima). In the northern part of the island there are considerable concentrations of industry around Kitakyushu, Fukuoka and Nagasaki; the southern part is still largely undeveloped.

Kyushu's highest peak is Mount Sobo (5768 ft/1758 m), in the center of the island; on the offshore island of Yakushima, to the S, however, Mount Miyanoura rises to a height of 6349 ft/ 1935 m. Thanks to its volcanic origin Kyushu has many hot springs, most of them in the four National Parks on the island (Aso National Park, Unzen-Amakusa National Park, Saikai National Park, Kirishima-Yaku National Park: see separate entries).

Kyushu's southerly situation gives it a warm climate throughout the year, varying slightly from N to S (mean annual temperature at Fukuoka 60·3 °F/15·7 °C, at Kagoshima 62·6 °F/17·0 °C). It is also warmed by the *Kuroshio Current.* Snow falls rarely, and only in the northern part of the island. Spring and summer come early, advancing from S to N. The rainy period also starts early (end of May), as do the autumn typhoons (August–September).

HISTORY. – The mainland cultures of China and Korea reached Japan by way of northern Kyushu. Legend ascribes special importance to an area in southern central Kyushu, for tradition has it that Ninigi-no-mikoto, grandson of the sun goddess Amaterasu-omikami, came down to earth on Mount Takachiho.

In the 13th c. the Mongols made two unsuccessful attempts to invade Kyushu, and in response to this threat massive works of fortification were built along Hakata Bay and on the Tsushima Islands. Towards the end of the 16th c. northern Kyushu was the base from which Toyotomi Hideyoshi's vessels sailed on his campaigns of conquest in Korea. Many of the Korean potters who were carried off to Japan later settled on Kyushu and established the fame of such pottery centers as Arita (see separate entry).

During the long period when Japan shut itself off from contact with foreign countries Kyushu formed its only link with the outside world; and when the Meiji Restoration opened up Japan for trade with other countries, particularly with the United States and Europe, Kyushu played an important part. – The town of Nagasaki (see separate entry) attained unhappy fame as the target of the second atomic bomb during the Second World War.

Matsue
まつえ

Prefecture: Shimane. – Population: 138,000.
Post code: J-690. – Telephone code: 0852.

(i) (central)
**Shimane-ken Tokyo Kanko Bussan
Assensho,**
Tetsudo Kaikan,
1-9-1, Marunouchi, Chiyoda-ku,
J-100 **Tokyo;**
tel. (03) 212 1091.

(local)
Matsue Tourist Information,
City Hall,
96, Suetugu-cho,
tel. 24 1111.

HOTELS. – **Western style:** *Hotel Ichibata,* 30,
Chidori-cho, 138 r., Japanese garden, thermal bath,
beach. – **Ryokan:** *Suimeiso,* 26, Nishichamachi, 51 r.;
Meirinkaku, 558, Kuniya-cho, 16 r.; *Horaiso,* 101,
Tonomachi, 14 r. – YOUTH HOSTEL: *Matsue YH,*
1546, Kososhi-machi, 82 b.

RESTAURANT. – *Minami,* 14, Suetsugu-Honmachi.

EVENTS. – *Oshiro-matsuri* (beginning of April),
Castle Festival; *Matsue-odori* (end of July), Summer
Festival, with fireworks; *Shrine Festival* in Temmangu
Shrine (end of July); *Toro-nagashi* (mid August), end
of Bon Festival, with paper lanterns on lake; *Shrine
Festival* in Takeuchi Shrine (end of August); *Taiko-
gyoretsu* (end of November), procession with large
drums; *Shrine Festival* in Matsue Shrine (beginning of
November).

TRANSPORTATION. – **Air:** from TOKYO (Haneda Air-
port) to Izumo (3 hours); from OSAKA to Izumo (1
hour). – **Rail:** from OSAKA (Shin-Osaka Station) JNR
Shinkansen line to Okayama (1¼ hours), then JNR
Hakubi and San-in lines (3½ hours); from OSAKA
(Central Station) JNR San-in line (6 hours); from
IZUMO JNR San-in line (30 minutes).

**Matsue, chief town of the prefec-
ture of Shimane and the largest city
in the historical region of San-in, lies
near the NW coast of Honshu on the
River Ohashi, which links Lake Shinji
to the W with the Naka-no-umi
Lagoon to the E. The town became
known through the work of the English writer Lafcadio Hearn, who
lived here at the end of the 19th c.
and who helped by his writings to
make Japan and Japanese culture
better known to the Western World.**

To the N of the town, on the Shimane
Peninsula, is a hilly coastal region which
forms part of the **Daisen-Oki National
Park** (see separate entry). Also included
in the National Park are the Oki Islands
lying between 25 and 50 miles off the

coast, the volcanic region around Mount
Daisen to the SE and the Izumo Peninsula
(see separate entry) to the SW, with the
Izumo-Taisha Shrine.

HISTORY. – The fief of Matsue was granted to Horio
Yoshiharu by Tokugawa Ieyasu in 1600 for his services in the Battle of Sekigahara, and Horio completed
the building of the castle in 1611, shortly before his
death. Under later rulers of the Kyogoku dynasty and
of the Matsudaira, who ruled the town for 234 years,
Matsue enjoyed a period of some prosperity.

Lafcadio Hearn (1850–1904) came to Matsue in May
1890 and taught for seven months in the secondary
school. Having married a Japanese wife and been
adopted by his parents-in-law, who gave him the
name of Koizumi Yakumo, he was accepted by
Japanese society. His "Glimpses of Unfamiliar
Japan" gives an account of his impressions.

SIGHTS. – 1 mile/1·8 km NW of the
station, on Mount *Kamedayama,* stands
Matsue Castle, built in 1607–11. The
three-storey *main tower* (rebuilt 1642)
contains a collection of old arms and
armor and material on the history of the
town. From the top floor there are fine
* views of the town, the hills to the N and
Lake Shinji to the W.

Matsue Castle

Around the castle is the *Shiroyama Park,*
famed for its show of cherry blossom and
azaleas in spring. Near by is the **Museum
of Culture** (*Matsue-kyodokan*), built in
1903 in the style of the Meiji period.

A pleasant walk (15 minutes) along the
castle moat to the N leads to a number of
old *samurai houses* (Bukeyashiki). Of
particular interest is the Shiomi House,
with furniture and furnishings. In the
same street is the *House of Lafcadio
Hearn,* with the **Yakumo-kinenkan,** a
memorial hall containing mementoes of
his stay in Matsue.

To the E, on higher ground, is the **Meimei-an**, a tea-house with an attractive *tea-garden* laid out for Matsudaira Harusato, who did much to promote the tea ceremony.

To the W of the town, on the S side of Mount *Asahi* (1122 ft/342 m), stands the **Gesshoji Temple**, built by Matsudaira Naomasa (1601–66), grandson of Tokugawa Ieyasu, with the tombs of the Matsudaira dynasty (1st to 9th generations).

To the S of the town lies the village of **Fudoki-no-oka**, which has much of interest to offer the archaeologically inclined. Here can be seen the traditional parcelling-out of land on a rectangular grid, old *burial mounds* (*futago-zuka*), reconstructions of *houses* of the Kofun period (3rd–7th c.) and the remains of a *provincial temple* (*koku-bunji*; 741). There is a *Museum* (Shiryo-kan) in the center of the village.

W of Fudoki-no-oka is the **Kamosu Shrine**, the *Main Hall* (Honden) of which is the oldest surviving building in the Taisha-zukuri style (1364). To the N of the shrine, 4½ miles/7 km S of the station (15 minutes by bus), can be found the **Yaegaki Shrine**, dedicated to the god of marriage, which features prominently in legend and poetry.

SURROUNDINGS. – W of the town lies *Lake Shinji, Japan's sixth largest lake (area 30 sq. miles/ 80 sq. km, circumference 30 miles/50 km), with a number of attractive little places on its shores. At the E end is *Matsue-onsen,* from which there is a fine *view of the lake. On the S side of the lake, 5 miles/ 8 km W of Matsue (bus, 30 minutes), is the spa of **Tamatsukuri-onsen**, with hot springs (122–158 °F/ 50–70 °C), a popular week-end resort.

To the E of Matsue stretches the **Naka-no-umi** Lagoon (area 38 sq. miles/99 sq. km, circumference 52 miles/83·5 km), which is linked with *Miho Bay* on the N but separated from it on the E by a broad spit of land. In the lagoon is the island of *Daikon* (area 2½ sq. miles/6 sq. km), with unusual lava formations at Osoe, in the SE.

Matsumoto
まつもと

Prefecture: Nagano. – Population: 195,000.
Post code: J-390. – Telephone code: 0263.
ⓘ (local)
Matsumoto Shiei Kanko Information,
1-1-1, Fukashi,
tel. 32 2814.

HOTELS. – **Western style:** *Matsumoto Dai-2 Tokyo Inn,* 1-176-7, Fukashi, 158 r.; *Matsumoto Town Hotel,* 2-1-38, Chuo, 108 r.; *Matsumoto Tokyu Inn,* at Central Station, 100 r.; *Hotel Sun Route,* 1-1, Agata, 90 r.; *Matsumoto Tourist Hotel,* 2-4-24, Fukashi, 88 r.; *Matsumoto Mount Hotel,* 3-2, Habaue, 72 r.; *Hotel New Station,* 1-1-11, Chuo, at station, 65 r.; *Matsumoto Green Hotel,* 1-5-11, Fukashi, 54 r.; *Hotel Iidaya,* 1-2-3, Chuo, 39 r.; *Hotel Yorozu-Ya,* 20 r. – **Ryokan:** Matsumoto Hotel Kagetsu Ryokan, 37 r.; *Ichiyama Ryokan,* 20 r.; Marumo Ryokan, 10 r.

IN ASAMA-ONSEN. – **Western style:** *Hotel Asamaen,* 24 r. – **Ryokan:** *Takanoyu Ryokan,* 52 r.; *Jimotoya Ryokan,* 34 r.; *Alpen Asamaso,* 27 r.; *Fujiminoyu,* 26 r.; *Yoshinoyu Ryokan,* 24 r. – YOUTH HOSTEL: *Asama-onsen YH,* 150 b.

TRANSPORTATION. – **Air:** from OSAKA (1¼ hours). – **Rail:** from TOKYO (Shinjuku Station) JNR Chuo line (3¾ hours); from OSAKA JNR Chuo line via NAGOYA (4 hours); from NAGANO branch line (1 hour); from ITOIGAWA JNR Oito line. – **Bus:** from Matsumoto Airport to city center (30 minutes); regional services to the Utsukushigahara Plateau and Kamikochi (April to October).

The university town of Matsumoto, situated in the Matsumoto Basin in central Honshu, is a good base for excursions to the Chubu-Sangoku National Park (see separate entry) and the Utsukushigahara Plateau, to the E of the town. The principal landmark of the town, which is much frequented by climbers, is the **Castle. There are many shops selling a variety of local craft products.

Matsumoto is linked by the JNR Oito line with Itoigawa, 65 miles/105 km away on the W coast of Honshu (Sea of Japan). The line runs along the E flank of the *Hida Mountains* (Northern Japan Alps), and the stations make good starting-points for the ascent of the peaks, some of them over 9800 ft/3000 m, in this central mountain region.

The town is the economic and communications center of the *Matsumoto Basin,* in which a considerable trade in the rearing of silkworms has developed since the end of the 19th c. Other industries are weaving, textiles, engineering and the processing of agricultural produce.

Matsumoto Castle

Station comes in 20 minutes to **Asama-onsen** (hot springs, many Japanese-type hotels). Scattered over a wide area to the S are the thermal resorts of *Oboke, Yamabe, Fujii, Iriyamabe* and *Tobira,* which together form the resort area of **Utsukushigahara-onsen.**

From Asama the bus continues to *Lake Misuzu,* a reservoir with a circumference of 2 miles/3 km. In summer this is much frequented by campers (boat trips, fishing), in winter by skaters. From the shores of the lake a cable-lift runs up a hill topped by an outlook tower (extensive views).

1 hour 40 minutes from Matsumoto the bus reaches the skiing area of *Asama,* with fine panoramic views of the Hida Mountains. This area is at its most attractive in May and June, when expanses of snow alternate with mountain azaleas in blossom.

Azumino is a picturesque upland region in the foothills of the Northern Japan Alps. Its main center, the little town of **Hotaka,** is 30 minutes from Matsumoto on the JNR Oito line.

In Hotaka is a *Museum of Art* (Rokuzan Bijutsukan), mainly containing works by the Japanese sculptor Ogiwara Rokuzan, whose Western style has earned him the name of the "Rodin of the East". From Hotaka Station it is a 45-minute walk (bicycles also available for hire) to the *Gohoden Wasabi-en,* a large horseradish farm in an idyllically beautiful valley.

SIGHTS. – ¾ mile/1 km NE of the station stands ** **Matsumoto Castle,** built in 1504, with one of the 12 castle towers in Japan which have survived without alteration. The black facing of its walls has earned it the popular name of "Crow Castle" (Karasu-jo). The castle, commanding a wide expanse of plain, is a classic example of the Hirashiro style of fortification, surrounded by a moat and walls. The six-storey * *main tower* is linked by corridors with an outwork to the N. From the top floor there is a fine view of the surrounding area.

Opposite the main tower is a *Folk Museum,* with 50,000 items of archaeological, historical and folk interest.

From the Castle it is a 10 minutes' walk to the *Kaichi Gakko School,* in a Western-style building erected in 1876. The oldest school of its kind, it contains a variety of material on the history of education in Japan, etc.

A bus (15 minutes) runs from the station to the **Matsumoto Museum of Folk Art.**

SURROUNDINGS. – To the E of the town lies the **Utsukushigahara Plateau,** at an altitude rising to over 6500 ft/2000 m, from which there are fine views of the Hida Mountains. The bus from Matsumoto

Matsushima Bay
まつしま

Prefecture: Miyagi.

ⓘ (central)
Miyagi-ken Tokyo Kanko Bussan Assensho,
Tetsudo Kaikan,
1-9-1, Marunouchi, Chiyoda-ku,
J-100 **Tokyo;**
tel. (03) 231 0944.

(local)
Miyagi-ken Tourist Information Center,
3-8-1, Honmachi,
J-980 **Sendai;**
tel. (0222) 21 1864.

HOTELS. – **Ryokan:** *Hotel Taikanso,* Matsushima-cho, 119 r.; *Matsushima Daiichi Hotel,* Matsushima-cho, 32 r. – YOUTH HOSTEL: *Matsushima YH,* in Nobiru, 94-1, Minami-akazaki, 124 b.

EVENTS. – *Matsushima Toro-Nagashi* (mid August), "Festival of Floating Lanterns", with fireworks.

TRANSPORTATION. – **Air:** from TOKYO (Haneda Airport) to Sendai (45 minutes). – **Rail:** from TOKYO (Ueno Station) to Omiya (30 minutes), then JNR New Tohoku–Shinkansen line (2¼ hours); or JNR Tohoku line to Sendai (4¼ hours), then JNR Senseki line to Matsushima-Kaigan (35 minutes). – **Bus:** from Sendai Airport to Sendai Station (10 minutes); from Sendai to Matsushima-Kaigan (1 hour). – **Boat:** round trips between Matsushima-Kaigan and Shiogama.

Matsushima Bay is the inner part of Sendai Bay, immediately S of the Ojika Peninsula on the E coast of Honshu. The name means "island of pines", referring to the pine-covered rocky islands and islets, more than 260 in number, which give this area its special character. The *scenery of the region, diversified by its varied rock formations and the bizarrely shaped trees which grow in its scanty soil, has long been re-nowned throughout Japan.

Together with Ama-no-hashidate (N of Kyoto on the W coast of Honshu) and Itsukushima in Hiroshima Bay, Mat-sushima is one of the three famous stretches of coastal scenery in Japan, the *sankei*.

The islands consist partly of volcanic tuffs, partly of white sandstone (which is also found in most of the coastal rock forma-tions). A few of the larger islands are in-habited, but the smallest are no more than rocks of a few square yards in extent. The waves have cut deeply into the rock, creating numbers of caves, tunnels, pin-nacles and arches. A few wind-battered pines contrive to cling to even the steepest walls of rock.

This has long been a popular holiday region for the Japanese, and along the 7½ mile/12 km stretch of coast running from N to S there are more than 40 Japanese-style hotels (*ryokan*). In spite of this it is essential to book accommodation in ad-vance – six months in advance for the period of the "Star Festival" (Tanabata-matsuri) of Sendai (see separate entry) at the beginning of August.

There are many viewpoints along the coast and on the islands from which to see the scenery of the bay and the islands – always changing as the light changes at different times of day and different seasons; but the highly formalized Japanese approach to scenery, in-fluenced by landscape-painting, distinguishes four particular viewpoints, the **Matsushima shi-daikan** ("the four most excellent views of Matsushima"):

Otakamori, a hill (348 ft/108 m) on the island of *Miyato* (pop. 1500), in the eastern part of the bay (1 hour from Matsushima Station by boat, or by road over a causeway).

Ogidani, a hill to the S of Matsushima Station in the central part of the bay (25 minutes' walk).

Tamonzan, a low hill on Cape Yugasaki, in the south-western part of the bay (30 minutes' boat trip from Shiogama).

Tomiyama, a hill 20 minutes' walk N of Rikuzen-Tomiyama Station (JNR Senseki line), 10 minutes by train from Matsushima Station. On the hill is the Daigyoji Temple (17th c.).

SIGHTS. – Near Matsushima-Kaigan Station, in the center of the bay, stands the **"Seaview Pavilion"** (*Kanran-tei*), a modest late 16th c. tea-house on a rock beside the pier. Originally part of Fushimi Castle, it was presented by Toyotomi Hideyoshi to his vassal Date Masamune (1567–1636). The sliding doors in the interior were painted by Kano Sanraku (1559–1635), a leading representative of the Momoyama style. As its name in-dicates, the pavilion has a beautiful view of the bay. In the garden is a small *museum* with mementoes of the Date family, which for some time during the medieval period was the most powerful princely family in north-eastern Japan.

A short distance N two short bridges lead on to a tiny islet covered with pines on which is the * *Godaido Temple,* built by Date Masamune (a tempting subject for photographers).

Inland, to the W (5 minutes' walk from Matsushima-Kaigan Station), an avenue of Japanese cedars leads to the **Zuiganji Temple**, founded in 828, which later became a center of the Rinzai sect (Myoshinji school). On either side of the avenue are *caves,* used by the monks as places for meditation. In one of the lar-ger caves (on the left, beyond the entrance to the temple) Abbot Hosshin, who had studied the new teachings in China, is said to have meditated after his return. The present buildings were erected by Date Masamune in 1609. Particularly notable are the *Middle Gate* (Haka-mon), the *Imperial Gate* (Onari-mon), the *living apartments* (Kuri), the *gallery* (Kairo) and the * *Main Hall* (Hondo), with sliding doors painted by artists of the Kano school. In the interesting Peacock Room is a wooden statue of Date Masamune, known as the "one-eyed Shogun" (*dokuganryu Shogun*), in full armor. There is also an interesting statue of Makabe Heishiro (the secular name of Abbot Hosshin).

¾ mile/1 km S of the Godaido Temple a red *wooden bridge* (Togetsukyo) leads on to the picturesque island of **Oshima**, with steep cliffs in which the waves have gouged out many *caves.* Buddhist figures in these caves show that they were once used as hermitages. To the NE of the Godaido Temple is another red wooden bridge leading on to the island of *Fukura,* which is noted for the variety of its vegetation (about 180 species).

The larger island of **Katsura** (pop. 600), to the SW (boat from Shiogama, 30 minutes), has a large beach.

SURROUNDINGS. – To the NE, beyond the island of Miyato, which bounds the bay in this direction, lies the port of **Ishinomaki** (pop. 120,000), situated at the mouth of the River *Kitakami* (50 minutes from Matsushima-Kaigan on the JNR Senseki line). In addition to fishing and the processing of fish products the town's main industry is paper-making.

From Ishinomaki there is a ferry service to the island of **Kinkazan,** 2½ miles/4 km SE of the Ojika Peninsula. The name means "gold flower", referring to the mica in the rocks which glitters in the sun. The whole island, which measures 2½ miles/4 km from E to W and 3 miles/5 km from N to S, is covered with dense vegetation, from which rugged crags rear up here and there. The animal life – unusually rich for Japan – includes red deer, monkeys and many species of birds.

Near the pier is the **Koganeyama Shrine,** dedicated to the Shinto divinities of prosperity and fortune. Behind the shrine is a path (1¼ miles/2 km) leading up to the summit of Mount *Kinkazan* (1460 ft/445 m) through beautiful scenery. From the top there are extensive *views: to the E the great expanse of the Pacific, to the W Matsushima Bay with its backdrop of wooded heights.

On the E coast, 3 hours' walk from the pier, is an unusual rock formation known as Senjojiki, with the appearance of rectangular blocks laid in parallel courses. – To the SE, 4½ miles/7 km from the Koganeyama Shrine, stands a lighthouse.

10½ miles/17 km NE of Ishinomaki, in Onagawa Bay, is the port of **Onagawa,** a center of deep-sea fisheries and particularly of whaling, with the Marine Laboratory of Tohoku University. Ferry to the island of Kinkazan (1¾ hours). – To the S of the harbour is the beginning of the Ojika Cobalt Road (toll), which runs down the middle of the *Ojika Peninsula* to end at the southern tip at the little town of *Ojika* which has a museum on the history of whaling.

Matsuyama

まつやま

Prefecture: Ehime. – Population: 410,000.
Post code: J-790. – Telephone code: 0899.
ⓘ (central)
Ehime-ken Tokyo Kanko Bussan Assensho,
Tetsudo Kaikan,
1-9-1, Marunouchi, Chiyoda-ku,
J-100 **Tokyo;**
tel. (03) 231 1804.

(local)
Tourist Section of Matsuyama City,
4-7-2, Nibancho;
tel. 48 6733.
Japan Travel Bureau,
Japan Travel Bureau Building,
Sanbancho;
tel. 31 2281.

HOTELS. – **Western style:** *Hotel Oku-Dogo,* 267, Sue-machi, 303 r., Japanese garden, thermal bath; *Business Hotel Taihei,* 3-1-15, Heiwadori, 85 r. – **Ryokan:** *Dogo Kokusai Hotel Yamatoya,* Dogo-Yunomachi, 113 r.; *Juen,* Dogo-Sagidanimachi, 77 r.; *Funaya,* Dogo-Yunomachi, 42 r. – YOUTH HOSTELS: *Oku-Dogo YH,* Sugitate-cho, 48 b.; *Shinsen-En YH,* 1-28, Dogo-imaichi, 35 b.

EVENTS. – *Tsubaki-matsuri* (beginning of January), Camellia Festival; *Dogo-onsen-matsuri* (mid March), in Dogo-onsen; *Castle Festival* (beginning of April); *Opening of Climbing Season* (beginning of July), at Ishizuchi Shrine; *Matsuyama Festival* (mid August), Summer Festival; *Funa-odori* (mid October), "Ship Dance", with miming on boats, on island of Gogoshima.

TRANSPORTATION. – **Air:** from TOKYO (Haneda Airport), 1½ hours; from OSAKA (45 minutes); from FUKUOKA (1 hour). – **Rail:** from TAKAMATSU JNR Yosan line (3 hours). – **Boat:** regular services (including hovercraft) from HIROSHIMA (2¾ hours or 1 hour).

Matsuyama, the largest city on the island of Shikoku and chief town of Ehime prefecture (formerly Iyo), lies on the NW coast. It is the economic center of the region and a market for the local agricultural produce (particularly oranges). It is also an educational center, with two higher educational establishments. The city's principal landmark is the well-preserved *Castle.

The principal industry is spinning. The most notable local craft product is porcelain (*Tobe-yaki*), which has been made here for more than 300 years.

HISTORY. – The original nucleus of the town lay 3 miles/5 km NE of the present site, in the area of the hot springs of Dogo-onsen. After the town passed into the hands of Kato Yoshiaki (1563–1631) the present-day town grew up round the castle which was now built. Later the town and the castle came under the control of the great Matsudaira family.

SIGHTS. – 550 yds/500 m E of the station, in the center of the city, is the densely wooded Mount *Katsuyama* or Shiroyama (433 ft/132 m), crowned by the *Castle, built in 1602–27, which has four gates with outworks. The three-storey *main tower* now houses a museum containing relics of the Matsudaira daimyos, in particular swords and armor. The area around the castle has been laid out as a beautiful park (cableway on E side of hill), seen at its best when the cherry trees are in blossom.

2½ miles/4 km NE of the station, on the slopes of a hill, is the ancient and famous health resort of *Dogo-onsen, with hot springs (alkaline, 115 °F/46 °C) which are mentioned as early as the 8th c. in the "Manyoshu Anthology" and which still attract large numbers of visitors. Many of the buildings – in particular the *Shinrokaku*, a three-storey wooden bath-house in Momoyama style – preserve something of the atmosphere of the past. Beyond the Shinrokaku is the *Yushinden*, a bath-house built for the Imperial family in 1899. A picture of spa life in the Meiji period is given in a short story by Natsume Soseki (1867–1916), "Botchan" ("Mother's Boy").

To the E of the resort stands the *Hogonji Temple*, built by the Emperor Tenchi (626–672), and to the S of this is *Dogo Park*, on the site of an old castle, which is at its most beautiful when the cherry trees are in blossom. At the end of March this is the scene of a festival with traditional dances and processions.

A short distance E of Dogo is the *Ishiteji Temple*, one of the 88 stations on the traditional pilgrimage route on Shikoku. Founded by Prince Ochi Tamazumi in 728, it was rebuilt in 1318 after a fire and is thus an example of the architecture of the Kamakura period, showing the characteristic mingling of Japanese and Chinese stylistic features. Particularly notable are the *Niomon Gate*, the *Hondo* (main hall), the *Gomado Hall*, a three-storey *pagoda* and the *bell-tower*.

SURROUNDINGS. – The town has two ports on the W coast – *Takahama*, also known as Matsuyama Kanko (ferry connections with Honshu and Kyushu), and *Mitsuhama*, farther S near the airport, which has plenty of local color (Asa-ichi morning market, seafood). – Rather more than a mile off the coast (ferry from Takahama, 10 minutes) lies the island of *Gogoshima*, with a magnificent show of peach and mandarine blossom in spring and the Funa-odori pantomime in October.

25 miles/40 km SE, inland, is the **Ishizuchi Quasi National Park**, a hilly area of some 41 sq. miles/107 sq. km.

The principal attraction of the park is the **Omogokei Gorge**, through which the River *Omogo* flows for a distance of 7 miles/11 km. The river's many windings, the rugged rock faces, the waterfalls and narrow passages combine with the lush green vegetation of the earlier part of the year or the vivid coloring of the fall to create scenery of every-changing beauty. The starting-point of a trip through the gorge is *Kammon* (bus from Matsuyama Station, 2¾ hours), from which the road continues past the *Kamehara Falls*, the *Kanayama Bridge* and the *Goraiko Falls*.

The highest point of the park, and of the island of Shikoku, is Mount **Ishizuchi** (6503 ft/1982 m), which is most conveniently reached from the industrial town of **Saijo** (pop. 55,000), 30 miles/50 km NE of Matsuyama. From Iyo-Saijo Station buses run to the lower station of a cableway, half-way up the mountain (20 miles/32 km, 1¼ hours), at the *Ishizuchi Shrine*, where the beginning of the pilgrimage and climbing season is celebrated in early July. – Another route to Mount Ishizuchi from the Omogokei Gorge is on the new expressway (toll) to *Tsuchigoya* (11 miles/18 km), from which the mountain can be climbed in 4 hours. The cableway takes 8 minutes. From the summit there are superb panoramic *views extending over much of Shikoku, the Inland Sea and the Pacific.

30 miles/50 km NE of Matsuyama, on the *Takanawa Peninsula*, lies the port of **Imabari** (pop. 124,000). Near the station is Fukiage Park. – 3 miles/5 km N, at the tip of the peninsula, rises Mount *Chikamiyama* (801 ft/244 m), from which there is a good *view of the whirlpool in the *Kurushima Strait* caused by the meeting of the tides from the Hiuchi-Nada Sea to the E and the Aki-Nada Sea to the W. – From Imabari there is a ferry service to the island of *Omishima*, 10 miles/16 km N (see under Inland Sea).

Mito
みと

Prefecture: Ibaraki. – Population: 220,000.
Post code: J-310. – Telephone code: 0292.
ⓘ (central)
   Ibaraki-ken Tokyo Kanko Information,
   Kokusai Kanko Kaikan,
   1-8-3, Marunouchi, Chiyoda-ku,
   J-100 **Tokyo**;
   tel. (03) 231 2642.

(local)
Ibaraki-ken Kanko Kyokai,
Ibaraki-ken Kankoka-nai,
1-5-38, Sannomaru;
tel. 21 8111.

HOTELS. – **Western style**: *Sannomaru Hotel*, 2-1-1, Sannomaru, 68 r.; beach; *Mito Keisei Hotel*, 1-4-73, Sannomaru, 52 r.; *Mimatsu Hotel*, 2-4-26, Miyamachi, 81 r. – **Ryokan**: *Umesato-kan*, 17 r.; *Izumi-so*, 15 r.; *Kame-ya Ryokan*, 14 r. – YOUTH HOSTEL: *Mito Tokuda YH*, 1127-2, Tomobe-machi, 12 b.

TRANSPORTATION. – **Rail**: from TOKYO (Ueno Station) JNR Joban line (1½ hours).

Mito, near the E coast of Honshu some 65 miles/100 km NE of Tokyo, is the chief town of Ibaraki prefecture and an important communications center. The castle which formerly dominated the town was almost

completely destroyed during the troubles which accompanied the Meiji Restoration in 1868.

HISTORY. – The fief of Mito passed to Tokugawa Yorifusa (1603–61), eleventh son of Tokugawa Ieyasu, in 1609. Yorifusa was the ancestor of one of the "three illustrious houses" (*gosanke*) from which the Shogun's deputies were selected (being thereby disqualified from succession to the Shogunate itself). Mitsukuni (1628–1700) founded a school of Chinese literature and military science (Mitogaku) in Mito; and here, under his aegis, scholars undertook the huge task of writing a history of the Japanese Empire, which was completed only in 1906 and comprised a total of 397 volumes.

SIGHTS. – In the center of the town, on a site formerly occupied by the castle is the *Kodokan Park*, named after the school (*Kodokan*: now a museum) founded by Nariaki (1800–60), 9th feudal Lord of Mito. Beyond the school-buildings are two shrines of the same period which – reflecting the pattern of education in those days – are dedicated respectively to a general, Kashima-Myojin, and the Chinese philosopher Confucius.

2 miles/3 km W of the station is the **Kairaku-en Garden** (or *Tokiwa Park*), originally laid out by Nariaki and later converted into a public park, which is now renowned more for the natural beauty of its 3000 plum trees (in blossom in February–March) than for the art of the landscape-gardener. The trees are not merely decorative: the fruit is preserved and, as *umeboshi*, features prominently on the Japanese menu. In Mito it is used in the making of pastries. – In the park is a reproduction of the *Kobun-tei*, a tea-house dating from the time of Nariaki.

SURROUNDINGS. – 7½ miles/12 km SE of the station is the seaside resort of **Oarai**. On a pine-covered hill near the Oarai-Isozaki Shrine is the *Joyo-Meiji Memorial Hall*, dedicated to the memory of the Emperor Meiji (1852–1912). – Farther N, on the coast, are the Japanese Atomic Energy Research Center (at Tokai) and the Center for Communications Satellites (at Takahagi).

15 miles/25 km W of Mito (JNR Mito line) is **Kasama** (pop. 31,000).

Kasama was the ancestral seat of the Makino family. It is now visited annually by more than a million pilgrims to the **Kasama-Inari Shrine** (1 mile/1·5 km N of station), the scene of a well-known Chrysanthemum festival at the end of October and beginning of November. – The traditional ceramic products of the area are known as *Kasama-yaki*.

In the south-western district of Inada is the *Sainenji Temple*, once the retreat of Shinran (1173–1262), the monk who founded the Jodo-shinshu sect and laid down its doctrine in the "Kyogyo-shinsho".

At *Kataniwa*, 4½ miles/7 km NW, is the **Ryogonji Temple** of the Rinzai sect, with a fine main gateway and a wooden statue of the Thousand-Handed Kannon.

At *Sakuragawa*, 6 miles/10 km W of Kasama, is the **Isobe Shrine**, the setting of a famous No play, surrounded by large numbers of ornamental cherry trees (the mountain cherry, *yamazakura*; in blossom beginning to middle of May). – A short distance W, to the N of Iwase Station, is a Buddhist temple of the Tendai sect, the **Tomiya-Kannon** or *Oyamaji*, with a fine three-storey pagoda of 1465.

15 miles/25 km SW of Kasama is Mount **Tsukuba** (2874 ft/876 m), which can be reached on the Kanto private line (running S from Iwase Station on the JNR Mito line; then 15 minutes' bus ride from Tsukuba Station). There are shrines both on the main peak, *Nyotai* ("female mountain") and on the subsidiary peak, *Nantai* ("male mountain"; 2854 ft/870 m), and on Nantai there are also a weather station and a revolving outlook platform (view over the Kanto Plain to Mount Fuji). There are cableways up both peaks; the ascent on foot is strenuous but rewarding (bizarre rock formations).

To the N of Tsukuba on the Kanto line is *Makabe*. ¾ mile/1 km SE of the station stands the **Denshoji Temple**, founded in 1268 by the Zen master Hosshin, a native of Makabe, after his return from China. The temple, now belonging to the Soto sect, contains statues of the famous 47 *ronin* of Ako, famed for their loyalty to their feudal lord (see under Tokyo, Sengakuji Temple). The cherry trees in the temple garden are in blossom in mid April.

25 miles/40 km NW of Mito, in Tochigi prefecture, is **Mashiko** (pop. 20,000), the best-known center of traditional ceramics in the Tokyo region. The development of the local pottery workshops began with the establishment of the first kiln by Otsuka Keizaburo in 1853, and was further promoted by Hamada Shoji (1894–1977), who, in association with the English potter Bernard Leach, made the local products widely known. Many of the workshops, more than 150 in number, which produce the local ware (*Mashiko-yaki*) can be visited, and some of them offer amateurs the opportunity of practicing the craft. – An interesting *pottery market* is held in May and October (dates variable).

Miyajima

みやじま

Prefecture: Hiroshima. – Population: 3600.
Post code: J-739-05. – Telephone code: 08294.

 (central)
Hiroshima-ken Tokyo Kanko Bussan Assensho,
Kokusai Kanko Kaikan,
1-8-3, Marunouchi, Chiyoda-ku,
J-100 **Tokyo**;
tel. (03) 215 5010.

(local)
Hiroshima City Tourist Information Office,
in Central Station,
Kokutetsu, Omote-guchi, Minami-ku,
J-730 **Hiroshima**;
tel. (0822) 61 1877.

HOTELS. – **Western style**: *Miyajima Grand Hotel*, 362, Miyajima-cho, 61 r. – **Ryokan**: *Kamefuku Ryokan*, 44 r.; *Iwaso Ryokan*, 15 r. – YOUTH HOSTEL: *YH Makoto Kaikan*, 756, Sairencho, 75 b.

EVENTS. – *Toshikoshi* (beginning of January), New Year Festival; *Kangen-sei* (mid June), boat procession at night, with portable shrines and music; *Tamatori-matsuri* (mid July), swimming contest around a sacred ball.

TRANSPORTATION. – **Rail**: from HIROSHIMA JNR Sanyo line to Miyajimaguchi (25 minutes) or Hiroshima Electric Railway (from Hiroshima Station) to Hiroden-Miyajima (1 hour). – **Boat**: from HIROSHIMA (Ujina) to Miyajima (25 minutes); ferry service between Miyajimaguchi and Miyajima (10 minutes).

**Miyajima (Shrine Island) is an island of some $11\frac{1}{2}$ sq. miles/30 sq. km in Hiroshima Bay, which opens off the Inland Sea. It is also known as Itsukushima after its famous shrine. Along with Matsushima Bay and Ama-no-hashidate it ranks among the three most celebrated stretches of coastal scenery in Japan.

From time immemorial this was a sacred island on which, until the Meiji Restoration, neither births nor deaths might take place and from which dogs were banned. Dogs are still not permitted, though this is now mainly for the protection of the many fallow deer on the island; and there is still no cemetery on Miyajima, so that burials must take place at Ono on the mainland, and even then the relatives of the dead must perform rites of purification before they may return to the "pure" island of Miyajima.

SIGHTS. – From the landing-stage a road flanked by stone lanterns leads (5 minutes) to the extensive complex of the ****Itsukushima Shrine**, which is dedicated to the Princesses Ichikishima-hime, Tagori-hime and Tagitsu-hime, daughters of the Shinto wind god Susanoo. This early Shinto shrine is first mentioned in 811. It was rebuilt in the time of Taira Kiyomori (1118–81) and was several times restored in subsequent centuries. The various buildings of the shrine rise out of the waters of a small bay, supported on piles; at high tide they appear to float on the water, presenting a picturesque and colorful spectacle with their red timber framing and their white walls. The individual buildings are linked with one another by covered gangways.

In accordance with Shinto practice, the **Principal Shrine** consists of a number of separate halls. Nearest

Itsukushima Shrine, Miyajima

55 yards

1 Honden	8 Fumyo-mon
2 Heiden	9 Honden
3 Haiden	10 Heiden
4 Haraideri	11 Haiden
5 Takabutai	12 Haraiden
6 Music pavilion	13 Araebisu Shrine
7 Okumi Shrine	14 Five-storey pagoda

the shore is the **Honden** (Main Hall), and beyond this, built out into the bay, are the **Offerings Hall** (*Heiden*), the **Prayer Hall** (*Haiden*), the hall for ceremonies of purification (*Haraiden*) and, at the far end, the **stage** (*Takabutai*) for cult dances (Bugaku, Kagura), flanked by two music pavilions. The dances (usually masked) are performed at the great festivals, in return for offerings to the shrine, and also on other occasions.

Exactly in line with the longitudinal axis of the principal shrine, 220 yds/200 m beyond the stage, is a red wooden **torii**, the largest in Japan (pillars 53 ft/16·20 m high, lintel 76 ft/23·30 m long). It was erected in 1875 in Ryobu style and bears an inscription by Prince Arisugawa (1835–95).

SW of the principal shrine are two other buildings, also on piles – the *Okuni Shrine* and the *Tenjin Shrine*, dedicated respectively to the god Okuninushi and to Sugawara Michizane (845–903), deified as Tenjin. This group of buildings is linked with the shore by a gangway and the boldly arched *Sori-bashi*, a red wooden bridge. – To the NW, on a platform just off the shore, is the oldest *No theater* in Japan, originally constructed in 1568 and restored during the Edo period. SW of this, on the mainland, stands the modern **Treasury**, fire- and earthquake-proof. Of the more than 4000 valuable objects preserved here (masks, armor, cult objects) 130 are classified as "national treasures"; of outstanding importance are the picture and manuscript scrolls recording the chronicles of the Taira dynasty, kept in a richly decorated chest. – To the

N of the Treasury is the *Daiganji Temple* of the Koyasan-Shingon sect, dedicated to Benzaiten, goddess of fortune. The temple contains a figure of the goddess, known as the Itsukushima Benten, and statues of Buddha and his disciples. – To the W, inland, lies Omoto Park, with an *Aquarium*.

To the NE of the principal shrine, in a small side bay, is the former *Hall of Morning Prayer* (Asazaya), now occupied by the shrine offices (exhibition of masks and costumes, weapons and pictures). A covered gangway leads to the *Marodo Shrine*, which is similar in structure and layout to the Principal Shrine.

From the Marodo Shrine there is another gangway to the shore. On a hill to the N is the * **Hall of a Thousand Mats** (*Senjokaku*), which actually has only some 450 tatami mats. The hall was built in 1587 by Toyotomi Hideyoshi, and since 1872, as the Hokoku Shrine, has been dedicated to his memory. It is said to have been constructed from the timber of a single camphor tree.

A beautiful path runs S from the Principal Shrine through the *Momijidani* ("Maple Valley"; several tea-houses) to the lower station of a cableway (1 mile/1·7 km; 50 minutes) up Mount **Misen** (1739 ft/ 530 m), the highest point on the island. Near the summit the *Gumonji-do Temple*, founded by Kobo-daishi in the early 9th c. offers a fine * view of the bay and of Hiroshima.

Japanese pilgrims walk round the island, making offerings at the "*Seven Beaches*" (Nanaura). For visitors a boat trip can be recommended (apply to shrine offices).

SURROUNDINGS. – There are ferry services (Setonaikai Kisen) to the other islands in the Inland Sea (see separate entry). The route runs via Hiroshima and Miyaura (island of Omishima) to Setoda (island of Ikuchi) and from there back to the mainland (Mihara, Onomichi).

Miyako Islands
See under Okinawa

Miyazaki
みやざき

Prefecture: Miyazaki. – Population: 270,000. Post code: J-880. – Telephone code: 0985.

(central)
Miyazaki-ken Tokyo Kanko Bussan Assensho,
Kokusai Kanko Kaikan,
1-8-3, Marunouchi, Chiyoda-ku,
J-100 **Tokyo;**
tel. (03) 216 9587.

(local)
Miyazaki-ken Tourist Information Office,
1-6, Miyata-cho;
tel. 25 4676.

HOTELS. – **Western style**: *Sun Hotel Phoenix*, 3083, Hamayama, Shioji, 302 r., Japanese garden, beach; *Miyazaki Kanko Hotel*, 1-1-1, Matsuyama, 201 r., Japanese garden; *Hotel Plaza Miyazaki*, 1-1, Kawahara-cho, 183 r., SP, beach; *Hotel Phoenix*, 2-1-1, Matsuyama, 118 r., Japanese garden, SP; *Miyazaki Daiichi Hotel*, 5-4-14, Tachibana-dori, Higashi, 152 r.; *Miyazaki Green Hotel*, 2-36-1, Ohashi, 70 r.; *Miyazaki Riverside Hotel*, 1-18, Kawara-cho, 30 r. – **Ryokan**: *Hotel Kandabashi*, Tachibana-dori, 110 r.; *Ryokan Rintokei*, Matsuyama, 71 r.; *Konanso*, Yodogawa, 64 r.; *Hotel Taigetsu*, Azumo-cho, 50 r.; *Hotel Nihombashi*, Hiroshima, 35 r.; *Miyazaki Grand Hotel*, Matsuyama, 33 r. – **Minshuku**: *Sasa*, 1482, Aoshima, 30 r., SP. – YOUTH HOSTELS: *YH Miyazaki-ken Seinen Kaikan*, 130 r., Umizoi, Oriuzako, 100 b.; *YH Hama-so*, 151, Azuma-cho, 100 b.; *YH Seiryu-so Bekkan*, 164, Azuma-cho, 50 b.; *YH Miyazaki-ken Fujin-Kaikan*, 1-3-10, Asahi, 50 b.

RESTAURANT. – *Suginoko Bekkan*, 2-1-4, Nishi, Tachibana-dori.

TRANSPORTATION. – **Air**: from TOKYO (Haneda Airport), 1½ hours; from FUKUOKA (1 hour). – **Rail**: from FUKUOKA (Hakata) JNR Nippo line (6½ hours); from KAGOSHIMA (Nishi-Kagoshima Station) JNR Nippo line (2½ hours). – **Bus**: from Miyazaki Airport to city center (10 minutes).

Miyazaki, chief town of Miyazaki prefecture, lies on the SE coast of Kyushu. It is a city of fine broad streets, traversed by the River Oyodo, with a mild climate and clean air which make it a pleasant place to stay. It lies in a predominantly agricultural region.

SIGHTS. – 2 miles/3 km N of the station (bus) is the **Miyazaki Shrine**, dedicated to Jimmu-tenno. Within the precincts of the shrine is the *Prefectural Museum*, with material of the Kofun period (*haniwa* figures, etc.). Adjoining is the **Heiwadai Park**, with the *Peace Tower* (1940). In a corner of the park is the *Haniwa-en Garden*, named after the copies of haniwa terracotta figures set up here.

SURROUNDINGS. – 6 miles/10 km S of Miyazaki lies the **Nichinan-kaigan Quasi National Park** (19 sq. miles/48 sq. km), which extends for some 30 miles/50 km along the Pacific coast. Off the coast near its northern end is the little island of *Aoshima (bridge; bus from Miyazaki, 20 minutes), covered with luxuriant tropical and subtropical vegetation. The sedimentary rocks round its coasts have been eroded by the waves into the form of an old-fashioned wash-board. On the mainland opposite the island is a well-stocked *Cactus Garden*. – Continuing S, the road (No. 220) crosses the *Horikiri Pass* and comes to the **Udo Shrine** (bus from Mizaky, 1½ hours), the principal buildings of which are in a sea-cave on *Cape Udo*.

Takachiho Gorge

Rocky coast, Aoshima

Farther SW is **Nichinan** (pop. 53,000), a town formed in 1950 by the amalgamation of the small towns of Aburatsu, Agata, Obi and Togo. In Obi are the remains of a castle belonging to the Ito family; the fishing harbor is in Aburatsu. – Off *Nango* is the island of **Oshima**, with an *Underwater Park* (banks of coral, fish, etc.; trips in glass-bottomed boats).

The S end of the park consists of a plateau lying at the height of about 1000 ft/300 m, projecting into the Pacific at **Cape Toi**. A herd of some 60 wild horses lives on the plateau. On the cape is a tall lighthouse from which there are extensive * views over the sea.

17 miles/27 km N of Miyazaki is *Saitobaru* (Tsuma Railway to Tsuma, then bus), notable for its 380 burial mounds of the Kofun period. The most important finds are displayed in the local museum.

From Miyazaki the JNR Nippo line runs N, keeping close to the coast, to **Nobeoka** (53 miles/85 km; pop. 135,000), the largest industrial town on the E coast of Kyushu. From here it is 2 hours by train (JNR Takachiho line) to *Takachiho*, on the south-western outskirts of the **Sobo-Katamuki Quasi National Park**. This is a region of unspoiled natural vegetation which provides a habitat for rare species of animals, reaching its highest points in Mount *Sobo* (5768 ft/1758 m) and Mount *Katamuki* (5256 ft/1602 m). Its main attraction is the * *Takachiho Gorge*, carved out by the River *Gokase* from the lava flows deposited by

Mount *Aso*. Many Japanese myths are associated with this gorge: the gods are said to have performed the world's first dance here, and the Iwato-kagura is still danced in honor of the sun goddess Amaterasu-omikami in the area around the Iwato Shrine between November and February. – The best base for the ascent of Mount **Sobo** (about 5 hours) is *Kobaru* (bus from Taketa on the JNR Hohi line).

Morioka

もりおか

Prefecture: Iwate. – Population: 231,000.
Post code: J-020. – Telephone code: 0196.
(i) (central)
Iwate-ken Tokyo Kanko Bussan Assensho,
Tetsudo Kaikan,
1-9-1, Marunouchi, Chiyoda-ku,
J-100 **Tokyo;**
tel. (03) 231 2613.

(local)
Iwate-ken Tourist Information Center,
10-1, Uchimaru;
tel. 51 3111.

HOTELS. – **Western style:** *Morioka Grand Hotel,* 1-10, Atagoshita, 50 r.; *Morioka Central Hotel,* 1-3-6, Saien, 40 r.; *Hotel Sun Route,* 7-19, Odori 3-chome,

189 r.; *Hotel Morioka Ace*, 2-11-35, Chuo-dori, 139 r.; *Morioka Rifu Hotel*, 18-5, Nasugawa-cho, 62 r. – YOUTH HOSTEL: *Morioka YH*, 1-9-41, Takamatsu, 96 b.

RESTAURANTS. – *Restaurant Wakana*, 1-3-33, Osawa, Kawahara; *Taga*, Kenmin Kaikan, 13, Uchimaru.

EVENTS. – *Chagu-chagu* (mid June), cavalcade of festively dressed children at Komagata Shrine.

TRANSPORTATION. – **Air**: from (Haneda Airport), 1½ hours. – **Rail**: from TOKYO (Ueno Station) to Omiya (30 minutes), then JNR New Tohoku–Shinkansen line (3¼ hours); also JNR Tohoku line via SENDAI (6¼ hours). – **Bus**: from Hanamaki Airport to city center (1¼ hours).

Morioka, chief town of Iwate prefecture and an important educational center (University) lies in northern Honshu, SE of Mount Iwate.

The city is noted for the manufacture of hardware, in particular the cast-iron kettles known as *nambu-tetsubin*. Other local products are lathe-turned wooden dolls (*kokeshi*) and the pottery of Kuji, to the N of Morioka (*Kuji-yaki*).

SIGHTS. – The central feature of the town, 1 mile/1·7 km SE of the station, is **Iwate Park**, with a monument to the poet Ishikawa Takuboku (1886–1912), who spent his early days in Morioka. The park occupies the site of the old Castle of Morioka.

Near here the River *Nakatsu* is spanned by the *Kaminohashi-giboshi*, a bridge dating from the same period as the castle, with rich 17th c. bronze ornament.

The **Regional Museum** (*Kyodo-shiryokan*; bus from station, 10 minutes) occupies a house of the Edo period, set in a beautiful garden, which belonged to the Nambu family. – 10 minutes' walk away is the **Ho-onji Temple**, probably built in 1732. In the main hall are small figures of the 500 ascetics (*rakan*), together with figures of Marco Polo and Kublai Khan.

Near the birthplace of Hara Kei, Japan's first middle-class Prime Minister (murdered by right-wing extremists in 1921), is the *Hara-Kei-kinenkan*, a memorial containing mementoes of Hara Kei and documents on the history of modern Japan.

SURROUNDINGS. – In the southern foothills of Mount *Iwate*, a quiescent volcano (see under Towada-Hachimantai National Park), lies the romantic little hill resort of **Amihari-onsen** (JNR Tazawako line to Shizukuishi, then bus, 50 minutes). – Farther W (Tazawako line) is *Lake Tazawa (area 6350 acres, depth 1395 ft/425 m) surrounded by densely wooded hills. The best view of the lake is from Mount *Koma* (5371 ft/1637 m: see under Towada-Hachimantai National Park).

S of Morioka is the agricultural market center of **Hanamaki** (pop. 68,000), with an airport. The poet and fairy-tale writer Miwazawa Kenji (1896–1933) was born here, and there is an exhibition devoted to him in the House of Culture. Every year from September 5 to 7 is celebrated the Hanamaki-matsuri festival, the climax of which is the Stag Dance (Shika-odori).

NW of Hanamaki (bus service) we reach the extensive resort area of **Hanamaki-onsenkyo**. At **Hanamaki-onsen** is a sport and recreation center (including winter sports); beautiful cherry trees on the banks of the River *Dai* and a large rose-garden laid out by Miyazawa Kenji. – To the W are **Dai-onsen** and **Namari-onsen**.

NE of Morioka (JNR Yamada line to Moichi, then JNR Iwaizumi line, 4 hours) is *Iwaizumi*, to the N of which in the large **Ryusendo Cave** can be seen stalactites and stalagmites, sinter formations, lakes, and waterfalls. At the entrance is the *Cave Museum* (Ryusenshindo-kagakukan).

Nagano
ながの

Prefecture: Nagano. – Population: 328,000. Post code: J-380. – Telephone code: 0262.

(central)
Nagano-ken, Tokyo Kanko Bussan Assensho,
Kokusai Kanko Kaikan,
1-8-3, Marunouchi, Chiyoda-ku,
J-100 **Tokyo**;
tel. (03) 214 5651.

HOTELS. – **Western style**: *Hotel New Nagano*, 828, Minami-chitosecho, 124 r.; *Nagano City Hotel Kikuya*, 2377, Gondoocho, 87 r.; *Hotel Aoki*, 1354, Suehiroocho, 76 r.; *Hotel Yama*, 2273, Gondoocho, 50 r.; *Hotel Sankeien*, 1477, Shindencho, 43 r.; *Nagano Palace Hotel*, 1326, Sekido-minami, Minami-nagano, 30 r. – YOUTH HOSTEL: *YH Kwoju-in*, Zenkoji, 479, Motoyoshi-cho, 30 b.

RESTAURANT. – *Nakajima Kaikan*, 1361, Suehiro, Minami-Nagano.

TRANSPORTATION. – **Rail**: from TOKYO (Ueno Station) JNR Shin-etsu line (3 hours); from NAGOYA JNR Chuo and Shinonoi lines (3½ hours).

Before becoming chief town of its prefecture in central Honshu the city of Nagano was known as Zen-

koji, after the well-known temple of that name. It is a center of silkworm culture and a market for the fruit grown in the surrounding area.

SIGHTS. – 1¼ miles/2 km from the station is the **Zenko-ji Temple**, founded in 623 by Zenko (or, according to another reading, Yoshimitsu), which is visited every year by large numbers of Buddhist pilgrims. The **Main Hall (1707) contains bronze * statues of the gods Amidanyorai, Kannon and Seishi which are believed to have come to Japan in 552 as gifts from a king of Korea, to have been thrown into a canal at Osaka by opponents of Buddhism, to have been recovered in 602 and finally brought to Nagano in 1598. The central figure is shown only every seven years (last in 1980).

SURROUNDINGS. – Nagano lies within easy reach of the highlands of central Honshu, with their peaks rising above 9800 ft/3000 m and their many lakes and hot springs, and with four National Parks.

To the N and E of the town are the two separate areas which make up the **Joshin-etsu-kogen National Park**. To the N are Mounts *Myoko* (8091 ft/2466 m), *Kurohime* (6736 ft/2053 m), *Togakushi* (6270 ft/1911 m) and *Iizuna* (6290 ft/1917 m), to the E Mount *Tanigawa* (6441 ft/1963 m) and two active volcanoes, *Shirane* (7094 ft/2162 m) and *Asama* (8340 ft/2542 m; last eruption April 1982). In this eastern section are the extensive skiing areas of *Sugadaira* and *Shiga-kogen* (numerous lifts). With its clear lakes and open birch forests the plateau attracts many summer visitors (boat rentals, golf-courses, several hotels). This part of the National Park is traversed by the *Shiga-Kusatsu-kogen Ridge Highway*, which connects **Yudanaka** in the N with **Karuizawa** (see separate entry) in the S, reaching a height of some 6550 ft/2000 m (bus services by JNR and private firms). – From Yudanaka a road crosses the *Kusatsu Pass* to the little mountain resort of **Kusatsu**, idyllically situated on a rocky slope above the River *Agatsuma*. The Yubatake and Sainokawara hot springs (140–153 °F/60–67 °C) contain sulphur, iron, alum and arsenic. The Onsen-matsuri festival is celebrated here on August 1–3.

From *Sesshogawara*, in the winter-sports area around Kusatsu, a cableway runs up Mount **Shirane** (or *Kusatsu-Shirane*). From the upper station it is a half-hour walk to the three craters of the volcano.

43 miles/70 km N of Nagano is **Takada** (JNR Shinetsu line), where an Austrian Major named von Lerch first introduced skiing into Japan. The main skiing area in this region, with its abundance of snow, is on Mount *Kanaya*, to the SW.

Nagana
ながさき

Prefecture: Nagasaki. – Population: 450,000.
Post code: J-850. – Telephone code: 0958.

(local)
Nagasaki City Tourist Information Office,
JNR Nagasaki Station;
tel. 23 7423 (English spoken).
Japan Travel Bureau,
Nagasaki-ekimae,
(at station);
tel. 23 1261.
Adachi Building,
1-7, Hama-cho;
tel. 22 0185.

HOTELS. – **Western style**: *Nagasaki Tokyu Hotel*, 18-1, Minamiyamate-machi, 226 r.; *Hotel New Tanda*, 2-24, Tokiwa-machi, 161 r.; *Nagasaki Grand Hotel*, 5-3, Manzai-machi, 126 r., Japanese garden; *Parkside Hotel*, 14-1, Heiwa-machi, 72 r.; *New Nagasaki Hotel*, 14-5, Daikoku-machi, 60 r.; *Nagasaki Heights Hotel*, 3-19, Kozen-machi, 50 r.; *Business Hotel New Port*, 16-12, Motofune-cho, 75 r.; *Nagasaki Plaza Hotel*, 13-10, Motofune-cho, 57 r.; *Business Hotel Dejima*, 2-13, Dejima-cho, 45 r.; *Business Hotel Futabaso*, 2-11, Aburaya-cho. 35 r.; *New Oriental Hotel*, 5, Dekidaiku-cho, 29 r.; *Hotel Kiri-so*, 6-46, Kajiya-machi, 25 r. – **Ryokan**: *Nagasaki Kokusai Hotel Nisshokan*, Nishizaka-machi, 111 r.; *Nagasaki Kanko Hotel Shumeikan*, Chikugo-machi, 65 r.; *Yataro*, Kazahashira-cho, 58 r.; *Hotel Hakuunso*, Kajiya-machi, 40 r.; *New Hotel Kuoso*, Manzai-machi, 26 r.; *Suwaso*, 7, Rokasu-machi, 17 r. – YOUTH HOSTELS: *Nagasaki Kenritsu YH*, 2, Tateyama-cho, 90 b.; *Nagasaki Oranda-Zaka YH*, 6-14, Higashiyamate-cho, 55 b.; *Nagasaki Nanpoen YH*, 320, Hamahira-cho, 20 b.

RESTAURANTS. – **Japanese cuisine**: *Kagetsu*, Maruyama-cho; *Fukiro*, Kaminishiyama-cho; *Waraku*, Tsuki-machi; *Matsutei*, Motoshikkui-machi; *Ichiriki*, Suwa-cho; *Tatsuta*, Motoshikkui-machi; *Yoneharu*, Yorozuya-cho; *Shoraku*, Okeya-cho; *Aoyagi*, Maruyama-cho; *Yosso*, Hamaichi-dori. – **Chinese cuisine**: *Tokaen*, Shinchi-cho; *Chukaen*, Shinchi-cho; *Fukuju*, Shinchi-cho; *Kairakuen*, Shinchi-cho; *Keikaen*, Shinchi-cho; *Toakaku*, Kajiya-cho; *Koyuten*, Furukawa-cho; *Tototei*, Junin-cho; *Kozanro*, Shinchi-cho. – **European cuisine**: *Ginrei*, Kajiya-cho. – **Russian cuisine**: *Harbin*, Kozen-cho.

EVENTS. – *Hata-age* (April–May), Kite Festival on the surrounding hills; *Peiron* (beginning of June), rowing regatta in harbor; *Bon-matsuri* (mid August), festival for the souls of the dead; *Okunchi-matsuri* beginning of October), procession with magnificent floats and dragon dance at Suwa Shrine.

TRANSPORTATION. – **Air**: from TOKYO (Haneda Airport), 1¾ hours. – **Rail**: from TOKYO (Central Station) JNR Tokaido–Shinkansen line to HAKATA (7 hours), then JNR Nagasaki and Sasebo lines (2½ hours). – **Bus**: from airport to city center (1 hour).

Nagasaki, chief town of its prefecture, lies on the NW coast of Kyushu in a fjord-like inlet, sheltered by off-

shore islands, which makes an excellent natural harbor. From the 16th c. to the end of the 19th it was the only Japanese port open to foreign shipping.

An important industrial city, Nagasaki is the main center of Japanese shipbuilding. The shipyards extend along the W side of Nagasaki Bay for several miles, with huge docks capable of accommodating the super-tankers and the gigantic container ships which are built here. Other major industries are engineering, steel-processing, pharmaceuticals, the photographic industry and the processing of agricultural produce and fish. Nagasaki is also one of Japan's principal exporting and importing ports.

HISTORY. – At the end of the 12th c. the territory of what is now Nagasaki, then a fishing village known as *Fukae-no-ura* or *Tama-no-ura*, passed into the hands of a feudal lord called Nagasaki Kotaro, whose name the city still bears. In 1571 the port was opened to European vessels in the East Indian trade, and Portuguese, Dutch and Spanish trading-posts were established here. Since the Japanese had no ships capable of sailing on the open sea they left the trade with China, the Philippines, Macao, Goa and from there to Europe to European seamen, particularly the Portuguese. Soon Christian missionaries began to preach the Gospel in Japan; but since the Japanese ruling classes feared, rightly or wrongly, that the Jesuits who established themselves in Nagasaki wanted to exert influence on the Government, and in addition objected to the Portuguese monopoly of trade and the beginnings of Westernization, Toyotomi Hideyoshi issued an edict against the missionaries in 1587, and in 1597 26 Christians were crucified.

This did not prevent the continuing development of trade, now exclusively in the hands of the Dutch and the Chinese. At first, however, the Dutch merchants and seamen were not allowed to go beyond the confines of the island (now attached to the mainland) of Dejima; it was some time before these restrictions were relaxed and the foreigners were permitted to send delegations to the Court at Edo.

In 1691 a German doctor named Engelbert Kaempfer (1651–1716) arrived in Nagasaki and, pretending to be a Dutchman, was able to travel into the interior of Japan, recording in his voluminous diaries much information about the manners and customs as well as the animal and plant life of the country. His observations, published posthumously (1777–79) under the title "History and Description of Japan", include a highly amusing account of his visit to the Court of the Shogun, whom he took for the Emperor. During the audience the Europeans were required to sing, dance and perform a variety of absurd actions – being evidently regarded as exotic curiosities. Kaempfer's book was the first objective and scholarly description of Japan by a European. Other accounts of travel in Japan were written by the Swedish botanist Carl Peter Thunberg (1743–1822), who visited Dejima in 1775, and the German doctor and scientist Philip Franz von Siebold (1796–1866), who lived in Nagasaki from 1823 to 1829.

With the opening-up of Japan to the West in the Meiji period the importance of Nagasaki declined sharply, since it now lost its monopoly in the import of European goods and ideas, though for a brief period it continued to attract Japanese anxious to learn about the European sciences and technologies which now became freely accessible.

Nagasaki Harbor

On August 9, 1945 one of the two atom bombs with which the American forces sought to break the already weakened Japanese will to resist (see under Hiroshima) was dropped on Nagasaki, causing fearful destruction and killing a large number of civilians (conservatively estimated at between 25,000 and 75,000). – In 1957 and 1982 catastrophic damage was caused by storms.

SIGHTS. – To the E of the station, on the slopes of Mount Nishizaka, is **Nagasaki Park** (*Nagasaki Koen*), formerly known as *Suwa Park*. On its SW side are the *Prefectural Library* and the **Museum of Art** (temporary exhibitions). In the park are *monuments* to Engelbert Kaempfer, Franz von Siebold and Carl Peter Thunberg as well as an Indian banyan tree (*Ficus bengalensis*) planted by General (ex-President) Ulysses S. Grant in 1879.

Adjoining the park on the NE is the *Suwa-jinja Shrine*, built in the mid 16th c. on the model of the shrines of that name in central Japan. A flight of 73 steps leads up to the shrine, from which there is a fine panoramic * view of the city and the port.

To the S of Nagasaki Park a number of bridges span the River Nakajima, including the Chinese-style *Megane-bashi* ("Spectacles Bridge") built by Abbot Nyojo in 1634. – E of this bridge is the so-called "Chinese Temple", the *Kofukuji Temple*, long frequented by the Chinese merchants in Nagasaki, which now belongs to the Obaku sect of Zen Buddhism. – A little way S of the Kofukuji stands the *Kodaiji Temple*, whose monks belong to the Soto school of Zen. This contains a Buddha figure 23 ft/7 m high and the tomb of Takashima Shuhan (1798–1866), who introduced Western weapon technology into Japan.

Farther S is the * **Sofukuji Temple**, also belonging to the Obaku sect which was founded in 1629 by a Chinese master of Zen. The buildings are thus good examples of the Late Ming style, in particular the *gate-tower*, which is decorated with a representation of the mythological paradise at the bottom of the sea, known as Ryugu. Other notable features are the second gateway, of unusual type, and the main hall. – To .the SW, on the *Oranda-saka* ("Dutch Hillside"), are numbers of early Western-style buildings flanking cobbled streets.

SW of the Kofukuji Temple, on the S side of the mouth of the Nakajima, is the former island of Dejima, now joined to the mainland and chiefly occupied by quays and port installations. The days of the Dutch merchants, who had a strictly guarded trading-post here from 1641 to 1854, are recalled by a warehouse in the style of the period, reconstructed in 1958, in the garden of which is a small museum.

To the N, beyond the Central Station, is a *memorial* to the 26 Christians (20 Japanese and 6 foreigners, including St Francis Xavier) who were crucified here on February 5, 1597 on the basis of an edict directed against Roman Catholics and particularly against the Jesuits. The area was first laid out as a park in 1949 on the 400th anniversary of St Francis Xavier's arrival in Japan; then in 1962, 100 years after the canonization of the martyrs, a memorial hall was erected with reliefs of the 26 saints.

S of Dejima on the road skirting the bay (1½ miles/2·5 km from the station) stands a Neo-Gothic church built in 1865 (restored after the last war), also dedicated to the memory of the martyrs. – To the W of this is *Glover's Mansion*, once the residence of a British merchant, which tourists are frequently told is the setting of Puccini's "Madame Butterfly". From the garden there is a fine *view of the harbor.

Sofukuji Temple, Nagasaki

1½ miles/2·5 km NW of the station (tram to Matsuyama-cho), in Hamaguchi-machi, lies the **Peace Park**, with a *memorial* marking the epicentre of the explosion of the atom bomb. At the S end of the park are the *International Hall of Culture* (Atom Bomb Museum), erected in 1955, and the *Peace Statue* (by Kitamura Seibo), almost

33 ft/10 m high. On the NE side of the park is the *Urakami Church* (1914; rebuilt 1959). In the park are displayed works of sculpture by sculptors of many nations.

On the W side of the bay rises Mount *Inasayama* (1089 ft/332 m; nature park), the top of which can be reached by cable-

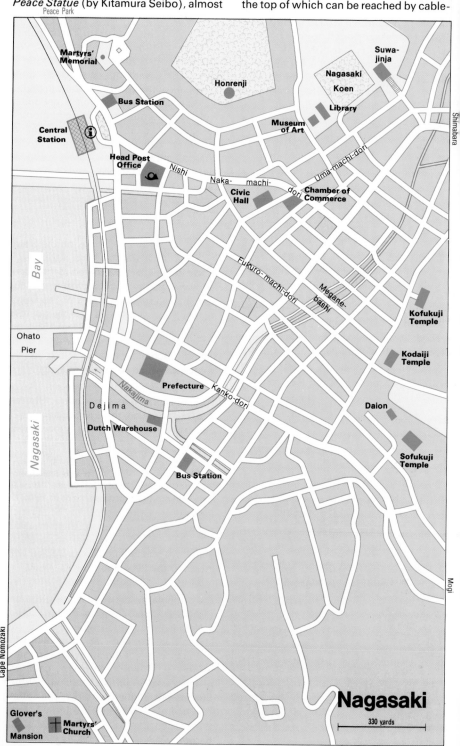

Nagasaki

Martyrs' Memorial, Nagasaki

way in 5 minutes (fine * views of the bay and the city, particularly after dark).

Interesting cruises round the port (50 minutes) are run from Ohato Pier No. 1.

SURROUNDINGS. – 7 miles/11 km SE of Nagasaki (bus, 30 minutes), in the wide sweep of *Chijiwa Bay*, is the picturesque little fishing port of **Mogi**, amid groves of mandarines and oranges. The loquat (Chinese *lo kwat, Eriobotrya japonica*) is also grown here. – From Mogi there is a ferry (1 hour 20 minutes) to *Tomioka* on the island of *Shimo* (Amakusa Islands).

There is also a bus service to the *Shimabara Peninsula* (see under Unzen-Amakusa National Park), between Chijiwa Bay and Shimabara Bay to the E.

12½ miles/20 km S of Nagasaki (90 minutes by bus) *Cape Nomozaki* extends far into the East China Sea (fine views of sea).

There are regular ferry services between Nagasaki and the *Goto Archipelago* (see under Saikai National Park) to the W, and the mainland port and naval base of **Sasebo** (pop. 251,000) to the N.

Nagoya

Prefecture: Aichi. – Population: 2,100,000.
Post code: J-450-466. – Telephone code: 052.

ⓘ (local)
Nagoya City Tourist Office,
Kokutetsu Nagoya-eki Kitaguchi;
tel. 541 4301 (English spoken).

HOTELS. – **Western style:** *Nagoya Kanko Hotel,* 1-19-30, Nishiki, Naka-ku, 505 r.; *Nagoya Miyako Hotel,* 9-10, 4-chome, Meieki, Nakamura-ku, 400 r.; *International Hotel Nagoya,* 3-23-3, Nishiki, Naka-ku, 266 r.; *Hotel Nagoya Castle,* 3-19, Hinokuchi-cho, Nishi-ku, 253 r., Japanese garden, SP; *Meitetsu Grand Hotel,* 2-4, Meieki 1-chome, Nakamura-ku, 242 r., Japanese garden; *Nagoya Terminal Hotel,* 2-1, 1-chome, Meieki, Nakamura-ku, 256 r.; *Hotel New Nagoya,* 7-35, 4-chome, Meieki, Nakamura-ku, 86 r.; *Nagoya Crown Hotel,* 1-8-3, Sakae, Naka-ku, 488 r.; *Daini Washington Hotel,* 3-12-22, Nishiki, Naka-ku,

216 r.; *Kanaya Hotel Kanko,* 23-22, Higashi-sakura 2-chome, 184 r.; *Daiichi Washington Hotel,* 3-18-28, Nishiki, Naka-ku, 216 r.; *Hotel Chiyoda,* 1-6-10, Nishiki, Naka-ku, 199 r.; *Nagoya Plaza Hotel,* 3-8-21, Nishiki, Naka-ku, 173 r.; *Tokyu Inn,* 2-17-18, Marunouchi, Naka-ku, 187 r.; *Nagoya Kanayama Washington Hotel,* 6-ban 25-go, Kanayama 4-chome, Naka-ku, 184 r.; *Nagoya Roren Hotel,* 1-8-40, Naka-ku, 140 r.; *Hotel Sun Route,* 1-8-5, Sakae, 126 r.; *Lions Hotel,* 22-35, 1-chome, Sakae, Naka-ku, 120 r.; *Hotel Rich,* 3-9, 2-chome, Sakae, Naka-ku, 105 r.; *Nagoya Green Hotel,* 1-8-22, Nishiki, Naka-ku, 105 r.; *Kanayama Plaza Hotel,* 3-7-15, Masaki-cho, Naka-ku, 68 r.; *Business Hotel Kiyoshi,* 1-3-1, Heiwa, Naka-ku, 56 r.; *Hotel Koyo,* 3-23-33, Sakae, Naka-ku, 23 r.

Ryokan: *Suihoen,* 4-1-20, Sakae, Naka-ku, 25 r.; *Maizurukan,* 8, Kitanegi-cho, Nakamura-ku, 23 r.; *Hasshokan,* 29, Ishizaka, Hiroji-cho, Showa-ku, 15 r. – YOUTH HOSTELS: *Nagoya YH,* 1-50, Kameiri, Tashiro-cho, Chikusa-ku, 100 b.; *YH Aichi-ken Seinen-Kaikan,* 1-18-8, Sakae, Naka-ku, 50 b; *YH Miyoshi Ryokan,* 5-8-3, Mieki, Nakamura-ku 18 b.

RESTAURANTS. – *Hasshokan Nakamise,* 2-12-20, Sakae, Naka-ku; *Kamone,* 2-7, Shirokabe-cho, Higashi-ku; *Suihoen,* 1-1, Minami-Buhei-cho, Naka-ku.

EVENTS. – *Archery Contests* (mid January), with collecting of lucky arrows, at Atsuta Shrine; *Fertility Festival* (mid March) at Tagata Shrine, procession with phallic symbols; *Shrine Festival* at Toshogu Shrine (mid April), procession with decorated floats and old puppets; *Atsuta-matsuri* (beginning of June), wrestling contests and parade of boats, at Atsuta Shrine; *Minato-matsuri* (mid July), Port Festival, with processions and fireworks; *Nagoya-matsuri* (mid October), procession in medieval costumes, with fireworks, etc.

VISITS TO FACTORIES. – Apply to *Tourist and Foreign Trade Section,* tel. 961 1111, ext. 2245, or *City Tourist information,* in Central Station, tel. 541 4301.

TRANSPORTATION. – **Air:** from TOKYO (Haneda Airport), 45 minutes; from SAPPORO (1½ hours); from KAGOSHIMA (1¼ hours); also from Fukuoka, Matsuyama, Oita, Kumamoto and Miyazaki. – **Rail:** from TOKYO (Central Station) JNR Tokaido–Shinkansen line (2 hours); from OSAKA JNR Tokaido–Shinkansen line (1 hour); also on JNR Tokaido, Chuo and Kansai lines. – **Bus:** from TOKYO JNR and Nihon–Kyuko services by Tomei Expressway (6 hours); from OSAKA and KYOTO by Meishin Expressway (2¾ hours or 3¼ hours).

Municipal Transport

Subway (Underground): Higashiyama line from Fujigaoka to Nakamura-koen; Meijo line from Ozone to Nagoyako and from Kanayama to Aratama; Tsurumai line from Joshin to Akaike.

Bus: some 150 routes.

Nagoya, chief town of Aichi prefecture and Japan's fourth largest city, lies in central Honshu. Its situation in the spacious Ise Bay, opening on to the Pacific, has favored the development of the port, which is

now the third largest in Japan (after Yokohama and Kobe). It is also an important industrial center.

The economic rise of Nagoya began with the Meiji reforms. Its main industrial activities are heavy industry, shipbuilding and automobile manufacture, together with chemicals and pharmaceuticals, textiles and ceramics (this last continuing a tradition established in the 12th c. in nearby Seto). Many factories and workshops can be visited.

Nagoya Castle

HISTORY. – Nagoya grew up around the castles built by the Imagawa and Oda families in the 16th c., and gained increased importance when Tokugawa Ieyasu built the large castle which still survives for his son Yoshinao in 1612 and appointed him as Governor of the province of Owari. The castle was also designed to be a stronghold of the Tokugawa in their conflict with the Toyotomi family. After Ieyasu's defeat of his enemies in 1614–15 the Owara-Tokugawa dynasty resided in Nagoya until 1868, when they were compelled to surrender their authority to the central government. – Soon afterwards there began the development of industry which laid the foundations of the city's prosperity. The air attacks of 1945 caused heavy damage in Nagoya, and the castle was largely destroyed. The post-war reconstruction gave the city a fine network of wide modern streets.

SIGHTS. – The **Castle** can be reached from the Central Station by subway (underground) (Higashiyama line). The *main tower*, 157 ft/48 m high, was rebuilt in 1959; on the gable are two gilded dolphins (*shachi*). It now houses a museum containing art treasures from the palace which was destroyed during the last war, including painted *wall screens and sliding doors and wall-paintings, mainly of the Kano school. From the fifth floor of the tower there are extensive *views of the city and the Nobi Plain. From the original castle there survive three *corner towers*, the second gateway and walls. – To the E of the castle tower is the *Ninomaru Garden*, with a tea-house.

A little way S of the Castle we come to the **Aichi Shrine** (formerly known as the *Gokoku Shrine*), rebuilt in 1952 and

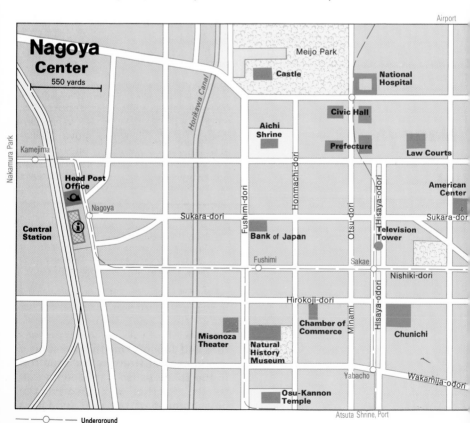

Nagoya
Center

550 yards

Airport

Meijo Park

Castle

National Hospital

Civic Hall

Aichi Shrine

Prefecture

Law Courts

Horikawa Canal

Nakamura Park

Kamejima

Head Post Office

Nagoya

Honmachi-dori

American Center

Central Station

Fushimi-dori

Sukara-dori

Otsu-dori

Hisaya-odori

Sukara-dori

Bank of Japan

Television Tower

Fushimi

Sakae

Nishiki-dori

Hirokoji-dori

Misonoza Theater

Chamber of Commerce

Minami

Hisaya-odori

Chunichi

Natural History Museum

Yabacho

Wakamija-odori

Osu-Kannon Temple

Atsuta Shrine, Port

— ○ —   **Underground**

dedicated to the victims of the war. – Farther S (Marunouchi, Naka ward), close together, are two other shrines: the **Toshogu Shrine**, founded in 1619 and rebuilt in 1952, which is dedicated to Tokugawa Ieyasu; and the **Nagoya Shrine**, founded by Daigo-tenno in 911 and moved here in 1876 from its original site within the precincts of the Castle. – In Hisaya-dori, a broad street running in a N–S direction to the E of the two shrines, stands the 590 ft/180 m high **Television Tower**, from the observation platform of which there is a magnificent panoramic *view. A little way S of this is the Sakae subway (underground) station.

2 miles/3 km E of the Castle (Shin-Dekimachi bus stop) the **Tokugawa Museum of Art** (*Tokugawa bijutsukan*) houses many treasures which belonged to the Tokugawa family of Nagoya, including pictures, porcelain, weapons and documents; particularly notable items are the 43 parts of the **"Genji-monogatari-emaki"**, a picture scroll by Fujiwara Takayoshi, and the *"Saigyo-mono-gatari-emaki"*, a scroll depicting scenes from the life of the priest Saigyo (1118–90). – Some ½ mile/800 m SW is the *Kenchuji Temple* of the Jodo sect, once the Owari-Tokugawa family temple.

On Mount *Kakuozan*, to the E of the city center, is the **Nittaiji Temple** (1904), which contains a gilded Buddha statue. From the hill there is a *view of the city. – A short distance E is the **Gokyaku-rakan Hall**, with 500 wooden figures of Buddha's disciples and, in a gallery, 18 statues of disciples by the 18th c. netsuke artist Kita Tametaka, who worked in Nagoya.

To the E of the city lies **Higashiyama Park** (*Higashiyama-koen*; subway station), 203 acres in extent, with the *Zoo*, the *Botanic Garden*, the *Observatory* and a 33 ft/10 m-high *statue of Kannon*. To the N are the large **Heiwa Park** ("Peace Park"), a cemetery containing the tomb of Oda Nobunaga (1534–82) and the *Temple of the Thousand-Handed Kannon* (Senju-Kannon) a gift from Thailand.

SE of the Central Station (Higashiyama subway (underground) line to Fushimi Station, then Tsurumai line to Osu-Kannon Station) is the **Osu-Kannon Temple** (or *Hoshoin*), rebuilt on the site of an earlier temple of 1612, with a large library which among much else possesses the earliest surviving copy of the historical work "Kojiki" (712). – To the E is the **Nanatsu Temple** or *Chofuku-ji*, founded in the village of Nanatsudera in 735 and moved to its present site in 1611, which contains *statues of Kannon and Seishi-bosatsu (Heian period).

Running W from the Central Station, the Higashiyama subway (underground) line ends at **Nakamura Park** (*Nakamura-koen*). A small bamboo grove (Taika-yabu) marks the site of the house in which Toyotomi Hideyoshi (1536–98) was born; and adjoining this is the *Hokoku Shrine*, built on the 300th anniversary of Hideyoshi's death. Near by is the *Myokoji Temple*, with the birthplace of Kato Kiyomasa (1559–1611), one of the great military commanders of his day; there is a monument to him in the Hokoku Shrine.

To the S of the city (Meijo subway (underground) line, Jingu-nishi Station) can be found the **Atsuta Shrine**, after the Ise Shrine (see under Ise-Shima National Park) the most important Shinto shrine in Japan. In this shrine one of the three Imperial insignia, the "grass-mowing sword" (*kusanagi-no-tsurugi*) was preserved.

In the Meiji-mura Open-Air Museum

In Japanese mythology the sword originally belonged to the storm god Susanoo. When the legendary hero Yamato-takeru set out to conquer the eastern provinces the sword was presented to him by the high priestess of the Ise Shrines, Yamato-hime. Then, when his enemies tried to kill him by setting the long grass on fire, he saved himself by mowing the grass with his sword. He then hung the sword on a mulberry tree, from which it was stolen by Princess Miyazu-hime. And finally, according to the legend, the brilliant flash of the blade set a cedar tree on fire. Hence, in popular etymology, the name of the shrine (*atsuta* = "burning field").

In the northern part of the wooded precincts is the principal shrine, **Hongu**, surrounded by an enclosing wall (no admission). To the E is the **Treasury**, a modern building which contains a large number of works of art (old and modern pictures, ceramics, jewelry, dramatic masks).

Some 550 yds/500 m NW of the shrine is a burial-mound, the **Shiratori-no misasagi** ("Tomb of the White Bird"), said to be the burial-place of Yamato-takeru, who is supposed to have turned into a white bird after his death.

To the S of the city lies the **Port** (terminus of the Meijo subway (underground) line), which has a water area of some 25,000 acres.

SURROUNDINGS. – 19 miles/30 km N of Nagoya (Meitetsu private line) is **Gifu** (pop. 408,000), chief town of a prefecture, situated at the foot of Mount *Inaba*. It is noted for the manufacture of paper parasols, lanterns, fans, etc. *Gifu Park*, laid out in 1888 on the banks of the River *Nagara*, has an aquarium. A cableway runs up Mount Inaba, on the summit of which is the restored Castle (museum; view).

A particular attraction for tourists is the **cormorant-fishing** (*ukai*) on the River Nagara. Every evening from May to October (except at full moon) the fishermen set out, accompanied by boats carrying spectators. The fish (*ayu*, a member of the salmon family) are attracted by the light of a fire burning in an iron basket at the front of the boat. The master of the boat (*usho*) directs the cormorants (who have a ring round their necks to prevent them from swallowing the fish) with the aid of a line. Each bird may catch anything up to 50 fish. This very ancient method of fishing was probably introduced from China.

To the E of Gifu (Meitetsu private railway line; also bus from Nagoya) is **Inuyama** (pop. 63,000), with Hakutei-jo Castle (1440). SE of the town the *Meiji-mura Open-Air Museum* includes some 40 buildings of the Meiji period brought here from all over the country, an old railway, etc. – The Meitetsu line continues to **Imawatari**, the starting-point for boat trips down the rapids on the River *Kiso*, which is particularly beautiful here (time to Inuyama about 1½ hours).

E of Nagoya (Meitetsu private railway, 30 minutes) lies the pottery town of **Seto** (pop. 120,000). The first pottery (unglazed) was produced here about 1200. The ware produced by Kato Toshiro in the 13th c. (Ko-Seto) is much prized. In the Fukagawa Shrine are two *koma-inu* figures (mythical dog-lions) attributed to Toshiro. The Kamo Shrine, to the N of the town, is dedicated to Kato Tamikichi, who introduced the Arita method of producing porcelain in 1807. The Suehiko Shrine was built for Toshiro, who is also commemorated by a monument (of porcelain) in Seto Park.

SE of Nagoya is *Mikawa Bay*, part of Mikawa Bay National Park. A good center from which to visit the park is the attractive resort of **Gamagori** (Meitetsu line from Nagoya, 1½ hours). The railway continues via *Toyohashi* to the *Atsumi Peninsula*, the most southerly part of the park (beautiful coastal scenery). From Toyohashi a bus runs via Mikawa-Tahara to **Cape Irako**, with the Irako Shrine and a cave. – Ferry to *Toba* (see under Ise-Shima National Park).

Nara

なら

Prefecture: Nara. – Population: 310,000.
Post code: J-630. – Telephone code: 0742.

 (central)
Nara-ken Tokyo Kanko Bussan Assensho,
Kokusai Kanko Kaikan,
1-8-3, Marunouchi, Chiyoda-ku,
J-100 **Tokyo**;
tel. (03) 216 5955.

HOTELS. – **Western style**: *Nara Hotel*, 1096, Takabatake-cho, 73 r., Japanese garden; *Hotel Yamatosan-so*, 27, Kawakami-cho, 51 r., Japanese garden. – **Ryokan**: *Kasuga Hotel*, Noborioji-cho, 52 r.; *People's Inn Hanakomichi*, 23, Konichi-cho, 29 r.; *Ryokan Nara Park*, Horai-cho, 27 r. – **Minshuku**: *Enraku*, 8, Konishi-cho, 50 r.; *Wakasa Ryokan*, 14, Oshiage-cho, 43 r. – YOUTH HOSTELS: *Nara YH*, Sogoundo-koen, 64, Handa-hiraki-cho, 120 b.; *YH Nara-ken Seishonen-Kaikan*, 72-7, Ikenokami, Hand-hiraki-cho, 54 b.

RESTAURANTS. – *Edosan*, 1167, Takahata-cho; *Kusanoe*, 151, Rokujo Higashi-cho; *Restaurant Garden Yamato*, 40-1, Nobioroji-cho; *Restaurant Kikusui*, 1130, Takahata Bodai-cho; *Sushitsune Honten*, 15, Hashimoto-cho.

EVENTS. – *Wakakusa-yama-yaki* (mid January), grass burning on Mount Wakakusa, with fireworks; *Setsubun* (beginning of February), Lantern Festival at Kasuga Shrine; *Oni-oi-shiki* (beginning of February), driving out of demons at Kofukuji Temple; *Omizu-tori* (beginning of March), drawing of water from sacred well, with torchlight parade, at Todaiji Temple;

Kasuga Festival (mid March) at Kasuga Shrine; *Hanae-shiki* (beginning of April), offering of flowers on Buddha's birthday at Yakushiji Temple; *Shomu-sai* (beginning of May), procession at Todaiji Temple; *Takigi-no* (mid May), performances of No plays by torchlight at Kofukuji Temple; *Lantern Festival* (mid August) at Kasuga Shrine; *On-matsuri* (mid December), procession in historical costumes at Kasuga Shrine.

TRANSPORTATION. – **Rail**: from KYOTO Kinki–Nippon private line (40 minutes); from OSAKA (Nanba Station) JNR Kinki–Nippon line (30 minutes).

Municipal Transport

There are numerous bus services from the Central Station to the principal sights in the city and surrounding area.

SIGHT	BUS STOP
Kofukuji Temple	Kencho-mae (10 minutes)
Nara National Museum	Hakubutsukan-mae (10 minutes)
Kasuga Shrine, Botanic Garden	Kasuga Taisha-mae (10 minutes)
Todaiji Temple, Mount Wakakusa	Daibutsu-mae (10 minutes)
Isuien Garden, Neiraku Museum	Hakubutsukan-mae (10 minutes)
Saidaiji Temple	Saidaiji-mae (10 minutes)
Heijo-kyuden	Heijo-kyu-ato (17 minutes)
Toshodaiji Temple	Toshodaiji-mae (14 minutes)
Yakushiji Temple	Yakushiji-mae (15 minutes)
Horyuji Temple	Horyuji-mae (40 minutes)

The city of ****Nara, celebrated as the cradle of Japanese culture, lies in central Honshu, to the S of Lake Biwa, surrounded by hills, forests and fields, with the Nara Basin extending to the S. With its wealth of ancient and historic buildings and its treasures of art it attracts more than a million visitors every year.**

Nara's historic old buildings lie in a particularly beautiful setting of which there are fine views from Mount Mikasayama. The climate varies over the year but in general is mild.

The city retains something of the atmosphere of a small town, and has practically no industry. Its best-known craft products are carved wooden dolls (*Nara-ningyo*), lacquerware (*Nara-shikki*), fans (*Nara-uchiwa*) and ceramics (*Akahada-yaki*).

HISTORY. – In the early centuries of the Empire, after its legendary foundation by Jimmu-tenno in the Yamato (Nara) basin, the site of the capital was changed after the death of each ruler: it was only during the reign of the Empress Gemmyo-tenno (661–721), in 710, that a permanent capital was established at *Heijokyo* (present-day Nara). In accordance with the town-planning principles of the Chinese T'ang era the new town, to the W of the present city center, was laid out on a rectangular grid, modelled on the layout of the Chinese capital of Ch'ang-an. With a total extent of 1¼ miles/2 km from N to S and 2½ miles/4·3 km from E to W, it was divided into an eastern and a western half by a broad street running S from the Imperial Palace. Nara rapidly developed into the political and cultural center of the country, and its importance was reflected in its population, which even in these early days reached 200,000. It remained the seat of Government for 74 years, giving its name to the **Nara period**. Under Government direction Japan adopted the Buddhist religion and was strongly influenced by the Chinese art of the T'ang period. Official embassies travelled to China, and monks came from there to teach in Japan, including Ganjin, who was invited by Shomu-tenno in 753. Subsequently various Buddhist sects gained influence in Japan, and Confucianism was also introduced, though on a smaller scale.

During the reign of the Empress Gemmyo-tenno a number of literary works were produced which are still of great value to historians – the "Kojiki", the earliest surviving work with a historical content (though its history is interwoven with legend), in 712; the "Fudoki", the earliest topography of Japan, written in Chinese script, in 713; the "Nihon-shoki", a Japanese chronicle based on Chinese models, in 720. The "Manyoshu", the oldest surviving anthology of poetry (4173 poems), was also produced during this period.

The Nara period reached its climax in the reign of Shomu-tenno (701–756), who commissioned the Daibutsu, a bronze statue of Buddha 52 ft/16 m high. The spread of Buddhism was promoted by an Imperial edict providing for the construction of provincial temples (*kokubunji*), and a special Government agency (the Shakyoshi) was set up to produce copies of Buddhist writings. Chinese influence led to the building of large temple complexes, and sculpture and painting were strongly influenced by Chinese forms and techniques, which themselves incorporated elements taken over from Indian culture. While the sculpture of the Suiko period (552–645) was still marked by severity and rigidity, the work now produced showed softer forms. Such influences are particularly evident in the Tempyo (Late Nara) period.

In 784 Kammu-tenno (737–806) transferred the capital from Nara to Nagaoka in order to put an end to the strong influence exerted on State policies by the Buddhist priesthood; but although Nara thus lost its political importance it has remained to this day Japan's leading center of culture. – In the course of time the town moved gradually eastward, so that the historic nucleus of Nara now lies on the outskirts of the modern city. – Since 1974 Nara has been twinned with the Chinese town of Xian, the ancient Ch'ang-an.

SIGHTS. – From the Central Station (JNR) Sanjo-dori, an important commercial and shopping street, leads to ****Nara Park**, the largest of its kind in Japan (1300 acres). Within the park, finely

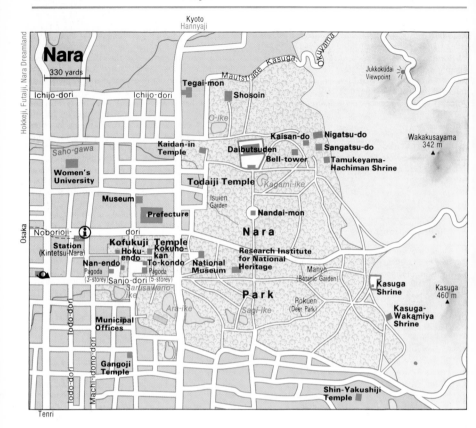

wooded with ancient trees, are many historic old buildings, and a further attraction is provided by the large numbers of tame roe deer which live here. – To the right of the entrance is *Sarusawa Pond* (circumference 1200 ft/360 m), with the five-storey pagoda of the Kofukuji Temple reflected in its waters. At the NW corner is the *Uneme Shrine*.

From the E side of the pond a path runs N to the ****Kofukuji Temple**, one of the Seven Great Temples of Nara.

Founded in 669 by Kagami-no-Himehiko, wife of Fujiwara-no-Kamatari, this was the Fujiwara family temple and the principal temple of the Hosso sect. Originally erected in Kyoto under the name of the *Yamashina-dera*, it was removed in 678 to Umasaka (S of Nara), and when the new capital was founded in 710 was transferred to its present site by Fubito, son of Kamatari, and renamed the Kofukuji. As the power of the Fujiwara family increased, so, too, did the importance of the temple, which in its heyday comprised a total of 175 buildings. Most of these, however, were destroyed during the fighting between the Minamoto and Taira families in the 12th c.

The surviving buildings can be seen from the former site of the great S gate. Among them is an octagonal hall, the **Nan-endo**, built by Fujiwara Fuyutsugu in 813 and rebuilt in 1741. Its principal treasure is a *statue of Fukukenjaku-Kannon*, carved in 1188 by Kokei, father of Unkei; also very fine are statues of the four celestial guardians and the six patriarchs of the Hosso sect. In front of the hall is a 9th c. *bronze

lantern with an inscription attributed to Kobo-daishi. – SW of this stands a three-storey ****pagoda**, a graceful structure of the Fujiwara period.

N of the Nan-endo is the ****Hoku-endo** (Northern Hall), also on an octagonal plan. This was originally built for the Empress Gensho in 721 in memory of Fubito, founder of the Kofukuji Temple, and rebuilt in 1208. It contains a wooden ***statue of Miroku-bosatsu* (1212), probably by Unkei. – To the E can be found the *Chu-kondo*, a hall built in 710 and rebuilt in 1819, with a wooden *statue of Shakyamuni.

The ****To-kondo** (East Hall), rebuilt in its original form in 1415 after repeated destructions, contains a 15th c. *statue of Yakushi-nyorai*, together with statues of Nikko-bosatsu and Gakko-bosatsu (probably 8th c.) and other sculpture.

Facing this hall, to the S, is a five-storey ****pagoda**, erected in 730 by Komyo, wife of Shomu-tenno, burned down five times and rebuilt in its original form in 1426. The second highest pagoda in Japan (164 ft/ 50 m), it is a notable example of Nara architecture; it contains statues of Amida-nyorai, Shakyamuni, Yakushi-nyorai and Miroku-bosatsu. – NE of the To-kondo is the ****Kokuhokan** or Treasury, built in 1959, which contains a variety of art treasures belonging to the temple. Particularly notable are a bronze *head of Buddha* (7th c.), a carved wooden group of the Juni-shinsho ("Twelve Celestial Generals"; Heian period), two No figures (Kongo and Misshaku), a statue of Ashura in dry lacquer technique (Early Nara period) and two **guardian figures (*Kongo-rikishi*).

To the E of the Kofukuji is the ****National Museum** (built 1895, extended 1972), which contains major works of art, particularly of the Nara period. There are periodically temporary displays of exhibits selected from the museum's large reserves.

Farther E we reach the *Research Institute for the National Heritage*, beyond which is a large red *torii* (Ichino-no torii) leading into the precincts of the Kasuga Shrine. The road, flanked by cypresses and cedars, passes the *Botanic Garden* (on left) and the *Rokuen Deer Park* (on right). In the Botanic Garden is a small stage for performances of *gagaku* and *bugaku* music. The roe deer who live in the deer park are regarded as emissaries of the gods, for according to tradition the Fujiwara who built the shrine invited the god Takemikazuchi-no-mikoto to Nara and he entered the town mounted on a roe deer. – The road to the shrine passes through the second *torii* (Ni-no torii) and continues between two rows of stone lanterns, some 3000 in all, which are lit twice a year on the occasion of the Mandoro festival. Then comes the *South Gate*, a single-storey structure of 1179, in the corridors of which hang elaborately decorated lanterns. Beyond the gateway is the **Heiden** (Cult Hall, 1650), and to the left of this the **Naoraiden** (Entertainment Hall), which dates from the same period. A flight of stone steps leads up to the Middle Gate (Chumon), from which roofed corridors lead off on both sides, enclosing the main buildings of the Kasuga Shrine.

The **Kasuga Shrine**, founded by Fujiwara Nagate (714–771), consists of four separate buildings and is dedicated to the divinities Takemikazuchi and Futsunushi and the ancestral gods of the Fujiwara family, Amenokoyane and his consort Hime-okami. The buildings are characteristic examples of the Kasuga-zukuri style, differing from early timber buildings in the red painting of the beams, the white facing of the walls and the curving roof-line. Until 1863 the buildings were pulled down every 20 years and re-erected in their orginal form, as is still the practice at the Ise Shrines; nowadays this process of renewal is confined to the roofs.

On the left stands the *Utsushidono* (Transfer Hall), in which the images of the various divinities are housed during the reconstruction of the shrine buildings. The covered passage leading from here to the main shrine, the **Nejiri-roka**, by the famous Hidari Jingoro (1594–1634), is decorated with fine carving. To the N of the Transfer Hall grows a tree, *Yadorigi*, on the trunk of which six other species have been grafted. Visitors may buy small paper "fortunes" – which may be good or bad. The paper is then tied to a branch, especially if the fortune is not a good one.

From the Kasuga Shrine another path flanked by stone lanterns runs S to the **Kasuga-Wakamiya Shrine**, probably founded in 1135, which is dedicated to the god Amenooshikumo, the son of Amenokoyane. The present buildings, in Kasuga-zukuri style, were erected in 1863.

The southern section of the low elongated Main Hall is occupied by the **Kaguraden** (Sacred Dance Hall, 1613), in which the ritual Kagura dances are performed in honor of Amaterasu, the ancestral divinity of the Imperial House. – The shrine festival *On-matsuri*, celebrated in December, is Nara's principal festival, attracting large numbers of visitors from far and wide. From the shrine a splendid procession in historical costumes wends it way through the town, and No and Kyogen plays are performed at the first *torii*.

SW of the main shrine can be found the **Treasury** (*Homotsuden*), built in 1973, which contains valuable works of art.

To the E of Nara Park rises *Mount Kasuga* (1509 ft/460 m), which is revered as the seat of the gods. The woods which cover its slopes have been untouched since time immemorial and are particularly beautiful in the fall. From the top of the hill there is a fine *view of the town and the Nara Basin.

Another good viewpoint is the grass-covered Mount *Wakakusa* (1122 ft/342 m), to the N, on which the Yama-yaki festival is celebrated in January.

Some 650 yds/600 m S of the Kasuga Shrine stands the *Shin-Yakushiji Temple**, founded by the Empress Komyo in 747 to secure the help of the gods in curing an eye complaint from which her husband Shomu suffered. The temple, a classic example of the Late Nara style, takes its name from the Healing Buddha (Yakushi) to whom it is dedicated. It contains a **statue of Yakushi-nyorai, carved from a single piece of wood, and a *statue of the Eleven-Headed Kannon, surrounded by 12 pottery figures of **guardian divinities (Juni-shinsho) – all masterpieces of Late Nara sculpture. The **Hondo (Main Hall) is the only part of the temple surviving from the Nara period; all the other buildings were destroyed at an early stage.

In the northern part of Nara Park, at the foot of Mount Wakakusa, is the **Tamukeyama-Hachiman Shrine**, founded in 749, which is dedicated to the war god Hachiman. This was probably originally built beside the Heijo Palace, to the W of the town, and was moved to its present site in 1251; the buildings now visible were erected in 1691 by a priest named Kokei. The central hall is dedicated to the Emperor Ojin (posthumously revered as Hachiman), the one on the left to his wife Hime-mikoto, the one on the right to his parents Jingu-Tenno and Chuai. To the S is the Treasury (*Hozo*), to the N the Sutra Hall (*Kyozo*).

> The **Azekura-zukuri** technique used in this shrine is a form of construction which creates a kind of "air-conditioning" system. The building is constructed of timber beams of triangular section fitted together without the use of nails. When the humidity of the air is high the wood expands, preventing air from entering the building, while in dry weather the wood shrinks and allows sufficient fresh air to enter. This produces a relatively stable climate within the building, to which the excellent state of preservation of the works of art it contains – some of them more than a thousand years old – can be attributed. This form of construction is found not only in the Tamukeyama-Hachiman Shrine but in buildings elsewhere in Japan.

To the W of the Tamukeyama-Hachiman Shrine stands the ****Todaiji Temple** (Great East Temple), one of the "Seven Great Temples of Nara". It is the principal temple of the Kegon sect of Buddhism and takes the leading place among the provincial temples (*kokubunji*) erected following Shomu-tenno's edict.

The central tenet of the Kegon sect – one of the oldest in Japan – which was founded by a Chinese priest, Dozen, in 736, is that every man can attain Enlightenment. The sect reveres the Rushana Buddha (Vairoçana), the original Buddha.

The building of the Todaiji Temple was begun in 745 at the behest of the Emperor Shomu, an ardent supporter of Buddhism. The statue of the Great Buddha (Daibutsu) was cast at Nara in 745–749, after the failure of earlier attempts made at the Shigaraki Palace S of Lake Biwa.

After its completion the temple was dedicated in 752 in the most splendid ceremony of the century, attended by Shomu (who by then had abdicated) with his wife and his daughter the Empress Koken, the entire Court and some 10,000 priests and worshippers. The head of the Buddha figure was broken off in a severe earthquake in 855 but was restored in 861. In 1180 Taira Shigehira destroyed the Great Buddha Hall (Daibutsuden), and the head and right hand of the statue were damaged by fire. The statue was restored under the direction of Abbot Chogen, and the completion of the work (1195) was celebrated in a ceremony attended by the Emperor Gotoga and the Shogun, Minamoto Yoritomo. In 1967 the Buddha Hall was burned down during a rising led by Matsunaga Hisahide. The statue was restored in 1692, the hall in 1709.

The **temple precinct** is entered by the ****Nan-daimon** (Great South Gate), a two-storey structure borne on 18 columns. Originally erected towards the end of the Nara period, it was destroyed by a typhoon in 962 and rebuilt in 1199. It is in the massive Tenjiku-yo style, which originated in India. In lateral niches in the external walls are two ***Nio statues** (guardian figures) 26 ft/8 m high, attributed respectively to Unkei and Kaikei and to Tankei. In niches in the rear

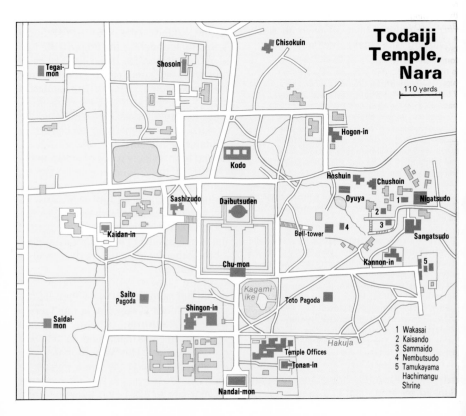

Todaiji Temple, Nara

110 yards

Chisokuin
Tegai-mon
Shosoin
Hogon-in
Kodo
Hoshuin
Chushoin
Sashizudo
Daibutsuden
Oyuya
Nigatsudo
Kaidan-in
Bell-tower
Sangatsudo
Chu-mon
Kannon-in
Saito Pagoda
Kagami-ike
Toto Pagoda
Saidai-mon
Shingon-in
Hakuja
Temple Offices
Tonan-in
Nandai-mon

1 Wakasai
2 Kaisando
3 Sammaido
4 Nembutsudo
5 Tamukayama Hachimangu Shrine

Guardian figure, Todaiji Temple, Nara

wall, standing on stone bases, are two *koma-inu figures (dog- or lion-like animals), typical examples of Chinese Sung art, which are said to be the work of a Chinese sculptor named Chinnakei.

Leading from the gate a path passes the Kagami-ike Pool (performances of Bugaku music at the Shomu-sai festival) to the **Hall of the Great Buddha (Daibutsuden). Although this has been rebuilt, following its repeated destruction, on a smaller scale (some two-thirds of the original size), it is still the largest timber building in the world (187 ft/57 m long, 166 ft/50·5 m wide, 160 ft/48·7 m high). Like the South Gate, it is in Tenjiku-yo style. At the ends of the roof-ridge are shibi (talismans designed to protect the building from fire). Within the hall is the **Great Buddha (Daibutsu), the Original Buddha, the work of a Korean sculptor, Kuninaka-no-Kimimaro. The bronze base (circumference 68 ft/20·7 m) is in the form of a lotus flower with 56 petals. The seated figure is the largest Buddha statue in Japan (53 ft/16·2 m high). 437 tons of bronze, 286 lb/130 kg of gold and 7 tons of wax were used in its casting. The raised right hand is in the semui-no-in position (mudra), the

"promise of peace", the left hand in the yogan-no-in position, the "fulfilment of wishes". The gilded wooden halo with representations of the 16 incarnations of the Buddha was added in the 17th c. The two figures in front of the statue, Nyoirin-Kannon (fulfiller of all wishes, on the right) and Kokuzo-bosatsu (divinity of wisdom and good fortune, on the left), date from the same period. In the rear part of the hall are statues of two of the four Celestial Guardians – to the left Komokuten, ruler over the West, who is depicted trampling on a demon who symbolizes all that hampers the Buddhist faith; to the right Tamonten, in a similar pose. Beside the figure of Komokuten is a model of the original temple; in front of Tamonten is a massive wooden column with a rectangular hole at ground-level. It is the popular belief that anyone who can creep through this opening is sure of admission to paradise.

Outside the Buddha Hall, to the right, is a seated figure of Binzuru, which is believed to cure any ailment if the patient touches the statue with one hand and the affected part with the other. In front of the hall is a masterpiece of Late Nara art (Tempyo period), an octagonal **bronze lantern with fine relief decoration.

330 yds/300 m W of the Buddha Hall we reach the *Kaidan-in Temple, founded in 754, several times destroyed by fire and rebuilt in its present form about 1730. In the center of the temple are statues of Shakyamuni and Taho-nyorai, in the corners **statues of the four Celestial Guardians in full armor. Keidan was originally the name given to the terrace on which priests were ordained, incorporating earth brought from China by Ganjin. Five hundred monks are said to have been ordained as priests here.

550 yds/500 m N is the Treasury (Shosoin), with the Azekura-zukuri method of "air-conditioning" (see box, p. 218). In this building (normally not open to the public) are preserved art treasures of inestimable value which originally belonged to the Emperor Shomu and after his death were presented to the Todaiji Temple by his widow and daughter. Many of the pieces of jewelry, weapons, pictures and sacred vessels come from the Middle and Near East. At the end of October and beginning of November the Treasury is ventilated, and during this period some of its contents are displayed in the National Museum in Nara. – Adjacent are two modern reinforced-concrete extensions.

To the E of the Buddha Hall stands an old *bell-tower, with a bell cast in 749, badly damaged in a typhoon in 989 and re-cast in 1239; it is the second largest bell in Japan (height 13 ft/3·9 m, diameter 9 ft/2·8 m). – Still farther E, on higher ground, is the Hall of the Second Month (Nigatsu-do), built in 752 by a priest named Jitchu, a disciple of Roben (first Abbot of the Todaiji, 689–773) and rebuilt in 1669 after a fire. The hall (not open to the public) contains two statues of the Eleven-Headed Kannon. It takes its name from the Omizu-tori water-drawing ceremony, which takes place in the second month of the lunar calendar (at present between March 1 and 14). Adjoining, to the S, is the **Hall of the Third Month (Sangatsu-do), the oldest surviving building within the temple precinct, erected by Roben in 733. The Prayer Hall (Raido) was added about 1200 (Kamakura period); the two buildings can be distinguished by the form of roof construction. The name of this hall comes from the reading of the "Hokke Sutra" (which is preserved in the hall) in the third month of the lunar calendar. In the center of the hall is the 12 ft/3·6 m high **Fukukenjaku-Kannon, a dry-lacquered statue attributed to Abbot Roben, with a crown

Great Buddha, Todaiji Temple

decked with 20,000 pearls and precious stones. It is flanked by pottery **figures of Nikko-bosatsu and Gakko-bosatsu (Nara period). To the side are **statues of Bonten and Taishakuten, also in dry-lacquer technique. Flanking the statue of Bonten are wooden *statues of Fudomyoo (on right) and Jizo-bosatsu (on left). In the four corners of the hall are **Celestial Guardians (dry lacquer).

In the rear chamber can be seen two **portable shrines (mikoshi) with figures of Benzaiten, goddess of love, and Kichijoten, goddess of fortune, and four guardian figures (dry lacquer). A pottery **figure of Shukongo-shin by Roben which is kept behind the Fukukenjaku-Kannon is shown only on the anniversary of Roben's death (December 16).

To the W of the South Gate of the Todaiji Temple lies the **Isuien Garden**, with (to the left of the entrance) the small **Neiraku Museum**, opened in 1969 (Chinese and Korean applied arts). The Isuien Garden is a landscaped garden in Shakkei style (the "borrowed landscape", in which the surroundings of the garden are incorporated in the total effect). In the nearer part of the garden are two tea-houses, the Seishuan and the Sanshutei, and a waiting-room (Teishuken). The rear part of the garden, laid out in 1899, has the South Gate of the Todaiji and Mount Wakakusa as its backdrop. On the island in the little lake is a stone from the founda-tions of the Buddha Hall; the stepping-stones are old millstones used in the manufacture of fabric dyes. In the thatched tea-house, the Hyoshintei, green tea is sometimes served.

1¼ miles/2 km outside the town center (bus service) one may visit the **Nara Dreamland**, a leisure and amusement center in Disneyland style, with "Adven-ture Land", "Fantasy Land", the "World of Yesterday and Tomorrow" and a miniature railway 2 miles/3 km long.

SURROUNDINGS of Nara

NW of the town are the excavated remains of the **Heijo-kyuden Imperial Palace** (bus from Nara Central Station, 15 minutes, or from Yamato-Saidaiji Station, 5 minutes). Originally occupying an area of 265 acres, this was the cultural and political center of the old capital of Heijokyo. When the seat of Govern-ment was transferred to Nagaoka in 784 the palace fell into ruin, and only the foundations are now visible.

The outlines of the **Daigokuden** (Hall of Cere-monies) can be traced. To the S of this there were 12 other buildings, including the **Choshuden** (As-sembly Hall). The whole complex was surrounded by a gallery or ambulatory with several gates. The ex-cavations brought to light moats, fountains and areas of paving; objects recovered during the excavations are displayed in the "Material Hall".

650 yds/600 m E of the Palace stands the *Hokkeiji Temple, founded by the Empress Komyo in the 8th c. The Main Hall was rebuilt in 1601. It contains a fine wooden **statue of the Eleven-Headed Kannon, believed to have been carved by an Indian sculptor. – Near by is the *Kairyuoji Temple, also founded by Empress Komyo. The only surviving buildings are the West Hall and Sutra Library (both partly rebuilt in the 12th c.) and a five-storey **pagoda.

NW of Yamato-Saidaiji Station is the **Akishino Temple, founded in 780. Most of the temple was burned down in 1135, only the Lecture Hall (Kodo) being spared. Later converted into the Main Hall (Hondo), this is a good example of the architecture of the Nara period. The dry-lacquer *statue of the divinity Gigeiten dates from that period; the well-known sculptor Unkei is believed to have had a hand in it. – A little way W of the station is another of the "Seven Great Temples of Nara", the **Saidaiji Temple (Great West Temple), built in 765 for Shotoku-tenno (previously the Empress Koken), the principal temple of the Shingon-Ritsu sect. Most of the buildings are modern.

The **Shakado** (Main Hall), N of the ruins of the East-ern Pagoda, dates from 1752. It contains a wooden *statue of Shakyamuni by the priest Eison (1201–90) and a statue of Monju-bosatsu of 1302. – SW of the Main Hall is another hall, the **Aizendo**, with seated figures of Aisenmyoo (1247) and Eison (Kamakura period).

The *Shiodo near the E gate has a number of *statues of the Late Nara (Tempyo) period, including the four Celestial Guardians (Tamonten in wood, the others in bronze); the figures of demons at the foot of the statues date from the foundations of the temple. There is also a 12th c. wooden statue of the Eleven-Headed Kannon. – To the E of the Main Hall is the **Shuhokan** (Treasury), with sculpture, paintings and calligraphy. The temple also possesses 12 *picture scrolls on silk with representations of guardian figures (Juni-shinsho).

NE of the temple is the tomb of the Emperor Seimu, a typical megalithic grave of the Kofun period.

To the W of the Saidaiji (Gakuen-mae Station), in a hilly and wooded region with many lakes, we find the Yamato-bunka Museum (sculpture, paintings, ceramics, lacquerware, etc. from the Asian countries).

The area SW of Nara, now a quiet agricultural region, was formerly an important intellectual spiritual center, as is shown by the presence of a number of temples which are among the oldest in the area and form an attractive contrast to the green rice-fields and peasant farms. They can be reached from Nara (Kintetsu-Nara Station) on the Nara line of the Kintetsu private rail-way to Yamato-Saidaiji, then the Kashihara line, going S.

A little way W of Amagatsuji Station is the tomb of the Emperor Suinin, a burial-mound on a keyhole plan set in the middle of a lake (Kofun period).

650 yds/600 m S of Amagatsuji Station is the **Toshodaiji Temple, the principal temple of the 30 temples of the Ritsu sect, founded in 759 by Ganjin.

The only buildings which survive from the original foundation are the Main Hall and Lecture Hall; the others are modern. – Entering by the **Nandaimon** (Great South Gate; reconstructed 1960), the visitor

Ganjin (Chinese form *Chien Chen*) was a high priest in China in the time of the T'ang dynasty who was invited to Japan by the Emperor Shomu-tenno to propagate the Buddhist faith. Ganjin set out for Japan in 742, but this and four other voyages were frustrated by pirate attacks, storms and shipwreck. During one of these voyages he lost his sight. It was not until 754, when he was 66 years old, that he finally reached Nara, where he taught in the Todaiji Temple and ordained priests. After the building of the Toshodaiji he moved to the new temple, where he died on May 6, 763.

Yakushi Trinity, Yakushiji Temple

comes to the **Kondo** (Main Hall), the largest and finest example of Tempyo architecture (49 ft/15 m by 95 ft/29 m). The pillared gallery is of classic beauty. The hall contains an 11 ft/3·3 m-high *seated statue of Rushana-butsu* (dry-lacquer technique) by two of Ganjin's Chinese pupils, T'an Ching and Szu T'o. The magnificent halo was originally decorated with 1000 small Buddha figures, of which 864 remain. To the left is a *Thousand-Handed Kannon* (dry lacquer, 18 ft/5·5 m high), to the right a *statue of Yakushi-Nyorai*, also in dry-lacquer technique, which are attributed to Ganjin's pupils Szu T'o and Jua Pao. The hall also contains two 5½ ft/1·7 m-high *wooden statues* (Bonten and Taishakuten) by Chun Fa-li and a seated wooden figure of Dainichi-nyorai (12 ft/3·7 m high) of the early Heian period.

Beyond the Main Hall we reach the **Kodo** (Lecture Hall), which was originally the assembly hall of the Heijo-kyuden Imperial Palace and was brought here when the temple was founded. The original style has been badly distorted by restoration work carried out by Chun Fa-li (759) and by later repairs. The finest piece of sculpture in this hall is the 8 ft/2·4 m-high figure of *Miroku-bosatsu* by Chun Fa-li. Note also the statues, carved from a single piece of cypress wood, of Jikokuten and Zochoten. – To the right of the Lecture Hall is a long building containing priests' quarters (*Higashimuro*, at N end) and the Cult Hall (*Raido*, S end). In front of this building is the **Drum Tower** (*Koro* or *Shariden*), where the Uchiwa-maki festival is celebrated in May.

To the E of the priests' quarters are two buildings in Azekura-zukuri technique – the **Kyozo** (Sutra Library) to the S, the **Hozo** (Treasury) to the N. The new Treasury, *Shinhozo* (1970), contains paintings, manuscripts and fragments of sculpture. – To the NW, surrounded by a wall, is the *Mieido* (Portrait Hall), which contains a dry-lacquer **statue of Ganjin** (30 in./80 cm high), carved in the year he died. The hall is open only on June 6. – From here a path leads to the *tomb of Ganjin*.

From the next railway station going S, Nishinokyo, it is a short distance to the **Yakushiji Temple** (which can also be reached by a walk of 800 yds/750 m from the Toshodaiji). Begun in 680, during the reign of the Emperor Temmu, this is – together with the Kofukuji – the principal temple of the Hosso sect.

During the construction of the temple, which lasted until 698, Temmu died and was succeeded by his wife in 687. After the transfer of the capital to Nara, in 718, the temple was moved to its present site by Asuka. It was damaged on several occasions, most severely during the Civil War of 1528.

Of the original buildings of the temple, which is one of the "Seven Great Temples of Nara", there survives only the East Pagoda; all the other buildings date from the Kamakura period or later. – The **Kondo** (Main Hall; restored 1600; rebuilt on the original foundations 1976) contains the famous *Yakushi Trinity* – a 8½ ft/2·6 m-high figure of Yakushi-nyorai (Lord of the Eastern Paradise) flanked by Nikko-bosatsu and Gakko-bosatsu. The statues, originally gilded, were blackened in a fire in 1528, and only the haloes are still gilded. The large bronze base of the central figure shows Chinese and Indian influences. All three statues date from 697, as does another *Yakushi Trinity* in the **Kodo** (Lecture Hall), beyond the Main Hall.

Obliquely opposite stands the three-storey *East Pagoda* (124 ft/37·9 m high), which is believed to have been built in 698. The smaller intermediate roofs give it the appearance of having six storeys. It is topped by a metal pinnacle (*sorin*). The pagoda is the only surviving example of Buddhist architecture of the Hakuho period.

Behind the pagoda is the *Toindo* (East Hall, 1285), which contains a 6 ft/1·9 m-high *bronze figure of Sho-Kannon* (or Kudara-Kannon) of about 600, a gift from the King of Paeckche (Korea). – On the other side of the pagoda is the **Bussokudo**, with a stone bearing a footprint of Buddha (*Bussoku-seki*).

Pagoda, Yakushiji Temple

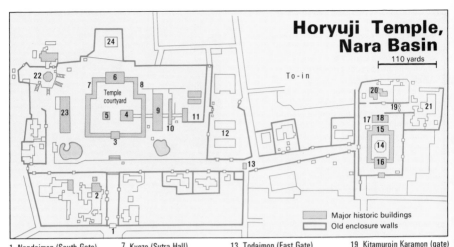

Horyuji Temple, Nara Basin

110 yards

To-in

Temple courtyard

Major historic buildings
Old enclosure walls

1 Nandaimon (South Gate)
2 Temple offices
3 Chumon (Middle Gate)
4 Kondo (Main Hall)
5 Five-storey Pagoda
6 Daikodo (Lecture Hall)

7 Kyozo (Sutra Hall)
8 Shoro (bell-tower)
9 Shoryoin
10 Tsumashitsu
11 Kofuzo (Small Treasury)
12 Daihozoden (Great Treasury)

13 Todaimon (East Gate)
14 Yume-dono
15 Eden (Picture Hall)
16 Raido
17 Shodo (bell-tower)
18 Dempodo

19 Kitamuroin Karamon (gate)
20 Kitamuroin Hondo
21 Chuguji Temple
22 Saiendo
23 Sangyoin
24 Kami-no-mido

To the right of the Main Hall is the *bell-tower*, with a Korean °bell. – The **Hozoden** (Treasury), which is open only from January 1 to 15 and from October 20 to November 10, contains two fine paintings of Kichijo-ten, goddess of beauty, and a Chinese priest.

**Nara Basin. – The Nara Basin (also known as the Yamato Basin) which extends to the S of the town is watered by tributaries of the River *Yamato*, which flows W from the plain and reaches the sea S of Osaka. In this area are numbers of other temples dating from the early period of Japan.

The **Hokkiji Temple** can be reached from Nara by a train from the Kintetsu-Nara Station which runs via Yamato–Saidaiji and Tamagatsuji (see above) to Kintetsu–Koriyama (15 minutes), from which it is a 20-minute bus ride to the temple. This was founded in 638 by a priest named Fukuryo, who thus fulfilled the last wish of Shotoku-taishi (574–622). It is also known as the Okamoto Temple, after the site of Shotoku-taishi's palace where the temple was built. The three-storey **pagoda, dating from 685, is in the style of the Early Nara period.

From here it is a 15-minute walk SW to the **Horinji Temple**, built in 621 by a son of Shotoku-taishi. The dominating feature of the *Kondo* (Main Hall) is the seated wood °statue of Yakushi-nyorai in the Toribusshi style, influenced by Chinese and Korean models. The hall also contains statues of Kichijo-ten, Sho-Kannon and Bishamonten of the Late Heian period. – In the *Kodo* (Lecture Hall) are painted wooden °statues of the Eleven-Headed Kannon 16 ft/ 4·8 m high), Kokuzu-bosatsu and Jizo-bosatsu.

¾ mile/1 km SW is the oldest completely preserved temple complex in Japan, the ****Horyuji Temple**, a magnificent example of the architecture of the Asuka period (552–645) with masterly works of art covering the whole range of Japanese history.

Yomei-tenno, the first Buddhist Emperor of Japan, was overtaken in 586 by a serious illness and ordered a statue of the Healing Buddha (Yakushi-Nyorai) to be made, but died before it was completed. In order to fulfil his wish Shotoku-taishi, the Emperor's son, caused the Horyuji Temple to be built in 607. As one of the "Seven Great Temples of Nara" this became the great center of Buddhism in Japan, from which the new faith was carried to all parts of the country. In those days the road from the Imperial Court to the coast passed the site of the temple.

The Horyuji, principal temple of the Shotoku sect, comprises 45 buildings erected between the Asuka and Momoyama periods, 17 of which are classified as "major national treasures". – The temple complex is divided into two parts – the To-in or Higashi-no-in (the eastern part), with 14 buildings, and the Sai-in or Nishi-no-in (the western part), with 31 buildings.

The main entrance to the **Sai-in** and to the whole temple precinct is the ****Nandaimon** (Great South Gate), which has been rebuilt several times, most recently in the Muromachi period, in 1438. From here

Horyuji Temple

Guardian figure, Horyuji Temple

a path leads past the temple offices to the **Chumon (Middle Gate), which dates from the foundation of the temple. The gate, with roofed corridors (*kairo*) on either side, differs from other gates in its use of columns to support the structure. Flanking the entrance, which is divided by columns, are two *guardian figures* (Nio), the right-hand one red as a symbol of light, the left-hand one black as a symbol of darkness. The two figures date from 711, and were thoroughly restored in 1964. – The corridors opening off the Middle Gate enclose the inner courtyard of the temple, on the right-hand side of which is the **Kondo (Main Hall), a two-storey wooden structure measuring 30 ft/9·1 m by 24 ft/7·3 m and 58 ft/17·8 m high. Dating from the Asuka period, this is claimed to be the oldest surviving wooden building in the world.

The inner walls of the hall were decorated with famous frescoes, comparable in style and execution with those in the Ajanta caves (India); but these were unfortunately destroyed by fire in 1949; there are photographs of the frescoes in the Great Treasury. In the hall are a number of 7th c. statues, the best known of which is the bronze **Shaka Trinity, cast by Tori-busshi in 623. In this group the principal figure, Shakyamuni, is flanked by Yakuo-bosatsu and Yakujo-bosatsu. To the right of the Trinity is a bronze **statue of Yakushi-nyorai*, cast in 607 for Yomei-tenno, to the left a bronze *statue of Amida-nyorai* (1232) and wood statues of the goddess Kichijo-ten and the war god Bishamonten, both dating from 1078. There are also wood **statues of the four Celestial Guardians* of the Late Asuka period, the oldest surviving figures of this kind.

On the left-hand side of the courtyard is a five-storey **pagoda 105 ft/32 m high dating from the foundation of the temple. At the corners of the roofs are talismans intended to ward off fires; in the lower part is an additional intermediate roof (*mokoshi*). On the ground floor are four terracottas depicting scenes from the life of Buddha – on the E side "Conversation between Yumia and Monju"; on the S side "Paradise of Miroku"; on the W side "Cremation of Buddha"; and on the N side "Buddha's Entry into Nirvana".

On the N side of the courtyard is the **Daikodo (Lecture Hall), the original structure of which was destroyed by lightning in 925 and rebuilt in 990. It contains a gilded wooden **Yakushi Trinity (the central figure being flanked by Mikko-bosatsu and Sakko-bosatsu) and *statues of the four Celestial Guardians.

To the W of the Lecture Hall is the **Kyozo (Sutra Hall), of the Tempyo period, with a wooden statue of the Korean priest Kanroku, who came to Nara in 607. – The bell-tower, **Shoro, was rebuilt in the Heian period; the bell is believed to date from the 8th c.

Immediately E of the courtyard stands the **Shoryoin (rebuilt 1121), dedicated to the soul of Shotoku-taishi, formerly the priests' quarters. In this hall is a **statue of Shotoku-taishi*, clad in the sumptuous ceremonial garments of the T'ang period and flanked by statues of various dignitaries, including the priest Eji.

Beyond the immediately adjoining building, the *Tsumashitsu*, we reach the small Treasury, the *Kofuzo, which contains some pieces of Buddhist sculpture, followed by the two buildings of the Great Treasury, the **Daihozoden**, built in 1941 on the 1320th anniversary of Shotoku-taishi's death. This contains outstanding works of art of different periods. Particularly notable are the figure of **Kudara-Kannon*, a Korean work whose smooth lines contrast with the rigid forms of Japanese sculpture of the same period; a wooden figure of the **Nine-Headed Kannon*; and a figure of **Yumetagai-Kannon*, who turns bad dreams into good ones (dating, like the Nine-Headed Kannon, from the Hakuho period). In the southern building of the Great Treasury are items from the Main Hall, including the **Tamamushi-no-zushi*, a miniature shrine 8 ft/2·4 m high which belonged to the Empress Suiko. The shrine owes its name to the *tamamushi*, a species of insect (*Chrysochroa elegans*) whose multi-colored wings were originally used to decorate certain parts of the shrine (no longer visible). The shrine has openwork bronze mounts and is decorated on all sides by Buddhist paintings on a black ground (on the front doors Celestial Guardians, on the side doors Bosatsus, on the back pagodas, stars and a phoenix). The shrine is a good example of the painting and decorative art of the Asuka period, as is another **miniature shrine* which belonged to Tachibana, Komyo's mother, and which contains an Amida Trinity of gilt-bronze.

SE of the Great Treasury is the **Todaimon (Great East Gate), the entrance to the other section of the temple precinct, the **To-in**, on a site occupied until 622 by Shotoku-taishi's Ikaruga Palace. After Shotoku's death the palace fell into ruin, and in 739, on the Emperor's orders, was replaced by the East Temple dedicated to Shotoku's family. – After passing along the corridor (*kairo*) the visitor comes to the **Yume-dono (Hall of Dreams), the oldest building in Japan on an octagonal plan, with a handsome bronze roof ornament. Shotoku-taishi is said to have meditated here when he met a difficult passage during study of the sutras; then – so the legend goes – a wise man from the East would appear to him and explain the passage which was troubling him. – The most notable work of art in this hall is the gilded wooden figure of **Guze-Kannon (or Nyoirin-Kannon), resembling Shotoku and said to have been carved by him (although all that can be said with certainty is that it is a work of the Tori-busshi school). The statue can be seen only from April 11 to May 5 and from October 22 to November 3. The hall also

Yume-dono (Hall of Dreams)

contains a *statue of the priest Gyoshin Sozu* (dry lacquer, Tempyo period) and a *pottery figure of the priest Dosen* (Heian period).

On the N side of the courtyard stands the *E-den (Picture Hall), with scenes from Shotoku's life. Adjoining this on the right is the *Shariden (Hall of the Ashes of Buddha), which, like the **bell-tower to the left, dates from the Kamakura period.

Immediately N of the Picture Hall we reach the **Dempodo (Prayer Hall), formerly the residence of Dowager Empress Tachibana, which came into the possession of the temple in 739. The hall contains sculpture of the Late Nara period – in the centre an *Amida Trinity (dry lacquer), flanked by two other wood *Amida groups. There is also some wood sculpture of the Heian period.

In the NE corner of the To-in is the Chuguji Temple, a nunnery of which the abbesses were originally members of the Imperial family. The temple contains an expressive wood figure of **Nyoirin-Kannon 6 ft/ 1.8 m high, said to be the work of Shotoku, and the **Tenjukoku Mandara, a fragment of the oldest known work of embroidery in Japan (7th c.). The mandara, originally 16 ft/4·8 m long, was worked by Shotoku's widow and her ladies-in-waiting and depicts scenes from life in the Asuka period.

The eastern part of the Nara basin is most conveniently reached on the JNR Sakurai line from the Central Station, Nara. – 6 miles/10 km E of Nara is Tenri (pop. 65,000), headquarters of the Tenri-kyo sect (founded 1838), with a Museum of Folk Art. 1 mile/1·5 km E of the station stands the Isonokami Shrine, with a two-storey gate and a fine Cult Hall. The shrine preserves a sword which according to legend was presented by the divinity Takemikazuchi-no-mikoto to the first Emperor of Japan, Jimmu.

The railway continues S to Miwa (40 minutes from Nara), near the Omiya Shrine (or Miwa Myojin), at the foot of Mount Miwa (1532 ft/467 m). Dedicated to the divinity Omonoushi, the shrine is claimed to be one of the oldest in the country, founded in the 1st c. B.C. It is linked with the Isonokami Shrine by an old road running past prehistoric burial-mounds and ancient settlements. – The next station on the line is Sakurai, from which a bus (25 minutes) can be taken to the Hase-dera Temple.

This temple, founded in 686, is the principal center of the Buzan school of the Shingon sect. The Main Hall, originally built by the Emperor Shomu and rebuilt in 1650, contains a 26 ft/8 m-high wooden statue of the Eleven-Headed Kannon. In front of the temple are a No stage and the Treasury (museum). – The temple is

a popular destination for excursions, particularly during the flowering period of the cherry trees (April–May) and the peonies. From the terrace there are fine *views of the surrounding hillsides.

From Sakurai the Osaka line of the Kintetsu private railway runs E to Muro-guchi-Ono Station, 5 miles/ 8 km S of which is the *Muroji Temple of the Shingon sect, built in 681 and restored by Kobo-daishi in 824. Within the beautiful temple precinct is a **pagoda 53 ft/16·2 m high. The temple is said to have been specially built for women, since access to the holy mountain of Koya-san (see separate entry) was long forbidden to them; and the Muroji accordingly became known as the "women's Koya-san".

The **Kondo (Main Hall) contains a wooden figure of **Juichimen-Kannon and seated figures of **Nyoirin-Kannon and **Shaka-nyorai, all dating from the Early Heian period.

From Sakurai there is also a bus service into the southern part of the Nara Basin. It is a half-hour run to the Tanzan Shrine, at the foot of Mount Tonomine, founded in 701 by a priest named Joe, eldest son of Fujiwara-no-Kamatari, and several times rebuilt (most recently in 1850). Near the entrance to the shrine stands a 13-storey *pagoda, unique of its kind in Japan. The interior of the shrine – which is known as the "Nikko Shrine of Kansai" – is notable for its simplicity. – Behind the pagoda is a path leading up to the summit of Mount Tonomine, on which is the tomb of Kamatari.

To the W of Sakurai is Kashihara (pop. 106,000; Sakurai railway line to Unebi Station), at the foot of Mount Unebi (653 ft/199 m), on which the legendary Jimmu-tenno is said to have built his palace; here, too, is his burial-mound. Near by is the Kashihara Shrine, dedicated to Jimmu-tenno and his wife Himetatara-Isuzu-hime, which was built in 1889 with timber from the Imperial Palace in Kyoto. Beyond this is the Empress's tomb. – NE of the shrine is the Archaeological Museum (Yamato-rekishikan), with finds from the Nara Basin, including Neolithic material.

A little way S of the museum is Kashihara-jingu Station (Yoshino line of the Kintetsu private railway), from which a bus can be taken (20 minutes) to the *Tachibana Temple of the Tendai sect, built on the supposed site of Shotoku-taishi's birthplace. Of the original large complex only the Main Hall (Kondo: rebuilt 1864) survives; it contains a wood *statue of Shotoku (Muromachi period). – To the N is the Asuka Temple or Angoin Temple (also reached by bus from Sakurai, 15 minutes), formerly the priests' quarters of the Hokoki Monastery, founded in 596 and moved to Heijokyo (Nara) in 718. The temple contains a *bronze statue of Shakyamuni (by Tori-busshi, 606).

From Kashihara-jingu there is also a bus service to the Okadera Temple (formerly known as the Ryugaiji), ¾ mile/1 km E of the Tachibana Temple. Originally the palace of the Emperor Tenchi, this was handed over to the Hosso sect in 663. It contains a pottery figure of *Nyoirin-Kannon (Heian period) and a seated wood figure of the priest Gien (d. 728), of the Nara period. – To the S of the Okadera two burial-mounds have been excavated (bus from Kashihara-jingu, 15 minutes). The Ishibutai Tomb (probably that of Soga-no-Umako) dates from the 7th c. SW of this tomb is the Takamatsuzuka Tomb, also of the 7th c., in which grave-goods showing Chinese and Korean influences were found; reproductions in the nearby Asuka-shiryokan (museum).

The return to Asuka can be on the Kintetsu private line from Asuka Station (19 miles/30 km).

Narita

なりた

Prefecture: Chiba. – Population: 72,000.
Post code: J-286. – Telephone code: 0476.

ⓘ (central)
**JNTO New Tokyo Airport
Tourist Information Center,**
Airport Terminal Building,
Narita Airport;
tel. 32 87 11.

(local)
Chiba-ken Tourist Information Center,
2, Ichibamachi,
J-280 **Chiba;**
tel. (0472) 22 9175.

HOTELS. – **Western style:** *Hotel Nikko Narita,* 500, Tokko, 535 r.; *Narita View Hotel,* 700 Kosuge, 515 r.; *Narita Prince Hotel,* 560, Tokko, 321 r.; *Holiday Inn Narita,* 320-1, Tokko, 254 r.; *Narita Airport Rest House,* in Passenger Terminal Building, Narita Airport, 210 r.; *Hotel New Tsukuba,* 847, Hanazaki-cho, 15 r. – **Ryokan:** *Ogiya,* 474, Saiwai-cho, 29 r.; *Wakamatsu Honten,* 355, Hon-machi, 14 r.

EVENTS. – *First Temple or Shrine Visit* (beginning of January), in Shinshoji Temple, Sogo-Reido, etc.; *Setsubun* (beginning of February), at Shinshoji Temple; *Cherry Blossom Festival* (beginning of April); *Hanamatsuri* (beginning of April), Buddha's birthday; *Gion-matsuri* (beginning of July), ceremonial procession; *Chrysanthemum Show* (November), at Shinshoji Temple and Sogo-Reido.

TRANSPORTATION. – **Rail:** from TOKYO (Keisei-Ueno Station) Keisei line (1¼ hours). – **Bus:** from New Tokyo International Airport JNR bus or Chiba-Kotsu bus to Narita Station (30 minutes).

The town of Narita, E of Tokyo, is noted for the Shinshoji Temple, one of the great Japanese pilgrimage centers, visited by more than seven million worshippers every year. In recent years the town has acquired increased importance from its proximity to Tokyo's new international airport: since the opening of the airport its population has increased by a third.

SIGHTS. – ¾ mile/1 km from the JNR station, by way of the lively and colorful **Omote-sando** shopping quarter, is the **Naritasan-Shinshoji Temple**.

The temple, dedicated to the light god Fudo, was founded in 939, during a rising instigated by Taira Masakado in the area of the present-day prefectures of Chiba and Ibaraki. The Emperor Sujaku had the statue of Fudo in the Jingoji Temple at Kyoto brought to Kozugahara (to the W of the Shinshoji) in order to secure the god's help in defeating the rebels. When the rebellion came to an end in 940 with the death of Masakado a temple was built in Kozugahara to house the statue, and in 1705 this was moved to its present site.

The most notable features within the 50 acres of the temple precinct are the *Niomon Gate,* the **Hall of the Three Saints,** the **Buddha Hall,** the **Hondo** (Main Hall, built 1963–68 in traditional style), a *bell-tower* and a three-storey *pagoda.* The temple attracts particularly large numbers of worshippers at New Year and the Setsubun festival (beginning of February).

Adjoining the temple precinct is **Naritasan Park** (41 acres), which is seen at its most beautiful when the cherry and plum trees are in blossom. In the park is a **Historical Museum,** in which are displayed some of the temple's treasures and archaeological material from the Boso Peninsula.

From the JNR station there are buses (20 minutes) to the **Sogo-Reido Shrine,** dedicated to Kiuchi Sogo (or Sakura Sogo, 1612–53). In defiance of a ban on direct appeals to the Shogun, Sogo presented to Tokugawa Ietsuna a petition on behalf of the peasants suffering from a failed harvest and high taxes. Although his mission was successful, he and five members of his family were condemned to death and executed. Scenes from Sogo's life are depicted in a memorial hall, the *Sogo Goichidai-Kinenkan;* adjacent to the hall is a small museum.

SURROUNDINGS of Narita

15 miles/25 km NE of the town, in the wide delta of the *Tone* (Japan's third longest river), is the river port of *Sawara* (pop. 49,000; JNR Narita line). ¾ mile/1 km SE of the station can be seen the house of the geographer Ino Tadataka (1745–1818), who surveyed the whole coastline of Japan (mementoes). – 2½ miles/4 km E of the station (bus, 15 minutes), set amid ancient trees, is the **Katori Shrine,** dedicated to the war god Futsunushi-no-mikoto. Its foundation is attributed to the first Emperor, Jimmu-tenno; the present buildings date from about 1700. From the rear terrace there are extensive *views of the **Suigo-Tsukaba Quasi National Park,** which can be reached from Sawara by bus (in summer also round trips by boat).

NE of Sawara, in a magnificent old cedar forest, stands the **Kashima Shrine,** dedicated to the war god Takemikazuchi-no-mikoto (bus from Katori Shrine via Sawara and Itako, 1¼ miles). Like the Katori Shrine and the nearby *Ikisu Shrine,* this is an ancient pilgrimage shrine. The buildings date from 1604–19; the museum contains a collection of arms and armor. A stone known as Kaname-ishi, to the rear of the shrine, is popularly believed to hold down a giant catfish, the cause of earthquakes.

Boso Peninsula. – To the S of Narita, bounding the E side of Tokyo Bay, the **Boso Peninsula** extends into the Pacific. This extensive agricultural area, mainly supplying the capital, is known as the "larder of Tokyo". Land is being reclaimed off the NW coast to permit the extension of the Keiyo industrial zone. The coastal regions in the southern part of the peninsula form the **Minami-Boso Quasi National Park**.

The best starting-point for a trip along the coast is the town of **Chiba**, on the W side of the peninsula (30 minutes from Narita on JNR Narita or Kashima line), from which the JNR Uchibo line runs S down the coast.

At **Kisarazu** (also reached by car ferry from Kawasaki) is the Shojoji Temple (440 yds/400 m W of station). – Near **Sanukimachi** Station is Mount *Otsubo* (394 ft/120 m), topped by a 184 ft/56 m-high statue of Kannon, which can be climbed by an internal staircase (*view of Tokyo Bay). There is also a bus from the station (30 minutes) to Mount *Kano* (1155 ft/352 m), with a 140 ft/42 m-high outlook tower from which there are *views of Tokyo Bay, the Fuji-Hakone region and the Nikko Hills. Near by stands the **Jinyaji Temple**, said to have been built by Shotoku-taishi (rebuilt in 16th–18th c.). – 10 minutes' walk away is the **Shiratori Shrine**, from which there is a view of the "Ninety-nine Valleys" (Kuju-kutani).

At **Kanaya** (also reached by ferry from Yokosuka on the Miura Peninsula) is a cableway up Mount *Nokogiri* (1079 ft/329 m), on the summit of which are an old temple, caves and some 1300 Buddhist sculptures.

The Uchibo railway line reaches its most southerly point at **Tateyama**. From the station there are buses (45 minutes) to **Shirahama**, at the southernmost tip of the peninsula; fine *view of the coastline from *Cape Nojima*.

The line now crosses the peninsula to **Awa-Kamogawa** on the E coast, with the Kyonin-ji Temple, founded in 1281 (bus from station, 5 minutes). Off the coast are a number of wooded islands. At Matsubara Beach we find the "Kamogawa Sea World" leisure center, with a dolphin show, etc. – From here the JNR Sotobo line runs N.

At **Awa-Amatsu**, on Mount *Kiyosumi* (1257 ft/383 m; bus, 25 minutes), is the Kiyosumi Temple, probably founded in 771, in which Nichiren, founder of the Nichiren sect, spent his novitiate. The Main Hall dates from the late Edo period. Within the temple precinct can be seen a bronze statue of Nichiren.

Awa-Kominato was the birthplace of Nichiren. The Tanjoji Temple (bus from station, 5 minutes), which is dedicated to him, was founded in 1276. The present buildings date from the early 19th c.

Katsuura is a fishing port (deep-sea fisheries) with an interesting morning market which has a tradition going back 300 years.

Naruto

なると

Prefecture: Tokushima. – Population: 65,000.
Post code: J-772. – Telephone code: 08868.

ⓘ (local)
Tourist Section of Naruto City,
170, Aza-higashiyama,
Minamihama, Muyacho;
tel. 5 1111.

HOTELS. – **Western style**: *Naruto Koen Hotel*, 190, Tosadomariura, Naruto-cho, 27 r.; *Naruto Prince Hotel*, Naruto-cho, 25 r.; *Hotel Otani*, Naruto-cho, 14 r. – **Ryokan**: *Naruto*, 45-4, Muya-cho, 42 r.; *Mizuno*, 101, Okazaki, 33 r., beach; *Shichishuen*, 65-8, Tosadomariura, Naruto-cho, 19 r. – YOUTH HOSTEL: *Naturo YH*, 149-12, Kitatono-cho, Hayasaki, Muyacho, 50 b., beach.

TRANSPORTATION. – **Rail**: from TAKAMATSU and TOKUSHIMA JNR Kotoku and Naruto lines (change at Ikenotani; 1½ hours and 30 minutes). – **Bus**: from TAKAMATSU (1½ hours); from TOKUSHIMA (30 minutes). – **Boat**: from KOBE hovercraft (1½ hours); from FUKURA (island of Awaji; 1 hour).

The port of Naruto lies at the NE tip of Shikoku, separated from the smaller island of Awaji by the **Naruto Strait (*naruto* = "roaring gateway"). In this arm of the sea, only 1400 yds/1·3 km across, which links the Inland Sea with the Pacific, the action of the tides gives rise to strong counter-currents and whirlpools.

SIGHTS. – ¾ mile/1 km E of the station lies the port area of **Okazaki**. Here, too, is the **Castle** (restored), which now houses a Museum of Ethnography. – The *Konaruto Bridge*, 482 yds/441 m long, links the town with the island of *Oge*, to the NE (bus from station, 20 minutes), on which is **Naruto Park**. From the northern tip of the island and from Mount *Naruto* (cableway from Senjojiki) there are impressive *views of the turbulent waters of the **Naruto Strait.

The different levels of the Inland Sea and the open Pacific give rise to violent whirlpools up to 65 ft/20 m in diameter and to strong currents reaching speeds of up to 11 knots. – Boat trips to the whirlpools from the harbor.

The *Naruto-Ohashi Bridge* (1780 yds/1630 m long), at present under construction, will link the islands of Naruto and Awaji (see separate entry).

SURROUNDINGS. – There is a railway line from Naruto to **Bando**, 7 miles/11 km SW, where German prisoners of war were confined during the First World

War. A **German House** (*Doitsu-kan*) was opened in 1972, with mementoes of the prisoner of war camp and a collection of German folk art. – Adjoining the German House stands the **Ryozenji Temple**, the first of the 88 pilgrimage temples of Shikoku. Farther N, at the foot of Mount Oasa (1775 ft/541 m), is the Oasahiko Shrine.

Niigata

にいがた

Prefecture: Niigata. – Population: 460,000.
Post code: J-950. – Telephone code: 0252.

ⓘ (central)
Niigata-ken Tokyo Kanko Bussan Assensho,
Kokusai Kanko Kaikan,
1-8-3, Marunouchi, Chiyoda-ku,
J-100 **Tokyo**;
tel. (03) 215 4618.

HOTELS. – **Western style:** *Bandai Silver Hotel*, 1-3-30, Bandai, 210 r.; *Hotel Niigata*, 5-11-20, Bandai, 126 r., Japanes garden; *Italia-ken*, 7-1574, Nishibori, 100 r., beach; *Niigata Silver Hotel*, 1-1-25, Benten, 98 r.; *Niigata Toei Hotel*, 1-6, Benten 2-chome, 46 r.; *Minato Hotel*, 1-3-12, Hanazone, 57 r.; *Hotel New Kohaku*, 1-2-6, Akashi, 37 r. – YOUTH HOSTEL: *Niigata Hiyoriyama YH*, 5932-591, Nishi-funamicho, 15 b.

RESTAURANTS. – *Atarashiya*, Furumachi-dori, Rokuban-cho; *Ikinaritei*, 573, Nishi-Ohata-cho; *Kinshabu*, 620, Nishi-Ohata-cho; *Nabejaya*, Hachibancho, Higashihori-dori.

EVENTS. – *Niigata Festival* (end of August), with great firework display.

TRANSPORTATION. – **Air:** from TOKYO (Haneda Airport), 50 minutes; from OSAKA (1 hour). – **Rail:** from TOKYO (Ueno Station) to Omiya (30 minutes), then JNR New Joetsu-Shinkansen line (1¾ hours), also JNR Tohoku, Jo-etsu and Shin- etsu lines (4¼ hours); from OSAKA JNR Tokaido, Kosei, Hokuriku and Shin-etsu lines (7¼ hours).

Niigata, chief town of its prefecture, is the largest port on the W coast of Honshu. The city is traversed by the River Shinano, which here flows into the Sea of Japan. The industrial installations (petrochemicals, etc.) lie to the E of the river, with the commercial quarter and the residential districts to the W. Many canals flow through the town, which is sheltered on the seaward side by a line of sandy hills. – After the opening-up of Japan in the 19th c. Niigata developed a considerable trade with Siberia.

SIGHTS. – From the station there is a bus (10 minutes) to the **Gokoku Shrine**, dedicated to the victims of the Second World War. From a viewpoint near the shrine there is, in clear weather, an extensive prospect extending as far as the island of Sado.

On the left bank of the Shinano is **Hakusan Park** (bus from station, 15 minutes), with the *Hakusan Shrine*. With its zoo and its various sports facilities, the park is the largest recreation area in the vicinity of Niigata. To the NW of the park is the *University*.

Near Terao Station on the JNR Echigo line (also reached by bus from Niigata Station, 25 minutes) is the **Niigata-yuen**, a flower garden which is at its best in spring (April–May); fine view of the Sea of Japan. – Another good viewpoint is Mount *Hiyoriyama*.

The **Cultural Museum** (*Hoppo-bunka-hakubutsukan*) can also be reached by bus from the station (45 minutes).

SURROUNDINGS. – Part of the coastal region to the S of the town falls within the **Sado-Yahiko Quasi National Park** (coach excursions from Niigata; also service buses to Yahiko). N of **Yahiko**, in a grove of cedars, stands the *Yahiko Shrine* (Lantern Festival on July 25). A cableway ascends Mount *Yahiko* (2093 ft/638 m), from which there are fine °views of the surrounding area.

To the S of Niigata is **Shirone** (pop. 35,000; private railway line from Niigata), which attracts many visitors to its Kite festival, the Takoage, at the beginning of June. This is a contest with huge paper kites (up to 23 ft/7 m long), in which the opposing parties, posted on opposite sides of the river, try to bring down their opponents' kites.

See also the island of **Sado**.

Nikko

にっこう

Prefecture: Tochigi. – Population: 25,000.
Post code: J-321-14. – Telephone code: 0288.

ⓘ (central)
Tochigi-ken Tokyo Kanko Busshan Assensho,
Kokusai Kanko Kaikan,
1-8-3, Marunouchi, Chiyoda-ku,
J-100 **Tokyo**;
tel. (03) 215 4050.

HOTELS. – **Western style:** *Nikko Lakeside Hotel*, 2482, Chugushi, 100 r., Japanese garden, beach; *Nikko Kanaya Hotel*, Kami-Hatsuishi-cho, 82 r., Japanese garden, SP; *Nikko Prince Hotel*, Shobugahama, Chugushi, 20 r., SP; *Chuzenji Kanaya Hotel*, 2482, Chugushi, 32 r. – **Ryokan:** *Nikko Green Hotel*, 9-19, Honmachi, 57 r.; *Namma Hotel*, at Yumoto-onsen (to NE), 73 r.; *Izumiya Ryokan*, at

Chuzenji-onsen (to W), 39 r.; *Nikko Grand Hotel*, Yumoto-onsen, 38 r.; *Oku-Nikko Onsen Hotel*, Yumoto-onsen, 24 r.; *Konishi Ryokan Bekkan*, Kamihatsuishi, 24 r. – YOUTH HOSTELS: *YH Yumoto Yama-No-le*, at Yumoto (to NE), 80 b.; *Nikko YH*, 1140, Tokorono, 50 b; *Nikko Daiyagawa YH*, 1075, Nakahatsuishi, 29 b.

EVENTS. – *Yayoi-matsuri* (mid April), transfer of portable shrines from the Futaarasan Shrine to the Takino-o and Hongu Shrines; *Gohan-shiki* (beginning of May), a festival at the Rinnoji Temple derived from the traditional ceremonies for the reception of princely visitors; *Ennen-no-mai* (mid May), cult dance in Rinnoji Temple imitating the old Dengaku dance of the Kamakura period; *Spring Festival* at Toshogu Shrine (mid May), with portable shrines, parades in old armor and archery contests; *Tohai-matsuri* (beginning of August), night pilgrimage from Lake Chuzenji to the Futaarasan Inner Shrine on Mount Nantai; *Autumn Festival* at Toshogu Shrine (mid October).

TRANSPORTATION. – **Rail**: from TOKYO (Ueno Station) JNR Nikko line (2¼ hours); from TOKYO (Asakusa Station) Tobu private line to Tobu-Nikko (sometimes necessary to change at Shimo-Imaichi; 1¾ hours). – **Bus**: several services in Nikko National Park.

The town of ** Nikko, situated on the edge of the Nikko National Park, is renowned for its sumptuous tombs. A popular Japanese catch-phrase is "Never say 'magnificent' [*kekko*] until you have seen Nikko."

The River *Daiya* separates the old town, to the E, from the new town (Nishi-machi or Iri-machi) on the W bank, with the principal sights.

SIGHTS. – From the JNR and Tobu line stations, which lie close to one another, it is a 15-minute walk to the red-lacquered Sacred Bridge, the * *Shinkyo* or Mihashi Bridge, which crosses the Daiya to the temples and shrines, set amid beautiful cedars.

This area of woodland and trees along the roads leading to the shrines were planted between 1625 and 1651 by Matsudaira Masatsuna, who – lacking the resources of other daimyos who contributed to the building of the shrine – made this more modest contribution to the mausoleum for Tokugawa Ieyasu. Some 13,000 of these trees still survive.

The Sacred Bridge (92 ft/28 m long, 24 ft/ 7·2 m wide), a reconstruction of the original bridge of 1636 which was destroyed by a flood in 1902, marks the spot where, according to the legend, a priest named Shodo (735–817) crossed the river on the backs of two gigantic snakes. Formerly used only by the Shogun and his suite, the bridge is now open only on shrine festivals. Visitors use the new bridge adjoining to reach the **Hongu Shrine** (or

Futaarasan-Hongu Shrine), one of the oldest of the Nikko shrines, founded by Shodo in 784. The present buildings, however, date only from the late 17th c., as does the **Shihonryuji Temple** beyond the shrine. In the Main Hall of the Shihonryuji are a figure of the Thousand-Handed Kannon and statues of Godaison and Shodo (the latter believed to be a self-portrait).

Taking the path which runs left beyond the bridge, we come into the pilgrims' road, *Omotesando*, leading to the Toshogu Shrine. This comes first to the * **Rinnoji Temple** of the Tendai sect, probably founded in 848 by a priest named Ennin (794–864; posthumously given the name of Jikaku-daishi) and modelled on a temple on the sacred mountain, Mount Hiei. The Abbot's Lodging (Hombo) and its garden can be seen by previous appointment. In the main hall, the *Sambutsu-do* (Hall of the Three Buddhas; 1648), are gilded statues, 26 ft/8 m high, of Amida-nyorai, the Thousand-Handed Kannon and Bato-Kannon (this last with a horse's head on her forehead, symbolizing her role as the patroness of animals) and portraits of Abbots Tenkai (1536–1643; posthumously named Jigen-daishi) and Ryogen (912–985; posthumously named Gansan-daishi). To the N, on higher ground, stands a 43 ft/13 m-high bronze column (*Sorinto*), set up by Tenkai in 1643 to ward off evil spirits. To the right of the column is the **Gohotendo**, a hall dedicated to the divinities Daikokuten, Bishamonten and Benzaiten.

The pilgrims' road continues to the ** **Toshogu Shrine**, Nikko's most important shrine. The 22 buildings to be seen here were erected at a time when architecture and applied art had reached a peak of achievement. Artists were summoned from all over Japan to play their part in creating a complex of supreme magnificence.

Some 15,000 craftsmen were employed on the construction of the Toshogu Shrine, most of them coming from Kyoto and Nara, where there was a great flowering of architecture at that period. The result was a complex of buildings with an over-lavish profusion of decoration, incorporating all the sumptuousness of the preceding Momoyama period. The practice of renewing the buildings of a shrine every 20 years meant that work was almost continuously in progress.

On his death in 1616 Tokugawa Ieyasu was buried on Mount Kunozan, but a year later, in accordance with his testament, his remains were moved to their last

Nikko, in its beautiful wooded setting

resting-place at Nikko. In the same year the Emperor granted him the posthumous style of Tosho-daigongen ("Incarnation of the Bodhisattwa illuminating the East"). The construction of his mausoleum was begun by his grandson Iemitsu only in 1634 and was completed in two years. Until the fall of the Shogunate in 1868 the superintendence of the mausoleum was the responsibility of a Prince of the Imperial House – who resided, however, in Edo (Tokyo) and visited Nikko only three times a year. – The shrine had a narrow escape from destruction during the Meiji Restoration, when a group of Tokugawa supporters entrenched themselves here. Fortunately, however – thanks to the mediation of Itagaki Taisuke – the buildings were evacuated without a fight.

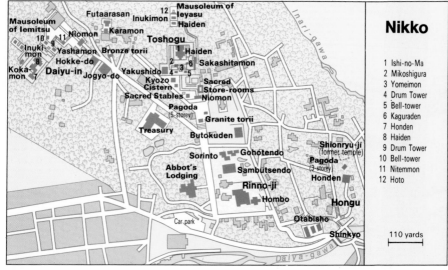

Nikko

1 Ishi-no-Ma
2 Mikoshigura
3 Yomeimon
4 Drum Tower
5 Bell-tower
6 Kaguraden
7 Honden
8 Haiden
9 Drum Tower
10 Bell-tower
11 Nitemmon
12 Hoto

110 yards

The visitor comes first to the *Staircase of the Thousand* (Sennin-ishidan), the farthest point to which ordinary people were formerly admitted. Beyond this is a 28 ft/8·4 m-high granite *torii*, with an inscription in the name of the Emperor Go-Mizunoo (1596–1680). To the left can be seen a five-storey **pagoda** of 1818. The staircase then continues up to the main gateway, the **Nio-mon** or *Omote-mon*, which gives access to a courtyard with *three sacred storehouses* and the stables for the sacred horses. The uppermost storehouse has a polychrome relief on the gable depicting an elephant, said to have been carved by Kano Tanyu (1602–74) after some literary model (elephants being unknown in Japan at that time). On the stables are carved figures of mon-keys, including the famous group of three ("See no evil, hear no evil, speak no evil"). At the far (NW) end of the courtyard is the granite basin of the sacred fountain, and beyond this the Sutra Library (**Kyozo**). Flanking the path are stone and bronze lanterns presented by former daimyos. A flight of steps leads up to the middle courtyard, with a *bell-tower* on the right and the *Drum Tower* on the left. One of the

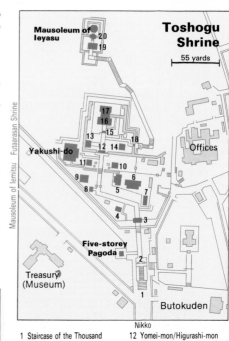

Toshogu Shrine

55 yards

Mausoleum of Iemitsu   Futaarasan Shrine

Mausoleum of Ieyasu

Yakushi-do

Offices

Five-storey Pagoda

Treasury (Museum)

Butokuden

Nikko

1 Staircase of the Thousand
2 Granite torii
3 Nio-mon (Omote-mon)
4 Stables of Sacred Horses
5 Upper store-room
6 Middle store-room
7 Lower store-room
8 Fountain
9 Kyozo (Library)
10 Bell-tower
11 Drum Tower
12 Yomei-mon/Higurashi-mon (Sunlight Gate/ Twilight Gate)
13 Mikoshi-gura
14 Kagura-den
15 Kara-mon
16 Haiden (Cult Hall)
17 Honden (Main Hall)
18 Sleeping cat
19 Haiden
20 Inuki-mon

In the Rinno-ji Temple, Nikko

bronze lanterns, presented by Holland in 1636, has the Tokugawa coat of arms upside-down. The bell was a gift from Korea. To the left of the Drum Tower is a large hall, the **Yakushi-do** (a reconstruction of the original, burned down in 1961). – At the entrance to the inner courtyard is the sumptuously decorated **Yomei-mon** ("Sunlight Gate"), which only highly placed and unarmed samurai were allowed to use. The gate is also called the "Twilight Gate" (Higurashi-mon) – the idea being that anyone seeing it is so fascinated that he remains contemplating it until twilight falls. The two-storey structure, supported on

Five-storey pagoda, Toshogu Shrine

(*tamagaki*) has a lower part of stone and an upper part of carved and painted woodwork with metal facings. Just within the gate is the *Haiden (Cult Hall), with portraits by Tosa Mitsuoki (1617–91) of 36 poets whose works are preserved in a manuscript by the Emperor Go-Mizunoo. The side rooms were used by the Shogun and his suite and by the Abbot of the Rinnoji Temple. – From here, by way of the **Ishi-no-ma* ("Stone Chamber" – so called because of its stone paving), we pass into the *Honden (Main Hall; 52 ft/16 m long, 33 ft/10 m wide, 46 ft/14 m high), which consists of the *Heiden* (room for offerings), the *Naijin* (inner room) and the *Nainaijin* (innermost room). In this last chamber can be seen the lavishly decorated and gilded shrine (Gokuden) in which Tokugawa Ieyasu is revered as a divinity and Toyotomi Hideyoshi and Minamoto Yoritomo as subsidiary gods. In the corridor to the right of the Main Hall is a famous wood-carving of a sleeping cat which is attributed to Hidari Jingoro. Beyond this we reach a handsome gate, the *Sakashita-mon*, which even highly placed samurai were not permitted to use.

From here a flight of 200 stone steps leads up to the **Mausoleum of Ieyasu**, with the *Inuki-mon* gate and, in front of this, two bronze *koma-inu* (dog- and lion-like creatures). Beyond the gate is the tomb, in the form of a small pagoda (rebuilt in 1683 after an earthquake).

12 columns, is overcharged with carving, lacquerwork and gilding. On the front is a tablet bearing its name in the hand of the Emperor Go-Mizunoo. The two ceiling-paintings of dragons are by Kano Tanyu and Kano Yasunobu (17th c.). In the interior is a column with bas-reliefs in the wrong place – a deliberate imperfection designed to ward off the envy of evil spirits (the "evil-averting column", *mayoke-no-hashira*).

Beyond the gate, on the left, is the **Mikoshi-gura**, a hall in which the portable shrines used on festival occasions are kept. To the right are the **Kagura-den** (the hall for cult dances) and the shrine offices. The entrance to the shrine proper is the **Kara-mon**, a Chinese-style gate, mainly in white and gold with fine carved decoration. The enclosure wall of the shrine

Between the five-storey pagoda at the entrance to the shrine and the main gate (Nio-mon) the road to the *Futaarasan Shrine branches off on the left.

The Futaarasan Shrine, founded by Shodo in 784 and rebuilt in 1619, is dedicated to the divine couple Onamuchi and Tagorihime and their son Ajisuki-takahikone, the divinities of Mount Nantai (formerly called Mount Futaarasan), to the W of Nikko. It consists of the Main Shrine, **Honsha**; an upper shrine, **Oku-miya**, on the summit of the hill; and the Middle Shrine, **Chugushi**, on Lake Chuzenji, built for the convenience of pilgrims who could not climb the hill.

The shrine consists of a *Cult Hall*, a Chinese-style gate (*Kara-mon*) and the *Honden* (Main Hall), where in return for an appropriate offering the Kagura cult dance will be performed by young girls.

Guardian figure, Toshogu Shrine

Yomei-mon gate, Toshogu Shrine

To the S of the Futaarasan Shrine are two halls belonging to the Rinno-ji Temple, the **Hokke-do** and the **Jogyo-do**, known as the Futatsu-do (Twin Halls). Built in 848 on the model of a building on Mount Hiei, they contain Buddhist statues from the Toshogu Shrine which were removed from that shrine during the Shinto renaissance of the Meiji period. – To the S, on Mount *Daikoku*, is another hall belonging to the Rinno-ji, the **Jigen-do**, dedicated to Tenkai (1536–1643), Chief Priest of Nikko and the confidant of Tokugawa Ieyasu. On the way to this we pass the *Amida Hall** (on left), the **Sutra Hall** (on right) and a *bell-tower*. Beyond the Cult Hall, which is surrounded by a wall, is the tomb of Tenkai.

Kego Falls, Lake Chuzenji

To the W of the main complex lies the **Daiyuinbyo**, the Mausoleum of Iemitsu, the 3rd Shogun.

Although this mausoleum was built only 16 years after the Toshogu Shrine, the trend towards the simpler style of the Edo period can already be seen. The colors are restricted to black and gold.

Beyond the first gate (*Nio-mon*) is a second gate (*Nitem-mon*), a two-storey structure with statues of the Buddhist gods Komokuten and Jikokuten (in niches in outer walls) and the wind and thunder gods (niches in interior). – In the middle courtyard are a *bell-tower* and a *Drum Tower*. Continuing through the third gate, *Yasha-mon* (also called Botam-mon, "Paeony Gate"), with representations of four Buddhist divinities, and the fourth gate (*Kara-mon*), in Chinese style, we come into the inner courtyard. In this are the *Cult Hall** and, linked with it by a corridor (*Ai-no-ma*), the *Main Hall** (*Honden*), which contains a seated figure of Iemitsu. At the entrance to the innermost court is the *Koka-mon*, a gate in the style of the Ming period, followed by another gate (*Inuki-mon*), beyond which is the inner Cult Hall and, on a higher level, the bronze tomb of Iemitsu.

SE of the Mausoleum of Iemitsu stands the **Treasury**, with many works of art from the various shrines.

The road W from the Futaarasan Shrine passes the *Takino-o Shrine**, with the tomb of the priest Shodo. Near the entrance is the *Shirai-no-taki* (waterfall).

SURROUNDINGS of Nikko

To the W of the town extends the *Nikko National Park** (543 sq. miles/1407 sq. km), which with its mighty peaks, ancient forests, wide expanses of moorland, lakes and waterfalls is one of the most beautiful and most visited regions in Japan.

There are numbers of waterfalls N and NW of Nikko. It is a 1½ hours' walk (bus service in summer) to the *Kirifuri-no-taki* (good view from observation plat-

form). Farther N, on the slopes of Mount *Maruyama*, lies a winter-sports area (several lifts). – To the W of the town (bus to Tanozawa stop, then a 40-minute walk) are the *Jakko Falls* (also called the Nunobiki Falls).

There is a bus service to the western part of the National Park. The road via *Umagaeshi* reaches *Lake Chuzenji**, below Mount *Nantai* (8150 ft/2484 m). On the eastern shore, at *Chuzenji-onsen*, are the *Kegon Falls* (330 ft/100 m high). This is a very popular holiday area; the autumn coloring is particularly fine on the S side of the lake, with the little towns of *Teragasaki* and *Matsugasaki*. On the E side is the *Chuzenji Temple* (also called the Tachiki-Kannon Temple), a dependency of the Rinno-ji Temple in Nikko; it contains a figure of the Thousand-Handed Kannon by Shodo. – The ascent of the extinct volcano of *Nantai* starts from the Middle Shrine (Chugushi), a dependency of the Futaarasan Shrine, with a fine Cult Hall (Heiden) and Main Hall (Honden). The crater region (440 yds/400 m in diameter) can be reached in about 4 hours; a small charge is made for the ascent. Near the summit is the Innermost Shrine (Okumiya).

From Chuzenji-onsen the bus route follows the N shore of the lake to *Jigokuchaya*, near which are the *Ryuzu Falls*. – The road then continues over the *Senjugahara Plateau*, with its rich Alpine vegetation, to *Nikko-Yumoto-onsen*, a popular summer and winter sports resort on **Lake Yunoko**, which offers excellent fishing. It then goes over the *Konsei Pass* (6641 ft/2024 m), descends to the **Ozegahara Plain**, a great expanse of moorland, and comes to *Lake Ozenuma*, at the W end of the National Park.

The north-eastern part of the park is also easily reached from Nikko by way of the health resort of *Shiobara-onsen*, which lies 15 miles/25 km N below Mount *Takahara* (to S) and the Nasu Range (to N). – The two peaks of Mount **Takahara**, *Keicho* (5794 ft/1766 m) and *Shaka* (5889 ft/1795 m), from which there are magnificent *views* of the mountain world, can be climbed from *Oku-Shiobara* (distance 5 miles/8 km).

At the foot of the **Nasu volcanoes** extends the resort area of *Nasu-onsenkyo*, with the resorts of *Nasu-Yumoto, Kita, Benten, Omaru, Sandogoya, Takao* and *Itamuro*. – The volcano region is reached on the *Nasu*

Plateau Toll Road. Kakkodaira is the starting-point of the relatively easy ascent (cableway to Tenguhana) of Mount **Chausu** (or *Nasu* 6290 ft/1917 m), from the summit of which there is a route to Mount *Asahi* (6244 ft/1903 m).

Noto Peninsula
のと

Prefecture: Ishikawa.

(central)
Ishikawa-ken Tokyo Kanko Bussan Assensho,
Kokusai Kanko Kaikan,
1-8-3, Marunouchi, Chiyoda-ku,
J-100 **Tokyo**;
tel. (03) 231 4030.

(local)
Ishikawa-ken Tourist Information Center,
2-1-1, Hirosaka,
J-920 **Kanazawa**;
tel. (0762) 61 1111.

HOTELS. – IN WAJIMA. – **Western style**: *Okunoto Grand Hotel Takasu-en*, 31-6, Aza, 2-Tsukada-cho, 120 r.; *Hotel Yashio*, 1, Sodegahama, Fugeshi-cho, 36 r.; *Young Inn Wajima*, 1-27, Kawai-cho, 26 r. – **Ryokan**: *Sosogi Ryokan*, A-35, Sosogi, Machino-machi, 47 r., beach; *Hosenkaku*, 2 Yada, Sugihira-machi, 43 r.; *Choju Kaku Bekkan Yonehisa*, 31-6, Aza, 2-Kawai-cho, 35 r., beach. – YOUTH HOSTELS: *Wajima Chorakuji YH* (temple), 7-104, Shinbashi-dori, 95 b.; *Konzoji YH* (temple), 32, Kanakura-ebu, Machino-machi, 60 b.; *Sosogi-Kajiyama YH*, 4-1, Sosogi-Kibe, Machino-machi, 60 b.

TRANSPORTATION. – **Rail**: from NAGOYA JNR Hokuriku line to Takaoka (4 hours), from there JNR Johana line to Shokawa Lakes and JNR Himi line to Himi; from OSAKA (Central Station) JNR Hokuriku line to KANAZAWA (3¼ hours), then JNR Nanao line via Nanao and Wakura to Anamizu (2 hours: from here JNR Noto line to Suzu, 1¼ hours) and Wajima (20 minutes). – **Bus**: from Suzu via Noroshi, Otani and Sosogiguchi to Wajima.

The Noto Peninsula reaches far out into the Sea of Japan on the N coast of central Honshu. Its western part is a green and hilly region with a rugged coastline and a harsh climate; the E side, with its many bays and inlets, is more sheltered. Much of the beautiful *coastal **region is included in the Noto Peninsula Quasi National Park.**

At the SE end of the peninsula, near Toyama Bay, is **Takaoka** (pop. 175,000), the industrial and commercial center of the region. Opposite the station is *Sakurababa Park*, from which a 200-year-old avenue of cherry trees leads to *Takaoka Park*, with the meagre remains of Takaoka Castle. – There is a bus service (1 hour) to the gorge of the River *Shokawa*, S of the town, with numerous man-made lakes (excursion boats).

The town of **Hakui** (pop. 29,000), on the *Chirihama* coast (W side of peninsula), is an important traffic junction on the railway from Kanazawa (see separate entry), a town noted for its silks. To the N of the town, near the sea, is the *Keta Shrine*, with a handsome Main Hall; and a short distance away from this is the *Myojoji Temple* of the Nichiren sect, with a fine Cult Hall (Kigando), Founder's Hall (Kaisan-do) and five-storey pagoda. Both of these can be reached by bus in about 20 minutes from Hakui Station.

To the N of Chirihama's 5 mile/8 km-long beach of white sand lies the Noto-Kongo area, 9 miles/15 km of rocky coast with picturesque rock formations (bus from Hakui).

From Hakui the JNR Nanao line runs NE to the lively port and commercial town of **Nanao** (pop. 50,000), a naval base of the Edo period which is now an important shipbuilding center, with yards belonging to the Kawasaki Corporation.

In *Nanao Bay*, to the N of the town, is the wooded island of **Noto** (boat service).

3 miles/5 km NW of Nanao, on *Cape Ben-ten*, is the well-known health resort of **Wakura-onsen**, with hot springs at temperatures of up to 194 °F/90 °C, a good center for excursions in the beautiful and much-indented coastal region. – Farther N is the little port of **Ogi** (bus from Anamizu, on the Nanao Railway; also boat from Nanao, 3 hours), near the beautiful *Tsukumo Bay*.

The town of **Wajima**, on the N coast (Nanao railway line), long noted for its lacquerware, is the port of departure of boat trips to the island of *Hekurajima*. It has an interesting morning market.

The island of **Hekurajima**, 30 miles off the coast (boat, 2 hours), is frequented in summer by large numbers of fishermen from Wajima in quest of shellfish and seaweed. Women divers (*ama*) frequently take part in the work.

There are buses from Wajima to the *Sosogi* (or Oku-Noto-Kongo) coastal region, to the NE, with its picturesque rock formations. In this area can be seen *Tokikunike*, one of the largest farmhouses in Japan (area 6720 sq. ft/624 sq. m). It was built during the Early Edo period by descendants of Taira Tokikuni, who was exiled to this region by Minamoto Yoritomo. – Near this, in the direction of the sea, is a *Regional Museum* (lacquerware).

Oga Peninsula
おが

Prefecture: Akita.
 (central)
Akita-ken Tokyo Kanko Bussan Assensho,
Tetsudo Kaikan,
1-9-1, Marunouchi, Chiyoda-ku,
J-100 **Tokyo;**
tel. (03) 211 1775.

(local)
Akita-ken Tourist Information Center,
4-1-1, Sanno,
J-010 **Akita;**
tel. (0188) 60 1702.

HOTELS. – IN OGA. – **Western style**: *Oga Hotel*, 13-1, Aza Kusakihara, Kitaura-Yumoto, 75 r., thermal bath, beach; *Oga Prince Hotel*, 70, Aza Ichinomorishita, Kitaura-Yumoto, 47 r., thermal bath, beach; *Oga Kanko Hotel*, 21, Aza Kusakihara, Kitaura-Yumoto, 42 r., thermal bath, beach. – **Ryokan**: *Hakuryukaku*, 86, Aza Kusakihara, Kitaura-Yumoto, 47 r., thermal bath, beach; *Manseikatu*, 37 r., thermal bath, beach; *Yuzankaku*, 27 r., thermal bath, beach. – **Minshuku**: *Miyajima-so*, 33, Aza Nukisawa, Togahama Shioya, 54 r., SP. – YOUTH HOSTELS: *Oga YH*, 85-1, Nakazato, Kitaura-Yumoto, 120 b., thermal bath; *Oga Chorakuji YH* (temple), Monzen, Funakawa-minato, 80 b., beach.

EVENTS. *Namahage* (end of December), parade of young men wearing demon masks.

TRANSPORTATION. – **Rail**: from TOKYO (Ueno Station) JNR Ou line to AKITA (7½ hours), then JNR Oga line to Oga (1½ hours) or Oga-onsen (45 minutes). – **Boat**: excursions from Monzen to Toga (50 minutes; May–October only).

The rocky *Oga Peninsula, 25 miles/ 40 km NW of Akita on the NW coast of Honshu, was formerly the hilly S end of a spit of land which extended NE almost to Noshiro. The Hachirogata Lagoon which it formerly enclosed has been drained and is now an attractive area of green rice-fields traversed by canals. The narrowest point of this almost exactly triangular peninsula, just to the W of Mount Kampu (1165 ft/

355 m), is only some 6 miles/10 km across. The steep´ W coast extends for 15 miles/25 km from Cape Nyudo in the N to Cape Shioze in the S. The highest peaks are Honzan (2349 ft/ 716 m), Kenashi (2208 ft/673 m) and Shinzan (1873 ft/571 m).

The rocky coast, deeply eroded by the sea, which in this area is often stormy, is a region of rugged stacks and cliffs, caves, natural arches and other picturesque rock formations. At many places fresh seafood is offered for sale, for the rocky promontories afford good fishing. A beautiful panoramic road winds its way along the *Oga-nishi-kaigan* corniche; the best view of the coastal scenery, however, is to be had from the sea (boat rental).

SIGHTS. – The road from Akita (see separate entry) comes first to the town of **Oga** (pop. 39,000), on the S coast of the peninsula. A short distance away, in a picturesque cove, is the fishing village of *Funakawa* (boat rental).

On the beautiful W coast is **Monzen**, from which during the season (May–October) there are boat trips to Toga, near Cape Nyudo (1¼ hours); other round trips can be arranged. Half an hour's walk from Monzen is the *Akagami-Goshado Shrine* – an excursion which involves climbing 999 steps.

Legend has it that the steps were built by demons who were to have their will with the local pretty girls if they completed a thousand steps by dawn. They were unable, however, to build the thousandth step.

From Monzen there are coach trips along the panoramic road to the N. A pleasant stopover is *Oga Suizokukan*, in beautiful Toga Bay (Aquarium). The health resort of **Oga-onsen**, to the N, is also an attractive place to stay. – On *Cape Nyudo* is a lighthouse.

The most interesting local custom is the *Namahage*, a traditional practice followed in all the towns and villages on the peninsula on December 31. The name comes from *nama*, the mark left on a certain part of the anatomy by sitting too long by the fireside, and *hage*, "remove".

Young men in shaggy straw cloaks and fearsome demon masks go round knocking at every door. The master of the house receives them in traditional festive garb; and after they have bowed to the household altar they begin to make threatening noises and growl, "Any lazy layabouts here?". Only after they have been appeased with rice-cakes and sake do they move on to the next house.

Ogasawara Islands (Bonin Islands)

See under Tokyo

Okayama

おかやま

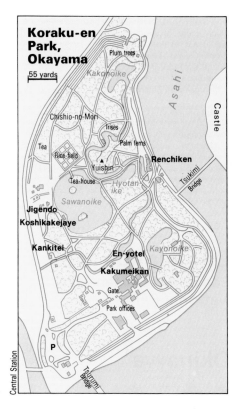

Koraku-en Park, Okayama

55 yards

Prefecture: Okayama. – Population: 552,000.
Post code: J-700. – Telephone code: 0862.

ⓘ (local)
Okayama-shi Kanko Information,
Okayama-eki,
(Central Station);
tel. 22 2912.

HOTELS. – **Western style**: *Okayama Royal Hotel*, 2-4, Ezu-cho, 200 r.; *Okayama Kokusai Hotel*, 1-16, 4-chome, Kadota Honmachi, 194 r., Japanese garden, SP; *Okayama Plaza Hotel*, 116, Hama, 85 r., beach; *Hotel New Okayama*, 25-1-1, Ekimae-cho, 82 r.; *Okayama Grand Hotel*, 2-10, Funabashi, 31 r.; *Okayama Business Hotel*, 1-1-1, Minamigata, 78 r.; *Okayama Park Hotel*, 2-5-12, Tamachi, 61 r.; *Okayama New Station Hotel*, 18-9, Ekimoto-machi, 44 r. – **Ryokan**: *Shinmatsunoe*, Ifuku-cho, 49 r. – YOUTH HOSTEL: *YH Okayama-ken Seinen Kaikan*, 1-7-6, Tsukura-cho, 65 b.

RESTAURANT. – *Koraku*, 2-1-25, Marunouchi.

TRANSPORTATION. – **Air**: from TOKYO (Haneda Airport), 2 hours. – **Rail**: from TOKYO (Central Station) JNR Shinkansen line via OSAKA (Shin-Osaka Station), 4¼ hours.

The town of Okayama lies in western Honshu on both banks of the River Asahi, which flows into the Inland Sea in Kojima Bay. It is the chief town of a prefecture and its economic and cultural centre. Bounded on the N by the foothills of the Chugoku Range, it is a good base from which to explore the beautiful surrounding area.

The city's industries include engineering, textiles and chemicals as well as the traditional craft of porcelain manufacture (Bizen-yaki).

SIGHTS. – 1 mile/1·5 km E of the station (bus) is the ****Koraku-en Park**, one of the three most celebrated landscaped gardens in Japan (the others being at Kanazawa and Mito). Commissioned in 1687 by Ikeda Tsunamasa, the local feudal lord, and completed in 1700, it is a typical example of a pleasure garden of the school of Kobori Enshu (1579–1647).

Within an area of 28 acres it contains tea-pavilions, pools, waterfalls and numbers of pine, maple, cherry and plum trees. The backdrop to the garden is formed by the **Castle**, beyond the river (Tsukimi Bridge), also known as "Crow Castle" (U-jo) on account of the black coloring of its walls. Of the original 16th c. Castle there survive only two outer towers; the rest was rebuilt in 1966 after its destruction during the Second World War.

1¼ miles/2 km NW of the station one reaches the *Ikeda Zoo*, with many species of native Japanese animals. From here a cableway runs up Mount *Kyoyama* (outlook tower).

Higashiyama Park 2 miles/3·5 km SE of the station offers fine *views of the city and Kojima Bay to the SW.

SURROUNDINGS. – 5½ miles/8·5 km W (JNR Kibi line) is **Kibitsu**, with the *Kibitsu Shrine*, dedicated to the legendary Prince Kibitsuhiko, which is believed to have been founded in the 4th c. The present buildings, erected in 1425, are in the Kibitsu-zukuri style characteristic of the Kibi region.

A bus runs S from Okayama along a 1704 yd/1558 m-long dike across the mouth of Kojima Bay to **Uno**, the port of **Tamano** (which lies farther W). From here there are boat services to Takamatsu (see separate entry) on Shikoku and to the island of Shodo (see separate entry). – 5 miles/8 km W of Uno is *Shibu-*

kawa Beach (bus, 25 minutes), a beach of white sand which is one of the most beautiful on the Inland Sea; it has extensive recreational facilities and a *Museum of the Sea* with an aquarium. – Farther W is Mount *Washuzan* (436 ft/133 m), with *views of the Inland Sea and the port of **Shimotsui** (ferry service to Marugame on Shikoku).

9 miles/14 km E of Okayama (JNR Ako line, 20 minutes) we reach **Saidaiji**, with the *Saidaiji Temple* of the Shingon sect, founded in 777. Here in February is celebrated the festival of Hadeka-matsuri (or Eyo, "Festival of the Naked Ones"), at which young men clad only in a loincloth go through a ritual purification ceremony in the River *Yoshii* at night and then try to catch one of the luck-bringing pieces of wood thrown into the darkness by the priests.

Oki Islands
See under Daisen-Oki
National Park

Okinawa
おきなわ

Prefecture: Okinawa.
Area of island: 484 sq. miles/1253 sq. km.
(i) (central)
Okinawa-ken Tokyo Kanko Bussan Assensho,
Kokusai Kanko Kaikan,
1-8-3, Marunouchi, Chiyoda-ku,
J-100 **Tokyo**;
tel. (03) 231 0848.

(local)
Okinawa Prefecture Federation of Sightseeing,
Sightseeing Building,
42-1, Asahi-machi,
J-902 **Naha**;
tel. (0988) 62 4716.

HOTELS. – IN NAHA. – **Western style**: *Okinawa Harbor View Hotel*, 2-46, Izumizaki, 345 r.; *Okinawa Grand Castle*, 1-132-1, Yamakawa-cho, Shuri, 305 r., SP; *Naha Tokyu Hotel*, 1002, Ameku, 280 r., SP; *Maruyama Kanko Hotel*, 3-6-10, Akatsuki, 73 r.; *Kanko Hotel Asato*, 455, Naha, 71 r., beach; *Pacific Hotel Okinawa*, 3-5-1, Nishi, 380 r.; *Naha Grand Hotel*, 228, Matsuo, 137 r.; *Hotel New Okinawa*, 266, Matsuo, 84 r. – **Ryokan**: *Green House*, 2-9-2, Nishi, 13 r., beach. – YOUTH HOSTELS: *Naha YH*, 51, Onoyama-cho, 100 b.; *YH Harumi-so*, 2-22-10, Tomari, 40 b.; *YH Tamazono-so*, 54, Asato, 30 b.

IN OKINAWA. – **Western style**: *Koza Kano Hotel*, 823, Moromisato, 87 r. – IN NAGO. – **Ryokan**: 115-3, Kise, 13 r., beach. – IN KUNGAMI. – YOUTH HOSTEL: *Maeda-Misaki YH*, 357, Yamada, Onna-son, 50 b., beach.

EVENTS. – *Juri-uma* (mid January), procession, with dances, at Naha-Tsuji; *Haryusen* (beginning of May),

boat race and pleas for good fishing at Tomari, Naha and Itoman; *Eisa* (mid July), dance festival for men in Okinawa; *Tug-of-War* (mid August) at Itoman, with rope 550 yds/500 m long; *Izaihu God Ceremony* (every 12 years; last in 1977) on Kudakajima ("island of the gods"), 4 miles/6 km E of southern Okinawa (women catch and smoke sea-snakes, *irabu*).

TRANSPORTATION. – **Air**: from TOKYO (Haneda Airport), 2½ hours; from OSAKA (2 hours); from FUKUOKA (1¼ hours). – **Bus**: from Naha International Airport to city center (15 minutes). – **Boat**: from TOKYO (46 hours); from OSAKA (38 hours); from KAGOSHIMA (20 hours).

****Okinawa lies some 300 miles S of Kyushu in a curving string of islands which separates the Pacific from the East China Sea. The prefecture of Okinawa includes not only the main island of Okinawa but also some 60 smaller islands with a total area of 922 sq. miles/2388 sq. km, taking in the Okinawa group, the Daito Islands far to the E and the Miyako and Yaeyama groups to the S. The name Ryukyu, which dates from the T'ang period, is applied to the Okinawa, Miyako and Yaeyama groups.**

The islands lie in a zone of subtropical climate with a mean annual temperature of 73°F/23°C and a rainy period in May and June. Summer temperatures last from March to November; in the fall there are frequent typhoons.

Most of the islands are of volcanic origin and surrounded by coral reefs, which color the water in varying hues according to their size and constitution, and with their abundance of tropical fish form ideal diving grounds. A number of nature parks and national parks have been established in the islands. – In 1975 the International Exposition of the Sea ("Expo '75") was held on Okinawa.

The main sources of revenue are fishing, agriculture, petrochemicals and tourism. Traditional craft products include *bingata* (a batik-printed fabric), *bashofu* (a fabric woven from plant fibers which is used in the making of kimonos) and coral jewelry.

MYTH and HISTORY. – According to legend Tenshin, ruler of all worlds, sent the divinity Amamikiyo down to earth, which was then entirely covered by water, and Amamikiyo brought from heaven stones and earth, from which he formed the islands.

There are various theories about the origin of the population of the islands; but there are strong indications that the first settlers were incomers from South-East Asia or the Pacific area. Finds of pottery point to

Okinawa – a coral island in the Pacific

a connection with the Japanese heartland during the Jomon period, and certain linguistic resemblances have also been identified.

The islands were known to Chinese seamen from the 3rd c. B.C. During the 12th and 13th c. three kingdoms were established, one of which submitted to the overlordship of the Chinese Ming dynasty in 1372. In the early 15th c. the three kingdoms were united, and extensive trading connections were established with China and Japan, and later with Korea and South-East Asia. As a result various cultural innovations reached Japan by way of the islands.

The period of rule by the House of Sho which began in 1429 and lasted for more than 400 years brought no political stability, since the islands remained within the sphere of interest of both China and Japan. In 1609 the Daimyo of Satsuma province, Shimazu, gained control of the islands, and the exploitation which now began led to increasing impoverishment. The Okinawa Islands were not fully incorporated in the Japanese Empire until 1879, after the Royal House of Ryukyu had been displaced.

In the closing months of the Second World War the islands were taken by American forces after bitter fighting. Thereafter the United States established large military bases; and although the islands were returned to Japan in May 1972, American units are still stationed there.

Okinawa

The main island of **Okinawa**, lying between latitude 26° 10' and 26° 50' N and between longitude 127° 40' and 128° 20' E, is the largest of the Ryukyu group, with an area of 484 sq. miles/1253 sq. km. The N of the island is hilly (Yonahadake, 1634 ft/498 m), and the main settlements

are concentrated in the flatter south. Some four-fifths of the population live within the built-up areas of Naha and Okinawa.

The chief town of the prefecture, **Naha** (pop. 300,000), the administrative, cultural and communications center of the southern Japanese islands, lies in SW Okinawa at the mouth of the River *Kokuba*. The town was completely destroyed during the Second World War and was rebuilt after the war in modern style.

The city's principal traffic artery is *Kokusai-o-dori*, a street 1 mile/1·6 km long lined with shops, department stores and restaurants. Between the harbors of Naha and Tomari stands the **Naminoue Shrine**, dedicated to the three ancestral gods of the Japanese Imperial House; view of the coast and the Kerama Islands. A short distance SE is the **Gokokuji Temple** of the Shingon sect, with a monument to a Protestant missionary named Bettelheim, from Pressburg (now Bratislava), who came to Naha in 1846, stayed there for several years and translated the New Testament into Japanese.

1¼ miles/2 km E is the **Sogenji Temple**, dedicated to the kings of Ryukyu, which was destroyed during the Second World War. All that remains is a stone gate, the *Sekimon*, which was restored in 1955. – Near by are the old potters' workshops of **Tsuboya** which are still in operation.

On a low hill 4 miles/6 km E of the town stands the *Shurei-no-mon*, a reconstruction (1958) of the original 16th c. gate. This was the second of six gates belonging to Shuri Castle, seat of the royal dynasty of Ryukyu from 1429 to 1879. – 220 yds/200 m W is the *Tama-udon, burial-place of the Sho family. Here, too, is a stone gate, the *Sonohiyan Utaki* (built 1511, restored 1957), where the kings of Ryukyu came to pray. – In the vicinity are the **Benzaiten Temple** (founded 1502, rebuilt 1968) and parts of the *Enryakuji Temple*, which dates from 1492. To the N of the Shurei-no-mon we find the **Okinawa Prefectural Museum** (folk art, etc.).

7½ miles/12 km S of Naha lies the port of *Itoman*, a deep-sea fishing center and scene of the annual Haryusen boat race. – To the S and SE extends the **Okinawa Battlefield Quasi National Park** (area 12 sq. miles/30·8 sq. km), with many memorials to the fallen. – 5 miles/8 km E of Itoman is the *Gyokusen-do* stalactitic cave.

4½ miles/7 km NE of Naha, on a hill commanding extensive views, are the ruins of **Urasoe Castle** and 6 miles/10 km farther NE, near the Pacific coast, the ruins of **Nakagusuku Castle**, with much of its 15th c. circuit of walls still preserved. From the park around the castle there are fine *views of the Pacific and the East China Sea. To the N, 10 minutes' walk away, stands the *Nakamura House*, a 200-year-old farmhouse built entirely of timber without the use of nails.

Gushikawa, on the Pacific coast, is noted for the fights between bulls held here on Sundays. It is reached by way of **Okinawa** (formerly known as *Koza*; pop. 98,000), the second largest town in the prefecture.

Bulls fighting, Gushikawa

The central and northern sections of the W coast, between *Nagahama Beach* and *Nago Bay* and between *Nakijin* and *Cape Hedo*, the northernmost tip of the island, form the **Okinawa Coast Quasi National Park** (area 26 sq. miles/67 sq. km), with beautiful beaches and magnificent facilities for water sports (glass-bottomed boats; snorkeling, etc.). – Part of this protected area forms the *****Okinawa Marine Park** (*Okinawa Kaichu*). On *Cape Fusena* in an *Under-*

water Observatory the fish living on the coral reef can be watched in their natural habitat.

The town of **Nago** (pop. 48,000; bus from Naha, 2½ hours), in Naha Bay, is a good base for excursions in northern Okinawa and to the Motobu Peninsula to the W. Near the center of the town are the ruins of its old Castle, surrounded by cherry trees (in blossom January–February). From here there are beautiful *views of the Kunigami Hills to the NE and the Motobu Peninsula.

The **Motobu Peninsula** extends for some 5 miles/8 km into the East China Sea. Here, from July 1975 to January 1976, was held the International Exposition of the Sea ("Expo '75"). The area occupied by the Exposition is now a park, with an aquarium, several exhibition pavilions and "Aquapolis", a steel structure anchored off the coast (observation platform, restaurant). – Near the N coast are the ruins of *Nakijin Castle*, residence of King Hokuzan in the 14th c. (bus from Nago to Oyadomari, then 15 minutes' walk). There are remains of ramparts and foundation walls. Fine * views of the East China Sea and the offshore islands.

Miyako Islands

The largest of the eight islands in the group is **Miyako** (68 sq. miles/176 sq. km; pop. 45,000), surrounded by coral reefs and largely covered by sugar-cane plantations. The economic and administrative center is **Hirara** (pop. 33,000), on the W coast. 165 yds/150 m S of the harbor stands a monument presented by the Emperor Wilhelm I of Germany to commemorate the rescue of shipwrecked German seamen in 1873. – The highest point on the island is Mount *Nobaru* (358 ft/109 m), on the western slopes of which is a *Botanic Garden*. Near by is the "*Taxation Stone*" (Bubakariisu), which was used from the 17th to the 19th c. to determine the islanders' liability for tax: only those reaching the height of the stone (4 ft 7 in/1·4 m) were required to pay tax.

The finest beach on Miyako is **Yonohamae**, on the S coast of the island, from which there is a view of the offshore island of *Kurima*.

Yaeyama Islands

To this group belong Ishigaki, Iriomote, Taketomi, Yonaguni and 15 smaller islands. – The island of *Ishigaki* has

Luxuriant vegetation in an Okinawa cove

beaches of white sand and luxuriant vegetation (palms, sugar-cane). The chief place on the island is **Ishigaki** (pop. 41,000), which has an interesting old samurai house, *Miyara-donchi* (1819), with a landscaped garden. – To the N of the town is Mount *Omoto*, the highest point in Okinawa prefecture (1723 ft/ 525 m). – Particularly beautiful is *Kabira Bay*, with many small islands and secluded sandy beaches. The much esteemed black pearls are cultivated here.

SW of Ishigaki lies the island of ****Iriomote**. A third of the island's area, together with the smaller islands of *Kohama, Taketomi, Kurojima, Aragusuku* and the *Nakanokan* group, form the **Iriomote National Park**. The most notable features of the park are the long coral reefs with their varied marine life and the dense primeval forest with its rich wild life (including the Iriomote wild cat).

The finest beach on Iriomote is *Haemida*, on Cape Haemida (S coast of the island). – From the port of **Funaura**, on the N coast, a footpath (20 minutes) runs S to a *grove of nipa palms*, continuing to the *Mariudo* and *Kampira Falls* on the River *Urauchi*.

The island of **Taketomi** (hovercraft from Iriomote) is noted for its "starry sand", formed from the calcareous skeletons of tiny marine creatures. One way of seeing the island is to make a tour in an ox-cart. – There is also a hovercraft service to the island of **Kohama**, with the developing holiday center of *Haimurubushi*, set amid subtropical woodland.

Osaka
おおさか

Prefecture: Osaka. – Population: 2,750,000.
Post code: J-530-556. – Telephone code: 06.
(i) (local)
Osaka City Tourist Information Office,
Umeda-machi
(at Central Station),
Kita-ku;
tel. 345 2189 (English spoken).

HOTELS. – IN KITA WARD. – **Western style:** **Royal Hotel*, 5-3, Nakanoshima, 1500 r., Japanese garden, SP; **Osaka Dai-ichi Hotel*, 1-9-20, Umeda, 478 r.; **Hotel Osaka Grand*, 3-18, 2-chome, Nakanoshima, 358 r.; *New Hankyu Hotel*, 1-35, Shibata 1-chome, 1029 r.; *Hotel Hanshin*, 3-30, Umeda 2-chome, 243 r.; *Hokke Club Osakaten*, 50, Togano-cho, 453 r.; *Osaka Tokyu Inn*, 2-1, Doyama-cho, 402 r.; *Osaka Tokyu Hotel*, 7-20, Chaya-machi, 340 r.; *Toko Hotel*, 1-3-19, Minami-mori-cho, 300 r.; *Umeda Os Hotel*, 50, Sonezakinaka 1-chome, 262 r. – IN HIGASHI WARD. – **Western style:** *International Hotel Osaka*, Hashizume-cho, Uchihon-machi, 394 r., Japanese garden; *Hotel Keikan Osaka*, 1-10, Tanimachi, 334 r.; *Hotel Osaka Castle*, 2-35, Kyobashi, 90 r.; *Lutheran Hotel*, 3-36, Tanimachi, 168 r. – **Ryokan:** *Hotel Hishitomi*, Honmachi, 60 r. – IN MINAMI WARD. – **Western style:** **Hotel Nikko Osaka*, 7, Nishino-cho,

Daihoji, 700 r.; *Holiday Inn Nankei Osaka*, 28-1, Kyuzawamon-cho, 230 r.; *Hotel Do Sports Plaza*, 3-12, Shiomachi-dori, 193 r.; *Ark Hotel*, 1-1-1, Nagaboribashi-suji, 246 r. – **Ryokan**: *Daikokuya Honten*, Soemoncho, 20 r.

IN NANIWA WARD. – **Western style**: *Hotel Nankai*, 2-680-1, Shinkawa, 214 r. – IN TENNOJI WARD. – **Western style**: *Osaka Miyako Hotel*, 110, Horikoshi-cho, 151 r. – IN ABENO WARD. – **Western style**: *Hotel Echo Osaka*, 1-4-7, Abeno-suji, 83 r. – IN OYODO WARD. – **Western style**: *Toyo Hotel*, 3-16-19, Toyosaki, 641 r., Japanese garden; *Plaza Hotel*, 2-2-49, Oyodo Minami, 575 r., Japanese garden, SP; *Mitsui Urban Hotel*, 3-18-8, Toyosaki, 405 r. – IN NISHI WARD. – **Western style**: *Park Hotel*, 19-16, Utsubo-honmachi, 1-chome, 153 r.; *New Oriental Hotel*, 2-6-10, Nishi-Honmachi, 119 r.

YOUTH HOSTEL. – *Osaka-Shiritsu Nagai YH*, in Higashi-Sumiyoshi ward, 450, Higashi-nagai-cho, 108 b.

RESTAURANTS. – IN KITA WARD. – **Western cuisine**: *Restaurant Hook Osaka-ten*, 10-20, Togano-cho; *Kyomatsu*, 1-3-38, Dojima; *Takoume*, 2-16-20, Sonezaki. – **Japanese cuisine**: *Aioiro*, 1-16-12, Tenjin-bashi; *Hon Miyake*, 3-2-4, Nakanoshima; *Kitano Yamatoya*, 9-20, Doyamacho; *Komaya*, 1-4-6, Sonezaki-Shinchi; *Nadaman*, in Osaka Royal Hotel, Tamaecho; *Rogetsu Bekkan*, 1-7-10, Sonezaki-Shinchi; *Shin Kiraku*, Shin Hanshin Building, 2-2-25, Umeda; *Tsurutei*, 1-2-21, Sonezaki-Shinchi; *Shori* (tempura), 1-1-9, Sonezaki-Shinchi; *Chikuyo-tei* (eel dishes), 1-1-43, Sonezaki-Shinchi; *Kita-Shinchi Sarashina* (noodle dishes), 1-2-20, Sonezaki-Shinchi. – IN HIGASHI WARD. – **Western cuisine**: *Edoyasu*, 5-33, Kitahama; *Restaurant Kagairo*, Meiji Seimei Building (9th floor), 5-1, Fushimi-machi. – **Japanese cuisine**: *Edogiku*, 2-41, Kawaramachi; *Gansuiro*, 2-49, Kawaramachi; *Hanasaku*, 5-20, Imabashi; *Kagairo*, 1-29, Kitahama; *Kitahachi*, 2-25, Imabashi; *Kitcho Shiten*, Kitcho Building, 2-46, Kita-Kyuhoji-cho; *Mimiu Honmachi-ten*, 5-36, Bingomachi; *Minokichi Senba-ten*, Yagi Building, 2-10, Minami-kyutaro-machi; *Nice*, Senba Center Building, 1-4, Senbachuo; *Sakau*, 4-4, Hiranocho; *Sentei* 5-2, Kita-Kyuhonmachi; *Kitamura* (sukiyaki), 46, Higashi-Shimizucho; *Yoshinozushi* (rice dishes), 4-13, Awajicho; *Amihiko* (eel dishes), 2-86, Kitahama. – IN MINAMI WARD. – **Western cuisine**: *Mato*, 16, Soemoncho. – **Japanese cuisine**: *Ichiju Issai Sangen*, 31, Kasayamachi; *Iroha*, 48, Soemon-cho; *Maruman Honke*, 30, Unagidani Nakanocho; *Matsumoto*, 10, Nishi-Yaguracho; *Nishiki*, 52, Soemoncho; *Rokuban*, 39, Soemoncho; *Shin-ichi*, 27, Soemoncho; *Shin Miura*, 19, Sakamachi; *Shiruyoshi*, 50, Higashi-Shimizucho; *Shoben Tango-tei*, 1-1, Namba-Shinchi; *Takouki*, 159, Minami-Sakamachi; *Toriyoshi*, 1-1547, Kawaramachi; *Yamatoya*, 16, Soemoncho; *Honmorita* (sukiyaki), 1-7, Namba-Shinchi; *Hon Fukuzushi*, 1-12, Shinsai-bashi-suji; *Izumoya* (eel dishes), 2-47, Shinsaibashi-suji; *Imai* (noodle dishes), 8, Nishi-Yaguracho.

EVENTS. – *Toka-Ebisu* (beginning of January), first visit to shrine and procession with women carried in palanquins, at Imamiya-Ebisu Shrine; *Doya-doya* (mid January), shrine visit with combat game between men asking for a good harvest, in Shitennoji Temple; *Hana-matsuri* (beginning of April), celebration of Buddha's birthday in Shitennoji Temple; *Shoryo-e* (mid April), festival commemorating the founder, Shotoku-taishi, with performances of Bugaku and Gagaku music, in Shitennoji Temple; **Osaka International Festival** (April–May), festival of music and drama in the Osaka Festival Hall and other theaters; *International Trade Fair* (April–May in alternate years: 1984, etc.); *Otaue-matsuri* (mid June), rice-planting festival at Sumiyoshi Shrine; *Summer Festival* at Ikutama Shrine (beginning of July); *Port Festival* (mid July), commemorating the opening of the port on July 15, 1868; * *Tenjin-matsuri* (middle to end of July), procession of decorated boats on the river, with fireworks, at Temmangu Shrine; *Sumiyoshi-matsuri* (July–August), procession to River Yamato with portable shrines, fish market in evening, at Sumiyoshi Shrine; *Takigi No* (beginning to middle of August), evening performances of No plays at Ikutama Shrine; *Shinno-matsuri* (middle to end of November), festival in Sukunahikona Shrine (first celebrated in 1822) in honour of the god of healing, Sukunahikona-no-mikoto.

TRANSPORTATION. – **Air**: from TOKYO (Narita International Airport and Haneda Airport), 1 hour; from FUKUOKA (1 hour); from SAPPORO (1¾ hours); from KAGOSHIMA (1 hour); from NAHA (Okinawa), 2 hours; also scheduled services from other countries. – **Rail**: from TOKYO (Central Station) JNR Tokaido–Shinkansen line via NAGOYA and KYOTO to Shin-Osaka (3¼ hours); from FUKUOKA (Hakata) JNR Tokaido–Shinkansen line via HIROSHIMA and OKAYAMA (4½ hours); also services on JNR Tokaido line and Sa-yo line (longer traveling times); from HAGI JNR San-in line via IZUMO and MATSUE to Osaka Station; from WAKAYAMA JNR Hanwa line to Tennoji Station; from NIIGATA JNR Hokuriku line via KANAZAWA and FUKUI to Osaka Station. – **Bus**: from Itami Airport to city center (25 minutes); also 124 routes within city. – **Boat**: ferry service on Inland Sea via Kobe, Sakaide, Takamatsu, Imabari and Matsuyama to Beppu (Kansai Steamship Co.; 15 hours); hovercraft via Kobe and Sakaide to Takamatsu (3¼ hours); via Kobe and Komatsushima to Kannoura (10¼ hours); via Kobe, Hiwasa and Kannoura to Muroto (Muroto Steamship Co.; 13½ hours); from Osaka-Minami to Hiroshima, Tokushima, Kochi (Shikoku) and Hyuga (Kyushu).

Municipal Transport

Subway (Underground)

Midosuji line from Abiko via Umeda and Shin-Osaka to Senri-chuo.

Tanimachi line from Higashi-Umeda to Tennoji.

Yotsubashi line from Nishi-Umeda to Suminoe.

Chuo line from Fukaebashi to Osaka-ko (Port).

Sennichi-mae line from Noda-Hanshin to Sin-Fukae.

Sakaisuji line from Tenroku (Tenjinbashi-suji – Roku-chome) to Dobutsuen-mae.

The **Osaka Loop Line** runs round the inner city.

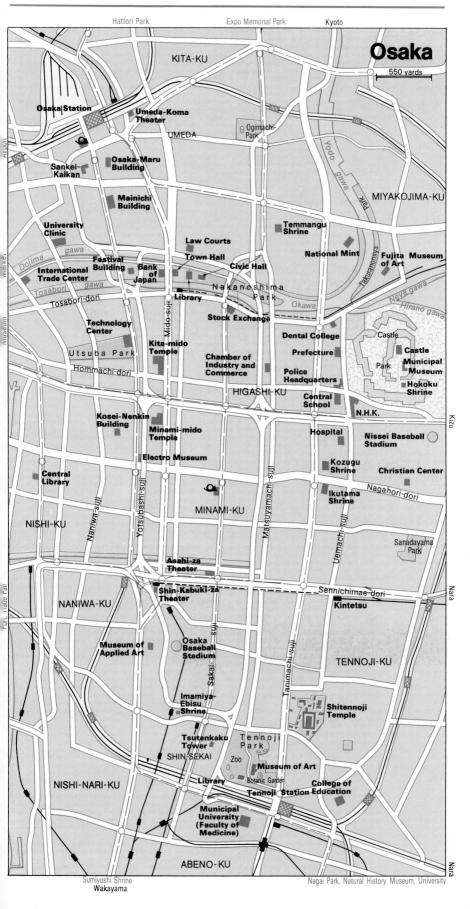

Hattori Park   Expo Memorial Park   Kyoto

Osaka

550 yards

KITA-KU

Osaka Station

Umeda-Koma
Theater

Ogimachi-
Park

UMEDA

MIYAKOJIMA-KU

Sankei-
Kaikan

Osaka-Maru
Building

Mainichi
Building

Temmangu
Shrine

University
Clinic

Dojima gawa

National Mint

Fujita Museum
of Art

Law Courts

Festival
Building

Bank
of
Japan

Town Hall

Civic Hall

International
Trade Center

Tosabori gawa

Nakanoshima
Park

Okawa

Tosabori-dori

Library

Stock Exchange

Technology
Center

Kita-mido
Temple

Utsuba Park

Dental College

Castle

Prefecture

Castle

Hommachi-dori

Chamber of
Industry and
Commerce

Police
Headquarters

Park

Municipal
Museum

Hokoku
Shrine

HIGASHI-KU

Central
School

Kosei-Nenkin
Building

N.H.K.

Minami-mido
Temple

Hospital

Nissei Baseball
Stadium

Electro Museum

Kozugu
Shrine

Christian Center

Central
Library

Nagahori-dori

Ikutama
Shrine

NISHI-KU

MINAMI-KU

Sanadayama
Park

Asahi-za
Theater

Shin-Kabuki-za
Theater

Sennichimae-dori

NANIWA-KU

Kintetsu

Museum of
Applied Art

Osaka
Baseball
Stadium

TENNOJI-KU

Imamiya-
Ebisu-
Shrine

Shitennoji
Temple

Tsutenkaku
Tower

Tennoji
Park

SHIN-SEKAI

Zoo

Museum of Art

NISHI-NARI-KU

Library

Botanic Garden

College of
Education

Tennoji Station

Municipal
University
(Faculty of
Medicine)

ABENO-KU

Sumiyoshi Shrine
Wakayama

Nagai Park, Natural History Museum, University

*Osaka, chief town of a prefecture and Japan's second largest city, lies on the S coast of western Honshu, at the point where the River Yodo flows into the wide sweep of Osaka Bay, which opens out into the Pacific. The bay is bounded on the SE by the Kii Peninsula and shut off from the Inland Sea to the W by the island of Awaji. Osaka is the industrial, commercial and administrative center of western Japan and a major part of the Hanshin industrial zone which extends to Kobe.**

The city lies in the delta of the Yodo, here ramifying into the network of watercourses and canals, spanned by more than a thousand bridges, which has earned Osaka the name of the "Venice of the East" and has provided conditions favorable to the development of trade. Although since the last war it has taken second place to Tokyo in the commercial field it is still a major business center, internationally as well as nationally.

For administrative purposes Osaka is divided into wards (*ku*) – Abeno, Asahi, Fukushima, Higashi, Higashi-Nari, Higashi-Sumiyoshi, Highashi-Yodogawa, Hirano, Ikuno, Joto, Kita, Konohana, Minami, Minato, Miyakojima, Naniwa, Nishi, Nishi-Nari, Nishi-Yodogawa, Oyodo, Suminoe, Sumiyoshi, Taisho, Tennoji, Tsurumi and Yodogawa. – The city has both State and private transportation services and a subway (underground railway).

The economy of Osaka is dominated by heavy industry (iron and steel, engineering, shipbuilding); chemicals, textiles, printing and the foodstuffs industry are also of importance. The port handles some 40% of Japan's foreign trade.

HISTORY. – The origins of Osaka go back to the mythological early days of the Japanese Empire. The Emperor Jimmu, after his legendary odyssey through the Inland Sea, is said to have landed at the mouth of the Yodo and called the place Naniwa ("rapid waves"). It is certain at any rate that the site, conveniently placed as it was, was occupied at a very early date: the Emperor Nintoku may have had a fortified residence in the area in the 4th c. During the 7th and 8th c. the Emperors also resided here, maintaining through the port of Naniwa political and economic relationships with Korea, then in the heyday of the early Korean kingdom.

In the 16th c. Toyotomi Hideyoshi strengthened the castle with new and powerful fortifications and compelled merchants from Kyoto and the trading-post of Sakai, S of Osaka, to take up residence within the territory he ruled.

During the bloody fighting for control of the Shogunate the castle was held in the summer of 1615 by Toyotomi Hideyoshi, and the *Siege of Osaka* by the forces of his rival Tokugawa Ieyasu, commanded by his son Hidetada, is one of the most celebrated episodes in the conflict for predominance in medieval Japan.

Although the Tokugawa shoguns had their residence in Edo they appointed a Governor (*Jodai*) of Osaka as their representative and protected and favored the increasingly powerful merchants of the town. The merchants for their part were generous patrons of the leading artists of the day, who did much notable work in the wealthy commercial city. Frequently their work expressed criticism of the decay of traditional manners and values resulting from the decline of the increasingly impoverished samurai. Commerce and industry, however, continued to flourish: during the Meiji period the population of Osaka had almost reached the half-million mark, and by the beginning of the Second World War it had risen to some 3,250,000.

In 1970 Osaka was host to the World Fair ("Expo 70"). The exhibition grounds are now a public park.

Sightseeing in Osaka

In YODOGAWA ward, N of the *Shin-Yodo*, a broad arm of the river, is the Shin-Osaka Station (on the Shinkansen line; starting-point of the San-yo and Kagoshima lines to Fukuoka). From here the Midosuji subway (underground) line runs S to Umeda Station, adjoining the Central Station.

The **Umeda** quarter, in KITA ward, is the city's commercial and entertainment center, at the hub of its busy traffic. In this area are the (underground) **Umeda Shopping Center**, near the station, and large numbers of restaurants and theaters. To the SE of the area, near the river, is the **Temmangu Shrine**, founded in 949 and dedicated to Sugawara Michizane; the present buildings are a reconstruction of 1901. The great shrine festival, the Tenjin-matsuri (July), is widely famed. – To the E of the shrine stands the **National Mint**, with a *museum* containing coins of many lands, ancient and modern. The surrounding area has one of the finest shows of cherry blossom in the city in spring. – On the other side of the river, in MIYAKO-JIMA ward, lies **Sakuranomiya Park**, with a landscaped garden and sports facilities (fine view of Osaka Castle).

At the S end of Kita ward, in the river, is the island of **Nakanoshima**, the real center

Osaka
Castle

110 yards

Uemachi

Keep

Municipal
Museum

Prefecture

Sakura-mon

suji

Ote-mon

Hokoku
Shrine

Police

N.H.K.

Nissei Stadium

Shogunate the castle was burned down by the retreating Tokugawa forces. The present buildings, in reinforced concrete, are a reconstruction of 1931.

The five-storey main tower or *Keep* (138 ft/42 m high), standing on a stone base 46 ft/14 m high, contains exhibitions on the history of the castle and the city. From the upper floors there are extensive views.

In the park are the **Municipal Museum** (history and culture) and the *Hokoku Shrine*, dedicated to Hideyoshi and his family.

of the city, with tower blocks, offices, hotels and part of the University. **Naka-noshima Park**, at the eastern tip of the island, the city's first public park, was opened in 1891.

Two broad boulevards running parallel to one another, Shinsaibashi-suji and Midosuji-odori, lead across the river into HIGASHI ward. In a park to the E of these streets stands **Osaka Castle**.

The original castle was built by Toyotomi Hideyoshi; completed in 1586 after three years' building, it was then the largest castle in Japan. Almost all Hideyoshi's military commanders were required to contribute stones for its construction: the largest of these is the stone known as *Higo-ishi*, near the S entrance (19 ft/ 5·9 m high, 48 ft/14·5 m long), brought by the celebrated General Kato Kiyomasa (1562–1611) from the island of Shodo (see Shodojima). – After Hideyoshi's defeat by the forces of Tokugawa Ieyasu in 1614–15 the castle was destroyed, but it was later rebuilt by the Tokugawa shoguns for reasons of prestige. When the Meiji Restoration ended the

The two boulevards continue into MINAMI ward, a popular entertainment quarter. The S end of the Shinsaibashi-suji is the liveliest shopping area in Osaka, and its southward continuation, Ebisu-bashi-suji, is lined with small shops and restaurants. – To the E of another wide street, Tanimachi-suji, stands the **Kozugu Shrine**, dedicated to the Emperor Nintoku, who resided in Osaka. The original buildings were destroyed during the Second World War; the hall was rebuilt in 1961. In the surrounding gardens is a historic old stone lantern; fine view of the city. 220 yds/200 m away is the tomb of the famous dramatist Chikamatsu Monzaemon (1653–1724).

The leading places of entertainment are in the southern part of Minami ward; among them are the *Shin-Kabuki-za Theater* (Kabuki plays), the *Kado-za* and *Naka-za*

Osaka Castle

Evening street scene, Osaka

Theaters and the *Asahi-za Theater* (Bunraku puppet plays). In the **Namba** district are several shopping centers, some of them underground.

To the W of Minami ward we come to NISHI ward on the eastern boundary of which, at the Yotsubashi subway (underground) station (Yosubashi line), is the *Municipal Electro Museum* (electrical apparatus, generators, high-frequency technology, atomic power; Planetarium on 6th floor). – Still farther W is MINATO ward. Near Bentencho Station (Osaka Loop Line) and the subway (underground) station of the same name (Chuo line) is the **Transport Museum**, opened in 1962 (land, air and sea transport; models of vehicles and aircraft). – The Chuo subway (underground) line ends at the **Port** (Osaka-ko Station), where are situated the exhibition grounds of the Trade Fair. The port was originally at the mouth of the *Ajikawa*, an arm of the Yodo which bounds the area on the N, but when this became silted up the port installations were moved to their present site and now extend into TAISHO and SUMINOE wards to the S.

Immediately S of the Namba quarter lies TENNOJI ward, on the northern edge of which, near Tanimachi-Kyuchome subway (underground) station (Tanimachi line), is the **Ikutama Shrine**, dedicated to the divinities Ikushima and Tarushima. The buildings were reconstructed after the Second World War; from the hill there is a *view of the city. – Tanimachi-suji continues S to **Tennoji Park** (Shitennoji-mae subway (underground) station, Tanimachi line), in which are the **Municipal Museum of Art**, the large **Zoo** and the **Botanic Garden** (hothouses), as well as various sports facilities. The hill of *Chausuyama*, a prehistoric tumulus, was the site of Tokugawa Ieyasu's camp during the Siege of Osaka. – Close by, to the NE, stands the *****Shitennoji Temple** (or *Tennoji Temple*).

The temple was founded by Prince Shotoku in 593, and is thus older than the Horyuji Temple at Nara; but following repeated destructions by fire nothing is left of the original temple. Most of the present buildings were erected after the Second World War on the basis of the original plans.

The South Gate (*Chumon*) gives access to the reconstructed temple precinct, with the five-storey *pagoda*, the **Kondo** (Main Hall) and the **Kodo** (Lecture Hall). To the E is the **Treasury**, which contains Shotoku-

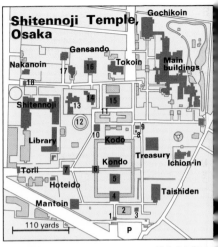

Shitennoji Temple, Osaka

1 Nandaimon	10 North bell-tower
2 Visitor Center	11 Kame-no-ike
3 South bell-tower	12 Maru-ike
4 Chumon	13 Kisshoin
5 Pagoda (5-storey)	14 Josen-in
6 Saijumon	15 Rokujido
7 Saidaimon	16 Eireido
8 Fudodo	17 Daikokudo
9 Kameisui	18 Nakanomon

taishi's sword and a copy of the Hokkekyo Sutra dating from the Late Heian period. – At the W entrance is a stone *torii* of 1294, the oldest of its kind in Japan.

Beyond the expressway on the W side of Tennoji Park, in NANIWA ward, lies the **Shin-Sekai** entertainment quarter, with the 340 ft/103 m-high *Tsutenkaku* outlook tower. A short distance N is the **Imamiya-Ebisu Shrine**, rebuilt in 1956.

From the nearby Daikoku-cho Station the JNR Nankai line runs S into SUMIYOSHI ward (Sumiyoshi-koen Station), where the port used to be before silting-up moved the coastline farther W. The stone base of a lighthouse on the E side of the Jusangenbori Canal is a relic of these earlier days. – To the E of the station is **Sumiyoshi Park**, one of the city's most popular open spaces, with mighty pines and camphor trees. Farther E again we find the **Sumiyoshi Shrine**, founded at Kobe in 202 and later moved to its present site. The shrine is dedicated to the four patron gods of seafarers. The entrance is flanked by many stone lanterns presented by worshippers. Painted red and white and roofed with cypress bark, the buildings (restored 1810) are in the pure Sumiyoshi (Shinto) style, with projecting saddle-roofs and crossed gable beams. The arched bridge within the precincts of the shrine is said to have been built by Yodogimi, Toyotomi Hideyoshi's wife.

SURROUNDINGS of Osaka

6 miles/10 km S of the city center is the town of **Saikai** (train from Namba to Mikunigaoka Station, Koya Line), where can be seen the *tomb of the Emperor Nintoku* (Daisen-ryo), a typical Kofun burial-mound on a "keyhole" plan covering an area of 52 acres (Kofun period 3rd–7th c.). The burial-mound proper is the circular part to the rear. Densely wooded, it is surrounded by three rings of moats. There are other burials in the vicinity.

Burial Mound of Emperor Nintoku   **Saikai**

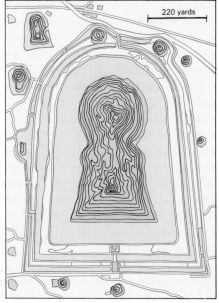

220 yards

NW of Osaka is the industrial city of **Nishinomiya** (pop. 410,000; JNR Tokaido line from Osaka, 20 minutes). On the N side of the town rises Mount *Kabuto* (1014 ft/309 m), at the foot of which lies *Koyoen Park* (swimming pool, Zoo, Botanic Garden). Half-way up the hill is the **Kannonji Temple** (or *Kabutoyama-daishi*), belonging to the Shingon sect, which is believed to have been founded in the 7th–8th c. It contains a wooden *statue of Nyoirin-Kannon (Late Heian period) and other notable pieces of sculpture. From the temple precinct, planted with cherry trees, there is a fine view of Osaka Bay.

The satellite town of **Senri**, N of Osaka, can be reached by subway (underground) (Midosuji line). From the subway (underground) station a bus can be taken to the **Expo Memorial Park** (650 acres), where the World Fair was held in 1970. In the park are the National Museum of Ethnology (Japanese folk art, etc.), a Japanese garden and various entertainment facilities. Near by is the International Museum of Art.

To the N of Osaka, farther inland, is **Toyonaka** (pop. 403,000; Hankyu–Takarazuka Railway, 20 minutes). In Hattori-Ryokuchi Park can be seen the Hattori-minka-shuraku Open-Air Museum, with old peasant houses from central Japan.

15 miles/25 km N of Osaka we reach the popular **Takarazuka** leisure center (JNR Fukuchiyama line or Hanyku-Takarazuka line), with a Zoo, a Botanic Garden and a variety theater.

20 miles/32 km N of Osaka (Keihan line from Yodoyabashi Station to Yawatacho), on Mount *Otokoyama*, is the *Iwashimizu-Hachiman Shrine* (cableway from station). The sumptuous Main Hall (Honden) is dedicated to the Emperor Ojin, revered as the war god Hachiman. At the shrine festival (mid September) costumes of the Heian period are worn. Behind the Main Hall can be seen a monument to Thomas Alva Edison (1934).

19 miles/30 km from Osaka, on the branch of the JNR Tokaido line which runs NE from the city, is **Yamazaki** Station, near which stands the **Myokian Temple**, with a fine 15th c. Shoin (Abbot's Lodging) and a * *tea-room, built by the celebrated master Sen-no-Rikyu (1521–91), which was frequented by Toyotomi Hideyoshi. In the vicinity is Mount *Tennozan*, the scene of a battle between Hideyoshi and Akechi Mitsuhide, who had killed Oda Nobunaga in the Honnoji Temple in Kyoto. On the slopes of the hill is the **Hoshakuji Temple** of the Shingon sect, dedicated to the Eleven-Headed Kannon, which is said to have been founded by a priest named Gyoki. The three-storey pagoda is a classic example of the architecture of the Momoyama period.

Oshima
See under Hakodate

Otaru
おたる

Prefecture: Hokkaido. – Population: 185,000.
Post Code: J-047. – Telephone code: 0134.
(i) (local)
Otaru Tourist Section,
2-12-1, Hanazono-cho;
tel. 32 4111.
Japan Travel Bureau,
at Central Station,
3-9-1, Inaho-cho;
tel. 23 3101.

HOTELS. – **Western style**: *Otaru International Hotel*, 3-9-1, Inaho, 54 r.; *Asari Grand Hotel*, 2-676, Asarigawa-onsen, 52 r., thermal bath; *Hokkai Hotel*, 1-5-11, Inaho, 42 r., Japanese garden; *New Green Hotel*, 3-5-14, Inaho, 90 r.; *Otaru Green Hotel*, 3-3-1, Inaho, 88 r.; *Business Hotel New Minato*, 2-10-10, Inaho, 73 r. – YOUTH HOSTEL: *YH Otaru Tenguyama*, 2-16-22, Mogami, 39 b.

RESTAURANT. – *Kaiyotei*, 4-7, Sumiyoshicho.

EVENTS. – *Skiing Competitions* (end of February) in Tenguyama skiing area; *Ushio-matsuri* (end of July), parades and folk-dancing in Otaru Park.

TRANSPORTATION. – **Rail**: from SAPPORO or HAKODATE JNR Hakodate line (40 minutes or 4 hours).

Otaru lies on the W coast of Hokkaido in Ishikari Bay, which opens off the Sea of Japan. Although it was founded only in the mid 19th c. it is one of the older settlements on Hokkaido. Conveniently situated both for trade with the Soviet Union and for the herring fisheries, it developed into a port of some consequence before the Second World War. The town is attractively situated, with great stretches of coastal scenery and ranges of hills to the S. – The name comes from the Ainu term *Ota oru nai*, ''river by the sandy beach''.

HISTORY. – The Matsumae family who controlled much of Ezo (the old name for Hokkaido) from the 16th c. onwards established a fishing village here to encourage the Ainu to fish for herring in the waters to the N. After the opening of the first railway line in Hokkaido (1880) the settlement developed into a flourishing commercial port, at first mainly engaged in shipping coal. The trade in industrial products now plays a predominant part, while the importance of the fisheries has declined.

SIGHTS. – The principal commercial and shopping street is Miyako-odori. – 1 mile/ 1·5 km S of the station, in hilly country, lies **Otaru Park** (82 acres), with pines, plum and cherry trees, and a variety of sports facilities (skiing in winter). From the hill there is an attractive view of the town.

NW of the station (bus) stands the **Otaru Museum**, housed in a British-style brick building (history, art). – 3 miles/5 km beyond this is the **Shukuzu Marine Park** (bus from station, 25 minutes), with the largest aquarium on Hokkaido and a museum in an old fisherman's house.

On the coast 1¼ miles/2 km NE of the town we come to **Temiya Park**, with a *cave* containing an inscription (still undeciphered) 6½ ft/2 m high by 15 ft/ 4·5 m long (copy at entrance to cave).

SURROUNDINGS. – Ishikari Bay to the W of the town is bounded by the **Shakotan Peninsula**, the coastal regions of which form the *Niseko-Shakotan-Otaru-kaigan Quasi National Park*. At Cape Nomanai on the NW coast of the peninsula there are sheer cliffs 820 ft/250 m high, much eroded by the sea. From *Capes Kamui* and *Shakotan*, at the N end of the peninsula, there are magnificent *views of the Sea of Japan. – **Ranshima** has a very beautiful beach, and 1 mile/ 1·5 km SE of the station is the *Oshoro Stone Circle* (diameter 92 ft/28 m), a prehistoric structure the purpose of which is unknown. – At *Yoichimachi*, to the W of the station, the *Fugoppe Cave*, discovered in 1950, has rock engravings which are estimated to be 1500 years old.

Rikuchu-kaigan National Park

りくちゅう海岸国立公園

Prefectures: Iwate and Miyagi.
Area: 47 sq. miles/123 sq. km.
(i) (central)
National Parks Association of Japan,
Toranomon Denki Building,
8-1, Toranomon 2-chome, Minato-ku,
J-105 **Tokyo;**
tel. (03) 502 0488.

HOTELS. – IN MIYAKO. – **Western style**: *Hotel Omiya*, on Jodogahama Beach, 47-5, Dai 4 Chiwari, Oaza, Sokei, 26 r., beach. – **Ryokan**: *Kumayasu Ryokan*, 2-5, Shin-machi, 26 r. – YOUTH HOSTELS: *YH Suehiro-Kan*, 7-27, Suehiro-machi, 70 b.; *Miyako Kimura YH*, 1-28, Kurada-machi, 70 b., beach.

IN KUROSAKI. – **Ryokan**: *Michiai*, 17, Shimo-mura, 2 Chiwari, Fudai-mura, 15 r., beach. – IN KAMAISHI. – **Ryokan**: *Shosen-Kaku*, 40 r. – IN OFUNATO. – **Western style**: *Ofunato Grand Hotel*, 29-1, Aza Marumori, Ofunato-cho, 25 r. – IN RIKUZEN-TAKATA. – YOUTH HOSTEL: *Rikuzen Takata YH*, 176-6, Sunamori-Kesen-machi, 96 b. – IN KESENNUMA. – **Western style**: *Kesennuma Plaza Hotel*, 1-1, Kashiwazaki, 45 r., beach.

TRANSPORTATION. – **Rail**: from TOKYO (Ueno Station) to Omiya (30 minutes), then JNR New Tohoku-Shinkansen line to Ichinoseki (2¼ hours) or Morioka (3¼ hours); also JNR Tohoku line via ICHINOSEKI (5¼ hours; from there JNR Ofunato line to Kesennuma, 2 hours) and MORIOKA (6½ hours; JNR Yamada line from there to Miyako, 2 hours) to Hachinohe (8¼ hours; JNR Hachinohe line from there to Kuji, 3 hours). – **Bus**: several routes within National Park. – **Boat**: round trips from Miyako.

The Rikuchu-kaigan National Park extends for more than 110 miles/ 180 km along the E coast at the northern tip of Honshu, an ever-changing landscape of cliffs, rock terraces and small coves and inlets (rias). – The vegetation consists predominantly of rhododendrons; the wildlife includes large numbers of sea-birds (gulls, petrels).

The best center from which to see the National Park is the town of **Miyako**, from which there are coach excursions to the most beautiful parts of the park. To the N of the town lies **Jodogahama Beach**, with its dark fringe of pines and its white sand one of the most beautiful beaches in the region. Other attractive beaches are at *Taro, Omoto* and *Kurosaki*, farther N. At

Kitayamazaki the cliffs reach a height of 985 ft/300 m.

The coasts in the southern part of the National Park are flatter, edged with dunes which are planted with pines. There is a particularly beautiful beach at **Goishi-kaigan.**

Rishiri-Rebun-Sarobetsu National Park

りしりれぶん さろべつ 国立公園

Prefecture: Hokkaido.
Area: 130 sq. miles/340 sq. km.
ⓘ (central)
National Parks Association of Japan,
Toranomon Denki Building,
8-1, Toranomon 2-chome, Minato-ku,
J-105 **Tokyo;**
tel. (03) 502 0488.

HOTELS. – IN WAKKANAI. – **Western style:** *Wakkanai Sun Hotel*, 3-7-16, Chuo, 38 r., *Hotel Soya*, 2-11-1, Daikoku-cho, 30 r., – **Minshuku:** *Saihoku*, 2-9-4, Chuo, 17 r., beach; *Hokuto*, 3-5-20, Horai, 13 r., beach. – YOUTH HOSTELS: *Komadori House YH*, 3-chome, Komadori, 100 b.; *Wakkanai YH*, 5-3-18, Horai, 40 b.

ON RISHIRI. – **Western style:** *Hotel Shibata*, Sakae-cho, Oshidomari, 36 r. – **Ryokan:** *Fujita Ryokan*, 115, Minatomachi, Oshidomari, 18 r.; *Ryokan Oosuga*, Minatomachi, Oshidomari, 17 r. – YOUTH HOSTELS: *Rishiri Choritsu YH*, 68, Izumi-cho, Kutsukata-aza, Rishiri-cho, 52 b.; *Rishiri Oshidomari YH*, 113, Oshidomari, Higashi-Rishiri-cho, 52 b.

ON REBUN. – **Western style:** *Rebun Hotel*, Kafuka, 36 r., beach; *Mitsui Kanko Hotel*, Kafuka, 31 r., beach. – **Ryokan:** *Kato Ryokan*, Kafuka, 24 r., beach; *Sakurai Ryokan*, Kafuka, 22 r., beach; *Mendon Ryokan*, Funadomari, 15 r., – **Minshuku:** *Hokkaido-so*, Tonnai, Kafuka, 15 r., beach; *Miyajima-so*, Teshikari, Kafuka, 15 r., beach. – YOUTH HOSTELS: *Rebun YH*, Tsugaru-cho, Kafuka, 80 b.; *Momoiwa-so YH*, Motocho, Kafuka, 74 b., beach; *Rebun Choritsu Funadomari YH*, Osonae, Funadomari, 56 b., beach.

TRANSPORTATION. – **Air:** from SAPPORO to Wakkanai (1 hour) and Oshidomari (on Rishiri; 1½ hours); from Wakkanai to Oshidomari (20 minutes; summer only). – **Rail:** from ASAHIKAWA JNR Soya line via Toyotomi to Wakkanai (4¼ hours). – **Bus:** from Toyotomi and Wakkanai to Sarobetsu Plain; round trip on Rishiri. – **Boat:** from Wakkanai to various coastal places on Rishiri; from Kutsukata and Oshidomari (Rishiri) to Funadomari and Kafuka (Rebun).

Rishiri-Rebun-Sarobetsu National Park, Japan's most northerly national park, takes in the Sarobetsu Plain at the northernmost tip of Hokkaido and the offshore islands of Rishiri and Rebun. This area, of particular interest to birdwatchers, can be reached from the port of Wakkanai.

Thanks to the warm Tsushima Current **Wakkanai** (pop. 60,000), in *Soya Bay*, is ice-free throughout the year. – S of the town are **Toyotomi** and the little seaside resort of *Toyotomi-onsen*. From Toyotomi Station there is a bus to the *Sarobetsu Plain*, with the **Sarobetsu Gensei Kaen**, a well-watered garden with sub-Arctic vegatation (azaleas, etc.).

Off the coast opposite the Sarobetsu Plain lies the almost exactly circular island of **Rishiri**, with the volcanic cone of Mount *Rishiri* (5640 ft/1719 m). A road encircles the coast (coach excursions round the island; rental of bicycles). There is good fishing to be had in *Lake Himenuma*, and pleasant walks to *Misaki Park* and *Kutsugata-Misaki Park*. The ascent of Mount Rishiri takes about 10 hours there and back; in the summit area there are rare species of sea-birds and Alpine plants.

6 miles NW is the island of **Rebun** (32 sq. miles/82 sq. km), known as the "Island of Flowers", from which a fine view of Mount Rishiri may be enjoyed. There is a beautiful beach at *Motochi-kaigan* and imposing cliffs at *Nishitomari-kaigan*.

Ryukyu Islands
See Okinawa

Sado
さ ど

Prefecture: Niigata.
Area of island: 331 sq. miles/857 sq. km. –
Population: 87,000.
ⓘ (central)
Niigata-ken Tokyo Kanko Bussan Assensho,
Kokusai Kanko Kaikan,
1-8-3, Marunouchi, Chiyoda-ku,
J-100 **Tokyo;**
tel. (03) 215 4618.

HOTELS. – **Western style:** *Hotel Osado,* 315-5, Oaza Shikabuse, Aikawa-cho, 147 r.; *Sado Grand Hotel,* 4918-1, Oaza Kamoutashiro, Ryotsu, 105 r., SP, beach; *Sado Green Hotel Kiraku,* 658, Aza Nishino, Oaza Harakura, 28 r., thermal bath, beach. – **Ryokan:** *Kubota Ryokan,* Aikawa-cho, 22 r.; *Yumoto-kan,* Sumiyoshi, 14 r., thermal bath; *Ryoso Kobune,* 11 r. – YOUTH HOSTELS: *YH Kazashima-kan,* 397, Katanoo, 29 b., beach; *Senkaku-so YH,* 369-4, Himezu, Aikawa-machi, 20 b.; *Sado Hakusan YH,* Yamada, 15 b.

TRANSPORTATION. – **Air:** from NIIGATA to Ryotsu (25 minutes; irregular). – **Boat:** from NIIGATA (1–2½ hours); from NAOETSU (3 hours).

The island of Sado, lying off the coast of eastern central Honshu in the Sea of Japan, is Japan's largest island after the four main islands (area 331 sq. miles/857 sq. km). It is traversed by two ridges of mountains running parallel to the E and W coasts, with the Kuninaka Plain between them. Most of the island is within the Sado-Yahiko Quasi National Park. Thanks to the warm Tsushima Current it has a very agreeable climate. The inhabitants live mainly by farming and fishing.

The vegetation in the southern part of the island consists mainly of camellias and groves of bamboos. – The best time to visit Sado is from April to October, since during the winter the crossing may be difficult because of storms.

HISTORY. – In spite of its proximity to the mainland, Sado had for many centuries practically no contact with the rest of Japan; and the island's place-names, customs and culture still show evidence of this independent development, which continued until the 13th c.

Until the 17th c. Sado was used as a place of exile for opponents of the central government – e.g. for the Emperor Juntoku (1197–1242), who failed in an attempt to overthrow the Kamakura Shogunate. The Buddhist monk Nichiren (1222–82), founder of the nationalistically oriented Nichiren sect, was also banished to Sado (1271–74). During his exile he wrote two of his fundamental theoretical works.

At the beginning of the 17th c. gold was discovered in the Aikawa area, giving a temporary boost to the island's economy.

The chief place on the island and the port used by the boats from Honshu is **Ryotsu** (pop. 21,000), from which there are buses to all parts of the island. To the S of the town, below Mount *Kimpoku* (3849 ft/1173 m), is the *Kamo Lagoon,* a sheet of water linked with the sea.

In the *Kuninaka Plain* with its extensive rice-fields there are a number of features of historical interest. 6 miles/10 km SW of Ryotsu is **Izumi**, with the former residence of the Emperor Juntoku, the Kuroki-gosho. – Near by in the village of **Niibo** stands the Komponji Temple, in which Nichiren stayed when he first arrived on the island. He later moved to the *Myosho-ji Temple,* on a hill to the SW, now a place of pilgrimage for members of his sect.

The town of **Aikawa** (pop. 14,000) became a boom town when gold was discovered in the area, with a population which at one time approached 200,000. Although the mines are now practically worked out, a certain amount of gold is still extracted. The red clay from the workings is used in the manufacture of the characteristic local pottery (*Mumyoi-yaki*). – A picturesque cliff-fringed coast extends from here to *Cape Hajikizaki,* at the northern tip of the island.

SE of Aikawa lies **Mano**, in the bay of the same name. Near the Mano Shrine is the burial-place of the Emperor Juntoku, and in the neighboring Myosenji Temple the tomb of Hino Suketomo, a follower of Godaigo-tenno. – In the *Ryuginji Temple,* also on the W coast, can be seen a bronze *statue of Kannon (Heian period).

At the southern tip of the island is the charming little port of **Ogi**, with the Rengebuji Temple, believed to have been founded in 808 by a priest named Kukai. In May the local fishermen in their wooden boats gather eelgrass, which is then dried on the beach. – Boat trip (recommended) to *Cape Sawazaki,* passing the rocky *Nansenkyo* coast.

Saikai National Park

さいかい
国立公園

Prefecture: Nagasaki.
Area: 94 sq. miles/243 sq. km.
 (central)
National Parks Association of Japan,
Toranomon Denki Building,
8-1, Toranomon 2-chome, Minato-ku,
J-105 **Tokyo;**
tel. (03) 502 0488.

(local)
Sasebo-shi Tourist Information Center,
1-3, Shirobae-cho,
J-857 **Sasebo**;
tel. (0956) 22 6630.

HOTELS. – IN AND AROUND SASEBO. – **Western style:**
Yumibaru Kanko Hotel, 506, Udogoe-cho, 60 r.;
Sasebo Green Hotel, 4-1, Miura-cho, 74 r. – **Ryokan:**
Gekka-so, 4-28, Miura-cho, 25 r. – YOUTH HOSTEL:
Hiradoguchi YH, in Hiradoguchi, 1111-3, Nakaze,
Okubomen, Taibra-cho, 100 b.

ON HIRADO. – **Western style:** *Hirado Kanko Hotel
Senrigahama Besso*, 100, Kawachi-cho, 143 r., –
Ryokan: *New Hirado Kaijo Hotel*, 2231-3, Okubo-
cho, 134 r., SP; *Kokusai Kanko Hotel Kishotei*, 2520,
Okubo-cho, 92 r.; *Hirado Wakigawa Hotel*, 1123-1,
Iwanoue-cho, 40 r.; *Hirado Kanko Hotel*, 2490,
Okubo-cho, 60 r.; *Miyashiya Ryokan*, 15 r.;
Kawamura Ryokan, 14 r.; *Ryokan Tokiwa*, 11 r. –
Minshuku: *Michishio*, 877, Sakitaka-cho, 26 r., SP.

ON FUKUE (Goto Islands). – **Western style:** *Goto Bus
Terminal Hotel*, 19-18, Fukue-cho, 56 r. – **Ryokan:**
Ohato Hotel, 1-33, Sakae-cho, 28 r.; *Suisenkaku*, 2-1,
Ideka-cho, 24 r. – **Minshuku:** *Goto*, 430, Masuda-
cho, 25 r., beach.

TRANSPORTATION. – **Rail:** from NAGASAKI JNR
Matsuura line or Sasebo line to Hiradoguchi (4
hours). – **Bus:** from Hiradoguchi to Hirado. – **Boat:**
from Sasebo to Hirado (1½ hours); ferry from
Hiradoguchi to Hirado (15 minutes).

**The *Saikai National Park lies at
the extreme western end of the
main Japanese group of islands. It
includes a small strip of the coast
of Kyushu, parts of the island
of Hirado, the Kujukushima Islands
(literally, the "Ninety-Nine Islands") and a number of small islands in the Goto (literally, "Five
Islands") Archipelago. The scenic
beauty of the National Park and its
features of historical interest have
made it one of the most popular excursions from Kyushu. The vegetation is subtropical, and stretches of
rugged coast alternate with beautiful beaches. Pearl-culture is practiced in some areas.**

Immediately off the NW coast of Kyushu
are the **Kujukushima Islands,** a closely
packed group of some 170 small islands
and islets, covered with subtropical
vegetation lying in the channel between
Kyushu and Hirado. There are cruises
around the islands from **Sasebo.**

The island of **Hirado** can be reached by
boats from Sasebo (about 1½ hours); there
are also ferries from Hiradoguchi (15
minutes) and a road bridge.

This hilly island (area 66 sq. miles/171 sq.
km), lying just over a third of a mile from the
coast of Kyushu, played an important part in
the 16th c., when Japan was first opened up to
foreign trade. When the first persecutions of
Christians began towards the end of the
century many converts sought refuge on Hirado
and built churches which externally looked like
temples.

The chief town, **Hirado** (pop. 30,000), in the
extreme NE of the island, was the first Japanese
port to become involved in trade with foreign
countries, and factories (trading stations) were
established here by Dutch and British merchants.
With the growth of the more conveniently
situated port of Nagasaki, however, Hirado lost
its commercial importance.

The town can easily be seen on foot. A short
distance N of the pier is the **Historical Museum**
(*Kanko-shiryokan*). On the low hill behind the
Museum are a number of monuments, including
one to the English pilot William Adams, who was
cast ashore in Japan in April 1600 and was
subsequently employed by Tokugawa Ieyasu to
build ships for the Japanese Navy and acted as
an intermediary between the Government and the
foreign factories in Hirado. – Some 220 yds/200 m
away are the remains of the
Oranda-Shokan-Ato, the Dutch factory.

To the S of the harbor is the **Matsuura Museum**
(*Matsuura-shiryokan*), with mementoes of the
princely Matsuura family which formerly ruled Hirado.
On a hill to the SE stands a Neo-Gothic church.

On Mount *Kameoka* is **Hirado Castle** (a modern
reconstruction of the original 18th c. structure), with
views of the sea and the bridge linking the island with
the mainland. Near by is the *Kokusai Cultural Center,*
a modern building in the shape of a ship.

The most westerly part of the National
Park is constituted by the **Goto Islands,**
lying some 30 miles off the coast of
Kyushu (boat services from Sasebo and
Nagasaki). The group consists of the five
large islands of Fukue, Naru, Wakamatsu,
Nakadori and Uku together with some
150 smaller islands and islets.

The island of **Fukue** (area 126 sq. miles/
327 sq. km) is an important stock-rearing,
farming and fishing area. There are beautiful beaches along the coasts and impressive cliffs on *Cape Osezaki*, to the SW.
The island has a *ruined castle*, a number of
old *samurai houses* and a Roman Catholic
church.

Sakata

さかた

Prefecture: Yamagata. – Population: 105,000.
Post code: J-998. Telephone code: 0234.

ⓘ (central)
Yamagata-ken Tokyo Kanko Bussan
Assensho,
Tetsudo Kaikan,
1-9-1, Marunouchi, Chiyoda-ku,
J-100 Tokyo;
tel. (03) 215 2222.

(local)
Yamagata-ken Kanko Kyokai,
Yamagata-ken Kankoka-nai,
2-8-1, Matsunami,
J-990 Yamagata;
tel. (0236) 31 9233.

HOTELS. – Western style: Kikusui Hotel, 2-4-21, Hiyoshi-cho, 16 r.; Sakata Tokyu Inn, 1-10-20, Saiwai-cho, 88 r.; Sakata Green Hotel, 1-6-10, Honmachi, 69 r.; Sakata Station Hotel, 1-9-6, Saiwai-cho, 25 r.

RESTAURANT. – Somaya, 1-2-20, Hiyoshimachi.

TRANSPORTATION. – Rail: from TOKYO (Ueno Station) JNR Shin-etsu line (6 hours); from NIITSU (nr Niigata) JNR Uetsu line and Rikuu-sai line (2¼ hours); from YAMAGATA JNR Ou line to Shinjo (1 hour), then Rikuu-sai line (1¼ hours).

Sakata, situated on the W coast of northern Honshu, is one of the most important ports on the Sea of Japan. In the Edo period it was already a market and entrepôt for the rice grown in the Shonai Plain, and the first large rice-store in Japan was built here in 1672. The development of industry gave the town a considerable economic boost. Its main industry is now the production of chemicals.

HISTORY. – The rice trade brought fabulous wealth and great landed possessions to two local merchant families, the Honma and the Abumiya. According to an old folk-song no man can be as wealthy as a Honma: all that can be hoped for is to be merely as rich as a daimyo. The wealth of the Abumiya family is described by the 17th c. writer Ihara Saikaku in his "Nihon Eitaigura".

SIGHTS. – 550 yds/500 m W of the station (bus, 5 minutes), in a house which once belonged to the Honma family, is the **Honma Museum of Art**, with books, pictures, sculpture and porcelain which belonged to the family. Attached to the Museum is a fine landscaped garden, the *Tsurumai-en*. – Farther W, on a low hill, lies **Hiyoriyama Park**, with an old wooden lighthouse; extensive * view of the mouth of the River *Mogami* and the Sea of Japan. – In the vicinity are the **Hie Shrine**, with the Kokyu Library, and the **Kaikoji Temple**, in which the mummified bodies of two monks, Chukai-shonin and Emmyokai-shonin, are preserved.

The residence of the Abumiya family (Edo period) is a 10-minute bus ride from the station.

SURROUNDINGS. – To the N of the town, on the borders of Yamagata and Akita prefectures, we reach the **Chokai Quasi National Park** (JNR Uetsu line from Sakata, 30 minutes). In the eastern part of the park rises Mount *Chokai* (also known, from the name of the old province, as Dewa-Fuji; 7317 ft/2230 m), the main peak in the Chokai volcanic chain running parallel to the coast. There is a bus from *Fukura* to the foot of the mountain (45 minutes), from which it is a 7 hours' climb to the top. An alternative route (about 5 hours) starts from *Kisakata* (N of Fukura on the JNR Uetsu line). From the summit there are panoramic *views of the Sea of Japan and the Oga Peninsula to the N and the island of Sado to the SW. – 20 miles off the coast lie the **Tobishima Islands** (boat from Sakata, 4 hours), with a number of caves gouged out by the waves. The islands are the home of black-backed gulls (a protected species).

E of Sakata, in the Valley of the *Mogami*, we reach **Furukuchi**, starting-point of boat trips through the rapids to the health resort of *Kusanagi-onsen*. The trip of 5 miles/8 km takes about 1½ hours (May–November). The beauty of the region was described by the 17th c. writer Matsuo Basho in his travel diary "Oku-no-Hosomichi".

To the S of Sakata (JNR Uetsu line, 30 minutes) the old castle town of **Tsuruoka** (pop. 99,000) was once the seat of the princely Sakai family and now an important center of the rice trade. In Tsuruoka Park, 1¼ miles/2 m SW of the station (bus, 10 minutes), are the remains of the old castle and the Shonai Shrine, dedicated to the Sakai family (cherry blossom in April). Near by stands the Chido Open-Air Museum, with historic old buildings from the town. – The Tsuruoka-Temmango Shrine, 1¼ miles/2 km from the station, is the scene in May every year of the Bakemono festival, a gay parade in which men wear women's dress and women wear men's clothes. – A short distance away is *Kurokawa*, with the Kasuga Shrine, where old No plays are performed during the Ogi festival (beginning of February).

NW of Tsuruoka, on the slopes of Mount *Takadate*, can be found the extensive complex of the *Zempoji Temple*, mostly dating from the Heian period. – On the coast (private railway from Tsuruoka, 30 minutes; bus, 40 minutes) is the popular little health resort of *Yunohama-onsen*. To the S of the town (bus, 1 hour) another small resort, *Atsumi-onsen* has a picturesque market held every morning at the Kumano Shrine.

Sapporo

さっぽろ

Prefecture: Hokkaido. – Population: 1,500,000.
Post code: J-060-064. – Telephone code: 011.

ⓘ (local)
Sapporo Travel Center,
in Central Station;
tel. 241 9285.
Tourist Section of Sapporo City,
Nishi 2-chome, Kita-Ichijo,
Chuo-ku;
tel. 211 2111.
Japan Travel Bureau,
Nippon Seimei Building,
Nishi 4-chome, Kita-Sanjo,
Chuo-ku;
tel. 271 4011 and 241 1281.
JTB Building,
Nishi 2-chome, Minami-Ichijo,
Chuo-ku;
tel. 261 8261 (English spoken).

HOTELS. – **Western style:** *Keio Plaza Hotel Sapporo*, 7, Nishi, Kita 5, Chuo-ku, 525 r.; *Sapporo Grand Hotel*, 4, Nishi, Kita-Ichijo, Chuo-ku, 521 r., Japanese garden; *Sapporo Zennikku Hotel*, Nishi 1-chome, Kita-Sanjo, Chuo-ku, 470 r., SP; *Hotel New Otani Sapporo*, 1-1, Nishi, Kita 2-jo, Chuo-ku, 340 r.; *Century Royal Hotel*, 5, Nishi, Kita-Gojo, Chuo-ku, 336 r.; *Sapporo Tokyu Hotel*, 4, Nishi, Kita-Yojo, Chuo-ku, 263 r.; *Sapporo Prince Hotel*, 11, Nishi, Minami-Nijo, Chuo-ku, 345 r.; *Hotel New Miyakoshi*, 3, Nishi, Kita-2, Chuo-ku, 124 r.; *Sapporo Park Hotel*, 3-11, Nishi, Minami-Jujo, Chuo-ku, 226 r., Japanese garden; *Sapporo International Hotel*, 4-1, Nishi, Kita-Yojo, Chuo-ku, 99 r.; *Sapporo Royal Hotel*, 1, Higashi, Minami-Shichijo, Chuo-ku, 88 r., Japanese garden; *Sapporo Washington Hotel*, Nishi 4-chome, Kita 4-jo, Chuo-ku, 523 r.; *Hotel Sunflower Sapporo*, Nishi 3-chome, Minami 5-jo, Chuo-ku, 238 r.; *Hotel Rich*, 3-10, Nishi 3-chome, Kitaichi-jo, Chuo-ku, 169 r.; *Business Hotel Soen*, Nishi, 14-chome, Kita 6-jo, Chuo-ku, 162 r.; *Hotel Highland*, 3-1, Nishi 8-chome,

Minami 6-jo, Chuo-ku, 147 r.; *Sapporo Plaza Hotel*, Nishi 1-chome, Minami 7-jo, Chuo-ku, 150 r.; *Sapporo Clark Hotel*, 11-21, Nishi, Kita-Shijo, Chuo-ku, 111 r.; *Susukino Green Hotel*, 2, Nishi, Minami-Shijo, Chuo-ku, 99 r.; *Ohdori Koen Hotel*, Nishi 8-chome, Ohdori, Chuo-ku, 88 r.; *Marushin Hotel*, Nishi 4-chome, Minami 1-jo, Chuo-ku, 74 r.; *Hotel New Frontia*, 9-chome, Nishi, Kita-Ichijo, Chuo-ku, 59 r.; *Business Hotel Lilac*, Nishi 7-chome, Ohdori, Chuo-ku 44 r.; *Business Hotel Marumatsu*, Nishi 3-chome, Minami 7-jo, Chuo-ku, 42 r. – **Ryokan:** *Hotel Shikanoyu*, in Jozankei-onsen, Minami-ku, 197 r.; *Jozankei Hotel*, in Jozankei-onsen, Minami-ku, 194 r.; *Shogetsu Grand Hotel*, in Jozankei-onsen, Minami-ku, 98 r.; *Hotel Maruso*, 3-3, Kitaichijo-Nishi, Chuo-ku, 38 r.; *Sapporo Daiichi Hotel*, 10, Odori-Nishi, Chuo-ku, 33 r. – YOUTH HOSTELS: *Sapporo Shiritsu Lions YH*, 1257-2, 18-chome, 1-jo, Miyanomori, Chuo-ku, 100 b.; *Nakanoshima YH*, 2-chome, 1-jo, Nakanoshima, Toyohira-ku, 70 b.; *Jozankei YH*, in Jozankei-onsen, 4-310, Higashi, Minami-ku, 56 b.; *Sapporo Miyagaoka YH*, 3-1, 14-chome, 1-jo, Miyanomori, Chuo-ku, 52 b.

RESTAURANTS. – *Bobaitei*, 7-12, Nishi 3-chome, Minami-Shichijo, Chuo-ku; *Hyosetsunomon Shinkan*, Nishi 2-chome, Minami-Gojo, Chuo-ku; *Kaiyotei*, Nishi 1-chome, Minami-Juichijo; *Kikuei*, Nishi 4-chome, Minami-Hachijo, Chuo-ku; *Muscat*, Koshiyama Building, Nishi 3-chome, Kita-Nijo; *Otemon*, Nishi 1-chome, Minami-Juichijo, Chuo-ku; *Sentozasho*, Nishi 3-chome, Minami-Shichijo, Chuo-ku.

EVENTS. – *Yuki-matsuri* (beginning of February), *Snow Festival*, with snow sculpture; *Hokkaido Shrine Festival* (mid June), procession with portable shrines and decorated floats; *Summer Festival* (end of August), a popular fair with Bon dances and fireworks.

WINTER SPORTS. – **Skiing** on Mounts *Arai, Moiwa* and *Teine* (where the Winter Olympic Games were held in 1972).

TRANSPORTATION. – **Air**: from TOKYO (Haneda Airport), 1½ hours; from OSAKA (1¾ hours); from NAGOYA

The O-dori boulevard, Sapporo

(1½ hours). – **Rail**: from TOKYO (Ueno Station) JNR Tohoku line to AOMORI (7 hours), then ferry to HAKODATE (4 hours) and from there JNR Hakodate line (4½ hours).

*Sapporo, chief town of the island and prefecture of Hokkaido, is one of the newest cities in Japan. It lies in the basin of the River Toyohira, which forms the southern part of the Ishikari Plain. Although Sapporo is slightly farther S than Florence the winters are cold, with an abundance of snow. The average summer temperature is about 71·1 °F/21·7 °C. – The 11th Winter Olympic Games were held here in 1972.**

The city's main sources of income are agriculture and forestry, the production of foodstuffs (including the brewing of beer) and fishing. The local craft products include woodcarving and embroidery, mostly reflecting Ainu traditions.

HISTORY. – Until the 19th c. the Sapporo region was inhabited solely by the "proto-Japanese" Ainu, from whose language the city's name is derived (*Sato poro petsu*, "long dry river-bed" – i.e. the valley of the Toyohira). In the middle of the century Japanese settlers came to Hokkaido and set about clearing the dense forests to win agricultural land. In 1871 the Meiji Government moved the State agency responsible for promoting settlement from Hakodate to Sapporo, and rapid progress was made with the development of the town, which was laid out on a regular grid plan, following the North American model. In 1886 Sapporo became the chief town of the prefecture. Its population reached the million mark in 1970, and since then has continued to increase.

SIGHTS. – NW of the Central Station is the campus of the **University of Hokkaido** (12 faculties), which developed out of the College of Agriculture (moved here from Tokyo in 1875). In the grounds of the Faculty of Agriculture is a *bust* of Dr William Smith Clark (1826–86), an American who founded the College of Agriculture and became its Dean. On the base is inscribed Clark's parting injunction to his students, "Boys, be ambitious." Near by is the Clark Memorial Hall (1960).

SW of the station is the **University Botanic Garden**, with an Alpine garden and hothouses. In the grounds is the *Ainu Museum* (or Batchelor Museum), in an English-style building erected in 1891, with collections illustrating all aspects of Ainu culture. Adjoining this museum is the *University Museum* (archaeology, ethnography and zoology; collection of birds assembled by the British ornithologist T. W. Blakiston).

Near the entrance to the Botanic Garden stands the brick-built *Prefecture* (1888). – 550 yds/500 m E is one of the city's landmarks, the **Clock-Tower** (1881), the only surviving Russian-style building in Sapporo. It contains a library and an exhibition illustrating the Japanese colonization of Hokkaido.

550 yds/500 m S of the Central Station, running across the city from E to W, runs

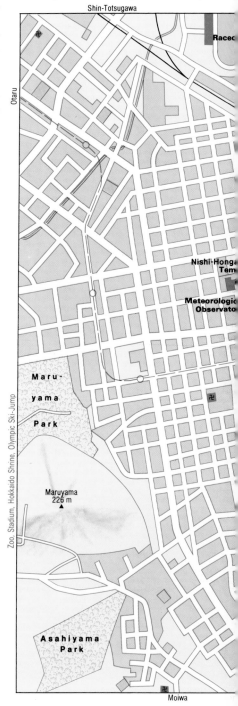

O-dori, a wide boulevard planted with trees and flower-beds which is the scene of Sapporo's famous Snow Festival at the beginning of February. At its E end is the 482 ft/147 m-high *Television Tower*, from the observation platform of which (295 ft/90 m) there is a fine view of the Ishikari Plain. Beneath the boulevard is a large shopping arcade. – 550 yds/500 m farther S, running parallel with O-dori, is a busy shopping street, Tanuki-koji,

known as the "Ginza of Sapporo". To the SE lies the entertainment quarter of SUSUKINO, with numerous bars and restaurants.

From the station there is a subway (underground) line via Susukino to **Nakajima Park**, which is bounded on the E by the River Toyohira. In the park are a landscaped garden, the Hassoan tea-house (brought here in 1918 from the

Clock-Tower, Sapporo

summit a panoramic road (toll) descends the S side of the hill (skiing area; several lifts).

SURROUNDINGS. – In the hilly regions SW of the city is the health resort of **Jozankei-onsen** (bus, 1 hour), which ranks after Noboribetsu as the most popular spa on Hokkaido. The *Nakayama-Toge Mountain Road* runs from Sapporo to here, continuing to *Lake Toya* in the **Shikotsu-Toya National Park** (see separate entry).

9 miles/15 km W of Sapporo is an excellent winter-sports area (bus, 1 hour), where the Winter Olympics were held in 1972. At the foot of Mount *Teine* (3360 ft/1024 m) lies the **Teine Olympic Area** (13 lifts, golf-course, swimming pool, etc.).

7 miles/11 km NE of Sapporo (bus, 40 minutes) **Nopporo-Shinrin Park** (area 8 sq. miles/20 sq. km) has a Memorial Tower (Hyakunen Kinen-to 330 ft/ 100 m high), erected in 1971 on the 100th anniversary of the settlement of Hokkaido, and a Historical Museum (Hokkaido Kaitaku Kinenkan).

Kohoan Temple in Shiga prefecture), various sports grounds and a swimming pool.

At the foot of the hills which rise to the W of the city is *Maruyama Park** (bus from station, 20 minutes), with sports facilities and a Zoo. The *Hokkaido Shrine* (founded 1869, present buildings 1964) in the northern part of the park, is particularly beautiful at cherry-blossom time (beginning of May). To the W of the park, on Mount *Okurayama*, can be seen the *Olympic ski-jumping platform*. On Mount *Maruyama* (742 ft/226 m) is *Maruyama Forest*, a statutorily protected area of natural forest with a variety of different species.

To the SW of the city (bus from station, 25 minutes) rises Mount *Moiwa* (1739 ft/ 530 m), with a cableway and chair-lift to the summit (extensive views). From the

Satsunan Islands
さつなんしょ島

Prefecture: Kagoshima.
(i) (central)
Kagoshima-ken Tokyo Kanko Bussan Assensho,
Olympic Building,
2-7-17, Ginza, Chuo-ku,
J-100 **Tokyo;**
tel. (03) 561 6701.

HOTELS. – ON TANEGASHIMA. – **Western style:** *Tanegashima Kanko Hotel*, Nishinoomote, 33 r. – YOUTH HOSTEL: *Tanegashima YH*, 1937-1, Nakanoshima, Minamitane-machi, 42 b.

ON YAKUSHIMA – **Western style:** *Miyanoura Kanko Hotel*, Miyanoura, Kamiyaku-cho, 15 r., beach; *Hotel Pine*, Onoaida-onsen, Yaku-cho, 22 r., thermal bath, beach. – **Ryokan:** *Tashiro-kan*, Miyanoura, Kamiyaku-cho, 16 r., beach; *Minamiso*, Minamitane-machi, 20 r. – YOUTH HOSTEL: *Yakushima YH*, 4469-62, Anbo, Yaku-cho, 50 b., beach.

TRANSPORTATION. – **Air:** from KAGOSHIMA to Tanegashima (35 minutes), Amami-Oshima (1¼ hours) and Yoron-to (1¾ hours). – **Boat:** from KAGOSHIMA to Nishi-no-Omote (Tanegashima; 3 hours), Miyanoura (Yakushima; 3½ hours), Naze (Amami-Oshima; 11 hours) and Yoron-to (21 hours); from NAHA (Okinawa) to Yoron-to (4 hours).

The Satsunan Islands, lying between latitude 31° and 27° N, are at the N end of the curving chain of islands which extends from the southern tip of Kyushu to the coast of Taiwan. The group includes the islands of Tanegashima and Yakushima, the Tokara Islands and the Amami Archi-

In Maruyama Park, Sapporo

Snow Festival, Sapporo

pelago. **The warm climate fosters rich subtropical vegetation, and the beautiful scenery of the islands, with their romantic coasts and deep-blue sea, attracts large numbers of visitors.**

Tanegashima (172 sq. miles/446 sq. km; pop. 25,000), the most northerly of the Satsunan Islands, is separated from Kyushu by the Osumi Strait. Portuguese seamen landed here in 1543, bringing the first firearms seen in Japan: whereupon the ruler of the island, Tanega Tokitaka had them copied and called the new weapons *Tanega-bo*. The Japanese Space Center is on Tanegashima, and in February 1981 the first Japanese rocket was launched from here, carrying an ETS-4 satellite into an elliptical orbit.

The ferries from Kagoshima put in at **Nishi-no-Omote** (pop. 25,000), on the NW coast, from which a bus route runs through the interior of the island, which is relatively flat, to *Cape Kadokura* in the extreme S (1 hour). On the cape are the *Misaki Shrine* and a monument to the first Portuguese seamen. There is an impressive stretch of coast, rugged and heavily eroded by the sea, at *Kumano*. – From Shimama one can take a boat to Yakushima.

The almost exactly circular island of **Yakushima** (194 sq. miles/503 sq. km) presents a striking topographical contrast to Tanegashima. With its 32 extinct volcanoes rising well above 3300 ft/1000 m,

it is known as the "Japanese Maritime Alps". The highest peak is *Miyanoura* (6349 ft/1935 m), its flanks covered with subtropical mountain plants. The mighty ancient cedars (*yaku-sugi*) are widely famed. – Yakushima is part of the **Kirishima-Yaku National Park** (see separate entry).

The **Tokara Islands** are a widely scattered group lying between Yakushima and Amami-Oshima and between the East China Sea and the Pacific.

Some 300 miles/500 km S of Kyushu are the **Amami Islands**, with a total area of 478 sq. miles/1237 sq. km and a population of 162,000. The mean annual temperature is 70°F/21°C.

The largest and most northerly of the Amami Islands is **Amami-Oshima** (274 sq. miles/709 sq. km), the hub of inter-island traffic. On the NW coast is the port of **Naze** (pop. 48,000). The rich subtropical natural vegetation alternates with sugar-cane, banana and pineapple plantations. The beaches of white sand are sheltered by coral reefs. The silk produced on the island (*Oshima-tsumugi*) has long been renowned. – From Naze there are boats to Tokunoshima and Okinoerabushima.

Popular tourist attractions on **Tokunoshima** are bullfights (i.e. fights between bulls) and the gay dance festival of Hachigatsu-odori, which is celebrated also on Tokunoshima's southern neighbor **Okinoerabushima**. Between them the two islands have more than a hundred stalactitic caves, and the *Shoryu-do* cave on Okinoerabushima is one of the largest of its kind in Asia. Impressive cliffs at *Inno-jo-buta*; beautiful bay at Sumiyoshi.

Yoron-to, the most southerly of the Satsunan Islands, is ringed by coral reefs with abundant marine

A beach on the island of Yoron-to (Satsunan group)

life and which offer excellent *diving grounds. The inhabitants live almost exclusively from the tourist trade. The most suitable form of transport is a bicycle (which can be rented). – From *Tchabana Bay*, on the N coast, a road runs S to the **Yunyu Botanic Gardens** in the interior of the island. From the *Kotohira Shrine*, situated on high ground, there are fine panoramic* views. To the SE are the 130 ft/40 m-high cliffs of *Yuukino-misaki*. – From here the road continues E to *Mingu-kan*, an old settlement of thatched wattle-and-daub cottages with a small local museum. – The coast road comes to **Yurinohama Beach**, from which there are trips in glass-bottomed boats (about 1 hour). Offshore are banks of "starry sand", formed from the skeletons of tiny marine creatures. There is also a small pottery manufactory on Yoron-to. The best shopping center for souvenirs, etc., is the *Yunyu-Ginza*. – Opposite Yoron-to lies **Okinawa** (see that entry), to which there are boat services.

Sendai
せんだい

Prefecture: Miyagi. – Population: 680,000.
Post code: J-980. – Telephone code: 0222.
(i) (local)
   Sendai City Tourist Information Office,
   JNR Sendai Station;
   tel. 22 3269 (English spoken).

HOTELS. – **Western style**: *Hotel Rich Sendai*, 2-2, Kokubun-cho, 242 r., beach; *Sendai Plaza*, 2-20-1, Honcho, 221 r.; *Sendai Hotel*, 1-10-25, Chuo, 89 r.; *Grand Hotel Sendai*, 3-7-1, Ichiban-cho, 77 r.; *Hotel Koyo*, 1-7, 4-chome, Ichiban-cho, 63 r.; *Sendai City Hotel*, 2-2-10, Chuo, 58 r., Japanese garden; *Sendai Central Hotel*, 2-1-7, Chuo, 43 r.; *Washington Hotel*, 3-1, Omachi, 2-chome, 270 r.; *Chisan Hotel*, 4-8-7, Chuo, 226 r.; *Green Hotel*, 2-5-6, Nishiki-cho, 210 r.; *Fujiya Hotel*, 8-9, Ichiban-cho 2-chome, 192 r.; *Hotel*

Sun Route, 10-8, Chuo 4-chome, 173 r.; *Tokyo Daiichi Hotel Sendai*, 2-3-18, Chuo, 154 r.; *Miyagi Daiichi Hotel*, 122, Higashi 7-bancho, 121 r.; *Royal Hotel*, 4-10-11, Chuo, 70 r.; *Sendai Oroshi Center Hotel*, 2-15-2, Oroshi-machi, 52 r. – **Ryokan**: *Miyako Hotel Bekkan*, 2-9-14, Honcho, 37 r. – YOUTH HOSTELS: *YH Chitose*, 6-3-8, Odawara, 70 b; *YH Sendai Akamon*, 61, Kawauchi-Kawamae-cho, 51 b.; *Sendai Onnai YH*, 1-9-35, Kashiwagi, 25 b.

RESTAURANTS. – *Gaslight Ginza*, in Washington Hotel; *Sendai Seiyoken*, Shin Sendai Building, 1-1-30, Omachi.

EVENTS. – *Dondo-matsuri* (mid January), burning of New Year decorations at Osaki-Hachimangu Shrine; *Shrine Festival* at Aoba Shrine (end of May), procession in medieval armor; *Tanabata* (beginning of August), Star Festival, with a tradition going back 700 years.

TRANSPORTATION. – **Air**: from TOKYO (Haneda Airport), 45 minutes; from OSAKA (2 hours). – **Rail**: from TOKYO (Ueno Station) to Omiya (30 minutes), then JNR New Tohoku–Shinkansen line (2 hours) or JNR Tohoku line (4¼ hours). – **Bus**: from TOKYO (Central Station) Tohoku–Kyuko express bus (8¼ hours); from Sendai Airport to city center (45 minutes).

The city of Sendai, once a castle town, lies in northern Honshu 6 miles/10 km from the Pacific coast. It owes its name as the "city of forests" to its *situation between wooded hills. Sendai is the chief town of Miyagi prefecture and the political, cultural and economic center of the Tohoku region.

The city's main industries are foodstuffs, woodworking, electrical apparatus and metal-processing. Traditional craft products are lacquerware and wooden dolls.

In the Botanic Gardens on Yoron-to

HISTORY. – In 1602 the powerful Daimyo Date Masamune (1566–1636) built Aobajo Castle, and Sendai became the center of one of the largest fiefs in northern Japan. The ambitious Masamune, known as the One-Eyed Shogun (*Dokuganryu Shogun*), was one of the last to hold out against the rising power of Toyotomi Hideyoshi; and it was only when Hideyoshi took Odawara Castle in 1590 and thus broke the resistance of Hojo Ujimasa that Masamune brought himself to swear an oath of allegiance to Hideyoshi. When, after Hideyoshi's death, Tokugawa Ieyasu was victorious in the struggle for his succession Masamune threw in his lot with the new ruler and took part in his Korean campaign and in the Siege of Osaka Castle in 1615. During the persecution of Christians initiated by the second Tokugawa Shogun, Hidetada, Masamune secured the liberation of the Franciscan friar Luis Sotelo (1574–1624), whom he later permitted to return to Europe together with an embassy he was sending to the West. – The history of the Date clan became famous through the Kabuki play "Sendai Hagi".

SIGHTS. – To the W of the station (bus, 15 minutes) is *Aoba Hill*, at the foot of which are the remains of ramparts – all that is left of Aobajo Castle. Relics and mementoes of the Date family are displayed in the **Museum** (*Sendai Shiritsu Hakubutsukan*). – Beyond the river is **Nishi Park**, with the Sakuragaoka Shrine, the Civic Hall and the Observatory.

To the W of the city (bus from station, 20 minutes) are the **Botanic Garden** of Tohoku University and, to the N of this, the *Zoo* (Yagiyama Dobutsu Koen).

SW of the city center, in a loop of the River *Hirose*, stands the **Zuihoji Temple**, with the Mausoleum of Date Masamune (Zuihoden), restored in recent times.

2½ miles/4 km NW of the station is the **Osaki-Hachimangu Shrine** (1607), a fine example of the architecture of the Momoyama period. The richly decorated *Main Hall* resembles that of the Zuiganji Temple in Matsushima (see that entry). – the **Rinnoji Temple**, dedicated to the Date clan (bus from station, 15 minutes), dates from the Meiji period.

NE of the city center (bus to Miyamae Gochome, 10 minutes) is the **Toshogu Shrine**, dedicated to Tokugawa Ieyasu, which was built by Date Tadamune.

1 mile/1·5 km E of the Central Station lies **Tsutsujigaoka Park**, seen at its best when the ancient cherry trees are in blossom. Adjoining the park are various sports grounds.

Near the Kita-Sendai Station (Senzan line) is the **Komyoji Temple**, within the precincts of which are the tomb of Hasekura Tsunenaga, who traveled to Europe on an official mission in 1613, and a monument to Luis Sotelo, who went with him.

SURROUNDINGS. – 4 miles/6 km S of the city (bus, 20 minutes) we come to the *Yaso-en*, a wild garden.

9 miles/15 km NE of Sendai (JNR Senseki line, 20 minutes) is **Tagajo**, where a castle is said to have been built about 724 to provide protection against the indigenous Emishi tribes. The site of the castle is marked by a monument erected about 760.

The Senseki line continues to **Shiogama** (pop. 60,000), a busy fishing port in the SW of *Matsushima Bay*. On a wooded hill 770 yds/700 m NW of Hon-Shiogama Station is the Shiogama Shrine, dedicated to the patron divinities of seafarers and expectant mothers. Among its treasures are an iron lantern presented by Izumi Saburo in 1187 and a sundial of 1783. – A colorful Harbor Festival is celebrated in Shiogama in mid August.

To the W of Sendai are two popular health resorts, which can be reached by bus. **Akiu-onsen** (50 minutes) has hot springs at a temperature of 131 °F/ 55 °C. From here a pleasant detour can be made up the *Natori* Valley for a distance of 9 miles/14 km to the 180 ft/55 m-high **Akiu-Otaki Falls**, near which is the romantic **Rairaikyo Gorge**. – The resort of **Sakunami-onsen** (55 minutes) also attracts many visitors on account of its hot springs (95–140 °F/ 35–60 °C).

See also **Matsushima**.

Setonaikai
See Inland Sea

Shikoku

Area of island: 7254 sq. miles/18,787 sq. km.
Population: 3,940,000.

Shikoku, the smallest of the four main Japanese islands and economically and culturally the least developed, lies to the S of western Honshu, separated from it by the Inland Sea. It is divided into four prefectures – Tokushima, Kagawa, Kochi and Ehime.

The climate of Shikoku, influenced by the Kuroshio Current, is in general warm and dry. The island lies in the path of the typhoons which are particularly frequent in autumn ("Taifun-Ginza"). – The interior of Shikoku is traversed by mountain ranges running from E to W, reaching their highest points in *Ishizuchi* (6503 ft/ 1982 m) and *Tsurugi* (6414 ft/1955 m). Both these ranges are in Quasi National Parks – tracts of rugged territory slashed by the wild and romantic gorges of the rivers Yoshino and Shimanto. The N coast, facing on to the Inland Sea, and the W coast, opposite Kyushu, are much indented by coves and inlets. The western coastal region forms the **Ashizuri-Uwakai National Park**.

Cape Ashizuri, the southernmost tip of Shikoku

A characteristic feature of Shikoku used to be the large numbers of white-clad pilgrims making their way to the island's 88 pilgrimage temples. Nowadays those making the pilgrimage, which lasts about two weeks, usually travel by bus.

All the **pilgrimage temples** are associated with *Kukai* (774–836), posthumously known by the name of Kobo-daishi, the priest – born in what is now Kagawa prefecture – who founded the Shingon sect. Participation in the pilgrimage, which has been popular since the Edo period, secures for the believer release from the cycle of rebirths.

See also *Ashizuri-Uwakai National Park, Kochi, Matsuyama, Naruto*, **Takamatsu, Tokushima** and **Uwajima**.

Shikotsu-Toya National Park
しこつとうや
国立公園

Prefecture: Hokkaido.
Area 381 sq. miles/987 sq. km.

(central)
National Parks Association of Japan,
Toranomon Denki Building,
8-1, Toranomon 2-chome, Minato-ku,
J-105 **Tokyo**;
tel. (03) 502 0488.

(local)
Toyako-onsen Tourist Association,
Abutacho-Yakuba-shisho,
J-049-57 **Toyako-onsen**;
tel. (01427) 5 6630.

HOTELS. – IN NOBORIBETSU. – **Western style**: *Noboribetsu Grand Hotel*, 154, Noboribetsu-onsen, 234 r., Japanese garden, thermal bath. – **Ryokan**: *Daiichi-Tatsimoto-kan*, 55, Noboribetsu-onsen-machi, 365 r., thermal bath; *Noboribetsu Prince Hotel*, Noboribetsu-onsen, 399 r.; *Daiichi Takimotokan*, Noboribetsu-onsen, 280 r.; *Noboribetsu-onsen Kanko Hotel Takinoya*, Noboribetsu-onsen, 72 r. – **Minshuku**: *Kikusui*, 220-5, Naka Noboribetsu-cho, 52 r. – YOUTH HOSTELS: *Kuttara-ko YH*, Noboribetsu-onsen-cho, 76 b.; *YH Akashiya-so*, Noboribetsu-onsen, 55 b.; *YH Noboribetsu-Ekimae*, 2-2-1, Noboribetsu-higashi-cho, 50 b.; *YH Ryokan Kanefuku*, 132, Noboribetsu-onsen, 40 b; *YH Noboribetsu Kannonji*, 119, Noboribetsu-onsen-cho, 25 b.

IN MURORAN. – **Western style**: *Business Hotel Muroran Royal*, 2-21-11, Nakashima-cho, 59 r.; *Muroran Daiichi Hotel*, 3-21-6, Nakashima-cho, 58 r.; *Hotel Ocean*, 14-19, Saiwai-cho, 53 r.; *Hotel Harbor*, 4-11, Sawa-machi, 42 r. – **Ryokan**: *Honda Ryokan*, 28 r.; *Osawa Ryokan*, 28 r.; *Fumino Ryokan*, 20 r.

IN NATIONAL PARK. – **Western style**: *Toya Kanko Hotel*, Aza-Toyako-onsen-machi, Abuta-cho, 148 r., thermal bath; *Toya-Ko Onsen Hotel*, 6, Aza-Toyako-onsen-machi, 121 r., thermal bath; *Hotel Sun Route*, Tomakomai, 1-2, Nishiki-cho 1-chome, 92 r.; *Shikotsu-Ko Grand Hotel*, Okotan Bangaichi, Shikotsu-ko, Chitose-shi, 34 r., thermal bath, beach. – **Ryokan**: *Ryokan Hifumi*, 24, Aza-Toyako-onsen-machi, Abuta-cho, 58 r., thermal bath. – YOUTH HOSTELS: *Showa-Shinzan YH*, 79, Sobetsu-onsen, Sobetsu-cho, 285 b., thermal bath; *Toya Kanko-kan YH*, 83, Sobetsu-onsen, Sobetsu-machi, 200 b., thermal bath; *Nakayama-toge YH*, Nakayama-toge, Kimobetsu-cho, 60 b.

TRANSPORTATION. – **Rail**: from SAPPORO JNR Chitose and Muroran lines to Muroran (Higashi-Muroran Station). – **Bus**: several routes in National Park.

The *Shikotsu-Toya National Park**, in western Hokkaido near Sapporo, contains in its three separate parts a whole range of beautiful volcanic landscapes, with crater lakes and many hot springs. The best places from which to visit it are Sapporo and Muroran, at the E end of the Uchiura Bay.

The largest section of the National Park lies at the very gates of Sapporo. An hour's bus ride from the city is the health resort of **Jozankei-onsen** (saline springs), on the River *Toyohira*, which rapidly developed into a thriving spa after the opening of the road from Sapporo in 1871. Beauty-spots in the vicinity of the resort are the *Shiraito-no-taki Waterfall*, the Nishikibashi Bridge and the crag of *Futami-Iwa*.

W of Jozankei-onsen, in the north-western section of the National Park, is an extinct volcano, *Yotei* (6211 ft/1893 m), below the N side of which lies the town of **Kutchan** (JNR Hakodate line from Sapporo, 2 hours). From here there is a bus service to *Lake Hangetsu*, from which it is a 4 hours' climb to the summit of the volcano; an alternative route is from the next station on the line, Hirafu. The three summit craters are known as "Father Cauldron", "Mother Cauldron" and "Little Cauldron". It is a 1¼ mile/2 km-walk round the main crater.

To the S of Jokanzai-onsen the road crosses the *Nakayama Pass* (2743 ft/ 836 m; *view) and comes to the crystal-clear *Lake Toya*, surrounded by mountains (bus, 1½ hours). In the middle of the almost exactly circular lake, which is 590 ft/179 m deep and does not freeze over even in severe winters, is the densely wooded island of *Nakanoshima* (or Oshima), surrounded by the much smaller islets of *Kannon, Manju* and *Benten*. On the SW side of the lake is the popular health resort of **Toyako-onsen** (hot springs at temperatures of up to 140 °F/ 60 °C), from which there are boats to Nakanoshima (20 minutes).

S of the lake are Mounts Usu and Showa-Shinzan, which can be climbed from **Sobetsu** on its southern shore (also reached by JNR Iburi line from Kutchan or Muroran line from Muroran to Date-Mombetsu, then Iburi line). It is 5 minutes by bus to the foot of the active volcano of **Showa-Shinzan** (1339 ft/408 m), which came into being only in 1944–45. At the bus stop there is a display illustrating the volcano's development, which was recorded in every detail. The climb takes an hour. – From the bus stop a cableway 1495 ft/1365 m long runs up to the base of the E side of Mount **Usu**, also an active volcano, which formed *Meiji-Shinzan* ("new mountain of the Meiji period"), on its northern flank, in a great eruption in 1910 and *Showa-Shinzan* ("new mountain of the Showa period", to the E, in 1944–45. In the summit region are *Great Usu* (2379 ft/725 m) to the E

and *Little Usu* to the W, which together with the heights of the *Byobuyama* range enclose *Lake Ginnuma*.

In **Usu** (also reached by the JNR Muroran line from Muroran), 1 mile/1·5 km N of the station, stands the oldest temple on Hokkaido, the *Zenkoji Temple* (1804), one of the three official missionary temples.

Outside this part of the National Park, on the *Etomo* Promontory which bounds *Uchiura Bay* on the E, lies the town of **Muroran** (pop. 162,000; bus from Sapporo, 3½ hours), which has a good natural harbor and an extensive industrial zone. 12 minutes' bus ride from the station is an aquarium, the *Muroran Suizokukan*. In the center of the peninsula rises Mount *Sokuryoyama* (655 ft/200 m), from which there are fine *views of the mountains of the National Park. *Cape Chikyu* at the S end of the peninsula has wave-eroded cliffs up to 330 ft/100 m high as well as a lighthouse (1920).

The Muroran railway line runs E to **Noboribetsu**, to the N of which is the health resort of **Noboribetsu-onsen** (also reached by a 1¼ hours' bus ride from Muroran through the beautiful *Momijidani* Valley – "Maple Valley"). Noboribetsu-onsen, surrounded by magnificent forests, is the largest resort on Hokkaido, with the Daiichi-Takimoto, a series of 40 basins supplied by ten different hot springs (113–199 °F/ 45–93 °C). The town has a *Hot Springs Museum* (with an associated research institute) and an *Ainu Museum*. – The hot springs rise in the **Jigokudani** ("Valley of Hell"), an area of volcanic rock formations 440 yds/400 m from the town. From here it is a short climb to *Lake Oyunuma*, a crater lake still bubbling with volcanic activity. From Mount *Hiyoriyama* (1201 ft/366 m) beside the lake, rises a column of sulphurous vapors. – E of Noboribetsu-onsen is Mount *Kuma* (1801 ft/549 m; cableway), with the Bear Ranch, the home of some 200 brown bears. In a beautiful setting under the E side of the hill lies *Lake Kuttara* (buses from Noboribetsu-onsen in summer, 25 minutes). There is also a bus service to **Karurusu-onsen** (hot springs, 100–133 °F/38–56 °C), situated in the *Chitose* Valley below Mount *Orofure* (4039 ft/ 1231 m).

The railway continues to the village of **Shiraoi**, situated near the coast on *Lake Porotoko*. 770 yds/700 m SW is an *Ainu settlement*, built in 1965 to maintain the traditions of the Ainu people. Although established with an eye to the tourist market, it is well worth visiting. The *Shiraoi-minzoku-shiryokan* Museum gives an interesting glimpse of the old way of life of the Ainu.

From **Tomakomai**, on the Muroran line, a road leads inland to beautiful **Lake Shikotsu**, in the section of the National Park which also includes Jokanzai-onsen (see above). The lake, which is 1190 ft/363 m deep and never freezes, lies between two active volcanoes, *Tarumae* (3360 ft/1024 m) to the S and *Eniwa* (4331 ft/1320 m) to the N. On the shores of the lake are two health resorts, *Shikotsu-kohan* and *Marukoma-onsen*, linked by a boat service (1¼ hours).

Mount **Tarumae** has erupted several times since the late 17th c., the 1909 eruption being particularly violent. The climb to the summit crater from *Morappu*, on the S side of the lake, takes about 45 minutes (bus to 7th staging-point in summer).

Mount **Eniwa** can be climbed from Shikotsu-kohan via *Poropinai* in 3 hours. The view from the summit extends as far as Sapporo. Some of the events in the 1972 Winter Olympics were staged here.

From here the bus can be taken back to Sapporo via Noboribetsu.

See also **Sapporo**.

Shimane
See under Daisen-Oki National Park

Shimonoseki
しものせき

Prefecture: Yamaguchi. – Population: 275,000.
Post code: J-750. – Telephone code: 0832.
ⓘ (central)
Yamaguchi-ken Tokyo Kanko Bussan Assensho,
Kokusai Kanko Kaikan,
1-8-3, Marunouchi, Chiyoda-ku,
J-100 **Tokyo**;
tel. (03) 231 4980.

(local)
Yamaguchi-ken TIC,
Ogori-eki, Ogori-cho,
Yoshiki-gun;
tel. (08397) 2 6373.

HOTELS. – **Western style**: *Shimonoseki Grand Hotel*, 31-2, Nabe-cho, 45 r.; *Sanyo Hotel*, 2-9, Mimosusogawa, 35 r., SP, thermal bath; *Tokyu Inn*, 4-4-1, Takesaki-cho, 128 r. – YOUTH HOSTEL: *Shimonoseki-Hinoyama YH*, 3-47, Mimosusosakawa-machi, 52 b.

TRANSPORTATION. – **Air**: from TOKYO (Haneda Airport) to Kitakyushu (1½ hours). – **Rail**: from TOKYO (Central Station) JNR Sanyo–Shinkansen line via OSAKA (Shin-Osaka Station) and HIROSHIMA (7 hours); from FUKUOKA (Hakata) via KITAKYUSHU (Kokura Station; 1¼ hours).

The large deep-sea fishing port of Shimonoseki lies at the western tip of Honshu, separated from the island of Kyushu by the Shimonoseki Strait, only 1100 yds/1000 m wide. Its major industries, in addition to fish-processing, are shipbuilding, chemicals and metalworking.

HISTORY. – The coastal waters off Shimonoseki were the scene of the important naval Battle of Dannoura (1185) in which the Taira forces were defeated by the Minamoto. Before the Meiji era Shimonoseki was the main base of the Choshu clan, who were opposed to the Shogunate's policy of opening up Japan, and in 1863 the Choshu fired on foreign vessels lying off the town, under the battle-cry "Revere the Emperor and drive out the barbarians": whereupon, in August 1864, American, French, British and Dutch naval forces bombarded the town and captured it within three days. – The 1895 Peace Treaty between Japan and China was signed at Shimonoseki.

SIGHTS. – On a hill 1½ miles/2·5 km E of Shin-Shimonoseki Station (bus, 10 minutes) is the **Kameyama-Hachimango Shrine**, dedicated to the legendary Emperors Chuai, Ojin and Nintoku and the Empress Jingu, who is believed to have sailed for Korea from here in the 3rd c. From the grounds of the shrine there is a fine *view of the Shimonoseki Strait. Behind the shrine stands the house in which the treaty between Japan and China was signed in 1895. – 550 yds/500 m NE, on Mount *Benishiyama*, is the **Akama-jingu Shrine**, dedicated to the boy Emperor Antoku (1178–85), which contains the tombs of Antoku, who was drowned in the Battle of Dannoura, and seven members of the Taira family.

The coastal area of *Dannoura*, a strip ¾ mile/1 km long, lies farther E (bus). The memory of the Battle of Dannoura is kept alive in many old tales; and the popular belief that the members of the Taira clan who lost their lives in the battle were transformed into marine creatures is reflected in the names *koheike* for a local species of fish and *heike-gani* for shrimps.

At Dannoura Station are the entrances to the *Kammon Tunnel* (1958) and the *Kammon Bridge*, which link Honshu with Kyushu. Here, too, is the lower station of a cableway up Mount *Hinoyama*, from the top of which there is a fine * view of the strait and the town of Kitakyushu on the far side.

3 miles/5 km E of the city center lies the district of CHOFU, once the home of samurai, which preserves some streets of old houses. The **Kozanji Temple**, founded in the 14th c., has a Main Hall of 1325; the other buildings are modern. To the left of the temple is a small museum. – 1 mile/1·5 km SW of Chofu Station stands the **Iminomiya Shrine**, dedicated to Chuai, Jingu and Ojin, and near this is the **Nogi Shrine**, dedicated to Nogi Maresuke (1849–1912), who committed suicide to accompany the Emperor Meiji in death; behind the shrine is the house in which he was born, now containing a small museum. – It is a 7-minute bus ride from the station to the coast at *Sotoura*, where there is an extensive recreational area and the large *Shimonoseki Aquarium*.

Shiretoko National Park

しれとこ
国立公園

Prefecture: Hokkaido.
Area: 160 sq. miles/414 sq. km.
ⓘ (central)
National Parks Association of Japan,
Toranomon Denki Building,
8-1. Toranomon 2-chome, Minato-ku,
J-105 **Tokyo**;
tel. (03) 502 0488.

HOTELS. – **Western style**: *Shiretoko Grand Hotel*, Aza-Utoro-Bangaichi, Shari-machi, 78 r., beach; *Shiretoko Kanko Hotel*, Aza-Yunosawa, Rausa, Mensahi-gun, 56 r., thermal bath. – **Ryokan**: *Ryokan Tanaka-ya*, Shari-machi, 24 r., beach; *Sakae-ya Ryokan*, Rausu, Menashi-gun, 16 r., thermal bath. – **Minshuku**: *Shinobu-kan*, Utoro, Shari-machi, 16 r., beach; *Green Shiretoko*, Utoro, Shari-machi, 14 r., thermal bath, beach; *Pereke*, Utoro, Shari-machi, 16 r., beach. – YOUTH HOSTELS: *Shiretoko YH*, Utoro-onsen, Shari-machi, 360 b., thermal bath, beach; *Utoro YH*, Utoro, Shari-machi, 120 b., beach; *Rausu YH*, 4, Hon-cho, Rausu-machi, 88 b., beach; *Iwaobetsu YH*, Iwaobetsu, Shari-machi, 23 b., beach. •

TRANSPORTATION. – **Rail**: from KUSHIRO and ABASHIRI JNR Semmo line to Shari. – **Bus**: from Shari to Shiretoko-Goko and Rausu. – **Boat**: ferry service from TOKYO to KUSHIRO (30 hours); boat from Utoro to Rausu (4½ hours; summer only).

The * Shiretoko Peninsula, most of which is included within the Shiretoko National Park, projects into the Sea of Okhotsk from the E coast of Hokkaido in the form of a narrow wedge 40 miles/65 km long. The dominant features of the landscape are two quiescent volcanoes, Rausu and Shiretoko.

This area, difficult of access until about 10 years ago, has now been opened up by the provision of excellent new roads. The best center is the seaside resort of Utoro on the NW coast. The traveling season is confined to the months of May to October.

From **Shari** Station (JNR Semmo line) a bus runs along the coast to **Utoro** (50 minutes) and on to the five **Shiretoko Lakes**. The most notable beauty-spots in this area are *Lake Rausu* (circumference (4 miles/6 km) and the *Kamuiwakka* and *Oshin-Koshin Falls*.

From Utoro there are boat trips round the peninsula to **Rausu** on the SE coast (4½ hours). For most of the way the coast is fringed with cliffs up to 650 ft/200 m high. Near Rausu is the health resort of *Rausu-onsen*. – A bus goes SW to *Nemuro-Shibetsu*, from which there are trains (JNR Shibetsu line) to Shibecha on the JNR Semmo line.

Shizuoka
しずおか

Prefecture: Shizuoka. – Population: 462,000.
Post code: J-420. – Telephone code: 0542.
ⓘ (central)
Shizuoka-ken Tokyo Kanko Bussan Assensho,
Kokusai Kanko Kaikan,
1-8-3, Marunouchi, Chiyoda-ku,
J-100 **Tokyo**;
tel. (03) 215 0612.

HOTELS. – **Western style**: *Shizuoka Grand Hotel Nakajimaya*, 3-10, Koya-machi, 117 r., beach; *Shizuoka International Hotel New Yashima*, 3-43, Higashi-Takajo-machi, 61 r.; *Shizuoka Washington Hotel*, 6-5, Minami-machi, 83 r.; *Shizuoka Green Hotel*, 5-6, Denma-cho, 72 r.; *Business Hotel Marusan*, 4-2-18, Komagata-dori, 41 r.; *Pacific Hotel*, 15-1, Aioi-cho,

33 r. – **Ryokan:** *Yashimaen*, Higashi-Takajo-machi, 19 r. – YOUTH HOSTELS: *YH Ishibashi Ryokan*, 405, Negoya, 60 b.; *YH Suigetsu-in-Sanso*, 648, Tawaramine, 20 b.

EVENTS. – *Shizuoka-matsuri* (beginning of April), procession in historical costumes at Sengen Shrine.

TRANSPORTATION. – **Rail:** from TOKYO (Central Station) JNR Tokaido–Shinkansen line (1½ hours); from NAGOYA JNR Tokaido–Shinkansen line (1¼ hours).

Shizuoka, chief town of its prefecture, lies on the S coast of Honshu, roughly half-way between Tokyo and Nagoya. It is the principal market for green tea (some 60% of total Japanese production) and is also an educational center, with a University and a College of Pharmacy. Characteristic local craft products are lacquerware and bamboo articles.

HISTORY. – During the Edo period the town, then called *Sumpu*, had a castle built by the Tokugawa which was the most westerly outpost of the capital, Edo (now Tokyo). The first Tokugawa Shogun, Ieyasu, lived here for 25 years.

SIGHTS. – In the northern part of the town is the site of the *Castle*, which was completely destroyed in 1945, leaving only some fragments of walls and moats. The site is now occupied by the *Civic Hall* (Sumpu Kaikan).

On the northern outskirts of the town, 1¼ miles/2 km from the station, is Mount *Shizuhata-yama*, which is renowned for its show of cherry blossom in spring (beginning of April). Below the S side of the hill can be found the **Sengen Shrine**, founded in the 17th c. (present buildings 19th c.). The ceiling-paintings are by artists of the Kano school. From the rear of the shrine a flight of steps leads up into a park from which there are fine *views of the town and surrounding area. – Near the Sengen Shrine, set in a beautiful garden, we find the **Rinzai-ji Temple** of the Rinzai sect, founded in the early 16th c. as the protective temple of the Imagawa clan who then ruled the province of Suruga. The temple's treasures include an Amida statue of the Kasuga school and drawings by Kano Tanyu (1602–74).

1½ miles/2·5 km S of the station (bus, 15 minutes) lies the excavation site of **Toro**. After the chance finds made here in 1943 an area of 41 acres was excavated to reveal a settlement of the Late Yayoi period (*c.* 2nd–3rd c.). The largest of the 12 houses brought to light (oval in plan and originally with thatched roofs) measured 39 ft/12 m by 36 ft/11 m. Subsidiary buildings on piles are thought to have been store-houses. The pattern of fields around the settlement pointed to rice-culture. Agricultural implements, domestic equipment and jewelry recovered during the excavations are displayed in the site museum.

SURROUNDINGS. – 6 miles/10 km S (bus to Kunozanshita, 35 minutes) we reach Mount *Kunozan*, which falls steeply down to Suruga Bay, in an area notable for the mildness of its climate. On the terraced slopes strawberries are grown. Tokugawa Ieyasu was buried here before his remains were transferred to Nikko, and on the summit of the hill, approached by a flight of 1150 stone steps, is the **Toshogu Shrine**, in the sumptuous Gongen-zukuri style, which was founded by his son Hidetada in 1617. The shrine contains various items which belonged to Ieyasu, including armor and swords. – Some distance below the shrine is the station of a cableway running up to the *Nihon-daira Plateau* with its extensive tea plantations. From here there are panoramic *views of Suruga Bay, Mount Fuji (to the NE), Mount Kunozan and the Pacific coast. The fir grove of *Miho-no-matsubara* to the E, fringing a long sandy beach, has been much celebrated in poetry and painting. – The plateau can also be reached direct from Shizuoka by bus or from Shimizu by train (JNR Shimizuko line).

To the N of Miho-no-matsubara lies the port of **Shimizu** (pop. 242,000). 3 miles/4·5 km S of the station, on higher ground, is the Ryugenji Temple. – Farther N we reach **Okitsu**, noted for its beautiful setting and mild climate, which during the Edo period was the 17th staging-point on the Tokaido Highway. From this period dates the Ryokan Minaguchi-ya, still serving its original purpose, which features in Oliver Statler's novel "The Inn on the Tokaido".

Shodojima
しょうどじま

Prefecture: Kagawa.
Area of island: 60 sq. miles/155 sq. km.
Population: 44,000.
(i) (local)
Shodojima Kanko Annai Center,
    tel. (08796) 212,

HOTELS. – **Western style:** *Shodoshima International Hotel*, 24-67, Tonosho-cho, Shozu-gun, 106 r., Japanese garden, beach; *Hotel New Kankai*, 1135, Tonosho-cho, Shozu-gun, 73 r., beach; *Hotel Kashiyama*, Uchinoumi-cho, Shozu-gun, 38 r. – **Ryokan:** *Kame-ya*, 16-3, Uchinoumi-cho, Shozu-gun, 38 r.; *Suimei-so*, 1171-6, Tonosho-cho, Shozu-gun, 36 r., SP, beach; *Kankai-Ro*, 24, Tonosho, Shozu-gun, 30 r., SP, beach. – **Minshuku:** *Mamamoto*, 850, Tonosho, Shozu-gun, 13 r., beach. – YOUTH HOSTELS: *Shodoshima Olive YH*, Nishimura, Uchinoumi-cho, Shozu-gun, 100 b.; *Shodo Shima YH*, Utsukushinohara-Kogen, Tonosho-cho, Shozu-gun, 50 b.

TRANSPORTATION. – **Boat**: from OKAYAMA (1¼ hours; hydrofoil 40 minutes); from OSAKA (6 hours); from KOBE (4½ hours); from UNO (45 minutes); from TAKAMATSU (35–70 minutes).

Shodojima is the largest island in the Inland Sea after Awaji. The southern part is covered by olive plantations; the rocky gorges in the N have long been a source of building stone – used, for example, in the construction of Osaka Castle (1586).

The boats from Okayama (Honshu) and Takamatsu (Shikoku) put in at **Tonosho** (pop. 23,000), from which there are coach tours of the island (4 or 6 hours). On a hill to the E of the harbor, commanding extensive views, is the *Peacock Garden*.

Peacock Garden, Tonosho (Shodojima)

In the center of the island is the impressive *Kankakei Gorge* ("cold misty valley"; bus from Tonosho), 5 miles/8 km long and 1¼ miles/2 km across. It is flanked by a range of hills with bizarrely eroded rock formations and a dense covering of maples, firs and azaleas (vivid autumn colors in November). From the valley bottom a cableway runs up to the *Shibocho* viewpoint, which affords a fine *prospect of this particularly beautiful part of the Inland Sea.

The COACH TOURS of the island (with Japanese-speaking guides) take in *Futagoura Bay*, the beach of *Myonan*, the *Silver Beach*, the quarry which produced the stone used in building Osaka Castle, the *Choshikei Monkey Park*, the Kankakei Gorge, the *Peace Park* and the *Kankakei Highway*, which offers a succession of beautiful views.

Takamatsu
たかまつ

Prefecture: Kagawa. – Population: 320,000.
Post code: J-760. – Telephone code: 0878.

ⓘ (central)
Kagawa-ken Tokyo Kanko Bussan Assensho,
Kokusai Kanko Kaikan,
1-8-3, Marunouchi, Chiyoda-ku,
J-100 **Tokyo**;
tel. (03) 231 4840.

(local)
Travel Information Center,
in Central Station;
tel. 51 6951.
Tourist Section of Takamatsu City,
1-8-15, Bancho;
tel. 21 8111.
Japan Travel Bureau,
Japan Travel Bureau Building,
7-6, Kajiyamachi;
tel. 51 2111.

HOTELS. – **Western style**: *Keio Plaza Hotel Takamatsu*, 5-11, Chuo-cho, 180 r., beach; *Takamatsu Grand Hotel*, 10-5-1, Kotobuki-cho, 136 r.; *Takamatsu International Hotel*, 2191, Kita-cho, 107 r., Japanese garden, SP; *Okura Hotel Takamatsu*, 1-9-5, Jyoto-cho, 350 r.; *Takamatsu Washington Hotel*, 1-2-3, Kawara-machi, 252 r.; *Hotel Tokuju*, 3-5-5, Hanazono-cho, 121 r.; *Takamatsu City Hotel*, 8-13, Kamei-cho, 45 r.; *Takamatsu Station Hotel*, 1-1-1, Kotobuki-cho, 26 r. – **Ryokan**: *Hotel Kawaroku*, Hyakken-cho, 75 r.; *Tokiwa Honkan*, Tokiwa-cho, 23 r. **Minshuko**: Sunaya Shiten, 1-12, Nishiuchi-machi, 69 r., SP. – YOUTH HOSTELS: *Kagawa-ken Yashima YH*, 34-1, Yashima-higashi-machi, 96 b.; *Takamatsu-Shi YH*, 531-3, Okamoto-cho, 52 b.; *Takamatsu Yashima-Sanso YH*, 77-4, Yashima-naka-machi, 50 b.; *YH Takamatsu Yuai-Sanso*, 2-4-14, Nishiki-cho, 32 b.

EVENTS. – *Okaya-matsuri* (beginning of May), in Tamura Shrine; *Great Shrine Festival* (beginning of August in alternate years) in Sumiyoshi Shrine; *Takamatsu-matsuri* (mid August), Summer Festival.

TRANSPORTATION. – **Air**: from TOKYO (Haneda Airport), 2 hours; from OSAKA (40 minutes). – **Rail**: from TOKYO (Central Station) JNR Tokaido–Shinkansen line to OKAYAMA (4½ hours), then JNR Uno line to UNO (35 minutes). – **Boat**: from UNO (1 hour); from OSAKA Inland Sea Line (6 hours).

Takamatsu, lying on the N coast of eastern Shikoku overlooking the Inland Sea, is the chief town of Kagawa prefecture and the second largest town on the island of Shikoku. Bounded on the S by wooded ranges of hills with a very agreeable climate, it is a popular tourist center. Much of the adjoining coast is within the Inland Sea National Park. – The town's main industries are paper-making, cotton goods and pharmaceuticals. Local craft products are lacquerware and fans.

SIGHTS. – In the N of the town are the harbor and the Central Station (JNR Yosan line). 330 yds/300 m E is **Tamamo Park**, with the remains of the *Castle*, built by Ikoma Chikamasa in 1587 – one of the very few moated castles in Japan. Also in the park are the *Hiunkaku Pavilion* (1917) and the Matsudaira family treasure. Magnificent views of the Inland Sea.

From the station there is a bus (10 minutes) to **Ritsurin Park**, which formerly belonged to the summer villa of the Matsudaira family. Based on the principle of the "borrowed landscape", this large landscaped garden (185 acres) incorporates the adjacent Mount Shiun in the total picture, which includes lakes, hills, groups of rocks and bizarrely shaped trees. Within the park are a *Zoo*, an Art Gallery, a Museum of Folk Art and a swimming pool.

SURROUNDINGS of Takamatsu

2½ miles/4 km off the coast (ferry service) is the island of **Megishima** or **Onigashima**. From the hills on the island there are charming views of the Inland Sea.

4 miles/6 km E of Takamatsu, reached by bus or tram, is the former island of **Yashima**, now connected with

In the Ritsurin Park, Takamatsu

the mainland of Shikoku by a tongue of land. At the S end of the plateau, on Mount *Nanrei* (cableway, 5 minutes), stands the **Yashimaji Temple**, which contains many mementoes of the conflicts between the Minamoto and Taira clans. – From Yashima Station a line runs N to Mount *Goken* or Yakuri (1214 ft/360 m; extensive views), on the slopes of which can be found the **Yakuriji Temple** (founded 827).

Farther E (Kotoku line from Takamatsu, 25 minutes) one reaches the **Shido Temple** of the Shingon sect, one of the 88 pilgrimage temples of Shikoku, founded in the late 7th c. It contains a wooden statue and a painting of the Eleven-Headed Kannon and a series of colored drawings illustrating the temple's history (the Shidodera-engi-zue). – Beyond this is *Sanuki-Tsuda*, from which an attractive footpath runs along the 2½ miles/4 km of white beach (Kinrin Park). 2 miles/3 km NW of the station, the **Chofukuji Temple** (built 824) has a 46 ft/14 m-high statue of Yakushi-nyorai dating from the Early Fujiwara period.

To the W of Takamatsu, on Mount *Shiramine* (1106 ft/337 m), is the Mausoleum of the Emperor Sutoku (1119–64). – The JNR Yosan line, running close to the coast, continues to **Sakaide** (pop. 66,000) and **Marugame** (pop. 72,000). ¾ mile/1 km S of Marugame Station are the remains of a castle built in 1597 (three-storey tower and two gates). The town is noted for the manufacture of fans. There are several ferry services over the Inland Sea to Honshu.

To the S of Marugame the JNR Dosan line branches off and runs SE to **Zentsuji** (40 minutes), birthplace of Kobo-daishi or Kukai (774–835), who founded the Shingon sect of Buddhism.

¾ mile/1·2 km W is the **Zentsuji Temple** founded by Kukai, the principal temple of the Shingon sect, with many buildings dating from the 17th c. The *Jogyoso Hall* contains a figure of Buddha. On the W side of the temple precinct stands a five-storey *pagoda* 150 ft/45·6 m high (rebuilt 1882) and the 14th c. Main Hall (*Kondo*), with a wooden statue of Yakushi-nyorai. The *Treasury* has manuscripts in Kukai's hand. The two large camphor trees in the outer precinct of the temple are said to date from the original foundation.

Farther S is **Kotohira** (which can also be reached from Takamatsu by the Kotohira private line and bus, 1 hour).

1¼ miles/2 km W of the station, on the slopes of Mount *Zozusan*, is the **Kompira Shrine** (or *Kotohira-jinja*), dedicated to the divinity Omononushi-no-mikoto, which is one of the great pilgrimage centers of Japan.

Takamatsu   Ritsurin Park

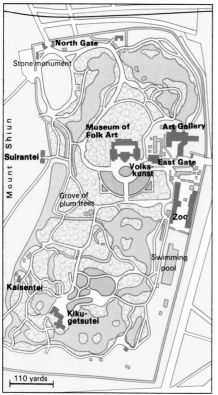

North Gate

Stone monument

Mount Shiun

Suirantei

Museum of Folk Art

Art Gallery

Volks-kunst

East Gate

Grove of plum trees

Zoo

Swimming pool

Kaisentei

Kiku-getsutei

110 yards

From the main gate (*Daimon*) a flight of 1300 steps leads up to the temple. The first building encountered is the old Abbot's Lodging (*Shoin*, 1659), the doors and walls of which were decorated by the landscape-painter Maruyama Okyo (1733–95). Beyond this, on the left, is the *Chadokoro* (Tea Hall), followed by the *Asahi-sha* (Hall of the Morning Sun), with early 19th c. woodcarving. Another flight of 785 steps leads up to the *Main Shrine*, with the Music Hall (for cult dances) and the Votive Hall (with numerous votive pictures). The Music Hall was rebuilt in Taisha-zukuri style in 1878, following the destruction during the Meiji Reform of many of the temple buildings, which had been erected in a medley of styles over the centuries. A third flight of 583 steps links the Main Shrine with the Inner Shrine (*Okusha*), set in a grove of cedars and camphor trees. – The annual shrine festivals are celebrated at the beginning of January and the beginning of October.

The next station on the Dosan line is **Shioiri**. ¾ mile/ 1·3 km NE of the station lies *Lake Mannoike*, which is thought to be the earliest reservoir (man-made lake) created in Japan (early 8th c.).

W of Shioiri is **Kan-onji** (37 miles/60 km from Takamatsu on the JNR Seisan bus route via Marugama). 1 mile/1·5 km N of the station we find *Kotohiki Park*, with cedars. At the foot of *Mount Kotohiki* is the *Kan-onji Temple*, a pilgrimage temple with a statue of Buddha and fine picture scrolls. From Mount Kotohiki there is a good view of a system of rock-cuttings (17th c.) representing an ancient coin with a rectangular hole in the middle and inscribed with four Chinese characters.

3 miles/5 km S of the city center of Takamatsu (20 minutes by rail) is the **Ichinomiya Temple** (701–703) and near this the **Honenji Temple** (the family temple of the Matsudaira clan), with a 13 ft/ 4 m-long reclining Buddha.

SW of Takamatsu (JNR Dosan line, 1 hour, or bus, 1½ hours) is *Awa-Ikeda*, a traffic junction which makes a good base for excursions into the **Tsurugi Quasi National Park**.

An attractive road (30 miles/50 km) runs via *Ori* and then follows the *Iya*, a tributary of the Yoshino, up through the *Iyadani Gorge* to *Sugeoi*. This area, which is particularly beautiful in the fall, is said to have provided a refuge in the 12th c. for members of the Taira clan who were being pursued by the Minamoto. There were formerly many rope bridges made from vegetable fibers spanning the rivers, but the only surviving example is the *Iya-no-Kazurabashi* Bridge at *Zentoku* (50 yds/45 m long, 46 ft/14 m high, 4½ ft/ 1·4 m wide). Near the bridge a road branches off to the *Oboke Gorge* (bus from Awa-Ikeda, 40 minutes) and the *Koboke Gorge*, which together form the largest gorge system on Shikoku. There are boat trips from Oboke through the wild and romantic scenery of the gorges (40 minutes).

Farther E is another section of the Quasi National Park centered on Mount **Tsurugi** (see Tokushima, Surroundings).

Takayama
たかやま

Prefecture: Gifu. – Population: 65,000.
Post code: J-506. – Telephone code: 0577.

ⓘ (local)
Hida Kanko Information,
1, Showa-cho
(in front of station);
tel. 32 5328.

HOTELS. – **Western style:** *Takayama Green Hotel*, 2-180, Nishino-isshiki-cho, 131 r.; *Hida Hotel*, 2-60, Hanaoka-cho, 48 r. – **Ryokan:** *Ryokan Seiryu*, 6, Hanakawa-cho, 25 r.; *Ryokan Hishuya*, 2581, Kamiokamoto-cho, 17 r. – **Minshuku:** *Iiyama-So*, 262-2, Honobu-cho, 200 r.; *Matsuyama Ryokan*, 5-11, Hanazato-cho, 107 r.; *Bunsuke*, 77, Shimo-ichino-cho, 35 r.; *Yamakyu*, 58, Tenshoji-machi, 28 r.; *Bugeyashiki*, 129, Nishi-machi, 20 r. – YOUTH HOSTEL: *YH Tenshoji*, 83, Tenshoji-machi, 150 b.

EVENTS. – *Takayama-matsuri* (mid April), also known as Sanno-matsuri, a procession with historic decorated floats and a puppet-show in the evening, at the Hie Shrine.

TRANSPORTATION. – **Rail:** from NAGOYA JNR Takayama line via GIFU (3 hours); from TOYAMA JNR Takayama line (1½ hours).

The small town of Takayama in central Honshu, to the W of the Hida range which forms part of the Chubu-Sangaku National Park, has preserved much of its old-world

An old farmhouse in Takayama

charm. Many old houses still demonstrate the skill of the local carpen-
ters, who were renowned in the
medieval period for their mastery
of their craft. Takayama is also
noted for its traditional pottery
(Shibukusa-yaki) and lacquerware
(Shunkei-nuri).

SIGHTS. – A little way E of the station is
the **Kokubunji Temple**, the oldest in
the town. Its Main Hall (1615) contains
a seated figure of the *Healing Buddha
(Yakushi-nyorai) and a *statue of Kannon; in the forecourt is a three-storey
pagoda (1807). – To the NE, beyond
the River *Miyakawa*, is the *Kusakabe-
mingeikan*, a house of traditional style,
built for a wealthy merchant about 1880,
which is now occupied by a local
museum. Near by is the *Yoshijima-ke*,
another house of the same period. On the
north-eastern outskirts of the town stands
the *Yatai-kaikan Hall*, in which the
elaborately decorated floats used in the
Takayama-matsuri festival are displayed.

Hida-Minzoku-mura Open-Air Museum

(exhibition of local history). – Every
morning at seven the local market is held
on the banks of the river.

SW of the station are the **Folk Museum**
(*Minzoku-kan*) and beyond this the
Hida-Minzoku-mura (or *Hida-no-
sato*) **Open-Air Museum** (bus, 10
minutes), with old peasant houses, etc.

SURROUNDINGS. – NW of Takayama is the village
of **Shirakawago** (Nohi bus service to Makido, 1½
hours, then JNR bus to Ogimachi, 1 hour), with a
number of old peasant houses brought here from
other areas.

See also **Chubu-Sangaku National Park**.

In the Kusakabe-mingeikan

In the center of the old town is the **San-
machi-suji**, with three little parallel
streets lined by old wooden houses and
shops. Here, too, one finds the **Municipal Museum** (*Kyodo-kan*), with a
collection of material on the history of the
town.

On the eastern outskirts of the town
(bus, 15 minutes) is the temple area,
Higashiyama-tera-machi, a low hill on
which are several small temples. – To the
S rises Mount *Shiroyama*, once the site of
a castle, on which is the **Shorenji
Temple**, with a Main Hall dating from
1504. – On the way back to the station we
pass the *Takayama-Jinya*, a group of
buildings of the Edo period, with
dwelling-houses and large store-houses

Tanegashima
See under Satsunan Islands

Tokushima
とくしま

Prefecture: Tokushima. – Population: 255,000.
Post code: J-770. – Telephone code: 0886.
(i) (central)
**Tokushima-ken Tokyo Kanko Bussan
Assensho,**
Tetsudo Kaikan,
1-9-1, Marunouchi, Chitoda-ku,
J-100 **Tokyo**;
tel. (03) 216 2081.

(local)
Tourist Section of Tokushima City,
2-5, Saiwai-cho;
tel. 22 1171.
Japan Travel Bureau,
1-29, Ryogoku-honmachi;
tel. 23 3181.

HOTELS. – **Western style**: *Tokushima Park Hotel*, 2-32-1, Tokushima-cho, 82 r.; *Awa Kanko Hotel*, 3-13-3, Ichiban-cho, 35 r.; *Shin Tokushima Hotel*, 1-20, Naka-dori-cho, 30 r.; *Hotel Kasuga*, 1-28, Terashima-Honcho-Nishi, 24 r.; *Tokushima Kokusai Hotel*, 1-22, Moto-machi, 40 r.; *Hotel Astria*, 2-26-1, Ichiban-cho, 25 r. – **Ryokan**: *Tokushima Grand Hotel Kairakuen*, 1-8, Igao-cho, 58 r.; *Kinsen-kaku*, 1-3, Otakiyama, Bisan-cho, 33 r.; *Yoshino-kan*, 2-18, Terashima-Honcho-Higashi, 22 r. – YOUTH HOSTEL: *Tokushima YH*, 7-1, Hama Ohara-machi, 80 b., beach.

EVENTS. – *Tokushima Festival* (beginning of April); *Awa-ningyo-joruri* (beginning of June and mid August), puppet-plays; *Awa-odori* (mid August), traditional dance festival.

TRANSPORTATION. – **Air**: from TOKYO (Haneda Airport), 2 hours; from OSAKA (Fukue Airport), 30 minutes. – **Rail**: from TAKAMATSU JNR Kotoku line (1½ hours). – **Bus**: from Tokushima Airport to city center (25 minutes). – **Boat**: from OSAKA (South Pier; 3½ hours); from KOBE (3½ hours; hovercraft 1¾ hours).

Tokushima, chief town of a prefecture, lies on the E coast of Shikoku, to the S of the outflow·of the River Yoshino into the Kii Strait. It is the administrative, economic and educational center of eastern Shikoku and is noted for the production of cotton fabrics and wooden articles.

SIGHTS. – In the heart of the town, ¼ mile/400 m E of the station, is a wooded hill, *Shiroyama*, most of which is occupied by **Tokushima Park**, with the remains (walls and an old bridge) of *Tokushima Castle* (built 1586). The garden attached to the castle, with rocks and pools, is a characteristic example of the landscape architecture of the Momoyama period, and affords a charming *view of the town. Adjoining the park is a Zoo.

660 yds/600 m SW of the station, on the eastern slopes of Mount *Otaki* (Bizan), lies the **Bizan Park**, with the **Prefectural Museum**, the 82 ft/25 m-high *Peace Pagoda*, erected in 1958 as a memorial to those who died in the Second World War, and the house once occupied by Wenceslão de Morães (1854–1929), a Portuguese naval officer who came to live here in 1893 and wrote a 16-volume work on Japan; his tomb is in the Cho-onji Temple. A cableway runs up the hill (915 ft/279 m), from which there is a panoramic *view of the Yoshino Delta, the Inland Sea and the hills. – Below the S side of the hill (1 mile/1·5 km S of the station) is the **Imbe Shrine**, believed to be the oldest in the town.

N of the station (bus, 10 minutes) we reach the **Kogenji Temple**, formerly the family temple of the princely Hachisuka clan, some of whom are buried here.

SURROUNDINGS of Tokushima

SW of the town are a number of old temples. – 5½ miles/9 km from the station (bus, 30 minutes) stands the *Jorokuji Temple* of the Soto sect, founded in the 8th c. The Kannondo Hall contains a wooden figure of Sho-Kannon, said to have been carved by the priest Gyoki (670–749). – The **Tatsueji Temple** (Mugi railway line to Tatsue), one of the 88 pilgrimage temples of Shikoku, has a fine painting of Buddha. – 8 miles/13 km SW is another pilgrimage temple, the *Kakurinji*, in a grove of ancient cedars. It contains a wooden statue of Jizo-Bosatsu. – 1½ miles/2·5 km farther S (bus from Tokushima, 30 minutes, then 30 minutes' walk), on the slopes of Mount *Nakatsumine* (2395 ft/730 m), we find the *Nyoirinji Temple*, principal temple of the Hoju-Shingon sect, with a wooden statue of the Nyoirin Kannon. The temple is situated in an area of forest with several waterfalls.

The JNR Mugi line runs S from Tokushima, following the coast, and in 15 miles/25 km (30 minutes) reaches the fishing port of **Anan** (also reached by bus, 1 hour), romantically situated in *Tachibana Bay*. 3 miles/4·5 km W of the station (bus, 10 minutes) is the **Yahoko Shrine**, which has two wooden *statues of Shinto divinities, probably of the Fujiwara period. – From here the **Muroto-Anan Quasi National Park** extends for some 55 miles/90 km SW along the coast to *Cape Muroto*. The scatter of little islands in Tachibana Bay, reminiscent of the coastal scenery at Matsushima (see that entry) on the NE coast of Honshu, has earned this region the name of "Awa-Matsushima". At *Hiwasa*, 15 miles/25 km S of Anan, turtles can be seen laying their eggs between mid May and mid August.

The JNR Tokushima line runs W up the *Yoshino* Valley to **Anabuki** (40 minutes), to the NE of which (bus, 15 minutes) are many *earth pyramids* 40–60 ft/12–18 m high formed by erosion. – From Anabuki the eastern part of the **Tsurugi Quasi National Park** can be reached on a road (bus 2½ hours), ascending the valley of the River *Anabuki*, which rises on Mount Tsurugi, and through the romantic *Tsurugikyo Gorge* (particularly beautiful in autumn) to **Misogibashi**, from which Mount **Tsurugi** (6414 ft/1955 m) can be climbed. 1¼ miles/2 km above the little town stands the **Ryukoji Temple**, near which are the **Tsurugisan Shrine**, with prayer-halls (overnight accommodation), and *Lake Fujinoike*. Large numbers of pilgrims come to the shrine at the annual shrine festival in mid July. From here there is a footpath (2½ miles/4 km) to the summit of Mount Tsurugi, with magnificent panoramic *views. The descent can be by way of *Minokoshi* and *Lake Meotoike* to **Tsurugibashi**, from which there is a bus (1¼ hours) to **Sadamitsu** on the JNR Tokushima line. Between Minokoshi and the 9th staging point on this route a cableway considerably shortens the ascent on this side. – For a description of the western part of the Tsurugi Quasi National Park see under Takamatsu.

Tokyo

とうきょう

Prefecture: Tokyo.
Population: 8,700,000 (city area); 12,000,000 (Greater Tokyo).
Post code: J-100-190. – Telephone code: 03.

ⓘ **Japan National Tourist Organization** (*JNTO*),
Tourist Information Center,
6-6-1, Yuraku-cho, Chiyoda-ku;
tel. 502 1461.
JNTO New Tokyo Airport Tourist Information Center,
Airport Terminal Building,
Narita Airport;
tel. (0476) 32 8711.

Tourist Section of Tokyo Metropolitan Government,
3-5-1, Marunouchi, Chiyoda-ku;
tel. 212 2404.
Tokyo Tourist Association,
2-10-1, Yuraku-cho, Chiyoda-ku;
tel. 212 8727.
Japan Travel Bureau,
Foreign Tourist Department,
1-13-1, Nihonbashi, Chuo-ku;
tel. 274 2693 and 274 3921.

Imperial Household Agency,
Sakashitamon Gate,
Imperial Palace.

EMBASSIES. – *United States of America*: 10-5, Akasaka 1-chome, Minato-ku, J-107, tel. 583 7141.

– *Canada*: 3-38, Akasaka 7-chome. Minato-ku, J-107, tel. 408 2101. – *United Kingdom*: 1, Ichiban-cho, Chiyoda-ku, J-102, tel. 265 5511.

HOTELS. – IN CHIYODA WARD – **Western style**: *°New Otani Hotel*, 4, Kioi-cho, 2067 r., Japanese garden, SP; *°Imperial Hotel*, 1-1-1, Uchisaiwai-cho, 767 r., Japanese garden; *°Hotel New Japan*, 2-13-8, Nagata-cho, 506 r., Japanese garden; *°Palace Hotel*, 1-1-1, Marunouchi, 407 r., Japanese garden; *°Marunouchi Hotel*, 1-6-3, Marunouchi, 210 r.; *Akasaka Tokyu Hotel*, 2-14-3, Nagato-cho, 566 r.; *Hotel Grand Palace*, 1-1-1, Iidabashi, 500 r.; *Tokyo Hilton Hotel*, 2-10-3, Nagata-cho, 469 r., Japanese garden, SP; *Akihabara Washington Hotel*, 1-8-3, Sakuma-cho, 320 r.; *Diamond Hotel Annex*, 25, Ichiban-cho, 312 r.; *Fairmont Hotel Tokyo*, 2-1-17, Kudan-Minami, 243 r., Japanese garden, SP; *Diamond Hotel*, 25, Ichiban-cho, 465 r., Japanese garden; *Hotel Kokusai Kanko*, 1-8-3, Marunouchi, 95 r.; *Hill Top Hotel* (Yamanoue Hotel), 1-1, Kanda-Surugadai, 75 r.; *Tokyo Station Hotel*, 1-9-1, Marunouchi, 62 r.; *Hotel Toshi Center*, 2-4-1, Hirakawa-cho, 55 r.; *Akasaka Prince Hotel*, 1, Kioi-cho, 42 r., Japanese garden, SP; *Tokyo Green Hotel Suidobashi*, 1-1-16, Misaki-cho, 324 r.; *Tokyo City Hotel*, 1-9, Nihonbashi-motomachi, 267 r.; *Tokyo Green Hotel Awajicho*, 2-6, Kanda-Awajicho, 226 r.; *Hotel Kayu Kaikan*, 3-1, Sanban-cho, 126 r.; *Tokyo YMCA Hotel*, 7, Kanda-Mitoshirocho, 100 r. – **Ryokan**: *Fukudaya*, 6-12, Kioi-cho, 14 r.

IN CHUO WARD. – **Western style**: *Tokyo Hotel Urashima*, 2-5-23, Harumi, 1001 r.; *Ginza Daiichi Hotel*, 8-13-1, Ginza, 803 r.; *Ginza Tokyu Hotel*, 5-15-9, Ginza, 447 r.; *Mitsui Urban Hotel Ginza*, 8-6-15, Ginza, 263 r.; *Holiday Inn Tokyo*, 1-13-7, Hatch-obori, 127 r.; *Ginza Nikko Hotel*, 8-4-21, Ginza, 112 r.; *Ginza Capital Hotel*, 3-1-5, Tsukiji, 530 r.; *Center Hotel Tokyo*, 2-52, Kabuto-cho, Nihonbashi, 116 r.;

Tokyo, with Fujiyama as a backdrop

Ginza Kokusai Hotel, 8-7-13, Ginza, 93 r. – **Ryokan**: Hotel Yaesu Ryumeikan, 1-3-22, Yaesu, 34 r.; Shinkomatsu, 1-9-13, Tsukiji, 13 r.

IN MINATO WARD. – **Western style**: *Hotel Okura, 2-10-4, Toranomon, 924 r., Japanese garden, SP; *Tokyo Prince Hotel, 3-3-1, Shiba Park, 477 r., Japanese garden, SP; Takanawa Prince Hotel, 13-1-3, Takanawa, 1010 r., SP; Shimbashi Daiichi Hotel, 1-2-6, Shimbashi, 1181 r.; Shinagawa Prince Hotel, 4-10-30, Takanawa, 1020 r.; Hotel Pacific, 3-13-3, Takanawa, 954 r., Japanese garden, SP; Takanawa Prince Hotel, 3-13-1, Takanawa, 458 r., Japanese garden, SP; Shiba Park Hotel, 1-5-10, Shiba, 370 r.; Hotel Takanawa, 2-1-17, Takanawa, 217 r., SP; Takanawa Tobu Hotel, 4-7-6, Takanawa, 201 r.; Tokyo Kanko Hotel, 4-8-10, Takanawa, 158 r., Japanese garden; Hotel Tokyukanko, 2-21-6, Akasaka, 48 r.; Hotel Tokyo, 2-17-8, Takanawa, 46 r., Japanese garden; Azabu Prince Hotel, 5-40-3, Minami-Azabu, 30 r., Japanese garden, SP; Miyako Inn Tokyo, 3-7-8, Mita, 403 r.; Atagoyama Tokyu Inn, 1-6-6, Atago, 269 r.; Akasaka Shampia Hotel, 7-6-13, Akasaka, 250 r.; Hotel Yoko Akasaka, 6-14-12, Akasaka, 245 r.; Marroad Inn Akasaka, 6-15-17, Akasaka, 206 r.; Hotel Ibis, 7-4-13, Roppongi, 200 r.;

Tokyo's great shopping street, the Ginza

Asia Kaikan (Asia Center), 8-10-32, Akasaka, 180 r.; *Tokyo Grand Hotel*, 2-5-3, Shiba, 165 r.; *Sun Hotel Shimbashi*, 3-5-2, Shimbashi, 119 r.; *Hotel Mates*, 2-9-5, Shiroganedai, 74 r.; *Keihin Hotel*, 4-10-20, Takanawa, 46 r.

IN SHINJUKU WARD. – **Western style**: *Keio Plaza Inter-Continental Hotel*, 2-2-1, Nishi-Shinjuku, 1485 r., Japanese garden, SP, several restaurants; *Century Hyatt Hotel*, 2-7-2, Nishi-Shinjuku, 800 r.; *Hotel Sun Light*, 5-14-1, Shinjuku, 72 r.; *Shinjuku Sun Park Hotel*, 3-22-15, Hyakunin-cho, 57 r. – IN BUNKYO WARD. – **Western style**: *Hotel Daiei*, 1-15, Koishikawa, 82 r.; *Suidobashi Grand Hotel*, 1-33-2, Hongo, 221 r.; *Tokyo Yayoi Kaikan*, 2-1-14, Nezu, 139 r.; *Hotel Sato*, 1-4-4, Hongo, 70 r. – IN TAITO WARD. – **Western style**: *Takara Hotel*, 2-16-5, Higashi-Ueno, 142 r.; SP; *Hokke Club Ueno Ikenohataten*, 2-1-48, Ikenohata, 176 r.; *Hotel Ogaiso*, 3-3-21, Ikenohata, 80 r.; *Ikenohata Bunka Center*, 1-3-45, Ikenohata, 38 r., – IN SUMIDA WARD. – **Western style**: *Ryogoku Pearl Hotel*, 1-2-24, Yokozuna, 212 r. – IN MEGURO WARD. – **Western style**: *Gajoen Kanko Hotel*, 1-8-1, Shimo-Meguro, 94 r., Japanese garden; *Hotel New Meguro*, 1-3-18, Chuo-cho, 31 r., Japanese garden. – IN SHINAGAWA WARD. – **Western style**: *Toko Hotel*, 2-6-8, NIshi-Gotanda, 265 r. – IN SHIBUYA WARD – **Western style**: *Hotel Sun Route Tokyo*, 2-3-1, Yoyogi, 548 r.; *Shibuya Tokyu Inn*, 1-24, Shibuya, 352 r.; *Hotel Sun Route Shibuya*, 1-11, Nanpeidai, 182 r.; *Shinjuku Park Hotel*, 5-27-9, Sendagaya, 199 r. – IN TOSHIMA WARD. – **Western style**: *Hotel Grand Business*, 1-30-7, Higashi-Ikebukuro, 292 r. – IN OTA WARD. – **Western style**: *Haneda Tokyu Hotel*, 2-8-6, Haneda-kuko, 307 r., Japanese garden, SP.

YOUTH HOSTELS. – *Ichigawa YH*, in Chiyoda ward, 1-6, Goban-cho, 128 b.; *Tokyo Yoyogi YH*, in Shibuya ward, 3-1, Yoyogi-kamizono, 150 b.

RESTAURANTS. – IN CHIYODA WARD. – **Western cuisine**: *Actress Restaurant*, 1-1-1, Yuraku-cho; *New Orient*, 1-1, Marunouchi, Tokyo Central Station Arcade; *Tony Roma*, 1, Sanban-cho. – **Japanese cuisine**: *Yaesu Chinzanso*, 1-8-3, Marunouchi. – IN CHUO WARD. – **Western cuisine**: *Benihana*, 1-1, Nihonbashi Muromachi; *Benihana of New York*, 6-3-7, Ginza; *Restaurant Shiki Coq d'Or*, 5-2-1, Ginza, Toshiba Building; *Royal Ginza-ten*, 6-2-1, Ginza. – **Japanese cuisine**: *Ginza Happo-en*, 6-4-7, Ginza; *Ginza Jisaku*, 7-6-16, Ginza; *Hamadaya*, 3-12, Ningyo-cho, Nihonbashi; *Izui*, 6-4-17, Ginza; *Jisaku*, 14-19, Akashi-cho, Tsukiji; *Kanetanaka*, 7-18-17, Ginza; *Kinsen*, 4-4-10, Ginzen, Kintetsu Building (5th floor); *Kitcho*, 2-32-8, Ningyo-cho, Nihonbashi; *Mita*, 6-7, Nakasu, Nihonbashi; *Zakuro*, 2-7-19, Kyobashi; *Ginza-yonchome Suehiro* (steaks), 4-4-10, Ginza, Kintetsu Building; *Steak House Hama Ginza-ten* (steaks), 7-6-12, Ginza, Polestar Building; *Suehiro Asahi Edobashi-ten* (steaks), 3-13-11, Nihonbashi; *Suehiro Tsukiji-ten* (steaks), 4-1-15, Tsukiji; *Okahan Hoten* (sukiyaki), 7-6-16, Ginza; *Hige-no-Tempei* (tempura), 1-6, Kyobashi; *Inagiku* (tempura), 2-6, Kayabacho, Nihonbashi; *Ten-ichi* (tempura), 6-7-16, Ginza. – IN MINATO WARD. – **Western cuisine**: *Akatombo*, 1-15-12, Toranomon; *La Marée*, 5-1-25, Minami-Aoyama; *Isolde & Tristan*, 3-2-1, Nishi-Azabu. – **Japanese cuisine**: *Aoyama Diamond Hall*, 3-6-8, Kita-Aoyama; *Colza* (steaks), 7-15-10, Roppongi; *Steak House Hama* (steaks), 7-2-10, Roppongi; *Hasejin Azabu-ten* (sukiyaki), 3-3-15, Azabudai; *Imaasa* (sukiyaki), 2-20-5, Shinbashi, Shinbashi-ekimae Building. – IN SHINJUKU WARD. – **Western cuisine**: *Restaurant Daitokai*, 4-11-8,

Takatanobaba; *Suzuya*, 1-23-15, Kabuki-cho. – **Japanese cuisine**: *Holytan*, 2-30-10, Kabuki-cho; *Kakiden*, 3-37-11, Shinjuku, Yasuyo Building (9th floor); *Kurawanka* 3-36-6, Shinjuku, Daian Building; *Shinjuku Gyuya* (steaks), 5-11-16, Shinjuku. – IN TAITO WARD. – **Western cuisine**: *Ueno Seiyoken*, 4-58, Ueno-koen. – **Japanese cuisine**: *Hamasei*, 2-2-8, Nishi-Asakusa; *Ichinao*, 3-8-6, Asakusa; *Izuei*, 2-12-22, Ueno.

EVENTS. – *Dezome-shiki* (beginning of January), parade by firemen, with acrobatic stunts; *Setsubun* (beginning of February), Spring Festival, at Asakusa-Kannon, Zojoji, Gokokuji and other temples; *Azuma-odori* (beginning to middle of April), geisha dances in Shimbashi-Embujo Theater; *Hana-matsuri* (beginning of April), celebration of Buddha's birthday, at Gokokuji and other temples; *Spring Festival* at Yasukuni Shrine (end of April); *Spring Festival* at Meiji Shrine (April–May), with old Court dances, performances of No plays and archery contests; *Kanda-matsuri* (mid May in odd-numbered years), at Kanda-Myojin Shrine, procession with two large portable shrines; *Sumo contests* in Kuramae-Kokugikan Sumo Hall (January, May and September); *Sanja-matsuri* (mid May), at Asakusa Shrine, procession with many portable shrines and parade of geishas; *Sanno-matsuri* (mid June), at Hie Shrine, procession with portable shrines and children's procession; *Hozuki-ichi* (beginning to middle of July), fair at Asakusa-Kannon Temple; *Bon-odori* (July–August), folk-dances at Tsukiji Honganji and Asakusa-Kannon Temples, Yasukuni Shrine, etc.; *Kakunori* (September–October), woodmen's festival, with balancing acts on logs in River Sumida; *Tokyo Festival* (beginning of October), with parades and a variety of events; *Oeshiki-matsuri* (mid October), procession of pilgrims carrying large lanterns to Hommonji Temple; *Autumn Festival* at Yasukuni Shrine (mid October); *Autumn Festival* at Meiji Shrine (October–November); *Motor Show* (odd-numbered years, beginning of November); *Nitten* (November–December), exhibition of contemporary Japanese art in Municipal Museum of Art, Ueno Park; *Shichi-go-san* (mid November), shrine visit by children of three, five and seven, at Meiji, Hie, Kanda-Myojin and other shrines; *Tori-no-ichi* (November), Cock Fair at Otori Shrine, at which lucky bamboo rakes are sold; *Gishi-sai* (mid December), festival at Sengakuji Temple commemorating the 47 *ronin*; *Toshi-no-ichi* (middle to end of December), New Year Fair at Asakusa-Kannon Temple.

For information about other events consult the "*Tour Companion*", a weekly tourist guide available free of charge at the Tourist Information Center and from hotels.

The *Teletourist Service* is a free tape-recorded telephone service of information about what's on in and around Tokyo: tel. 503 2911 (English) and 503 2926 (French).

SHOPPING. – The largest shopping areas are Tokyo's principal commercial street, the **Ginza** (Chuo ward; 1 mile/1·5 km long), *Omotesando Avenue*, the streets around Shinjuku Station and the districts of *Kabukicho* (Shinjuku ward), Aoyama and Roppongi (Akasaka quarter, Minato ward) and Akihabara (Chiyoda ward).

TRANSPORTATION. – **Air**: The new international airport at Narita (37 miles/60 km NE) is used by international flights, Haneda Airport (southern outskirts of city) by domestic services and flights from

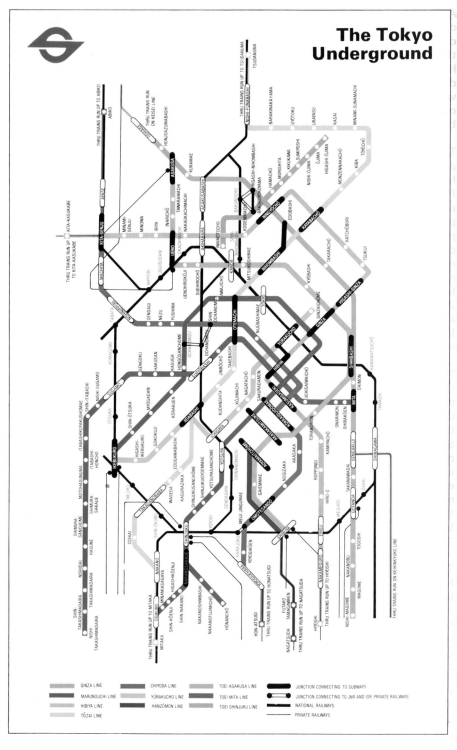

The Tokyo Underground

Taiwan. – **Rail**: Central Station for the Shinkansen line, Ueno Station for northern Japan, Shinjuku Station for the W of the country. – **Boat**: Most passenger services go to Yokohama (see that entry), 19 miles/30 km S.

There are MOTORWAYS from Tokyo to Nagoya (Tomei Expressway), Lake Yamanaka (Chuo Expressway) and Sendai (Tohoku Expressway).

From **Narita International Airport** (*New Tokyo International Airport*, NTIA) there are buses and express trains to Keisei-Ueno Station and express buses to Tokyo City Air Terminal and Haneda Airport.

**Tokyo, the Japanese capital, lies on the S coast of eastern central Honshu. The rivers Sumida,

Arakawa and Tama flow through the city area into Tokyo Bay, which opens off the Pacific. Together with the cities of Kawasaki and Yokohama to the S, Tokyo forms the industrial complex of Keihin. It ranks with Mexico City and Shanghai as one of the world's largest cities, both in area and in population.

This megalopolis is the political, industrial and commercial center of Japan. The focal point of the city is the Imperial Palace; most of its industry (mainly electrical appliances, electronics, optical products, precision engineering, textiles, printing and publishing) is located in the coastal area; the city center is the commercial and business quarter; while the residential areas are increasingly moving to the periphery. Greater Tokyo consists of 23 wards (*ku*), 26 towns, 7 communes and 8 villages (some of these being on the Izu and Ogasawara Islands, which are administered as part of Tokyo).

The division of the city into separate business and residential districts means that its main traffic routes are thronged twice daily with swarms of commuters. Around the main traffic junctions of Shinjuku, Shibuya, Ikebukuro and Ueno large new developments or sub-centers have come into being, and with the introduction of earthquake-proof structural techniques many high-rise buildings have been erected since 1963, and "super-high-rise" buildings (i.e. 35 storeys or more) since 1968.

Tokyo now has relatively few "old inhabitants" (*Edokko*, families who have lived here for three generations), and compared with other Japanese towns it has few historic buildings. Remains of an older Tokyo are to be found mainly in the Asakusa, Ueno, Shitaya and Fukagawa districts.

HISTORY. – The earliest traces of human occupation in the Tokyo area are the 5000-year-old shell mounds (*omori*) found in Shinagawa ward, in the SW of the city. There is evidence of agriculture in the 3rd c. B.C., but the oldest settlements so far identified are villages of the 8th c. A.D. on the lower course of the River Tama. The old name of Tokyo, **Edo**, was originally applied to a fishing village which first appeared on the stage of history in 1457, when Ota Dokan built a castle on the site of the present Imperial Palace. After being held for a time by the Uesugi family Edo became in 1524 the seat of the Odawara-Hojo clan, and in 1590 passed into the hands of Tokugawa Ieyasu as part of the fief of Kanto. It then became the administrative center of the fief, and after Ieyasu's appointment as Shogun in

1603 developed into the political center of the whole country. In order to ensure the loyalty of his vassals and the daimyos the Shogun laid down that their families must live in Edo.

Although two-fifths of the town was destroyed in a great fire in 1657 Tokyo had a population of some 1,200,000 in the 18th c., making it the largest city in the world. Severe damage was also caused by numerous earthquakes, and frequent earth tremors are still recorded in this tectonically unstable area.

The 15th Tokugawa Shogun, Yoshinobu, was compelled to yield up his power to the Emperor Meiji, who in 1868 transferred his residence from Kyoto to Edo, now renamed **Tokyo** ("Eastern Capital"). – The 1923 earthquake caused heavy damage, and during the Second World War 800,000 houses were destroyed by air attack; but reconstruction was soon under way, and Tokyo's development as one of the great cities of the world continued. – The 18th Summer Olympic Games were held in Tokyo in 1964.

Sightseeing in Tokyo

Chiyoda ward

CHIYODA ward is the center of both the old and the modern Tokyo, with the Imperial Palace, the principal public buildings and private institutions and the Central Station (terminus of the Shinkansen line).

W of the Central Station is the **Marunouchi** quarter, in which are many banks, department stores, the headquarters of the Japanese National Railways (JNR) and the Head Post Office. On the N side of the district (Otemachi subway (underground) station) is the **Postal**

In the Marunouchi business quarter

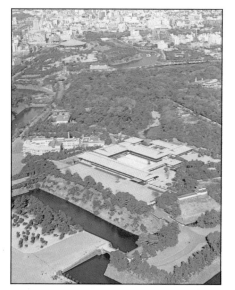

Bird's-eye view of the Imperial Palace

Museum, with a collection of postage stamps and displays illustrating the Japanese postal system. To the S of the station stands the **Town Hall**, an eight-storey building designed by the well-known architect Kenzo Tange. In front of it is a bronze statue of Ota Dokan, builder of the 15th c. Castle. – A short distance W, in the Kokusai Building, is the *Imperial Theater* (Teikoku Theater). – Near the *Chamber of Industry and Commerce*, beyond a moat, lies the Kokyo Gaien, the square in front of the **˙˙Imperial Palace**.

From this square the "Double Bridge" (*Nijubashi*) gives access to the palace grounds which are sur-

rounded by massive walls. The palace is not open to the public, but the palace gardens are open on January 2 and April 29 (the Emperor's birthday) and can be seen at other times with a special authorization from the Imperial Household Agency. – The Imperial Palace suffered damage during the Second World War but was rebuilt in its original form, using reinforced concrete.

The eastern part of the gardens, the **Higashi-Gyo-en**, which contains a number of old buildings, is freely open to the public. To the N, on the far side of the street which runs through this area, lies **Kitanomaru Park**, which is particularly beautiful during the cherry-blossom season. On the intervening street is the **National Museum of Modern Art** (20th c. art) and farther N the **Science Museum** (technology and the natural sciences; atomic energy, space travel). Near the northern boundary of the park stands the **Nippon Budokan**, an octagonal hall built for the 1964 Olympics and which now accommodates sporting and other events.

Nippon Budoka Hall

Nijubashi, the Double Bridge, in the grounds of the Imperial Palace

On *Kudan Hill*, to the NW of the park outside the moat which surrounds it, can be found the **Yasukuni Shrine**, dedicated to those who died fighting for Japan. On the way to the shrine we pass a bronze statue of Omura Masujiro (1825–69), a statesman of the Early Meiji period. Near the south gate are two *komainu* (mythological animal figures) and a stone *torii* some 40 ft/12 m high, and at the entrance to the inner shrine is a bronze *torii*.

To the S of the Kokyo Gai-en lies **Hibiya Park**, the first Western-style park in Japan, opened in 1903, in which are a Neo-Gothic hall built in 1929, the *Hibiya-kokaido*, and the *Hibiya Library*. – To the W of the park stretches the **Kasumigaseki** district, where one can see the **Parliament Building** (*Kokkai-gijido*), a granite structure erected in 1936 with

In the street running W from the Parliament Building and the National Library, on left, we find the **Suntory Museum of Art** (old Japanese art and applied art), and a short distance beyond this, in a park, the **Akasaka Palace**, now used for the accommodation of State guests. The palace, an earthquake-proof structure, was built in 1899–1909 on the site of the residence of the Kii-Tokugawa family, in which the Emperor stayed while the Imperial Palace was being rebuilt. It is in late 18th c. French style, and contains a large collection of oil-paintings by Japanese and French artists (on first floor). – To the N of the Suntory Museum and the E of the Akasaka Palace, beside the New Otani Hotel, lies a small park, the **Shimizudani-Koen**, containing a monument to Okubo Toshimichi, one of the leading figures of the Meiji Restoration. – Still farther N is the *Church of St Ignatius* (1949; R.C.).

Meiji Shrine   In the Meiji Shrine

Parliament Building

a tower 213 ft/65 m high. Farther W is the **Hie Shrine** (or *Sanno-sama*), dedicated to the divinity Oyamakuni, originally founded in the Early Edo period and rebuilt in 1959 after its destruction during the Second World War. The shrine festival in mid June is one of the best-known Tokyo festivals. – N of the Parliament Building stands the six-storey **National Library** (*Kokkai-toshokan*: 2,500,000 volumes, periodicals, records, microfilm archives), beyond which are the *Supreme Court* and the **National Theater** (*Kokuritsu-gekijo*), opened in 1967, with two houses (Kabuki, Bugaku and Gagaku; No, Bunraku and Kyogen).

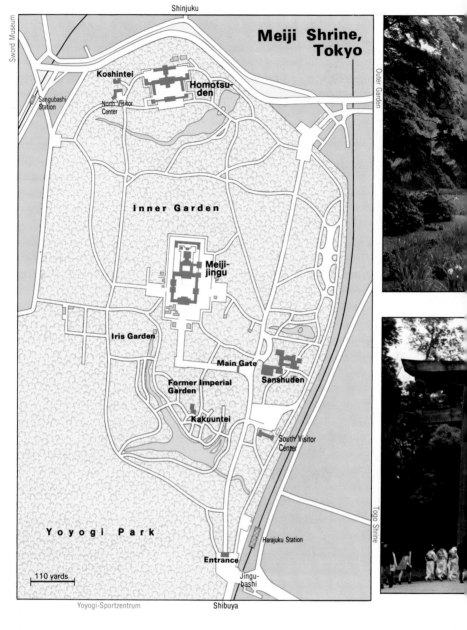

Meiji Shrine, Tokyo

To the W of the Akasaka Palace are other large parks (reached by train from Central Station to Sendagaya Station). S of the railway line is the **Outer Garden of the Meiji Shrine**, in which can be found the **Meiji Memorial Gallery**, with pictures in Western and traditional Japanese style depicting the principal events of the Meiji era. Also in the gardens are the large **National Stadium** and other sports facilities. – 1 mile/1·5 km S, near the Aoyama Cemetery, is the **Nezu Art Gallery** (art and applied art of Japan, China and Korea).

Shibuya ward

In this ward, immediately W of Chiyoda ward, is the **Inner Garden of the Meiji Shrine** (179 acres; Harajuku Station), most of the trees and bushes in which were gifts from all over Japan. Notable among the many festivals and ceremonies celebrated here are the birthday of the Emperor Meiji (beginning of November) and the performances of Court dances and music (May and November). In the southern part of the park are a *lake* and the **Iris Garden**. In the center stands the *Meiji Shrine, dedicated to the Emperor Meiji and his wife. Begun soon after the Emperor's death and completed in 1920,

Iris Garden, Meiji Shrine

it is one of the most frequented pilgrimage centers in Japan. The buildings, plain and simple in style, were largely destroyed in 1945 but were rebuilt in 1958 in their original form. The *torii* at the entrances are in cypress wood from Mount Ari on Taiwan. – Near the small lake at the N end of the park is the *Treasury* of the shrine, which contains personal possessions of the Emperor.

NW of the Inner Garden is the **Sword Museum** (Sangubashi Station), with swords both ancient and modern.

Adjoining the Inner Garden on the S is the **Yoyogi Sports Center**, built as the Olympic Village for the 1964 Olympics. In the grounds of the Center is a bronze bust of the pioneer flyer Tokugawa Yoshitoshi (1884–1963); the biplane which he flew is in the Transportation Museum (see below). – A short distance E is the **Ota-Ukiyoe Museum**, with a large collection of colored woodcuts. In this area are many fashion shops.

Chuo ward

To the E of the Central Station is the CHUO ward, the best-known part of which is the **Ginza**. Tokyo's best shopping area, this also has very many restaurants, bars and places of entertainment. On Sundays and public holidays – when the shops are open – the Ginza becomes a pedestrian precinct.

The **Ginza** occupies an area on the banks of the River Sumida which began to be drained in the 17th c. Thereafter it rapidly developed into an important trading quarter in which the *chonin* (craftsmen

Torii in Inner Garden of Meiji Shrine

Yoyogi Sports Center

Kabuki-za Theater

The Ginza at night

and merchants) had their establishments. The name Ginza (*gin*, "silver", and *za*, "place") comes from the national mint, which Tokugawa Ieyasu transferred here from Shizuoka in 1612.

Near the Higashi-Ginza subway (underground) station is the **Kabuki-za Theater** (2600 seats; stage 177 ft/54 m wide). The first performance of a Kabuki play here was in 1889; there are now performances throughout the year. The **Shimbashi-Embujo Theater**, a short distance S, puts on performances of traditional dances (Azuma-odori) and Bunraku puppet-plays throughout the year.

550 yds/500 m SE of the Kabuki-za Theater is the **Nishi-Honganji Temple** of the Judo-Shinsu sect, founded in 1630 but several times (most recently in 1923) destroyed by fire and rebuilt in 1935 in a mingling of old and modern styles. – To the S, on the banks of the river, is the **Tsukiji Market**, which handles some 90% of the fish consumed by the people of Tokyo. The best time to see the market is between 4 and 8 a.m. (stout footwear advisable).

Opposite the market, surrounded on three sides by water, are the **Hama-rikyu Gardens**, in which the Tokugawa family once had a summer villa. – On the far side of the river are two man-made islands. On the more southerly of the two, near the

Harumi Pier bus stop, is the *International Trade Center* (temporary exhibitions). – On another area of reclaimed land to the S, in Koto ward, is the **Oceanographic Museum** (1974), in the form of a ship's hull (history and future prospects of oceanography). – On the more easterly of the two islands, **Yumenoshima**, is **Tokyo Heliport**.

To the N of the Ginza, in Chuo-dori, we find the **Bridgestone Gallery** (Western art, contemporary Japanese painting). Farther along the street we reach the *Nihonbashi Bridge* (built 1603, last rebuilt 1911), formerly regarded as the city's central point, from which distances to other places in Japan were reckoned. It is now overspanned by a multi-lane motorway, much to the detriment of its amenity. – To the SE is the **Yamatane Museum** (Japanese painting since the Meiji era).

Koto ward

From Nihonbashi Station the subway (underground) (Tozai line) can be taken to the Monzen-Nakacho Station, over the river in KOTO ward. 660 yds/600 m N of this station lies the **Kiyosumi-koen**, a beautiful landscaped garden in the construction of which rocks from all over the country were used.

Taking a train or the subway from the Central Station to Ochanomizu Station, we come on the S of the canal to the **Surugadai** quarter on Surugadai Hill. At the E end stands the Orthodox *Cathedral of St Nicholas* (built 1884, restored 1929), and to the E of this, near the railway line, the **Transportation Museum** (history of Japanese transport since 1872). – To the N of the canal is the **Yushima Seido**, a hall dedicated to the Chinese philosopher Confucius, which was originally built in 1690 and several times rebuilt after fires; in its present form it dates from 1935. It contains a bronze bust of Confucius. In the school which was formerly attached to the shrine a number of Japanese statesmen received their Confucian training. To the W is the *School of Medicine*. – N of the Yushima Seido is the **Kanda-Myojin Shrine** (present buildings 1934), where the lovely Kanda-matsuri festival is celebrated in mid May.

Farther N on the subway line from the Central Station is Korakuen Station, at the *Korakuen, a garden originally laid out by Tokugawa Yorifusa in 1626 and remodelled by his son Mitsukuni. This is one of the finest landscaped gardens in the city, showing Chinese influence in its

In the Korakuen Garden

layout. On the island in the lake stands a small *temple* dedicated to Benten, goddess of fortune; the arched bridge leading to the island is known as the Full Moon Bridge, since the arch and its reflection in the water form a complete circle. – To the E of the gardens is the most popular sports

and recreation area in the city (park, swimming pool, stadium and a variety of other facilities for sport and recreation). – NE of the subway (underground) station is the *Kodokan Judo Hall* (training facilities).

Taito and Sumida wards

N of Chiyoda ward, reached by train or subway (Ueno Station), is TAITO ward. The main-line Ueno Station is the terminus of the lines to northern Honshu. Immediately W of the station lies *Ueno Park* (207 acres). This large open space, originally belonging to a daimyo, was taken over by the Shogunate in the 17th c. and opened to the public in 1878.

The main entrance to the park is at the SE corner, near the station of the Keisei private line to Narita. A broad flight of steps leads up on to Sakuragaoka (Cherry-Tree Hill), on which are a statue of Saigo Takamori (1827–77) and a monument to the Shogitai (supporters of the Shogunate who were killed during the Meiji Restoration).

The S end of the park is occupied by *Lake Shinobazu* (circumference 1¼ miles/2 km; boat rental), in which, on a tongue of land, is the **Benten Temple**. The lake is renowned for its show of lotus blossom in August. At its NW corner is an *Aquarium* (fish, amphibians, reptiles), from which there is a monorail to the Zoo. To the E of the Zoo monorail station stands the **Toshogu Shrine**, a richly decorated building dedicated to Tokugawa Ieyasu (erected 1627, renovated 1651). Along the path leading to the shrine are more than 250 stone lanterns presented by daimyos. The *Main Shrine*, in Gongen-zukuri style, is reached by way of the *Kara-mon* gate, beyond which are a five-storey *pagoda* and a well-known *bell-tower*.

The **Zoo**, on the W side of the park, has some 850 species of animals, mostly in open enclosures; special displays are put on from time to time. – To the N is the large **Municipal Gallery of Art** (changing exhibitions). Beyond this is the **Horyuji Treasury** (*Horyuji Homotsu-kan*: weapons, furniture, etc.), to the rear of which is an attractive garden with three old pavilions. To the W, outside the park, is the *National College of Art*.

The massive building at the N end of the park is the ** **National Museum** (originally the Imperial

National Museum

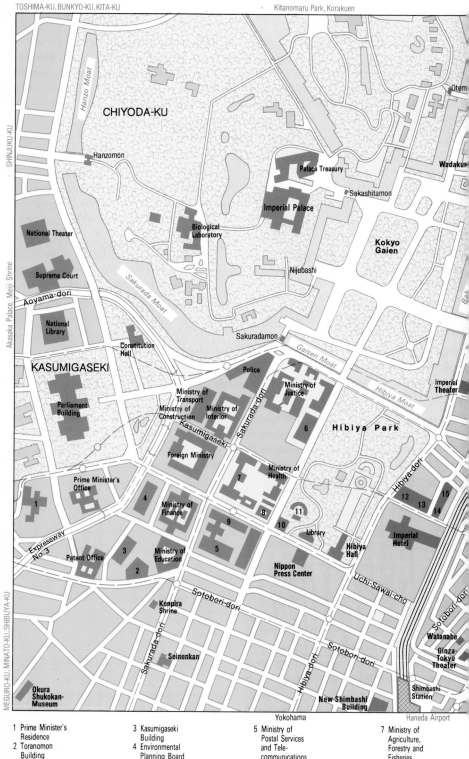

1 Prime Minister's
   Residence
2 Toranomon
   Building

3 Kasumigaseki
   Building
4 Environmental
   Planning Board

5 Ministry of
   Postal Services
   and Tele-
   communications
6 Supreme Court

7 Ministry of
   Agriculture,
   Forestry and
   Fisheries
8 Family Court

Museum), with 25 rooms containing temporary exhibitions on the history and art of the Far East. The site
was occupied until 1868 by the Kan-Eiji Temple, then
Edo's principal Buddhist temple, which was re-
erected in 1975 on a new site not far from the park. –
To the SE is the *Gallery of Antiquities* (Toyokan:
material from China and Korea), and beyond this the
***National Museum of Natural Science** (zoology,

botany, geography, physics, chemistry, astronomy,
meteorology, oceanography). In front of the Museum
can be seen a statue of the bacteriologist Hideyo
Noguchi (1876–1928).

The adjoining ***National Museum of Western Art**,
housed in a reinforced concrete building designed
by Le Corbusier (1959), contains the collection of

Omiya, Sendai
Ueno Park, TAITO-KU, ARAWAKA-KU

Tokyo Center

225 yards

International Post Office
Postal Museum
Bank of Japan
Mitsukoshi department store
Nippon Building
Nippon Steel
Etai-dori
JNR
Sotobori-dori
Etai-dori
Yamatane Museum
Maruzen bookshop
Chuo-dori
Showa-dori
Takashimaya department store
17 16
Marunouchi Bldg.
Central Station
Daimaru department store
Yaesu-dori
tsubishi Building
Head Post Office
MARUNOUCHI
Bridgestone Gallery
Yaesu-dori
Town Hall
Sotobori-dori
cho
n
JNTO
Tokyo Theater
Ginza-yu
Asahi Press
Namiki-dori
Central Art Gallery
Showa-dori
Ginza Church
Chuo-dori
Fuji Bldg.
ling
Nichido Gallery
Harumi-dori
Ginza Tower
CHUO-KU
ahi Building
Canon Building
GINZA
Kabuki-za Theater
Jisaku
Harumi-dori
Ginza-Tokyu-Hotel
Togeki Building
Showa-dori
Minolta Bldg.
Nissan Bldg.
19
Nishi Honganji
SUMIDA-KU
KOTO-KU
KOTO-KU

Hama-rikyu, International Trade Center

9 Ministry of Trade
  and Industry
10 District Court
11 Hibiya Concert
   Hall
12 Nissei Theater
13 Takarazuka
   Theater
14 Yurakuza
   Theater
15 Hibiya
   Theater
16 Shin-Marunouchi
   Building
17 Tokyo Kaijo
   Building
18 Nichigeki Theater
19 Shimbashi-
   Embujo Theater

Western sculpture and painting assembled by the industrialist Matsukata Kojiro, including works by Cézanne, Degas, Monet and Rodin. – Immediately S of the Museum is the **Civic Hall** (*Bunka-kaikan*; 1961), which is used for concerts, drama and conferences. Beyond this is the *Japanese Academy of Art*. – From here, passing the *Kiyomizu Temple*, we return to the main entrance.

Outside the SW corner of Ueno Park is the **Yushima-Tenjin Temple**, founded in the 14th c. which is surrounded by a small garden planted with plum trees. – Continuing N, and passing on the left the campus of Tokyo University, we come to the **Nezu Shrine**, dedicated to the

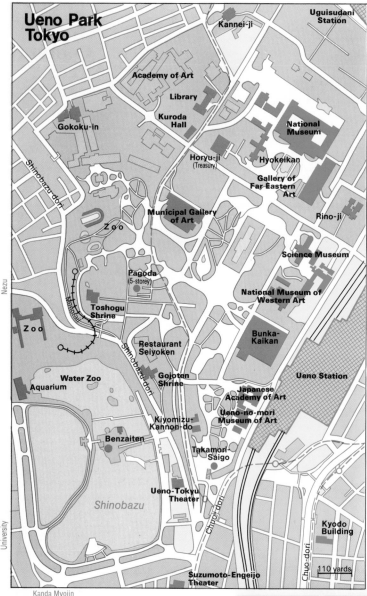

Ueno Park Tokyo

Kannei-ji
Uguisudani Station
Academy of Art
Library
Kuroda Hall
Gokoku-in
National Museum
Shinobazu-dori
Horyu-ji (Treasury)
Hyokeikan
Gallery of Far Eastern Art
Nezu
Municipal Gallery of Art
Zoo
Rino-ji
Pagoda (5-storey)
Science Museum
Toshogu Shrine
Zoo
National Museum of Western Art
Restaurant Seiyoken
Shinobazu-dori
Bunka-Kaikan
Gojoten Shrine
Water Zoo Aquarium
Japanese Academy of Art
Ueno Station
Kiyomizu-Kannon-do
Ueno-no-mori Museum of Art
Benzaiten
Takamori-Saigo
University
Shinobazu
Ueno-Tokyu Theater
Chuo-dori
Kyodo Building
Chuo-dori
110 yards
Suzumoto-Engeijo Theater
Kanda Myojin
Asakusa

Layout of National Museum

Shrine in Asakusa-Kannon Temple

four Shinto divinities and Sugawara Michizane (845–903); it can also be reached by subway (underground) (Yushima Station). The shrine is said to have been founded about the beginning of the Christian era; the present buildings date from 1706. Within the precincts of the shrine are several thousand azalea bushes (in flower towards the end of April).

To the E of Ueno Station (subway (underground) to Asakusa Station) is the *Asakusa-Kannon Temple (*Sensoji Temple*), the principal temple of the Sho-Kannon sect of Buddhism. It is approached by a street (Nakamise) lined

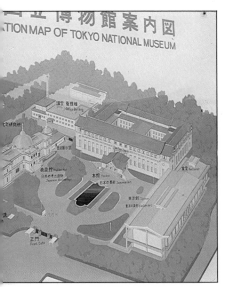

Outside the Asakusa-Kannon Temple

with souvenir shops. The temple is said to have been founded by three fishermen who brought up a statuette of Kannon in their nets. The large Kannon Hall of 1651, destroyed during the war, was rebuilt in its original form in reinforced concrete in 1958. The temple's treasures are housed in the Hozomon Gate (also restored). – The surrounding district of **Asakusa** is a popular entertainment quarter, with many cinemas, theaters and restaurants.

From Asakusa the subway (underground) (Toei–Asakusa line) continues S. At Kurumae Station is the **Kuramae-Kokugikan Sumo Hall**, the headquarters of sumo wrestling (13,000 seats; contests in January, May and September); adjoining the hall is a small *Sumo Museum*. – To the S of the river, in

SUMIDA ward, is the **Tokyo-to Ireido** (Ryogoku rail station), a memorial to the victims of the 1923 earthquake and the air attacks of the Second World War. The three-storey pagoda contains the remains of the 40,000 people who perished in the devastating fire which followed the earthquake. – From here we can return to the city center by rail.

Minato and Meguro wards

MINATO ward lies to the S and SW of the city center. Its principal sights can be seen by using the subway (underground).

550 yds/500 m N of Kamiyacho subway (underground) station (Hibiya line) is the **Okura-Shukokan Museum** (arts and crafts of the Far East). 330 yds/300 m NE is the **Radio Museum** (development of radio and television in Japan). – The subway (underground) line continues through the **Roppongi** district, a favorite residential area with foreigners, with

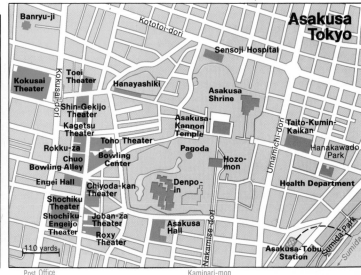

many diplomatic missions, and an entertainment quarter (restaurants, bars, nightclubs, etc.).

At Hiroo subway (underground) station is *Arisugawa Park*, commemorating Prince Arisugawa. – To the E of this is the **Zempukuji Temple**, said to have been founded by Kobo-Daishi (rebuilt after the Second World War). The temple treasury contains several manuscripts in Kobo-Daishi's hand together with pictures and woodcarving. Within the temple precinct is a huge old ginkgo tree. There is also a monument with a bronze tablet commemorating the American diplomatic representative Townsend Harris, who lived here for some considerable time.

1 mile/1·5 km S, near Meguro Station, we come to the **National Park for Natural History Studies** (50 acres), with an abundant growth of vegetation. – A little way SW of the station, in MEGURO ward, is the **Rakanji Temple** (1695), noted for its statues of the 500 *rakan* (disciples of Buddha), only some 300 of which still survive. – Near by stands the **Meguro-Fudo Temple** (*Ryusenji*) of the Tendai sect (rebuilt after war damage), which is dedicated to the fire god Fudo. On the celing of the Main Hall is a painting of a dragon by Kawabata Ryushi (1885–1966). Within the temple precinct can be seen a *waterfall* in which ascetic worshippers bathe in winter.

The Toei-Mita subway (underground) line also runs into Minato ward. At Shibakoen Station is **Shiba Park**, and to the N of this the **Zojoji Temple** (the precinct of which formerly included the park). Founded in 1393, this is the principal temple of the Jodo sect in the Kanto district. Notable features are the main gate (Sammon), the large bell and the figure of a Black Buddha. The temple also possesses an account, illustrated by pictures, of the life of Honen, founder of the sect. The Main Hall is a reinforced-concrete structure of 1974. – Near here rises the *Tokyo Tower, an openwork steel tower 1100 ft/330 m high resembling the Eiffel Tower in Paris. There are observation platforms at heights of 490 ft/150 m and 820 ft/250 m (*views of Tokyo, Tokyo Bay and the Boso and Izu peninsulas). At the foot of the tower, which is topped by a television and telecommunications aerial, is a *museum*, with exhibits illustrating the development

Graves of the *ronin* in the Sengakuji Temple

of electronics and a collection of wax figures.

Farther S (Toei-Asakusa subway (underground) line from Mita Station to Sengakuji) stands the *Sengakuji Temple, widely famed as the burial-place of the 47 *ronin*, who are still revered as supreme examples of steadfast loyalty. Their graves are in the courtyard of the temple, and there are mementoes and wooden effigies of the *ronin* in the temple museum. – Still farther S is the **Tozenji Temple**, which housed the British Embassy for a brief period in 1861.

From Gotanda subway (underground) station the Ikegami railway can be taken to Ikegami Station, near which can be found the **Ikegami-Hommonji Temple**, a major center of the Nichiren sect. In the well-wooded temple precinct are the graves of two of Nichiren's disciples, Nichiro and Nichirin, and the painter Kano Tanyu (1602–74). Of the old temple buildings only the five-storey pagoda (1607) and the Sutra Hall survived the Second World War. The great Oeshiki festival is celebrated here on the anniversary of Nichiren's death in October.

Well to the S of the city, on Tokyo Bay, is **Haneda Airport**. Until the opening of the new international airport at Narita this airport handled not only domestic flights and freight traffic (as it still does) but also all international passenger traffic to Tokyo.

Tokyo Tower

Shinjuku, Bunkyo and Kita wards

The northern and north-western wards of Tokyo can be reached by rail (Yamanote line) or by various subway (underground) lines.

Adjoining Chiyoda ward on the NW is SHINJUKU ward, a "sub-center" (*shin-toshin*) of the megalopolis of Tokyo. During the Edo period this was the site of a posting-station on the historic Kashu road. The area around the large **Shinjuku Station** (*plaza laid out by Junzo Sakakura, 1966) is now one of the busiest traffic junctions in the city, with several department stores and shopping arcades and a variety of places of entertainment. Here the townscape is dominated by a series of modern *high-rise blocks including the *Shinjuku Mitsui Building* (696 ft/ 212 m high), the *Shinjuku Sumitomo Building* (656 ft/200 m), the *Shinjuku Center Building*, the *Shinjuku Nomura Building*, the *Yasuda Kasai Kaijo Building* and the *Keio Plaza Intercontinental* and *Century Hyatt* hotels. Further skyscrapers are under construction.

Skyscrapers in the Shinjuku "sub-center"

A short distance SE of Shinjuku Station lies the *Shinjuku Gyoen, a park (144 acres) which was formerly the private property of the Emperor but was taken over by the State after the Second World War. Part of the park is laid out in classic Japanese style (cherry blossom in April, chrysanthemums in November); other parts are in French and in English style. There is a hothouse containing many tropical plants.

From Otemachi subway (underground) station, near the city center, the Tozai line runs NW to Waseda Station in the N of Shinjuku ward, near which is the private **Waseda University**, founded in 1882. On the campus can be found the **Tsu-bouchi Theater Museum**, named after the Japanese translator of Shakespeare, Shoyo Tsubouchi (1859–1935).

Near Gokokuji subway (underground) station (Yurakucho line), in BUNKYO ward, stands the **Gokokuji Temple**, headquarters of the Buzan school of the Shingon sect and one of the city's largest temples. The hill behind the temple has been since 1873 the burial-place of the Imperial family; the stone lanterns are copies of the finest lanterns at Kyoto and Nara. The temple has an amber statue of Kannon, probably from India, and the treasury contains a mandala of the Kamakura period. To the E of the temple lies the grave of the English writer Lafcadio Hearn (1850–1904). – ½ mile/ 800 m S of the Gokokuji Temple we reach **St Mary's Cathedral** (R.C.), designed by the well-known Japanese architect Kenzo Tange. The bells in the 203 ft/ 62 m-high tower were a gift from the Federal Republic of Germany.

¾ mile/1 km NW of the Gokokuji Temple, in the **Ikebukuro district**, the recently built complex called **Sunshine City** possesses the 790 ft/240 m-high *Sunshine City 60 Building*, Tokyo's tallest skyscraper.

1 mile/1·5 km E of the Gokokuji Temple (from the city center Marunouchi subway (underground) line to Myogadani Station) the **Koishikawa Botanic Garden** (40 acres), belongs to Tokyo University and contains 6000 different species of plants, including trees dating from the 17th c., when the garden was established. There are still remains of the landscaped garden which was attached to the Shogun's Palace. – To the N, near Komagome Station (JNR Yamanote line), is the *Rikugien Garden, a characteristic landscaped garden of the feudal period.

From Ueno Station the JNR Keihin-Tohoku line runs to Oji, in KITA ward, near which can be found the interesting *Paper Museum (paper-making and paper products).

SURROUNDINGS of Tokyo

Tokyo Disneyland. 6 miles/10 km from the city center on Expressway No. 9 (Tozai subway (underground) line to Urayasu Station) is **Tokyo Disneyland** (1 Maihama, Urayasu-shi, Chiba-ken 272-01. Telephone 54 2511), opened in April 1983, which has behind it the proven expertise of more than 28 years of Disney experience in the theme park industry. For the Japanese and for tourists from all over Asia and the Pacific region, the long-awaited opening of Tokyo

Tokyo Disneyland © 1983 Walt Disney Productions

Disneyland has become a reality. Many of the most popular attractions and restaurants found in the established theme parks of the USA are incorporated into the Tokyo project, as well as several entirely new attractions, such as "Pinocchio's Daring Journey", "The Eternal Seas" and "Meet the World". In addition to the attractions, there are up to 300 entertainers appearing daily in stage shows, musical performances and parades; and, of course, Mickey Mouse and all the other Disney characters can be found greeting visitors and signing autographs. There are more than 27 places to eat, ranging from snack bars to elaborate gourmet restaurants.

In contrast to "Main Street USA" of Disneyland and "Walt Disney World", Tokyo Disneyland has a **"World Bazaar"** through which visitors will pass on their way to Adventureland, Fantasyland, Tomorrowland and Westernland. The World Bazaar is totally under cover and fully protected from the weather. It features a main street, courtyards, shops, boutiques, restaurants and entertainment – all reminiscent of America at the turn of the century, at a time when the gas lamp was giving way to electric light. As visitors stroll down this "main thoroughfare" into the plaza, Cinderella Castle comes into view; in this plaza will be found transport, an antique Fire Engine, an Omnibus and a Horseless Carriage – all reminiscent of the same period.

Adventureland has a mixture of attractions. Based on Disney's Academy Award winning "True-life Adventure" films, the "Jungle Cruise" is a trip along a winding river amid lush vegetation. Visitors sail past a safari camp, the ruins of an ancient temple guarded by monkeys, through the rain forests of the Amazon and into the Congo along the rapids of the Nile complete with hippos and crocodiles. It is a trip far from civilization, in the remote jungles of Asia and Africa, using the "wonderland of nature's own design".

Above the "Jungle Cruise" landing visitors may board the "Western River Railroad", an authentic full-size steam train. From the train they can experience other views of the "Jungle Cruise", see both the American "old west" and the world as it was when only prehistoric animals roamed the earth.

Adventureland is also the site of the "Enchanted Tiki Room". This magical room is a vine-covered "theater-in-the-round" housing over two hundred multicolored birds performing a musical luau (a Hawaiian-style party).

One of the most popular Disney attractions, the "Pirates of the Caribbean" is also here. It is a twenty minute trip through a pirate raid on a Caribbean seaport, including singing, rowdy sailors and the firing of cannon to port and the splashing of water off the starboard bow. "Pirates of the Caribbean" is one of the most sophisticated and technologically advanced entertainments ever conceived as a permanent attraction.

Westernland expressed Americana and the "wild west" themes with adventures designed to give visitors a feeling of having lived during the pioneer days of America. Perhaps the most romantic of all – the cruise on the "Mark Twain Riverboat" – lets visitors sail on the waters of the Rivers of America in a stern-wheel paddle steamer or, if they prefer a more primitive way, they can conquer the river in an authentic Indian war canoe.

The Rivers of America surround an authentic "Tom Sawyer Island" complete with Injun Joe's Cove, Tom Sawyer's Treehouse, Fort Sam Clemens and suspension and barrel bridges. To explore the island visitors will board "Tom Sawyer Island Rafts" next to the Riverboat Landing.

Westernland also features the longest running show in the world – the "Golden Horseshoe Revue". With the first performance in the USA in 1955 and five shows daily since, the revue, complete with a can-can show, is listed in the Guinness Book of World Records as the longest running production of its kind in show business history. Advance reservations are necessary for this attraction.

Another favorite is the "Country Bear Jamboree", a depiction of the United States in the late 1800s. Starring bears in the leading roles, this Vaudeville-style musical is presented in a most humorous and entertaining way.

Fantasyland is where one will become part of the famous Disney stories and films. Visitors will ride through "Snow White's Adventure" in the Seven Dwarfs' mining car; fly through the air with Peter Pan to Never Never Land; and experience "Pinocchio's Daring Journey" in a new attraction created expressly for Tokyo Disneyland. In the "Mickey Mouse Revue", comedy and music will be featured as Mickey and other Disney characters "come to life" to perform all the Disney favorite adventures.

"It's a Small World" is an enclosed water cruise through a hundred nations, represented by some five hundred animated dolls with songs in their native languages.

Another attraction of note is the "Haunted Mansion" complete with leaded windows, mahogany paneling and inhabited by "999 ghosts and goblins". Visitors board specially designed omnicars of the Mansion, incorporating special lighting effects, details of which are unbelievably real. Included in these Fantasyland attractions are "Dumbo, the Flying Elephant" and Cinderella's Golden Carousel, which will be enjoyed by children of all ages. To take the scenic route into Tomorrowland visitors board an authentic Swiss Alpine cable car and view Tokyo Disneyland from a height of 70 ft/22 m. Directly below them people can be seen at the wheel of miniature racing cars in the "Grand Circuit Raceway".

Tomorrowland gives a glimpse into the future and explores the possibilities of progress. "Space Mountain" is a simulated ride through space, complete with multi-colored strobe lights and holographic asteroid shower. This realistic space trip is housed in a cone shaped superstructure which can be seen from the heart of Tokyo. If visitors prefer to experience a more "down to earth" flight, they can board "Star Jets" and control their own altitude as they whirl high above Tomorrowland.

Also in Tomorrowland are two original attractions; one is called "Meet the World", a unique presentation covering Japan's history and the impact she has made in the world; the other, "The Eternal Sea", enables visitors to explore man's newest frontier through Disney's unique 200° theater. In "Magic Carpet Round the World" the theatre experience is even more spectacular as Disney's "360° Circle-Vision" will take visitors to all the famous sights of the world.

Tokyo Disneyland will never be complete, always adding new attractions and shows to provide a combination of nostalgia and disbelief, of reality and fantasy.

37 miles/60 km NE of Tokyo, at the foot of Mount *Tsukuba* (2874 ft/876 m) is *Tsukuba Science City, the most modern and one of the largest centers of scientific work in the world.

This "test-tube town" (present population over 20,000) designed by Fumihiko Maki has been growing for some years on a green-field site of some $10\frac{1}{2}$ sq. miles, and now has over 1650 buildings (including some ultra-modern high-rise blocks), a central "spine" area and extensive pedestrian zones. Already something like a third of all national research institutes are based here, and there is also a University (a "glass mountain") with 23 research departments and 6 teaching departments. Altogether there are more than 3000 scientists and some 9000 students. The town is well equipped with residential accommodation, shopping centers, schools, recreational facilities and places of entertainment.

The technical and scientific resources available to this large "think tank", which will probably not be completed until near the end of the century, include laboratories with all the most modern equipment (wind tunnels, electron microscopes, lasers, etc.), a seven-storey reinforced-concrete building with an earthquake simulator, a road over 4 miles/6 km long for road tests and a 420 yd/380 m-long tunnel for experiments in noise reduction, ventilation and lighting. Among many other projects for research it is planned to study the possibility of the increasing automation of factories by the use of robots.

See also **Fuji-Hakone-Izu National Park, Fuji Lakes, Fujiyama, Hakone, Izu Peninsula, Kamakura, Narita** and **Yokohama**.

Boso Peninsula: see under Narita (Surroundings).

The **Ogasawara Islands** or **Bonin Islands**, which administratively belong to Tokyo, are an archipelago of small islands in the Pacific lying between 600 and 750 miles/1000 and 1200 km S of the Japanese coast. After a period of American occupation following the Second World War they were returned to Japan in 1968, and in 1972 were declared a National Park.

The islands (twice-weekly boat service from Tokyo, 40 hours) are covered with luxuriant subtropical vegetation and have beaches of white sand and picturesquely indented coasts. They are divided into four sub-groups, the **Muko, Chichi, Haha** and **Kazan** (or **Iwojima**) groups. The name of the archipelago as a whole comes from Ogasawara Sadayori, who discovered the islands in 1593.

The largest of the islands, with an area of barely 10 sq. miles/25 sq. km, is **Chichijima** ("Father Island"). The best beaches are on the W coast (Kohama Bay). There is good fishing all round the coast.

Hahajima ("Mother Island"), 3 hours S of Chichijima, is also popular with fishermen.

Tottori
とっとり

Prefecture: Tottori. – Population: 135,000.
Post code: J-680. – Telephone code: 0857.
(i) (local)
Tottori-shi Kanko Information
Higashi Shinaji-cho
(outside Central Station);
tel. 22 3318.

HOTELS. – **Western style**: *Hotel New Otani Tottori*, 2-153, Ima-machi, 143 r., beach; *Hotel Taihei*, 628, Sakae-cho, 82 r. – **Minshuku**: *Yamamasaya*, in Iwami (to E), 1435-1, Hamayuyama, 12 r.

RESTAURANT. – *National Kaikan*, 252, Eiraku-onsen-machi.

TRANSPORTATION. – **Air**: from TOKYO (Haneda Airport), 2 hours; from OSAKA (45 minutes). – **Rail**: from KYOTO JNR San-in line via OSAKA (4 hours); from OKAYAMA JNR Tsuyama and Imbi lines ($2\frac{1}{2}$ hours).

Tottori, chief town of a prefecture and a university town, lies on the N coast of western Honshu in the San-in district. It is noted for its woodworking and paper-making industries. From the visitor's point of view it makes a good base from which to see the nearby National Park.

SIGHTS. – 1 mile/1·7 km NE of the station, on higher ground, lies **Kyusho Park**, in which are the remains of a 16th c. castle. Farther in the same direction is the **Kannon-in Garden**, with the Kannon-in Temple and, near by, the *Ochidani Shrine*, dedicated to Tokugawa Ieyasu. – 220 yds/200 m from the station can be found an interesting *Museum of Folk Art.*

SURROUNDINGS. – To the N of the town the River *Sendai* flows into the Sea of Japan. In this area (bus, 20 minutes) are great expanses of dunes, lying on both sides of the river. The eastern part of the area falls within the **San-in-kaigan National Park**, which extends eastward for almost 50 miles/80 km. Among the chief attractions in this region of varied scenery are the stretch of coast at *Kasumi*, Uradome Beach and the resort of *Kinosaki*. The San-in railway line from Tottori runs along the coast.

There are excellent beaches at *Uradome, Tajiri* and *Ajiro*. Off the little bays lie isolated rocks and islands with caves eroded by the sea. – Inland lies the health resort of **Hamasaka-onsen** (bus from Hamasaka Station, 25 minutes), which offers good walking in summer and skiing in winter. – **Kasumi** lies in a particularly attractive area. 1 mile/1·5 km S of the station is the *Daijoji Temple* of the Shingon sect, probably founded in the 8th c., which has many works by the painter Maruyama Okyo (1733–95). – From March to November there are boat trips along the coast.

Kinosaki-onsen lies in the hills in a beautiful park-like landscape. Near the Onsenji Temple is a cableway up Mount *Daishi* (*view of the estuary of the River Maruyama). – Farther inland, on the banks of the *Maruyama*, is **Gembudo**, near which, in columnar basalt formations, are five caves (*Gembu-do*). Carved on the rock face are the three Chinese characters spelling *gem-bu-do*. – The railway continues to the **Toyooka** junction.

Towada-Hachimantai National Park
とわだ
はちまんたい
国立公園

Prefectures: Akita, Aomori and Iwate.
Area: 322 sq. miles/833 sq. km.

(i) (central)
National Parks Association of Japan,
Toranomon Denki Building,
8-1, Toranomon 2-chome, Minato-ku,
J-105 **Tokyo**;
tel. (03) 502 0488.

(local)
Towada-Hachimantai Tourist Association,
33 Shimonakajima, Hanawa,
J-018-53 **Kazuno**;
tel. (01862) 3 2019.

HOTELS. – AROUND LAKE TOWADA. – **Western style**: *Towada Kogen Hotel*, Yakiyama, Towada-machi, 49 r., thermal bath; *Towada-Kohan Grand Hotel*, 16, Yasumiya Aza-Towada, Oaza Okuse, Towada-Kohan-machi, 37 r., thermal bath, beach; *Towada Kanko Hotel*, 16-9, Yasumiya Aza-Towada, Oaza Okuse, Towada-Kohan-machi, 29 r., beach; *Hotel Sun Plaza*, in Towada, 1-6, Higashi-Sanban-cho, 50 r.; *Towada Green Hotel*, in Towada, 20-74, Nishi-Sanban-cho, 22 r. – **Ryokan**: *Homei-kan*, in Towada, Okuse, 35 r., beach; *Hoo-kaku*, Yakeyama, Towada-machi, 19 r., thermal bath; *Oirase-so*, in Towada, Okuse, 15 r.; *Kuriyama*, 62, Yasumidaira, Towada-ku, 12 r., beach. – YOUTH HOSTELS: *YH Hakubutsukan*, Yasumiya, Towada-Kohan, Towada-machi, 200 b., beach; *Towada YH*, Hakka, Towada-Kohan, Towada-machi, 100 b.; *Oirase YH*, Yakeyama, Towada-machi, 80 b.; *Nishi-Towada YH*, 18, Nagasakashita, Itadome, 60 b.

IN AND AROUND NATIONAL PARK (southern section). – **Western style**: *Hachimantai Rising Sun Hotel*, 590-226, Yoriki, Matsuo-mura, 60 r., thermal bath; *Hachimantai Kanko Hotel*, 5-2-1, Midorigaoka, Matsuo-mura, 57 r., thermal bath. – YOUTH HOSTELS: *Hachimantai YH*, 5-2, Midorigaoka, Matsuo-mura, 150 b.; *YH Matsukawa-so*, in Matsukawa-onsen, Matsuo-mura, 77 b., thermal bath. – IN MORIOKA: see that entry.

TRANSPORTATION. – **Rail**: from TOKYO (Ueno Station) to Omiya (30 minutes), then JNR New Tohoku-Shinkansen line to Morioka (3¼ hours) and Aomori (2½ hours); from AOMORI or MORIOKA JNR Rohoku line to MISAWA, then private line to Towada. – **Bus**: several services into the two sections of the National Park from AOMORI, Towada-Minami, Hachimantai, Misawa, Odate, etc.

The Towada-Hachimantai National Park, at the northern tip of Honshu, is divided into two separate sections. The northern section includes the area around **Lake Towada, while the southern section consists of the Hachimantai Plateau, with Mounts Iwate, Nyuto and Koma. The natural beauty of these regions, with their magnificent forests, crystal-clear lakes and volcanic cones, is still largely untouched.

To the S of the coastal town of **Aomori** (see that entry) are the Hakkoda Mountains. Buses run through this region to Sukayu-onsen and *Tsuta-onsen* (3½ hours).

Sukayu-onsen is a good base from which to see the **Hakkoda Mountains**, a range of eight extinct volcanoes, the highest of which is **Odake** or *Sukayu* (5200 ft/1585 m). The dense forests in this area are particularly beautiful in autumn. From the summit of Mount Odake the *view reaches to the Sea of Japan in the W and the Pacific in the E.

Lake Towada, in the Towada-Hachimantai National Park

The bus continues through the beautiful **Valley of the *Oirase*, flowing between tree-covered crags. The 9 mile/14 km long section between *Yakeyama* and **Nenokuchi**, on the E side of Lake Towada, is particularly fine.

Lake Towada is a large crater lake (area 23 sq. miles/59 sq. km, depth 1100 ft/334 m) surrounded by primeval forest, with a road following its shores. From the S side two promontories reach out into the lake, forming three deep bays, *Higashi-no-umi* ("East Lake"), *Naka-no-umi* ("Middle Lake") and *Nishi-no-umi* ("West Lake"). – The River Oirase flows into the lake at Nenokuchi, from which a bus (20 minutes) runs up Mount *Towada* (3458 ft/1054 m; *view of lake), descending to **Utarube** on Higashi-no-umi. From here it is worth making the detour along the promontory to Mount *Ogura* (2034 ft/620 m; view). – The road round the lake now comes to the largest place in this area, **Yasumiya** (also reached by boat from Nenokuchi, 1½ hours), with a bronze statue of Takamura Kotaro (1883–1956) and the Towada Museum. From here a road leads NW along the second promontory, passing Gozengahama Beach, to the *Towada Shrine*. – The shore road continues round Nishi-no-umi to **Wainai** (or *Oide*), with a well-known trout farm, from which a road goes S to the *Hakka Pass* (2123 ft/ 647 m; *view).

The southern section of the National Park can be reached from Hachimantai or Morioka. Its volcanic heights and widely scattered settlements are a favourite resort of climbers and winter-sports enthusiasts. The many hot springs have led to the development of various health resorts.

From **Hachimantai** (JNR Hanawa line) a road (the middle section of which is the Hachimantai–Aspite toll road; bus) crosses the **Hachimantai Plateau** which occupies the northern part of the region to **Koma** (JNR Tohoku line). Near the road, at the foot of *Mount Yakeyama*, a volcano 4482 ft/1366 m high, are the health resorts of **Tamagawa-onsen** (hot spring, 208°F/98°C), **Goshogake-onsen** (steam baths) and **Fukenoyu-onsen**.

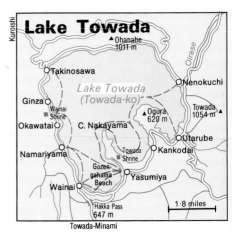

From **Morika** (see that entry), outside the National Park to the E, the JNR Tohoku line runs to *Takizawa*, from which a bus (40 minutes) can be taken to *Yanagisawa*, below the E side of the quiescent volcano of **Iwate** (6697 ft/ 2041 m). It is well worth climbing Mount Iwate – which has two peaks, Higashi-Iwate to the E and Nishi-Iwate to the W – for the sake of its rich mountain vegetation and the magnificent *view from the summit. An alternative route for the descent is down the SW flank to *Amihari-onsen*.

The JNR Tazawako line, running W from Morioka, passes close to *Lake Tazawa*. From Tazawako Station there is a bus (July–October) to the 8th staging-point on the route up Mount **Koma** (5371 ft/ 1637 m), from which it is an hour's climb to the summit (*view of Lake Tazawa). – *Lake Tazawa*, one of Japan's deepest lakes (1395 ft/425 m), lies outside the National Park.

Tsukuba
See under Tokyo

Tsuruga
つるが

Prefecture: Fukui. – Population: 65,000.
Post code: J-914. – Telephone code: 07702.
(central)
Ⓘ**Fukui-ken Tokyo Kanko Bussan Assensho,**
Kokusai Kanko Kaikan,
1-8-3, Marunouchi, Chiyoda-ku,
J-100 **Tokyo**,
tel. (03) 211 8054.

HOTELS. – **Western style**: *Kanko Hotel*, 2-8, Kawasaki-cho, 33 r.; *Kanko Hotel Kitaguni*, 1-3, Nakagogo, 25 r.

EVENTS. – *Ebisu-Daikoku Tsunahiki* (mid January), a popular festival; *Sounomairi* (mid July), procession at Kehi Shrine; *Kehi-no-Nagamatsuri* (beginning of September), procession at Kehi Shrine.

TRANSPORTATION. – **Rail**: from TOKYO (Central Station) JNR Tohoku–Shinkansen line to MAIBARA (3½ hours), then JNR Hokuriku line (30 minutes); from OSAKA JNR Kosei and Hokuriku lines (1¾ hours).

The port of Tsuruga in western central Honshu, to the N of Lake Biwa, lies at the head of the deep inlet of Tsuruga Bay – a favored situation which gave it special importance from an early period as a gateway to Korea. It is still a considerable port, with a variety of industries.

SIGHTS. – A short distance N of the station, surrounded by thousands of cherry trees, is the **Kanagasakigu Shrine**, dedicated to the two sons of the Emperor Godaigo. – 1 mile/1·5 km N is the **Kehi Shrine**. The timber used in the uprights of the torii is said to have drifted here from the island of Sado in the 17th c.

6 miles/9 km NW of the station we find the **Jogu Shrine**, which has an old bell said to have been brought back by Toyotomi Hideyoshi from his Korean campaign. The stone known as *Omi-ishi* is noted for giving out a sound when it is touched.

3½ miles/5·6 km W on the shores of Tsuruga Bay lies **Matsubara Park**, with a fir grove containing the tomb of Takeda Kounsai (1803–65) who was executed here together with his companions for resisting the Tokugawa policy of opening up Japan.

SURROUNDINGS. – To the W of the town, beyond the promontory bounding Tsuruga Bay, we come to the **Wakasawan Quasi National Park**. This area can be reached on the JNR Obama line, which in 15 miles/25 km reaches **Mikata**. Between this little town and the coast are the *Five Mikata Lakes* (Mikata-goko), which are linked with one another by various streams and channels. A charming road (bus, 35 minutes) runs up Mount *Baijo* (1296 ft/395 m), on the summit of which is the *Uwase Shrine*; * view of the lakes.

The largest town in *Wakasa Bay* is **Obama** (pop. 34,000), where the well-known *Wakasa-nuri* lacquerware is produced. Worth seeing are a number of interesting temples – the Jingu-ji; the Myotsu-ji, with a three-storey pagoda; the Mantoku-ji, with a beautiful garden; the Myoraku-ji, which has a statue of the Thousand-Handed Kannon; and the Renge-ji, with a bronze statue of the Healing Buddha (Yakushi-nyorai). – Boat trips to the picturesque *Sotomo* coastal region (rocks, caves, waterfalls).

At the W end of Wakasa Bay is the beautiful coastal scenery of **Ama-no-hashidate** (see that entry).

Tsushima Islands
See under Fukuoka

Tsuwano

つわの

Prefecture: Shimane. – Population: 8000.
Post code: J-699-56. – Telephone code: 08567.

(i) (central)
**Shimane-ken Tokyo Kanko Bussan
Assensho,**
Tetsudo kaikan,
1-9-1, Marunouchi, Chiyoda-ku,
J-100 **Tokyo**;
tel. (03) 212 1091.

HOTELS. – **Western style:** *Tsuwano Kanko Hotel
Shinkan*, 82-3, Ushiroda, 30 r. – **Ryokan:** *Yoshinoya*,
Ushiroda, 33 r.; *Koraku Ryokan*, 76, Ushiroda, 25 r.;
Wata-ya Ryokan, Ushiroda, 12 r. – **Minshuku:**
Hiroshima-ya, Ushiroda, 30 r.; *Tsuwano*, Ushiroda, 28
r. – YOUTH HOSTEL: *Tsuwano YH*, 819-ko,
Washihara, Tsuwano-cho, 14 b.

TRANSPORTATION. – **Rail:** from TOKYO (Central
Station) JNR Shinkansen line to *Ogori* (6 hours),
then JNR Yamaguchi line (1¼ hours).

**The little town of * Tsuwano, once a
castle town, lies at the western tip
of Honshu, 40 miles/60 km NE of
Yamaguchi. It still preserves many
old buildings, including burghers'
houses and samurai houses, recall-
ing its earlier days. During the
medieval period the town was held
successively by the Yoshimi,
Sakazaki, and Kamei families, who
fostered artistic activity in
Tsuwano, which now attracts large
numbers of visitors, particularly in
spring and in the fall.**

SIGHTS. – A good way of seeing the town
is on a bicycle (which can be rented at the
station). The old samurai houses, flanked
by canals, are to be found in the center
of the town (Tonomachi). – On a hill
beyond the station, surrounded by cherry
trees, is *St Mary's Memorial Church*,
commemorating 153 Christians who were
martyred in the village of Urakami for their
faith.

Near the station is the **Yomeiji Temple**,
with the Tomb of Mori Ogai, one of the
leaders of the Meiji Restoration, and the
mausoleum of the Kamei family.

To the S of the station, housed in the former Princely Academy, is the **Historical
Museum** (*Yoro-kan*), with a collection
of arms and armor, etc. Adjoining it is the
Museum of Folk Art (*Kyodo-kan*),
with exhibits illustrating the history of the
town and various items which belonged
to its princely families.

W of the town is Mount *Shiroyama* (extensive views), with the sumptuous **Inari
Shrine**. A cableway runs up to the
remains of Tsuwano Castle, now surrounded by a park.

It is a 10-minute bus ride to the
Washihara-Hachimangu Shrine, with
a race-track 260 yds/240 m long which is
used in the Yabusame equestrian festival
celebrated in April every year.

Unzen-Amakusa National Park

うんぜん
あまくさ
国立公園

Prefectures: Nagasaki, Kumamoto and Kagoshima.
Area: 99 sq. miles/256 sq. km.

(i) (central)
National Parks Association of Japan,
Toranomon Denki Building,
8-1, Toranomon 2-chome, Minato-ku,
J-105 **Tokyo**;
tel. (03) 502 0488.

(local)
Unzen Tourist Association,
Obama-cho,
J-854-06 **Unzen**;
tel. (095773) 3434.

HOTELS. – **Western style:** *Ariake Hotel*, in Unzen-
onsen, 116 r., Japanese garden, SP, thermal bath;
Kyushu Hotel, in Unzen-onsen, 106 r., Japanese garden, SP, thermal bath; *Amakusa Kokusai Hotel*, 996,
Oaza-Hirose, Hondo-cho, 72 r., SP, beach; *Unzen
Kanko Hotel*, in Unzen-onsen, 62 r., Japanese garden,
thermal bath; *Amakusa Grand Hotel*, 1-21, Suwa-
cho, Hondo, 47 r. – **Ryokan:** *Hotel Toyokan*, Obama-
machi, 130 r.; *Miyazaki Ryokan*, Obama-machi, 111
r.; *Fujiya Ryokan*, Obama-machi, 92 r.; *Yumoto Hotel*,
Obama-machi, 72 r.; *Hosenkan*, Obama-machi, 69 r.;
Unzen Hotel, in Unzen-onsen, 65 r., thermal bath;
Hotel Honda, Obama-machi, 63 r.; *Unzen New Grand
Hotel*, 299, Unzen, 50 r., thermal bath; *Unzen Park
Hotel*, Obama-machi, 50 r., – YOUTH HOSTELS: *YH
Seiun-so*, 500-1, Unzen, 300 b., thermal bath;
Amakusa YH, 180, Hondo, Hondo-cho, 60 b.

TRANSPORTATION. – **Rail:** from NAGASAKI JNR
Nagasaki line to ISAHAYA (25 minutes), then Shimabara
private line via Shimabara and the E coast of the
peninsula to Kazusa; from FUKUOKA (Hakata) to
Isahaya (2¼ hours). – **Bus:** from Isahaya via Obama to
Unzen; from Kumamoto to Hondo (Amakusa; 2½
hours). – **Boat:** from MISUMI (Uto Peninsula) to
Shimabara.

**The * Unzen-Amakusa National Park,
at the extreme western end of the**

main Japanese group of islands, includes the central section of the Shimabara Peninsula and the Amakusa Islands, just off Kumamoto. The area is bounded by the Ariake Sea, Chijiwa Bay and Yatsushiro Bay.

The backbone of the Shimabara Peninsula is formed by the **Unzen Massif**, which attracts large numbers of visitors in spring for the azaleas and in the fall for the vividly colored foliage. The volcanic origin of the range is reflected in the presence of numerous geysers, fumaroles and bubbling pools of mud.

From **Obama**, on the W coast of the peninsula, a road runs through the Unzen Massif to Shimabara. Below the S side of Mount Myoken is **Unzen-onsen** (hot springs at temperatures of up to 203 °F/ 95 °C). Near the town are the fumaroles of *Unzen-jigoku* and ¾ mile/1 km NE a golf-course. There is a bus service to the *Nitta Pass* (3610 ft/1100 m) from which a cableway ascends Mount *Myoken* (4377 ft/1334 m). From the top of Myoken there is a path (1 hour) to the summit of Mount *Fugen* (4462 ft/ 1360 m), on which is the Fugen Shrine. From both peaks there are superb *views of the Ariake Sea to the N, Mount Aso to the E, the Kirishima Range to the SE and the Amakusa Islands to the S.

Half-way down the E side of the peninsula lies the old castle town of **Shimabara** (pop. 47,000). The Castle (¼ mile/400 m W of the station), built in 1615 and reconstructed in 1964, now houses a museum on the history of Christianity in Japan. Beyond the Castle is the Seibo Museum, with works by the artist Kitamura Seibo. To the W of this is an old street with samurai houses. – Off the harbor can be seen the *Tsukumojima Islands*, formed in 1792 by an eruption of the *Mayuyama* Volcano W of the town.

The Shimabara private railway line continues S along the coast, coming in 17 miles/28 km to *Harajo*. 550 yds/500 m E of the station we find the ruins of *Hara Castle*, where in 1637 the Christians put up their last resistance to the troops of the Tokugawa Shogunate. The siege of the castle ended with the death of some 20,000 Japanese Christians.

To the S of the Shimabara Peninsula, beyond the Hayasaki Strait, are the **Amakusa Islands**. At the NE end of the group, just off the Uto Peninsula, is the little island of **Oyanoshima**, followed towards the SW by **Kamishima** and **Shimoshima**.

On the E coast of Shimoshima is **Hondo**, the administrative center of the Amakusa Islands, which in earlier days played an important part in the diffusion of Christianity. The site of the castle is now occupied by the *Sennin-Zuka Park* (Christian Memorial Park), with a memorial to those who died in the 1637 Rising and a museum. Here, too, is a well-known figure of Kannon with the Infant Jesus (Kannon, usually depicted in female form, being seen as representing the Virgin). – Other features of interest are the *Meitokuji Temple*, the *Giobashi* Bridge and the Aquarium.

From Hondo a road runs via the port of **Oniike**, in the NE of the island, to **Tomioka**, near which are some picturesque stretches of coastal scenery, and on to the resort of **Shimoda** (which has a number of hot springs). – From Hondo a bus runs S (2¼ hours) to the busy fishing port of **Ushibuka** (pop. 25,000).

Uwajima
うわじま

Prefecture: Ehime. – Population: 75,000.
Post code: J-798. – Telephone code: 0895.
(i) (central)
   Ehime-ken Tokyo Kanko Bussan Assensho,
   Tetsudo Kaikan,
   1-9-1, Marunouchi, Chiyoda-ku,
   J-100 **Tokyo**;
   tel. (03) 231 1804.

   (local)
   Tourist Section of Uwajima City,
   1, Akebono-cho;
   tel. 24 1111.
   Japan Travel Bureau,
   in Bus Center,
   1-3-20, Marunouchi;
   tel. 22 0703.

HOTELS. – **Western style**: *Uwajima Kokusai Hotel*, 4-1, Nishiki-cho, 40 r.; *Uwajima Daiichi Hotel*, 1-3-9, Chuo-cho, 52 r. – **Ryokan**: *Jonan-so*, 273-2, Shirahama, 20 r. – YOUTH HOSTEL: *YH Mannen-so*, Nametokoyama, Meguro Matsuno-machi, Kita-Uwa-gun, 120 b.

EVENTS. – *Yatsushida-dori* (end of October), procession with large animal figures at Uwatsushiko Shrine; *Fights between bulls* (January, April, July, August, October, November).

TRANSPORTATION. – **Rail**: from MATSUYAMA JNR Yosan line (2 hours). – **Boat**: ferry from BEPPU via Yawatahama (6 hours).

The port of Uwajima, on the W coast of Shikoku, lies in an outstandingly beautiful stretch of *coastal scenery. It has a mild climate in which citrus fruits flourish, while the sea offers rich fishing grounds and excellent conditions for pearl-culture.

SIGHTS. – 750 yds/700 m SW of the station (bus, 5 minutes), on a hill 260 ft/80 m high, is the main tower of the old Castle. – 1¼ miles/2 km SW of the station can be found the beautiful landscaped garden of **Tensha-en**, created in the 19th c. for the summer residence of the Date family. – In Gotenmachi, not far away, is the **Date Museum** (*Date-hakubutsukan*), with weapons, picture scrolls and other items which belonged to the Date family.

1¼ miles/2 km SE of the station is the **Uwatsushiko Shrine** (annual festival at end of October). On a hill beyond the shrine lies **Atago Park** (*view of town and surrounding area).

¾ mile/1 km N of the station stands the *Bull-fighting Stadium*, in which bull-fights (*togyu*: i.e. fights between bulls) are held six times a year, following a tradition which dates from medieval times; the rules are similar to those of sumo wrestling.

SURROUNDINGS. – 19 miles/30 km N (bus, 1 hour) lies the port of **Yawatahama** (pop. 44,000), from which there are ferry services to the E coast of Kyushu (Beppu and Usuki). Around the town are mandarine plantations and terraced fields. – 10 miles/16 km farther N rises Mount *Kinzan* (2690 ft/820 m), on the summit of which (*view) is the **Kinzan-Shussekiji Temple**.

To the W of Yawatahama the narrow **Sadamisaki Peninsula**, 32 miles/52 km long, projects into the sea, separating the Inland Sea from the Bungo Channel. Between *Cape Sada* (ferry from Yawatahama, 1½ hours) and *Cape Jizo* is the *Hoyo Strait*, only 9 miles/15 km wide. From the much-indented coast of the peninsula there are beautiful views of the Inland Sea.

9 miles/15 km NE of Yawatahama we reach the old castle town of **Iyo-Ozu** (pop. 39,000). 1 mile/1·5 km SW of the station are the remains of the Castle. From June to September visitors can watch the catching of fish by specially trained cormorants on the River *Hiji*.

Wakayama

わかやま

Prefecture: Wakayama. – Population: 405,000.
Post code: J-640. – Telephone code: 0734.
(central)
(i) **Wakayama-ken Tokyo Kanko Bussan Assensho,**
Kokusai Kanko Kaikan,
1-8-3, Marunouchi, Chiyoda-ku,
J-100 **Tokyo**;
tel. (03) 231 2041.

(local)
Wakayama-ken Kanko Renmei,
Wakayama-ken Kanko-ka-nai,
1-1, Komatsubara-dori;
tel. 23 6111.

HOTELS. – **Western style:** *Wakayama Tokyu Inn*, 7-1, Minami-Migiwa-cho, 137 r.; *Wakayama Green Hotel*, 48, Shinsaika-machi, 27 r.; *Business Inn Kasuga*, 4-1, Sugino-Baba, 26 r. – Ryokan: *Aoi-kan*, 13, Juniban-cho, 27 r., – YOUTH HOSTEL: *YH Wakayama-ken Seinen-kan*, 1-14-2, Chikko, 40 b.

TRANSPORTATION. – **Rail**: from OSAKA (Tennoji Station) JNR Hanwa line (1 hour); from Nanba Station Nankai Private line to Wakayama-shi (1 hour).

The old castle town of Wakayama, now the chief town of a prefecture, lies in western Honshu, on the W coast of the Kii Peninsula opposite Shikoku. It was from an early period a gateway into the interior of Japan, and is now a busy commercial and industrial town (textiles, etc.). The nearby * Wakanoura coast is a popular holiday area.

SIGHTS. – In the city center is the **Castle** built by Toyotomi Hideyoshi in 1585, surrounded by a park. The three-storey main tower was rebuilt in 1958 after its destruction during the war. – 2½ miles/4 km S of the station (bus) lies the **Akiba-yama Park**, which contains a number of shrines.

SURROUNDINGS. – To the S of Wakayama (25 minutes by bus) is the well-known seaside resort of *Wakanoura, with beautiful coastal scenery (view of the island of Awaji: see that entry). Near the town stands the **Kimiidera Temple**, founded in 770 by a Chinese priest named Iko, which is the headquarters of the Guse-Kannon sect and one of the pilgrimage temples of the western provinces. Notable features are the main gate, bell-tower, pagoda, a wooden statue of the Eleven-Headed Kannon and other sculpture. Within the temple precinct are large numbers of cherry trees.

12½ miles/20 km S of Wakayama (JNR Kisei line) we reach the port of **Shimotsu**. 1 mile/1·7 km E of the station is the Chohoji Temple of the Tendai sect, with the tombs of the daimyos of Wakayama. The offshore island of *Bentenjima* (boat, 15 minutes) offers good fishing.

NW of Wakayama (Nankei-Kada private railway line, 25 minutes) is **Kada**, which has a beautiful beach.

To the N and NE are a number of other interesting temples, which can be reached by the JNR Hanwa line. – 5 miles/8 km E of *Kii* Station is the **Negoroji Temple** of the Shingi-Shingon sect, founded in 1126. The relic shrine (*tahoto*) was renewed in 1515. In the Main Hall (Daishido), built in 1391, can be seen a portrait of the founder, Kakuban (or Kokyo-daishi). Beautiful cherry blossom at the beginning of April.

The next station on the line is *Izumi-Hashimoto*, near which are the **Mizuma-Kannon Temple** of the

Tendai sect (2½ miles/4 km) and the **Ko-onji Temple** or Kozumi-Kannon Temple (3 miles/4·8 km), which has many works of Buddhist sculpture in its hall (Kannon-do).

The Temple of the Shingon sect at **Kumeda** was founded in the early 8th c. – 9 miles/14 km S is *Mount Ushitaki*, covered with maple forest (particularly beautiful in the fall) and with many waterfalls. the **Dai-Itokuji Temple** of the Tendai and Shingon sects was founded in the 7th c.

Yaba-Hita-Hikosan Quasi National Park

やばひた
ひこさん
国定公園

Prefectures: Fukuoka and Oita.
Area: 329 sq. miles/852 sq. km.

(central)
National Parks Association of Japan,
Toranomon Denki Building,
8-1, Toranomon 2-chome, Minato-ku,
J-105 **Tokyo**;
tel. (03) 502 0488.

Oita-ken Tokyo Kanko Bussan Assensho,
Kokusai Kanko Kaikan,
1-8-3, Marunouchi, Chiyoda-ku,
J-100 **Tokyo**;
tel. (03) 231 5096.

HOTELS. – IN YABAKEI AREA. – **Ryokan**: *Ryokan Hasumitei*, in Nakatsu, 3-2, Honmachi, 19 r.; *Chomeikan*, in Hon-Yabakei-cho, 1646, Sogi, 17 r.; *Takamotoya Ryokan*, in Nakatsu, 1691, Edamachi, 13 r.; *Yabakei Kanko Hotel*, in Kamoyoshi-onsen, Shin-Yaba, 13 r.; *Rokumeikan*, in Yabakei-cho, 3152, Shin-Yaba, 12 r.; *Chikushitei Bekkan*, in Nakatsu, 1692, Edamachi, 9 r.; *Sankoken*, in Yamakuni-cho, 41-3, Morizane, 9 r. – YOUTH HOSTELS: *Yamakuniya*, in Yabakei-cho, 1933-1, Sogi, 50 b.; *Fumon-in*, in Nakatsu, 978, Teramachi, 20 b.

IN HITA. – **Ryokan**: *Grand Hotel Mikuma*, 1-3-19, Kuma, 57 r.; *Hita Grand Hotel*, 1-3-8, Kuma, 50 r.; *Hita Gajoen Hotel*, 1-1, Ueno-cho, 46 r.; *Kameyamatei Hotel*, 1-3-10, Kuma, 43 r.; *Yorozuya*, 1-3-12, Kuma, 24 r.; *Sansuikan*, 3-23, Kawara-cho, 20 r.; *Hotel Hinokumaso*, 2-4-7, Kuma, 18 r. – YOUTH HOSTEL: *Hita YH*, in Oyama, Nishi-Oyama, 50 b.

ON MOUNT HIKOSAN. – **Ryokan**: *Rokosuke Bekkan Takasu Kogen Hotel*, 1339, Hikosan, 17 r.; *Ryokan Chuokan*, 1336, Hikosan, 10 r.

TRANSPORTATION. – **Rail**: from KITAKYUSHU (Kokura Station) Hita–Hikosan line to Hikosan (1½ hours); from OITA or FUKUOKA (Hakata) JNR Kyudai line to Hita (2 hours or 1½ hours). – **Bus**: from NAKAT-SU (2 hours); from FUKUOKA (Bus Center at Nishitetsu Station) to Hita (2½ hours).

The * Yaba-Hita-Hikosan Quasi National Park – a region of mountains, deep gorges, waterfalls and dense forests – lies in north-eastern Kyushu.

On the borders of Fukuoka and Oita prefectures rises Mount *Hikosan* (3940 ft/ 1200 m; bus from Hikosan Station, 20 minutes), with the **Hikosan Shrine** on one of its five peaks. The bus goes up to the *torii* at the entrance to the extensive precincts of the shrine.

Set in a dense grove of cedars, the shrine was founded in the 7th c. by a priest named En-no-Ozuno. It was one of the earliest centers of Shintoism on Kyushu, and with the fusion of Shintoism and Buddhism rose to considerable importance as a center of the ascetic Shugendo sect. There are said to have been several thousand monks here in the later 16th c., and the abbots not infrequently came from the Imperial family. With the renaissance of pure Shintoism during the Meiji period the shrine lost its influence, but it remains a classic example of the hill shrines of the Shugendo sect.

In the *Hita Basin* on the SW border of the Quasi National Park lies the town of **Hita** (pop. 65,000), a popular summer holiday resort which also has some industry (woodworking). Between May and October the local people fish in the River *Mikuma* with trained cormorants.

From Hita there are buses (45 minutes) to the little potters' town of **Onda**, in a romantic setting near the border of the prefecture. The pottery produced here is mainly coarse ware for domestic use; pottery fair at the beginning of October. To visit the Pottery Museum (Togei-kan), apply to one of the potters' workshops. – 15 miles/25 km from Onda (taxi) is **Koishiwara** (also reached from Fukuoka by bus, 2½ hours; change at Haki), which also has many potters' workshops (fairs in April–May and at the beginning of October).

S of Hita (bus, 1 hour), in the beautiful Valley of the River *Tsuetate*, the health resort of **Tsuetate-onsen** has several hot springs (up to 208°F/98°C). From here there is a road to *Uchinomaki* in the **Aso National Park** (see that entry).

A road runs NE from Hita through a particularly beautiful part of the Quasi National Park (bus). At **Yamakuni** it reaches the River *Yamakuni* and follows it downstream. At **Kakizaka** the River *Yamautsuri* comes in from the SE to join the Yamakuni.

The Yamautsuri flows through the *Shin-Yabakei Gorge*, into which a road branches off here. The most beautiful part of the gorge begins at **Fumonjibashi** (5 miles/8 km). At **Hitome-Hakkei** is a viewpoint which affords a magnificent * prospect. 2 miles/3 km beyond this is **Utsukushidani**, where the autumn coloring is especially fine.

Beyond Kakizaka the main road traverses the *Yabakei-kyo Gorge, with impressive steep rock faces, side gorges and luxuriant vegetation. The road runs through the *Ao-no-Domon Tunnel*, said to have been cut by a priest named Zenkei, who spent 30 years on the task, completing it in 1764.

At **Nakatsu** (pop. 64,000) the Yamakuni flows into the Inland Sea. An industrial town and market center for the local agricultural produce, it was the birthplace of Fukuzawa Yukichi (1835–1901), who played a leading part in the introduction of Western ideas into Japan and founded a school in Edo (Tokyo) which developed into the Keio-Gijuku University. There is a monument to him in a park ¾ mile/1 km NW of the station, and near this stands the house in which he lived, now serving as his memorial.

Yaeyama Islands
See under Okinawa

Yakushima
See under Satsunan Islands

Yamagata
やまがた

Prefecture: Yamagata. – Population: 245,000. Post code: J-990. – Telephone code: 0236.

(i) (central)
Yamagata-ken Tokyo Kanko Bussan Assensho,
Tetsudo Kaikan,
1-9-1, Marunouchi, Chiyoda-ku,
J-100 **Tokyo**;
tel. (03) 215 2222.

(local)
Yamagata-ken Kanko Kyokai,
Yamagata-ken Kankoka-nai,
3-4-51, Hatago-cho;
tel. 31 9233.

HOTELS. – **Western style**: *Yamagata Grand Hotel*, 1-7-40, Hon-cho, 79 r.; *Hotel Onuma*, 2-1-10, Kojirakawa-machi, 72 r., Japanese garden; *Zao Echo Hotel*, in Zao-onsen, 117, Sandogawa, 61 r., thermal bath; *Hotel Zao Garden*, in Zao-onsen, 1118-15, San-dogawa, 30 r., thermal bath; *Hotel Jurin*, in Zao-onsen, 814, Uenodai, 30 r., thermal bath; *Hotel Yamagata*, 1-1, Saiwai-cho, 86 r.; *Green Hotel*, 1-3-12, Kazumi-cho, 64 r.; *Hotel Zao*, in Zao-onsen, 963, Yujiri, 55 r.; *Hotel Sakaiya*, 1-14-10, Kazumi-cho, 51

r.; *Yamagata Business Hotel*, 5-12-7, Nanoka-cho, 34 r.; *Business Hotel Sanko*, 3-5-21, Hatago-cho, 25 r. – **Ryokan**: *Takamiya Annex Unkai-so*, in Zao-onsen, 934-2, Kawamae, 28 r., thermal bath; *Shinzan-so Takamiya*, in Zao-onsen, 26 r., thermal bath. – **Minshuku**: *Ginrei Honten*, in Zao-onsen, 52 r.; *Ohira-sanso*, in Zao-onsen, 51 r. – YOUTH HOSTELS: *YH Kashiwaya Michinoku-so*, in Zao-onsen, 60 b.; *Minami-Zao YH*, 59-17, Kashiwagiyama, 50 b.; *YH Zao Yama-No-Ie*, in Zao-onsen, Dokko-numa-han, 30 b.

RESTAURANTS. – *Chitosekan*, 4-9-2, Nanoka-machi; *Kishokaku*, 2-8-81, Yakushi-machi; *Mimasu*, 2-3-7, Nanoka-machi.

EVENTS. – *Hanagasa-matsuri* (beginning of August), dancing procession through the streets of the town.

TRANSPORTATION. – **Air**: from TOKYO (Haneda Airport), 1¼ hours. – **Rail**: from TOKYO (Ueno Station) JNR Ou line (4½ hours); from SENDAI JNR Senzan line (1½ hours).

*Yamagata, in north-eastern Honshu, is chief town of a prefecture and one of Japan's best-known winter-sports resorts, appropriately twinned with the Austrian resort of Kitzbühel. The best skiing area is on Mount Zao (there are seven peaks), SW of the town. The town's principal products are cast-iron articles (kettles, etc.), wooden dolls (*kokeshi*) and fruit.

SIGHTS. – In **Kajo Park** (10 minutes' walk N of the station) are the remains of a castle built by Shiba Kaneyori in the 14th c. and the **Prefectural Museum** (*Yamagata-ken-ritsu hakubutsukan*). – There is a bus service (15 minutes) to the **Senshoji Temple** of the Jodo sect, with the Tomb of Tokuhime, a concubine of Toyotomi Hidetsuku, who was condemned to death for high treason.

1¼ miles/2 km NE of the station is **Chitose Park**, in which are the *Yakushido Temple* (8th c.) and a large sports ground. – From the densely wooded *Chitose Hill*, 2½ miles/4 km E of the station, there is a fine *view of the town and the Yamagata Plain. At the foot of the hill stands the **Banshoji Temple**, which is believed to date from the 7th–8th c.

SURROUNDINGS of Yamagata

To the E of the town extends the **Zao Quasi National Park** (155 sq. miles/400 sq. km). The volcanic massif of Mount Zao (buses from Yamagata, 1 hour), the main skiing area in this region, consists of three peaks – Kumano (6040 ft/1841 m), Goshiki (5492 ft/1675 m) and Katta (5771 ft/1759 m). The snow-laden trees are known as the "snow monsters of Zao".

S of Yamagata (rail service) is **Kaminoyama**, from which a 16 mile/26 km-long toll road, the Zao Echo Line, passes through the Quasi National Park by way of Mount Katta to *Togatta-onsen*. From the Kattadake bus stop a cableway runs up Mount *Katta*. The summit of Mount *Kumano* can be reached in 40 minutes.

The principal resort in the Zao Massif is **Zao-onsen** (bus from Yamagata, 45 minutes), which has the additional attraction of its hot springs. There are a number of cableways and numerous ski-lifts in the area. – A cableway runs up Mount *Jizosan* (5693 ft/ 1735 m), leaving only a short climb to the summit. Between Jizosan and the neighboring peak of *Sanpokojinyama* (5588 ft/1703 m) lies the *Zao Shizen Shokobutsu-en*, a landscaped garden which is at its best from June to September. Adjoining the garden is a statue of Jizo, patron god of travelers, which was erected in 1775 for the protection of climbers.

From Zao-onsen it is a half-hour bus ride to the *Zao-bo Dair Kogen* plateau, and a 20-minute ride to *Senningawa Yuhodo*, on the River Senningawa. Near the Zao-sancho bus stop lies *Lake Okama*, a crater lake 130 ft/40 m deep.

Kaminoyama-onsen, one of the three most beautiful health resorts in the Tohoku district, lies S of Yamagata on the railway (20 minutes). Near the station is the Kaisendo Museum (arms and armor, lacquerware). Tsukioka Park, in which are the ruins of a castle, is famous for its cherry blossom.

The railway continues to the textile town of **Yonezawa** (pop. 93,000). From the station there are buses to Matsugasaki Park, once the site of a castle belonging to the powerful Uesugi family. In the park can be seen the Uesugi Shrine, dedicated to Uesugi Harunori (1756–1822), who established a silk factory in the town. The mausoleum of the Uesugi family can also be reached by bus (15 minutes).

N of Yamagata (rail, 25 minutes; bus, 40 minutes) is **Yamadera**, with the *Yamadera Temple* (also known as the Risshakuji Temple), the largest temple of the Tendai sect in northern Japan. The temple, probably founded about 860 by a priest named Ennin, lies within a large precinct on a hill, approached by a flight of 1000 steps. On the slopes of the hill are numerous caves, in one of which (near the Founder's Hall, the Kaizando) the founder is said to have died.

9 miles/14 km N of Yamagata is **Tendo** (pop. 52,000; JNR Ou line, 25 minutes), once a castle town held by the Tendo family, later the residence of Oda Nobunaga's descendants. In Maizuru Park are the ruins of the castle and the Kenkun Shrine, dedicated to Oda Nobunaga. Tendo is noted as the place of manufacture of the Japanese board-game *shogi*. Near the town is *Tendo-onsen*, which has a Museum of Folk Art (Tendo-mingeikan).

See also **Bandai-Asahi National Park**.

Yamaguchi

やまぐち

Prefecture: Yamaguchi. – Population: 120,000.
Post code: J-753. – Telephone code: 08392.

(central)
ⓘ **Yamaguchi-ken Tokyo Kanko Bussan Assensho,**
Kokusai Kanko Kaikan,
1-8-3, Marunouchi, Chiyoda-ku,
J-100 **Tokyo;**
tel. (03) 231 4980.

(local)
Yamaguchi-shi Kanko Information,
2-6, Sodayu-cho
(in Central Station);
tel. 4 6949.

HOTELS. – **Western style**: *Hotel Tokiwa*, 4-6-4, Yuda-onsen, 53 r., thermal bath; *Hotel Tanaka*, Yuda-onsen, 53 r.; *Matsudaya Hotel*, 3-6-7, Yuda-onsen, 40 r., thermal bath; *Business Hotel Shinyo*, 1-1-3, Yuda-onsen, 70 r.; *Business Hotel Sanai*, 1154-9, Sento-cho, 44 r., thermal bath. – **Ryokan**: *Kamefuku Ryokan*, 4-5-2, Yuda-onsen, 88 r., thermal bath; *Mizuno Ryokan*, 4-1-5, Yuda-onsen, 84 r., thermal bath; *Nobara Ryokan*, 3-7-8, Yuda-onsen, 40 r., Japanese garden, thermal bath. – YOUTH HOSTEL: *Yamaguchi YH*, 801 Miyanokami, 25 b.

TRANSPORTATION. – **Air**: from TOKYO (Haneda Airport) to the Ube (1½ hours). – **Rail**: from TOKYO (Central Station) JNR Sanyo–Shinkansen line to OGORI (6 hours), then JNR Yamaguchi line (30 minutes). – **Bus**: from Ube Airport to Ogori (30 minutes), then JNR Yamaguchi line.

Yamaguchi is the chief town of the most westerly prefecture on Honshu. From the 14th c. onwards, under the patronage of the Ouchi family, it developed into a major center of artistic activity, which received fresh stimulus during the Onin Wars (1467–77) through the influx of many artists from the toubled areas, including the painter Sesshu (1420–1506). Only a few old buildings remain to bear witness to the former splendor of this "Kyoto of the West".

SIGHTS. – On a hill 1 mile/1·5 km NW of the station lies **Kameyama Park**, which commands extensive views and which is particularly beautiful when the cherry trees and azaleas are in flower and when the trees take on their vivid autumn coloring. In the park are bronze statues of members of the Mori family, who played important parts in bringing about the Meiji Reform. Here, too, is the Neo-Romanesque *St Francis Xavier Memorial Church* (1950: St Francis Xavier worked as a missionary in Yamaguchi from 1551 onwards).

2½ miles/4 km N of the station is the **Joeiji Temple**, with a Zen garden designed by Sesshu. – The **Rurikoji Temple** has a fine five-storey pagoda of 1405.

1½ miles/2·5 km NE of the station is the **Daidoji Temple**, where St Francis Xavier preached the Gospel. It has a 20 ft/6 m-high granite cross and a bust of the Saint (1926).

SURROUNDINGS. – To the S of Yamaguchi (bus, 12 minutes) lies the well-known health resort of **Yuda-onsen** (hot springs, 86–158 °F/30–70 °C), in a beautiful setting. On the N side of the town is Kumano Park, seen at its best at cherry-blossom time and in the fall. The local festival takes place at the beginning of April.

12¼ miles/20 km N of Yamaguchi the River *Abu* flows through the **Chomonkyo Gorge**. Between Chomonkyo Station and *Uzugahara* is a romantically picturesque stretch of country, with waterfalls, caves and dense forest.

19 miles/30 km NW (bus, 1 hour) we come to the **Akiyoshi Plateau Quasi National Park**, in which is the extensive stalactitic cave of * *Akiyoshi-do. Of the cave system's total length of 6 miles/10 km a stretch 1100 yds/1 km long is open to the public. From the exit at *Kurotani* there is a road to the *Akiyoshi Plateau*, with a variety of karstic features. A bus can be taken back to the entrance to the cave.

Yokohama

よこはま

Prefecture: Kanagawa. – Population: 2,900,000.
Post code: J-220. – Telephone code: 045.

ⓘ (local)
Yokohama International Welcome Association,
Silk Center Office,
1 Yamashita-cho, Naka-ku;
tel. 641 5824 (English spoken).
Yokohama City Air Terminal Office,
2-3, Ono-machi, Kanagawa-ku;
tel. 459 4880.

HOTELS. – **Western style:** *New Grand Hotel,* 10, Yamashita-cho, Naka-ku, 197 r., SP; *Yokohama Tokyu Hotel,* 1-1-12, Minami-Saiwai-cho, Nishi-ku, 219 r.; *Hotel Sun Route Yokohama,* 2-9-1, Kita-Saiwai-cho, Nishi-ku, 150 r.; *Satellite Hotel Yokohama,* 76, Yamashita-cho, Naka-ku, 105 r.; *Silk Hotel,* 1, Yamashita-cho, Naka-ku, 81 r., Japanese garden; *Hotel Aster,* 87, Yamashita-cho, Naka-ku, 72 r.; *Bund Hotel,* 1-2-14, Shin-Yamashita, 60 r.; *Shin Yokohama Hotel,* 3-8-17, Shin-Yokohama, Kohoku-ku, 50 r.; *Yokohama Prince Hotel,* 3-13-1, Isogo, Isogo-ku, 37 r., Japanese garden, SP; *New Otani Inn Yokohama,* 4-81, Sueyoshi-cho, Naka-ku, 267 r. – YOUTH HOSTEL: *Kanagawa YH,* 1, Momijigaoka, Nishi-ku, 60 b.

RESTAURANTS. – *Italian Quarter,* Shin Sotetsu Building, 1-5, Minami-Saiwai-cho, Nishi-ku; *Kokonotsuido,* 1319, Tayamachi, Totsuka-ku; *Restaurant Kaori,* 6-111, Chojamachi, Nishi-ku; *Restaurant Rosen Cavalier,* Shin Sotetsu Building, 1-5, Minami-Saiwai-cho, Nishi-ku; *Steak House Belle Air,* 1100, Imai-cho, Hodogaya-ku; *Yokohama Seiyoken,* Shine Sotetsu Building, 1-5, Minami-Saiwai-cho, Nishi-ku.

In Yokohama harbor

EVENTS. – *First Shrine Visit* (beginning of January) at Iseyama and other shrines; *Port Festival* (beginning of May), with processions; *Iseyama Shrine Festival* (mid June); *Anniversary of Opening of Port* (June 2); *Firework Display* in Yamashita Park (mid July).

TRANSPORTATION. – **Rail:** from TOKYO (Central Station) JNR Yokosuka line (30 minutes); also from Yurakucho Station JNR Keihin–Tohoku line (40 minutes), from Shimbashi Station via Shinagawa Station JNR Yokosuka line (30 minutes) and from Shibuya Station Toyoko private line (40 minutes). – **Bus:** from Narita International Airport (1½ hours).

Yokohama, Japan's second largest city, lies in eastern central Honshu immediately S of Tokyo, with which it forms the Keihin industrial complex (Tokyo-Kawasaki-Yokohama). It is the chief town of Kanagawa prefecture, the country's largest commercial port and the principal gateway to Japan for visitors arriving by sea, as well as a major industrial center (shipbuilding, engineering, automobile construction, petrochemicals, etc.).

The city is divided into 14 wards (*ku*) Asahi, Hodogaya, Isogo, Kanagawa, Kanazawa, Kohoku, Ko-nan, Midori, Minami, Naka, Nishi, Seya, Totsuka and Tsurumi. The district of Yamashita-cho (also known as the Bund), bordering on the port area, is the business quarter. Yamate-machi (the Bluff), to the S of this, is the residential area favored by foreigners. Good shopping areas are Isezaki-cho, Yoshida-machi and Noge-machi (all in Naka ward). Isezaki-cho is also an entertainment quarter.

HISTORY. – Yohohama is a very young city. After Commodore Perry arrived in Tokyo Bay with his "black ships" and signed the Treaty of Kanagawa (1854) which opened Japan up to Western trade the little fishing village rapidly developed into a busy port and commercial town. In 1859 the first foreigners settled in Yokohama, including Townsend Harris, the first American diplomatic respresentative in Japan. By 1889 the population of the town had risen to over 120,000.

SIGHTS. – SE of the Central Station, near the city center, is Sakuragicho Station, from which the principal sights can be reached. – To the W of the station, in the northern part of Naka ward, is the **Iseyama Shrine** (1870), dedicated to the patron god of the city, which is one of the Great Shrines of Ise. It has a cypress-wood *torii* 33 ft/10 m high. A little way N of the shrine lies the **Kamon-yama Park**, which is famous for its show of cherry blossom (mid April). In the park is a statue of the politician Ii Naosuke (1815–60), who played a major part in the opening up of Japan. – SW of the Iseyama Shrine, on the slopes of a hill commanding extensive views, is **Nogeyama Park**, in which are a Zoo and a swimming pool. To the SE of the park the busy shopping street, *Isezaki-cho*, leads back into the center of Naka ward.

SE of Sakuragicho Station (5 minutes' walk) stands the **Prefectural Museum**, housed in an imposing late 19th c. building (history, natural history). Farther SE a brick building with a tower (1917), now a *Memorial Hall* commemorates the opening of the port. By the hall is a monument to Okakura Tenshin, Yokohama's best-known sculptor. – In **Yokohama Park**, adjoining the *Civic Hall*, is a large Stadium.

NE of Yokohama Park is the **Port** (boat trips round the harbor several times daily). At the end of *Osanbashi Pier* the nine-storey **Silk Center** houses the Yokohama International Welcome Association, the Post Office, various airline offices, the Silk Hotel and the *Silk Museum*. Along the harbor front to the SE extends **Yama-shita Park** (view of harbor). Moored in the harbor is the old trans-oceanic liner "Hikawa Maru", now a museum (aquaria of tropical fish). To the SW rises the *Marine Tower*, 348 ft/106 m high, erected on the 100th anniversary of the opening of the port; it affords an extensive ∗view of the city (particularly impressive at night). – 550 yds/500 m W lies

Yokohama's Chinatown

Yokohama's **Chinatown** (*Chukagai*), with many restaurants, shops and places of entertainment.

To the S, beyond the River Nakamura, is the busy shopping street *Motomachi*, which marks the beginning of the foreigners' quarter of Yokohama, YAMATE-MACHI (the *Bluff*). Near the end of Motomachi can be found the *Foreigners' Cemetery*, and to the E of this is the **Minato-no-mieru-oka Park**, from which there is a fine view of the harbor.

On the south-eastern outskirts of the city the beautiful ∗**Sankei-en Garden** (bus from station, then 10 minutes' walk) contains a number of historic old buildings brought here from other parts of the country. Among them are a 500-year-old three-storey *pagoda* from the Tomyoji Temple at Kamo (Kyoto); the *Rinshun-kaku* (1649), a villa from the Kii Peninsula which belonged to a branch of the Tokugawa clan; the *Choshu-kaku*, a tea-pavilion built by Tokugawa Iemitsu; the *Yanohara-ke*, an 18th c. farmhouse; and the *Tenzuiji Juto Sayado Temple* (1592), from Daitoku-ji (Kyoto). At the S end of the park is the *Hasseiden* (1933), a hall containing statues of the Eight Sages (Shakyamuni, Confucius, Socrates, Christ, Shotoku-taishi, Kobo-daishi, Shinran and Nichiren).

From the Central Station the Keihin-Kyuko private line and the subway (underground) run SW to the **Gumyo-ji**

Temple of the Shingon sect, the oldest in the city. It contains a 9th c. wooden *statue of the Eleven-Headed Kannon. – To the E of the temple (20 minutes' walk from Makita subway (underground) station) the **Santondai Archaeological Museum** houses material recovered by excavation in the Yokohama area.

A short distance NE of the Central Station, in KANAGAWA ward, is the **Hongakuji Temple** of the Soto sect, which in 1856 became the temporary residence of the United States Consul-General. The Japanese-American Commercial Treaty was signed here in 1858. – NE of the Central Station (JNR Tohoku line to Tsurumi Station) stands the *Sojiji Temple* of the Soto sect, originally built in 1321 in what is now Ishikawa prefecture and re-erected on its present site after a fire in 1898. It is one of the principal Zen temples in Japan, the mother house of some 15,000 dependent temples. Within the temple precincts are a number of educational establishments.

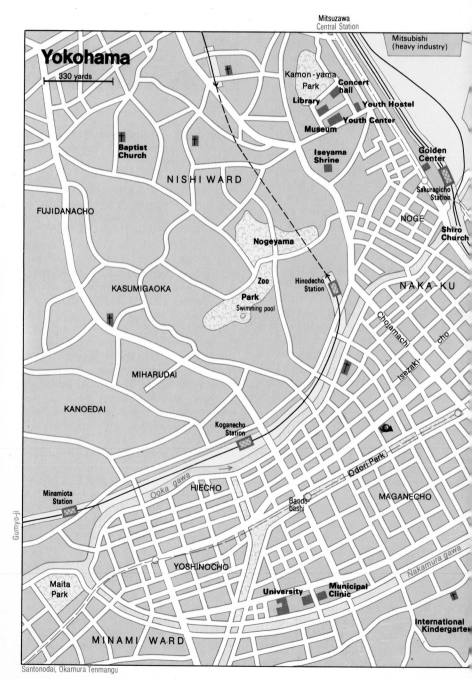

SURROUNDINGS. – At **Matanocho**, SW of Yokohama, can be found **Yokohama Dreamland**, a Disneyland-type amusement park (area 163 acres) opened in 1963, with a variety of entertainments, an open-air theater, an ice-rink and a hotel (JNR Odakyu line to Ofuna, Fujisawa, Totsuka or Chogo, then bus).

From the Central Station the Keihin-Kyuko private line runs S, passing the Gumyo-ji Temple (see above), to **Kanazawa-Bunko** (11 miles/18 km), to the E of which is the **Shomyoji Temple** of the Shingon-Ritsu sect, founded by Hojo Sanetoki in 1260. In the Main Hall is a wooden *statue, 6 ft 3 in./1·9 m high, of a Miroku-bosatsu (1276); the bell-tower contains a bronze bell of 1301. The nearby *Kanazawa-bunko Library*, established by Sanetoki in 1275 contains

various objects from the temple precinct and a large collection of old manuscripts and documents (many of which disappeared after the collapse of the Kamakura Shogunate).

Yoron-to
See under Satsunan Islands

Silk Exchange

ectural useum

Shimin Hall

ANNAI

Center Building

YMCA   Yokohama

Civic Hall   Park

nnai
tion   Stadium

High School

MATSUKAGECHO

hojamachi

Shinko Pier

Osanbashi Pier

Harbor

Silk Center

Municipal Offices

Conference Center
Industry and Commerce Center

Prefecture

Bank of Japan

Kanagawa Center of Culture

Hikawa Maru

Yamashita Pier

Yamashita Park

Marine Tower

Hepburn House

YWCA

Chinatown
YAMASHITACHO

Motomachi

Ishikawacho Station

Minato-no-mieru-oka

Foreigners' Cemetery

Motomachi

British Hall

Park

International School

CLIFF SIDE   Swimming pool

Language Center

R.C. Church

YAMATE-MACHI

Yamate Park

KASHIWABA

NAKA WARD

Negishida

Yoshino-Kumano National Park

よしのくまの 国立公園

Prefectures: Nara, Mie and Wakayama.
Area: 214 sq. miles/554 sq. km.

(i) (central)
National Parks Association of Japan,
Toranomon Denki Building,
8-1, Toranomon 2-chome, Minato-ku,
J-105 **Tokyo;**
tel. (03) 502 0488.

HOTELS. – **Western style:** *Yoshino Hotel Honnkan,* 2340, Yoshinoyama, Yoshino-cho, 40 r., thermal bath. – **Ryokan:** *Shin-Yoshino-onsen Tatsumi-ya,* 403, Yoshinoyama, Yoshino-cho, 33 r., thermal bath; *Chikurin-in gunpo-en,* 212, Yoshinoyama, Yoshino-cho, 25 r.; *Takarano-ya,* Yoshinoyama, Yoshino-cho, 13 r., thermal bath. – YOUTH HOSTEL: *YH Yoshinoyama Kizo-in* (temple), 1254, Yoshinoyama, Yoshino-cho, 60 b.

TRANSPORTATION. – **Rail:** from OSAKA (Abeno-bashi Station) Kinki–Nippon private line to Yoshino (1¼ hours); from WAKAYAMA (Wakayamashi Station) JNR Wakayama line to Yoshinoguchi (1¾ hours), then Kintetsu–Yoshino private line to Yoshino.

The *Yoshino-Kumano National Park,* **situated on the Kii Peninsula, which reaches out into the Pacific from western central Honshu, takes in the mountains of the Yoshino region and the deep gorges of the Kumano region. Many of the temples and shrines once visited by swarms of pilgrims can still be seen. During the Nara period this territory, then remote and inaccessible, was the haunt of the mountain ascetics of the Shugendo sect.**

The isolated north-western section of the National Park consists of the **Yoshino Mountains,** which rise above the little town of Yoshino. The mountains are widely famed for their cherry trees – some 100,000 in all, in four large groves, which are in blossom at varying times, depending on altitude, between the beginning and the end of April. Nearest the upper station of the cableway is the *Shimo-no-Sembon* ("Lower Thousand Trees"), which is followed by *Naka-no-Sembon* ("Middle Thousand Trees"), *Kami-no-Sembon* ("Upper Thousand Trees") and *Oku-no-Sembon* ("Inner Thousand Trees"). The Cherry Blossom Festival (Hanao-eshiki) is celebrated in mid April. The tradition has it that the trees were originally planted by a priest named Enno-Ozunu in the 7th c. and dedicated to the mountain divinity Zao-Gongen.

Near *Yoshino* is the **Yoshino Shrine,** dedicated to the Emperor Godaigo, with the tomb of Murakami Yoshiteru (d. 1333), a vassal of Prince Morinaga who was killed while defending the Prince. – From the lowest cherry grove a road runs up to the *Kimpusenji Temple,* the original buildings of which were destroyed by fire in 1348 and replaced in the 15th c. The Main Hall (Zaodo), 112 ft/34 m high, is one of the tallest timber buildings in Japan. The two guardian figures at the entrance are attributed to Unkei and Tankei (12th–13th c.). To the right of the hall there once stood the palace of the Southern Dynasty (14th c.). – From here the road runs S to the nearby **Yoshimizu Shrine** and the **Katte Shrine.**

Higher up, to the left of the road, stands the **Nyoirinji Temple.** At the entrance are inscribed a poem by Kusunoki Masatsura (1326–48) and the names of 143 of his men who were killed in a battle with Ashikaga forces. Beyond the temple is the tomb of the Emperor Godaigo. – Farther S the *Chikurin-in Temple* has a garden designed by the tea-master Sen-no-Rikyu (1522–91). The *Tenno-bashi* Bridge leads to the *Saruhikizaka* viewpoint (*view of the eastern slopes of Mount Yoshino and the upper cherry grove). Beyond this a road branches off to the *Yoshino-Mikumari Shrine,* founded in the early 17th c. by Toyotomi Hideyori.

The road continues past the *Kimpu Shrine* to the grove of the "Inner Thousand Trees", in which is the **Kokeshimizu Shrine,** once the hermitage of the 12th c. priest Saigyo (1118–90).

Another, much larger, part of the National Park takes in the Omine Hills to the SE of Yoshino, with Mounts Sanjo, Misen, Odaigahara and Shaka, and the Toro Gorge.

The best base from which to climb Mount Sanjo (3½ hours) is **Dokawa** (Kinki–Nippon private railway line to Shimoichiguchi, then bus, 2 hours).

On the summit of Mount **Sanjo** (5643 ft/1720 m) are a number of temples, in particular two dedicated to the divinity Zao-Gongen and En-no-Ozunu, the first ascetic to take up his quarters on the mountain. The temples attract large numbers of pilgrims, for whom accommodation is provided from the beginning of May to the end of September. From the summit there are fine * views of the Kii Peninsula, reaching on clear days as far as Mount Fuji. The descent can be by an alternative route leading to Yoshino (8 hours).

Farther SE, on the borders of Nara and Mie prefectures, is Mount **Odaigahara** (5561 ft/1695 m). A toll road 10 miles/ 16 km long leads up to the summit (bus from Yamato-Kamiichi over the Obamine Pass, 3 hours). The area around the source of the River Miya, on the E side of the mountain, is one of the finest gorges in Japan. In the **Osugidani Gorge**, between *Dainichigura* and *Dokura-no-taki*, are several waterfalls, the best known of which is the *Senbiro-no-taki*. On the summit of Mount Odaigahara, a plateau 2 miles/3 km by 1¼ miles/2 km in extent, covered with forest and grassland, are a temple, a weather station and a number of mountain huts. The River *Kitayama*, which rises in the summit area, flows S through the Toro Gorge.

The Kumano area, in the southern part of the National Park, can best be reached from Shingu or Katsuura on the JNR Kisei line.

At **Shingu** the River *Kumano* flows into the Pacific. The town has an active woodworking industry. The Kumano-Hatayama Shrine is one of the principal Shinto shrines in the region (festival mid October). From here there is an attractive run along the Shichirimihama coast to Kumano. – NW of Shingu lies a very beautiful stretch of country, with gorges, rapids and luxuriant vegetation. Boats sail up the Kumano as far as this area.

In the upper part of its course the *Kitayama*, which joins the *Totsu* at *Miyai*

to form the River Kumano, flows through the romantic * **Toro Gorge**. The lower part of the gorge is called *Toro-Hatcho* ("water 8 *cho* deep") and has many stretches of rapids; and above this are *Kami-Toro* ("Upper Toro") and *Oku-Toro* ("Inner Toro").

From *Miyai* it is worth making a detour to **Hongu** (bus, 30 minutes) to see the Kumano-Hongu Shrine, one of the three great Kumano shrines (festival mid April). From Hongu there is a bus service to the pretty health resort of **Yunomine-onsen**, 2½ miles/4 km SW.

Near *Kii-Katsuura* is **Nachi**, with the 425 ft/130 m-high * *Nachi Falls* (bus from village, 20 minutes). At the top of the steps leading down to the falls is the 7th c. **Seigantoji Temple** of the Tendai sect, dedicated to Nyoirin Kannon – the starting-point of the pilgrimage to the 33 temples dedicated to Kannon in the western provinces. Near by is the * **Kumano-Nachi Shrine** (4th c.), another of the three great Kumano shrines (festival mid July).

The JNR Kisei line now continues along the coast. S of Katsuura, outside the National Park, is the whaling port of **Taiji** (Whaling Museum in Kujirihama Park; bus from station). A short distance N we come to the health resort of **Yukawa-onsen** (hot spring, 86–108 °F/30–42 °C), in a deep and peaceful inlet.

At the tip of the peninsula is the small fishing port of **Kushimoto**. To the S is *Cape Shionomisaki* (lighthouse), off the E coast of which is the island of *Oshima* (ferry from Kushimoto, 10 minutes). Here, too, are the *Hashikui-Iwa Islands*, a group of some 30 rocky islets covered with trees.

Practical Information

Decorated float in the Gionmatsuri festival, Kyoto

When to Go

The best times to visit Japan are the spring (end of March to mid May) and the fall (autumn) (mid October to beginning of December). The great length of the country from north to south means that it can still be quite cold in northern Japan in March, at a time when the cherry trees are already coming into blossom in the south. The *cherry blossom* and the *autumn coloring* (see map, pp. 310–11) of Japan are among the country's particular attractions, and many places are renowned for the beauty of the display they offer at these seasons.

In the plains summers are hot and sometimes wet; at this time of year the seaside resorts and the upland regions have a more agreeable climate. The level of rainfall in the rainy season (*tsuyu, bai-u*; June–July) is lower in the northeast than in the south. The typhoon season begins in September, in the south as early as July. – During the winter central and northern Japan are under deep snow; in some areas the winter-sports season continues into May. The west coast of Honshu is particularly cold, with an abundance of snow, while temperatures on the east coast and in lowland areas seldom fall below freezing-point. – The Okinawa islands, lying far to the south-west of the main Japanese islands, occupy a special position, with a mean annual temperature of 73 °F/23 °C.

Autumn colors

Since the Japanese themselves are great travelers and there are large numbers of foreign visitors during the main vacation season it is advisable to book accommodation well in advance – several months in advance for the period from December 21 to January 5 and the winter-sports season. The peak holiday periods for the Japanese themselves are the "golden week" in May and the "silver week" in November, the Bon Festival (July 13–15) and the summer vacation (mid July to end of August).

Weather

Japan, lying off the Asian mainland, extends for 1735 miles/2790 km from north to south; moreover it is broken up by mountain ranges, and is exposed by its long coastline to maritime influences. All these factors combine to produce wide climatic variations – though the major part of the country falls within the temperate zone.

In winter cold air masses coming from the Polar regions advance on Japan from Siberia, bringing abundant falls of snow in the north-west, while in the south-west there is heavy rain. Beyond the central upland regions and along the Pacific coast there are day temperatures in winter of up to 50 °F/10 °C and there is little snow.

Cherry blossom

In southern Japan spring comes in February, with very changeable weather during the transitional period from winter to spring. – Summer brings high temperatures and – as a result of the meeting of polar and tropical air masses – an abundant rainfall. – In autumn, after the typhoon season, the humidity of air is low and the temperature still pleasantly warm.

For a more detailed account of climatic conditions in Japan, see pp. 14–18.

Place (from north to south)	AT = air temperature in °F (°C) PR = precipitation in inches (mm) HA = humidity of air in % RD = number of days with rain			**The Weather in Japan at a Glance**												
	Spring (April)				**Summer (July)**				**Fall (October)**				**Winter (January)**			
	AT	PR	HA	RD	AT	PR	HA	RD	AT	PR	HA	RD	AT	PR	HA	RD
Sapporo	43·0 (6·1)	4·6 (118)	68	9	68·4 (20·2)	2·5 (64)	80	9	50·7 (10·4)	3·5 (90)	74	13	22·8 (−5·1)	4·1 (104)	75	16
Sendai	49·3 (9·6)	1·7 (42)	67	8	71·8 (22·1)	3·3 (85)	86	13	57·2 (14·0)	6·7 (170)	77	9	33·1 (0·6)	5·2 (132)	71	6
Tokyo	56·3 (13·5)	1·9 (49)	66	10	77·4 (25·2)	4·8 (122)	79	10	62·4 (16·9)	5·5 (140)	74	11	39·4 (4·1)	8·0 (203)	57	5
Kyoto	55·6 (13·1)	2·2 (56)	67	7	79·0 (26·1)	5·7 (145)	76	8	62·1 (16·7)	9·4 (239)	74	5	38·3 (3·5)	4·8 (122)	72	5
Hiroshima	55·4 (13·0)	2·0 (51)	71	10	77·9 (25·5)	6·1 (156)	82	8	62·2 (16·8)	10·9 (276)	75	6	39·4 (4·1)	4·4 (111)	71	7
Fukuoka	57·0 (13·9)	3·0 (77)	74	10	79·7 (26·5)	5·3 (134)	80	11	63·1 (17·3)	9·9 (252)	76	7	41·5 (5·3)	3·9 (100)	69	12
Okinawa	69·4 (20·8)	4·8 (122)	79	10	82·8 (28·2)	5·6 (142)	82	9	75·4 (24·1)	6·9 (174)	74	9	60·8 (16·0)	5·9 (149)	70	13

Dress, Baggage

Dress should be adapted to the time of year: the seasons in Japan are broadly comparable to European or North American seasons. During the rainy period and the typhoon season protection against rain is, of course, essential. – Visitors traveling on their own will be well advised to keep their baggage to a minimum and to take cases of manageable size. Since the baggage racks in trains and buses are designed to take the relatively small cases used by the Japanese, large items of baggage may give rise to problems.

Time

Japanese Standard Time is 14 hours ahead of Eastern Standard Time (New York) and 9 hours ahead of Greenwich Mean Time (8 hours ahead of British Summer Time). There is no Summer Time in Japan.

Electricity

Electric current in Japan is mostly 100 volts A.C. Hotels are likely to have outlets for 220 volts as well. – Since Japanese sockets are different from European ones, an adaptor will be required for electric razors, etc.

Visiting Cards

Visiting cards play an important part in Japanese life and are exchanged on every conceivable occasion. Visitors should have their names transcribed into the Japanese syllabic script (Katakana): the printing of such cards is a facility provided by Japan Air Lines (JAL) for their passengers.

Travel Documents

Visitors from the United Kingdom require only a valid **passport** (no visa) to enter

● **Cherry Blossom**
● **Fall Coloring**

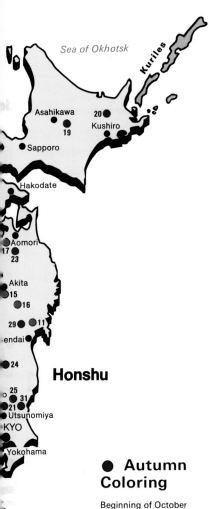

Sea of Okhotsk

Kuriles

Asahikawa   20
        19 Kushiro

Sapporo

Hakodate

Aomori
17
23

Akita
15
16

29   11
endai

24

Honshu

25
31
21
Utsunomiya
KYO

Yokohama

en Izu Islands

O c e a n

● Cherry Blossom

End of March

1 Omura
Nagasaki prefecture
Omura Park

2 Fukuoka
Fukuoka prefecture
Nishi Park

3 Kochi
Kochi prefecture
Castle

4 Imabari
Ehime prefecture
Hashihama Park

5 Kimiidera
Wakayama prefecture
Kimiidera Temple

6 Nakatsugawa
Aichi prefecture

Beginning of April

7 Iwakuni
Hiroshima prefecture
Kintai Bridge

8 Onomichi
Hiroshima prefecture
Senkoji Park

9 Kyoto
Kyoto prefecture

10 Maruoka
Fukui prefecture
Castle

11 Gembikei
Iwate prefecture

12 Nara
Nara prefecture

13 Iida
Nagano prefecture

14 Kambayashi
Nagano prefecture

15 Akita
Akita prefecture
Senshu Park

16 Kakunodate
Akita prefecture

17 Hirosaki
Aomori prefecture
Castle

Beginning of May

18 Takada
Niigata prefecture
Takada Park

● Autumn Coloring

Beginning of October

19 Sounkyo Gorge
Hokkaido prefecture

20 Lake Akan
Hokkaido prefecture

21 Oku-Nikko
Tochigi prefecture

22 Kamikochi
Nagano prefecture

Mid October

23 Lake Towada
Aomori prefecture

24 Bandai-kogen
Fukushima prefecture

25 Shiobara-keikoku
Tochigi prefecture

26 Usui Pass
Gumma prefecture

27 Kurobe-keikoku
Toyama prefecture

28 Tachikue-kyo
Shimane prefecture

End of October

29 Narugo-kyo
Miyagi prefecture

30 Mount Myogi
Gumma prefecture

31 Fukuroda Falls
Ibaraki prefecture

32 Shosen-kyo
Yamanashi prefecture

33 Kyoto
Kyoto prefecture

34 Nara
Nara prefecture

35 Komatsu
Ishikawa prefecture

36 Nakayama-Shichiri
Gifu prefecture

37 Sumata-kyo
Shizuoka prefecture

38 Akame-Shijuhachi Falls
Mie prefecture

39 Mount Daisen
Tottori prefecture

40 Nagato-kyo
Yamaguchi prefecture

41 Omogo-kei
Ehime prefecture

42 Takachiho-kyo
Miyazaki prefecture

Beginning of November

43 Tonomine
Nara prefecture

44 Kanka-kei
Kagawa prefecture

45 Yaba-kei
Oita prefecture

Mid November

46 Mino-o
Osaka prefecture

47 Butsuji
Hiroshima prefecture

48 Miyajima
Hiroshima prefecture

Japan for a stay of up to 180 days provided that they do not engage in any remunerative activity in Japan. Canadian visitors require no visa for a stay of up to 90 days. Australian and United States citizens require a visa but are exempted from payment of the visa fee.

Visitors who intend to stay for more than 90 days in Japan are required to apply to the local authority of their place of residence for registration as an alien.

To drive a car in Japan an **international driving license** is required. It is advisable for visitors to take their national driving license as well.

Medical insurance should be taken out before leaving home to cover the cost of any treatment required while in Japan.

Inoculations, etc.

Smallpox and cholera inoculations are not required except for visitors from infected areas.

It is recommended that visitors should have typhoid and polio vaccination.

If you are traveling via South-East Asia, with stopovers en route, you should check the inoculation, etc., requirements for the countries concerned.

Customs Regulations

Personal effects and holiday gear can be taken into Japan without payment of duty. A written declaration of personal effects is only required for visitors arriving by ship, for unaccompanied baggage or for those bringing in articles in excess of the duty-free allowances.

The duty-free allowances are: 500 grams of tobacco or 400 cigarettes or 100 cigars; three bottles (76 decilitres) of alcoholic liquor; two watches valued at no more than 30,000 yen; and other goods to a total market value of not more than 100,000 yen.

Currency

The Japanese unit of currency is the **yen** (¥). There are banknotes for 500, 1000,

5000 and 10,000 yen and coins in denominations of 1, 5, 10, 50, 100 and 500 yen.

Exchange Rates
(subject to fluctuation)

100 yen=US $0·36	US $1=275 yen
100 yen=£0·25	£1=400 yen

There are no restrictions on the amount of either Japanese or foreign currency that may be taken into Japan; it is advisable, however, to declare the amount of foreign currency taken in. – On leaving Japan visitors can take out up to 5 million yen and foreign currency up to the amount declared on entry.

Foreign currency can be changed into yen at any bank or official exchange office on production of the visitor's passport. A receipt will be given by the bank or exchange office. Any unused yen can be changed back to a total of 3 million yen; higher amounts can be changed back only on production of the exchange receipt or receipts.

It is advisable to take money in the form of travelers' checks. In the larger towns shops and hotels usually accept the major credit cards (American Express, Americard, Visa, Diners Club, Master Charge, Carte Blanche, etc.).

Eurocheques cannot be cashed in Japan.

Postal and Telephone Services

Head post offices and telephone and telegraph counters are open daily from 8 a.m. to 8 p.m. Other post offices are closed on Saturday afternoons. In small towns post offices are open from 9 a.m. to 5 p.m.

All post offices and postal services can be identified by this symbol.

Telegrams can be written in the Latin alphabet and handed in at telegraph counters in post offices and railway stations. – Telegrams to foreign countries are accepted at telegraph counters in post offices, telephone offices and the offices of Kokusai Denshin Denwa (KDD) in Tokyo, Kyoto and Osaka. The rate per word is 118 yen to the United States, 192 yen to the United Kingdom, and 108 yen to Canada. KDD also put through telephone calls to foreign countries: in Tokyo and Yokohama dial 0051, in the Kanto area (03) 211 5511 (for Europe and North America), in the Kansai area (06) 945 11 22. Hotel operators will also place calls. A 3-minute call to the United States or Canada costs 2430 yen, to the United Kingdom costs 2700 yen.

Postal rates. – Letters within Japan cost 60 yen (up to 25 grams), to North America 150 yen air mail or 110 yen surface mail, to Europe 170 yen air mail (up to 10 grams) or 110 yen surface mail (up to 20 grams). Postcards cost 40 yen within Japan, 100 yen air mail or 80 yen surface mail to North America, 110 yen air mail or 80 yen surface mail to Europe.

Telephoning. – Most towns in Japan have an automatic dialing system. There are three kinds of public telephones, identified by different colors.

Red telephones: local and inter-city calls; accept up to six 10-yen coins.

Blue telephones: local and inter-city calls; accept up to ten 10-yen coins.

Yellow telephones: mainly inter-city; accept up to ten 10-yen coins and up to nine 100-yen coins.

Unused 10-yen coins will be returned on termination of the call.

Getting to Japan

Practically all visitors to Japan from Europe and North America now travel by air. The most direct route is via Anchorage (Alaska), flying from London over the North Pole, but a variety of alternative routes are possible, with stopovers on the way if desired. From Europe it is possible to fly via Paris and Moscow or on the South-East Asian route via Rome and the Middle East; from North America there are alternative routes by way of either the North or the South Pacific. – There are no regular passenger services by sea to Japan from Europe or North America, though there are some passenger-carrying freighter services from North America.

Japan Travel-Phone is a new telephone information service in English (started in 1982) designed to help foreign visitors to Japan. This service puts callers in touch with English-speaking members of the staff of the Tourist Information Center who can provide information, advice or the services of an interpreter.

The Travel-Phone service operates throughout Japan except in central Tokyo or Kyoto, and can be called either from a private telephone or from a blue or yellow public telephone. To make a call:
  – if calling from a public telephone, put in a 10-yen coin;
  – dial 106;
  – when the operator replies, ask, in English, for "collect call, T.I.C., please".
The operator will then transfer the call to an appropriate member of the staff. On completion of the call the 10-yen coin will be returned.

In Tokyo the Tourist Information Center can be contacted by dialing 502 1461, in Kyoto by dialing 371 5649. Calls in these areas are charged for (10 yen).

Travel in Japan

By Road

Japan has a well-developed road system, with some 1370 miles/2200 km of motorways (on which tolls are charged) and 25,000 miles/40,000 km of national highways. In the larger towns and their immediate surroundings signposting is in Japanese and English; but in the country areas foreign drivers are likely to have some difficulty in finding their way since signposts are almost exclusively in Japanese.

In Japan traffic travels on the left, as in Britain. Road signs are generally in line with international standards.

Visitors intending to travel by car should apply to the Japan Automobile Federation (see below under Information) for

══ Motorways
── Trunk roads

Hokkaido

Sea of Japan

Sado

Niig

Kanazawa Toyama

Oki

Gifu

Matsue Tottori

Kyoto Nagoya

Himeji Kobe

Nara

Hiroshima Okayama

Ise Hamam

Tsushima

Shimonoseki

Osaka

Kitakyushu

Sea Takamatsu

Wakayama

Fukuoka Inland

Matsuyama

Goto Islands

Kumamoto

Naga-
saki

Shikoku

Kyushu

Kagoshima

Tanegashima

*East China
Sea*

Yakushima

Ryu-kyu Islands

Naha Okinawa

Pacific

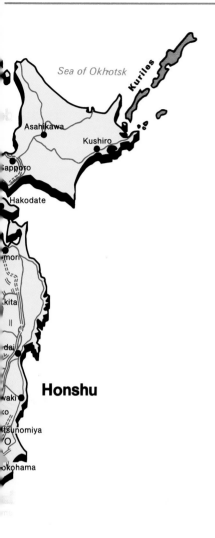

Sea of Okhotsk

Kuriles

Asahikawa

Kushiro

apporo

Hakodate

mor

kita

dai

Honshu

waki

ko

tsunomiya

O

okohama

Izu Islands

Ocean

details of traffic regulations. Given the language difficulties, however, most visitors will probably prefer to rely on public transport or to take organized tours.

By Air

The principal Japanese airports are Tokyo-Haneda (domestic services) and the new international airport of Tokyo-Narita, some 40 miles/60 km NE of the city center. There are direct flights from London and other European airports as well as from North American airports.

The national airline, **Japan Air Lines** (*JAL*), flies a number of domestic services as well as an extensive network of international services. Other domestic services are flown by *All Nippon Airways* (ANA), *Toa Domestic Airlines* (TDA) and *Nihon Kinkyori Air Lines* (NKA). There are also a number of smaller companies mainly providing local services – *South West Airlines* (SWAL: Okinawa Islands), *New Central Airlines* (NCA: Niigata), *Nippon Naigi Airlines* (NNA: Kagoshima) and *Nagasaki Airways* (NAW: Nagasaki). – Map of Japanese airports: pp. 320–1.

By Rail

Thanks to their punctuality, speed, cleanliness and comfort the Japanese railways are the most used form of public transport for travel within Japan. The State system, **Japanese National Railways** (*JNR*), has a network of 13,000 miles/21,000 km extending into the remotest parts of the country. Particularly notable are the *Shinkansen* high-speed trunk lines, which until 1981 could boast the fastest train in the world. The Shinkansen "bullet train" from Tokyo to Fukuoka (Hakata), the speed of which is now exceeded only by the French TGV, covers the 731 miles/1177 km between the two cities in just under 7 hours, at an average speed of 112 m.p.h./180 km p.h., with a maximum speed of 130 m.p.h./210 km p.h. A journey on the Shinkansen from Tokyo to Kyoto, passing Mount Fuji, is one of the high spots of a visit to Japan. New Shinkansen lines from Tokyo (feeder service from Ueno Station to Omiya) to Morioka and from Tokyo to Niigata came into service in 1982. – Between Tokyo and

Rail Services

——— **Main lines**
——— **Shinkansen**

Hokkaido

Sea of Japan

Sado

Nii

Kanazawa
Toya
Na

Oki

Gifu

Yonago
Himeji
Kobe
Kyoto
Nagoya
Okayama
Nara

Masuda
Hiroshima

Tsushima
Toba

Shimonoseki
Osaka

Kitakyushu
Sea Takamatsu
Wakayama

Hakata
(Fukuoka)
Matsuyama

Beppu
In-
land
Uwajima

Goto Islands
Kumamoto

Naga-
saki
Nakamura

Kyushu
Shikoku

Kagoshima

Tanegashima

*East China
Sea*

Yakushima

Ryu-
kyu
Islands

Naha
Okinawa

Pacific

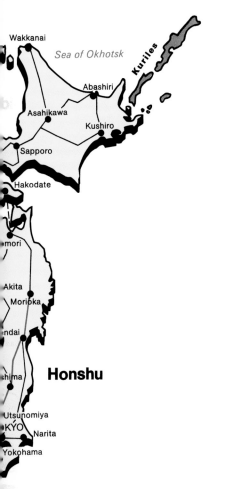

Wakkanai
Sea of Okhotsk
Kuriles
Abashiri
Asahikawa
Kushiro
Sapporo
Hakodate

mori

Akita
Morioka
ndai

hima   **Honshu**

Utsunomiya
KYŌ   Narita
Yokohama

n Izu Islands

Ocean

The Shinkansen super-express

Fukuoka there are also the Hikari and Kodama trains, which provide a service at 20–30-minute intervals. The Hikari stops only at Nagoya, Kyoto, Shin-Osaka, Okayama, Hiroshima and Kokura, while the Kodama has 27 intermediate stops and takes correspondingly longer for the journey between Tokyo and Fukuoka. – In addition to these fast trains there are also ordinary express trains (*tokkyu*), fast stopping trains (*kyuko*) and local trains (*futsu*).

Advance reservation is advisable, particularly on the Shinkansen trains. Seat reservation tickets, sleeper tickets and the supplementary tickets required for "green cars" (the former first class) can be obtained at the green-striped ticket windows in railway stations and offices of the Japan Travel Bureau (JTB).

Japan Rail Pass

Foreign visitors to Japan can obtain a **Japan Rail Pass** allowing unlimited travel on all JNR lines, buses and ferries for a period of 7, 14 or 21 days. There are two kinds of Rail Pass, green and ordinary, green being the equivalent of first class. Prices for a green pass are 30,000 yen for 7 days, 48,000 yen for 14 days and 64,000 yen for 21 days, and for an ordinary pass 21,000 yen, 33,000 yen and 44,000 yen. Children from age 6 up to and including age 11 pay half price.

A Japan Rail Pass can be purchased only through a JAL office or authorized travel agency outside Japan, which will issue a voucher exchangeable for a Rail Pass on arrival in Japan (at the JNR Information and Ticket Office, Tokyo-Narita International Airport, or JNR Travel Service Centers in Tokyo, Yokohama, Nagoya, Kyoto, Osaka, Hiroshima, Sendai, Niigata, Fukuoka/Hakata, Kumamoto, Nishi-Kagoshima and Sapporo).

A feature of Japanese stations is the marking of compartment numbers and doors on the platform. The trains stop exactly by these marks.

There are also a number of private railway companies serving the area around the larger towns. The fares are often significantly lower than on the JNR. During the main travel season advance booking is advisable.

Bicycle rental at railway stations. – At many JNR stations bicycles can be rented at very reasonable charges. This is a convenient way of seeing towns in which the distances between the various sights are relatively short – though it may sometimes be difficult for visitors who know no Japanese to find their way around. – Bicycles can be rented at the following stations:

Abashiri and Lake Saroma
Hokkaido prefecture
Hamasaroma Station, Yumo line
May 1 to October 31, 8.30 a.m. to 5 p.m.
Sights: Lake Saroma, Cape Kimuaneppu, Ryugu-Kaido Wild Flower Garden.

Lake Towada and Oirase Valley
Aomori prefecture
Bus stop for Nenokuchi and Towadako-onsen
April 15 to November 10, 8.30 a.m. to 5 p.m.
Sights: Lake Towada, Oirase Valley, Choshi Falls.

Oga Peninsula
Akita prefecture
Hadachi Station, Oga line
April 28 to October 31, 8.30 a.m. to 5 p.m.
Sights: Mount Kampu, Hachirogata Lagoon, bizarre rock formations on beaches.

Lake Tazawa
Akita prefecture
Tazawako Station, Tazawako line
April 28 to October 31, 8 a.m. to 5.30 p.m.
Sights: Lake Tazawa, Tazawako Hills, Nyuto health resort, Gozanoishi Shrine.

Chusonji Temple
Iwate prefecture
Hiraizumi Station, Tohoku line
March 25 to November 10, 8 a.m. to 5.30 p.m.
Sights: Chusonji Temple, Konjikido Hall, Motsuji Temple, Gembikei Gorge.

Urabandai
Fukushima prefecture
Inawashiro Station, Banetsu-Saisen line
April 1 to November 20, 8 a.m. to 5.30 p.m.

Suigo
Ibaraki prefecture
Itako Station, Kashima line
Throughout year, 8 a.m. to 5 p.m.
Sights: Iris Garden, Katori Shrine, Kashima Shrine, Lake Kasumigaura.

Lake Hamana
Shizuoka prefecture
Bentenjima Station, Tokaido line
March 1 to November 30, 8.30 a.m. to 5.30 p.m.
Sights: Lake Hamana, health resort of Kanzanji, Honkoji Temple, Flower Park.

Tojimbo
Fukui prefecture
Awarayumachi bus stop
March 10 to November 30, 8 a.m. to 5 p.m.
Sights: columnar basalt formations, Maruoka Castle, health resort of Awara.

Lake Biwa and Omi-Hachiman
Shiga prefecture
Omi-Hachiman Station, Tokaido line
March 1 to November 30, 8.30 a.m. to 6 p.m.
Sights: Chomyoji Temple, Azuchi Castle, Lake Biwa, Kibo-ga-Oka Bunka Park, Omi-Hachiman Folk Museum.

Ishiyama Temple and Shigaraki
Shiga prefecture
Ishiyama Station, Tokaido line
March 1 to November 30, 8.30 a.m. to 6 p.m.
Sights: Ishiyama-dera Temple, Takeba-Taisha Shrine, Iwama-dera Temple, Shigaraki potters' workshops.

Sagano and Arashiyama
Kyoto prefecture
Saga Station, San-in line
Throughout the year, 8 a.m. to 5 p.m.
Sights: Tenryuji Temple, Daikakuji Temple, Kinkakuji Temple, Ninnaji Temple, Ryoanji Temple, Gioji Temple, Nembutsudera Temple, Nison-in Temple, Arashiyama area.

Ama-no-Hashidate
Kyoto prefecture
Amanohashidate Station, Miyazu line
March 15 to November 30, 8.30 a.m. to 6 p.m.
Sights: Coastal region, Monjuyama Park, Kasamatsu Park, Tango Folk Museum.

Banshuji
Okayama prefecture
Banshu-Ako Station, Ako line
March 1 to November 30, 8.30 a.m. to 6 p.m.
Sights: Ako Castle, Oishi Shrine, Ako Salt Museum, Cape Ako-misaki.

Kibiji
Okayama prefecture
Bichu-Takamatsu and Higashi-Soja stations, Kibi line
Throughout the year, 8 a.m. to 5.30 p.m.
Sights: Kibitsu Shrine, Bichu Kokubunji, Saijo-Inari.

Hiroshima-Miyoshi
Hiroshima prefecture
Miyoshi Station, Geibi line
Throughout the year, 8 a.m. to 6 p.m.
Sights: Wakamiya Park, Hogenji Temple.

Yamaguchi
Yamaguchi prefecture
Yamaguchi Station, Yamaguchi line
Throughout the year, 8 a.m. to 6 p.m.
Sights: Kameyama Park, Rurikoji Temple, Joeiji Temple.

Takamatsu and Yashima
Kagawa prefecture
Takamatsu Station, Yosan line
Throughout the year, 8.30 a.m. to 6 p.m.
Sights: Ritsurin Park, Takamatsu Castle, Honenji Temple, Mount Goken.

Kochi and Urado Bay
Kochi prefecture
Kochi Station, Dosan line

Throughout the year, 8 a.m. to 5 p.m.
Sights: Kochi Castle, Godaisan Park, Katsurahama Park, Sekkeiji Temple, Tosa Shrine.

Nichinan Coast
Miyazaki prefecture
Aoshima Station, Nichinan line
Throughout the year, 8.30 a.m. to 6 p.m.
Sights: Aoshima Island, Cactus Park, Horikiri Pass.

By Boat

There are many ferry services (some of them carrying cars) linking the main Japanese islands with the numerous smaller ones. On the shorter crossings there are hydrofoils and motor launches, on the longer routes in the Inland Sea and to Okinawa luxury ships.

The Inland Sea ferries ply on the following route: Osaka–Kobe–Sakate–Takamatsu–Imabari–Matsuyama–Beppu.

Important Ferry Services			
From	To	Time	
		Hrs	Mins
Tokyo	Kushiro	33	
Tokyo	Oshima	4	
Tokyo	Hachijojima	11	
Tokyo	Kochi	21	10
Aomori	Hakodate	4	
Niigata	Ryotsu	2	30
Gamagori	Toba	1	20
Osaka	Beppu	15	
Osaka	Hiroshima	11	
Uno	Takamatsu	1	
Nagasaki	Fukue	4	45
Misumi	Shimabara	1	
Kagoshima	Osaka	20	
Kagoshima	Naha	23	30

Funiculars and Cableways

The mountains and highland regions of Japan are well supplied with funiculars and cableways, numbers of which were established after winter sports were introduced to Japan by the Austrian Major von Lerch.

City Transport

For the payment of fares on the various forms of municipal transport 10-, 50- and 100-yen coins are required. Fares vary according to the distance traveled.

Map of airports served by domestic flights: pp. 320–1.

Trams and buses. – In recent years the number of *trams* in service has been considerably reduced. Where trams are still operating the fare is normally 100 yen. Direction boards and all notices, etc., are in Japanese. This is true also of *buses*, which are the main form of public transport in all Japanese towns. The fare – usually 100 yen – is put into a machine on entering the bus.

Subways (Undergrounds). – Tokyo, Osaka, Nagoya, Yokohama, Fukuoka and Sapporo have subway (underground) systems, much the largest system being that of Tokyo, with ten lines. The lines are distinguished by different colors and by names, which are shown on the individual trains. It is easy for foreigners to find their way round the system with the help of an English-language plan; the names of the stations are given in both Japanese and Latin script. Beside the name of the station are shown the names of the next station in both directions. Tickets are obtained from automatic machines near the entrance gate; fares vary with distance, as shown on the machine (usually only in Japanese). In case of uncertainty the best plan is to take the cheapest ticket (100 yen) and pay any excess at the exit gate or the "fare adjustment counter". Tickets are collected at the exit.

Suburban transport

Both Japanese National Railways and various private companies run rail and bus services linking the larger cities with their suburbs. There are also local services between Tokyo and Yokohama and between Kyoto, Osaka and Kobe.

Taxis

There are usually taxi ranks at railway stations, airports and the larger hotels. The fare is shown on the meter; it is not usual to give tips. At night (11 to 5) there is a 20% surcharge; but it is quite likely that at night or in bad weather the driver will demand – from Japanese as well as foreigners – a much higher amount. In these circumstances it is a common practice for the prospective passenger to indicate by raising two or three fingers that he is prepared to pay twice or three times the regular fare.

Airports served by Domestic Flights

Hokkaid‹

Sea of Japan

Sado

Oki

Tsushima

Goto Islands

Kyushu

Shikoku

East China
Sea

Tanegashima

Yakushima

Ryu-kyu Islands

Okinawa

1 Wakkanai
2 Rebun
3 Rishiri
4 Mombetsu
5 Asahikawa
6 Memambetsu
7 Sapporo
8 Obihiro
9 Kushiro
10 Okushiri
11 Hakodate
12 Aomori
13 Misawa
14 Akita
15 Hanamaki
16 Sendai
17 Yamagata
18 Niigata
19 Tokyo (Haneda)
20 Oshima
21 Miyakejima
22 Hachijojima
23 Matsumoto
24 Toyama
25 Komatsu
26 Fukui
27 Nagoya
28 Osaka
29 Shirahama
30 Tottori
31 Yonago
32 Izumo
33 Ube
34 Hiroshima
35 Okayama
36 Takamatsu
37 Matsuyama
38 Kochi
39 Tokushima
40 Tsushima
41 Iki
42 Fukuoka
43 Kitakyushu
44 Fukue
45 Nagasaki
46 Kumamoto
47 Oita
48 Miyazaki
49 Kagoshima
50 Tanegashima
51 Yakushima
52 Kikaishima
53 Amami-Oshima
54 Tokunoshima
55 Okinoerabushima
56 Yoron-to
57 Agunijima
58 Okinawa
59 Ishigaki
60 Miyako

Most taxi-drivers speak only Japanese, and it is, therefore, advisable for foreigners to carry a piece of paper with their desired destination written in Japanese script. The Japanese system of street naming and house numbering is so complicated that it is quite usual for taxi-drivers to have to ask the way from some local resident. Passengers need not expect the driver to help them in getting into or out of the taxi, even if they have a lot of luggage. The doors of taxis are opened and closed automatically. – It is better not to travel by taxi at peak hours, particularly in Tokyo, in view of the frequent bottlenecks.

Language

Relatively few Japanese speak any foreign language, and the foreign visitor is also presented with the formidable barrier of a script which is completely strange to him. Tourist guides and the staff of the larger hotels speak English, and it is sometimes possible to get the services of an English-speaking student as a guide. The English spoken by Japanese can sometimes be difficult to follow; and visitors for their part should be careful to speak as clearly and distinctly as possible. – The average Japanese citizen, particularly of the older generation, is unlikely to have much English; nor are taxi-drivers or public transport staff.

The origins of the **Japanese language** are not known with certainty. In spite of the similarity of the script it has no connection with Chinese. It is now generally assigned to the Ural-Altaic language group, to which the Mongol and Turkic languages also belong; but there are also indications, particularly in the phonetic field, of links with the languages of the South Seas. Japanese is an agglutinating language in which the component elements are only loosely affixed to the stem. Phonetically it is notable for its richness in vowels; the words, predominantly of two syllables, usually show an alternation of vowel and consonants. This characteristic is most easily seen in a Latin transcription: in the spoken language it is less evident, since the speech melody produced by the stressing of particular syllables which is familiar in European languages is much less marked in Japanese.

Formally, Japanese shows a strong differentiation of a very characteristic kind.

Apart from local dialects there are various different levels of speech and forms of expression related to the social status or sex of the person speaking. The language is also rich in polite formulae which indicate the exact social relationship between the person speaking and the person addressed.

Written Japanese

Japanese was first given a written form about the 4th c. A.D., using Chinese characters. In the written Chinese language the words, which are normally monosyllabic, are represented by ideograms which give not the sound but the meaning of the word; but since Japanese is quite different from Chinese both etymologically and grammatically it was not possible to use the Chinese characters in the same way as in Chinese, as indicators of meaning. Accordingly the characters were used, irrespective of their meaning, to render similarly sounding syllables of the polysyllabic Japanese language. This frequently gave rise to the difficulty that several complex Chinese characters had to be used to write a single Japanese word; and in consequence there was an increasing trend towards using certain elements of these characters to represent particular syllables. A continuing process of simplification led to the development by the 12th century of a syllabary capable of representing all the sounds of the Japanese language. This was the **Hiragana** script which is still in use.

Japanese also uses another syllabary, **Katakana**, which was developed only a little later than Hiragana. It, too, was derived from the Chinese script, but it is more angular than the rounded Hiragana and also includes some variant characters. Accordingly it is used – like italics in the Latin alphabet – for emphasis or for words taken over from foreign languages.

The **Kanji** script is quite different from these syllabaries. It consists of characters which correspond in meaning to the Chinese ideograms from which they are derived. These are used to write substantives, verbs and adjectives, but give no information about the sound of these words; accordingly the pronunciation and the inflections (which are lacking in Chinese) are indicated by the addition of Hiragana signs. – The adoption of this system of characters gave rise to a problem which still features prominently in modern Japanese. The monosyllabic Chinese language has a large number of words which are identical in phonetic content and require to be differentiated in the spoken language by their varying tones but in the written language are quite clear and distinct. This kind of acoustic differentiation is quite alien to Japanese, which has thus acquired large numbers of homophones distinguishable in meaning only by the writter character or the context. There is the further difficulty that words pronounced differently may have the same meaning, so that a Kanji character may have two different pronunciations, one Chinese and the other Japanese. This is why in the course of a conversation the Japanese are frequently compelled to refer to the written character in order to be sure that the speakers mean the same thing. For the same reason a television news bulletin, for example, is accompanied by subtitles supporting and clarifying the spoken text.

The modern Japanese script is a mixture of Kanji, Hiragana and Katakana, each being used in accordance with the characteristics which have been sketched out above. The standard form is a combination of Kanji and Hiragana (one for the sense, the other for the sound), with Katakana for foreign words (Japanese has many loan-words taken over from English, French and German) and for emphasis. Telegrams are written solely in Katakana.

This complex system calls for the use of a much greater number of individual characters than are required, for example, in a Western language. The school curriculum requires a knowledge of 881 Kanji characters; an adult of average education knows some 2500 characters; while in scientific and literary works some 4000 characters are in use. Altogether there are perhaps something like 10,000 Kanji characters. – The number of phonetic or syllabic signs is very much smaller: the "Table of Fifty Sounds" comprises 46 characters (in Hiragana and Katakana) and 25 standardized combinations. Figures are usually given in their Arabic form.

The traditional method of writing is in vertical columns from right to left. In recent years the practice has also developed of writing in horizontal lines from left to right, on the Western model; and both forms may be used together (e.g. in newspapers).

Transcription

The phonetic structure of the Japanese language lends itself without difficulty into transcription in the Latin alphabet, as set out in the "Table of Fifty Sounds". The standard method of transcription, as used in this Guide, was laid down by a committee of scholars in 1885 and is known as the **Hebonshiki romaji**, after the American philologist Hepburn. There is also another form of romanization recommended for official use, the *Kunreishiki romaji*.

Pronunciation

In the Hebonshiki romanization the consonants are pronounced as in English, the vowels as in Italian. One or two particular points should, however, be noted:

Vowels are always short unless marked to indicate length.

Double **consonants** are pronounced double – i.e. given twice the length of a single consonant, sometimes with a slight phonetic separation between the two.

The letter e is pronounced roughly like the first e in "better", never given the obscure sound of the second e. Short i and u between consonants and at the end of a word are frequently almost inaudible (so that miruku, for example, does not sound very different from "milk"). – The letter s is always unvoiced (as in "so"); w is like the English w, f like the English f (but with no contact between the lower lip and the upper teeth); r is somewhere between r and l; in ng the letters are always pronounced separately (as in "ungodly"); and initial y almost disappears.

Useful words and phrases

It is useful to know at least a few words of Japanese, and the Japanese themselves are always delighted when a visitor attempts a few words in their language.

English	Japanese
Good morning	ohayo gozaimasu
Good day	konnichiwa
Good evening	kombanwa
Good night	oyasuminasai
I am British	watakushiwa Igirisujin desu
I am American	watakushiwa Amerikajin desu
I am Canadian	watakushiwa Kanadajin desu
I am glad to meet you	hajime mashite
What is your name?	onamae wa nanto osshaimasuka?
My name is ...	... to moshimasu
Please	dozo
Thank you	arigato gozaimasu
Not at all	do itashi mashite
Excuse me	shitsurei
Yes	hai
No	iie
Goodbye	sayonara
Yesterday	kino
Today	kyo
This morning	kesa
This evening	komban
Tomorrow	asa
Where is ...?	... wa dokodesuka?
Where is the post office?	yubinkyoku wa dokodesuka?
Where is the bank?	ginko wa dokodesuka?
Where is the station?	eki wa dokodesuka?
Where is the department store?	depato wa dokodesuka?
Where is the taxi rank?	takushi noriba wa dokodesuka?
Where is the left luggage office (checkroom)?	nimotsu azukarijo wa dokodesuka?
Where is the youth hostel?	yusu hosuteru wa dokodesuka?
Where is the lavatory (toilet, washroom)?	toire wa dokodesuka?
Let me see this, please	koro wo misete kudasai
What does that cost?	ikura desuka?
That is too dear	takasugimasu
Please show me something cheaper	mo sukoshi yasui no wo misete kudasai
I'll take this	kore wo kudasai
Color film (for prints)	purinto yo kara firumu
Color film (for slides)	suraido yo kara firumu
Tape-recorder	tepu-rekoda
Camera	kamera, shashin-ki
Watch	tokei
Craft product	mingeihin
Souvenir	miyagehin
Doll	ningyo
Toy	omocha
Cigarettes	tabako
Restaurant	resutoran
Clear soup	konsome
Cream soup	potaju
Salt	shio
Pepper	kosho
Cake	keki
Coffee	kohi
Black tea	kocha
Beer	biru
Milk	miruku
Bread	pan
Menu	menyu

English	Japanese
Beauty salon	bi-yoin
Hairdresser's	rihatsuten
Tourist information office	kanko annaijo
Hotel	hoteru
Bill	kanjo
Doctor	isha
Airport	hikojo
Subway, underground railway	chikatetsu
Porter	akabo
Ticket window	kippu-uriba
North	kita
East	higashi
South	minami
West	nishi
Left	hidari
Right	migi
Block (in city)	cho, chome
District (of city)	machi
Ward (of city)	ku
Town, city	shi
Village	mura
Sub-prefecture (rural district)	gun
Prefecture	ken

Numbers

0	zero
1	ichi
2	ni
3	san
4	shi, yon
5	go
6	roku
7	nana, shichi
8	hachi
9	kyu
10	ju
100	hyaku
1000	sen
10,000	ichi-man
31,520	san-man ni-sen go-hyaku ni-ju

The Japan National Tourist Organization produces an excellent booklet, the "Tourist's Handbook", which contains a useful selection of phrases likely to be required in everyday situations and of possible replies to inquiries. It may help visitors out of the embarrassment of being unable to communicate with people they encounter on their sightseeing.

Those who want to go into Japanese a little more thoroughly will find some language guides listed among the suggestions for further reading at the end of this Guide.

Guides

English-speaking guides, either for parties or for individual visitors, can be obtained through travel agencies and the larger hotels. There are also associations of voluntary guides – often students or people who have taken a language course – who will be glad of the opportunity to speak English.

Information: **Japan Guide Association,**
Shin-Kokusai Building,
3-4-1, Marunouchi,
Chiyoda-ku,
J-100 **Tokyo**;
tel. (03) 213 2706.

Yokohama YMCA,
1-7, Tokiwa-cho,
Naka-ku,
J-220 **Yokohama**;
tel. (045) 662 3721.

Tourist Information Center,
Kyoto Tower Building,
Higashi-Shikojicho,
Shimogyo-ku,
J-600 **Kyoto**;
tel. (075) 371 5649.

Nara YMCA,
2-14-1, Kunishi-cho,
Nishidai-ji,
J-630 **Nara**.

Teijin Educational System Co. Ltd
(*TESCO*),
Aoyama Building,
1-2-3, Kita-Aoyama,
Minato-ku,
J-100 **Tokyo**;
tel. (03) 404 7003.

International 3 F Club,
4-37-13, Hongo,
Bunkyo-ku,
J-100 **Tokyo**;
tel. (03) 812 7700.

Manners and Customs

Although the Japanese way of life is increasingly becoming assimilated to that of the Western World, particularly in the cities, much importance is still attached to the **etiquette** of Japanese life, reflecting traditions many centuries old. Japanese politeness is proverbial: thus a Japanese will never directly contradict anyone he is talking to, but will try to find an indirect and conciliatory way of expressing his view. Impatience or any display of irritation or disapproval is regarded as a loss of face, and civilized communication is conducted with smiles and external composure.

When greeting anyone it is not usual to shake hands; instead, the two parties bow to one another. – Great importance is attached to correctness of *dress* (though in this respect Western influence is constantly gaining ground). Men should avoid wearing shorts or garish shirts. – On entering a Japanese house or a temple visitors take off their outdoor shoes and put on slippers; rooms floored with reed mats (*tatami*) should be entered only in stockinged feet.

Visiting cards are exchanged in Japan much more frequently than in Europe, and visitors should, therefore, make sure that they have a supply of cards, bearing their name in Katakana, the Japanese syllabic script. In all the larger towns there are printers who will supply cards for visitors. (See also p. 309.)

Tipping is not normal in Japan. Hotel and restaurant bills include an appropriate service charge, and tips need only be given where some special service has been rendered by hotel staff (or by taxi-drivers, etc.). In Japanese-style hotels (*ryokan*) it is usual to give the maid a tip at the beginning or end of the guest's stay; but it is regarded as lacking in tact to hand money over openly. – Foreign visitors should be careful not to over-indulge in alcohol, since this would involve a loss of face.

Maikos (trainee geishas)

Contrary to an opinion widely held in Europe, Japanese **geishas** are highly skilled entertainers – that and nothing more. Their function is to create an easy and relaxed atmosphere at any social occasion, and they have received a thorough training to equip them for this role. Their skills include not only witty conversation but playing musical instruments, dancing, etc. To be invited to a geisha party is a great honor – though a foreigner who knows no Japanese will get only the merest inkling of the charm and quality of the entertainment. He can perhaps more easily get at least a superficial impression of what a geisha party is like by going to one of the parties organized by the Japan Travel Bureau in Tokyo and other cities.

Health

Many Japanese doctors speak English. Treatment by a doctor usually also includes the dispensing of any medicines required. If hospital treatment is required the hospitals run by various Christian bodies can be recommended.

Accommodation

During the main travel seasons (April–May and September–November) and the Japanese holiday periods (July–August and December–January) there is a very heavy demand for accommodation, and it is advisable to book several months in advance for all categories of accommodation. Even the remoter holiday areas attract large numbers of visitors during these periods.

Western-style hotels. – In all the larger towns and the principal tourist centers there are hotels providing the highest international standards of comfort and amenity and first-class service. In most cases they will have speciality restaurants and shopping arcades; and frequently there will also be a carefully tended Japanese garden. The rooms in such hotels are fully air-conditioned and equipped with television. Tariffs are on an international level.

A total of 339 Western-style hotels are members of the *Japan Hotel Association* (JHA), but there are also large numbers of other Western-style hotels with rather lower standards of amenity and considerably lower tariffs. – A new type of Western-style hotel has

Keio Plaza Hotel, Tokyo

developed in recent years – the *business hotel,* which provides simple but comfortable rooms at very reasonable rates. There are 296 hotels of this kind all over Japan.

Japanese-style hotels (*ryokan*). –

These are very different from Western-style hotels – with tatami mats on the floors, sliding screens dividing up the rooms, no beds during the day but a mattress laid out by the maid at night. Traditionally, meals are served in the rooms.

On entering a ryokan the guest must take off his outdoor shoes and put on the slippers which will be waiting for him; and when he goes into a room floored with tatami mats he must take off the slippers and walk in his stockinged feet. The maid accompanies him to his room, serves a welcoming cup of tea and asks when he wants his evening meal. In his room he will find a *yukata*, a cotton kimono which is the normal wear within the hotel and in the garden, and even in the street in hot spring resorts.

The communal Japanese bath – now almost always taken by men and women separately – is an occasion for relaxation. The bathers soap themselves thoroughly before entering the bath, rinse themselves down and then plunge into the extremely hot water of the pool.

Room in a ryokan

Traditionally, the chambermaid will serve the guest's meal in his room after his bath and will then withdraw, returning later to lay down a mattress on the floor – the soft mattress on the hard floor making a very comfortable bed.

A pleasant experience not to be omitted is a stroll in the garden of a ryokan – often a masterpiece of landscaping in the smallest of areas.

Some ryokans are reluctant to accept bookings from foreign visitors because of ignorance of their language and lack of experience in dealing with them. The best plan, therefore, is to make bookings through a Japanese travel agency. The *Japan Ryokan Association,* to which 2371 such establishments belong, is making increased efforts to encourage its members to adapt themselves to meet the requirements of foreign visitors – though this is sometimes achieved at the expense of the traditional Japanese style.

Information: **Japan Ryokan Association,**
                       8-3, Marunouchi 1-chome,
                       Chiyoda-ku,
                       J-100 **Tokyo;**
                       tel. (03) 231 5310.

Guest-houses (*minshuku*). –

A minshuku, usually family-run, offers a perfectly acceptable and reasonably priced alternative to a hotel or ryokan. They are found all over the country, and there is usually a reservation desk at the main railway station. Bookings can also be made through the Japan Travel Bureau and the Minshuku Center. Foreign visitors cannot rely on finding English-speaking staff in these establishments.

Information: **Japan Minshuku Association,**
                       New Pearl Building,
                       2-10-8, Hyakunincho,
                       Shinjuku-ku,
                       J-100 **Tokyo;**
                       tel. (03) 371 8120.

                       Japan Minshuku Center,
                       c/o Kotsu Kaikan,
                       2-10, Yurakucho,
                       Chiyoda-ku,
                       J-100 **Tokyo;**
                       tel. (03) 371 8222.

A ryokan

People's hotels (*kokumin shukusha*). – These establishments, now some 340 in number, were established on the initiative of the Government. Situated exclusively in resorts and holiday areas, they are open also to foreign visitors. The guests' rooms are usually in Japanese style, while the public rooms tend to follow the Western pattern. The standard of amenity is generally lower than in the Western-style hotels and ryokans, but these hotels provide excellent holiday accommodation in areas of great scenic attraction. It is advisable to book through a Japanese travel agency.

Vacation villages (*kokumin kyuka mura*). – There are 31 vacation villages (some of them with people's hotels) situated in National Parks, offering reasonably priced accommodation in beautiful surroundings together with a wide range of recreational facilities (sports grounds, water sports, skiing, attractive footpaths for walkers, camp sites). Accommodation can be booked through the Japan Travel Bureau or other agencies, but it is in great demand during the main holiday periods.

Information: **National Vacation Village Corporation,**
Tokyo Kotsu Kaikan Building,
1F, 10-1, Yurakucho 2-chome,
Chiyoda-ku,
J-100 **Tokyo**;
tel. (03) 216 2085.

Osaka JNR Station,
Umedamachi, Kita-ku,
J-530 **Osaka**;
tel. (06) 343 0131.

Youth hostels. – Japan has some 560 Youth Hostels, most of them in scenically attractive areas. Apart from 76 State-run hostels they are all privately owned. There is no age limit on their use, and no limit on the time that can be spent in any one hostel. Many hostels have family rooms, and often there will be a camp site associated with the hostel.

Hostellers must be in possession of an International Youth Hostels membership card. Advance booking is advisable; there is a central reservation office in Tokyo with a computer covering most Japanese Youth Hostels.

Information: **Japan Youth Hostels, Inc.,**
Hoken Kaikan Building (2nd floor),
1-2, Ichigaya-Sadoharacho,
Shinjuku-ku,
J-100 **Tokyo**;
tel. (03) 269 5831.

Food and Drink

To the visitor who sets out to understand and appreciate the special characteristics of Japanese cuisine, experience with the cuisine of other countries he may have visited will be of little help. Apart from a very few dishes in which foreign influences may be suspected, traditional Japanese cuisine is so different from that of other countries that comparisons are not really possible. This distinctiveness is expressed in the whole attitude to a meal, which is seen as a unity of taste, appearance and table setting, in which each of the three factors is of equal importance. Japanese cuisine can be best appreciated if the visitor allows his eye as well as his palate to participate in the experience, and while enjoying the food – as to the quality of which he need have no reservations, for the Japanese are gourmets by nature – also takes pleasure in the beauty of Japanese tableware.

The staples of Japanese cooking are rice, fish, eggs and vegetables. Naturally enough in a country with such an extent of coastline, fish predominates over meat, which is generally expensive. Fish, on the other hand, is available all year round in great variety and at all price levels, and can be recommended to the foreign visitor as the basis of his meal.

The traditional Japanese **breakfast** (*asa-gohan*) consists of rice, a raw egg, bean-paste soup (*misoshiru*), pickles (*tsukemono*), dried seaweed

Seafood

(*nori*), frequently fish, and the inevitable soy sauce which features on every Japanese menu. *Green tea* is drunk at breakfast as at all other meals.

Lunch is usually a light meal – frequently a mere snack of a kind familiar in the West. For those who want something a little more substantial there are *noodles* (served either hot or cold), rice patties with fish or other garnishing (*sushi*) or boiled rice with slices of fish or meat (*donburi*). For those who require a packed meal there is the *obento* – a combination of rice, fried fish or meat and pickles packed in a wooden box; this provides a tasty meal at a very reasonable price. Packs of this kind, often including local specialities, are on sale at all Japanese railway stations.

The main meal of the day is **dinner** (*ban-gohan*), which in Japanese households is a combination of native and Chinese cuisine. Here again the essential elements are rice and soup, together with fish (or meat) and vegetables, varying according to taste. In addition to green tea *rice wine* (*sake*) may be drunk with this meal – an ideal accompaniment to the food, particularly when taken hot – or one of the excellent Japanese *beers* (*biru*).

Etiquette requires that you should not pour out your own drink but should serve your neighbor, who will do the same for you. The various dishes are served together, not in sequence: thus soup is not a prelude to the meal but is taken with the main dish.

The Japanese Menu

Sukiyaki: This very tasty dish, now internationally known, is cooked at the table, like fondue. The ingredients – wafer-thin slices of beef, various vegetables, *shirataki* noodles and bean curd (*tofu*) – are simmered in a cast-iron frying-pan in a mixture of soy sauce, sugar and rice wine. The taste is enhanced by the addition of a light beaten raw egg.

Teppan-yaki: a dish similar to sukiyaki made of boiled fish with various vegetables.

Tempura: prawns, slices of fish and various vegetables dipped in a batter of wheaten flour and egg and fried in vegetable oil. The freshly made tempura is then dipped in a soy sauce seasoned with ginger and grated horse-radish (daikon) before eating.

Tempura

Sushi: rice patties savored with vinegar, garnished with prawns, slices of raw or cooked fish, egg, fish-roe, etc., and briefly dipped in soy sauce before eating. The patties may also be wrapped in dried seaweed.

Shabu-shabu: another type of fondue in which thinly cut beef, bean curd, mushrooms and vegetables

are cooked in boiling stock and dipped in a vinegar sauce before eating.

Mizutaki: slices of chicken, pork and beef, together with other ingredients, simmered in a special stock and, like shabu-shabu, dipped in a vinegar sauce before eating.

Kaiseki: a set meal which combines the three features of Japanese cuisine – taste, decorative presentation and fine tableware. Time-consuming to prepare, it is often served during the tea ceremony. Particular care is devoted to preserving the natural aroma of the various ingredients – fish, vegetables, seaweed, mushrooms, etc.

Sashimi: Regarded as a particular delicacy, this is a selection of raw fish, which is dipped briefly in a soy sauce seasoned with *wasabi* (a type of mustard) before eating. It may not immediately appeal to the foreign visitor but is well worth trying. The delicate flesh of tuna is particularly good.

Yakitori: kebabs of poultry and vegetables grilled over a charcoal fire and frequently basted with a special sauce during the process.

Yakitori

Kabayaki: eel grilled over a charcoal fire and basted with a special sauce; usually served on rice. As tasty as yakitori.

Noodles: served either hot or cold, in soup or with a sauce.

Soba: long buckwheat noodles, eaten hot or cold.

Udon: thick buckwheat noodles.

Ramen: Chinese soup noodles, used as an ingredient in soups.

Drinks

Green tea: Drunk without milk or sugar, this may at first seem rather strange, but it goes very well with Japanese food.

Sake: a wine made from fermented rice with an alcohol content of about 15%. Drunk either warm or cold, it enhances the taste of Japanese food admirably. There are three grades – very different in taste and quality.

Beer: Beer has been brewed in Japan since the 19th century and is now a very popular drink. The best-known brands (mostly lagers with a relatively low hop content) are *Kirin, Sapporo, Asahi, Suntory* and *Orion*.

Wine: made only on a fairly small scale since the end of the 19th century at Kofu (Yamanashi prefecture) below the N side of Mount Fuji. Japanese wines (white and red; dry) are expensive. Wine is also imported from the European wine-producing countries, and Australia.

Restaurants

There is hardly a country in the world whose national cuisine is not represented in Japan. French, Italian, German, Chinese, Russian, Indian and Thai compete for attention with the numerous Japanese speciality restaurants – in the street, on the upper floors of high-rise blocks, in underground arcades. Hotel restaurants tend to be more expensive. Faithful representations of the various dishes in a display window simplify selection and ordering which the foreigner can do by merely pointing.

An agreeable Japanese practice is to provide hot damp napkins (*oshibori*) for freshening up the face and hands. The use of chopsticks (*ohashi*), however, may give the uninitiated visitor some difficulty. It is perfectly in order to make matters a little easier by raising the bowl or plate to the mouth, and when eating noodle soups slurping is unavoidable. Each kind of food is served in a particular kind of dish – rice in a porcelain bowl, soup in a lacquer (or now plastic) bowl with a lid, fish and meat on porcelain or ordinary china plates.

A Japanese meal

In Western restaurants there will be a menu in English and the normal Western cutlery; the bill is usually paid at the cash desk on leaving. In snack bars and department stores vouchers for the dishes required are bought at the entrance.

Tips are not obligatory; in the better-class restaurants a service charge of 10–15% is added to the bill. Where the bill comes to more than 2000 yen a tax of 10% is payable.

Speciality restaurants

Japanese:

Sushi restaurants: In these the customers normally sit at a counter, ordering the *sushi* (rice patties) they want, one at a time, so that they are always freshly prepared – though it is also possible to order a selection of different patties at the same time.

Tempura restaurants: Here, too, the customers usually sit at the counter and are served directly by the chef.

Yaki restaurants (grills): The tables have a built-in hotplate or grill on which dishes such as sukiyaki are cooked. Some of these restaurants have a charcoal grill near the entrance on which yakitori are prepared.

Many of these restaurants, though small and crowded, have a pleasantly cosy atmosphere: at any rate they are an experience which no visitor should miss. In addition there are plenty of places – in the street, in department stores, in railway stations – where it is possible to have a quick snack or bowl of soup noodles.

Foreign:

Chinese restaurants: numerous in towns of any size, with food of excellent quality.

Western restaurants: entirely in the style to which Western visitors will be accustomed.

Cafés offer a range of Western-style snacks and impressively large ices and sundaes (usually more impressive in appearance than in taste).

Eating with Chopsticks

In the larger restaurants and in hotel restaurants it is usually possible to have Western-style cutlery. The normal implements, however, are chopsticks (*ohashi*), which come in a variety of types, from plain natural wood or bamboo to artistically lacquered or ivory models. In view of the different tastes of the various ingredients of a dish it makes sense to pick out small pieces of each with the chopsticks.

The use of chopsticks is not nearly so difficult as it may appear at first sight. They are held in the right hand, the lower stick lying between the thumb and forefinger and resting on the tip of the ring finger, while the upper one is held by the thumb, middle finger and ring finger and can thus be manoeuvred by them. – The chopsticks must never be left standing in the rice, for that implies a ceremonial funeral meal.

Traditional Sports

The traditional Japanese sports, apart from *sumo*, are grouped together under the name *budo* (the "way of the knight"). All these types of sport are based on the philosophy of Zen, which seeks to achieve complete harmony between body and mind and is no less important to the practitioner of the sport than the sport itself.

Aikido

Aikido, a form of self-defense known since the 12th century, was given its present form by Ueshiba Morihei (1883–1970). Weapons are used only if the opponent is armed. The result of the contest does not depend on physical strength but on complete control of the body.

Training centers: **Aikikai,**
102, Wakamatsu-cho,
Shinjuku-ku,
J-100 **Tokyo;**
tel. (03) 203 9236.

Tenshin-Dojo,
1-10-8, Juso-Higashi,
Yodogawa-ku,
J-530 **Osaka.**

Judo

Judo, a sport which has become increasingly popular in the West, is a development of the jujutsu or jujitsu practiced by the samurai. The object in judo is to use your opponent's strength for your own advantage. Only holds or throws are permitted. The level of skill attained by a judo adept (*judoka*) is indicated by the color of his belt. In international judo there are seven weight classes. Visitors can watch training sessions at the centers listed.

Training centers: **Kodokan Judo Hall,**
16-30, Kasuga-cho 1-chome,
Bunkyo-ku,
J-100 **Tokyo;**
tel. (03) 811 7154.

New Japan Judo Association,
4-15-11, Nagata, Joto-ku,
J-530 **Osaka;**
tel. (06) 961 0640.

Karate

Karate has become known in the West through such spectacular feats as the breaking of bricks with the heel of the hand, the value of which as a sporting technique is disputed.

In karate (literally "empty hand") all parts of the body may be used for striking. The sport is probably of Chinese origin.

Information: **Zennihon Karatedo Renmei**
(National Karate Federation),
Sempaku Shinkokai Building,
1-15-16, Toranomon, Minato-ku,
J-100 **Tokyo;**
tel. (03) 503 6637.

Training centers: **Kyokushin-kei, Hombu Dojo,**
3-3-9, Nishi-Ikebukuro,
Toshima-ku,
J-100 **Tokyo;**
tel. (03) 948 7421.

Nippon Karate Kyokai,
6-1, 1-chome, Ebisu Nishi,
Shibuya-ku,
J-100 **Tokyo;**
tel. (03) 462 1415.

Kendo fighters

Kendo

Kendo, originally a form of swordfighting, is now practiced with bamboo sticks. The contestants wear a mask to protect their head and face and a breastplate of leather and bamboo.

Kendo is included in the training programme of the police. Visitors are admitted to training sessions.

Information: **Metropolitan Police Board,**
Public Relations Center,
3-5, Kyobashi, Chuo-ku,
J-100 **Tokyo;**
tel. (03) 561 8251.
Training sessions are held on even-numbered days of the month; closed Mondays and Thursdays.

Kyudo

Kyudo, the ancient Japanese sport of archery, is still a popular activity. An asymmetrical bow 7½ ft/2·25 m long is used. The purely sporting aspect is of less importance, however, than the element of meditation. Kyudo schools and training halls are frequently attached to temples, and in the course of centuries a number of different schools of thought have been developed.

Information: **All-Japan Kyudo Federation,**
Kishi Memorial Hall,
1-1-1, Jinnan, Shibuya-ku,
J-100 **Tokyo**;
tel. (03) 467 3111.

Sumo

Sumo is the national sport of Japan, a form of wrestling practiced by men weighing between 250 lb/113 kg and 350 lb/159 kg in which the object is to force the opponent out of the ring or make him touch the ground with any part of his body other than his feet. The contest, which frequently lasts no more than a few seconds, is preceded by a ritual of purification.

Sumo stadiums: **Kuramae Kokugikan,**
2-1-9, Kuramae, Taito-ku,
J-100 **Tokyo.**
Contests in January, May and September.

Osaka Prefectural Gymnasium,
2, Shinkawa-machi, Naniwa-ku,
J-530 **Osaka.**
Contests in March.

A sumo contest

Aichi Prefectural Gymnasium,
1-1, Ninomaru, Naka-ku,
J-450 **Nagoya.**
Contests in July.

Fukuoka Kokusai Center,
84-3, Chikuko-Honcho,
Hakata-ku,
J-810 **Fukuoka.**
Contests in November.

Hot spring

Sumo wrestlers

Hot Springs

The volcanic activity which is omnipresent in Japan has given rise to numerous hot springs, around which health resorts (*onsen*) have grown up. In addition to spa or thermal treatment in the narrow sense, most of these resorts offer a variety of recreational and sporting facilities which draw many week-end visitors and vacationers. – These resorts are busy throughout the year, and early booking is essential almost everywhere.

National Parks in Japan
国定公園

 Legend: see p. 334

Hokkaidd

Sea of Japan

Sado

Niiga

Kanazawa

Toyam
14

Oki
20

16

Gifu

15

Matsue

19

Kyoto

Nagoya

Hamamat

Himeji Kobe

Nara

Okayama

Hiroshima

Ise

Tsushima

21

Osaka

17

Shimonoseki

Wakayama

Kitakyushu

Takamatsu

Goto Islands

Fukuoka

Matsuyama

18

25

22

Kumamoto

23

Naga-
saki

24

Shikoku

Kyushu

Kagoshima

26

Tanegashima

East China
Sea

Yakushima

Ryu-kyu Islands

Naha

Okinawa

Pacific

27 Iriomote

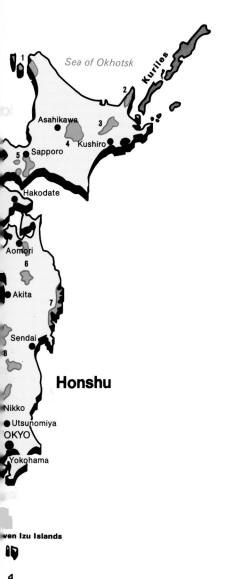

Sea of Okhotsk

Kuriles

Asahikawa 3

Kushiro 4

Sapporo 5

Hakodate

Aomori 6

Akita 7

Sendai 8

Honshu

Nikko

Utsunomiya

OKYO

Yokohama

ven Izu Islands

Ocean

Beaches

Although Japan, including the subsidiary islands, has a coastline of more than 15,000 miles/25,000 km, most of the beaches are concentrated on the Boso and Miura peninsulas in the Tokyo area, the Izu Peninsula, Ise Bay and Osaka Bay (all on the south coast of Honshu), southern Kyushu and the Okinawa Islands. This reflects the fact that most of the Japanese coasts are rocky and much indented, making access to the sea difficult.

Winter Sports

The most popular winter sport in Japan is **skiing**. Most of the good skiing areas are on Hokkaido – the 11th Winter Olympics were held at Sapporo in 1972 – and northern and central Honshu. Many winter-sports resorts also have hot springs and thus offer a combination of attractions.

Skiers in central Japan

National Parks

Japan has at present 27 National Parks, distributed over the whole country. These parks are established in areas of great natural interest and beauty but also frequently contain monuments of cultural interest such as temples and shrines. Coastal waters and islands are also included within National Parks where appropriate, and almost the whole of the Inland Sea has been declared a National Park.

Covering altogether more than 7700 sq. miles, the National Parks occupy 5·35% of the total area of Japan. A further 3% is occupied by *Quasi National Parks*. – Since

Japan has less room to spare than the countries of Europe and North America many of the National Parks consist of a number of separate sections.

1 Rishiri-Rebun-Sarobetsu National Park
Area: 131 sq. miles/340 sq. km
Prefecture: Hokkaido

2 Shiretoko National Park
Area: 160 sq. miles/414 sq. km
Prefecture: Hokkaido

3 Akan National Park
Area: 338 sq. miles/875 sq. km
Prefecture: Hokkaido

4 Daisetsuzan National Park
Area: 895 sq. miles/2319 sq. km
Prefecture: Hokkaido

5 Shikotsu-Toya National Park
Area: 381 sq. miles/987 sq. km
Prefecture: Hokkaido

6 Towada-Hachimantai National Park
Area: 322 sq. miles/833 sq. km
Prefectures: Aomori, Akita, Iwate

7 Rikuchu-kaigan National Park
Area: 47 sq. miles/123 sq. km
Prefectures: Iwate, Miyagi

8 Bandai-Asahi National Park
Area: 732 sq. miles/1897 sq. km
Prefectures: Yamagata, Niigata, Fukushima

9 Nikko National Park
Area: 543 sq. miles/1407 sq. km
Prefectures: Fukushima, Tochigi, Gumma, Niigata

10 Joshin-etsu-kogen National Park
Area: 729 sq. miles/1889 sq. km
Prefectures: Gumma, Niigata, Nagano

11 Chichibu-Tama National Park
Area: 469 sq. miles/1216 sq. km
Prefectures: Saitama, Tokyo, Yamanashi, Nagano

12 Ogasawara National Park
Area: 25 sq. miles/64 sq. km
Prefecture: Tokyo

13 Fuji-Hakone-Izu National Park
Area: 472 sq. miles/1223 sq. km
Prefectures: Kanagawa, Yamanashi, Tokyo, Shizuoka

14 Chubu-Sangaku National Park
Area: 656 sq. miles/1699 sq. km
Prefectures: Niigata, Toyama, Nagano, Gifu

15 Southern Alps National Park
Area: 138 sq. miles/358 sq. km
Prefectures: Nagano, Yamanashi, Shizuoka

16 Hakusan National Park
Area: 183 sq. miles/474 sq. km
Prefectures: Toyama, Ishikawa, Fukui, Gifu

17 Ise-Shima National Park
Area: 201 sq. miles/520 sq. km
Prefecture: Mie

18 Yoshino-Kumano National Park
Area: 214 sq. miles/554 sq. km
Prefectures: Mie, Nara, Wakayama

19 San-in-kaigan National Park
Area: 35 sq. miles/90 sq. km
Prefectures: Kyoto, Hyogo, Tottori

20 Daisen-Oki National Park
Area: 123 sq. miles/319 sq. km
Prefectures: Tottori, Okayama, Shimane

21 Inland Sea National Park
Area: 254 sq. miles/659 sq. km
Prefectures: Yamaguchi, Hiroshima, Okayama, Hyogo, Kagawa, Ehime

22 Ashizuri-Uwakai National Park
Area: 42 sq. miles/109 sq. km
Prefectures: Kochi, Ehime

23 Aso National Park
Area: 282 sq. miles/731 sq. km
Prefectures: Kumamoto, Oita

24 Unzen-Amakusa National Park
Area: 99 sq. miles/256 sq. km
Prefectures: Nagasaki, Kumamoto, Kagoshima

25 Saikai National Park
Area: 94 sq. miles/243 sq. km
Prefecture: Nagasaki

26 Kirishima-Yaku National Park
Area: 176 sq. miles/456 sq. km
Prefectures: Miyazaki, Kagoshima

27 Iriomote National Park
Area: 48 sq. miles/125 sq. km
Prefecture: Okinawa

Meeting a Japanese Family

The Japanese **Home Visit Program** offers visitors an opportunity of seeing how ordinary people live by spending a few hours with a Japanese family. This facility, which operates entirely on good-will (i.e. there is no charge), is offered in ten cities – Tokyo, Kagoshima, Kobe, Kurashiki, Kyoto, Nagoya, Osaka, Otsu, Sapporo and Yokohama.

Application should be made at least one day in advance to one of the offices listed below. It is possible to apply by telephone, but a personal application is preferable, since the offices can provide information about local sights and how to get to the family's house; in some cases, too, they issue a card of introduction. They will try to meet the visitors' preferences as to the kind of family they would like to meet.

Punctuality is essential: if you find that you cannot get there at the time agreed the family should be warned by telephone. There is no obligation to take any gifts to the family offering hospitality, but this would be a polite gesture.

On entering the house visitors must take off their outdoor shoes and put on the slippers which will be waiting for them. These in turn must be taken off when entering any room floored with tatami (straw mats). During the visit tea and cakes will be served.

All the offices listed have English-speaking staff.

Contact addresses: **Tourist Information Center,**
Kotani Building,
6-6, Yuraku-cho 1-chome,
Chiyoda-ku,
J-100 **Tokyo**;
tel. (03) 502 1461.

Yokohama International Welcome Association,
Silk Center Building,
1, Yamashita-cho, Naka-ku,
J-220 **Yokohama**;
tel. (045) 641 5824.

Kanagawa Prefectural Tourist Association,
1, Yamashita-cho, Naka-ku,
J-220 **Yokohama**;
tel. (045) 681 0007.

Tourist and Foreign Trade Section,
Nagoya City Office,
3-1-1, San-no-maru, Naka-ku,
J-450 **Nagoya**;
tel. (052) 961 1111.

Tourist Section,
Otsu City Office,
3-1, Goryo-cho,
J-520 **Otsu**;
tel. (0775) 23 1234.

Tourist Section, Department of Cultural Affairs and Tourism,
Kyoto City Government,
c/o Kyoto Kaikan, Okazaki,
Sakyo-ku,
J-600 **Kyoto**;
tel. (075) 771 6051.

Osaka Tourist Association,
c/o Foreign Trade and Tourist Department,
Osaka Municipal Office,
Senba Center Building No. 2,
1-4, Senba-cho, Higashi-ku,
J-530 **Osaka**;
tel. (06) 261 3948.

Osaka Tourist Information Office,
Higashiguchi,
JNR Osaka Station,
3-1-1, Umeda-cho, Kita-ku,
J-530 **Osaka**;
tel. (06) 345 2189.

Tourist Section,
Kobe City Office,
6-7, Kano-cho, Ikuta-ku,
J-650 **Kobe**;
tel. (078) 331 0252.

Tourist Section,
Kagoshima City Office,
11-1, Yamashita-cho,
J-890 **Kagoshima**;
tel. (0992) 24 1111.

Sapporo Tourist Association,
Sapporo City Hall,
Nishi-2, Kita-2, Kita-Ichijo,
Chuo-ku,
J-060 **Sapporo**;
tel. (011) 211 3341.

Kurashiki Association for International Friendship,
c/o Kurashiki Kokusai Hotel,
1-1-44, Chuo,
J-710 **Kurashiki**;
tel. (0864) 24 3593.

Visits to Factories

Many Japanese firms, from small craft workshops to large corporations, open their doors to overseas visitors, giving them the opportunity of seeing something of the production process and the everyday life of the workers. Some of the firms run conducted tours with explanations in English and issue informative leaflets. The craft workshops in particular often have shops for the sale of their products.

Contact addresses can be obtained from the Japan National Tourist Organization or from local information bureaus.

Calendar of Events

In spite of the great increase of Western influences in recent years the Japanese still cling to their ancient traditions, particularly in the numerous religious festivals with their gorgeous paraphernalia and rich costumes.

Since many festivals are related to the lunar calendar, exact dates cannot be given.

January

Nation-wide	*Shogatsu*, the first visit to the local shrine in the New Year (decorated streets; beginning of month)
Kitakyushu	*Mekari-shinji* (January 1)
Fukuoka	*Tamaseseri* (beginning of month)
Matsuyama	*Tsubaki-matsuri* (Camellia Festival; beginning of month)
Hiraizumi	*Ennen-no-Mai* (dancing; mid month)
Izu	*Atami ume-matsuri* (mid month)
Nagoya	*Archery contests* (mid month)
Nara	*Wakakusa-yama-yaki* (mid month)
Okinawa	*Juri-uma* (procession; mid month)
Osaka	*Toka Ebisu* (with procession; mid month)
Sendai	*Dondo-matsuri* (burning of New Year decorations; mid month)
Tsuruga	*Ebisu-daidoku Tsunashiki* (popular festival; mid month)
Akita, Yokote	*Bonten-matsuri* (procession; mid month)

February

Nation-wide	*Setsubun-matsuri* (end of winter, with visit to temple; beginning of month)
Hokkaido (Abashiri, Asahikawa, Mombetsu, Obihiro, Sapporo)	*Snow Festival* (with great displays of snow sculpture; beginning of month)
Abashiri	*Ryuhyo-matsuri* (Drift-Ice Festival; beginning of month)
Hakone	*Ume-matsuri* (Plum Blossom Festival; beginning of month)
Kobe	*Tsuinashiki* ("Spirits' Dance"; beginning of month)
Nara	*Lantern Festival* (beginning of month)
Yokote	*Kamakura-matsuri* (children's festival in snow houses; mid month)
Otaru	*Skiing contests* (end of month)

March

Nation-wide	*Hina-matsuri* (Doll Festival for girls; beginning of month)
Nara	*O-mizutori* (Festival of Fire and Lights; beginning of month) *Kasuga-matsuri* (dance festival; mid month)
Matsuyama	*Dogo-onsen-matsuri* (mid month)
Nagoya	*Fertility Festival* (mid month)

April

Nation-wide	*Hana-matsuri* (Buddha's birthday; beginning of month)
Hakone	*Sakura-matsuri* (Cherry Blossom Festival, Odawara; beginning of month)
Himeji	*Rice-Planting Ceremony* (beginning of month)
Kochi	*Doronko Festival* (beginning of month)
Matsue	*Oshiro-matsuri* (Castle Festival; beginning of month)
Matsuyama	*Castle Festival* (beginning of month)
Narita	*Cherry Blossom Festival* (beginning of month)
Shizuoka	*Shizuoka-matsuri* (procession; beginning of month)
Tokushima	*Tokushima Festival* (beginning of month)
Kamakura	*Kamakura-matsuri* (beginning to middle of month)
Lake Biwa	*Shrine Festivals* at Otsu and Hikone (mid month)
Himeji	*Spring Festival* (mid month)
Kobe	*Shinkosai* (Spring Festival; mid month)
Nagoya	*Shrine Festival* (mid month)
Nikko	*Yayoi-matsuri* (procession, with decorated floats; mid month)
Takayama	*Takayama-matsuri* (procession; mid month)

May

Arita	*Porcelain Fair* (beginning of month)
Chichibu-Tama National Park	*Hinode-matsuri* (festive procession in Fujimine; beginning of month)
Fukuoka	*Hakata-dontaku* (procession; beginning of month)
Hakodate	*Cherry Blossom Festival* (beginning of month)
Hakone	*O-shiro-matsuri* (procession, Odawara; beginning of month) *Kintoki-matsuri* (at Sengokugahara; begining of month)
Hiraizumi	*Azuma Kudari Gyoretsu* (procession; beginning of month)

Karatsu	*Castle Festival* (beginning of month)	Nagoya	*Atsuta-matsuri* (wrestling contests and procession of boats; beginning of month)
Kitakyushu	*Minato-matsuri* (popular festival; beginning of month) *Numagaku* (historical festival; beginning of month)	Kanazawa	*Hyaku-mangokumatsuri* (procession; mid month)
		Miyajima	*Kangen-sei* (boat procession at night; mid month)
Nikko	*Gohan-shiki* (beginning of month)	Morioka	*Chagu-chagu Umakko* (equestrian procession; mid month)
Okinawa	*Haryusen* (regatta; beginning of month)		
Takamatsu	*Okaya-matsuri* (beginning of month)	Osaka	*Rice-Planting Festival* (mid month)
Yokohama	*Port Festival* (beginning of month)	Sapporo	*Hokkaido Shrine Festival* (mid month)
Asahikawa	*Cherry Blossom Festival* (mid month)	Tokyo	*Sanno-matsuri* (procession; mid month)
Hakone	*Tsutsuji-matsuri* (Azalea Festival, Kowakidani, mid month)	Yokohama	*Shrine Festival* (mid month)
Izu	*Kurofune-matsuri* (at Shimoda; mid month)	**July**	
		Nation-wide	*Tanabata* (Star Festival; beginning of month)
Nara	*Takigi-no* (evening performances of No plays; mid month)	Kamikochi	*Yama-biraki* (opening of climbing season; July 1)
Nikko	*Ennen-no-mai* (cult dance; mid month) *Spring Festival* (mid month)	Hirosaki	*Nebuta-matsuri* (beginning of month)
		Izu	*Tarai nori kyoso* (contest in wooden tubs on river, Ito-onsen; beginning of month) *Genji-ayame-matsuri* (at Izu-Nagaoka-onsen; beginning of month)
Kagoshima	*Soga-don no Kasayaki* (ceremonial burning of paper parasols; end of month)		
Kobe	*Port Festival* (end of month) *Nanko-matsuri* (procession; end of month)	Matsuyama	*Opening of Climbing Season* (beginning of month)
		Narita	*Gion-matsuri* (procession; beginning of month)
Kyoto	*Mifune-matsuri* (boat festival; end of month)	Chichibu	*Kawase-matsuri* (shrine festival)
Sendai	*Shrine Festival* (end of month)	Kitakyushu	*Gion-taiko* (procession; mid month)
		Kyoto	*Gion-matsuri* (with decorated floats; mid month)

Heron dance, Tsuwano

		Miyajima	*Tamatori-matsuri* (swimming contest for a sacred ball; mid month)
June		Nagoya	*Minato-matsuri* (Port Festival; mid month)
Yokohama	*Port Festival* (anniversary of opening of port; June 2)	Okinawa	*Eisa* (men's dance festival; mid month)
		Tsuruga	*Sounomairi* (procession; mid month)
Kyoto	*Takigi-no* (evening performances of No plays; beginning of month)	Yokohama	*Firework display* (mid month)
		Kitakyushu	*Tobata Gion* (Lantern Festival; mid month) *Kurozaki Gion* (Lantern Festival; end of month)
Nagasaki	*Peiron* (rowing regatta; beginning of month)	Abashiri	*Orochon Fire Festival* (end of month)
		Hakone	*Kojo-sai* (Lake Festival; end of month)

Matsue	Matsue-odori (Summer Festival; end of month) Shrine Festival (end of month)
Osaka	Tenjin-matsuri (procession of boats; end of month)
Otaru	Ushio-matsuri (processions, with folk-dancing; end of month)

August

Nation-wide	Bon Festival (lantern festival for the dead; beginning of month)
Hiroshima	Peace Festival (anniversary of dropping of atomic bomb; August 6
Akita	Kanto-matsuri (beginning of month)
Aomori	Nebuta-matsuri (beginning of month)
Hakodate	Port Festival (beginning of month) Summer Festival (at Yunokawa-onsen; beginning of month)
Hakone	Taiko Hyotan-matsuri (at Miyanoshita; beginning of month) Torii-matsuri and Ryuto-sai (on Lake Ashi; beginning of month)
Izu	Ito Anjin-sai (festival commemorating William Adams, Ito; beginning of month)
Kochi	Yosakoi Festival (with processions; beginning of month)
Kushiro	Port Festival (beginning of month)

Matsushima	Tanabata-matsuri (Star Festival; beginning of month)
Nikko	Tohai-matsuri (pilgrimage by night; beginning of month)
Sendai	Tanabata-matsuri (Star Festival; beginning of month)
Takamatsu	Great Shrine Festival (beginning of month, alternate years)
Yamagata	Hanagasa-matsuri (dance through the streets; beginning of month)
Hakone	Daimonji-yaki (Festival of Lights; mid month)
Hiraizumi	Daimonji-okuribi (Fire Festival; mid month)
Izu	Shrine Festival at Mishimi-Taisha Shrine (mid month)
Kyoto	Daimonji (Fire Festival; mid month)
Matsue	Toro-nagashi (mid month)
Matsushima	Toro-nagashi (Festival of Floating Lanterns; mid month)
Matsuyama	Matsuyama Festival (mid month)
Nagasaki	Bon Festival (festival for souls of dead; mid month)
Nara	Lantern Festival (mid month)
Okinawa	Tug of War (mid month)
Takamatsu	Takamatsu-matsuri (Summer Festival; mid month)
Tokushima	Awa-odori (historical dance festival; mid month)
Kochi	Shinane-matsuri (end of month)
Matsue	Shrine Festival (end of month)
Niigata	Niigata Festival (end of month)
Sapporo	Summer Festival (end of month)

September

Tsuruga	Kehi-no-Nagamaturi (shrine festival; mid month)
Fukuoka	Hojo-e (shrine festival; mid month)
Kamakura	Shrine Festival at Tsurugaoka-Hachiman Shrine (mid month) Menkake-gyoretsu (masked procession; mid month)
Kumamoto	Hojo-e (with procession in old armor; mid month)
Kagoshima	Myoen-ji mairi (procession; end of month)

Festival decoration of paper fish

Kamakura	*Takigi-no* (evening performances of No plays; end of month)
October	
Asahikawa	*Kotan-matsuri* (Ainu Festival at Kamui-Kotan; beginning of month)
Kochi	*Ryoma-matsuri* (beginning of month)
Nagasaki	*Okunchi Festival* (procession, with dragon dance; beginning of month)
Fukuoka	*Shrine Festival* at Sumiyoshi Shrine (mid month)
Himeji	*Kenka-matsuri* (mid month)
Matsuyama	*Funa-odori* (Ship Dance; mid month)
Nagoya	*Nagoya-matsuri* (mid month)
Nikko	*Autumn Festival* (mid month)
Tokyo	*Oeshiki-matsuri* (temple festival; mid month)
Kyoto	*Jidai-matsuri* (commemorating foundation of town; end of month)
Uwajima	*Yatsushida-dori* (procession with animal figures; end of month)
November	
Narita	*Chrysanthemum Show*
Hakone	*Daimyo-gyoretsu* (procession, Hakone-Yumoto; beginning of month)
Kagoshima	*Ohara-matsuri* (beginning of month)
Karatsu	*Okunchi-matsuri* (procession; beginning of month)
Matsue	*Taiko-gyoretsu* (procession; beginning of month) *Shrine Festival* (beginning of month)
Nation-wide	*Shichi-go-san* (shrine visit by children; mid month)
December	
Chichibu	*Chichibu-Yo-matsuri* (shrine festival; beginning of month)
Kushiro	*Snow Festival* (with snow sculpture; beginning of month)
Nara	*On-matsuri* (procession; mid month)
Tokyo	*Toshi-no-ichi* (fair; mid month)
Oga	*Namahage* (procession with demon masks; end of month)

Folk Arts and Crafts

Following a period at the end of the 19th century when the old traditional crafts were in danger of being driven out by the development of industry, efforts were made in the early years of the new century to revive the old techniques. A leading part was played in this movement by Yanagi Soetsu (1889–1961), who assembled a priceless collection of folk art from all over Japan and, with the potters Kawai Kanjiro and Hamada Shoji, founded in 1931 the Japanese Folk Art Society (Nihon Mingei-kyokai) and, two years later, the Museum of Folk Art (Nihon Mingei-kan) in Tokyo.

Making Hakata dolls

In spite of the flood of industrial souvenirs and the inevitable degeneration of art into kitsch there is still a wide range of traditional craft products showing the old characteristic style, loving attention to detail and quality. A survey of present-day craft production is offered by the Nitten Exhibition in Tokyo (November–December).

Shopping and Souvenirs

Japan offers a wide range of both industrial and craft products, and foreign visitors have the additional advantage of being able to purchase a variety of articles duty-free. Shops selling duty-free goods have a sign at the entrance, "Tax free"; and when a visitor makes a purchase in one of these shops the assistant will complete an official form ("Record of Purchase of Commodities Tax-Exempt for Export") and insert it in the purchaser's passport. The saving may be from 5 to 40 per cent.

The following articles can be bought duty-free:
- articles made of, or incorporating, precious metals, precious stones or ivory;
- pearls;
- cloisonné work;
- furs;
- sporting guns;
- electronic products including radio and television sets, tape-recorders, record-players, etc.;
- cameras and ciné cameras, projectors, field-glasses, etc.;
- watches;
- smokers' requisites.

In the larger shops (with fixed prices) the following credit cards are accepted: American Express, Americard, Visa, Diners Club, Master Charge, Carte Blanche.

A particularly wide range of duty-free articles can be found in the
Japan Taxfree Center,
5-8-6, Toranomon,
Minato-ku,
J-100 **Tokyo**
(near the Tokyo Tower).

Before buying any technical appliance make sure that you will be able to have it serviced at home, and, in the case of an electrical appliance, that it can be adjusted to take the right voltage. It is well to remember also the limits set by aircraft baggage allowances and customs regulations at home.

Porcelain (*yaki*), which was known in Japan at an early period and after the Korean campaigns of Toyotomi Hideyoshi in 1592–98 was decisively influenced by Korean potters, is available in great variety, always marked by simplicity of form and pleasing but never over-stressed decoration. The many manufactories have display and sale rooms, organize conducted tours of their works and in some cases offer facilities for amateurs to practice the craft. The main centers for the manufacture of porcelain are Mashiko (Tochigi prefecture), Seto and Tokoname (Aichi), Tajimi and Toki (Gifu), Kanazawa (Ishi-

kawa), Shigaraki (Shiga), Kyoto, Imbe (Okayama), Hagi (Yamaguchi), Arita and Karatsu (Saga) and Sarayama (Oita).

The traditions of **lacquerware** are still carried on in the old centers of production – Tokyo, Kyoto and Kanazawa – and there are also lacquer workshops in Takamatsu and Nagoya. Simpler type of lacquerware for everyday use are produced in Fukushima, Ishikawa, Toyama and Wakayama prefectures.

Of the various lacquerwork techniques the most important is that known as *makie* ("scatter picture"), in which gold or silver dust is scattered on a coat of lacquer while it is still wet and is then covered with further coats; these upper coats are then polished with charcoal until the pattern reappears. – There are also lacquerwares with inlays of various kinds, mainly mother-of-pearl but also precious metals, coral, ivory and semi-precious stones. The technique of lacquer-carving (*tsuishu*) was replaced at an early stage by the simpler process of carving the wood and then covering it with lacquer (*kamakura-bori*).

There are a variety of techniques for the dyeing of **textiles**, and in Japan tie-dyeing (*kokechi*), batik-work (*roketsu*) and the stencil technique (*kyokechi*) came into use at an early period. Patterned *kokechi* fabrics are produced mainly on Okinawa and in Kumamoto, Kagoshima, Ehime, Shimane and Niigata prefectures. The principal dyeing centers are Kyoto and Kanazawa, together with Tokyo and the prefectures of Miyagi and Yamagata. – Aomori in northern Japan is famed for its embroidery, with geometric patterns on a dark ground, and on Hokkaido appliqué work of the type formerly produced by the Ainu can still be found.

Japanese **paper** is used in a variety of ways – in the making of dolls and brightly colored boxes, in wall screens and sliding doors and in the intricately folded creations of origami work.

The art of paper-making seems to have come to Japan from China in the early 7th century. The main centers of paper-making are now in the prefectures of Iwate (Higashiyama, Yanagifu), Niigata (Oguni), Nagano (Matsumoto), Saitama, Gifu, Fukui and Kanazawa and in the cities of Tokyo and Kyoto.

The small carved objects known as **net-suke** which first appeared in the 15th century were originally designed for use as toggles to secure a cord attached to a waist-belt from which purses, writing materials, etc., could be suspended. They became very popular in the 17th century and reached their heyday about 1800. Netsuke (known as "hand-flatterers" because of their smooth surface) were made of bamboo, wood, ivory, lacquer-work, porcelain, precious stones or occasionally other materials. They are now much sought after by collectors, and old specimens are hard to find. Even modern netsuke are not by any means cheap.

A material which lends itself to varied uses is **bamboo**, which can be carved or plaited to produce, for example, hats, baskets, chopsticks, etc.

In the field of **metalware** mention must be made of the bronze vases produced in Kyoto and Tokyo and the cast-iron kettles and water-containers of Morioka and Kyoto. Among the finest products of the metalsmith's craft are the swords produced mainly in the 14th century which now command very high prices indeed.

Souvenir figures

In addition to the actual centers of production the following central sales points offer a wide range of traditional arts and crafts:

Kokusai Kanko Kaikan,
1-8-3, Marunouchi, Chiyoda-ku,
J-100 **Tokyo**
(sales and information offices of the individual prefectures).

Bingoya,
69, Wakamatsu-cho, Shinjuku-ku,
J-100 **Tokyo.**

Kyoto Handicraft Center,
Kumano-Jinja-Higashi, Sakyo-ku,
J-600 **Kyoto.**

Opening Times

Shops are open daily (including the week-end) from 10 a.m. to 8 p.m. *Department stores* are also open on Saturdays and Sundays from 10 a.m. to 6 p.m., but are closed on one weekday.

Head post offices are open from 8 a.m. to 8 p.m. Monday to Saturday, from 8 a.m. to 12 noon on Sundays. Other post offices are open from 9 a.m. to 5 p.m. Monday to Friday and 9 a.m. to 12.30 p.m. on Saturdays; they are closed on Sunday.

Banks are open from 9 a.m. to 3 p.m. Monday to Friday, 9 a.m. to 12 noon on Saturdays.

Public Holidays	
January 1	New Year's Day
January 15	Adults' Day
February 11	National Foundation Day
March 20 or 21	Spring Equinox
April 29	Emperor's Birthday
May 3	Constitution Day
May 5	Children's Day
September 15	Respect for the Aged Day
September 23 or 24	Autumn Equinox
October 10	Health and Sports Day
November 3	Culture Day
November 23	Thanksgiving Day

Information

Japan National Tourist Organisation
(*JNTO*),
6-6, Yuraku-cho 1-chome,
J-100 **Tokyo**;
tel. (03) 502 1461.

167 Regent Street,
London W1;
tel. (01) 734 9638.

Rockefeller Plaza,
630 Fifth Avenue,
New York, NY 10111;
tel. (212) 757 5640.

333 North Michigan Avenue,
Chicago, IL 60601;
tel. (312) 332 3975.

1519 Main Street, Suite 200,
Dallas, TX 75201;
tel. (214) 741 4931.

1737 Post Street,
San Francisco, CA 94115;
tel. (415) 931 0700.

624 South Grand Avenue,
Los Angeles, CA 90017;
tel. (213) 623 1952.

2270 Kalakaua Avenue,
Honolulu, HI 96815;
tel. (808) 923 7631.

165 University Avenue,
Toronto, Ont. M5H 3B8;
tel. (416) 366 7140.

Central Information Offices of the Japanese Prefectures and Cities in Tokyo

Most of the 47 prefectures (-*ken*) and the largest cities have information bureaus in Tokyo which have English-speaking staff and supply information leaflets, etc., in English. They are grouped in two main offices, the Kokusai Kanko Kaikan and the Tetsudo Kaikan, and four individual offices.

Kokusai Kanko Kaikan,
1-8-3, Marunouchi, Chiyoda-ku,
J-100 **Tokyo**.

Prefecture	Telephone
Aomori	216 6010
Chiba	216 6017
Fukui	211 8054
Fukuoka	231 1750
Gumma	231 4836
Hiroshima	215 5010
Hokkaido	214 2481
Hyogo	231 1864
Ibaraki	231 2642
Ishikawa	231 4030
Kagawa	231 4840
Kanagawa	231 3901
Miyazaki	216 9587
Nagano	214 5651
Nagasaki	231 2046
Nara	216 5955
Niigata	215 4618
Oita	231 5096
Okayama	231 2687
Okinawa	231 0848
Osaka	212 3943
Saga	216 6596
Saitama	215 2031
Shiga	231 6131
Shizuoka	215 0612
Tochigi	215 4050
Toyama	216 2068
Wakayama	231 2041
Yamaguchi	231 4980
Yamanashi	231 0760

City	
Kobe	231 1861
Kyoto	216 3691
Osaka	231 1843

Tetsudo Kaikan,
1-9-1, Marunouchi, Chiyoda-ku,
J-100 **Tokyo**.

Prefecture	Telephone
Aichi	213 2907
Akita	211 1775
Ehime	231 1804
Gifu	231 1775
Iwate	231 2613
Kochi	212 1981
Mie	211 2737
Miyagi	231 0944
Shimane	212 1091
Tokushima	216 2081
Tottori	211 8286
Yamagata	215 2222

Thus the address of the Aomori prefecture information office, for example, is as follows:

Aomori-ken Tokyo Kanko Bussan Assensho,
Kokusai Kanko Kaikan,
1-8-3, Marunouchi, Chiyoda-ku,
J-100 **Tokyo**;
tel. (03) 216 6010.

Other prefectures:

Fukushima
Nittobo Building,
6-1, Yaesu, Chuo-ku,
J-100 **Tokyo**;
tel. (03) 273 8311.

Kagoshima
Olympic Building,
2-7-17, Ginza, Chuo-ku,
J-100 **Tokyo**;
tel. (03) 561 6701.

Kumamoto
5-3-15, Ginza, Chuo-ku,
J-100 **Tokyo**;
tel. (03) 571 2059.

Kyoto
Todofuken Kaikan,
2-4, Hirakawa-cho, Chitoda-ku,
J-100 **Tokyo**;
tel. (03) 261 3469.

Japan Travel-Phone
(Tourist information service in English): see p. 313

Japan Automobile Federation
3-5-8, Shiba Park, Minato-ku,
J-100 **Tokyo**;
tel. (03) 436 2881.

Diplomatic and Consular Offices

United States of America
Embassy:
10-5, Akasaka 1-chome,
Minato-ku,
J-107 **Tokyo**;
tel. (03) 583 7141.

Consulates:
5-26, Ohori 2-chome,
Chuo-ku,
J-810 **Fukuoka**;
tel. (092) 751 9331.

10, Kano-cho 6-chome,
Ikuta-ku,
J-650 **Kobe**;
tel. (078) 331 6865.

2129, Gusukuma,
Urasoe City,
J-901-21 **Naha**, Okinawa;
tel. (0988) 77 8142.

Sankei Building (9th floor),
4-9, Umeda 2-chome,
Kita-ku,
J-530 **Osaka**;
tel. (06) 341 2754.

Kita 1-jo, Nishi 28-chome,
Chuo-ku,
J-064 **Sapporo**;
tel. (011) 641 1115.

United Kingdom
Embassy:
1, Ichiban-cho,
Chiyoda-ku,
J-102 **Tokyo**;
tel. (03) 265 5511.

Consulates:
Holme Ringer and Co. Ltd,
9-9, Minato-machi,
Moji-ku,
J-801 **Kitakyushu**;
tel. (093) 331 1311.

Hong Kong and Shanghai Bank Building,
45, Awaji-machi 4-chome,
Higashi-ku,
J-541 **Osaka**;
tel. (06) 231 3355.

Canada
Embassy:
3-38, Akasaka 7-chome,
Minato-ku,
J-107 **Tokyo**;
tel. (03) 408 2101.

Airlines

Japan Air Lines (*JAL*)
International flights:
Daini Tekko Building,
1-8-2, Marunouchi,
Chiyoda-ku,
J-100 **Tokyo**;
tel. (03) 747 1111.

Domestic flights:
5-37-8, Shiba, Minato-ku,
J-100 **Tokyo**;
tel. (03) 456 2111.

There are *JAL* desks at all airports in Japan.

Offices in United States:
555 West Seventh Street,
Los Angeles, CA 90014;
tel. (213) 620 9580.

JAL Building,
655 Fifth Avenue,
New York, NY 10022;
tel. (212) 838 4400.

150 Powell Street,
San Francisco, CA 94102;
tel. (415) 982 8141.

919 17th Street N.W.,
Washington, D.C. 20006;
tel. (800) 223 5405.

Also at Anchorage, Atlanta, Boston, Chicago,
Cincinnati, Cleveland, Dallas, Denver, Detroit,
Honolulu, Houston, Miami, Minneapolis,
Philadelphia, Portland, St Louis, San Diego, San
Jose and Seattle.

Offices in United Kingdom:
Rotunda (16th floor),
150 New Street,
Birmingham B2 4PA;
tel. (021) 643 1368.

Stock Exchange House,
69 St George's Place,
Glasgow G2 1BT;
tel. (041) 221 6227.

8 Hanover Street,
London W1R 0DR;
tel. (01) 408 1000.

20 St Ann's Square,
Manchester M2 7HG;
tel. (061) 832 2807.

Offices in Canada:
Suite 336, 131 Ninth Avenue S.W.,
Calgary, Alberta T2P 1K1;
tel. (800) 663 3316.

Suite 725, Alexis Nihon Plaza,
1500 Atwater Avenue,
Montreal, Quebec H3Z 1X5;
tel. (514) 861 1521.

111 Richmond Street,
West Toronto, Ontario M5H 2G4;
tel. (416) 364 7226.

777 Hornby Street,
Vancouver, B.C.;
tel. (604) 688 6611.

All Nippon Airways (*ANA*),
1-8-1, Haneda Kuku, Ota-ku,
J-100 **Tokyo**;
tel. (03) 747 5111.

Toa Domestic Airlines (*TDA*),
2-2, Haneda Kuku, Ota-ku,
J-100 **Tokyo**;
tel. (03) 747 8111.

South West Air Lines (*SWAL*),
306-1, Aza Kagamizu,
J-902 **Naha**, Okinawa;
tel. (0988) 57 2111.

Nippon Kinkyori Air Lines (*NKA*),
2-2-6, Roppongi,
Minato-ku,
J-100 **Tokyo;**
tel. (03) 7586 8931.

New Central Air Lines (*NCA*),
J-950 **Niigata;**
tel. (0252) 75 4352.

Nippon Naigai Airlines (*NNA*),
Airport,
J-890 **Kagoshima;**
tel. (09955) 8 2021.

Nagasaki Airways (*NAW*),
Airport,
J-850 **Nagasaki;**
tel. (09575) 3 7114.

Emergency Calls

Police   **110**
Fire, Ambulance   **119**

International Telephone Codes

From the United States or Canada to
Japan   **011 81**
From the United Kingdom to Japan
                                   010 81

Calls from Japan to the countries of
the West are put through by
Kokusai Denshin Denwa Co. Ltd
(*KDD*), **Tokyo;**
tel. (03) 211 5111.

For international calls from **Tokyo**
and **Osaka** dial   **00 51**

A three-minute call to the United
States or Canada 2430 yen; to the
United Kingdom 2700 yen.